Advances in Business Financial Management

A Collection of Readings

Second Edition

Advances in Business Financial Management

A Collection of Readings

Second Edition

PHILIP L. COOLEY
Trinity University

The Dryden Press
Harcourt Brace College Publishers

Fort Worth Philadelphia San Diego New York Orlando Austin San Antonio
Toronto Montreal London Sydney Tokyo

Acquisitions Editor Shana Lum
Developmental Editor Stacey Sims
Project Editor Ann Rickerman
Art Director Bill Brammer
Production Manager Carlyn Hauser
Art & Literary Rights Editor Adele Krause
Electronic Publishing Coordinator Ellie Moore
Product Manager Craig Johnson
Marketing Assistant Kelly Whidbee
Cover Design Lora Knox

Copy Editor Cynthia Sheridan
Text Type 10/12 Janson Text

Address for Editorial Correspondence
The Dryden Press, 301 Commerce Street, Suite 3700, Fort Worth, TX 76102

Address for Orders
The Dryden Press, 6277 Sea Harbor Drive, Orlando, FL 32887
1-800-782-4479, or 1-800-433-0001 (in Florida)

ISBN: 0-03-015717-X

Library of Congress Catalog Card Number: 95-69072

Printed in the United States of America

5 6 7 8 9 0 1 2 3 4 066 9 8 7 6 5 4 3 2 1

The Dryden Press
Harcourt Brace College Publishers

To Miss Esther Berry

Preface

Advances in Business Financial Management, Second Edition, is a readings book designed for undergraduate and graduate students taking their first or second course in finance. Each of the 48 articles in this collection lies within the intellectual grasp of beginning students of finance. None of the articles contains complicated mathematics or statistics. The articles focus on the concepts of finance, not on methodology.

Instructors can use this book to supplement textbooks and casebooks on business financial management. *Advances in Business Financial Management*'s content adds depth to the material covered in such books, offering a perspective that they cannot provide. A textbook is necessarily limited in its depth of coverage because of the need for breadth, and a casebook presents finance problems with only limited information on their solution. Providing selected readings greatly enriches the educational process by taking students closer to the leading edge of knowledge. Readings also add variety to class activities, thereby increasing the interest of students.

Advances in finance usually appear first in journals sponsored by diverse professional groups, government agencies, universities, and corporations. Later, having stood the test of time, the advances may appear in textbooks. Staying abreast of the ideas in these far-flung publications is a formidable task even for dedicated scholars. This collection of articles eases the task and provides a convenient compendium for students and instructors.

Selection Process

The criteria for selecting an article for this book comprise a complex mixture of requirements, but include two overriding requirements: (1) the article must be accessible to students taking their first course in finance, and (2) the article must add to the understanding of ideas that are usually presented in introductory finance courses. Most of the articles have explicit implications for improving financial decision making, and several of them report on financial practices in the business world. Because this book focuses on the advances in business financial management, the articles are of recent vintage. I retained some classics—they are favorites with whistling clear messages and I could not let them go.

All 48 articles have survived the winnowing of hundreds of candidate articles. Finance professors from around the country, many of whom used the first edition in their classes, offered several suggestions for the second edition. In addition, I searched approximately 100 journals in finance, economics, accounting, banking, general business, law, real estate, insurance, and international business. More than 200 articles surfaced from the search process, and 48 were selected from the following sources:

Business Credit
Business Horizons
Business Review
Economic Perspectives
Economic Quarterly
Economic Review
Financial Analysts Journal
Financial Management
Financial Practice and Education
Harvard Business Review
Interfaces
Journal of Accountancy
Journal of Applied Corporate Finance
Journal of Cash Management
Journal of Commercial Bank Lending
Journal of Economic Perspectives
Journal of Finance
Journal of Financial Economics
Journal of Financial Education
Journal of Portfolio Management
Management Accounting
McKinsey Quarterly
Review
Sloan Management Review
Strategic Management Journal

A subset of the articles in this edition are available to instructors who prefer to adopt a customized version of the reader. For information, contact your local Dryden sales representative.

Special Feature

I have included several discussion questions at the conclusion of each article to enhance its use in teaching and learning. In total, the book contains 330 questions, averaging about 7 per article. Experience shows that students greatly appreciate the questions, which guide them in testing their comprehension. Instructors may wish to assign the questions for written responses, or they may use them to structure classroom discussion.

Organization of the Book

Like the first edition, this edition contains seven parts covering the major topics of business financial management. Although the parts follow the progression of ideas found in many textbooks, they can be rearranged to suit the purpose of the reader. Moreover, understanding an individual article does not depend on the particulars of preceding articles.

In brief, the following titles and subtitles describe the subject matter and organization of the book:

Part 1. Business Financial Management and Its Environment
Great ideas in finance, morality and ethics, executive compensation, and agency theory.

Part 2. Valuation and the Cost of Capital
Stock and bond returns, efficient markets, diversification, duration, corporate debt levels, and capital structure.

Part 3. Capital Budgeting
Corporate practice, capital efficiency, corporate strategy, real options, and theory of capital budgeting.

Part 4. Managing Working Capital
Innovations, commercial paper, repurchase agreements, negotiable CDs, trade credit, factoring, inventory control, and bank loans.

Part 5. Analyzing and Planning Financial Performance
Analyzing financial statements, financial ratios, liquidity measures, statement of cash flows, growth industries, and sustainable growth.

Part 6. Institutional Features of Long-Term Financing
Junk bonds, security design, preferred stock, initial public offerings, dividend policy, and stock dividends.

Part 7. Special Topics
Futures contracts, interest rate swaps, market for corporate control, leveraged buy-outs, corporate bankruptcy, global financial markets, and Japanese corporations.

Acknowledgements

This collection of readings owes its existence to the authors of the articles. I am grateful to the authors for allowing me to share their insights and clarity of thought with a new and wider audience. My gratitude also extends to the publishers of the articles for their permission to reprint the material.

The Dryden Press is the leading publisher of finance books for a good reason—its people. I thank the following Dryden team for bringing this book to fruition: Lyn Hastert, Shana Lum, Ann Rickerman, Stacey Sims, Bill Brammer, Carlyn Hauser, and Adele Krause. I also thank my assistant Diana Gomez for her dedication and commitment to meeting deadlines.

Many finance professors offered encouragement for this project and suggested articles for inclusion, which greatly improved the finished product. To these colleagues, I express a resounding thank you:

Raj Aggarwal
John Carroll University

Reena Aggarwal
Georgetown University

James S. Ang
Florida State University

H. Kent Baker
American University

William L. Beedles
University of Kansas

Brian L. Belt
University of Missouri

Joe M. Brocato
Tarleton State University

Tylor Claggett, Jr.
Wake Forest University

Wallace Davidson, III
Southern Illinois University

Allan C. Eberhart
Georgetown University

M. E. Ellis
St. John's University

Douglas R. Emery
Binghamton University

Gary W. Emery
University of Oklahoma

Gail E. Farrelly
Rutgers University

Eurico J. Ferreira
Indiana State University

John D. Finnerty
McFarland Dewey & Co.

Joseph E. Finnerty
University of Illinois

Jack Clark Francis
Baruch College

George M. Frankfurter
Lousisiana State University

Philip W. Glasgo
Xavier University

Benton E. Gup
University of Alabama

Clark A. Hawkins
New Mexico State University

Anthony F. Herbst
University of Texas at El Paso

John S. Jahera, Jr.
Auburn University

Michael D. Joehnk
Arizona State University

James M. Johnson
Northern Illinois University

O. Maurice Joy
University of Kansas

Richard Kolodny
University of Maryland

Chuck C. Y. Kwok
University of South Carolina

Gene E. Laber
University of Vermont

Scott C. Linn
University of Oklahoma

Thomas E. McCue
Duquesne University

Fred W. McKenna
University of S. Alabama

Victoria B. McWilliams
Arizona State University/West

Rodney H. Mabry
University of Tulsa

Jeff Madura
Florida Atlantic University

Arvind Mahajan
Texas A&M University

Richard D. Marcus
University of Wisconsin—Milwaukee

Barry R. Marks
University of Houston—Clear Lake

Larry J. Merville
University of Texas—Dallas

William T. Moore
University of South Carolina

Charles R. Moyer
Wake Forest University

Tarun K. Mukherjee
University of New Orleans

Glenn Petry
Washington State University

William J. Petty
Baylor University

Jack S. Rader
Financial Management Association

Rodney L. Roenfeldt
University of South Carolina

William L. Sartoris
Indiana University

Frederick C. Scherr
West Virginia University

Jacky C. So
Southern Illinois University

Meir Statman
Santa Clara University

Jerry L. Stevens
University of Richmond

Robert A. Taggart
Boston College

Emery A. Trahan
Northeastern University

Jack W. Trifts
Rollins College

George W. Trivoli
Jacksonville State University

James C. Van Horne
Stanford University

John M. Wachowicz, Jr.
University of Tennessee

Michael C. Walker
University of Cincinnati

James W. Wansley
University of Tennessee

Daniel T. Winkler
University of North Carolina—Greensboro

Jeffrey G. Wyatt
Miami University

John T. Zietlow
Indiana State University

A Concluding Note

The final judge of this readings book is you the reader. I am hopeful that students and instructors will share my conviction on the usefulness of these readings in furthering our understanding of finance. Personally, I will judge the book a success if both students and instructors share the magic of enlightenment from its use. I invite you to suggest articles for inclusion in the next edition.

Philip L. Cooley
San Antonio, Texas
August 1995

The Dryden Press Series in Finance

Amling and Droms
Investment Fundamentals

Berry and Young
Managing Investments: A Case Approach

Bertisch
Personal Finance

Brigham
Fundamentals of Financial Management
Seventh Edition

Brigham
Fundamentatls of Financial Management: The Concise Edition

Brigham, Gapenski, and Shome
Cases in Financial Management: Dryden Request

Brigham and Gapenski
Cases in Financial Management: Module A

Brigham and Gapenski
Cases in Financial Management: Module B

Brigham and Gapenski
Cases in Financial Management: Module C

Brigham and Gapenski
Financial Management: Theory and Practice
Seventh Edition

Brigham and Gapenski
Intermediate Financial Management
Fifth Edition

Brigham, Aberwald, and Gapenski
Finance with Lotus 1-2-3
Second Edition

Chance
An Introduction to Derivatives
Third Edition

Clark, Gerlach, and Olson
Restructuring Corporate America

Clauretie and Webb
The Theory and Practice of Real Estate Finance

Cooley
Advances in Business Financial Management: A Collection of Readings
Second Edition

Cooley
Business Financial Management
Third Edition

Dickerson, Campsey, and Brigham
Introduction to Financial Management
Fourth Edition

Eaker, Fabozzi, and Grant
International Corporate Finance

Evans
International Finance: A Markets Approach

Fama and Miller
The Theory of Finance

Gardner and Mills
Managing Financial Institutions: An Asset/Liability Approach
Third Edition

Gitman and Joehnk
Personal Financial Planning
Seventh Edition

Greenbaum and Thakor
Contemporary Financial Intermediation

Harrington and Eades
Case Studies in Financial Decision Making
Third Edition

Hayes and Meerschwam
Financial Institutions: Contemporary Cases in the Financial Services Industry

Hearth and Zaima
Contemporary Investments: Security and Portfolio Analysis

Johnson
Issues and Readings in Managerial Finance
Fourth Edition

Kidwell, Peterson, and Blackwell
Financial Institutions, Markets, and Money
Sixth Edition

Koch
Bank Management
Third Edition

Leahigh
A Pocket Guide to Finance

Maisel
Real Estate Finance
Second Edition

Martin, Cox, and MacMinn
The Theory of Finance: Evidence and Applications

Mayes and Shank
Financial Analysis with Lotus for Windows

Mayes and Shank
Financial Analysis with Microsoft Excel

Mayo
Financial Institutions, Investments, and Management: An Introduction
Fifth Edition

Mayo
Investments: An Introduction
Fourth Edition

Osteryoung, Newman, and Davies
Small Business Finance

Pettijohn
PROFIT+

Reilly
Investment Analysis and Portfolio Management
Fourth Edition

Reilly and Norton
Investments
Fourth Edition

Sears and Trennepohl
Investment Management

Seitz and Ellison
Capital Budgeting and Long-Term Financing Decisions
Second Edition

Siegel and Siegel
Futures Markets

Smith and Spudeck
Interest Rates: Principles and Applications

Weston, Besley, and Brigham
Essentials of Managerial Finance
Eleventh Edition

The Harcourt Brace College Outline Series

Baker
Financial Management

Contents

PART

I

Business Financial Management and Its Environment

A Portfolio of Nobel Laureates: Markowitz, Miller, and Sharpe

Hal R. Varian

Finance is one of the great success stories of quantitative economics. A recent ad in *The Economist* for a "mathematical economist" described an "excellent opportunity for numerate individual with background in capital markets." In today's market, numeracy pays!

But it was not always so. According to Robert Merton (1990):

> As recently as a generation ago, finance theory was still little more than a collection of anecdotes, rules of thumb, and manipulations of accounting data. The most sophisticated tool of analysis was discounted value and the central intellectual controversy centered on whether to use present value or internal rate of return to rank corporate investments. The subsequent evolution from this conceptual potpourri to a rigorous economic theory subjected to scientific empirical examination was, of course, the work of many, but most observers would agree that Arrow, Debreu, Lintner, Markowitz, Miller, Modigliani, Samuelson, Sharpe, and Tobin were the early pioneers in this transformation.

Three of these pioneers of quantitative finance have now been justly honored: Harry Markowitz, Merton Miller, and William Sharpe received the Nobel Prize in Economic Science in 1990.

From today's perspective it is hard to understand what finance was like before portfolio theory. Risk and return are such fundamental concepts of finance courses that it is hard to realize that these were once a novelty. But these esoteric theories of the last generation form the basic content of MBA courses today.

The history of the quantitative revolution in finance has recently been summarized in Bernstein (1992). Here I attempt to provide a very brief history of this

---

At the time of this writing, Hal R. Varian was the Reuben Kempf Professor of Economics and Professor of Finance at the University of Michigan, Ann Arbor, Michigan.

Source: *Journal of Economic Perspectives* (Winter 1993, Vol. 7 No. 1, pp. 159–169). Reprinted with permission.

enterprise, drawing upon the work of Bernstein and the accounts of the Nobel laureates in Markowitz (1991), Miller (1991) and Sharpe (1991). Readers interested in more detailed accounts of the development of modern financial theory should consult these works.

Harry Markowitz

Harry Markowitz was born in 1927 in Chicago. He attended the University of Chicago and majored in economics. He found the subject appealing enough to go on to graduate school and eventually arrived at the thesis stage. While waiting to see Jacob Marschak he struck up a conversation with a stockbroker who suggested that he might write a thesis about the stock market. Markowitz was excited by this idea and started to read in the area.

One of his first books was *The Theory of Investment Value* by John Burr Williams, (1938). Williams argued that the value of a stock should be the present value of its dividends—which was then a novel theory. Markowitz quickly recognized the problem with this theory: future dividends are not known for certain—they are random variables. This observation led Markowitz to make the natural extension of the Williams' theory: the value of a stock should be the *expected* present value of its dividend stream.

But if an investor wants to maximize the expected value of a portfolio of stocks he owns, then it is obvious that he should buy only one stock—the one that has the highest expected return. To Markowitz, this was patently unrealistic. It was clear to him that investors must care not only about the expected return of their wealth, but also about the risk. He was then naturally led to examine the problem of finding the portfolio with the maximum expected return for a given level of risk.

The fact that investors should care about both the risk and the return of their investments is so commonplace today that it is hard to believe that this view was not appreciated in 1952. Even Keynes (1939) said, "To suppose that safety-first consists in having a small gamble in a large number of different [companies]... strikes me as a travesty of investment policy." Luckily, Keynes was not held in high repute in Chicago, even in those days, and Markowitz was not deterred from his investigations.

Markowitz posed the problem of minimizing the variance of a portfolio taking as a constraint a required expected return. This way of posing the problem contained two significant insights. First, Markowitz realized that the mathematics could not pick out a single optimal portfolio, but rather could only identify a set of *efficient* portfolios—the set of portfolios that had the lowest possible risk for each possible expected return. Secondly, Markowitz recognized that the appropriate risk facing an investor was *portfolio* risk—how much his entire portfolio of risky assets would fluctuate.

Today, we pose the problem of portfolio selection as a quadratic programming problem. The choice variables are the fractions of wealth invested in each of the available risky assets, the quadratic objective function is the variance of return on the resulting portfolio, and the linear constraint is that the expected return of the portfolio achieve some target value. Variables may be subjected to nonnegativity constraints or not, depending on whether short sales are feasible.

The first-order conditions for this quadratic programming problem require that the marginal increase in variance from investing a bit more in a given asset should be proportional to the expected return of that asset. The key insight that arises from this first-order condition is that the marginal increase in variance depends on both the variance of a given asset's return plus the *covariance* of the asset return with all other asset returns in the portfolio.

Markowitz's formulation of portfolio optimization leads quickly to the fundamental point that the riskiness of a stock should not be measured just by the *variance* of the stock, but also by the *covariance*. In fact, if a portfolio is highly diversified, so that the amount invested in any given asset is "small," and the returns on the stocks are highly correlated, then *most* of the marginal risk from increasing the fraction of a given asset in a portfolio is due to this covariance effect.

This was, perhaps, the central insight of Markowitz's contribution to finance. But it is far from the end of the story. As every graduate student knows, the first-order conditions are only the first step in solving an optimization problem. In 1952, linear programming was in its infancy and quadratic programming was not widely known. Nevertheless, Markowitz succeeded in developing practical methods to determine the "critical line" describing mean-variance efficient portfolios. The initial work in his thesis was described in two papers, Markowitz (1952, 1956) and culminated in his classic book (Markowitz, 1959).

When Markowitz defended his dissertation at the University of Chicago, Milton Friedman gave him a hard time, arguing that portfolio theory was not a part of economics, and therefore that Markowitz should not receive a Ph.D. in economics. Markowitz (1991) says, "...this point I am now willing to concede: at the time I defended my dissertation, portfolio theory was not part of Economics. But now it is."

William Sharpe

Markowitz's model of portfolio selection focused only on the choice of *risky* assets. Tobin (1958), motivated by Keynes' theory of liquidity preference, extended the model to include a riskless asset. In doing so, he discovered a surprising fact. The set of efficient risk-return combinations turned out to be a straight line!

The logic of Tobin's discovery can be seen with simple geometry. The hyperbola in Figure 1 depicts the combination of mean returns and standard deviation of returns that can be achieved by the various portfolios of risky assets. Each set of risky assets will generate some such hyperbola depicting the feasible combinations of risk and return.

The risk-free return has a standard deviation of zero, so it can be represented by a point on the vertical axis, $(0, R_0)$. Now make the following geometric construction: draw a line through the point $(0, R_0)$ and rotate it clockwise until it just touches the set of efficient portfolios. Call the point where it touches this line

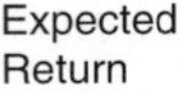
FIGURE 1

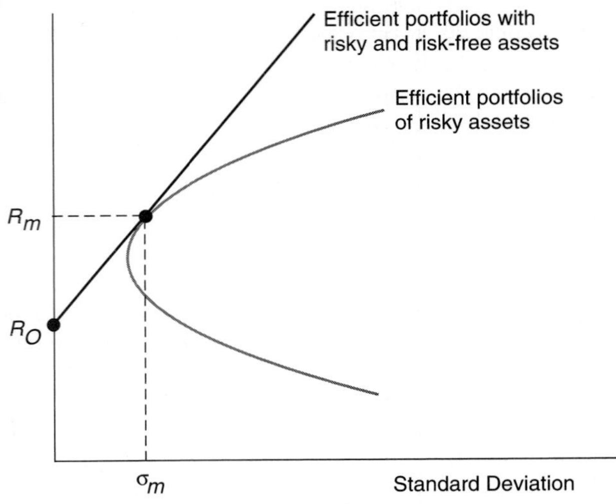

$(\sigma_m, \overline{R}_m)$. Now observe that every efficient portfolio consisting of risky assets and the riskless asset can be achieved by combining only two portfolios—one portfolio consisting only of the risk free asset, and one consisting of the portfolio that yields the risk-return combination $(\sigma_m, \overline{R}_m)$.

For example, if you want an expected return and standard deviation that is halfway between $(0, R_0)$ and $(\sigma_m, \overline{R}_m)$, just put half of your wealth in the risk-free asset and half in the risky portfolio. Points to the right of the risky portfolio can be achieved by leverage: *borrow* money at the rate R_0 and invest it in the risky portfolio.

Tobin's discovery dramatically simplified portfolio selection: his analysis showed the *same* portfolio of risky assets is appropriate for everyone. All that varies is how much money you choose to put in risky assets and how much you choose to put in the riskless asset. Each investor can limit his investment choices to two "mutual funds:" a money market fund that invests only in the riskless asset (e.g., Treasury bills) and another fund that invests only in the magical portfolio that yields $(\sigma_m, \overline{R}_m)$.

But one still needs to determine just which stocks, and which proportions of stocks, comprise the magic portfolio *m*—and that is a difficult and costly computation. The next contribution to portfolio theory was a simplified way to perform this computation. William Sharpe was a doctoral student at UCLA, one of the first students there to take courses in both economics and finance. When it came time to write a thesis, Fred Weston suggested that he talk with Harry Markowitz, who was then at RAND. Markowitz became Sharpe's unofficial thesis advisor and put him to work trying to simplify the computational aspects of portfolio theory.

Sharpe explored an approach now known as the "market model" or the "single factor" model. It assumes that the return on each security is linearly related to a single index, usually taken to be the return on some stock market index such as the S&P 500. Thus the (random) return on asset *a* at time *t* can be written as

$$R_{at} = c + bR_{mt} + \epsilon_{at}$$

where R_{mt} is the return on the S&P 500, say, and ϵ_{at} is an error term with expected value of zero. In this equation *c* is the expected return of the asset if the market is expected to have a zero return, while the parameter *b* measures the sensitivity of the asset to "market conditions." A stock that has $b = 1$ is just as risky as the market index; if the S&P index increases by 10 percent in a given year, we would expect this stock to increase by $c + 10$ percent. A stock that has $b < 1$ is less volatile than the market index, while one with $b > 1$ is more volatile. Sharpe's motivation in formulating this model was empirical: most stocks move together, most of the time. Hence, it is natural to think that a single factor (or small number of factors) determines most of the cross-sectional variation in returns.

This linear relationship can easily be estimated by ordinary least squares, and the estimated coefficients can be used to construct covariances, which, in turn, can be used to construct optimal portfolios. Sharpe's approach reduced the dimensionality of the portfolio problem dramatically and made it much simpler to compute efficient portfolios. Problems that took 33 minutes of computer time using the Markowitz model took only 30 seconds with Sharpe's model. This work led to Sharpe (1963) and a Ph.D. thesis.

Later, while teaching at the University of Washington, Sharpe turned his attention to equilibrium theory in capital markets. Up until this point portfolio theory was a theory of individual behavior—how an individual might choose his investments given the set of available assets.

What would happen, Sharpe asked, if everyone behaved like Markowitz portfolio optimizers? Tobin had shown that everyone would hold the same portfolio of risky assets. If Mr. A had 5 percent of his stock market wealth invested in IBM, then Ms. B should invest 5 percent of *her* stock portfolio in IBM. Of course, they might have different amounts of money invested in the stock market, but each would choose the same portfolio of risky assets. But Sharpe then realized that if everyone held the same portfolio of risky assets, then it would be easy to measure that portfolio: you just need to look at the *total* wealth invested in IBM, say, and divide that by the total wealth in the stock market. The portfolio of risky assets that was optimal for each individual would just be the portfolio of risky assets held by the market.

This insight gave Sharpe an empirical proxy for the risky portfolio in the Tobin analysis: in equilibrium it would simply be the market portfolio. This observation has the important implication that the market portfolio is mean-variance efficient—that is, it lies on the frontier of the efficient set, and therefore satisfies the first-order conditions for efficiency.

Some simple[1] manipulations of those first-order conditions then yield the celebrated Capital Asset Pricing Model (CAPM):

$$\overline{R}_a = R_0 + \beta_a (\overline{R}_m - R_0).$$

In words, the expected return on any asset *a* is the risk-free rate plus the risk premium. The risk premium is the "beta" of the asset *a* times the expected excess return on the market portfolio.

The "beta" of an asset turns out to be the covariance of that asset's return with the market return divided by the variance of the market return. This is simply the theoretical regression coefficient between the return on asset *a* and the market return, a result remarkably consistent with the single-factor model proposed in Sharpe's thesis.

Meanwhile, back on the east coast, Jack Treynor and John Lintner were independently discovering the same fundamental pricing equation of the CAPM. Treynor's work was never published; Sharpe (1964) and Lintner (1965) remain the classical citations for the CAPM.

The Capital Asset Pricing Model was truly a revolutionary discovery for financial economics. It is a prime example of how to take a theory of individual optimizing behavior and aggregate it to determine equilibrium pricing relationships. Furthermore, since the demand for an asset inevitably depends on the prices of all assets, due to the nature of the portfolio optimization problem, it is inherently a *general* equilibrium theory.

Sharpe's two major contributions, the single factor model and the CAPM, are often confused. The first is a "supply side" model of how returns are generated; the second is a "demand side" model. The models can hold independently, or separately, and both are used in practice.

Subsequent research has relaxed many of the conditions of the original CAPM (like unlimited short sales) and provided some qualifications about the empirical observables of the model. Sharpe (1991) provides a brief review of these points. Despite these qualifications, the CAPM still reigns as one of the fundamental achievements of financial economics, taught in every finance textbook and intermediate microeconomics text.[2]

Merton Miller

In 1990 Merton Miller was named a Distinguished Fellow of the American Economic Association in honor of his many contributions. He has worked on a variety of topics in economics and finance, but the idea singled out by the Nobel Committee was one of his early papers on corporate finance. Portfolio theory and the CAPM focus on the behavior of the demanders of securities—the individual investors. Corporate finance focuses on the suppliers of the securities—the corporations that issue stocks and bonds.

---

[1] Sharpe's proof of the CAPM was given in a footnote.

[2] Or at least, the good ones.

Merton Miller joined Carnegie Tech in 1952 to teach economic history and public finance. In 1956, the dean asked Miller to teach corporate finance in the business school. At first Miller wasn't interested, since finance was then viewed as being a bit too grubby for an economist to dabble in. But after appropriate inducements, Miller sat in on the corporate finance class in the fall and started to teach it the following term.

One of the major issues in corporate finance, then and now, was how to raise capital in the best way. Broadly speaking a firm can issue new equity or new debt to raise money. Each has its advantages and disadvantages: issuing debt increases the fixed costs of the firm, while issuing equity dilutes the shares of the existing shareholders. There were lots of rules of thumb about when to do one and when to do the other. Miller started to look at some data to see if he could determine how corporate financial structure affected firms' values.

He found, much to his surprise, that there was no particular relationship between financial structure and firm value. Some firms had a lot of debt; some had a lot of equity, but there didn't appear to be much of a pattern in terms of how the debt-equity ratio affected market value.

It has been seriously suggested that there should be a *Journal of Negative Results* which could contain reports of all those regressions with insignificant regression coefficients and abysmal R-squares. If such a journal had existed, Miller might well have published his findings there. But there was no such journal, so Miller had to think about *why* there might be no relationship between capital structure and firm value.

Franco Modigliani, whose office was next to Miller's, had been working on some of the same issues from the theoretical side. He was concerned with providing microeconomic foundations for Keynesian models of investment. Building on previous work by Durand (1952), Modigliani had sketched out some models of financial structure that seemed to imply that there was no preferred capital structure. Miller and Modigliani joined forces, and the world of corporate finance has never been the same.

Miller and Modigliani considered a simple world without taxes or transaction costs and showed that in such a world, the value of a firm would be independent of its capital structure. Their argument was a novel application of the arbitrage principle, or the law of one price. Since the MM theorem has been described at least twice in this journal (Miller, 1988; Varian, 1987), I will give only a very brief outline of the theorem.

The easiest way to think about the MM theorem, in my view, is that it is a consequence of value additivity. Consider any portfolio of assets. Then value additivity says that the value of the portfolio must be the sum of the values of the assets that make it up. At first, this principle seems to contradict the insights of Markowitz about portfolio diversification: certainly an asset should be worth more combined in a portfolio with other assets than it is standing alone due to the benefits of diversification.

But the point is that asset values in a well-functioning securities market *already* reflect the value achievable by portfolio optimization. This is the chief insight of the Capital Asset Pricing Model: the equilibrium value of an asset depends on how it covaries with other assets, not on its risk as a stand-alone investment.

In any event, the principle of value additivity is even more fundamental than the Capital Asset Pricing Model, since it rests solely on arbitrage considerations. If a slice of bread and a piece of ham were worth more together as a sandwich than separately, everyone would buy bread and ham and make sandwiches—for a free lunch! The excess demand for bread and ham would push up the price of each, restoring the equilibrium relationship that the value of the whole has to be the sum of the value of the parts.

From this observation, the MM theorem follows quickly. The value of the firm is defined to be the sum of the values of its debt and its equity. If the firm could increase its value by changing how much of its cash flow is paid to bondholders and how much to stockholders, any individual investor could construct a free lunch. The investor would buy a fraction f of the outstanding stocks and the same fraction f of the outstanding bonds which would give him a fraction f of the total cash flow. He could then repackage this cash flow in the same way as the firm could, thereby increasing the value of the total portfolio—and violating value additivity.

This sort of "home-made leverage" argument is one way to prove the MM theorem. But it is a particularly powerful way since it doesn't appeal to any particular model of consumer or firm behavior. It rests solely on the principle of arbitrage—there can be no free lunches in equilibrium.

The theory of the MM proposition is solidly established. The controversies all arise from the assumption of a frictionless world: in particular, no costs to bankruptcy, no asymmetric information, and no taxes. The latter is probably more important than the former. In the United States, at least, interest payments on debt are tax deductible while dividends to shareholders are taxed at both the corporate and individual level.

Since the MM proposition showed that debt and equity were perfect substitutes in the absence of taxes, the favorable tax treatment given to debt should imply that all firms are 100 percent debt-financed. This is contrary to fact—although for a while in the 1980s it looked as though it might come true. Miller (1988), and the comments on this article by Bhattacharya, Modigliani, Ross, and Stiglitz, describe the current state of research on the MM theorem. Suffice it to say that there is still doubt about exactly which frictions are the most relevant ones.

I happened to have lunch with Merton Miller in October 1990, the weekend before the Nobel prize winners were announced. Part of the lunchtime conversation was devoted to speculation about who might win the Nobel Prize in Economics that year. Mert thought that someone from Chicago might well receive the prize that year, and he suggested a few worthy possibilities—his own name not among them, of course. He was awarded the Nobel prize two days later. His 1990 forecast was a bit like the MM theorem itself—it was right in principle, but the details were a little off!

Summary

In reviewing the work of these three economists, we see a common thread of theory and empiricism running through their research. It isn't enough just to formulate a theory of portfolio choice—you've got to find a feasible way to compute optimal portfolios as well. It isn't enough to formulate a theory of capital market equilibrium—the theory should be estimated and tested. It isn't enough just to look at a scatterplot of firm values and debt-equity ratios—we need a theory for why there should or should not be a relationship among these variables.

Financial economics has been so successful because of this fruitful relationship between theory and data. Many of the same people who formulated the theories also collected and analyzed the data. This is a model that the rest of the economics profession would do well to emulate.

References

Bernstein, P., *Capital Ideas.* New York: The Free Press, 1992.

Durand, D., "Costs of debt and equity funds for business: Trends and problems of measurement," *Conference on Research in Business Finance,* 215–47. New York: National Bureau of Economic Research, 1952.

Keynes, J. M., "Memorandum for the estates committee," Kings College, Cambridge, May 8, 1939. In Moggridge, D., *Collected Writings of John Maynard Keynes, Vol. XII,* 66–68. New York: Cambridge University Press, 1983.

Lintner, J., "The valuation of risky assets and the selection of risky investments in stock portfolios and capital budgets," *Review of Economics and Statistics,* February 1965, 47, 13–37.

Markowitz, H., "Portfolio selection," *The Journal of Finance,* March 1952, 7, 77–91.

Markowitz, H., "The Optimization of a Quadratic Function Subject to Linear Constraints," *Naval Research Logistics Quarterly,* 1956, 3.

Markowitz, H., *Portfolio Selection: Efficient Diversification of Investment.* New York: Wiley, 1959.

Markowitz, H., "Foundations of portfolio theory," *Journal of Finance,* June 1991, 46, 469–77.

Merton, R., *Continuous Time Finance.* Oxford: Basil Blackwell, 1990.

Miller, M., "The Modigliani-Miller propositions after thirty years," *Journal of Economic Perspective,* Fall 1988, 2:4, 99–120.

Miller, M., "Leverage," *Journal of Finance,* June 1991, 46, 479–88.

Sharpe, W., "A simplified model for portfolio analysis," *Management Science,* 1963, 9, 277–93.

Sharpe, W., "Capital asset prices: A theory of market equilibrium under conditions of risk," *Journal of Finance,* September 1964, 19, 425–42.

Sharpe, W., "Capital asset prices with and without negative holdings," *Journal of Finance,* June 1991, 46, 489–509.

Tobin, J., "Liquidity preference as behavior towards risk," *Review of Economic Studies,* February 1958, 25, 65–86.

Varian, H., "The arbitrage principle in financial economics," *Journal of Economic Perspectives,* Fall 1987, 1:2, 55–72.

Williams, J. B., *The Theory of Investment Value,* Cambridge: Harvard University Press, 1938.

Questions

1. Harry Markowitz says, "...this point I am now willing to concede: at the time I defended my dissertation, portfolio theory was not part of Economics. But now it is." Describe *portfolio theory*, Markowitz's principal contribution to financial economics.
2. Describe each of the following steps in Harry Markowitz's reasoning:
   - The value of a common stock is the *expected* present value of its dividend stream.
   - Investors care not only about the expected return on their wealth, but also about the risk.
   - Efficient portfolios have the lowest possible risk for each possible expected return.
   - The relevant risk facing an investor is *portfolio* risk.
   - The riskiness of a common stock is not measured just by *variance* of the stock, but also by *covariance* of the stock with all other stocks in the portfolio.
3. James Tobin extended Harry Markowitz's model of portfolio selection to include a *riskless asset*. In doing so, he discovered a surprising result. Use Figure 1 to explain Tobin's discovery.
4. William Sharpe developed the *market model* to simplify the computations of portfolio theory. The key estimate of the market model is the coefficient of R_{mt}, denoted as b and called the *beta coefficient*, or more simply, *beta*. What does beta mean? Why is beta a useful measure of risk?
5. William Sharpe developed the *capital asset pricing model* (CAPM), which identifies the risky portfolio in James Tobin's analysis as the *market portfolio*. The relevant measure of risk in Sharpe's CAPM is beta (often estimated using historical rates of return in the market model).
   a. Define the following CAPM variables: $\overline{R}_a$, R_0, $\overline{R}_m$, and β_a.
   b. Prior to development of the CAPM, risk premiums were based largely on judgment and intuition. How is the risk premium of a common stock calculated according to the CAPM?
   c. Draw a graphic representation of the CAPM, placing *expected return* on the vertical axis and *beta* on the horizontal axis. (*Hint:* The relationship between $\overline{R}_a$ and β_a is a straight line intersecting the vertical axis at R_0.)
6. Merton Miller and his colleague Franco Modigliani imagined a simple world without taxes or transaction costs. What is MM's conclusion about a corporation's capital structure in this imaginary world? How does the introduction of corporate taxation to this imaginary world change MM's conclusion? Why?
7. "If a slice of bread and a piece of ham were worth more together as a sandwich than separately, everyone would buy bread and ham and make sandwiches—for a free lunch! The excess demand for bread and ham would push up the price of each, restoring the equilibrium relationship that the value of the whole has to be the sum of the value of the parts." Explain how this observation relates to MM's conclusion on corporate capital structure in the imaginary world.

Markets and Morality

HARRY M. MARKOWITZ

There are many obvious ways in which a society's rules of right and wrong influence the quality of life it provides. Where littering is not almost universally frowned upon, all live in a world of litter. Where "excuse me" and "thank you" are passé, all live in a rude world.

The consequences of rules of right and wrong are sometimes subtler. A few years ago a friend of mine in the financial industries asked me to have dinner with him and a Russian émigré mathematician he was thinking of hiring. It was the time when Gorbachev's policies seemed to promise to save the U.S.S.R. and the world. I was disturbed to hear the Russian mathematician predict that the Gorbachev reforms would not succeed.

"The basic problem is the Russian people's attitude toward profit," he explained. "If there are goods one place that are needed someplace else, and if someone makes a profit moving these goods from the one place to the other, he is considered greedy and evil. They do not ask 'what is it that will make these goods move from where they are to where they are needed?'"

In fact the Gorbachev reforms did not succeed. The Soviet economy crumbled despite its great and varied resources. The distribution system, in particular, performed abysmally. When economic collapse had proceeded far enough, Gorbachev took drastic action: He froze bank accounts, causing much distress among those who had managed to save anything.

The purpose of this harsh move was to frustrate those Gorbachev believed, or said he believed, were the true culprits: The blackmarketeers! Thus in Gorbachev's mind, or at least in his words to the Soviet people, the source of the Soviet ill was the greedy, evil people who seek to benefit from the misfortunes of others by moving goods from where they are to where they are needed, not out of altruism but out of avarice.

At the time of this writing, Harry M. Markowitz was the Marvin Speiser Distinguished Professor of Finance and Economics at Baruch College, City University of New York, in New York. This article is a slightly modified version of the Robert Weintraub Memorial Lecture delivered at Baruch College on April 17, 1991.

My own views are much closer to the gospel according to Adam Smith. In a free market each economic entity—each individual or firm—seeks to buy cheaply what it needs and sell dearly what it has. It does so in pursuit of its own self interest. According to the McDonald's commercial, "They do it all for you." But everyone over five years old knows they do it for their own profit.

The force that keeps McDonald's adapting its menus to changing consumer tastes, and keeps it from setting its prices astronomically high, is the fact that customers can go elsewhere: Buy a Burger King, make themselves a peanut butter and jelly sandwich, or whatever. The fact that many hope to make a decent living, or even an obscene fortune, as restaurant owners induces them to open restaurants of various kinds: fast food franchises; pricey French restaurants; big and small, cheap and expensive Chinese, Mexican, Indian, Italian, diner and deli and sandwich shop. Some succeed; some struggle and fold. In this way, Adam Smith's "invisible hand" distributes restaurants of various sorts, throughout big cities, small towns, suburbs, and here and there in the countryside.

While it is at it, it does the same for pharmacies, dry cleaners, small and large grocery stores, small and large department stores, clothing stores of great variety, and so on. All are there because they seek their own well-being. But to profit from me, the consumer, they must seek to please me; otherwise I will buy my groceries or my hi-fi or my car from a competitor.

Admittedly, the invisible hand can be clumsy. It beckons far too many people to each new fad. Even where no laws are broken, or laws are strictly enforced, the invisible hand can be unfair; it does not necessarily reward the nicest and punish the meanest, but rewards the person who can best hit a baseball, move an audience, or produce an acceptable product at the lowest price. The invisible hand is heartless, sometimes abandoning regions and occupations that are no longer needed or, at least, no longer needed at the levels at which they once thrived.

But, comparing East Germany with West Germany, Eastern Europe with Western Europe, Taiwan and Hong Kong with mainland China, many have come to agree with those of us who read Adam Smith years ago and were persuaded. Markets are smarter than bureaucrats. Granted that the invisible hand is clumsy, heartless, and unfair, it is ever so much more deft and impartial than a central planning committee.

My own deep conviction about this flows from several sources. Partly it came from reading Adam Smith; partly it came from arguing with my economics professor, Milton Friedman, then deciding that, for the most part, he was right; and partly it came from a lifetime of struggling with the use of computers and analysis to help humans make decisions. Much progress has been made in the field or fields that address such problems, variously called systems analysis, operations research, management science, artificial intelligence, decision systems, and normative economics. The computer can play a great game of chess; it can help manage a portfolio or analyze a manufacturing facility. But no way is it ready to run an economy.

I am therefore disappointed that Gorbachev did not give market economics a chance. I am hopeful that Yeltsin will do so if he has the opportunity: that he will quickly move to allow markets to set prices, and allow individuals to become wealthy, even wealthier than a commissar, provided they do so, not by fraud, collusion, or coercion, but by persuading others to buy their goods and services.

They should even be allowed to become wealthy by performing the arbitrage function of moving goods from where they are to where they are most needed, as long as they do not attempt to prevent others from doing the same. More generally, they should be allowed to become wealthy by buying things, or contracting to buy things, in places, times or forms where they are cheap and selling the same or similar things in places, times and forms where they are dear, again provided that they not restrain others from doing the same.

A Blanket Condemnation

I am also disappointed by the indiscriminate way in which many Americans use the accusation of "greed" as an explanation of economic events. For example, when the Persian Gulf war broke out, many Americans accused the oil companies of greed in raising gasoline prices before they used up their inventories of prewar oil. A New York politician recently expressed continued indignation at the rise in gasoline prices that occurred during the Gulf war, and even suggested that there be legislation to outlaw substantial price rises during supply disruptions.

I personally doubt that the oil companies chose the start of the Gulf war as a time to collude: to call each other and say "Let's use the war as an excuse to fix prices at a high level." I believe that each figured, either intuitively or by formal calculation, that the present value of their profits would be greatest if they did not continue to sell cheaply what they would have to replace dearly. The resulting rise in prices was the market's signal to the consumer that he or she should conserve.

As to the windfall gain reaped by oil companies and others who held oil when the Gulf war broke out, I believe that this windfall should be viewed as follows: The holding of oil is a risky investment. Sometimes holders of oil experience windfall gains, sometimes windfall losses. If, on average, the returns from holding oil more than compensate the holders for the risks they incur, then oil companies, speculators, and others would increase their holdings, thus setting aside oil for the future.

In the case of oil companies, and others in the oil business, holdings of oil are also part of working inventories. Because I believe that Adam Smith's invisible hand is ever so much more deft than central planners, I argue that each participant should be allowed to choose the level of oil stock he, she, or it thinks best for it. Windfall gains are part of the returns to the business, windfall losses are part of its costs. Leave it to the invisible hand to assure a reasonable allocation of resources partly by tempting resources into areas where profits, on average, are greater than elsewhere considering the risks involved.

Among those who consider the existence of "greed" to be an adequate explanation of economic ills, the oil companies are considered as saints as compared to the greedies who roam Wall Street. For example, the cover of *Liar's Poker*, a book about Salomon Brothers by Michael Lewis, shows a dollar bill with a picture of John Gutfreund, head of Salomon. Inscriptions on the dollar include

"In Gutfreund We Trust" and "Wall Street Greed." The back cover of Connie Bruck's book, *Predators' Ball*, about Drexel and Milken, excerpts a *New York Times* book review. According to the review, "The *Predators' Ball* dramatically captures the philosophy of greed that has dominated Wall Street in the 1980s." More generally, when one hears of the "greedy generation" one is supposed to equate this with the yuppies of the 1980s, especially those associated with the financial industries.

This blanket condemnation of "the greedies" of the 1980s fails to distinguish between those who committed crimes and those who simply pursued their own self-interest well within legal boundaries. Included in the latter, law-abiding class of participants, for example, are some very bright "rocket scientists" who used statistics and option pricing theory to develop mortgage products that, quite usefully, brought new sources of funds into the home mortgage market, as well as handsome profits into their own pockets.

The blanket condemnation of the "greedies" of the 1980s fails to distinguish between the complaint that too many people sought to maximize their own well-being, as Adam Smith would have us all do, legally, and the complaint that too much leverage was used in the 1980s. If the latter is the true complaint, blanket condemnation of "the greedies" fails to ask whether the reason for excess leverage was the fact that slick salespeople disguised the true risks of the junk bonds they sold. Or was it the fact that unwise laws structured institutions so that they were induced, and sometimes compelled, to take high risks?

Specifically, by the early 1980s many savings and loans were in bad shape because they had been structured to borrow short term and lend long term. Their short-term borrowings were called customer deposits, and their long-term lending included home mortgages; whatever the names or forms of the instruments, the S&Ls were set up to play the very risky game of borrowing short term and lending long term. The riskiness of this structure became apparent in the late 1970s when the short-term rates at which they borrowed rose above the long-term rates at which they had lent. Many became essentially bankrupt.

New legislation then sought to solve S&L problems by letting them "grow" out of them. It let them attract money by offering high rates and then let them invest this money at still higher rates. These high-yielding investments were mostly in real estate and partly in junk bonds. These were risky investments. Because of deposit insurance, the S&Ls could gamble with little risk to themselves. If they won, they kept the winnings. If they lost, the U.S. taxpayer paid most of the losses. As it turned out, frequently they lost.

Thus, even if S&L management had kept scrupulously within the law, and had acted purely in the interest of their institutions, the S&L debacle was inevitable. I agree we should pursue those who broke the laws. But I do not ascribe the S&L mess to a more widespread pursuit of self-interest during the 1980s than in the 1970s or 1960s or even in the 1770s when Adam Smith first published. Adam Smith said that we all pursue our self-interest. He did not say that the invisible hand would work when one person makes the decisions and gets the gains while another bears the cost. In particular it will not work if one party, in the present case S&L management, places the bets and collects the winnings if any, while another party, the U.S. taxpayer, pays the losses.

The blanket condemnation of the greedies of the 1980s blurs other important distinctions. It lumps together people who were remarkably stingy with those who were remarkably generous, either with public donations to good causes or with quiet private help to others in need. It lumps together those whose sole interest in life was the winning of the finance game, as measured by their accumulating wealth, and those who played the game well, accumulated fortunes, but found time for other interests.

It lumps together those who committed well-defined crimes and who deserved the punishment they got, and perhaps more, with those who were arrested conspicuously, left waiting for the next round of charges, then had their cases dropped as all a big mistake; and those whose crimes had been civil offenses before, but now were elevated to criminal offenses—by the prosecutors; and those whose connection with inside information was so remote as hardly to admit of insider trading, and so said the Supreme Court in one crucial case, but still they are part of the list of indictments and some convictions that prosecutors claim as their trophies.

All these the blanket condemnation smears with one ugly green stain as the greedy generation of the 1980s. I would like to examine some of these distinctions more closely, partly in fairness to many in the financial industries in the 1980s, and partly as a possible guide to those who plan to be associated with the financial industries in the future. But before that I would like to correct two misimpressions that I may be giving.

First, because much of my discussion concerns making money, you may think that I think that maximizing well-being is the same as maximizing wealth. This is not so. Economic theory describes the economic individual as maximizing "utility." As the world is uncertain, he or she is assumed to maximize *expected* utility. "Utility" is another name for well-being, quantified in a certain manner.

In economic theory it is sometimes convenient to assume that an individual's utility depends only on the amount he or she spends on consumption. But this is not necessary in theory, nor true in fact. I believe that most find, as I do, that once some moderate needs for food and shelter are satisfied, utility depends more on how you spend your time than on how much money you make. If a person hated to sell vacuum cleaners and loved to carve wooden ducks, and could make a fortune doing the former and a decent living doing the latter, then the person's utility would be maximized as a duck carver, not in selling vacuums.

As for myself, I find that I get a great deal of pleasure out of the vain game of trying to discover research results that others would pay attention to. Fortunately, there has always been someone willing to pay me at least a living wage to do just that.

The maximization of expected utility has many more dimensions than this rough sketch attempts to outline. I just want to make the point that the level of one's wealth is but one of these dimensions and, beyond a point, perhaps one of the less important ones.

A second misimpression I would like to correct is this. Because I have emphasized the efficacy of markets as compared to bureaucrats, you may think I think that markets can run themselves without the aid of laws and law enforcement. This is not the case. Laws and law enforcement are needed to assure me that the meal I buy at the restaurant is not poisoned, and the airplane I fly on is well-maintained; that vendors who wish me to buy from them do so by inducing me, not coercing me, and they allow others to do the same; that those who manufacture things for my use pay their full costs, including the costs of cleaning up the mess they make; that if I deposit money with a bank or pay a premium to an insurance company the banker or insurance company owner will not, literally or figuratively, go to Las Vegas to gamble with my money.

These two things now said, I would like to return to the alleged greedies of the 1980s. I feel that we should draw distinctions that the blanket condemnation blurs. For one, we should distinguish between illegal behavior and the pursuit of one's welfare within the law. For another, we should distinguish between areas where the financial markets worked quite well and brought us products of great value, as compared to areas where the markets seemed to fail us. In the latter case we should consider whether the failure is because Adam Smith's invisible hand is unable to function well when the entities to be bought and sold involve debt, equity, companies, and pieces of companies. Or is the market failure attributable to illegal behavior, or to legal behavior within unwise laws?

I would like to organize my remarks around two product areas of major importance in the 1980s. One is mortgage bond products as pioneered at Salomon Brothers; the other is junk bonds, that is, high-yield high-risk bonds, whose market was dominated by Milken at Drexel.

Liar's Poker

Liar's Poker is the story of Salomon Brothers, especially Salomon Brothers in the 1980s, as told by Michael Lewis, a young man who entered Salomon Brothers early in 1985 as a trainee, and left it three years later when he decided that making *that* much money wasn't *that* important. When he speaks generally, he speaks of the greed that permeated and dominated Salomon Brothers. When he describes specific individuals and actions, we find that some are mean and some are kind, some are stingy and others generous, some you can trust and some you cannot. Indeed, laying aside the pace of the trading floor and the dollar amounts being dealt with, the individuals described seem no more or less than human, as one might find in any large organization, even a university.

Lewis considers his to be a tale of greed. I view the same events and find in them the triumph of two great ideas: The first is Adam Smith's invisible hand at its clumsy but beneficent best; and the second is option pricing theory as first developed by Black and Scholes, and by Robert Merton, and as applied and enhanced by the "rocket scientists" whom Salomon Brothers had gathered. I will attempt a thumbnail sketch of some of the major forces and events that Mr. Lewis describes and explain my view of them.

Mr. Lewis was one of 127 to enter the Salomon Brothers' 1985 training program, then its largest training class to date. The class that followed was "twice as large again." Many more applied, but were not accepted into the program. Salomon Brothers was not the only investment bank that attracted applicants. Mr. Lewis tells us that "Forty percent of the thirteen hundred members of Yale's graduating class of 1986 applied to one investment bank, First Boston, alone." So, as the prospect of great gains had sent the forty-niners rushing to California one-hundred-and-some-years before, the new seekers of fortune sought to mine the gold of Wall Street.

The mortgage-backed bond did not become a great source of profit for Salomon Brothers until the 1980s, but its cause was championed within Salomon Brothers by Bob Dall as early as 1977. By February 1979, Lewie Ranieri, who started in the mailroom but was by then an energetic trader and salesman, was officially placed in charge of mortgage operations. In the early days the problem was marketing, convincing potential suppliers of the mortgages that would back the bonds and potential buyers of the bonds that the mortgage bond was in each of their interests. Ranieri traveled the country with his message, sometimes crossing paths with Mike Milken, who was in the process of convincing institutions of the value of lowly rated, high-yield bonds.

Eventually the mortgage bond business blossomed, thanks in part to a tax break that Congress passed in September 1981. This tax break made it highly desirable for S&Ls to sell their old mortgages, now at a loss because of the rise in interest rates, and use the proceeds for other investments, even the mortgages sold by other S&Ls.

In the following years the mortgage bond market continued to grow. It also changed character. Lewis quotes Samuel Sachs, longtime mortgage bond salesman, as saying, "They wheeled in the rocket scientists, who started to carve up mortgages into itty-bitty pieces. The market became more than the five things that Lewie [Ranieri] could hold in his brain at any one time."

One problem with mortgage bonds from an investor's viewpoint is that individual mortgage borrowers have the right to pay down or pay off their mortgages. They are more inclined to do so if interest rates fall so they can refinance at lower rates. Thus the mortgage pool that backs a mortgage bond can shrink in an unpredictable way. It is impossible to compute an exact maturity or duration for the pool or the bond.

Worse, the bond will pay down at the wrong time, when interest rates fall, so that the bondholder must reinvest this return of capital at lower rates. The interest rate that the investor should insist upon before investing in mortgage bonds should reflect the value of the *option* that the individual mortgage borrowers have for paying off their mortgages at their discretion. It is no trivial matter to evaluate this option.

The Collateralized Mortgage Obligation, or CMO, was invented at Salomon and First Boston to help deal with this basic problem. A given CMO is backed by a pool of hundreds of millions of dollars worth of ordinary mortgage bonds. The CMO issues certificates to its investors, but not all with the same claims to the interest and principal payments from the mortgage pool. The certificates are divided into what are called "tranches." The rights of the different tranches vary from one CMO to another.

A fairly simple one might work as follows: All mortgage prepayments go to the first tranche until that tranche is completely paid off; they then go to the second tranche until that one is paid off; and finally to a last, third tranche. In some CMOs, all tranches receive interest payments; in other CMOs some tranches receive interest only (referred to as IOs), whereas others receive principal only (called POs). There is still no certainty of exact dates of payoff, but investors can choose among tranches with longer or shorter duration, and with interest only, principal only, or both.

Lewis tells us that sixty billion dollars worth of CMOs were sold between June 1983 and January 1988. This money, which came from investors abroad as well as in the United States, was used to finance U.S. home mortgages.

Lewis contrasts the refinement of analysis that lay behind some mortgage products with the crudeness of some of the traders who bought and sold these products. "For each step forward in market technology [the mortgage product traders] took a step backward in human evolution. As their number grew from six to twenty-five, they became louder, ruder, fatter, and less concerned with their relations with the rest of the firm."

My own view is that the fact that the invisible hand could work its magic through mere humans is an essential part of Adam Smith's insight. Not many thousands of years ago, men like this would have clubbed each other over hunting rights. A few hundreds of years ago they would have hacked each other with axes and swords. Now they yelled at trainees while they sat at the hub of a vast communications network and brought together the supply and demand of home mortgages on a worldwide scale.

Lewis tells us that as mortgage products became more complex "inevitably Ranieri fell out of touch....The trading risks were managed by mere tykes, a few months out of a training program, who happened to know more about Ginnie Mae 8 percent IOs than anyone else in the firm. That a newcomer... should all of a sudden be an expert wasn't particularly surprising, since the bonds in question might have been invented only a month before.... Part of the reason young people got rich was that the 1980s was a period of constant change. A young brain leaped at the chance to know something his superiors did not. The older people were too busy clearing their desktops to stay at the frontiers of innovations."

At first, Salomon Brothers had a great advantage over other investment banks in the mortgage product area. This advantage was temporary, no matter what Salomon Brothers did, as it could maintain no monopoly over bright young people with a knowledge of statistics and math. As it was, its own policies facilitated the spread of competition. Bright young people could see that they were bringing millions of dollars of profit to Salomon Brothers, and felt that their annual bonuses should reflect this. This conflicted with Salomon caps on bonuses as a function of how long the person had been there.

As Lewis describes it, "Now, a peach-fuzzed youth (from Gutfreund's perspective) would emerge from the firm's training program, be sent to chase a new opportunity in the mortgage market, reap tens of millions of dollars in profits, and then demand a cut of what he had produced. Gutfreund had no intention of paying anyone 'a cut.' He entertained a notion that X was enough, and his notion was rooted in an era when paying a million dollars to a second-year trader was unthinkable."

But other investment banks were delighted to bid away many of Salomon Brothers' young stars. As other investment banks built their own capabilities, customers gained the ability to shop around. Profit margins narrowed in mortgage products, as they had earlier for equities when fixed commission rates were abolished.

In short, I take the story of mortgage products at Salomon as an example of Adam Smith's thesis, that individuals seeking their own self-interest through the marketplace will promote the common good, even if some of them are fat, loud, and rude.

The Predators' Ball

Now let us turn to the junk bond market under Milken at Drexel. I find Connie Bruck's detailed account of the Milken era quite plausible, and will use it as my principal source of facts concerning Milken activities.

In the 1980s Milken engaged in illegal behavior and near-illegal behavior, not just on rare occasions of compliance lapses, but as a regular part of doing business. Part of this illegal and near-illegal behavior had, as its purpose, the suppression of competition in the junk bond business.

For example, in 1985 the board of directors of Wickes decided to do a debt underwriting through Salomon Brothers, who had been trying to break into the junk bond business. After Milken learned of the forthcoming underwriting, Saul Steinberg, a close associate of Milken, accumulated 10.4% of Wickes' stock, and duly reported this to the SEC. Then Milken had a Saturday breakfast meeting with Sandy Sigoloff, president of Wickes. According to a Wickes director, "Mike told Sandy what Saul held, what Drexel had, and how, when you combined that with whatever other pockets Mike might have placed stock in, it meant they would have control of the company." In the next few days Drexel became comanager and then sole manager of the Wickes underwriting.

Ms. Bruck notes that if Steinberg, Drexel, and perhaps "other pockets" did plan to act in concert, they were in violation of securities laws by not filing with the SEC as a group. Ms. Bruck provides other examples of what she describes as "the brass-knuckles, threatening, market-manipulating Cosa Nostra of the securities world." (Lorraine Spurge has sent me a quite different account of this Wickes underwriting. See the appendix.)

A small part of Milken's illegal or near-illegal activities involved his association with Ivan Boesky. My dictionary defines greed as "excessive or reprehensible acquisitiveness." The word is so overworked that I hesitate to use it. But it does seem that Milken was as excessively acquisitive as one could get, and Boesky about as reprehensible.

Because Boesky is usually associated with words "greed," "insider trading," and "arbitrageur," I cannot resist saying a few words in defense of the perfectly respectable business of doing arbitrage. I must confess that this is in part self-defense, because for three years I was in the arbitrage business.

In "index arbitrage," as an example, the arbitrageur looks for times when the price of a "futures contract" for a stock index is out of line with the appropriate sum of prices of the individual stocks that make up the index. The arbitrageur then buys the one and shorts the other. (To short means to sell—not sell something you own but something you borrow for the duration of the short position.)

When prices of the futures contract and the individual stocks come back into line, or at the expiration of the futures contract, the positions are closed out. If no problem is encountered in executing the in and out trades, then a profit is assured. In normal times the existence of arbitrage keeps the corresponding prices from drifting too far out of line with each other. (October 19, 1987, is an example of not normal times.) Currency arbitrage is an older form of arbitrage, which keeps the rate at which you can trade yen for dollars, dollars for pounds, and pounds for yen from becoming too inconsistent.

The arbitrage fund that I managed from 1969 to 1972 watched for times when a convertible bond was undervalued as compared to the stock it could be converted into, according to our model. We bought the bond and shorted the stock in sufficient amount so we were not concerned with whether the price of the stock rose or fell, but only that the bond stop being undervalued as compared to the stock. The possibility of convertible arbitrage, and arbitrage involving stocks and options, which became more common after I left the business in 1972, helps keep the prices of related securities from wandering too far out of line.

Index, currency, convertible, and option arbitrageurs play their arbitrage games for the profit of their clients, their firms, or their own accounts but, in any case, for their own profit. We can still ask, "Do they nevertheless serve a social purpose?" Their purpose is a subtler version of the purpose served by the Soviet blackmarketeers who sought profit by moving goods from where they were to where they were needed.

Imagine that a quarter did not necessarily sell for twenty-five pennies nor a dollar for one hundred pennies, but that four quarters could always be exchanged (eventually) for a dollar and vice versa. Then arbitrageurs would watch for moments when quarters could be traded for dollars via pennies at other than an exact four-to-one ratio, and would take advantage of this discrepancy by buying the relatively underpriced one and selling the overpriced one. This would tend to keep prices in line. It would also supply quarters to the marketplace when greater demand made their price relatively high, and absorb them when lesser demand made it relatively low.

Admittedly, this may seem like a rather fussy fine-tuning of the price system. It seems, at least to me, to be a good thing rather than a bad one to have prices of related things be closely linked, and to have a bit more supply of what is momentarily in greater demand, and a bit more demand for what is momentarily in greater supply.

So far I have not discussed the kind of arbitrage that Boesky practiced, called merger arbitrage or risk arbitrage. A simplified example will serve to illustrate. Suppose that Company A agrees to buy Company B, and B agrees to be bought. At the time of the discussions between A and B, A's stock sells for $150 per share, B's for $100 per share. A agrees to exchange one share of its $150 stock for each share of B's $100 stock. Upon the announcement of the deal, let us assume that A's stock stays at $150 while B's rises to $140.

If you owned neither stock, and you were sure that the deal would go through, you could assure yourself a $10 profit by shorting (that is, selling) one share of A at $150 and buying one share of B at $140. When the deal goes through, your share of B would become a share of A, which you would use to cover your short position.

This procedure is safer than just buying a share of B because, in a falling market for example, the price of both A and B might fall, so the share of B would be worth less than $140 even if the deal goes through. With the arbitrage, i.e., with the selling of A at $150 and the buying of B at $140 right from the start, you have the $10 profit when the share of A is exchanged for the share of B, no matter what their prices at the time of the exchange.

There is one risk, however. Sometimes deals do not go through. Suppose that happens to the A–B deal when you've already sold A at $150 and bought B at $140. B will fall in price, say, down to $110. (It probably won't fall all the way back to $100 because of the prospect of other acquisition talks.) Suppose A's price stays at $150. Then you will have lost $30 where you thought you would make $10.

It is clear what a great value inside information would be for merger arbitrageurs. First, if they knew of the A–B acquisition before it was announced they could buy B at $100 (without bothering to short A, because the rise in B's stock because of the announcement would almost surely be greater than any fall due to moves in the market). Second, if merger arbitrageurs had set up a short-long A–B hedge and learned that the deal would fall through, they could close out the hedge before this was announced. Thus inside information is very valuable to the merger arbitrageur, but it is not legal to act upon. It is much less likely that any kind of inside information would be of value to other sorts of arbitrageurs.

The proposition, "Inside information is especially useful to merger arbitrageurs," does not imply the proposition, "All merger arbitrageurs use inside information." For a reduced sentence, Ivan Boesky implicated Marty Siegel, among others, and Marty Siegel implicated three arbitrageurs in prominent positions. The three were arrested with great fanfare, one led away in tears and handcuffs. One of the three was eventually convicted of having learned that a merger for which he had an arbitrage might not go through, and acting on this information. This is indeed a crime, or at least a securities law violation, and deserved some kind of punishment.

But it is not a pattern of buying and selling inside information as with Boesky, Siegel, and Levine. As for the other two arbitrageurs who had been arrested based on Siegel's information, after much delay it was decided that no charges would be brought, that there had been a miscommunication between Siegel and the prosecutors.

I agree with those who feel that if the prosecutor had been less politically motivated he would have prepared his case first and made his arrests second. A blanket hue and cry among people to root out the greedies of Wall Street only encourages such irresponsible behavior. In our country, with its checks and balances, it is important for law enforcement agencies to search for criminal behavior and prosecute it. It is equally important for citizens to speak out—yell out—when law enforcement fails to act responsibly.

Returning to Michael Milken and the junk markets, as I noted already, Milken engaged in illegal activities, in part to maintain a near monopoly in junk bonds. One use of this monopoly was to obtain high fees for junk bond underwritings. Implicitly, part of the fee was in the form of warrants, that is, the right to buy the issuing company's stock at a fixed price, which would prove highly valuable if the stock price rose. Frequently Drexel insisted to the issuer that the warrants were needed to induce prospective buyers to buy the bonds. In fact most of the warrants went to Drexel employees, favored Drexel clients, and investment partnerships controlled by Milken.

But the chief complaint about junk bonds is not that Drexel charged too much for them; rather it is that they were used for purposes that were destructive rather than constructive, that they weakened the American economy rather than strengthening it. I believe this to be true, but there are exceptions. Let us first note where junk bonds were constructive, and then examine an area where they were counterproductive.

One use of junk bonds is to finance the capital needs of companies that are not large enough or strong enough to warrant an investment-grade rating from bond rating services. Below, when we consider the harmful effects of junk bonds, I note that many people became gamblers on junk bonds without their knowledge or consent. Leaving that consideration aside, and assuming for now that the demand for junk bonds came from those who were willing to bear more risk for greater return, then the use of junk bonds to finance the capital needs of companies below investment grade is surely commendable.

Only a small minority of companies command investment-grade ratings. When other companies issue bonds, their bonds are, by definition, "junk"—that is, below investment grade. The junk bond market provides a major source of capital—in addition to equity and bank financing—for these companies. Clearly the junk bond market serves a useful purpose in bringing together supply and demand for such higher-risk, therefore higher-yield, securities.

The chief complaint about junk bonds is that they were used to finance highly leveraged deals, either management leveraged buyouts or hostile takeovers. The extent of the leverage is illustrated by Ms. Bruck's description of Nelson Peltz's 1985 hostile takeover of National Can, financed by Milken's junk bonds.

> Five hundred sixty-five million dollars was a towering debt load for $100 million of equity to carry. And Peltz pointed out that even the $70 million from Triangle at the equity base came from its earlier offering of junk. 'We put the hundred million in the sub [the subsidiary… formed for the buyout]. But it was all debt! We called it equity here, but it was debt over here. Do you understand the leverage in this deal? It was eleven to one!'

Part of the standard takeover strategy is to attempt to reduce the debt once the target firm is acquired. One way to do that is to sell off subsidiaries or divisions that are not essential to the core business. This is not necessarily a bad thing. In some hostile takeovers the stock of the company is sufficiently undervalued as compared to the underlying assets so that a corporate raider can buy the company at a high price (compared to the stock's recent market price), sell off pieces of the company, pay off most of the debt, and thus acquire the core business for almost nothing.

For example, Carl Icahn bought ACF, a railcar-leasing company in 1984 for $410 million, in part financed by Milken's junk bonds. He sold off unprofitable pieces of the company for a total of $400 million, and was left with the core business, which someone later referred to as "a gem, a cash cow." In general in such situations, either the market has set an irrationally low value on the company or, as corporate raiders often contend, the market reflects the poor way an entrenched management is using resources.

It seems to me that this point is well-taken. Such raids, and the threats of such raids, tend to put a bound on how inefficient management can become in widely held corporations where no individual or small group considers itself the company's owner.

But in highly leveraged deals such as Peltz's takeover of National Can, the sale of inessential assets still leaves the company highly in debt. Another source of debt reduction is the company's cash flow. To increase the cash flow available for debt reduction, the raider, now owner of the company, reduces research, employment, and maintenance. Sometimes, some of this makes the firm more efficient.

For example, when KKR took over RJR–Nabisco they saved a good deal of money by ending the firm's research into a smokeless cigarette. The general consensus is that the firm did not hurt its future by doing so. When Icahn took over ACF, its operations were in the Midwest but it maintained a 173-person headquarters unit in New York. Neither he, nor a consultant he hired, nor the people in the Midwest could figure out what headquarters did for the firm. So he fired them, with no apparent effect.

But beyond a point, cutting research, maintenance, and staff diminishes the value of the firm. I speak now of the value of the whole firm, independently of how claims to the firm are divided between stockholder and bondholder. The present value of the firm depends on its ability to generate revenues in excess of costs not only this year, but also next year and the years that follow. This in turn depends on maintaining and improving products, processes, plant, equipment, and staff. Given the levels of debt that had to be paid down, I imagine that the raiders, now owners, of the highly leveraged companies had to cut back research, maintenance, and staff to the point where firm value fell.

If so, then somebody had to lose, because total expected value fell and risk increased for the firm. Let us consider whether someone failed to calculate their own self-interest properly when they did their part in putting together the takeover. Consider then, who lost: not the old stockholders, as they were bought out at a favorable price. Not Drexel or Milken; they received large fees plus warrants. Not the raider; he received a highly advantageous gamble. If things went well, his highly leveraged bet would have an extremely high payoff. If they went poorly, then for the most part it was not his own money that was at stake—in any case, not all of his own money if he played his cards right—and, in the meantime, he enjoyed the perks of his large enterprise.

Old bondholders lost if the firm had any, because the quality and therefore the price of their old bonds fell as the firm became more risky. Perhaps better bond covenants could protect bondholders against such increases in firm risk at their expense. The people who were laid off lost. But it is hard to see how to protect them in this kind of situation without passing laws that generally restrict a firm's ability to lay off workers. This may seem like kindness in the short run, but in the long run it would lead to a rigid and less productive economy—therefore a much smaller pie for all to share.

What about the investors in the junk bonds? Were they winners or losers? Here we must distinguish between those who chose to invest in junk bonds and those who had their funds put at risk in these bonds without their knowledge or consent. If someone invests in a high-yield investment fund, then they have made a decision to seek the rewards and bear the risks of the junk bond. They have little or no cause to complain if they lose.

But Milken's vast sources of funds for junk bonds were not such high-yield investment trusts; rather they were pension plans, S&Ls, and certain kinds of insurance companies. I direct my remarks to the latter two, partly because the problem to be discussed is most clear-cut in these instances.

Earlier I noted how the S&L structure encouraged gambling behavior by the S&L management with S&L funds. The risks they took were in real estate and junk bonds. The game was structured so that if bets were won on average, then the S&L and its management gained; if they lost, then the U.S. taxpayer lost.

A similar game was available to some insurance companies. A good example is Fred Carr's First Executive Corp. As Ms. Bruck tells us in *Predators' Ball*, Fred Carr was one of Milken's best customers for junk bonds, a reliable source of funds when Drexel needed to close deals quickly.

The money with which Carr bought junk bonds was mostly the reserves of insurance policyholders. In a sense, some of these policyholders shared some of the high returns that First Executive received, as this allowed Carr to attract them by offering better terms than elsewhere, just as S&Ls were able to attract money with high yields. Other policyholders did not elect to join Executive Life; rather they did so automatically when their companies funded their pension plans by buying Executive Life annuities or Guaranteed Investment Contracts (GICs). As in the case of the S&Ls, Fred Carr bore little of the risk of the junk bonds.

The risk was borne principally by the policyholders. Of course, the policyholders were not warned of this risk. They were provided no notice saying, "This policy is backed by risky investments. It may or may not pay off in full." Policyholders with First Executive's New York unit, Executive Life of New York, are probably not in trouble because of New York's stricter regulatory supervision, but those with its California unit have not been allowed to redeem or "surrender" their policies, and some may face some diminishment of benefits.

This situation raises regulatory and moral questions. On the regulatory side, it is clear that, in general, we should try to eliminate situations where one party makes the decisions and reaps the gains, while someone else pays the costs or suffers the losses. One example of this concerns pollution, where someone manufactures a product and receives its price, while someone else pays part of the cost of the product in terms of bad air, water, or land. Another example is the kind we have discussed here, where one party gets the return, and the other gets the risk. The individual needs protection against such financial risk, as we need protection against bad food, unsafe planes, and the like.

The moral question is this: Suppose you find yourself in a situation where you can legally gain the reward and stick other people with the risk. Should you? It is easy enough for me to tell you not to do it, to find some other way to make money. But will it change your action when the time comes?

Perhaps you should weigh this in your decision. Some day many people you put at risk without comparable reward may lose, get mad, seek retribution. Even if what you did to them was legal, some regulator or prosecutor may look at everything else you did to see if anything can be used to embarrass or punish you. Is it worth it?

Summary

To summarize, crimes were committed in the financial industries during the 1980s. But, as longtime readers of the business press can attest, crimes were committed in other industries in the 1980s, and in both the financial and other industries before January 1, 1980, and after December 31, 1989. I know of no study that shows that, per person with comparable opportunity, the financial industries of the 1980s had more lawbreakers than other industries or other times. I do not say this as an excuse for lawbreakers. On the contrary, I wish the best of success to the SEC and other responsible law enforcement agencies in trying to achieve a more honest, therefore a better, securities market.

It is also true that members of the financial communities have been the victims of overzealous prosecutors. It is this that makes me feel that the blanket condemnation of the greedies of the 1980s is not just silly, but destructive.

I believe that the chief complaint about Wall Street in the 1980s is not concerned with lawbreaking, but with highly leveraged hostile takeovers. I now hold the hypothesis that excesses in this area were primarily due to the availability for this purpose of large pools of money—such as S&L deposits and insurance reserves—whose ultimate owners or guarantors could be stuck with risk with little or none of the reward, without their knowledge or consent. I conjecture that without these pools of money the junk bond would mostly be a vehicle for bringing together those who need funds, but do not have an investment-grade rating, with those who seek higher return, understanding that it comes with higher risk.

As for those students learning about financial theory and practice, I assume that is in pursuit of their own self-interest. I hope that, in choosing an education in finance, they have considered their talents and interests, as well as the fact that they have to earn a living. I hope they understand that there is no guarantee that financial industries will flourish, or that jobs on Wall Street always await. I hope that all that we teach is valuable, including, for example, risk analysis, accounting, financial instruments, statistics, math, financial data bases, and computers.

An education in finance should not change fine human beings for the worse.

Appendix

Lorraine Spurge is a former Drexel Burnham Lambert employee, associate of Michael Milken, and now president of Knowledge Exchange, Inc. Ms. Spurge's account of the Wickes underwriting differs in some important respects from that of Ms. Bruck in her book. A summary of Ms. Spurge's account follows (private communication):

November 30, 1984. "Reliance (controlled by Saul Steinberg) purchased five million shares of when-issued Wickes common stock, over the counter, from Drexel at 3.9375 per share."

January 8, 1985. "Reliance bought a second block of five million shares of when-issued Wickes common stock, over the counter."

February 11 or 12, 1985. "Wickes made the decision to use Salomon as their underwriter."

March 22, 1985. Reliance filed a 13D with SEC. "The reason Reliance filed their 13D in March and not in January is that the stock they purchased was when-issued, being issued at the recapitalization of Wickes post bankruptcy. It is unnecessary to file a 13D on when-issued stock because it is not a valid security until issued. An investor doesn't have a settlement date and doesn't pay for the security until it is issued and has an effective date."

"Salomon did not respond well to news of the Steinberg investment. After hearing the news, Salomon's investment bankers left California and returned to their New York office for consultation. This action obviously concerned Sigoloff."

March 23, 1985. "Sigoloff arranged a meeting at Drexel to discuss Steinberg's filing and Wickes' pending financing."

"Drexel expressed the view that Steinberg's filing didn't represent any threat to Wickes or their pending financing. Rather it reflected Steinberg's interest in investing in their company. Michael and the other people at Drexel did discuss different financing options and their expertise in executing those options."

March 25, 1985. "Salomon filing of the prospectus with the SEC was planned for [this day] (this was unbeknownst to DBL)." "[Saul] Steinberg called Sigoloff himself to tell him that Reliance had no intention of acquiring the company and his investment was purely a vote of confidence in the current Wickes management team."

March 28, 1985. "Wickes met with DBL's corporate finance professionals numerous times following the Saturday 3/23 meeting to discuss the Wickes financing. The Salomon people were obviously annoyed with the introduction of a second underwriter."

"On Thursday March 28 Sigoloff... called to speak with Mike and Aaron [Eshman] to tell them that he selected Drexel as the sole underwriter of the transaction. According to Sigoloff, Salomon had apparently refused to comanage a deal with Drexel."

Questions

1. What is Adam Smith's "invisible hand?"
2. The "four Ps" of marketing comprise product, price, promotion, and place. Company managers decide on what *products* to sell and *promote* at specified *prices* in different *places.* Which of the four Ps does Gorbachev apparently believe to be an unnecessary business activity? Do you agree with him? Why?
3. *Greed* may be defined as an "inordinate or all-consuming and usually reprehensible acquisitiveness especially for wealth or gain." Some people deride the 1980s as the

decade of greed. What were the events of the 1980s that lead to such scorn? Do you agree with the labeling of the 1980s as the decade of greed? Explain.

4. Although Markowitz favors free-market solutions to economic problems, he notes the usefulness of law and law enforcement in product markets and financial markets. What are some examples that he notes?
5. The collateralized mortgage obligation (CMO) was invented at Salomon Brothers and First Boston Corporation. What are CMOs? In what way did CMOs provide a career advantage for recent college graduates, the so-called rocket scientists?
6. *Arbitrage* may be defined as the simultaneous purchase and sale of the same or equivalent security, commodity contract, insurance, or foreign exchange on the same or different markets in order to profit from price discrepancies. Markowitz discusses index arbitrage, currency arbitrage, convertible arbitrage, and merger arbitrage. Explain how these types of arbitrage are consistent with the preceeding definition. What is the social purpose of arbitrage?
7. Michael Milken and Ivan Boesky engaged in what type of illegal and unethical activities?
8. Michael Milken sold millions of dollars of junk bonds to savings and loan associations (S&Ls). What are junk bonds and S&Ls? What is wrong with S&Ls investing in junk bonds?

Economics and Ethics: The Case of Salomon Brothers

Clifford W. Smith, Jr.

The 1990s have produced what appears to be an unprecedented focus on the ethics of the business community. The media have pronounced the 1980s the "decade of greed," prominent financiers are being prosecuted with zeal (if with notably few sustainable convictions), professional organizations are reviewing their codes of conduct, and many business schools are starting courses in ethics.

The source of the problem, many assert, is a deplorable loss of "values" in a materialistic society made still more mercenary by the market forces unleashed by "deregulation." Proposed solutions are more education, tighter regulations, and stiffer penalties for illegal conduct.

But are people in financial markets today really less ethical than their forebears? And are education, regulation, and penalties the most promising solutions to the apparent problem?

In addressing these questions, I will offer an economist's perspective. Like other sciences, good economics is "value-free." This does not mean economists do not share the values of their society, only that the primary aim of economics is to describe and predict human behavior, not prescribe it. Such predictions of behavior can then be used to design more effective public or corporate policies.

Classical economics begins with the assumption that people follow their perceived self-interest, weighing the expected benefits against the costs of alternative courses of action, and then choosing the one where the net benefits appear greatest. This is not to say that ethical considerations do not enter into this personal calculus. For most people, violating one's code of self-conduct imposes a great "cost" in the form of lost self-esteem. And even if one's sense of self-worth is not bound up with a personal code, the regard of one's friends and colleagues surely acts as a major restraint on unethical behavior. In economists' parlance, a good reputation is an important component of one's "human capital." The same

---

At the time of this writing, Clifford W. Smith, Jr., was the Clarey Professor of Finance at the University of Rochester's William E. Simon Graduate School of Business Administration.

Source: From Bank of America *Journal of Applied Corporate Finance.*

is true of large corporations: a company's "reputational capital," including its record for product safety, fair treatment of employees, and compliance with environment and workplace regulations, is a valuable asset—one that contributes to current and future corporate profits by improving the terms on which the company contracts with its customers, employees, and suppliers. And, given all the academic evidence that indicates the stock market is forward-looking, the value of such reputational capital is reflected in *current* stock prices.

In this article, I use the recent case of the Salomon Brothers' treasury bond scandal to illustrate two very basic, but largely neglected, points about the relation between ethics and economics in free markets:

First, private markets provide powerful economic incentives for ethical behavior—and hence important safeguards for consumers—by imposing substantial costs on institutions and individuals that depart from accepted standards. Under most circumstances, good ethics is good economics.

Second, poorly designed policies—those that give individuals or companies strong incentives to "cheat" the system—produce unethical behavior. This lesson applies to public as well as corporate policies.

The Salomon Bidding Scandal

Some Background

When auctioning Treasury bonds, the U.S. Treasury awards them first to the highest bidder at its quoted price, then moves to the next highest bidder. This process continues until the issue is exhausted. If the Treasury receives more than one bid at the price that exhausts the issue, it allocates the remaining bonds in proportion to the size of the bid. Treasury auction rules limit the amount of an issue sold to a single bidder to 35% of the issue.

In June 1990, Paul Mozer, the head of Salomon's Government-bond trading desk, submitted bids for more than 100% of an auction of four-year notes. Under the Treasury's rules, if Mozer's bid ended up tied with other bids at the market-clearing price, Mozer's bidding strategy would increase Solly's share of the issue. Although a treasury official warned him about excessive bidding after the auction, in July Mozer again bid for more than 100% of a Resolution Trust Corporation 30-year bond issue. The Treasury rejected the bid and instituted a 35% ceiling on bids by a particular buyer.

In December 1990, Mozer submitted bids for 35% of a four-year note auction. But he also submitted another bid for $1 billion under the name of Warburg Asset Management, a Salomon Brothers' customer, without the customer's authorization. The two bids represented 46% of the issue. Mozer repeated this tactic in eight other auctions thereafter.

In April, the Treasury sent a letter to Mercury Asset Management, a Warburg affiliate, reminding them that the combined bids of affiliated firms should not exceed 35% of the issue. After Mozer obtained a copy of the letter, he realized his unauthorized bid in Warburg's name had attracted the Treasury's attention; and he informed Salomon Chairman John Gutfreund, President Thomas Strauss,

Vice Chairman John Meriwether, and General Counsel Donald Feuerstein of his illegal bid in the February auction. But no immediate action was taken by Salomon's management.

In June, the Securities Exchange Commission and the Justice Department issued subpoenas to Salomon and some of its clients for their records involving auctions. Salomon initiated a review of its government-bond operations and in August disclosed its illegal bids during the period between December and May.

Legal and Regulatory Penalties

On August 18, 1991, the Treasury Department announced it had barred Salomon from bidding in government securities auctions for customer accounts (although it did allow the firm to continue bidding for its own account). Nine months later, on May 20, 1992, Salomon settled with the government. They agreed to pay $122 million to the Treasury to settle charges that it violated securities laws and $68 million for claims made by the Justice Department. The firm also established a $100 million restitution fund for payments of private damage claims that might result from the 50 or so civil lawsuits it was facing from the scandal. (Unclaimed amounts in this fund revert to the Treasury, not Salomon.) Salomon also announced it would take a second quarter charge-off of $185 million in addition to the $200 million reserve for potential liabilities from the scandal it had already established.

At the same time, the Federal Reserve Bank of New York announced that, although it had decided to retain Salomon's designation as a primary dealer, the firm's authority to trade with the Bank would be suspended in the months of June and July. Analysis estimated this suspension could cost Salomon as much as $4 billion in trading volume. It also barred the firm's traders from potentially valuable trading information derived from daily contact with the Fed's Open Market Desk.

Market-Imposed Costs

While these legal and regulatory penalties are considerable, they represent only a fraction of the total costs imposed on the firm. During the week in August 1991 that the information about the illegal bids was released, Salomon Brothers' stock price dropped by fully one third, representing a $1.5 billion loss in market value. Such a loss suggests the market expected Salomon to bear costs far in excess of the fines and other costs arising from expected legal and regulatory sanctions.

To provide a clearer understanding of the market forces that impose sanctions on parties to unethical behavior, I now focus on the costs imposed through private mechanisms in the period between public disclosure of the illegal bids in August 1991 and the settlement in May 1992.

The size of the market-imposed costs of unethical behavior depends on the extent to which information about such behavior is widely and rapidly distributed among potential as well as actual customers. The Wall Street community is a small, highly interactive group; and gossip is a major avocation of its members.

Thus, news of the illegal bids was widely distributed on Wall Street almost immediately.

Financial transactions, moreover, are among the events most closely scrutinized by the business media. Salomon's illegal bids were the subject of lead stories in the financial press throughout the week in which they were disclosed. On August 19, 1991, for example, *The Wall Street Journal* carried seven different stories about the event. Thus, information about this scandal was widely distributed to the business community after its initial disclosure.

Within days of the news release, Moody's Investors Service put Salomon on its credit watch list. Before the end of August 1991, Moody's had downgraded Salomon's debt rating on their $7 billion long-term debt and $6.6 billion commercial paper issues.[1]

Effect on Salomon's Underwriting Business

Different facets of Salomon's business can be expected to be affected differently by the scandal. To understand why this is so, it is necessary to offer a brief digression into the economics of information.

When the quality of a product or service is difficult to determine prior to purchase, buyers will reduce their demand prices to reflect the uncertainty they face. The quality of some products and services is much more difficult to know in advance; in economists' language, there are higher "information costs" in selling such products. For example, the quality of an individual airplane ticket is really known only after the plane has landed and the passengers have retrieved their luggage. In other transactions, quality can be readily determined. For example, in the case of a buyer for Kodak negotiating a purchase of silver, quality can be confidently and inexpensively ascertained prior to purchase by assay. In such cases, the seller's reputation is relatively unimportant, and unethical behavior by one of the firm's employees would have little negative effect on the future viability of the business.

Thus, one major determinant of the extent of potential customer defections is the difficulty of determining the quality of Salomon's various products. The damage to Salomon's reputation from the bidding scandal reduced the expected value of its underwriting business in large part because the "quality" of underwriter services is very difficult to ascertain prior to purchase.

Indeed, the extent of such information costs in underwriting securities is an important reason why very few companies choose to market new issues without the help of an investment banker. In the absence of a reputable underwriter, potential investors would be concerned that the issuer knows something about the firm's future prospects that, if disclosed, would adversely affect the value of the securities. Because companies issue new securities infrequently, it is difficult for them to argue credibly that such adverse information does not exist. By

[1] For a discussion of the valuable monitoring and information dissemination function performed by credit information services, see Lee J. Wakeman, "The Real Function of Bond Rating Agencies," *Chase Financial Quarterly*, Vol. 1 (1981), pp. 18–25.

employing an underwriter who regularly markets new securities, the issuer effectively obtains the underwriter's "certification" that all material information has been released; and such certification in turn raises the price of the issue.[2]

The damage to Salomon's reputation not only impaired its ability to "certify" the value of new issues (since unsupervised improper dealings presumably could have spread beyond the Treasury desk), but actually raised concerns about whether the firm would survive.[3] And such doubts about the firm's viability further exacerbated the firm's credibility with potential customers. Given increased uncertainty that Salomon would be around in a year's time, the firm, would-be investors *might* reason, has greater incentives to put together bad deals just to collect enough fees to stay afloat—never mind concerns about its long-term reputation. The perceived cost of *forgone* future business from irresponsible underwriting to a firm on the verge of extinction is far less than the costs of a bad deal to a sound, well-established firm. Thus, the more uncertainty about the future of the firm, the less effective are the normal restraints on cheating (notably, the anticipated value of future, especially repeat, sales).[4]

As *The Wall Street Journal* reported some nine months after initial disclosure of the scandal:

> Salomon continues to be shunned by many corporate clients in receiving lead-management mandates for stock underwriting, even amid a record volume of new stock and bond issues. 'We did not participate on the investment banking side to the extent we would have expected [before the scandal] .... and that hurt us,' Warren E. Buffet, Salomon interim Chairman, said."

For example, prior to the scandal Salomon ranked fifth among Wall Street firms in stock underwriting with a January to July 1991 market share of 7.8 percent. But after the scandal Salomon dropped to tenth with a January to May 1992 market share of only 2.2 percent.

Economic theory also suggests, however, that Salomon's *bond* underwriting business should be less affected by the scandal than its stock underwriting. Because stock values are far more sensitive than bond prices to undisclosed adverse information, the demand for underwriter *certification* services (as opposed to marketing and distribution services) is correspondingly greater in stock underwriting. And, sure enough, in contrast to the plunge in revenues from its stock underwriting business, Buffet characterized the firm's bond underwriting business in the first quarter of 1992 as "highly satisfactory."

---

[2] See Booth, James R. and Richard L. Smith, II (1986), "Capital Raising, Underwriting and the Certification Hypothesis," *Journal of Financial Economics*, Vol. 15, pp. 261–281; and Smith, Clifford W., Jr. "Investment Banking and the Capital Acquisition Process," *Journal of Financial Economics*, Vol. 15 (1986), pp. 3–29.

[3] For example *The New York Times* (9/29/91) ran an article titled "Warren Buffet's Stickiest Wicket: Making Sure Salomon Survives."

[4] See Benjamin Klein and Keith Leffler, "The Role of Market Forces in Assuring Contractual Performance," *Journal of Political Economy*, Vol. 89, No. 41 (1981).

Yet underwriting *volume* only tells part of the story. Clients' demand *prices* for Salomon's services were also reduced. For example, *The Wall Street Journal* reported,

> To combat client defections, Salomon is bidding aggressively for the right to underwrite bond and stock offerings by corporations.... Some competitors groan that Salomon is cutting prices to win bond issues.

In short, business the firm retained likely had smaller spreads and was thus less profitable than before.

Effect on Other Business

Major customers, including the World Bank and the State of California, suspended trading with Salomon. The illegal bids must raise questions among customers about the effectiveness of their representation if they continued to employ Salomon as a broker.

One area of Salomon's business unlikely to be directly affected by the scandal is Salomon's *principal* transactions (trading using the firm's own cash). But even this part of their business was indirectly affected. To ease liquidity pressures resulting from the scandal, Salomon liquidated almost one third of its asset portfolio, substantially reducing the firm's asset trading capacity. In fact, principal transactions fell by 33% in the first quarter of 1992.

Trading in derivatives such as futures and options was relatively unaffected. As reported in *The Wall Street Journal*, "Derivatives positions have risen steadily for Salomon Brothers; last year they climbed by $140 billion or 22%, mostly in the second half, to a total of $786 billion by year's end" (6/2/92). The increase, however, was concentrated entirely in *exchange-traded* financial futures, which rose $170 billion in 1991. Credit and liquidity problems that constrained other asset trading were less important in exchange-traded derivatives.[5] In fact, deterioration of Solly's credit standing disqualified the firm as an acceptable counterparty for certain over-the-counter derivative transactions such as swaps. This constraint in turn limited Salomon's ability to offer customers certain structured transactions such as dual-currency bonds and other hybrid securities.

The scandal also apparently changed management's view of other risks. For example, Warren Buffett instructed Salomon's Phibro Energy unit to sever all ties with a major client of long standing, Marc Rich and Co. He evidently concluded that the firm could not risk another scandal involving transactions with a customer whose head had been a fugitive from the U.S. since 1983.

In late October 1991, Salomon announced it had settled a class-action lawsuit stemming from the buyout of Revco Drug Stores, Inc. Salomon agreed to

---

[5] For an explanation, see Clifford W. Smith, Charles W. Smithson, and D. Sykes Wilford, *Managing Financial Risk* (Harper Collins, 1989).

pay nearly $30 million to security holders in Revco's $1.25 billion buy-out. The bidding scandal could have contributed to a less favorable settlement for at least two reasons: (1) it promised to consume enough management attention that Salomon would settle to eliminate the distraction; and (2) the firm's bargaining position was impaired because Salomon's credibility at trial was undermined by the scandal.

Labor Markets

The individual at the center of the scandal, Paul Mozer, was suspended from his Salomon duties in August. Not only does he face potential criminal penalties for his actions, he has also been named as a defendant in lawsuits filed by Salomon customers. He probably has ruined his career, could lose much of his accumulated wealth, and could spend a substantial amount of time in prison.

Salomon Chairman Gutfreund, President Strauss, Vice-Chairman Meriwether, and General Counsel Feuerstein were asked by the Board to resign. This action also was demanded by New York Fed President, Gerald Corrigan, for Salomon to remain a primary dealer in the Treasury market. While the requested resignations largely reflect top management's failure to take action following the April meeting, these gentlemen also were the top executives most responsible for monitoring the activities of subordinates to insure such illegal actions do not occur. Some of these individuals could also face additional regulatory penalties. For example, *The Wall Street Journal* reported that, "According to individuals with knowledge of the SEC's actions, it plans to charge Mr. Gutfreund and Mr. Strauss with failing to supervise Mr. Mozer and others" (*WSJ*, 5/21/92).

In the wake of the scandal, Salomon has lost many valued employees. To help keep others, Salomon took the unusual step of guaranteeing that the 1992 pay pool for its stock-research group would be at least 20% higher than the 1991 pool. While this was motivated in part by a desire to shelter valuable employees from events outside their control, it also likely reflects an increase in "reservation" wages by employees who now saw themselves as working for a riskier firm.

Building coordinated teams of employees throughout the organization is a time-consuming task that takes years to accomplish. Salomon's personnel losses in response to the scandal will likely affect the firm's productivity and competitiveness for years.

Salomon's Actions

As suggested earlier, when the quality of products and services is difficult to determine prior to purchase, buyers discount their demand prices to reflect the uncertainty they face. For this reason, sellers have incentives to provide credible assurance to potential customers that they will not cheat in order to raise the prices commanded by their products and services.

To reassure potential customers after the scandal became public, Salomon made several important changes:

First, the board removed the employees implicated in the scandal. Mozer as well as other members of his group (down to the clerk that submitted the illegal bids) were suspended. Gutfreund, Strauss, Meriwether and Feuerstein were asked to resign. Furthermore, the firm's board forced the resignation of Salomon's outside counsel, Wachtell, Lipton, Rosen and Katz. This law firm had conducted the internal investigation into the scandal beginning in early July, but they did not approach the government until a month later.

Second, the board appointed Warren Buffett as interim chairman. This is a dramatic example of an outside board member performing an invaluable role in corporate governance.[6] By moving quickly to appoint a respected outside board-member like Mr. Buffett as interim Chairman, the Salomon board sent a strong message to the market that this behavior is unlikely to be repeated.

Third, Salomon appointed Deryck Maughan as new Chief Operating Officer. Since Mr. Maughan had just transferred from Tokyo to New York, his appointment helped assure that the new senior management team would not be implicated in the scandal and thus would not be diverted from dealing with containing the costs imposed on the firm by the scandal.

Fourth, the firm moved quickly to liquidate assets, pay off bank loans, and reduce borrowing in the commercial paper market. Such actions, by reducing leverage, forestalled potentially serious liquidity problems.

Fifth, the firm publicly announced that it was beefing up its internal controls by forming a compliance committee and by hiring Coopers and Lybrand to institute a compliance review of its securities operations.[7]

How to Prevent Future Scandals (or Bad Policy Breeds Bad Ethics)

The central thesis in this discussion has been that private markets impose potentially significant costs on individuals and firms that engage in unethical behavior. This helps explain why ethical behavior is so widely observed in markets: ethical behavior is profitable. I also believe that more widespread understanding of such costs would lead to fewer ethical-conduct violations.

Economic analysis also suggests that public policy-makers concerned about the "integrity" of U.S. financial markets should focus less on the enforcement of regulations and more on reform of such regulations designed to align them with the financial incentives of market participants. The current bidding rules in the Treasury auctions hold out strong incentives for participants to "game" the system. First, as the Salomon case illustrates, by employing a multiple price (or

---

[6] Academics have argued that outside board members monitor internal management decisions and that large active investors like Mr. Buffet can play an important role in policy formulation. See, for example, Eugene F. Fama, "Agency Problems and the Theory of the Firm," *Journal of Political Economy*, Vol. 88, No. 2, (1980), pp. 288–307.

[7] This is consistent with the Watts/Zimmerman argument that a public accounting firm's value ultimately depends on maintaining a reputation for competence and independence. Ross Watts and Jerold L. Zimmerman, *Positive Accounting Theory*, (Prentice Hall: Englewood Cliffs, NJ, 1986).

"discriminatory") auction that charges bidders their announced "reservation prices," the current system provides strong incentives for bidders to seek ways around the imposed bidding limits. Perhaps even more destructive, the system also provides powerful incentives for bidders to collude when setting their bid prices. Such collusion—or just fear of the possibility of such collusion by others—causes the Treasury to raise less money than it would by substituting the single-price auction advocated by Milton Friedman two decades ago.

In such a single-price system, now almost universally advocated by economists, the entire block of securities would be allocated to the top bidders at the market-clearing bid. In a single-price auction, participants would bid differently; their optimal strategy would be simple—they would just bid what they thought the securities were worth. In multiple-price auctions, bidders must also forecast the other bids in determining their optimal strategy. Moving to a single-price system would reduce the "winner's curse" problem that, although inherent in all kinds of auctions, is exacerbated by multiple-price auctions.[8]

Economic theory and evidence suggest that adopting a single-price auction would reduce the Treasury's total funding cost.[9] The expected cost savings, moreover, would be supplemented by reductions in government monitoring costs resulting from the reformed structure of incentives. Indeed, had the Treasury spent more time worrying about the incentives to cheat built into their bidding procedures, this entire unfortunate set of events might never have occurred.

Similarly, a corporate board concerned about the ethical conduct of the firm's employees would do better to spend less time exhorting its human resources managers to search like Diogenes, for "an honest man." It should instead pay more attention to potential conflicts of interest among the firm's management, employees, customers, creditors, and shareholders. For example, Sears would almost certainly not be facing the widely reported consumer indignation and legal sanctions from unnecessary auto repairs had it anticipated the (quite predictable) effect of its compensation plan on its managers and employees: Sears' commission scheme encouraged its employees to *rip off* customers! Incentives work. If you adopt a compensation plan that pays employees for unethical behavior, then unethical behavior is exactly what you will get.

Questions

1. "Like other sciences, good economics is value-free." Do you agree with this statement?
2. *Ethics* may be defined as a group of moral principles or set of values—in other words, principles of right and wrong action or good and bad character. If you commit an unethical act and no one knows it, what potential cost do you incur? What if your best friend knows it? What if your boss knows it?

---

[8] The winner's curse refers to the fact that there is no double message associated with a winning bid. The good news is that you own the object you bid for; the bad news is that you paid more than others were willing to bid.

[9] See Paul R. Milgrom, "Auctions and Bidding: A Primer," *Journal of Economic Perspectives*, Vol. 3 (1989), pp. 3–22; and Paul R. Milgrom and Robert J. Webber, "A Theory of Auctions and Competitive Building," *Econometrics*, Vol. 50 (1982), pp. 105–114.

3. Describe the rule violations committed by Paul Mozer, the head of Salomon Brothers' government-bond trading desk. What was the reaction of Solly's upper management? The Securities and Exchange Commission and the Justice Department? The Treasury Department? The Federal Reserve Bank of New York? The stock market? Moody's Investors Service?
4. "When the quality of a product or service is difficult to determine prior to purchase, buyers will reduce their demand prices to reflect the uncertainty they face." Identify examples of this phenomenon.
5. Consistent with the economics of information, most companies employ investment bankers to help with the issuance of common stock. Explain this fact using the terms *reputational capital* and *certification*. In what way did the damage to Salomon's reputation affect its stock underwritings? Its bond underwritings? Its employees?
6. Trillions of dollars worth of securities change hands each year. Many of the transactions take place over the telephone, based solely on the participants' word. Yet securities fraud, based on the highest estimates, contaminate only a fraction of one percent of these transactions. Why is ethical behavior so widespread among investors, brokers, dealers, and investment bankers?

An Overview of the Executive Compensation Debate

GREGG A. JARRELL

In recent years, executive pay has come under heavy criticism from many quarters. Graef Crystal's 1991 book, *In Search of Excess*, has contributed much to the recent popular outcry over high executive pay. Subsequent events have attracted first the media, then politicians, to this issue. Notable among these events was the much-publicized trip to Japan, in January of 1991, of President Bush and several top auto executives for the ostensible purpose of encouraging the Japanese to compete less effectively in the U.S. auto market. This ill-advised and ineffectual mission became simply another occasion for the press to contrast the high recent compensation of the American CEOs with both the recession and layoffs in the auto industry and with the relatively low pay of their more successful Japanese CEO counterparts. Within months, several Congressmen were proposing measures that would limit top executive pay using crude formulas based apparently on what they had learned in the press about Japanese CEO pay levels.

Also fueling the public outrage were several well-publicized examples of astronomical pay during 1991 and 1992 in which top executives cashed out their stock options. The booming stock market contributed to a number of such cases of lucrative stock-based CEO pay at the same time working-class citizens were seeing the recession reduce growth in their real earnings. This contrast became the central focus of many media stories pointing up the fundamental inequity of the entire system for setting executive pay. Such stories in turn helped provoke further criticism of the performance of managers and directors of public companies. The mounting criticism has resulted in significant pay disclosure reforms being passed by the Securities and Exchange Commission (SEC), numerous shareholder proxy challenges, and a campaign promise by President-elect Clinton to take more dramatic regulatory steps to discourage "excessive" executive

---

At the time of this writing, Gregg A. Jarrell was a professor of finance and economics at the University of Rochester's Simon School of Business.

Source: From Bank of America *Journal of Applied Corporate Finance.*

pay, such as limiting corporate tax deductibility to executive compensation below $1 million yearly.

My purpose here is to reflect on the executive pay controversy, and on recently enacted and proposed reforms, in light of the relevant academic literature. During the last decade, academic economists have produced a considerable body of work on managerial pay and performance, both theoretical and empirical. In fact, economists have long been among the leading critics of executive pay and of the effectiveness of directors in setting pay and monitoring executive performance. But, although many academic critics of executive pay practices are now applauding recent policy reforms, I fear there is a fundamental inconsistency between the "populist" reforms now being proposed in the political sector and the policy implications of the scholarly research. Indeed, I challenge the conclusion reached by academic critics of executive pay that the existing body of scholarly research implies that the current system of setting executive pay needs major reform.

I start by describing traditional practice in the U.S. for setting executive pay and then review the positions of each of three different groups of commentators on the executive pay debate. The first group are political reformers—activists seeking to use the political process to reform the system of determining executive rewards. Next I review some of the research of financial economists, and then the work of accounting economists, as it bears on the political debate. I close with an assessment of the central policy implications of academic studies, and then contrast these policy implications with the assumptions underlying the policy reforms being pushed by political activists.

Traditional Executive Pay Practices

The compensation of top executives in the U.S. is typically composed of salary, bonus, and long-term incentives. Salary generally accounts for about half of total compensation, with the rest fairly evenly split between bonus and long-term incentives. Executive salary payments are pre-determined contractually and do not appear to be directly tied to year-to-year company performance. So the strength of the pay-for-performance relationship of most executive pay plans depends on the specific features of the bonus and long-term incentive plan.

The annual bonus is commonly based on accounting-earnings performance over the year, although other accounting measures may also be used as triggers. The most common formula is to make the bonus pool for top executives a fixed percentage of profits in excess of a specified return on capital. The exact definitions of earnings and return to capital vary somewhat across companies, but most plans specify a lower bound on earnings or the return to capital. According to data from The Conference Board, the percentage of companies having annual bonus plans rose steadily from under 40% in 1960 to 99% in the late 1980s.

Long-term incentives usually link payouts directly to the financial performance of the company through the use of stock options, stock appreciation rights, restricted stock or phantom stock. According to The Conference Board survey, over 80% of company plans use stock options; and this has held roughly constant 1960 to the late 1980s. Restricted stock and phantom stock plans have increased from 20% in 1980 to about 35% in the late 1980s. Long-term performance plans reward executives in cash or stock for attaining long-term, multi-year accounting goals, typically formulated as growth in earnings-per-share over three to five years. The use of long-term performance plans has increased sharply, rising from under 10% of plans in 1974 to nearly 40% by the late 1980s.

As a general rule, the "incentive" or "variable" pay of top executives—that portion over and above fixed salary—appears to depend much more heavily on accounting measures of performance than on stock-price performance. For example, a study by Kevin Murphy of U.S. companies during the period 1975–1984, reported that annual bonus payouts accounted for over 25% of total executive compensation, while stock options accounted for only about 10% on average.[1] In recent years, the option component has probably increased somewhat. But it is nevertheless important to keep in mind that the recent highly-visible cases of huge annual payouts were almost always the result of executives' choosing to exercise options granted years ago. Such options became so valuable only because of significant stock-price increases achieved since the time of grant.

According to a survey of the CEO compensation of the 1,000 largest U.S. public companies by the United Shareholders Association, the average salary and bonus for 1991 was $901,000. In addition, about 30% of these CEOs received salary and bonus payments for 1991 in excess of $1 million. These figures exclude payouts from stock options and other long-term incentive plans, as well as any dividends or capital gains from owning stock in their company.

Political Activists and Their Reform Agenda

The political activists include shareholder-rights organizations, institutional investors and their lobbying associations, some shareholder-value consultants, and certain politicians and regulators. Each of these groups have called for new policies to correct an assumed market failure in the labor market for CEOs. Such groups apparently share the assumption that corporate boards of directors, and other potential competitive forces for CEO discipline, have failed to provide a rigorous reward-and-punishment system for top corporate management that would be consistent with a genuinely competitive marketplace. The usual arguments are that shareholders are too diffuse and ill-informed to use the proxy machinery to monitor top management effectively, and that the board is successfully neutralized by most CEOs (who are usually also Chairmen of the Board).

The symptoms of this market failure allegedly include numerous incidents of egregiously large financial rewards to certain CEOs, widespread and steady pay raises for CEOs even when corporate performance is poor, infrequent dismissals of top management by the board (and then only for the most highly-publicized and long-run failures of policy), and across-the-board excessive rewards in the

---

[1] Kevin Murphy, "Corporate Performance and Managerial Remuneration: An Empirical Analysis," *Journal of Accounting and Economics*, 7 (1985), 11–42.

form of financial rewards and perquisites for top management of large American companies. Critics of the system point out that CEO pay rose about 7% in 1991, even as profits declined about 7%. They rail against the perennial handful of cases of multimillion dollar payouts received as a result of exercising options, and they complain that the pay of U.S. top executives as a ratio of the pay of average workers is roughly double the ratio for top executives in Japan.

If such critics are correct in charging that our labor market for top management is badly flawed, then the economic ramifications are indeed quite serious. Although the actual pay levels of top CEOs are only a trivial fraction of a typical large company's total stockholder equity, such a market failure implies that the wrong executives (or, alternatively, the right executives with the wrong incentives) have the decision rights over the allocation of a large fraction of America's corporate resources. Given the possibility of such a market failure, the current debate would seem to deserve the serious attention it has been receiving in the media, corporate boardrooms, and universities.

In response to pressure from political activists, the SEC recently enacted new disclosure rules governing executive compensation. It also liberalized certain proxy rules to provide institutional investors with more leverage over corporate policy through the use of the proxy machinery. The new disclosure rules, which generally become effective in 1993, mandate the use of tables, graphs, and reports (in place of the narrative description of plans used in the past) to both describe and *justify* executive compensation. In addition, companies are required to present a stock performance graph—a line graph comparing the firm's stock returns over the last five years to the returns of both the general market and a relevant peer group of companies.

This policy solution reveals how political activists and the SEC view the problem of executive compensation. They believe that the market failure can be corrected, at least in part, by new disclosures of pay levels and of stock-price performance, in combination with new proxy leverage for institutional shareholders. The theory is that the institutional shareholders, armed with the necessary data on pay and performance, can offer counter-balancing power to top management by using the proxy machinery to discipline and monitor the board of directors. The new regulations are clearly intended to harness the growing power of institutional investors to represent the interests of all shareholders and to prod the board of directors into performing more diligently its function of monitoring and disciplining top management.

The new disclosure rules also impose significant burdens on the use of stock options—burdens that presumably reflect regulators' conclusion that options have been a special source of compensation abuse. The new rules require that companies estimate and publish the potential realizable value of options granted to executives. Ostensibly, the rules allow companies to avoid valuing options; instead they can simply show end-of-term values based on assumed annual appreciation rates for the stock price of 5% and 10%, compounded annually. But because this end-value approach will involve disclosing some very large numbers, it is safe to predict that most firms will choose instead to use present value option pricing models, such as the SEC-approved Black-Scholes model, to place a value on the options it grants to its executives. It is also likely that the new rules will discourage the use of options and stock appreciation rights, since the disclosure "costs" of substitute long-term incentive plans are much lower. I also expect the new SEC rules will virtually eliminate the practice of re-pricing options, since to do so now triggers extremely burdensome disclosure requirements.

Political activists applaud the new SEC rules for encouraging greater institutional investor involvement and board oversight of executive compensation practices. In my view, however, the new SEC disclosure rules show more concern with reducing *levels* of executive compensation than promoting a stronger link between pay and performance. Promoting greater pay-for-performance linkage is given lip service, but the political impetus behind the new regulatory measures is the populist anger at high executive pay. The goal of pay for performance is desired only insofar as it leads to reduced levels of executive compensation. After all, the SEC rules discourage the use of options, which have been the most effective and popular method of linking executive pay with stock-price performance over the last decade. Further, proposed reforms include President-elect Clinton's promise to discourage public firms from paying executives compensation in excess of $1 million. Indeed, many executives are following the lead of Walt Disney's Michael Eisner and Frank Wells, who last week exercised stock options worth about $187 million to protect shareholders from a possible large tax bill in the future. Clearly, regulations of this kind are not passed out of a concern for pay-for-performance linkage, but rather to satisfy the populist demand for equity.

The Perspective of Financial Economists

In 1984, the University of Rochester hosted a conference on executive pay to promote and disseminate scholarly research on what was then a subject treated with fascination by the media but neglected by academics. Kevin Murphy, whose 1985 study was cited earlier, presented data based on 1,200 firms over a ten-year period showing that executive pay was positively (and significantly) correlated to shareholder returns over two five-year periods (1975–79 and 1980–84).[2] Not only were salary and bonus strongly related to stock performance, but factoring in the wealth changes stemming from executive stock holdings shows that total compensation is rather dramatically affected by shareholder returns. This research convinced Murphy that "Top Executives Are Worth Every Nickel They Get," the title of his 1986 *Harvard Business Review* piece.[3] At the same conference, a study by Ann Coughlan and Ronald Schmidt corroborated Murphy's results and found further that top executive turnover was significantly higher during 1978-80 in companies with relatively low stock returns.[4] Taken together, the research presented at the Rochester Conference seemed to refute

[2] Ibid.

[3] Kevin J. Murphy, "Top Executives Are Worth Every Nickel They Get," *Harvard Business Review* (March-April 1986), 125–132.

[4] Anne T. Coughlan and Ronald M. Schmidt, "Executive Compensation, Management Turnover, and Firm Performance: An Empirical Investigation," *Journal of Accounting and Economics* (1985) p. 43.

popular media critics of executive pay by showing that the cross-sectional pattern of executive reward and shareholder performance generally reflected an efficient labor market.

But this early conclusion from the Rochester Conference research apparently was not widely accepted by financial economists. Indeed, this conclusion of an efficient labor market for top CEOs was somewhat inconsistent with the blizzard of research being produced by financial economists on mergers and takeovers throughout much of the 1980s. One of the main messages of the takeover studies was that much of the booming M&A activity resulted from an *inefficient* top-management labor market. This market suffered from large "agency costs" arising from the conflict between the survival instincts of incumbent CEOs and the interest of outside shareholders in stock-price maximization. More precisely, this literature attributed to agency costs and an inefficient executive labor market much of the value-destroying conglomerate merger activity, the resistance by target incumbents to hostile takeovers promising large premiums to their shareholders, and the huge gaps in value between stock prices and takeover prices. In this sense, the M&A research, which dominated the activity of financial-economic scholars during this time, was at odds with the conclusion of the fledgling executive-pay literature that the executive labor market exhibited strong signs of economic efficiency.

This tension between the academic literature on executive pay and corporate restructuring was completely eliminated, however, with the publication of research by Michael Jensen and Kevin Murphy in 1990.[5] Using data, methodology, and results that are remarkably similar to those of Murphy's 1985 study cited earlier, the conclusion coming out of the Rochester conference was essentially reversed. The Jensen and Murphy research also found that pay and turnover rates are significantly linked to shareholder returns, but they changed their focus from this relationship to a new measurement of pay for performance: namely, the dollar change in CEO compensation for every $1,000 change in total shareholder wealth. The finding of Jensen and Murphy, using a large sample of CEOs and a long time period, was that total executive compensation increases about $3.00 for every $1,000 increase in shareholder wealth.

Although this result was perfectly consistent with the earlier findings of a positive relation between *percentage* stock returns and CEO pay, computing this relation as the change in dollar compensation to the change in total dollar shareholder wealth apparently convinced Jensen and Murphy that the typical executive's stake in changes in shareholder wealth is not sufficient to align the financial interests of top management with shareholders. They reached the same "cup is now half empty" conclusion in examining executive turnover rates. Although they reported in earlier work that turnover is higher when shareholder returns are lower, they asserted in 1990 that the actual probability of being dismissed was

[5] Michael C. Jensen and Kevin J. Murphy, "Performance Pay and Top-Management Incentives," *Journal of Political Economy*, 98, No. 2 (1990), 225–264. See also Michael C. Jensen and Kevin J. Murphy, "CEO Incentives—It's Not How Much You Pay, But How," *Harvard Business Review*, (May–June 1990), 138–153.

so low that the market for top executives must be extremely inefficient and uncompetitive.

Jensen and Murphy then concluded their 1990 study by speculating that the failure of the CEO labor market is a long-term result of the interaction of mandated disclosure of executive pay and egalitarian principles misapplied by the press and political forces. As they stated in a *Harvard Business Review* article,

> By aiming their protests at compensation levels, uninvited but influential guests at the managerial bargaining table (the business press, labor unions, political figures) intimidate board members and constrain the types of contracts that are written between managers and shareholders. As a result of public pressure, directors become reluctant to reward CEOs with substantial (and therefore highly visible) financial gains for superior performance. Naturally, they also become reluctant to impose meaningful financial penalties for poor performance. The long-term effect of this risk-averse orientation is to erode the relation between pay and performance and entrench bureaucratic compensation systems.[6]

Thus, the findings of financial economists such as Jensen and Murphy appear to support political reformers' general assessment that the U.S. executive compensation system is badly flawed. But Jensen and Murphy's assessment of the fundamental *cause* of the problem—namely, the inadequate link between pay and performance—is, of course, worlds apart from the thinking of political reformers. Whereas political reformers seek caps on executive pay, the solution proposed by Jensen and Murphy is *larger* potential payoffs to CEOs for outstanding stock performance (as well as lower payoffs and greater probability of dismissal, for substandard performance). The message of Jensen and Murphy is that providing CEOs with larger stakes in future shareholder wealth gains using new "super-linkage" compensation contracts would spur them to create more shareholder value, which in turn would trigger large financial rewards to CEOs. This solution, as suggested, is completely at odds with the policy goals of political reformers.

The View of Accounting Economists

There is a relatively new accounting literature—stemming largely from the work of Ross Watts and Jerry Zimmerman at the University of Rochester in the late 1970s and early 1980s—that uses the principles of economic reasoning to explain the development of accounting standards and corporate choices among different accounting methods.[7] The basic premise of such "positive" accounting theory is that accounting methods, in the absence of tax or regulatory consequences,

---

[6] Michael C. Jensen and Kevin J. Murphy, "CEO Incentives—It's Not How Much You Pay, But How," *Harvard Business Review*, (May–June 1990), p. 139.

[7] For an introduction to and summary of such work, see Ross Watts and Jerrold Zimmerman, (1986), *Positive Accounting Theory*, Prentice Hall, (Englewood Cliffs, NJ).

evolve over time so as to provide more cost-effective measures of managerial performance. In this view, the accounting measure of earnings has come to be the nearly universal measure of firm performance because it is the most efficient, or cost-effective measure of managerial performance yet devised.

Based on this reasoning alone, it can hardly be a criticism of modern CEO compensation contracts that they rely heavily on accounting earnings to evaluate managerial performance. Indeed, the accounting literature generally defends the traditional practice of basing executive bonuses and long-term incentive plans on accounting earnings. For example, one such defense presents evidence to support the widely-held view that the use of earnings shields executive compensation from market-wide fluctuations in equity values that are not caused by expected changes in fundamentals.[8]

Even so, critics of executive compensation practices often cite such accounting studies *precisely because* they show that accounting earnings are only marginally related to stock returns on a year-to-year basis. These critics therefore categorically reject any pay plans tied to earnings as failing to meet their pay-for-stock-performance standards.

But, in a recently completed working paper,[9] my Rochester colleague Frank Dorkey and I found that, after grouping the data into five-year averages, accounting earnings and stock returns are very significantly correlated. In fact, for a sample of 576 large firms covering 1963–1990, five-year changes in accounting-based performance measures—especially earnings per share before extraordinary items—had a higher positive correlation with five-year individual company stock returns than with changes in the broad stock market index over the same period.[10]

We also find, using five-year averages, that the accounting returns are not strongly related to the market index. This evidence that longer-term accounting measures are not influenced much by macroeconomic "noise," but are highly correlated with market-adjusted individual firm stock returns, provides support for the widespread use of accounting measures in incentive-pay contracts. This kind of evidence also explains why Kevin Murphy (1985) and others consistently find that actual yearly executive compensation (whether just salary and bonus, or including stock compensation) is positively and significantly correlated with yearly stock returns. Although most annual incentive pay is linked directly to accounting earnings and not stock returns, there is a strong enough correlation between net-of-market stock returns and accounting earnings that, in the final analysis, annual executive pay turns out to be significantly related to yearly stock returns.

---

[8] See Richard J. Sloan, "Accounting Earnings and Top Executive Compensation," Ph.D. Dissertation for Simon Business School, University of Rochester, 1991. Sloan also reviews some possible reasons why options indexed to measure only net of market (or industry) stock returns are not rationally used as substitutes for accounting earnings. These reasons include costs, such as tax losses, disadvantageous reporting requirements, and adverse-incentive costs.

[9] Gregg J. Jarrell and Frank C. Dorkey, "The Longer-Term Relation Between Accounting Performance and Stock Returns," *Working Paper*, (Bradley Policy Research Center, University of Rochester, 1992).

[10] This finding is consistent with the work of Sloan, cited in note 8.

Conclusion

Academic research on executive pay has consistently shown that both pay and turnover rates are positively related to stock returns. In large samples, these positive correlations between pay and performance are statistically significant according to the usual standards. Accounting research has consistently shown that accounting earnings and stock returns are also positively related, and in a statistically significant way. Indeed, my own recent research shows that five-year average company stock returns are more highly correlated with earnings-per-share than with returns to the value-weighted market portfolio. Moreover, earnings are not influenced greatly by the macroeconomic "noise" reflected in stock returns. Consistent with this evidence, traditional pay practice is to base most bonus payments on accounting performance, and to supplement bonuses with stock options designed to link long-term stock returns with executive pay.

The empirical findings of the academic research would thus appear to lend significant support to the view that common practice for rewarding top executives is consistent with both competitive markets and the basic principle of pay-for-performance. Yet there is much criticism of allegedly excessive executive pay and widespread concern that the market for selecting and rewarding top executives is uncompetitive and inefficient. Recent SEC disclosure reforms on executive pay, increased regulatory burdens placed on the granting of new options to executives, and calls for new tax penalties on executive pay packages above $1 million testify to the political weight behind these criticisms.

Why is economists' collective testimony to the competitiveness of the CEO labor market not being heard in the policy debate? The main reason may be that some academics themselves ignore it, or at least contribute to its misinterpretation. Financial economists in particular complain that the degree of pay-for-performance linkage revealed in the historical data is inadequate. This charge is made in good faith even though it is not analytically rigorous. After all, noting that executives receive only a small (but nonetheless statistically significant!) fraction of changes in total shareholder wealth is not sufficient grounds to conclude that top executives are not paid in relation to their marginal product.

Total shareholder wealth is influenced by the productivity of CEOs, but rarely is it accurate to equate the two. Common practice in the U.S. and elsewhere is to rely on accounting earnings directly to set incentive pay, but to supplement this with stock options. This would seem to be perfectly consistent with setting pay that reflects the measurable, controllable marginal productivity of CEOs.

Academic critics of executive pay might be correct when they claim that the market operates uncompetitively, but the empirical record reviewed here does not persuasively support that claim. In fact, I think that the academic record provides important signs that the market operates with reasonable efficiency overall. More important, however, the academic complaints about the inefficiency of the CEO labor market have unintentionally contributed to the recently enacted and proposed policy reforms. This is unfortunate, because the policy implications of the academic criticism are just the opposite of those intended by most policy reformers. The academic critics are actually calling for greater pay-for-performance linkage. Because of the improvements in performance expected to accompany greater pay for performance, such changes are expected to lead to much *higher*, not lower, executive pay on average. In contrast, the actual policies enacted and proposed are designed to cap CEO pay. To the extent they succeed in so doing, they will contribute over time to a reduced pay-for-performance linkage.

Questions

1. Describe the components of a typical compensation package for a chief executive officer (CEO) of a large corporation.
2. Why do critics (e.g., Ralph Nader, Mark Green, and Michael Kinsley) charge that executive compensation is excessive?
3. In what way do the following factors serve to constrain the level of executive compensation: (1) potential proxy fight, (2) outside members of the board of directors, (3) takeover threat, (4) SEC disclosure requirements, and (5) shareholder activist groups.
4. In your opinion, which is the more important issue: (1) the level of executive compensation or (2) the link between executive compensation and corporate performance? Explain.
5. Michael Jensen and Kevin Murphy, using a large sample of CEOs and a long time period, found that total executive compensation increases about $3 for every $1,000 increase in shareholder wealth. Do you believe that this positive relationship between compensation and shareholder wealth is sufficient to align the interests of executives with shareholders? Explain.
6. What is the advantage of tying executive compensation to some measure of accounting earnings instead of stock price?
7. Assume that the president of General Motors Corporation owns less than one percent of GM's common stock. Does it follow that GM's president will be relatively unmotivated by self-interest to maximize GM's stock price? Explain.
8. When heavyweight champion Michael Tyson fought challenger Michael Spinks, Tyson earned more than $20 million; Spinks earned "only" $13 million. Tyson knocked out Spinks only 91 seconds into the fight. How is it possible for Tyson and Spinks to earn more money for one boxing match than most top executives earn for several years of work?

Owners versus Managers: Who Controls the Bank?

LORETTA J. MESTER

> "Let's remember when we talk about hostile takeovers, the hostility is between the managements of the two organizations, not between the shareholders of either. In fact, the problem that exists is that too often, in my judgment, the managements try to protect themselves from, in effect, their own shareholders, who are essentially their bosses."

Alan Greenspan, Chairman of the Federal Reserve Board, testifying before the Senate Banking Committee in February 1988 on Bank of New York's hostile-takeover bid for Irving Bank.

On October 5, 1988, Bank of New York's year-long struggle to take over the Irving Bank Corporation ended when Irving announced it would accept BONY's tender offer. While not the first hostile takeover in the banking industry, the BONY-Irving transaction is the largest the industry has experienced to date. Although Irving claimed during the battle that such hostile takeovers would "promote serious instability in the industry," the Federal Reserve has taken the position that it will treat hostile bids no differently from friendly bids in assessing whether or not to permit a takeover.

Why do some managers, as Chairman Greenspan stated, try to "protect themselves" from their own shareholders? If managers are hired to act on behalf of the stockholders, the firm's owners, then why wouldn't the goals of both always be aligned? Or if managers were inclined to act on their own behalf and not on the owners' behalf, why wouldn't the market ensure the replacement of such managers and so deter any self-serving actions?

The agency theory of the firm can be used to analyze the relationship between a firm's owners and managers. It asks whether there are sufficient mechanisms in place that will induce managers to take actions in the best interests of

---

At the time of this writing, Loretta J. Mester was a senior economist in the Banking and Financial Markets Section of the Federal Reserve Bank of Philadelphia's Research Department.

Source: Reprinted from *Business Review*, Federal Reserve Bank of Philadelphia, (May/June 1989).

owners, or whether managers will be able to act in their own interests at the expense of owners. If agency problems exist, are there ways in which owners can control managers?

The conventional theory of the firm makes no distinction between the managers of a firm and its owners: the firm is treated as a single entity that acts to maximize its stock market value (and so its long-run economic profits). But this view applies only to small firms that are tightly run by entrepreneurial owners willing to take risks. Many firms today, including banks, are complex organizations. More banks are members of holding companies, holding a larger percentage of assets than ever before.[1]

At the same time, ownership of the bank is becoming more dispersed—that is, most shareholders own only a small fraction of the bank's shares. In today's larger, more complex banking corporation, decisions are made not by a single individual but by officers and directors, who do not, without inducement, have the same goals as the stockholders. Because outside directors on the bank's board have no managerial responsibilities, their goals are less likely to differ from those of the stockholders they represent. But inside directors are managers whose goals do differ from bank owners. And more control in the hands of inside directors means more chance of conflict, or so-called agency problems.

Recent empirical studies of the banking industry indicate that agency problems do exist. Agency theory suggests certain prescriptions that would help minimize the conflict between bank managers and bank stockholders. These prescriptions include the Fed's position on treating hostile takeovers no differently from friendly takeovers.

The Owner-Manager Relationship Is a Principal-Agent One

The relationship between bank owners and bank managers is just one example of a principal-agent relationship. A principal delegates an agent to take some action on his behalf, often because the agent is an expert. A person who hires a real estate agent to sell his house, a performer who hires an agent to find her interesting acting roles, or a litigant who hires an attorney to try his case in court are all principals who are hiring agents. In fact, the word "attorney" means agent. (See the Bibliography for several excellent articles on agency theory.)

Several principal-agent relationships are found in banks. The bank acts as an agent for its depositors: when depositors place their money in a bank account rather than investing directly in firms, they are delegating to the bank the responsibility of monitoring the performance of each firm to which the bank lends depositors' money.[2] Borrowers are also agents for the bank: typically, the

---

[1] In 1987, 68.3 percent of commercial banks were in bank holding companies (BHCs), holding 91.9 percent of the industry's assets. This is a substantial increase from 1977, when 26.5 percent of banks were in BHCs, holding 68.2 percent of the assets.

[2] Mitchell Berlin discusses the role of the bank as a delegated monitor in "Bank Loans and Marketable Securities: How Do Financial Contracts Control Borrowing Firms?" *Business Review* (July/August 1987) pp. 9–18.

firm selects the projects it will develop with the money it has borrowed. But banks can also be thought of as agents for borrowers, since the bank works on the firm's behalf in obtaining funding for the firm's project. Finally, as in other kinds of firms, the managers of the bank act as agents for the bank's owners, making decisions about the bank's everyday operations.

Because the agent can be a specialist, there are efficiency gains in the principal-agent relationship. Rather than doing some job for himself, the principal is better off hiring an agent who is an expert in the field. However, these gains must be weighed against the problems that arise in the principal-agent relationship. Problems can arise if the goals of the agent differ from the goals of the principal, and if the agent and principal have different information relevant for the decisions the agent is supposed to make on behalf of the principal. Both conditions must be present for there to be a problem. Suppose, for instance, that the agent had the same goals as the principal. In this case there would be no problem—the agent, in working on his own behalf, would also be doing what the principal wants.

But the goals of the principal and agent are not always aligned. For example, an attorney who is paid a flat fee regardless of the outcome of a case might not put forth her best effort to win on the litigant's behalf. Of course, if the litigant could see how hard the attorney was working and knew enough law to determine whether the attorney was pursuing the best strategy to win, then the litigant could fire the attorney for shirking. Knowing this, the attorney would be compelled to work hard in order to get paid. But typically the principal is ignorant of some relevant information—the litigant can't tell how hard the attorney is working and, even if he could, he doesn't know enough law to determine whether the attorney is doing the best possible job. (If the litigant knew enough law, he wouldn't have to hire the attorney.)

The benefits in the principal-agent relationship derive from the specialized knowledge of the agent. But the fact that the principal and agent have different information causes a problem if the two have different goals. One way to solve the problem is to bring the aims of the agent in line with the aims of the principal. For example, if instead of paying the attorney a flat fee, the litigant paid a fee contingent on the outcome of the case, then the attorney would have the incentive to try her best to win. (Many contracts between attorneys and their clients are written this way.)

The two conditions necessary for a principal-agent conflict—divergent goals and different information—are present in the owner-manager relationship. The owners of widely held firms want to maximize their firm's market value. Typically, these owners hold a portfolio of stock in many firms. If their portfolios are well diversified, they won't be concerned about the riskiness of any one firm.[3] Managers, however, have their own goals that may not coincide with value maximization. Managers want to maximize their own welfare, which may mean

[3] In fact, if the owners of a firm that is leveraged can declare bankruptcy and have limited liability, they may want to take on more risk. The owners would benefit from a risky action if it paid off, but could declare bankruptcy and avoid the full cost of the action if it didn't.

diverting some of the firm's resources for their own use. For example, managers may want to spend money on perquisites like large staffs and expensive offices—so-called expense preference behavior.

In addition, managers of large firms are often paid more than managers of small firms. While this could be related to the greater difficulty of managing a large firm, it also gives a manager the incentive to maximize the firm's size rather than its value. For example, a loan officer's compensation might be tied to the number of loans he makes, not to their quality and so not to the value produced by his portfolio. The manager of a large firm may also find that he has better employment opportunities than the manager of a small firm—another incentive to maximize size rather than value.

Unlike diversified shareholders of widely held firms, managers will be concerned about the riskiness of the firm. The manager may have developed skills and studied techniques that can't easily be used in another firm. If so, then if the firm goes bankrupt, the manager would suffer a high cost by losing his job. Since a manager can't be diversified like the firm's owners can be (that is, he can't hold a portfolio of employers), he may take on less than the value-maximizing amount of risk.[4]

Just as in the litigant-attorney relationship, it is difficult for the firm's owners to see all the actions the manager takes on their behalf. And even if owners see the actions, it is difficult for them to know if these actions are proper for the situation, since managers know more about the firm than the owners. (Recall that one reason to hire a manager is for his expertise.) Therefore, unless controlled, managers will not always act to maximize the wealth of shareholders. Managers will divert resources for their own use to provide themselves with perks and will act too conservatively in order to avoid the risk of unemployment.

Owners versus Managers in Banks

These same issues characterize the owner-management relationship in today's large, complex banking organization. But the conflicts between owners and managers can also explain why small banks often act in a very risk-averse manner. In these small banks, the owners are the managers. They can be thought of as owners who also manage their bank, but it's better to view them as managers who also own the bank. That is, their interests are closer to those of a typical manager than to those of shareholders in a widely held firm. Owner-managers in small banks often have a taste for managing and therefore try to act in a manner that would preserve their positions as bank managers. This would include acting very conservatively—maintaining high capital-to-asset ratios, for example—in order to avoid bankruptcy.[5]

---

[4] However, there are reasons why managers might take on more risk than the shareholders would like. For example, a manager who directs a risky project that turns out to be successful may increase his attractiveness to other firms. See Stiglitz [6]. Also, if the firm is near bankruptcy, a manager has nothing to lose by taking on a very risky project in an attempt to keep the firm solvent and retain his job. So he has the same incentives as stockholders in leveraged firms that are near bankruptcy. See Eric Rasmussen, "Mutual Banks and Stock Banks," *Journal of Law and Economics* 31 (October 1988) pp. 395–421.

[5] For example, in 1987, the capital-to-asset ratio of banks with assets of at most $100 million was 11.64 percent, while that of banks with assets of over $1 billion was 8.15 percent.

Banking is a regulated industry, and the regulators want to ensure its safety and soundness. Thus, it might seem that regulators would prefer the objectives of managers, since managers prefer less risk. However, regulators also want to ensure an efficient banking industry. They don't want to support bad managers who divert bank resources for their personal use. To the extent that the goals of managers and owners can be aligned, bad management would be weeded out and the industry would become more efficient. Regulations already in place, such as risk-based capital requirements, can help control risk-taking in banking.[6]

The fact that banks are regulated adds another place for the conflict between owners and managers to emerge. Periodically, banks must report their balance sheet information to regulators. Shareholders of the bank have an incentive for *downward window dressing*, that is, taking actions at the end of a reporting period that allow the bank to report lower values for assets and liabilities than their average values over the reporting period. Downward window dressing reduces the cost of meeting capital requirements, lowers the cost of deposit insurance (which is based on the bank's reported liabilities), and may reduce the cost of capital to the bank by raising the bank's apparent capital adequacy ratio and thereby making the bank look safer. So, downward window dressing raises the value of the bank, which is the aim of shareholders.

Managers, on the other hand, have an incentive for *upward window dressing*, since their compensation is often tied to the size of the bank. Also, since upward window dressing reduces the reported capital adequacy ratio, regulators may then require a capital infusion into the bank that would lower the chance of bankruptcy and the risk of managers losing their jobs.[7] Thus, in regulated firms like banks, the direction of window dressing, expenditures on perks, and risk-taking behavior are three areas where the conflict between owners and managers may appear.

What Controls the Behavior of Managers?

While managers and owners have divergent goals, it is not clear that managers can pursue their own goals at the expense of owners. There are some controls that limit the ability of managers to follow the beat of their own drummer. These controls fall into two groups: labor market controls and capital market controls.

Labor Market Controls

Managers want to act in their own best interests; however, if their interests can be made to coincide with those of stockholders, then by acting for themselves they will be acting for stockholders. For example, if a manager's compensation is tied to the value of the firm's stock, then she will want to act to raise the value

[6] But some regulations, such as flat-rate deposit insurance, exacerbate the conflict between bank managers and stockholders over the optimal level of risk-taking.

[7] This is discussed in Allen and Saunders [8].

of the stock—which is what the owners want. But even though more corporations are including stock in managerial compensation packages, bank size rather than performance still appears to be the largest determinant of pay scales in the banking industry.[8,9] Perhaps a better incentive for a manager is her reputation. Managers with good reputations will have an easier time finding other jobs, if they need to, and will have better employment opportunities than managers with poor reputations.

Capital Market Controls[10]

Other controls on the behavior of managers work through the capital markets. One potential control on managers is the stockholders' meeting. However, these meetings are rarely effective since they are usually controlled by management. Also, stockholders who are well diversified usually don't bother to attend the meetings and vote since they don't have very much of their wealth tied up in any one firm. Good management is what economists call a public good—all the stockholders benefit from good management, but no individual stockholder has an incentive to ensure that management is good because the personal gain from doing so is not great enough. Other shareholders can get a "free ride" if one shareholder decides to become an active participant in the stockholder meetings. Large shareholders, however, can exert control on the management—they find it worth their effort—but usually have to be compensated in some way for taking on the risk of not being diversified; for example, they may receive a high fee for being on the board of directors.[11]

One control on the management of nonfinancial corporations involves banks themselves. Like large shareholders, banks have an incentive to monitor the performance of firms to which they have made substantial loans, in order to avoid default. Unlike equity holders, who cannot control their funds once invested, banks have more control of their funds: they set the terms of their loans and can decide not to reinvest in the firms once the loans mature.

The interbank loan market and certificate of deposit (CD) market provide a similar control on banking firms, especially money-center banks, which rely greatly on purchased funds. Federal funds transactions (overnight interbank loans) are not collateralized, so banks that find themselves in trouble (perhaps due to the negligence of management) must pay a premium for such funds. Also, the large, negotiable CDs of large banks trade on a no-name basis. That is,

---

[8] This was reported by J. Richard Fredericks and Jackie Arata in *Montgomery Securities Annual Banking Industry Compensation Review*, May 5, 1987. In studying compensation at 33 banks in 1985 and 1986, they found no correlation between the compensation of the top five highest-paid employees and the performance of the bank.

[9] Joseph Stiglitz [5] observes that most stock-option plans were instituted not so that managers would bear more risk, but as supplements to their salaries. Thus, the incentive effects of these plans are questionable. However, a Bank Administration Institute survey of 839 banks with assets under $500 million found a positive correlation between bank performance and the presence of an annual bonus program. Of course, it is not clear which came first, the award program or better performance. See W. Frank Kelly, "Bank Performance and CEO Compensation," *Bank Administration* 62 (November 1986) pp. 52–56.

[10] Most of the discussion in this section and the next follows Stiglitz [5] and Jensen [2].

[11] See Stiglitz [5], p. 144.

even though CDs differ with respect to the quality of the issuing bank, dealers quote a single price for large-bank CDs and don't specify names when trading them. However, if a bank is in trouble, traders will refuse to trade the bank's CDs on a no-name basis. Once singled out, the bank will have to pay a premium for funds. (Continental Illinois, for example, was dropped from the no-name list when it ran into trouble in 1982.) In addition to hurting shareholders (by lowering the market value of the bank), these "punishments" have a direct negative impact on managers by hurting their reputations, by reducing the amount available for perquisites, by lowering compensation to the extent it is tied to market performance, and by increasing their chance of unemployment due to bankruptcy.

The Threat of Takeover Is a Capital Market Control on Managers

The 1980s have seen a new wave of corporate mergers, acquisitions, and takeovers. The pros and cons of these takeovers are being debated, especially the extensive use of debt financing characteristic of recent takeovers, and the wealth transfers from employees (many of whom lose their jobs) to shareholders of the acquired firm (who gain the takeover premium).

A potential benefit of a well-functioning takeover market is that the threat of a takeover, in which management is usually replaced, can discipline managers to act in the interests of the firm's shareholders. The idea here is that if the firm's market value could be enhanced with better management, then someone could purchase the firm by buying the outstanding shares from the current shareholders. He could then remove the bad management, make the proper decisions to maximize the firm's value, and gain from that increase in value.

For several reasons, however, this takeover threat won't necessarily be effective in controlling management. And even if takeovers are effective in replacing bad management, there are several ways in which managers can avoid this discipline.

For instance, takeovers may not work because of information problems. A firm may be performing poorly because the current management is bad or because the past management was bad. That is, management might be doing the best it can given what it has to work with. Only the insiders of a weak firm know which is the case, and if they hold enough stock in the firm to determine the outcome of any takeover attempt, they'll sell only if the offer is more than the firm is worth. In other words, successful takeovers will be overpriced takeovers, in which case the new stockholder will not gain.

As with the stockholders' meetings, there are free-rider problems associated with takeovers. Suppose takeovers work and eliminate inefficient management; then the shareholders who didn't sell their shares get a free ride and gain from the firm's increased stock price. Each shareholder reasons this way, believing she doesn't have enough stock to affect the success of the takeover attempt. Therefore, it is in her interest to hold onto her shares. If everyone does this, the takeover won't be successful.

Another free-rider problem occurs if it is costly to find badly managed firms, which are good takeover targets. Someone who has expended the resources to find such a firm and then makes a bid thereby announces to other potential bidders that the firm is a good target. The ensuing bidding war drives to zero any expected profits from taking over the firm, so the first bidder who expended the resources to find the target firm earns a negative expected profit, even if he's successful in taking over the firm. Therefore, there is no gain in finding good takeover targets.[12]

While extreme, these cases point out that it is not easy to complete a successful takeover. However, if bidders can find a way to keep some of the gains from a successful takeover for themselves (rather than sharing them with others) they will have an incentive to search out firms with inefficient management and attempt a takeover.[13] But even if the takeover market would otherwise work smoothly, there are ways in which managers of targeted firms can deter takeovers. By thwarting potential acquirers, these actions help entrench managers who may not be acting in the shareholders' interests.[14]

For example, managers of a targeted firm can swallow a *poison pill*, that is, they can take some action that will make the firm an unattractive candidate for takeover. The action is something that the firm wouldn't do if it were not threatened with a takeover. One poison pill is for the targeted firm itself to take over another firm in order to increase the possibility of antitrust litigation if its potential acquirer succeeds. Other poison pills include financial restructuring of the firm, issuing "poison pill preferred stock" that raises the cost of a takeover, or selling off some assets that attracted the bidder.

In the Bank of New York-Irving fight, Irving's board voted a poison pill that gave shareholders certain rights to buy stock at half price in the event of a hostile merger. They added a "flip in" amendment that allowed the measure even if the hostile investor did not attempt an immediate merger. BONY filed suit against this defense and a state court invalidated it. The decision was appealed and the Appellate Division of the New York Supreme Court upheld it, which led to the takeover's final resolution.

Another way a firm can prevent a takeover involves *greenmail.* The payment of greenmail refers to a targeted stock-repurchase plan in which managers repurchase the stock of a subgroup of shareholders at a premium over the market price. Greenmail can be used to avert a takeover—if offered enough, the potential acquirer will sell the shares it has accumulated back to management. Usually, the potential acquirer also signs an agreement prohibiting the purchase of any of the firm's stock for a period of time, sometimes as long as five years.

---

[12] Event studies find that in recent takeovers the excess returns to acquired firms are usually positive, while those to acquiring firms are often negative or zero. See Robert Schweitzer, "How Do Stock Returns React to Special Events?" in a forthcoming issue of this *Business Review.*

[13] See Andrei Shleifer and Robert W. Vishny [4].

[14] These defensive tactics may, however, actually improve the takeover market. Eliminating a bidder can help solve the bidding-war free-rider problem discussed above and encourage other firms to study the possibility of taking over the firm. The increased likelihood of more bids may be enough to compensate shareholders for the elimination of a potential acquirer and the costs of discouraging him. See Andrei Shleifer and Robert W. Vishny, "Greenmail, White Knights, and Shareholders' Interest," *Rand Journal of Economics* 17 (Autumn 1986) pp. 293–309.

Like greenmail, *golden parachutes* can be used to deter takeovers by raising their cost. A golden parachute is a large severance payment made to top managers who are replaced after a takeover. By lowering the costs to managers of losing their jobs, the parachutes also hinder the threat of takeover in controlling managers. They may also induce the manager to cave in and sell the firm at too low a price, or even to seek out buyers for the firm. On the other hand, the parachutes may benefit shareholders by facilitating a takeover. If the managers who have to decide whether or not to fight the takeover have golden parachutes, they will be less inclined to fight—and this can benefit shareholders. Also, by lowering the costs to managers of investing in education and training worth little outside the firm, the parachutes may increase the efficiency of managers.

On balance, then, whether golden parachutes are harmful or beneficial to stockholders depends on who receives them and how they are structured. If the parachutes are paid to the managers involved in negotiating the terms of the takeover with a potential acquirer, and if their value is tied to the increase in the firm's market value that may occur after a takeover, then parachutes benefit shareholders. Otherwise, they are probably detrimental to shareholders.

In general, restrictions on the type or number of potential acquirers of a firm make takeovers less likely and limit the ability of the takeover threat to discipline management. For example, there are two principal ways for a corporation to acquire a commercial bank. It can either acquire a controlling interest in the bank's stock or it can merge with the bank. But mergers are prohibited between nonbank corporations and commercial banks, and some states restrict corporate acquisitions of bank stock. Also, banks in states that prohibit branching are less attractive merger partners than are banks in branching states, all else equal, and prohibition of interstate banking eliminates out-of-state banks as potential bidders, making takeovers less likely. Thus, in banking, the threat of takeovers may not ensure that managers work on behalf of their shareholders.[15] However, the recent breakdown of these restrictions—for example, regional interstate banking pacts—suggests that the takeover threat should become more effective in the future.

How Effective Are the Control Mechanisms in the Financial Services Industry?

Although there are many potential mechanisms for ensuring that managers act on behalf of stockholders, these controls are imperfect and costly. Just how well do these controls work in the financial services industry? Are managers able to pursue their own goals at the stockholders' expense, or are they disciplined to act in a way that maximizes the value of the firm? Empirical studies suggest that there are agency problems in financial firms: managers are able to pursue their own interests and do not always act in an efficient, value-maximizing manner. (The Bibliography includes references to the studies discussed below.)

[15] This is the focus of Christopher James [11].

Several studies of the commercial banking industry find evidence that managers spend excessively on perquisites, such as large staffs. That is, they spend more than the profit-maximizing amount. Michael Smirlock and William Marshall present evidence that larger banks, whose management is presumably harder to control, exhibit such expense preference behavior. In a study of states that limit the acquisition market for banks by limiting the amount of bank stock a corporation can own, Christopher James finds that bank managers in these states spend more on perquisites than do managers of banks in states that permit corporate holdings of bank stock. This is evidence that takeovers can discipline managers.[16]

In a study last year, the author investigated the savings and loan industry for evidence of expense preference behavior. Savings and loans are organized either as stock-issuing institutions or as mutual institutions. Although the owners of a mutual S&L are, in theory, its depositors, these owners have virtually no control over management. Thus, managers of mutual S&Ls should be more able to follow their own pursuits than managers of stock S&Ls. The author's study finds that the mutual S&Ls are operating with an inefficient mix of inputs and outputs. While this could be due to the impact of regulations and to the fact that mutual S&Ls are not able to issue stock in order to expand, it is more likely evidence that managers are consuming some of the firm's resources as perquisites.

In addition to spending excessively on perquisites, managers have the incentive to act more conservatively than shareholders would like and to engage in upward window dressing. Anthony Saunders, Elizabeth Strock, and Nickolaos G. Travlos find evidence that banks with diffuse ownership—that is, no one shareholder holds a large number of shares—are more conservative than other banks whose shareholders can be expected to exert more influence on the decisions of managers. Linda Allen and Anthony Saunders find evidence of upward window dressing in banks located in states with takeover barriers and in banks whose managers have no large equity holdings.

To sum up these studies, in cases where the agency theory predicts that managers of financial firms will work on their own behalf rather than on the shareholders' behalf, there is evidence that they do so.

Prescriptions to Remedy Agency Problems

There is evidence that managers of financial firms are able to pursue their own interests rather than the interests of shareholders. The agency theory of the firm suggests several ways in which the goals of managers and shareholders could be better aligned, which would lead to higher efficiency and help resolve agency problems.

---

16 However, the methodology of the studies by Smirlock and Marshall and by James, as well as that of earlier banking studies, is critiqued in Loretta J. Mester, "A Testing Strategy for Expense Preference Behavior," *Working Paper 88-13/R*, Federal Reserve Bank of Philadelphia, December 1988.

Bank managers and directors could be encouraged to own stock in the companies they manage. In this way, they would directly benefit from the decisions they make that increase the market value of the bank. Since outside directors' goals are more coincident with shareholders', increasing the power of outside directors to remove managers could induce better behavior by managers. But this may not have much effect if it is difficult to find directors with enough knowledge to determine whether the management should be replaced. Finally, decreasing the barriers to takeovers—including state prohibitions on corporate acquisition of commercial bank stock, laws prohibiting interstate banking and branching, and laws restricting hostile takeovers—will increase the effectiveness of the takeover threat as a device to control managers; so will the Federal Reserve's position to treat hostile takeovers in banking no differently from friendly takeover bids.

Some argue that today's takeovers are too often funded by high-risk junk bonds or other sources of debt that can lead to macroeconomic instability by increasing the number of bankruptcies when a recession hits.[17] And there is evidence that while shareholders of the target firm gain in a takeover, their gain is at the expense of employees who lose their jobs or are forced to take wage cuts.[18] Clearly, not all takeovers are in the best interests of society. However, it should be remembered that an actual takeover is not necessary to induce managers to act efficiently—the *threat* of a takeover is what is needed. If restrictions on takeovers are reduced, making the possibility of a takeover a real threat to inefficient managers, these managers will be induced to maximize the value of their firms. Easing restrictions on takeovers could actually lead to a reduction in the number of acquisitions by reducing the number of inefficiently managed firms, which are among the prime takeover targets.

Bibliography

There are many excellent articles on the agency theory of the firm. Several of the articles cited in the text are included in this bibliography.

[1] Kenneth J. Arrow, "The Economics of Agency," in *Principals and Agents: The Structure of Business*, John W. Pratt and Richard J. Zeckhauser, eds.(Boston: Harvard Business School Press, 1985) pp. 1–35. This is an excellent overview of the principal-agent relationship. In fact, all of the articles in this book are recommended.

[2] Michael C. Jensen, "Takeovers: Their Causes and Consequences," *The Journal of Economic Perspectives* 2 (Winter 1988) pp. 21–48. An excellent overview of the takeover as a capital market control on managers, this article discusses such potential takeover deterrents as greenmail and golden parachutes.

[3] Michael C. Jensen and William H. Meckling, "Theory of the Firm: Managerial Behavior, Agency Costs and Ownership Structure," *Journal of Financial Economics* 3 (1976) pp. 305–360. This article discusses agency theory and the financial structure of firms.

[17] See F.M. Scherer, "Corporate Takeovers: The Efficiency Arguments," *Journal of Economic Perspectives* 2 (Winter 1988) pp. 69–82.

[18] See Shleifer and Vishny [4].

[4] Andrei Shleifer and Robert W. Vishny, "Value Maximization and the Acquisition Process," *The Journal of Economic Perspectives* 2 (Winter 1988) pp. 7–20. The authors review the agency theory of the firm and the role of hostile takeovers in disciplining managers.

[5] Joseph E. Stiglitz, "Credit Markets and the Control of Capital," *Journal of Money, Credit, and Banking* 17 (May 1985) pp. 133–152. This is an excellent introduction to the conflicts between owners and managers, and the effectiveness of certain controlling devices.

[6] Joseph E. Stiglitz, "Ownership, Control, and Efficient Markets: Some Paradoxes in the Theory of Capital Markets," in *Economic Regulation: Essays in Honor of James R. Nelson*, Kenneth D. Boyer and William G. Shepherd, eds. (East Lansing, MI: Michigan State University Press, 1981) pp. 311–340. The author discusses managerial incentives for risk-taking.

[7] "The Symposium on Takeovers," in *The Journal of Economic Perspectives* 2 (Winter 1988), includes several papers, in addition to those by Jensen and by Shleifer and Vishny, on the role of takeovers as an external control mechanism.

Empirical studies of agency problems in financial firms include:

[8] Linda Allen and Anthony Saunders, "Incentives to Engage in Bank Window Dressing: Manager vs. Stockholder Conflicts," *Working Paper No. 471*, Salomon Brothers Center for the Study of Financial Institutions, Graduate School of Business Administration, New York University, June 1988.

[9] Franklin R. Edwards, "Managerial Objectives in Regulated Industries: Expense-Preference Behavior in Banking," *Journal of Political Economy* 85 (1977) pp. 147–162.

[10] Timothy H. Hannan and Ferdinand Mavinga, "Expense Preference and Managerial Control: The Case of the Banking Firm," *Bell Journal of Economics* 11 (Autumn 1980) pp. 671–682.

[11] Christopher James, "An Analysis of the Effect of State Acquisition Laws on Managerial Efficiency: The Case of the Bank Holding Company Acquisition," *Journal of Law and Economics* 27 (April 1984) pp. 211–226.

[12] Loretta J. Mester, "Agency Costs in Savings and Loans," *Working Paper No.88-14/R*, Federal Reserve Bank of Philadelphia, November 1988.

[13] Anthony Saunders, Elizabeth Strock, and Nickolaos G. Travlos, "Ownership Structure, Deregulation and Bank Risk Taking," *Working Paper No. 443*, Salomon Brothers Center for the Study of Financial Institutions, Graduate School of Business Administration, New York University, October 1987.

[14] Michael Smirlock and William Marshall, "Monopoly Power and Expense-Preference Behavior: Theory and Evidence to the Contrary," *Bell Journal of Economics* 14 (Spring 1983) pp. 166–178.

Questions

1. Adolf Berle and Gardiner Means wrote a famous book entitled *The Modern Corporation and Private Property* (1932). In their book, the authors coin the phrase "separation of ownership and control." They also note a "centripetal force on economic power but a centrifugal force on ownership" among U.S. corporations. Explain the meaning of these quotations.

2. Michael Jensen and William Meckling state: "Stripped to its essentials, the corporation is simply a legal fiction that serves as a nexus of contracts." Chief Justice Marshall (1819) states: "A corporation is an artificial being, invisible, intangible, and existing only in the contemplation of law." In what sense is the corporation a legal fiction, an artificial being, invisible, and intangible? How does the corporation serve as a nexus of contracts?
3. The potential conflict of interest between corporate managers (agents) and shareholders (principals) is an agency problem. Agents and principals may have different goals and different levels of expertise. What are examples of problems that might arise?
4. In what ways does the labor market lessen the agency problem between corporate managers and shareholders?
5. In what ways does the capital market lessen the agency problem between corporate managers and shareholders?
6. Describe the following tactics for resisting corporate takeovers: (a) poison pill, (b) greenmail, and (c) golden parachutes.
7. MFAB, Inc. is a metal fabricating company with five plants located in three midwestern states. The company manufactures brackets, braces, and duct work. More than 500 employees work in each of MFAB's plants. Greenville Metal, a southeastern company, has agreed to acquire MFAB, Inc. for $35 million. To justify the price, Greenville Metal will have to close MFAB's Ohio plant, which produces the same products as Greenville Metal's North Carolina plant. The plant closing will cause 550 employees to lose their jobs. In your opinion, should Greenville Metal be prevented from acquiring MFAB, Inc. and closing the Ohio plant? Defend your answer.

PART

II

Valuation and the Cost of Capital

The Equity Premium: Stock and Bond Returns Since 1802

JEREMY J. SIEGEL

Since 1926, the compound real value-weighted return on all stocks listed on the New York Stock Exchange has averaged 6.4 per cent per year, while the real return on Treasury bills has averaged only 0.5 per cent.[1] This means that the purchasing power of a given sum of money invested (and reinvested) in stocks from 1926 to 1990 would have increased over 50 times, while reinvestment in bills would have increased one's real wealth by about one-third. Using these historical returns, it would take 139 years of investing in Treasury bills to double one's real wealth while it would take only 11 years of stock investment. Money managers often use these figures persuasively to convince investors that, over long periods of time, equity has no match as a wealth builder.

The return on stocks in excess of the return on short-term bonds is called the **equity premium.** Because stocks are generally riskier than fixed income investments, it is to be expected that the return on stocks would exceed that on bonds. However, in 1985 Rajnish Mehra and Edward Prescott demonstrated that stocks, despite their risk, appear to offer investors *excessive* returns, while bonds offer puzzlingly low returns.[2] The excessive return on equity is termed the "equity premium puzzle." Investors would have to be extraordinarily risk-averse, given the documented growth and variability of the economy, to accept such low returns on bonds while equity offered such superior returns. Such extreme risk-aversion appears to be inconsistent with data that reveal investor choice under uncertainty.

At the time of this writing, Jeremy J. Siegel was a professor of finance at the Wharton School at the University of Pennsylvania.

Source: Reprinted, with permission, from *Financial Analysts Journal*, January/February 1992.

[1] The average compound real return on the S&P 500 has been 6.7 per cent over the same period. Very small stocks (bottom quartile of capitalization) have performed better, averaging 8.2 per cent compound real return since 1926.

[2] R. Mehra and E. Prescott, "The Equity Premium: A Puzzle," *Journal of Monetary Economics* 15 (1985), pp. 145–61. The time period covered by Mehra and Prescott was 1889–1978. The returns on stocks and bonds were very similar to the returns since 1926.

Many theories have been offered to explain the equity premium puzzle.[3] The data that Mehra and Prescott analyzed covered a sufficiently long period of time and were derived from well documented sources. Thus no one questioned the validity of their return data.

I extended the time period analyzed by Mehra and Prescott back to 1802, while updating the returns on stocks and bonds to 1990. My analysis demonstrates that the returns from bonds during most of the 19th century and after 1980 were far higher than in the period analyzed by Mehra and Prescott. The equity premium is not nearly as large when viewed over this extended time span as it is in the post-1926 period. These data suggest that the excess return of stocks over bonds may be significantly smaller in the future than it has been over the past 65 years.

Long-Term Asset Returns

William Schwert has developed historical stock price series dating back to 1802; there are also some fragmentary data on stock returns dating to 1789.[4] In order to analyze asset returns since 1802, I divided the data into three subperiods. The first period, running from 1802 through 1870, contains stocks of financial firms and, later, railroads. The second period, running from 1871 through 1925, comprises the period studied by the Cowles Foundation.[5] The last subperiod, from 1926 to the present, coincides with the development of the S&P 500 stock index and contains the most comprehensive data on stock prices and other economic variables.[6] I use the Schwert data for the first subperiod and a capitalization-weighted index of all NYSE stocks for the second and third subperiods.

The early stock indexes were not as comprehensive as those constructed today. From 1802 to 1820, the stock index consisted of an equally weighted portfolio of stocks of several banks in Boston, New York and Philadelphia. An insurance company was added later, and in 1834 the portfolio became heavily

---

[3] Some rely on non-standard preference functions; see, for example, G.M. Constantinides, "Habit Formation: A Resolution of the Equity Premium Puzzle," *Journal of Political Economy* 98:3 (1990), pp. 519–43; A. Abel, "Asset Prices under Habit Formation and Catching up with the Joneses," *American Economic Review* 2:80 (1990), pp. 38–43; S. Benninga and A. Protopapadakis, "Time Preference and the Equity Premium Puzzle," *Journal of Monetary Economics*, January 1990; and P. Weil, "The Equity Premium Puzzle and the Risk-free Rate Puzzle," *Journal of Monetary Economics*, November 1989. Others rely on individual stocks and segmented asset holdings; see N.G. Mankiw, "The Equity Premium and the Concentration of Aggregate Shocks," *Journal of Financial Economics* 17 (1986), pp. 211–19 and N.G. Mankiw and S.P. Zeldes, "The Consumption of Stockholders and Non-Stockholders," *Journal of Financial Economics* 29 (1991), pp. 97–112. See A. Abel, "The Equity Premium Puzzle," Federal Reserve Bank of Philadelphia *Business Review*, September-October 1991, for a summary.

[4] G. William Schwert, "Indexes of United States Stock Prices from 1802 to 1987," *Journal of Business* 63:3 (1990), pp. 399–426. R. Ibbotson and G. Brinson, *Investment Markets: Gaining the Performance Advantage* (New York: McGraw Hill, 1987 p. 73) report that the Foundation for the Study of Cycles, in Pittsburgh, has published data from an internal stock index entitled "Historical Record: Stock Prices 1789–Present," *Data Bulletin* 1975–1. However, attempts to obtain documentation for this series have not been successful.

[5] A. Cowles, *Common Stock Indexes, 1871–1937* (Bloomington, IN: Principia Press, 1938).

[6] In the 1970s and 1980s, Roger Ibbotson and Rex Sinquefield analyzed data on inflation, stock and bond returns since 1926 (see *Stocks, Bonds, Bills, and Inflation, 1991 Yearbook* (Chicago: Ibbotson Associates, 1991)). Several authors (see for example J.W. Wilson and C.P. Jones, "A Comparison of Annual Common Stock Returns: 1871–1925 with 1926–85," *Journal of Business*, April 1987, and "Stock, Bonds, Paper, and Inflation, 1870–1985," *Journal of Portfolio Management*, Fall 1987) have extended much of the data back to 1872.

weighted toward railroad stocks. The Cowles index consisted of all stocks listed on the New York Stock Exchange and recorded, for the first time, dividend payments. The Cowles index is spliced to modern indexes, which calculate averages for all classes of common stock.

Stock Returns

Figure A displays what one dollar invested in various asset classes in 1802 would have accumulated to by the end of 1990. These series are referred to as total return indexes, because they assume that all cash flows, including interest and dividends as well as any capital gains, are continually reinvested in the relevant asset. Total return indexes differ from standard stock market indexes such as the S&P 500, which do not include the reinvestment of cash flows. These standard indexes are called capital appreciation indexes.[7]

FIGURE A TOTAL NOMINAL RETURN INDEXES, BEFORE TAXES, 1802–1990

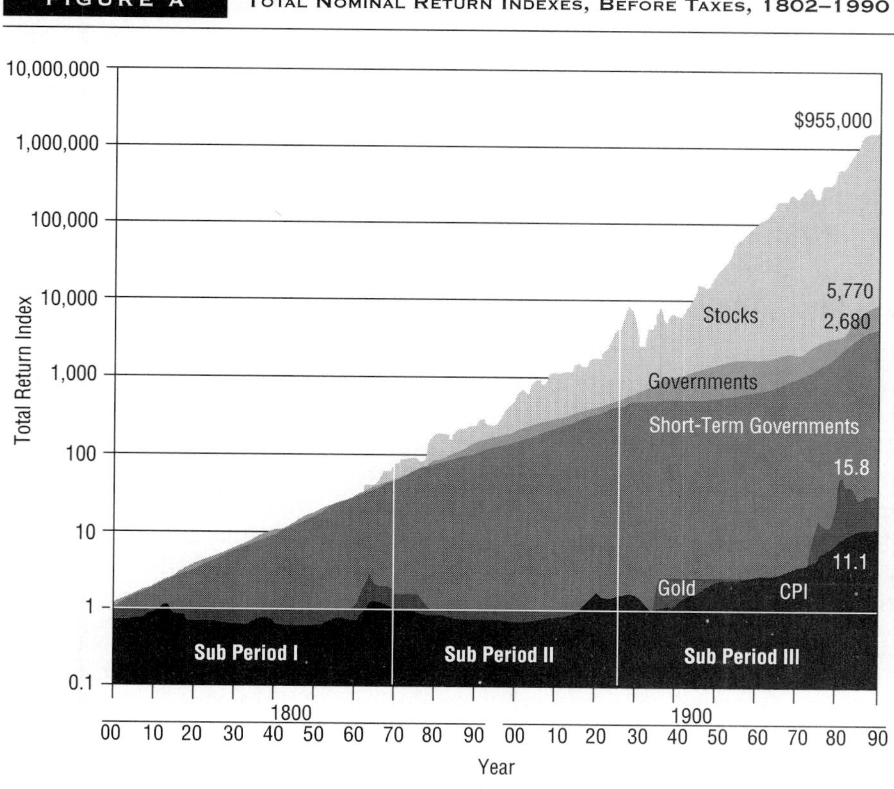

[7] Standard stock indexes do, however, reflect increases in the value of shares resulting from reinvestment of retained earnings and changes in the capitalization of expected earnings.

Figure A indicates that, in terms of total return, stocks have dominated all other asset classes since 1802. Over the entire period, equities achieved a compound annual nominal rate of return of 7.6 per cent per year; at this rate, the nominal value of equity approximately doubles every 9.5 years. Figure A also demonstrates that nominal stock returns have also increased over time. The average compound rate of return on stocks was 5.8 per cent from 1802 through 1870, 7.2 per cent from 1871 through 1925 and 9.8 per cent from 1926 through 1990.[8] Table I gives the stock returns in each subperiod.

The average nominal *arithmetic* (or mean) return on stocks is 9.0 per cent per year over the entire period. Although this can be interpreted as the expected return on stocks over a 12-month period, it cannot be converted into a compound annual rate of return over periods longer than one year. Because of the mathematical properties of return calculations, the compound rate of return to a buy-and-hold strategy is measured by the geometric, rather than the arithmetic, return.[9]

The power of compound returns is clearly evident in the stock market. One dollar invested in 1802, with all dividends reinvested, would have accumulated to nearly $1 million by the end of 1990. Hypothetically, this means that $3 million, invested and reinvested over these past 188 years, would have grown to the incredible sum of $3 trillion—nearly equal to the entire capitalization of the U.S. stock market in 1990!

Three million 1802 dollars—equivalent to about $35 million in today's purchasing power—was a large—but certainly not overwhelming—sum of money to the industrialists and landholders of the early 19th century.[10]

Long-Term Bonds

In comparing past with future bond returns, it is important to choose securities whose risk characteristics match closely. There was an active market for long-term U.S. government bonds over most of the 19th century except for the years 1835 through 1841, when prior budget surpluses eliminated all federal government debt outstanding. Sidney Homer presented a series of long-term government yields in his classic work, *A History of Interest Rates.*[11] Long-term government bond issues were not numerous during the 19th century; maturities generally ranged from three to 20 years, although some bonds had no fixed duration.[12] Figure B displays the interest rates on long-term U.S. government bonds,

---

8 The data from the Foundation for the Study of Cycles (found in Ibbotson and Brinson, *Investment Markets, op. cit.*) show a compound return of 7.95 per cent from 1802 through 1870 and 7.92 per cent from 1789 through 1870.

9 The geometric or compound return is the nth root of the one-year returns; it is always less than the average or mean arithmetic return, except when all yearly returns are equal. The geometric return can be approximated by the arithmetic mean minus one-half the variance of the individual yearly returns.

10 S. Blodget, Jr. (*A Statistical Manual for the United States of America*, 1806 ed., p. 68) estimated that wealth in the U.S. was $2.45 billion in 1802. Total wealth today is estimated at nearly $15 trillion, of which about $4 trillion is in the stock market.

11 S. Homer, *A History of Interest Rates* (New Brunswick, NJ: Rutgers University Press, 1963).

12 The first federal government debt was the Hamilton refunding 6s of 1790, "redeemable at the pleasure of the government at 100 in an amount not exceeding 2% a year."

TABLE I Stock Market Returns (standard deviations in parentheses)*

Period	Total Nominal Return (%)		Total Real Return (%)		Nominal Capital Appreciation (%)		Real Capital Appreciation (%)		Dividend Income	Average Tax Rate	Total Real After-Tax Return (%)	
	A	G	A	G	A	G	A	G	(%) A	(%) A	A	G
1802–1990	9.0	7.6	7.8	6.2	4.0	2.5	2.8	1.2	5.0	6.8	7.3	5.8
	(17.8)		(18.4)		(17.6)		(18.1)		(1.0)		(18.1)	
1871–1990	10.3	8.6	8.3	6.5	5.3	3.6	3.3	1.6	5.0	10.8	7.6	5.9
	(18.9)		(19.3)		(18.6)		(19.0)		(1.3)		(18.9)	
1802–1870	6.8	5.8	6.9	5.7	1.8	0.7	1.9	0.6	5.0	0.0	6.9	5.7
	(15.4)		(16.6)		(15.4)		(16.5)		(0.0)		(16.6)	
1871–1925	8.4	7.2	7.9	6.6	3.1	1.9	2.7	1.3	5.2	0.7	7.9	6.6
	(15.6)		(16.6)		(15.9)		(16.9)		(1.1)		(16.6)	
1926–1990	11.9	9.8	8.6	6.4	7.1	5.0	3.9	1.8	4.8	19.3	7.4	5.3
	(21.1)		(21.2)		(20.4)		(20.5)		(1.4)		(20.7)	
1946–1990	12.0	11.1	7.4	6.2	7.4	6.5	3.0	1.9	4.6	24.4	6.0	4.9
	(14.6)		(15.6)		(13.8)		(14.8)		(1.4)		(14.8)	
1966–1981	7.3	6.2	0.4	-0.7	3.1	2.1	-3.5	-4.6	4.2	26.4	-0.9	-1.8
	(15.1)		(14.3)		(14.3)		(13.8)		(1.3)		(13.5)	
1966–1990	10.7	9.6	4.6	3.5	6.3	5.3	0.6	-0.6	4.3	25.9	3.3	2.2
	(15.1)		(15.2)		(14.4)		(14.6)		(1.2)		(14.3)	
1982–1990	16.7	15.9	12.3	11.4	12.1	11.3	7.9	7.0	4.6	25.1	10.5	9.8
	(13.1)		(13.5)		(12.7)		(13.0)		(1.0)		(12.7)	

* A = arithmetic mean; G = geometric mean.

FIGURE B LONG-TERM INTEREST RATES, 1802–1990

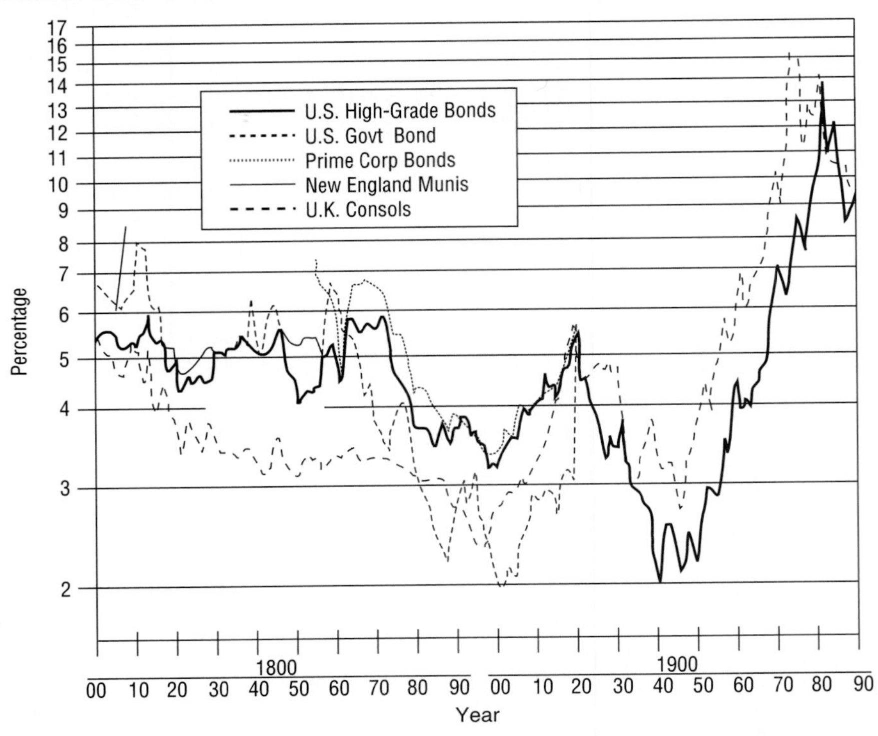

joining the Homer series with the Ibbotson and Sinquefield series, which begins in 1926.[13]

Despite the good data on federal government bond yields, there are persuasive reasons why high-grade municipal bonds may be more representative of high-quality bonds during much of the 19th and early 20th centuries. Some of the municipal bonds issued during the early 19th century, particularly those of the Commonwealth of Massachusetts and the City of Boston, were considered of higher quality than those of the federal government and thus traded at lower yields.[14] Risk of default on federal government bonds increased during both the War of 1812 and the Civil War, hence yields on federal debt rose above the yields on comparable high-grade municipals.[15] Furthermore, these high-grade municipals promised to pay interest and principal only in gold, thereby avoiding the

---

[13] Ibbotson and Sinquefield, *Stocks, Bonds, Bills, op. cit.*

[14] See Homer (*A History, op. cit.*, pp. 296 and 301) and J.G. Martin (*Boston Stock Market*, 1871) for a description of these municipals. The lower yield for municipals was not due to any tax advantage, because tax considerations did not emerge until the early 20th century.

[15] The Greenback period, when the government issued notes not redeemable in specie, provides a fascinating episode in monetary theory. For further discussion, see R. Roll, "Interest Rates and Price Expectations During the Civil War," *Journal of Economic History*, June 1972.

"bimetal" option, which gave the federal government the right to redeem the principal in either gold or silver. This option may have biased the yields on federal government bonds upward.[16]

There is another reason why municipal bond yields should sometimes be substituted for federal government bonds. From the Civil War to 1920, the yields on federal government bonds were biased downward because banks were permitted to issue circulating bank notes against government bonds held as reserves. These rights, called "circulation privileges," motivated banks to bid the prices of federal bonds up above the prices of comparable high-grade securities. The effect of this bias is evident in Figure B. In 1920, circulation privileges were abolished, and the yield on federal government bonds jumped to the level of high-grade municipals.[17]

To avoid the noted problems with federal government bond yields, I constructed a high-grade series that uses the minimum yield on Treasury bonds and high-grade municipal bond yields from 1800 to 1865 and high-grade municipal yields from 1865 to 1917. This is the high-grade bond series depicted in Figure A. Table II summarizes the statistics.

Short-Term Bonds

Treasury bills, or short-term governments, did not exist before 1920. Data on commercial paper rates dating back to the 1830s are available from Macaulay, but during the 19th century commercial paper was subject to a high and variable risk premium, as Figure C shows.[18] These premiums often developed during or just prior to liquidity and financial crises (marked by NBER-designated recessions). There were also defaults on this paper, but there is insufficient information to correct the yield series for these defaults. Despite the obvious shortcomings of the data, there are few other short-term rates available for the early 19th century, and those that are available cover very short periods.

To remedy this deficiency, I constructed a synthetic short-term government series that removes the risk premium on commercial paper.[19] I did so by using the relation between short and long-term interest rates that prevailed in Britain during the 19th century, where the yields for long and short-term bonds were

---

[16] For a discussion of the issues involved in the bimetal standard and the potential distortion in yields see P.M. Garber, "Nominal Contracts in a Bimetallic Standard," *American Economic Review*, December 1986.

[17] The magnitude of this distortion can be seen by examining the yields in 1917–20 on government bonds issued with and without circulation privileges (see Homer, *A History*, *op. cit.*, Table 46). The yield differential between bonds with and without circulation privileges ranged from 50 to 100 basis points.

[18] F.R. Macaulay (*The Movements of Interest Rates, Bond Yields, and Stock Prices in the United States since 1956* (New York: National Bureau of Economic Research, 1938)) reported rates for choice 60 to 90-day commercial paper after 1856, while data from 1831 through 1856 were collected from E.B. Bigelow (*The Tariff Question*..., (Boston, 1862)), which covers "Street rates on First class paper in Boston and New York at the beginning, middle, and end of the month." The paper floated in Boston is said to be of three to six months in duration. See Macaulay, p. A341, for a more detailed discussion of these sources.

[19] For details of the construction of U.S. short-term rate series, see J.J. Siegel, "The Real Rates of Interest from 1800–1900: A Study of the U.S. and U.K.," *Journal of Monetary Economics*, forthcoming.

TABLE II FIXED INCOME RETURNS (STANDARD DEVIATIONS IN PARENTHESES)*

	Long-Term Governments							Short-Term Governments				
	Coupon	Nominal Return (%)		Real Return (%)		Real After-Tax Return (%)		Rate (%)	Real Return (%)		Real After-Tax Return (%)	
Period	(%) A	A	G	A	G	A	G	A	A	G	A	G
1802–1990	4.7	4.8	4.7	3.7	3.4	3.2	2.9	4.3	3.1	2.9	2.8	2.6
	(1.8)	(5.4)		(8.5)		(8.4)		(2.2)	(6.2)		(6.3)	
1871–1990	4.5	4.7	4.5	2.8	2.5	2.1	1.8	3.7	1.8	1.7	1.4	1.2
	(2.3)	(6.5)		(8.5)		(8.3)		(2.5)	(4.7)		(4.8)	
1802–1870	4.9	5.1	5.0	5.2	4.9	5.1	4.8	5.2	5.4	5.1	5.4	5.1
	(0.4)	(2.7)		(8.3)		(8.2)		(1.1)	(7.6)		(7.6)	
1871–1925	4.0	4.5	4.4	4.0	3.8	3.9	3.7	3.8	3.3	3.1	3.2	3.1
	(0.6)	(2.9)		(6.3)		(6.3)		(0.9)	(4.8)		(4.8)	
1926–1990	5.0	4.9	4.6	1.8	1.4	0.6	0.2	3.7	0.6	0.5	-0.2	-0.3
	(2.9)	(8.4)		(9.9)		(9.4)		(3.4)	(4.3)		(4.2)	
1946–1990	5.9	4.9	4.5	0.5	-0.1	-1.1	-1.6	4.9	0.4	0.3	-0.8	-0.9
	(3.1)	(9.6)		(10.5)		(9.5)		(3.3)	(3.6)		(3.3)	
1966–1981	7.2	2.8	2.5	-3.9	-4.2	-5.6	-5.9	6.9	-0.1	-0.2	-1.9	-1.9
	(1.8)	(6.9)		(7.9)		(7.5)		(2.9)	(2.0)		(2.0)	
1966–1990	8.2	7.4	6.8	1.6	0.9	-0.7	-1.3	7.2	1.3	1.2	-0.5	-0.6
	(2.2)	(11.5)		(12.5)		(11.3)		(2.5)	(2.7)		(2.5)	
1982–1990	10.0	15.7	14.9	11.3	10.5	7.9	7.3	7.9	3.7	3.7	1.8	1.8
	(1.8)	(13.2)		(13.3)		(11.7)		(1.6)	(1.8)		(1.4)	

* A = arithmetic mean; G = geometric mean.

FIGURE C SHORT-TERM INTEREST RATES, 1802–1990

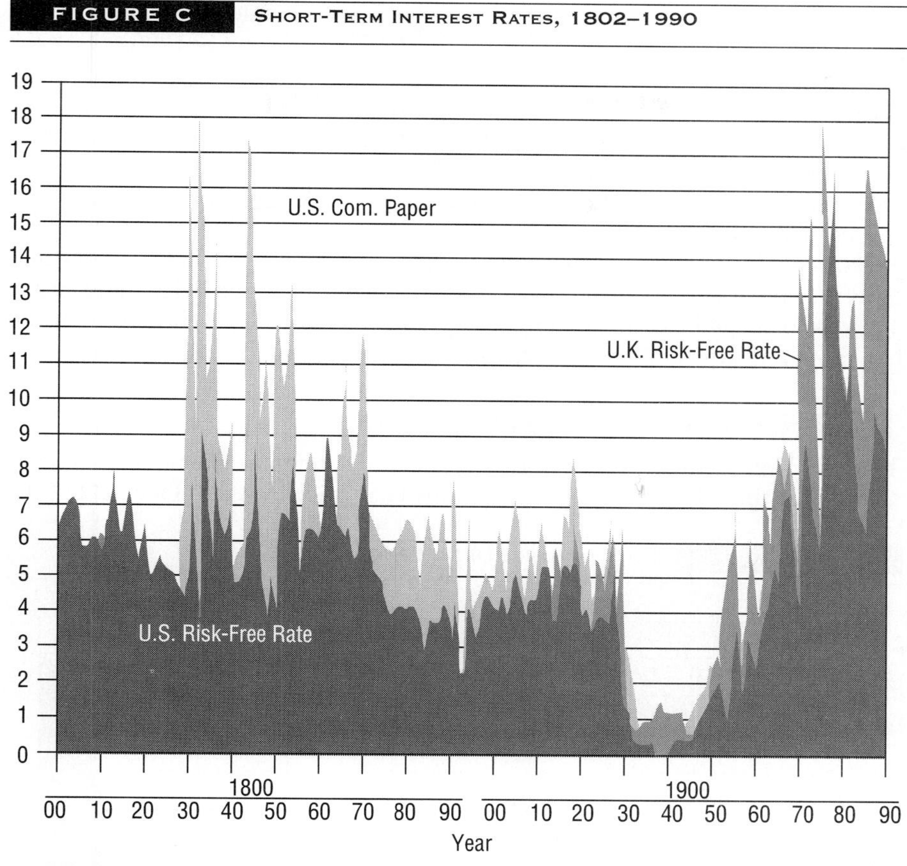

more representative of high-grade securities. The construction of the U.S. series assumes that the term structure of high-grade interest rates was the same over concurrent five-year periods in the U.S. and in the U.K. Figure C shows the short-term, risk-free series, along with other available short-term rates.

It is clear from Figure A that the total return indexes for fixed income assets fall far short of that for equity. With reinvestment of coupons, an initial investment of $1 in long-term bonds in 1802 would have yielded $5,770 in 1990; the same investment in risk-free, short-term assets would have yielded $2,680. Both these returns are less than 1 per cent of the sum accumulated in stocks over the entire period.

Gold and Commodities

The gold series represents the value of gold measured at the market price. Until the mid-1960s, this price was controlled by the government; furthermore, U.S. citizens were not allowed to hold gold in monetary form between 1933 and 1970. Gold has nonetheless been a key asset in world monetary history and many investors still consider it an important hedge asset. One dollar of gold bullion purchased in 1802 would have been worth $15.80 by the end of 1990.

The Consumer Price Index (CPI), provided for comparison, represents the value of a basket of widely diversified goods that could be stored costlessly, with no depreciation.[20] Consumer prices increased about 11-fold from 1802 to 1990, almost all of the appreciation coming in the last subperiod. Table III summarizes the returns for gold and commodities over the various time periods.

Note that, by the end of the first subperiod, 1802–70, the accumulations in government bonds, bills and stocks were virtually identical. It is in the second and especially the third subperiod that stocks clearly dominated fixed income assets. The return on gold is clearly dominated by bonds and stocks over the entire period, but its appreciation did surpass bonds (but not stocks) over the past 65 years.

The Price Level and Asset Returns

The behavior of price levels is critical to any interpretation of asset price movements over time. Figure D displays various U.S. price indexes. They all tell the

FIGURE D PRICE INDEXES, 1802–1990

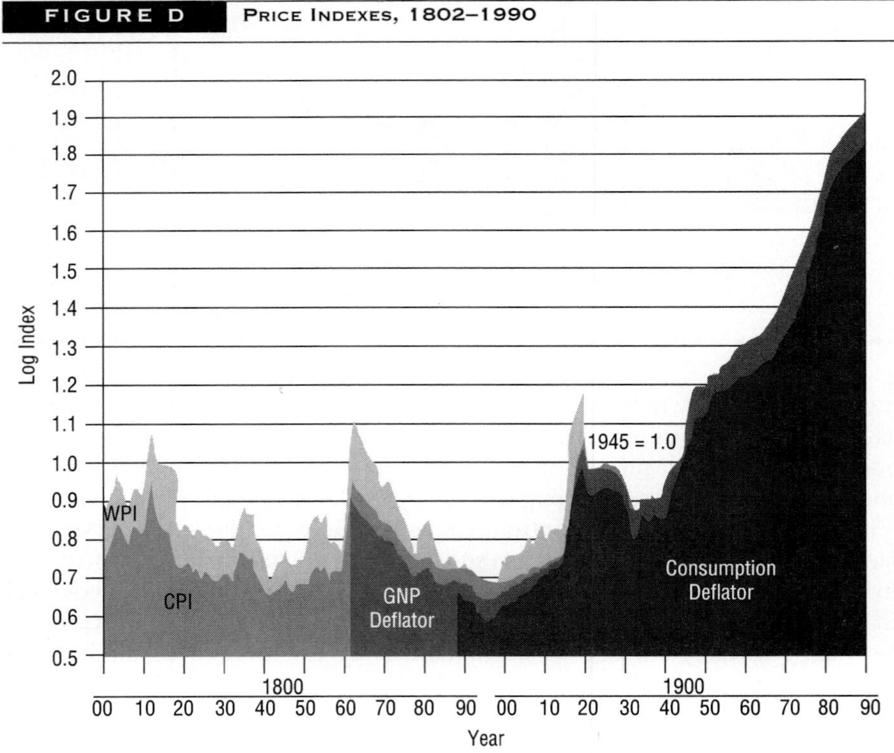

[20] The CPI includes services that cannot be stored. Since World War II, commodity prices have risen slower and service prices faster than the CPI. When futures markets exist, investors can buy futures, putting up margin in interest-bearing Treasury bills. This may result in returns higher than the CPI.

same story. Before World War II, the price level displayed no overall trend. Since the war, the price level has increased steadily. Prices accelerated until the 1980s, when the rate of inflation slowed. The CPI in 1990 was nearly seven times its 1945 value. Over the entire period, prices increased at an average compound annual rate of 1.3 per cent. Inflation averaged 0.1 per cent per year in the first subperiod and 0.6 and 3.1 per cent in the second and third subperiods. Table III gives the statistics.

Over long periods of time, increases in the price level are strongly associated with increases in the money supply. Throughout the 19th and the early part of the 20th centuries, the money stock was closely tied to the amount of gold held by the Treasury and central bank. The abandonment of the gold standard, a process that started in 1933 but gained momentum in the post-World War II period, reduced constraints on the monetary authority's issuance of money. Chronic inflation, which cannot occur under a gold standard, became the norm in the postwar period.

Figure E depicts total *real* return indexes—total (nominal) return indexes deflated by the price level. Because of inflation, real returns are much more modest than nominal returns, especially in the final subperiod. One dollar invested in equities in 1802 would have accumulated to $86,100 of constant purchasing power, or real dollars, by 1990.

Over the same period, one dollar would have accumulated to $520 in real dollars if invested in long-term governments, to $242 in real dollars if invested in short-term governments, and to only $1.42 if invested in gold. A dollar of hoarded currency, which pays no return and whose value is eroded by inflation, would have left an investor with only 9 cents of purchasing power in 1990.[21]

Taxes and Returns

Figure F displays the total return index corrected for both federal taxes and inflation. Average federal income tax rates were taken from studies by Robert Barro and Chaipat Sahasakul and are reported in Table I.[22] Because no state or local taxes are considered, tax rates before 1913, when the federal income tax was instituted, are set at zero. It is assumed that dividends and interest income are taxed at the average marginal tax rate prevailing in the year they were earned and that capital gains are taxed (and losses remitted) at one-fifth the prevailing average marginal tax rate.[23] The reduced tax rate on capital gains arises primarily from the deferment of taxes on gains accrued but not realized and secondarily from the lower tax rate on realized gains.

Because a significant part of the returns on equity has been earned through capital gains, while virtually all the returns on bonds are in the form of taxable interest, the returns on equity are taxed at a lower effective rate than those on

---

[21] An investor would actually have done far better hoarding paper money than gold bullion. The first U.S. currency, a one dollar U.S. note issued in 1862, now catalogues for $1000 in uncirculated condition, while earlier colonial paper goes for even more. Of course, gold coins have also increased in value far more than bullion.

[22] R.J. Barro and C. Sahasakul, "Measuring the Average Marginal Tax Rate from the Individual Income Tax," *Journal of Business* 56 (1982), pp. 419–52 and "Average Marginal Tax Rates from Social Security and the Individual Income Tax," *Journal of Business* 59 (1986), pp. 555–66.

[23] This adjustment is consistent with research done by A. Protopapadakis, "Some Indirect Evidence on Effective Capital Gains Tax Rates," *Journal of Business* 56 (1982), p. 127–38.

TABLE III Economic Variables (standard deviations in parentheses)*

	Prices							Output				S&P 500 (per share)			
	CPI (%)		WPI (%)		GNP Deflator (%)		Gold (%)	Real GNP (%)		Industrial Production (%)		Real Earnings (%)		Real Dividends (%)	
Period	A	G	A	G	A	G	A	A	G	A	G	A	G	A	G
1802–1990	1.5	1.3	1.4	1.0	—	—	2.3	—	—	—	—	—	—	—	—
	(6.1)		(9.0)				(14.8)								
1871–1990	2.1	2.0	2.0	1.6	2.3	2.2	3.3	3.5	3.3	5.5	4.0	6.0	3.0	3.9	3.1
	(5.0)		(8.1)		(5.3)		(17.7)	(5.6)		(17.7)		(25.7)		(12.8)	
1802–1870	0.4	0.1	0.4	-0.1	—	—	0.5	—	—	—	—	—	—	—	—
	(7.5)		(10.3)				(7.0)								
1871–1925	0.7	0.6	0.7	0.2	0.9	0.7	-0.2	3.8	3.7	5.6	4.1	6.5	2.1	2.5	1.6
	(5.1)		(9.6)		(5.5)		(1.2)	(4.9)		(18.2)		(31.9)		(13.4)	
1926–1990	3.2	3.1	3.1	2.9	3.5	3.4	6.2	3.2	3.0	5.4	4.0	5.6	3.7	5.2	4.4
	(4.7)		(6.4)		(4.7)		(23.6)	(6.1)		(17.4)		(19.1)		(12.1)	
1946–1990	4.6	4.5	4.3	4.1	4.9	4.9	7.4	2.6	2.5	3.7	3.5	7.1	6.1	6.4	6.2
	(3.9)		(5.3)		(4.0)		(26.5)	(4.3)		(6.1)		(14.9)		(5.9)	
1966–1981	7.0	7.0	6.8	6.7	6.6	6.6	22.0	2.8	2.8	3.4	3.3	7.6	7.0	5.8	5.7
	(3.3)		(4.2)		(2.1)		(39.2)	(2.3)		(5.1)		(10.8)		(4.5)	
1966–1990	6.0	5.9	5.2	5.2	5.6	5.6	13.4	2.8	2.8	3.2	3.1	4.7	3.9	5.4	5.3
	(3.1)		(4.1)		(2.2)		(34.4)	(2.3)		(4.9)		(12.7)		(3.7)	
1982–1990	4.0	4.0	2.5	2.5	3.9	3.9	-2.0	2.8	2.8	2.8	2.7	-0.4	-1.4	4.6	4.6
	(1.2)		(2.1)		(1.0)		(13.4)	(2.4)		(4.6)		(14.3)		(1.6)	

* A = arithmetic mean; G = geometric mean.

FIGURE E TOTAL REAL RETURN INDEXES, BEFORE TAXES, 1802–1990

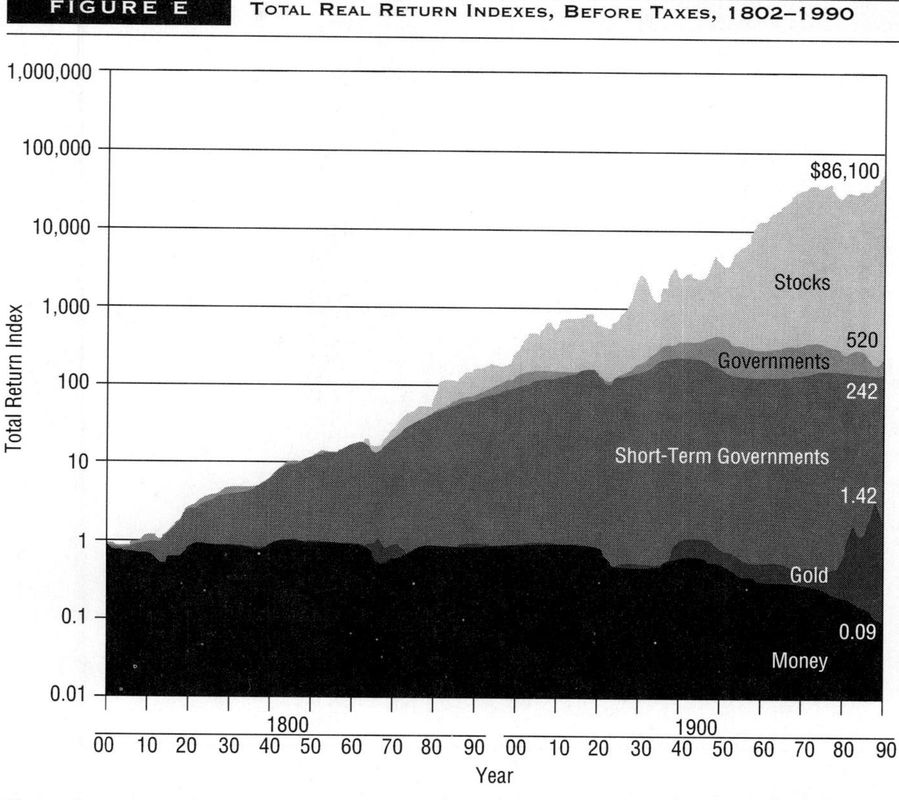

fixed income securities. In the third subperiod, 1926–90, when taxes became significant, the compound after-tax real return on stocks is reduced by 1.1 percentage points, to 5.3 per cent; the after-tax real return on short-term bonds is reduced by 0.8 percentage points, to -0.3 per cent, while the return on long-term government bonds falls 1.2 percentage points, to 0.2 per cent.

These results indicate that, on an after-tax basis, investors rolling over long-term bonds in the third subperiod have barely kept up with inflation, while those rolling over short-term bonds have fallen behind inflation. In fact, investors in short-term bonds have earned *no* after-tax real return from 1900 through 1990. Over the same period, the after-tax real return index for equities increased 90-fold!

Trends in Returns

Figure G displays 30-year centered moving averages of compound real rates of return on stocks, short and long-term government bonds.[24] One of the striking aspects of these data is the relative constancy of the real returns on equity across all the subperiods. In the first subperiod, the average geometric real return on equity is 5.7 per cent; it is 6.6 per cent in the second subperiod and 6.4 per cent

[24] The averaging period is progressively shortened to 15 years at the end points of these series.

FIGURE F **TOTAL REAL RETURN INDEXES, AFTER TAXES, 1802–1990**

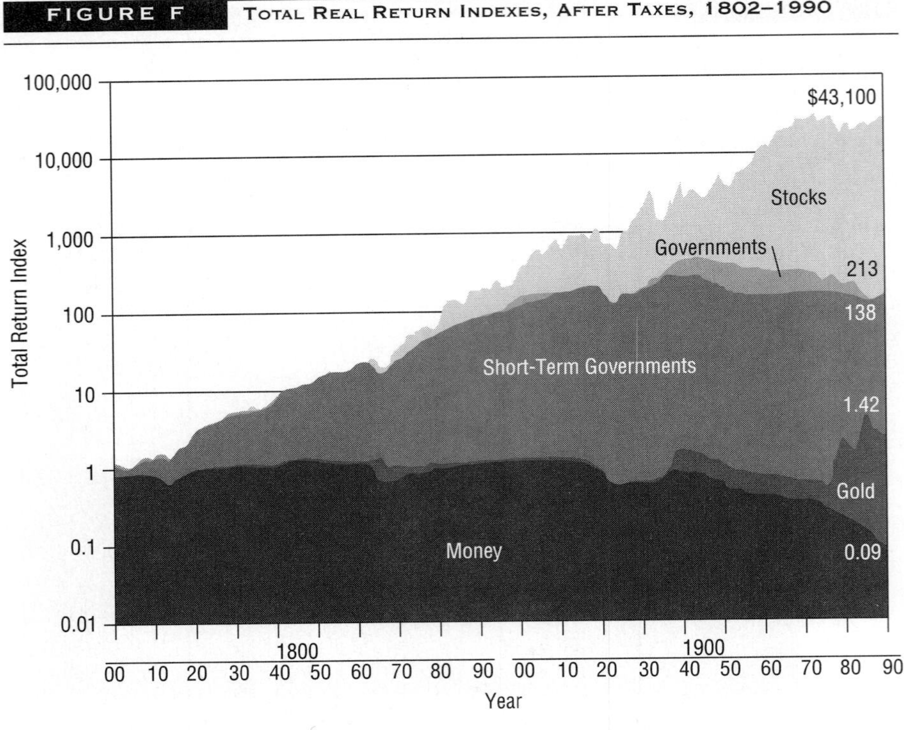

in the third.[25] These figures imply that although inflation increased substantially in the third subperiod, the nominal return on equity increased by an almost identical amount, so the return after inflation remained essentially unchanged. To the extent that stocks are claims on *real* assets, they might be expected to be good hedges against inflation over the long run.[26]

As noted, the average real compound rate of return on stocks over the entire period has been 6.2 per cent. Over every 30-year period from 1802 through 1990 there have been only two when the compound real annual rate of return on stocks fell below 3.5 per cent, and those occurred in the depths of the Depression, in 1931 and 1932. The periods of the highest real returns on stock ended in the early 1960s, when the real compound annual return exceeded 10 per cent.

The most striking pattern in Figure G is the decline in the average real return on fixed income assets. In all 30-year periods beginning with 1888, the year that Mehra and Prescott began their analysis, the real rate of return on short-term government securities has exceeded 2 per cent in only three periods,

---

[25] If the stock data from the Foundation for the Study of Cycles (see footnote 4) are considered, the real compound annual return in equity from 1802 to 1870 is 6.8 per cent.

[26] In the short run, stocks have proved poor hedges against inflation. This is particularly true if inflation is induced by supply shocks, which affect the productivity of capital. See E.F. Fama, "Stock Returns, Real Activity, Inflation and Money," *The American Economic Review*, September 1981.

FIGURE G REAL RETURNS ON STOCKS AND BONDS, 1802–1990 (30-YEAR CENTERED GEOMETRIC MOVING AVERAGE)

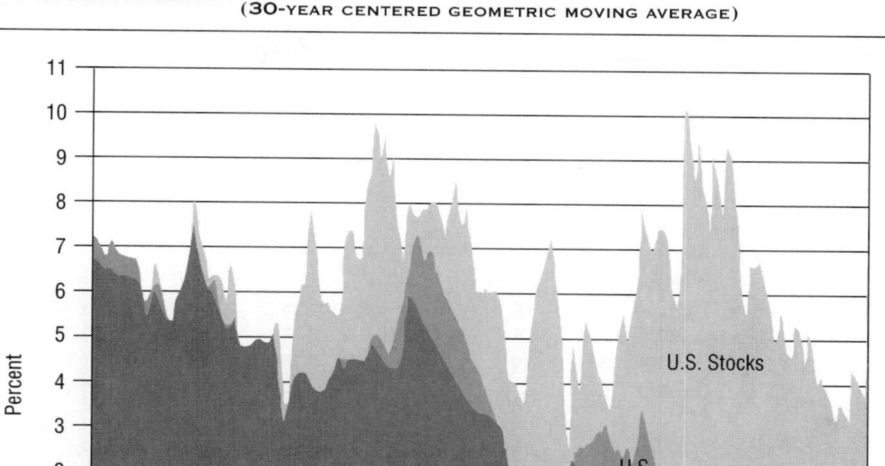

ending in the Depression years 1932–34. Since the late 19th century, the real return on bonds and bills over any 30-year horizon has almost never matched the average return of 4.5 to 5 per cent reached during the first 70 years of our sample period. Since 1878, the real return on long-term bonds has never reached 4 per cent over any 30-year period; it exceeded 3 per cent in only six years. One has to go back to the 1831–61 period to find any 30-year period where the return on either long or short-term bonds exceeded that on equities. The dominance of stocks over fixed income securities, so evident from Figures A, E and F, is borne out by examining long-term holding-period returns.

Table IV compares the compound returns on stocks, long and short-term bonds. Over the entire period, stocks outperformed short-term bonds 57.7 per cent of the time on a year-to-year basis but 88.8 per cent of the time over 30-year horizons. Since 1871, over horizons of 20 years or longer, stocks have under-performed short-term assets only once and have outperformed long-term bonds 95 per cent of the time. Even with holding periods as short as five years, stocks have outperformed long and short-term bonds by a four-to-one margin since 1926 and a three-to-one margin since 1872. In contrast, in 1802-71, stocks outperformed short or long-term bonds only about one-half the time over any holding period.

TABLE IV HOLDING-PERIOD RETURNS ON STOCKS, LONG BONDS AND SHORT BONDS

Holding Period	Time	Stock Return > Long Bond (%)	Stock Return > Short Bond (%)	Long Bond > Short Bond (%)
	1802–1870	49.3	49.3	34.8
	1871–1925	56.4	60.0	65.5
1 Year	1926–1990	67.7	69.2	86.2
	1802–1990	57.7	59.3	61.4
	1871–1990	62.5	64.7	76.5
	1802–1870	52.9	48.5	44.1
	1871–1925	58.2	61.8	56.4
2 Years	1926–1990	75.4	69.2	60.0
	1802–1990	62.2	59.6	53.2
	1871–1990	67.5	65.8	58.3
	1802–1870	47.7	49.2	43.1
	1871–1925	67.3	67.3	60.0
5 Years	1926–1990	78.5	80.0	61.5
	1802–1990	64.3	65.4	54.6
	1871–1990	73.3	74.2	60.8
	1802–1870	46.7	43.3	46.7
	1871–1925	83.6	83.6	60.0
10 Years	1926–1990	83.1	83.1	56.9
	1802–1990	71.1	70.0	54.4
	1871–1990	83.3	83.3	58.3
	1802–1870	54.0	60.0	46.0
	1871–1925	94.5	100.0	52.7
20 Years	1926–1990	95.4	98.5	64.6
	1802–1990	82.9	87.6	55.3
	1871–1990	95.0	99.2	59.2
	1802–1870	55.0	52.5	40.0
	1871–1925	100.0	100.0	60.0
30 Years	1926–1990	100.0	100.0	63.1
	1802–1990	88.8	88.1	56.3
	1871–1990	100.0	100.0	61.7

Trends in the U.K.

In the 19th century, as London emerged as the world's financial center, capital markets in Great Britain were far more developed than in the U.S. The British consol, depicted in Figure B, is a security that pays interest only; it was first floated in 1729. The consol has long been used by economists to construct a continuous and homogeneous long-term interest rate series stretching over 250 years. British short-term interest rates are represented, with some exceptions, by the open-market rate at which high-quality commercial paper is discounted.[27] Figure H shows the 30-year average real returns on U.K. short and long-term bonds.

There is remarkable similarity in the yield trends in the U.K. and the U.S. The sharp decline in the real yields on fixed income securities in the U.S. was closely mirrored in the U.K. Statistical tests cannot reject the hypothesis that the return process was identical for both long and short-term real interest rates in the U.S. and the U.K. over the entire period.

Explanations of Trends

Although the data demonstrate that returns on equities have compensated investors for increased inflation over the postwar period, the returns on fixed

FIGURE H REAL RETURNS ON U.K. BONDS, 1802–1990 (30-YEAR MOVING AVERAGE)

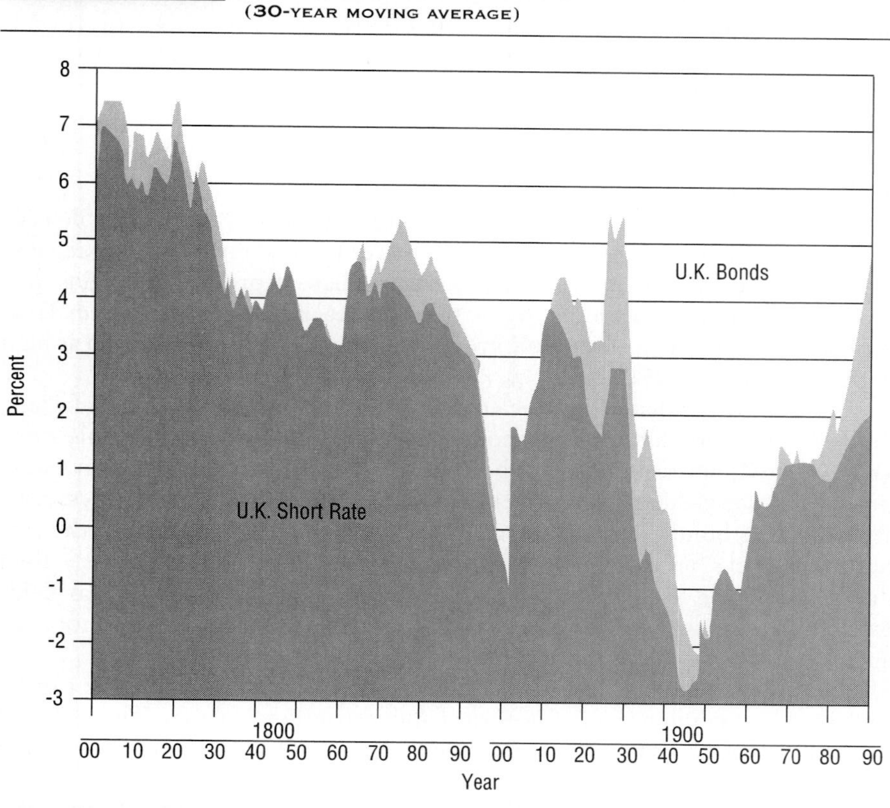

[27] These series can be found in Homer (*A History*, *op. cit.*, Table 23). He describes the paper as of "nonuniform maturity of a few months" before 1855 and thereafter "three month bills." These series are based on data compiled by the NBER from British Parliamentary papers and from various editions of *The Economist* (1858–1900). Details are contained in Siegel "The Real Rate of Interest" *op. cit.*

income securities have not. One possible explanation is that lenders did not anticipate inflation during much of the period.

One could argue that a large part of the increase in the price level since World War II, especially since 1970, was unanticipated, hence bondholders did not have a chance to adjust their required returns. The progressive abandonment of the gold standard only slowly reduced investors' convictions about the stability of the long-run price level.

Unanticipated inflation certainly lowered the real return on long-term bonds. Buyers of such instruments in the 1960s and early 1970s could scarcely have imagined the double-digit inflation that followed. But unanticipated inflation is less important for short-term bonds. The inflationary process, although increasingly subject to long-term uncertainty, has been quite persistent and inertial in the short run. Short-term investors thus have a better opportunity to capture the inflation premium in the rate of interest as they roll over their investments. Short-term bonds should therefore provide better protection against unanticipated inflation than longer-term bonds. Of course, this protection is not perfect; unanticipated inflation may account for up to one percentage point of the decline in real yield on short-term bonds over the sample period.[28]

Other Factors

Other factors influence the real rate of interest. Slower or more variable economic growth, for example, will generally lower the real rate investors demand to hold fixed income assets. Slower growth may have depressed real yields over short periods of time, including the 1970s, when real returns on short-term Treasury bills were negative. Economic growth in general, however, has been as high in the 20th as in the 19th century.

There is no evidence that the economy has become more volatile. In fact, Table III suggests that the real economy has actually been more stable since World War II, but real rates have been very low in this period. Intuition would suggest that the yield differential between risky assets such as stocks and less risky assets such as bonds would be smaller, the less risky the economy. If the real return on stocks has remained constant (and this is what the data suggest), then the real return on fixed income should have risen. The decline in the real yields on bonds suggests that changing variability of the real economy can not adequately explain the decline in real returns.

Perhaps the low real interest rates during much of this century can be explained by a combination of historical and institutional factors. The 1929–32 stock market crash and the Depression left a legacy of fear; most investors clung to government securities and insured deposits, driving their yields down. Redistribution policies undertaken by the government subsequent to the Depression may also have lowered real rates by shifting wealth to more risk-averse segments of the population. Furthermore, during World War II and the early postwar

---

[28] This has been suggested to me by some preliminary work done by Charles Calomaris.

years, interest rates were kept low by the Federal Reserve. Because of its inflationary consequences, this policy was abandoned in 1951, but interest rate controls, particularly on deposits, lasted much longer.

Finally, one cannot ignore the development of the capital markets, which transformed a highly segmented market for short-term instruments in the 19th century into one of the world's most liquid markets in this century.

The Equity Premium

The decline in the real return on fixed income investments has meant that the advantage of holding equities, which have experienced a remarkably steady real return, has increased over time. The equity premium, plotted in Figure I, has trended up over the last 200 years and was particularly high in the middle of this century. The premium, computed from real geometric returns, averaged 0.6 per cent in the first subperiod, 3.5 per cent in the second, and 5.9 per cent in the third.

FIGURE I EQUITY RISK PREMIUM, 1802–1990 (30-YEAR CENTERED GEOMETRIC MOVING AVERAGE)

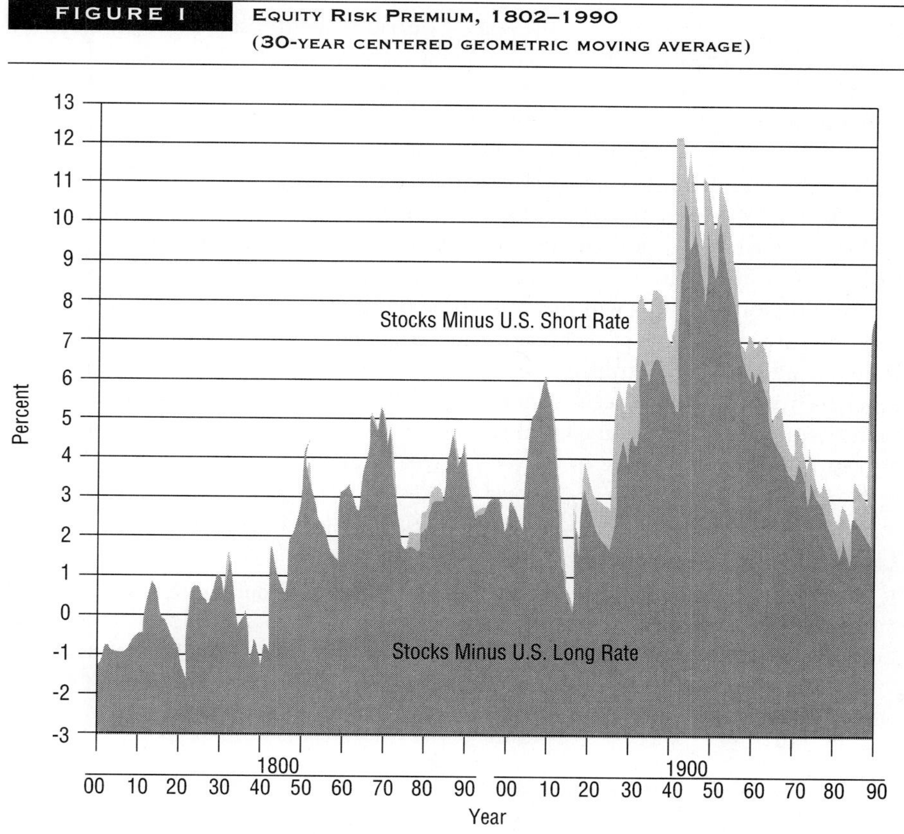

The primary source of this equity premium has been the fall in the real return on bonds, *not* the rise in the return on equity. Nonetheless, it is not unreasonable to believe that the low real rates on bonds may, on occasion, have fueled higher equity returns, because the costs of obtaining leverage were so low. The highest 30-year average equity return occurred in 1931–61, a period that also experienced very low real returns on bonds.

One might take an even broader view of the superior returns on equity. Certainly investors in 1802 (or even 1872) did not universally expect the United States to become the greatest economic power in the next century. This was not the case in many other countries. What if one had owned stock in Japanese or German firms before World War II? Or consider Argentina, which, at the turn of the century, was one of the great economic powers. In some sense, the returns on U.S. stocks might not be representative of the broader international context.[29]

Conclusions

The high real interest rates in the 19th century may have reflected the possibility that the U.S. would default on its bonds or abandon the gold standard. Since the inflation shocks of the 1970s, fear of outright default has been replaced by an inflationary premium in nominal interest rates. Future inflation may be caused by growing U.S. government deficits or by inflationary policies pursued by the Federal Reserve in response to political pressures or economic crises.

The last 10 years represent only about 5 per cent of the total time examined in this study, but the period since 1980 contains the highest real long-term bond returns during any consecutive 10-year period since 1884 and the highest real short-term bond returns since the 19th century (excepting the sharp deflationary periods of the Depression). It is not unreasonable to assume that the current higher real rates will turn out to be more characteristic of future returns than the unusually low real rates of the earlier part of this century. If they do, then the advantage of holding equities over bonds will shrink from the levels reached over the past several generations. The holders of fixed income investments should enjoy enhanced real returns in the future. Equities, however, still appear to be the best route to long-term wealth accumulation.[30]

Questions

1. Suppose that you invest \$100, then suffer a 50 percent loss during the first year and a 50 percent gain during the second year, leaving you \$75. Your average arithmetic (or mean) return is zero: (-50% + 50%)/2 = 0. But you have lost 25 percent of your investment during the two years! Your geometric (or compound) return is negative 13.4 percent:

---

[29] Of course, even on a worldwide basis, who might have expected the triumph of capitalism and market-oriented economies 100 or even 50 years ago? We may be living in the golden age of capitalism, the fortunes of which may decline in the next 100 years (or sooner)!

[30] I thank Peter Scherer and Ashish Shah for their research assistance.

$$FV = PV(1 + i)^n$$
$$\$75 = \$100(1 + i)^2$$
$$i = -13.4\% \text{ per year compounded annually}$$

Alternatively, the geometric return (GR) is:

$$GR = [(1 + i_1)(1 + i_2)]^{1/n} - 1$$
$$= [(1 - 0.50)(1 + 0.50)]^{1/2} - 1$$
$$= -13.4\% \text{ per year compounded annually}$$

Use the preceding ideas to calculate the arithmetic and geometric return for the following annual returns: First year, -5%; Second year, -8%; Third year, 40%.

2. For the period 1802 through 1990, what was the arithmetic average annual nominal return on common stock? What was the compound annual nominal return on common stock? Compare and contrast the meaning of these two rates of return.
3. "The power of compound returns is clearly evident in the stock market. One dollar invested in 1802, with all dividends reinvested, would have accumulated to nearly $1 million by the end of 1990." Substantiate this statement with calculations. (Due to rounding error in the nominal rate of return, your answer will vary slightly from the author's answer in Figure A.)
4. Fill in the following table of compound returns for the period 1802 through 1990:

	Nominal Annual Return (%)	Real Annual Return (%)
Common stock	______	______
Long-term government bonds	______	______
Short-term government bonds	______	______
Gold	______	______
Consumer price index	______	N/A

5. Compare and contrast Figure A with Figure E.
6. What differences can you observe between the patterns of long-term and short-term interest rates? (See Figures B and C.)
7. What was the compound annual inflation rate as measured by the CPI from 1802 to 1870, 1871 to 1925, and 1926 to 1990? How much of the purchasing power of an 1802 dollar would have been eroded by 1990?
8. Interpret the findings in Table IV, noting the impact of longer holding periods.
9. Describe the equity premium displayed in Figure I. In your opinion, are bonds or equities better for long-term wealth accumulation?

Hunting the Stock Market Snark

O. Maurice Joy

"Just the place for a Snark!" the Bellman cried,
As he landed his crew with care;
Supporting each man on the top of the tide
By a finger entwined in his hair.

"Just the place for a Snark! I have said it twice:
That alone should encourage the crew.
Just the place for a Snark! I have said it thrice:
What I tell you three times is true."

—Lewis Carroll
The Hunting of the Snark

This article, much like Lewis Carroll's poem, recounts a tale of hunting; only the tale that is about to unfold describes the ancient, persistent search for stock market inefficiencies.

Efficiency means different things to different people. Sometimes the word is used in its economic allocative sense, referring to a condition where resources have been distributed in some best way. Sometimes the word is used in an engineering sense of minimum cost of operations. To those interested in the stock market, efficiency means you cannot "beat" the market. In other words, the market, the entire accumulation of investors, is so smart in its collective totality, that you cannot get rich, except accidentally or illegally, from trading profits. Competition for information about stocks is so keen and widespread that the market correctly prices stocks, on average. More formally, the stock market is efficient if it is impossible to make an abnormal profit—a profit too large given

---

At the time of this writing, O. Maurice Joy was the Joyce C. Hall Distinguished Professor of Business Administration at the University of Kansas.

Source: Reprinted from "Hunting the Stock Market Snark," by O. Maurice Joy, *Sloan Management Review*, Spring 1987, pp. 17–24, by permission of publisher.

the riskiness of the stock—by using a given information set. Contrariwise, a market *inefficiency* occurs when it can be shown that some "beat-the-market" scheme works.

The Stock Market Snark

> *"But oh, beamish nephew, beware of the day,*
> *If your Snark be a Boojum! For then*
> *You will softly and suddenly vanish away,*
> *And never be met with again!"*

The snark is a mysterious and rarely seen beast. We are never told exactly what it is or what it looks like. We are never sure if the elusive snark exists until the very end of the poem. And even then, its existence is only dimly revealed through indirect evidence. Nonetheless, the hunting expedition is launched with a colorful cast of characters. Stock market inefficiencies are also mysterious, rare, and dimly seen, and the hunting crew is equally colorful, ranging from Joe Granville to computer-wielding academicians.

There is another striking similarity. If a snark were a member of the species boojum, the hunter would *vanish* when snark and hunter met. The stock market analogy seems clear here, at least up to a point. If a stock market snark—a market inefficiency—is encountered, and it is a boojum, it too should vanish. Exactly how it vanishes is debatable. In one interpretation, the market may be thought of as becoming more efficient with the passage of time, or seasoning, so that abnormal trading profits vanish under natural competitive pressures. In a second interpretation, the stock market snark may disappear because new evidence may convince us that what appeared to be a market inefficiency was illusory. Many articles refuting market inefficiency findings are of this latter kind.

To complete the analogy one should consider what becomes of the financial researcher, our hunter, when stock market snarks, boojum or otherwise, are encountered. Actually, the analogy is badly strained here. No researchers have been reported missing, although any hunter who found a truly lucrative inefficiency might prefer to vanish into the land of private profit making. And, while it is tempting to argue that one's manuscript or academic respectability vanishes when the snark turns out to be a boojum, that, too, is pushing the comparison too far. In any event we will now go hunting the stock market snark. We should not forget that determining whether snarks are boojums is of great importance to the hunting story.

Predicting the Future: Preparations for the Journey

> *"He had bought a large map representing the sea,*
> *Without the least vestige of land:*
> *And the crew were much pleased when they found it to be*
> *A map they could all understand."*

Prediction of future events is an important task of many disciplines, and this is particularly true of the stock market. Two points can be made about predicting stock market returns. First, it is difficult to do successfully. Second, it is relatively easy to *claim* success. These two points are important individually, but taken together they spotlight a vexing problem. Apart from religion, macroeconomics, and foreign policy, it is hard to find fields of human endeavor that rival security analysis for its mixture of large stakes and unsubstantiated claims of prediction expertise. Claims of predictive success abound in the stock market arena, both on the professional side and in the academic literature. Such claims, nonetheless, cry out for verification or, more scientifically, falsification tests.

Only in the past quarter-century has the finance discipline been able to test predictive stock market claims in a scientific fashion. One may ask why it has taken so long to address properly this issue. There are three reasons.

First, although we have long possessed financial data, only since the 1960s have we begun to collect systematically large bodies of data that are, in any sense, accurate. The advent of the COMPUSTAT and Center for Research in Security Prices (CRSP) data tapes has opened doors for a variety of stock market research studies. The second reason is the capacity growth in computers in the middle years of this century. Prior to that growth, lack of data-handling facilities severely limited our ability to analyze large data collections. Finally, it has only been in the past three decades that the finance area developed the theoretical and statistical expertise necessary to perform reliable predictive tests. The change in tenor of the academic finance literature since the 1950s has been startling, and was a requisite development of that testing.

Three Versions of Market Efficiency

"Come, listen, my men, while I tell you again
The five unmistakable marks
By which you may know, wheresoever you go,
The warranted genuine Snarks."

Earlier, an efficient market was defined as one where securities are "properly" priced based on a given information set. This assertion, known as the *efficient market hypothesis* (EMH), is predicated on a particular information set. There are three versions of the EMH, one for each proposed base or set of information:

- *Weak form efficiency:* the information base is the collection of past stock prices (or rates of return).
- *Semistrong form efficiency:* the information base is any publicly available source of data.
- *Strong form efficiency:* the information base is insider information.

While this structure is somewhat awkward—for example, semistrong efficiency subsumes weak form efficiency—it has two admirable features. First, this ordering structure allows us to compartmentalize where inefficiencies are found. More important, each of the three information sets can be linked directly to a major stock market evaluation philosophy. The links, which can be used to push our hunt along, are

- weak form efficiency—*technical analysis,*
- semistrong form efficiency—*fundamental analysis,* and
- strong form efficiency—*insider trading.*

Hunting the Snark with Technical Analysis

"We have sailed many months, we have sailed many weeks,
(Four weeks to the month you may mark),
But never as yet ('tis your Captain who speaks)
Have we caught the least glimpse of a Snark!"

In its most common form, technical analysis involves examining historical records of stock price behavior, identifying recognizable patterns that precede price movements, and then watching for repetitions of these patterns. The underlying rationale is that history repeats itself, and a careful student of history can profit from that fact.

The original Dow Theory is the forerunner of modern technical analysis. In several *Wall Street Journal* editorials written between 1900 and 1902, Charles Dow argued that stock market activity could be thought of as three-phased: primary movements, secondary movements, and daily fluctuations. He analyzed charts of industrial and railroad stock price averages to identify primary and secondary phases. Modern technical analysis techniques that use price or price and volume patterns are direct descendants of the Dow Theory. Other approaches to technical analysis have appeared in recent years. These include use of advance/decline lines, short sales, and odd lot ratios. All of these techniques share the underlying premise of the existence of a recognizable historical rhythm.

One of the first instances of a scientific test of market efficiency was Louis Bachelier's 1900 doctoral dissertation, *Theory of Speculation.* Bachelier developed a sophisticated mathematical theory of stock price behavior based on the notion that price changes (rates of return) are independent over time. The rate-of-return series, if this thesis were true, would have no memory: tomorrow's price change would not be related to today's price change. This proposal never fails to startle stock market students on first encounter, and it has an important implication for hunting snarks with technical analysis: history repeats itself only accidentally and not in a predictable way. Bachelier's work was mainly theoretical in nature, but he did some rough testing of the idea on the French bond market that seemed to verify the theory. Unfortunately, because Bachelier's work was in French, the English-speaking investment community was never aware of it until it was translated over half a century later. The English version is reprinted in Cootner.[1]

The decades of the 1930s, 1940s, and 1950s marked the beginning of sophisticated testing of the EMH. These early tests were statistical explorations of dependencies of changes in price indices rather than of individual stocks. Tests were performed on both commodity and stock market series. Most of them supported the conclusion that price changes, or rates of return, were independent over time; however, a subset of results seemed to indicate statistical dependencies strong enough to violate the EMH.

While there was some evidence that hinted of snarks, it was soon found that averaging across stocks' rates of return, which is inherent in price indices, can introduce false correlations. On reexamination, the early work on indices were examples of just such a phenomenon. The conclusion was that, if these indices were snarks, they were boojums because they disappeared. In the 1950s' terminology, academic researchers were frequently describing stock market price movements as resembling a "random walk," which, by definition, is unpredictable. A broad collection of these studies was compiled by Cootner.[2]

Another influential article appeared at the end of the 1950s. Harry Roberts, a University of Chicago statistician, made the previous statistical criticism of technical analysis understandable to all parties by directly confronting "charting." Roberts suggested that charted price patterns may be only statistical artifacts that have no historical rhythm, and therefore no predictive capability.[3] To illustrate his point, Roberts generated purely random price patterns, pictorially compared them to actual price patterns, and found the two sets to be indistinguishable. His moral is quite clear: we often see a snark where none exists.

The 1960s was a crucial decade for testing technical analysis. Two main lines were pursued: one involved "derivative statistical" properties of rate-of-return series; the other looked at the profitability of "trading rules" using technical analysis techniques. Foremost among the former kind of research were two articles by Eugene Fama of the University of Chicago.[4] Fama properly focused on individual securities rather than on indices. He collected an impressive assembly of data and performed many sophisticated computer tests. He concluded that stock price changes were independent over time, which is consistent with the EMH.

At the same time work progressed on the trading rules front. "Filter rules" were used to identify stocks that were over- or under-valued. A filter rule is

---

[1] P. Cootner, *The Random Character of Stock Market Prices* (Cambridge: MIT Press, 1967).

[2] Ibid.

[3] H. Roberts, "Stock Market Patterns and Financial Analysis: Methodological Suggestions," *Journal of Finance*, March 1959.

[4] E.F. Fama, "The Behavior of Stock-Market Prices," *Journal of Business*, January 1965, pp. 34-105; E.F. Fama, "Tomorrow on the New York Stock Exchange," *Journal of Business*, July 1965, pp. 285–299.

merely a mechanical trading rule. For an investor using an X% filter, the trading rule would go like this: if the price of a stock increases by at least X%, buy the stock and hold it until its price declines by at least X% from a subsequent high price, at which time simultaneously sell the stock and go short. This process is repeated over time. Price changes of less than X% are ignored.

Filter rule tests have two advantages over the kind of derivative statistical property work conducted by Fama. First, the rules tested were more like the techniques that technical analysts actually use. Thus, these investigations more nearly corresponded to tests of security analysis as practiced by stock market technicians. Second, these tests raised the notion of economic significance of the results rather than just statistical significance. The variable of interest in these tests was profitability, which provided a clearer interpretation of the results and their practical implications.

Some of the first filter results looked very promising for technical analysis. In particular "small X" filter rules appeared to uncover some very large snarks. But after these results were analyzed more closely—with more attention given to some important details that originally were not accounted for—several shortcomings were uncovered. The main one concerned transaction costs, including broker fees, clearinghouse fees, and transfer taxes. To overcome the EMH, the filter rule must generate profits large enough to completely cover these unavoidable trading costs. This is particularly important in small X filter rules where many trades are triggered by the low value of X. Researchers found that when transaction costs were included in the analysis, filter rules could not generate sufficient profits to cover these costs.[5] Once again, if these were snarks, they were boojums.

With the close of the 1960s two things became clear: technical analysis was discredited academically; several dozen technical analysts were employed on Wall Street. Since that time, little academic research has been done in the technical analysis area: it is considered a dead subject academically. Today, it still seems clear: technical analysis is discredited academically; several dozen technical analysts are still employed on Wall Street.

Why technical analysis still thrives today in the face of all the evidence that it does not work is an interesting question. One answer may be that Wall Street does not pay much attention to academic research. But that is, at best, only partly true. We know Wall Street does pay attention to academic research. For example, many of the tenets of modern portfolio management have become widely accepted and practiced by the professional investment community.

Perhaps the answer is that technical analysis tests are not very good. Yet the research papers that are most damaging to technical analysis are of an exacting and careful nature. It is an impressive and compelling set of tests. The only apparent weakness in this body of empirical literature is that perhaps the tests have not been directed enough to specific technical analysis schemes that are actually practiced. That is, academicians may have inferred too much from the

---

[5] E.F. Fama and M.E. Blume, "Filter Rules and Stock-Market Trading," *Journal of Business*, January 1966, pp. 226–241.

tests. Few research papers, for instance, have investigated the companion role that trading volume plays in conjunction with price movements. Yet that role is central to many technical analysis schemes.

Of course, another explanation for the continued use of technical analysis is closely akin to that expressed by Julian Huxley in a similar context: "Mythology, religion, and superstition all flourish when men must make decisions about matters over which they have no control."

Hunting the Snark with Fundamental Analysis

"It's a Snark" was the sound that first came to their ears,
And seemed almost too good to be true.
Then followed a torrent of laughter and cheers:
Then the ominous words "It's a Boo—"

Fundamental analysis refers to analyzing the underlying economic factors that determine stock price movements. Security analysts who are fundamentalists attempt to search out information that reflects future cash flow prospects for companies and how those prospects will be viewed (capitalized) by the marketplace. Historically, this is the oldest and most respectable form of evaluation. It has been for many years, and is today, the dominant form of security analysis.

One of the most influential proponents of fundamental analysis in this century was the late Benjamin Graham. His research output spanned the decades from the 1930s to the 1960s: several editions of his books were primers for generations of security analysts.[6] Because most of Graham's writing preceded the use of computers in security research, his work has not received much attention in the empirical literature. Yet many of the statistical tests performed in recent years have been related to his earlier writings.[7] A direct test of his approach is described below.

An early stock market research pioneer who began his work in the precomputer days was J.W. Meader, who approached the valuation topic using regression analysis.[8] Using a valuation formula that involved volume, book value, net working capital, earnings, and dividends, Meader developed a regression model that appeared to explain stock prices very well. This, in turn, offered the possibility of identifying misvalued securities.

As Meader repeated his work from 1930 to 1940, a curious result occurred. In any one year, Meader could "explain" the structure of stock prices quite well using his collection of variables. The model, however, proved incapable of "predicting" stock price changes, which was, of course, what Meader was interested in doing. He was discouraged by the results of his work.

---

[6] B. Graham, *The Intelligent Investor* (New York: Harper & Row, 4th ed., 1973).

[7] B. Graham, D. Dodd, and S. Cottle, *Security Analysis* (New York: McGraw-Hill, 4th ed., 1961).

[8] J.W. Meader, "A Formula for Determining Basic Values Underlying Common Stock Prices," *The Analyst*, 29 November 1935.

Another, much simpler, type of research began to appear in the 1960s. Graham argued for years that investors should not buy stocks with high price-to-earnings (P/E) ratios. Using annual earnings to form P/E ratios, researchers found that stocks with low P/E ratios outperformed stocks with high P/E ratios. These studies appeared to offer clear sightings of snarks. This was surprising not only to academicians, who believed the semistrong version of the EMH, but also to many market professionals, who, while they believed in inefficiencies, viewed the P/E ratio strategy as too naive to be useful.

Empirical studies are inherently fragile, as their results are wholly dependent on the skill with which the data has been collected and explored. The early P/E studies were flawed in two important ways. One of the main tenets of finance is that risk and return are closely related. Therefore, the finding that low P/E stocks offer higher returns than high P/E stocks is not sufficient by itself to demonstrate market inefficiency. It may mean merely that low P/E stocks are riskier than high P/E stocks, and the extra return on the low P/E stocks is fair compensation only for the extra risk. This simple, but important, point is crucial to understanding fully what the snark hunt is all about: We found a market inefficiency only when we uncovered a stock selection scheme that offered a rate of return in excess of the rate of return from an equally risky investment alternative. In other words, we must find a scheme that offers excess rates of return on a fully risk-adjusted basis. The early P/E studies failed to adequately satisfy that requirement.

A second major criticism relates to data integrity. Often the data was collected in ways that introduced biases toward inefficiency in the results. Some studies, for example, were not careful in noting earnings announcement dates. Therefore, some earnings used in P/E studies had not been announced publicly. This introduced an insider trading profit unrelated to P/E trading rules based on publicly available data. Consequently, it was difficult to determine if the reported results were representative of real-world circumstances.

P/E ratio work continued to progress in the 1970s. Researchers began to use more timely earnings, namely, the quarterly earnings announced in unaudited interim earnings reports. Some attention focused on *changes* in quarterly earnings.[9] The results from these studies looked very interesting, pointing to market inefficiencies. By now, however, the academic community had learned to scrutinize any claims of success in snark hunting.

In the past, when attention was given to test refinement, the apparent inefficiencies always disappeared. Similar expectations were held here, at least in the academic community, as empirical work intensified in the 1970s. As the problems of the earnings studies were reexamined in later work, however, the anomalous findings remained.

One of the most prestigious academic finance journals, and the one most skeptical of snarks, the *Journal of Financial Economics,* dedicated a double issue (June/September 1978) to the "anomalous evidence regarding market efficiency."

---

[9] O.M. Joy, R.H. Litzenberger, and R.W. McEnally, "The Adjustment of Stock Prices to Announcements of Unanticipated Changes in Quarterly Earnings," *Journal of Accounting Research* 15 (1977): 207–225.

For the most part, the issue recounted snark sightings that were pervasive and difficult to dismiss. In June 1983, the journal elaborated on a similar issue that emphasized the surprising finding that stocks of small firms seemed to offer excessively large risk-adjusted rates of return. Today, this finding is referred to as the "size" or "small cap" effect.

Today, snark sightings abound. Besides the size effect, among the techniques that appear to offer uncommonly high risk-adjusted rates of return are stocks with low P/E ratios[10] and stocks with unexpectedly large announced earnings.[11] In a similar vein Graham's investment advice recently has been tested. Over the years Graham consistently recommended stocks with relatively modest P/E ratios and debt levels that were not excessive and that were of reasonable size with good industry positions. The results of this test confirmed Graham's advice.[12] Warren Buffet offers updated testimony to Graham's wisdom.[13]

Results like these are hardly surprising to Wall Street. For years professional analysts have claimed that research on the EMH has overstated the case for efficiency. Therefore, recent findings have vindicated the long-standing Wall Street view that expertise in fundamental analysis is rewarded.

What about the other side of this issue? What do proponents of the efficient market theory have to say about the recent spate of apparently successful snark hunts? Three main criticisms are raised.

The first criticism, which is an old one, concerns transaction costs. Narrowly defined, transaction costs refer to the costs of buying and selling stocks. Several market inefficiency studies have incorporated these cost estimates. However, in a beat-the-market strategy there may be other kinds of transaction costs involved as well, such as opportunity costs for time spent on administering the scheme, computer usage costs, and differential bid/ask spreads on stocks. These are difficult to measure accurately. Even the more careful recent studies have not accounted fully for all such costs.

The second major objection to snark sightings is that today's easy access to computers and data tapes has led to extensive "data mining," where researchers repeatedly dig through the same data until they find their snark. Uncovered empirical oddities may be sample-specific and have no predictive success outside of those samples.

Perhaps the most compelling argument, however, is one raised by Ray Ball.[14] He correctly notes that any test of the EMH is predicated on an expectations model of stock price behavior. Consequently, any such test is unavoidably a joint test of market efficiency *and* the validity of the underlying expectations model. Ball interprets the results of the various tests not as indications of inefficiencies,

---

[10] S. Basu, "The Relationship between Earnings' Yield, Market Value, and Return for NYSE Common Stocks: Further Evidence," *Journal of Financial Economics* 12 (1983): 129–156.

[11] R.J. Rendleman, Jr., C.P. Jones, and H.A. Latané, "Empirical Anomalies Based on Unexpected Earnings and the Importance of Risk Adjustments," *Journal of Financial Economics* 10 (1982): 269–287.

[12] H.R. Oppenheimer and G.G. Schlarbaum, "Investing with Ben Graham: An *Ex Ante* Test of the Efficient Market Hypothesis," *Journal of Financial and Quantitative Analysis*, September 1981, pp. 341–360.

[13] W. Buffett, "Up the Inefficient Market: Graham & Dodd Is Alive and Well on Wall Street," *Barron's*, 25 February 1985.

[14] R. Ball, "Anomalies in Relationships between Securities' Yields and Yield-Surrogates," *Journal of Financial Economics* 6 (June/September 1978): 106–126.

but as evidence that the current widely used expectations model, which is based on market betas, is flawed.

Ball's criticism cuts across all forms of snark sightings, including P/E ratios, size, earnings surprises, and Graham's procedures. The simplest version of the model misspecification that Ball suspects involves risk. If extant models understate risk for certain types of stocks (e.g., low P/E stocks), then observed risk-adjusted returns are overstated for those stocks.

Ball's analysis is a good example of Kuhn's theory of what happens during a breakdown of a major research paradigm within a scientific discipline.[15] Inference becomes more difficult than in normal times, and beliefs are diffused. One may not agree with all aspects of Ball's criticism, but he has raised debatable points that are central to further investigation in this area. To claim market inefficiencies today requires a reconciliation of Ball's issues.

In summarizing the evidence on fundamental analysis, three points seem clear:

- Snarks have been reported, and not all have been shown yet to be boojums. Several anomalies have yet to be explained.
- Wall Street believes in snarks.
- The majority of the academic community does not believe in the existence of snarks. The final line of defense is Ball's model misspecification criticism.

Hunting the Snark with Insider Information

("That's exactly the method," the Bellman bold
In a hasty parenthesis cried,
"That's exactly the way I have always been told
That the capture of Snarks should be tried!")

The last version of the EMH is concerned with insider information. Can someone with insider information beat the market? This is the "strong form" of the EMH.

This issue always strikes market professionals as ludicrous. Who could not beat the market if one possessed insider information? Does anyone think Ivan Boesky didn't? Actually, this version of the EMH was never intended to be a hypothesis in the sense that the weak and semistrong versions were. No one, including the staunchest proponent of market efficiency, ever believed that insiders could not beat the market. Rather, this version was intended to provide a benchmark of where market efficiency broke down. In other words, this insider trading case could provide a contrast to the technical and fundamental analysis cases, where insider information was not available.

---

15 T.S. Kuhn, *The Structure of Scientific Revolutions* (Chicago: University of Chicago Press, 1969).

While the results are not as voluminous as they are in the preceding two cases, they are about what was expected. Corporate officers, who presumably have access to privy information, have traded with excess economic profits. Some merger studies have reflected the same phenomenon. However, insider trading is, by definition, illegal. Therefore, while it is profitable, this game is illicit, perilous, and not available to the average investor.

Perhaps the most important part of this EMH version is the work that shows who does not get insider information. Over the years there has been a series of tests concerning mutual fund performance. These are important because mutual funds supposedly employ sophisticated analysts and may, because of their connections, have access to insider information.

Tests have shown that mutual funds do not outperform the market by more than the expenses charged to their customers. That is, mutual funds apparently can beat the market in a risk-adjusted return sense without considering transaction costs to the mutual fund investors. But once the investors' transaction costs, mutual fund management fees, and load costs are considered, the funds do not outperform the market.[16] These results are, of course, fully consistent with the EMH. This does not imply, however, that mutual funds are a bad investment: the valuable service they *do* provide is broad diversification.

So What Is a Snark?

> *"They sought it with thimbles, they sought it with care;*
> *They pursued it with forks and hope;*
> *They threatened its life with a railway-share;*
> *They charmed it with smiles and soap."*

Apparently, Lewis Carroll himself did not know what a snark was, so snark hunting has been a murky business from the very beginning. However, two things seem clear today about the stock market version of the snark:

- While acceptance of the possibility of snarks seems to have increased within the academic community, most academics have never seen snarks and never expect to. Moreover, if ever there were such a thing as snarks, academicians would view them as boojums.
- The professional investment community, on the other hand, believes that snarks are everywhere, and those that are boojums are always those found by the other guy.

Why does this difference in attitudes and beliefs exist? Academicians are, by training, skeptical, and rightly so. Tests finding market inefficiencies are

[16] N. Mains, "Risk, the Pricing of Capital Assets, and the Evaluation of Investment Portfolios: Comment," *Journal of Business,* July 1977.

flawed in various ways. The attitude that tighter proof of snark finds is required is consistent with conservative scientific principles regarding hypothesis testing. At this point, the burden of proof is on the snark hunters to provide more illuminating pictures of their quarry.

It is also worth remembering that while the practice of finance may be ancient, the science of financial theory is in its infancy. Moreover, communication between theory and practice is sometimes limited. Given that the EMH is reasonably correct, the trickle down of that idea from theory to practice will take a long time. We have seen only the first phase of this movement.

Finally, we should never expect academic and professional attitudes to correspond perfectly in stock market research. Every profession has its optimistic and pessimistic groups, and in investments, the professional community will always be, by nature, more optimistic than the academic community about beating the market. Indeed, one of the primary reasons the market is relatively efficient today is that professional investors are keen to beat the market.

Attitudes within the two camps will no doubt change in the future. On the academic side, the theory will be improved to the point that even more snarks will be identified as boojums. However, academic opinion probably will be more attuned to the possibility of *temporary* market inefficiencies than they are today. Programmed trading is one such instance. On the professional side, Wall Street will rediscover the EMH. The basic idea of market efficiency will be elevated from that of a theoretical curiosity to a more fundamental and lasting common belief that serves as a powerful standard of comparison against which security analysts and portfolio managers must measure up. We are, in fact, already seeing that today in the increased use of index comparisons. Of course, Wall Street *always* will believe in snarks.

In the interim, what does all this mean for investors from a practical standpoint? First, according to the EMH, get-rich schemes are almost always fraudulent: Joe Granville and friends notwithstanding, it is hard to beat the market. Second, don't churn your account. Trading schemes that involve high portfolio turnover rates are doomed to failure because of transaction costs. Third, more adventuresome investors may wish to consider the relatively conservative segment of the snark literature. Benjamin Graham's strategies, low P/E strategies, and the like are anomalous and do not require churning. An investment strategy that prudently uses such elements can possibly enhance investment performance. But we should never forget that today's snark is likely to be tomorrow's boojum.

Questions

1. What is "the stock market snark"?
2. When a stock market is operationally efficient, does it necessarily follow that stock prices will reflect fundamental (true) values? Explain.
3. Describe the three versions of the efficient market hypothesis.
4. Compare and contrast technical analysis with fundamental analysis.

5. Some researchers using fundamental analysis claim to have discovered "snarks" in the stock market. Describe these snarks.
6. "But we should never forget that today's snark is likely to be tomorrow's boojum." What does this statement mean?

The Minimum Number of Stocks Needed for Diversification

GERALD D. NEWBOULD AND PERCY S. POON

A risk-averse investor seeking to improve investment performance by reading investment textbooks will learn the important distinction between diversifiable risk and non-diversifiable risk. The textbooks will then typically recommend that a portfolio of between *eight* and *twenty* stocks is the minimum necessary to eliminate diversifiable risk. (See Exhibit 1.)[1] In our view, this common recommendation, which originates from the work of Evans and Archer [3], seriously understates the minimum number of stocks that a risk-averse investor should aim for as a portfolio. This article argues that it may be desirable to have *substantially more than 20 stocks* in a portfolio to eliminate diversifiable risk.

The article first briefly reviews investment texts to show the pervasiveness of the standard recommendation to invest in eight to twenty stocks, and then argues that the standard recommendation is flawed—briefly, the standard recommendation is based upon the average risk that results from a very large number of equal-number stock portfolios. An individual investor, however, does not have a large number of such portfolios; the investor normally has one portfolio in any particular universe of stocks, and the risk outcome on this one portfolio could be other than the statistical average. Section II analyzes returns on the Standard & Poor's (S&P) 500 to demonstrate the variability of portfolio returns. The empirical results from analyzing these data lead to a recommendation that substantially more than 20 stocks may be needed to nearly eliminate diversifiable risk, depending on the weighing scheme used to construct portfolios and the personal risk preference. A final section provides a summary.

At the time of this writing, Gerald D. Newbould was the Hilton Distinguished Professor and Percy S. Poon was an assistant professor of finance at University of Nevada, Las Vegas, NV. We would like to thank the participants at the UNLV Finance Research Seminar. The research grant from the First Interstate Bank Institute for Business Leadership at UNLV is gratefully acknowledged.

Source: *Financial Practice and Education* (Fall 1993, pp. 85–87). Reprinted with permission.

[1] The eight-to-twenty stock recommendation in the textbooks is based on naive or random diversification. Therefore we will not discuss other methods of achieving diversification, such as the Markowitz method.

EXHIBIT 1 RECOMMENDATIONS FOR MINIMUM NUMBER OF STOCKS IN A PORTFOLIO

Source[a]	Exhibit 2 or Similar	# of Stocks
[12]	p. 100	8 – 16 (p. 99)
[6]	p. 698	8 – 20 (p. 697)
[4]	na[b]	10 – 15 (p. 231)
[8]	p. 14	10 – 15 (p. 144)
[7]	na	10 – 20 (p. 674)
[13]	na	12 – 15 (p. C16)
[9]	p. 288	12 – 18 (p. 288)
[1]	na	12 or more (p. 335)
[14]	p. 111	15 – 20 (p. 110)
[5]	p. 153	20 (p. 154)
[10]	na	20 (p. 218)
[2]	p. 139	20 (p. 139)

[a] See References.
[b] Not Available.

The Standard Recommendation

The risk of a portfolio is determined by the risks of the individual stocks, the relationships (covariances) between the individual stocks, and the percentage of the portfolio money invested in each of the stocks. The risk of a portfolio can be graphed against the number of stocks in the portfolio to show the reduction in risk due to diversification. To illustrate this, the S&P 500 was chosen as a possible universe of stocks from which to construct portfolios, and the market value of each company was used as the stock's weight in each portfolio. Then 1,000 portfolios in each category (i.e. 1,000 one-stock portfolios, 1,000 two-stock portfolios, etc.) were constructed over the period January 1988 to December 1990.[2] Using volatility of monthly returns, average risk on each sized portfolio was measured; Exhibit 2 shows the results. The steep fall of the curve shows *average* diversifiable risk being reduced as the number of stocks in the portfolio increases. Exhibit 2 is similar to that which appears in many textbooks, as listed in Exhibit 1.

Exhibit 1 also cites the interpretations provided by the various authors of what this curve implies. The minimum number of stocks recommended by these authors for a risk-efficient portfolio varies from a low of eight to a high of twenty. Some authors imply that further diversification is unnecessary; others are emphatic: "Further spreading of the portfolio's assets is *superfluous diversification* (author's emphasis) and should be avoided" [4, p. 231]. Even without such clear guidance, our interpretation of these recommendations is that the investor with,

[2] Since the estimation period was a fairly consistent bull market, our analysis would understate the volatility of portfolio risk.

EXHIBIT 2 AVERAGE PORTFOLIO RISK

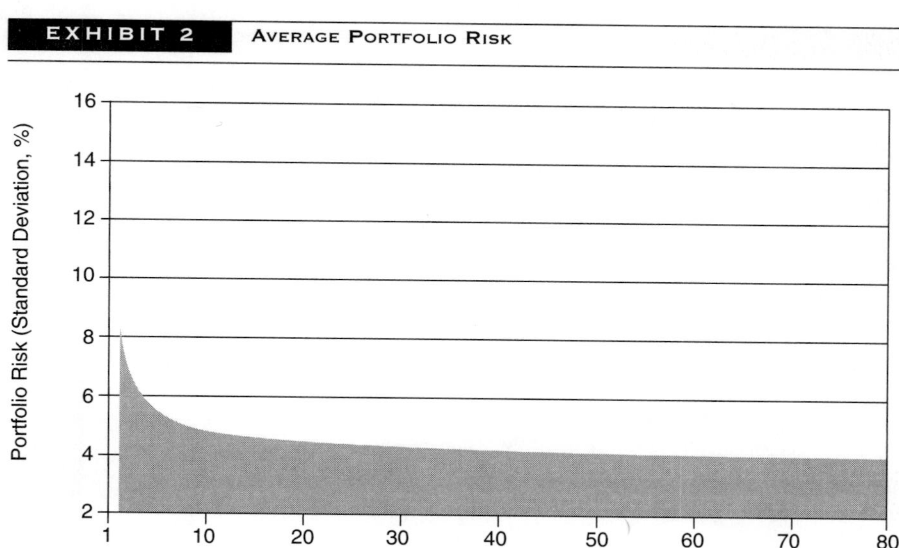

say, $10,000, would be indifferent in terms of risk between buying, say, ten random S&P stocks and investing in an S&P index fund. (Note that the whole discussion is in terms of risk; returns are not being analyzed, so professional management fees and transaction costs are not being considered.)

However, the flaw in these recommendations lies in overlooking the fact that an investor typically has but one portfolio (in any particular universe of stocks), and so perhaps should be unwilling to jeopardize his/her funds on the basis of the *average* outcome of a large number of equal-size portfolios chosen from that same universe. Having but one portfolio from a particular universe, the investor has to face the fact that the risk on *his/her* portfolio can be slightly, or even substantially, above or below the average. Briefly, the standard recommendations hide the fact that a range of outcomes underlies every point on the curve in Exhibit 2.

The Proposed Recommendation

To illustrate the range of risk that is hidden by Exhibit 2, Exhibit 3, with similar axes to Exhibit 2, shows the curves that would statistically accommodate 99 percent, 95 percent, and 90 percent confidence intervals of the 80,000 simulated portfolios. The effect of portfolio size on reducing diversifiable risk is still clear in the new exhibit—for any pair of curves does converge; but notice how risk reduction is delayed. Diversifiable risk is not effectively eliminated at eight, 10, 15, or even at 20 stocks. The upper and lower limit curves become virtually parallel only at a portfolio size much greater than 20 stocks.

EXHIBIT 3 UPPER AND LOWER CONFIDENCE LIMITS OF PORTFOLIO RISK

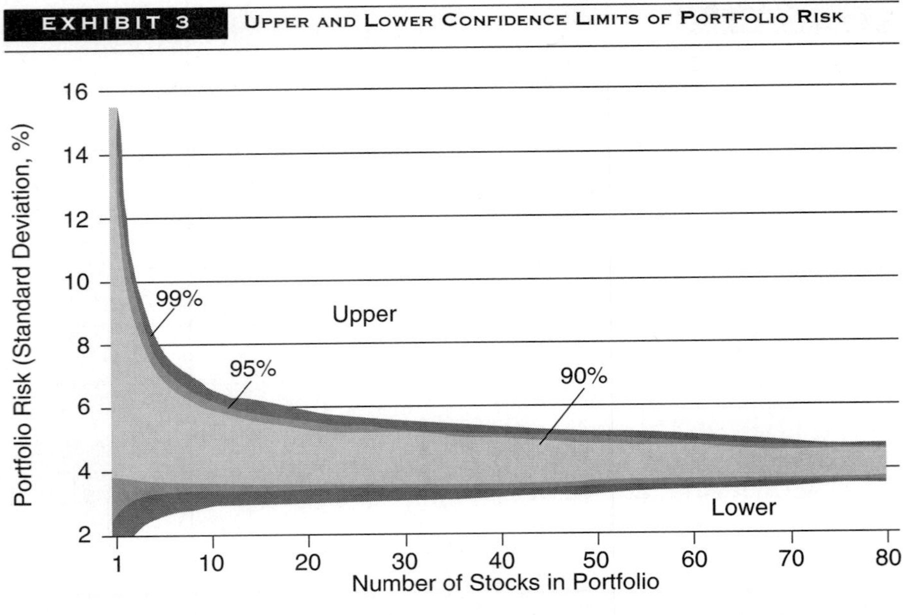

Perhaps a more illustrative procedure than Exhibit 3 is to assign the mean risk on a portfolio a value of 100 and express possible portfolio risks as a percentage of this. (Some Exhibit 2s are in fact constructed this way.) Exhibit 4 gives some examples. Thus the one-stock portfolio risk, when compared with the average one-stock portfolio, has a 0.5 percent chance of being 185 percent greater than the average, a 2.5 percent chance of being 164 percent greater than the average, and a 5 percent chance of being 154 percent greater than the average. Perhaps the best way to read Exhibit 4 is to choose a probability level at which the typical investor would feel comfortable and then run down that column until the percentage risks are also acceptable. While this must essentially be a personal decision (different investors have different degrees of "risk-aversion"), it would seem that the usual recommendation of eight to 20 stocks is a severe underestimate of the minimum size needed to diversify with comfort. The actual minimum number of stocks for an investor would depend on the universe of stocks being analyzed, the personal risk preferences, and the desired confidence intervals.

Two other points should be noted. Firstly, a conclusion that at least 30 stocks is the appropriate minimum has been arrived at previously, but by a different route. Statman [11] argued that diversification should be increased as long as the average marginal benefits (risk reduction) exceed the average marginal costs (transaction costs of buying more stocks) [p. 354]. Essentially, Statman was exploiting the slope in Exhibit 2 that continues between the usual recommendation (eight to 20 stocks) and the final leveling out of the *average* curve. As noted above, our argument that the minimum size is much greater than 20 stocks is

EXHIBIT 4 UPPER RISK RANGES OF MEAN PORTFOLIO RISK

	Upper Confidence Limit			
# of Stocks	**99%**	**95%**	**90%**	**Mean Risk[a]**
1	185	164	154	100
8[b]	141	131	126	100
10[b]	137	128	124	100
12[b]	135	127	123	100
15[b]	133	125	121	100
20[b]	130	123	119	100
30	127	121	118	100
40	124	118	115	100
50	121	116	114	100
60	119	114	112	100
70	116	112	110	100
80	115	111	110	100

[a] The mean risk of each size portfolio is standardized at 100.

[b] These are the recommendations for the minimum number of stocks in a portfolio, in many textbooks. See Exhibit 1.

based purely on the premise that an investor cannot afford to gamble on the probability of his or her being the average investor and should, if truly risk-averse, consider the range of risk outcomes that underlies the average.

Secondly, the 500 stocks used in our study had an equal chance of being selected for any portfolio, but once selected a stock was weighted in the portfolio according to the market value of the company. If investors weight their stock selections equally, it is possible that mean risk or convergence of risk range in Exhibit 3 might be different. The 80,000-portfolio simulation was rerun using equal probability of selection and equal weight once selected. The results are summarized in Exhibit 5. With equal weights, mean portfolio risk is higher but the deviation of risk is lower. However, Exhibit 5 does not appear to change our conclusion that the minimum number of stocks needed for diversification is substantially more than 20.

Summary

The recommendation that owning eight to 20 stocks achieves a risk-efficient portfolio pervades the investment literature. The risk-averse investor using this recommendation will find that in reality his/her portfolio is exposed to a range of risk which could be substantially different from the average. Probably there would be little consolation to the investor with an eight-stock portfolio experiencing a risk that was 141 percent of the risk on the average eight-stock portfolio if he/she was told that there was another investor at the other end of the distribution balancing him/her out—yet this is what the standard recommendation is doing. To recognize that each individual investor is risk averse on *his/her*

EXHIBIT 5 MARKET-VALUE WEIGHTED VERSUS EQUAL WEIGHTED PORTFOLIOS

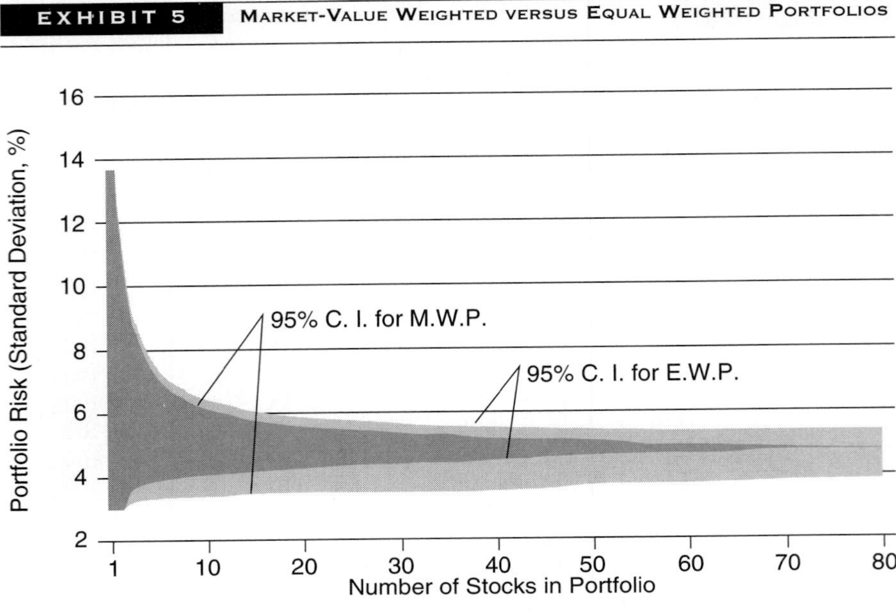

own individual portfolio outcome (and not merely risk averse on the *average* of all investors' outcomes), the standard diagram, Exhibit 2, should, in our view, be modified to conform to Exhibit 3. The empirical results from analyzing the S&P 500 data indicate that the recommendation would place the minimum number of stocks needed to achieve diversification much higher than 20 stocks. The actual number would depend upon the particular universe of stocks being analyzed, the weighting scheme used to construct portfolios, and the individual investor's desired confidence intervals and risk preference.

References

1. J. Bamford, J. Blyskal, E. Card, and A. Jacobson, *Complete Guide to Managing Your Money*, Mount Vernon, NY, Consumers Union, 1989.
2. R.A. Brealey and S.C. Myers, *Principles of Corporate Finance*, 4th ed., Hightstown, NJ, McGraw-Hill, 1991.
3. J.L. Evans and S.H. Archer, "Diversification and the Reduction of Dispersion: An Empirical Analysis," *Journal of Finance* (December 1968), pp. 761-767.
4. J.C. Francis, *Investments: Analysis and Management*, 5th ed., Hightstown, NJ, McGraw-Hill, 1991.
5. D.W. French, *Security and Portfolio Analysis*, Columbus, OH, Merrill, 1989.
6. L.J. Gitman and M.D. Joehnk, *Fundamentals of Investing*, 4th ed., New York, NY, Harper & Row, 1990.

7. G.A. Hirt and S.B. Block, *Fundamentals of Investment Management*, 3rd ed., Homewood, IL, Irwin, 1990.
8. E.A. Moses and J.M. Cheney, *Investments: Analysis, Selection, and Management*, St. Paul, MN, West, 1989.
9. F.K. Reilly, *Investment Analysis and Portfolio Management*, 3rd ed., Chicago, IL, The Dryden Press, 1992.
10. W.F. Sharpe and G.J. Alexander, *Investments*, 4th ed., Englewood Cliffs, NJ, Prentice Hall, 1990.
11. M. Statman, "How Many Stocks Make a Diversified Portfolio?" *Journal of Financial and Quantitative Analysis* (September 1987), pp. 353-363.
12. R.A. Stevenson, E.H. Jennings, and D. Loy, *Fundamentals of Investments*, 4th ed., St. Paul, MN, West, 1988.
13. The Rewards and Pitfalls of High Dividend Stocks, *The Wall Street Journal*, August 2, 1991.
14. B.J. Winger and R.R. Frasca, *Investments: Introduction to Analysis and Planning*, 2nd ed., New York, NY, Macmillan, 1991.

Questions

1. What is the distinction between diversifiable and nondiversifiable risk of a common stock?
2. Why does the standard deviation of portfolio return decline as the number of different common stocks in the portfolio increases? (See Exhibit 2.)
3. How many different common stocks in a portfolio do investment textbooks typically recommend for substantial reduction in diversifiable risk? Describe the weakness in this recommendation, according to the authors.
4. Based on Exhibit 4 and your personal risk preferences, how many different common stocks would you prefer to have in your portfolio? Explain.

The Use of Bonds in Financial Planning

David W. Cornell and J. Gregory Bushong

Bonds traditionally have been the province of institutional investors. However, as individuals seek to diversify their portfolios and add an element of certainty to future investment returns, bonds have become increasingly popular. This article examines bond characteristics, pricing, investment risk and ways to protect against that risk—information that can be extremely useful to CPAs and their clients in structuring investment portfolios designed to meet long-term needs.

Bond Characteristics

Bonds are fixed-income securities. The bond contract (indenture) calls for payment of principal (par value) at maturity and periodic interest payments during the bond term. Interest payments are determined by multiplying the bond's par (face) value by the interest rate (coupon rate) called for in the contract. Generally, interest payments are made semiannually, and bond terms run from one to several years.

Bond prices are based on the amount and timing of future cash flows from the bond and the current market rate of interest. Future cash flows include interest during the bond term and return of par value at maturity (or sales proceeds if the bond is sold before maturity).

Bond prices generally are based on the assumption the bond will be held to maturity. The bond price is the present value of interest payments plus the present value of the return of par at maturity, determined using the current market interest rate. If the market rate is greater than the coupon rate, the bond will

---

At the time of this writing, David W. Cornell was assistant professor of accounting at the Henry W. Bloch School of Business and Public Administration, University of Missouri, Kansas City, Mo; J. Gregory Bushong was assistant professor of accounting at the University of Kentucky, Lexington.

trade below par (at a discount). If the market rate is less than the coupon rate, the bond will trade above par (at a premium). If the coupon and market rates are equal, the bond will trade at par. There is an inverse relationship between changes in the market rate and bond prices: As the market rate increases, the bond's price decreases, and as the market rate decreases, the bond's price increases. Exhibit 1 shows how bonds are priced and how market rate changes affect prices.

Bond Risk

To judge whether a bond is a good investment, investors must consider the risk characteristics of the entity issuing the bond (default risk) and the risk of a change in interest rates (interest rate risk).

EXHIBIT 1 DETERMINING BOND PRICES

Bond price = Present value of future cash flows
= Present value of par + present value of interest payments

Example 1: Bond purchased to yield coupon rate

Assumptions:

- $10,000 fact amount.
- 12% coupon rate, which equals the market interest rate.
- 10-year bond, annual interest payments.

	Amount of cash flow	Factor	Present value
Principal	$10,000	.3220(1)	$ 3,220
Interest	1,200	5.6502(2)	6,780
Bond price			$10,000

Example 2: Bond purchased at a premium

Assumptions:

- Same as example 1, except the market rate and yield to maturity are 8%.

	Amount of cash flow	Factor	Present value
Principal	$10,000	.4632(3)	$ 4,632
Interest	1,200	6.7101(4)	8,052
Bond price			$12,684

(1) The $10,000 is received at the end of 10 years, and the factor is the present value of $1 received in 10 years at 12% interest.

(2) $1,200 is received at the end of every year for 10 years, and the factor is the present value of an ordinary annuity of $1 for 10 years at 12% interest.

(3) The $10,000 is received at the end of 10 years, and the factor is the present value of $1 received in 10 years at 8% interest.

(4) $1,200 is received at the end of every year for 10 years, and the factor is the present value of an ordinary annuity of $1 for 10 years at 8% interest.

Executive Summary

- INSTITUTIONS ARE NOT the only potential investors in bonds. Bonds can help individual investors meet a variety of goals. CPAs can help their clients by explaining the role bonds should play in the financial planning process.
- BONDS ARE FIXED-INCOME securities issued by federal, state and local governments and their agencies and by corporations. They pay periodic interest at a specified rate during the bond term and return the full amount of principal at maturity.
- THE POSSIBILITY OF default by the issuer is one risk bond investors face. Another risk is the possibility of changes in prevailing interest rates, which includes reinvestment and price risk.
- TO PROTECT AGAINST reinvestment and price risk, bond investments can be immunized; that is, the bond duration is equal to the investor's desired holding period.
- CAREFULLY SELECTED and managed, a bond portfolio can play an important role in a diversified investment plan, with little or no unnecessary risk being taken.

Default risk and types of bonds. Different entities issue bonds at different levels of default risk. Generally, the higher the default risk, the greater the rate of return. Lowest-risk bonds are issued by the U.S. Treasury. Since principal and interest on such bonds are guaranteed by the U.S. government, these bonds have essentially no default risk.

States, municipalities and other political subdivisions issue general obligation bonds, which—although backed by the issuer's full faith and credit—have an increased level of default risk. Municipalities also issue revenue bonds, which are serviced by income from specific revenue-producing projects such as toll bridges. Revenue bonds often carry a higher risk than general obligation bonds since their repayment depends on the project's success. Interest received on municipal bonds is free of federal income tax.

Nongovernment entities also issue bonds (e.g., debentures). These bonds' default risk depends on the issuer's ability to service the debt, which in turn depends on the issuer's financial condition and the business risks it faces. Default risk can be lowered by adding covenants to the bond indenture. Covenants provide safeguards to bondholders by restricting business activities.

Interest rate risk. Interest rate risk, the risk the market rate will change, is inherent in all bonds. If interest rates change while bonds are held, the actual return on the investment will differ from the expected yield. The two components of interest rate risk are

• *Reinvestment risk.* Reinvestment risk occurs when interest payments during the bond term cannot be reinvested at the market rate. Exhibit 2 illustrates this risk. In example 1, interest is reinvested at the market rate and the bond is held to maturity.

EXHIBIT 2 GROWTH OF A BOND INVESTMENT HELD TO MATURITY

Example 1: Constant market rate of interest

Assumptions:

- $10,000 par value.
- 12% coupon rate, which equaled the market rate at the time of purchase.
- Interest payments are reinvested at 12%.
- 10-year bond, annual compounding.

	Cash receipts from bond	Interest earned on interest payments received	Future value
Interest payments	$12,000[(1)]	$9,058	$21,058
Par value	10,000	—	10,000[(2)]
	$22,000	$9,058	$31,058[(3)]

Example 2: Decrease in market rate of interest

Assumptions:

- Interest payments are reinvested at 9%.
- Other assumptions are the same as those in example 1.

	Cash receipts from bond	Interest earned on interest payments received	Future value
Interest payments	$12,000[(4)]	$6,232	$18,232
Par value	10,000	—	10,000[(5)]
	$22,000	$6,232	$28,232[(6)]

(1) $1,200 per year is received at the end of each year for 10 years.
(2) The par value is received at maturity; therefore, the future value is equal to the cash received.
(3) $31,058 is the future value of the initial purchase price of $10,000 at 12% compounded annually for 10 years.
(4) $1,200 per year is received at the end of each year for 10 years.
(5) The par value is received at maturity; therefore, the future value is equal to the cash received.
(6) $28,232 is the future value of the initial purchase price of $10,000 at 10.9% rate compounded annually for 10 years.

In example 2, however, interest receipts are reinvested at 9% instead of 12%. This results in interest payments having a lower future value. As such, the bond investment's future value is lower than that implied by the market rate at purchase, and the return on the investment is lower than the expected 12%.

If rates rise during the bond term, the future value of the bond investment will be greater than the yield implied by the purchase price. The higher the coupon rate and the longer the period of time until maturity, the greater the impact of changes in the reinvestment rate on both future value and yield.

In both of exhibit 2's examples, the future value of the principal is equal to the bond's par value ($10,000), because the bond was held to maturity. Not all bonds, however, are held to maturity and if they are not, investors experience price risk.

• *Price risk.* Price risk occurs when bonds are sold on the open market. Price is determined by the market interest rate at the time of sale. Since a bond's price changes when interest rates change, investors may not receive par value upon sale. In other words, when bonds are sold before maturity, the investor's final proceeds and the return on the investment may differ from those expected at the time the bonds were purchased. Exhibit 3 illustrates price risk.

The assumptions in exhibit 3 are the same as those in example 2, exhibit 2, except the bonds are 20-year bonds and are sold at the end of the 10th year. In exhibit 3, the proceeds are determined by discounting future cash flows at the market rate. Since the coupon rate is higher than the market rate, the bond sells at a premium. This results in a yield of less than 12%, but the yield is greater than that in example 2, exhibit 2, because the amount received for the bonds is greater than par, lessening the effect of the lower return on reinvested interest.

As exhibit 3 illustrates, the two components of interest rate risk move in opposite directions. A decrease in the market interest rate has a negative reinvestment risk and a positive price risk. This implies the future value of reinvested interest payments will decrease due to a decreased reinvestment rate, but it also implies the bond's sales price will increase. The opposite is true if interest rates increase while the bond is held. An investor can avoid interest rate risk altogether by using the two components to offset each other. By eliminating interest rate risk, investors can immunize the bond against future interest rate changes.

Bond Immunization

A bond investment is immunized when reinvestment and price risks completely offset each other, leaving the investment's future value unchanged regardless of changes in the market rate. An investment is immunized when the bond's duration equals the desired investment horizon.

EXHIBIT 3 GROWTH OF A BOND INVESTMENT SOLD BEFORE MATURITY

Assumptions:

- $10,000 par value.
- 20-year bond, annual compounding, sold after 10 years.
- 12% coupon rate which equaled the market rate at the time of purchase.
- Interest payments are reinvested at 9% and the market rate of interest at the time the bond is sold is 9%.

	Cash receipts from bond	Interest earned on interest payments received	Future value
Interest payments	$12,000(1)	$6,232	$18,232
Par value	10,000	—	11,925(2)
	$22,000	$6,232	$30,157(3)

(1) $1,200 per year is received at the end of each year for 10 years.

(2) The amount received when the bond is sold is the present value of the remaining interest payments ($7,701) plus the present value of the par value ($4,224) discounted at 9%.

(3) $30,157 is the future value of the initial purchase price of $10,000 at 11.7% compounded annually for 10 years.

Bond Duration

Duration is the weighted average time from investment in the bond until receipt of cash flows from the investment. The investment horizon is the length of time an investor wishes to hold the bond. Exhibit 4 gives the formula for computing duration and an example of how it is determined.

The bonds in exhibit 4 have a 12% coupon rate, which equaled the market rate at the time they were purchased and the duration determined. If the market rate remains 12% throughout the bond term, the investment's yield will be 12%, regard-

EXHIBIT 4 DETERMINING DURATION

$$\text{Duration} = \frac{\sum \frac{c_t(t)}{(1+i)^t}}{\sum \frac{c_t}{(1+i)^t}}$$

Where:
t is the time period in which the cash flow occurs
c_t is the cash flow payment that occurs in period t
i is the market yield on the bond

- The denominator is the present value of the cash flows at the time the bond is purchased, which is equal to the price of the bond.
- The numerator is the present value of the cash flows at the time the bond is purchased weighted by year of receipt.

Assumptions:
- $10,000 par value.
- 12% coupon rate, which equaled market value at issue date.
- 10-year bond, annual compounding.

Year	Cash flow	Present value	Weighted present value
1	$ 1,200	$ 1,070	$ 1,070
2	1,200	957	1,914
3	1,200	854	2,562
4	1,200	763	3,052
5	1,200	681	3,405
6	1,200	608	3,648
7	1,200	543	3,801
8	1,200	485	3,880
9	1,200	433	3,897
10	11,200	3,606	36,060
	$22,000	$10,000	$63,289

$$\text{Duration} = \frac{63{,}289}{10{,}000} = 6.33 \text{ years}$$

less of the investment horizon. However, if the market rate changes and the bonds are held to maturity, the return on the investment will differ from that expected.

Use of Duration to Immunize Bond Investments

Bond investments can be immunized by investing in bonds with a duration (as computed in exhibit 4) equal to the investment horizon. Once the investment has been made, the investor must reinvest all interest upon receipt at the market rate then applicable and must sell the bond at the end of the investment horizon. The investment then yields the future value expected at purchase. This is true regardless of market rate changes because the two components of interest rate risk offset each other.

Exhibits 5 and 6 illustrate two alternative investment strategies. Exhibit 5 uses the duration strategy; exhibit 6 uses the maturity strategy. The difference in the two is the time to maturity. The maturity strategy equates the time to maturity with the investment horizon. The duration strategy ignores the time to maturity and instead equates the duration with the investment horizon.

EXHIBIT 5 FUTURE VALUE BY TYPE OF CASH FLOW DURATION STRATEGY

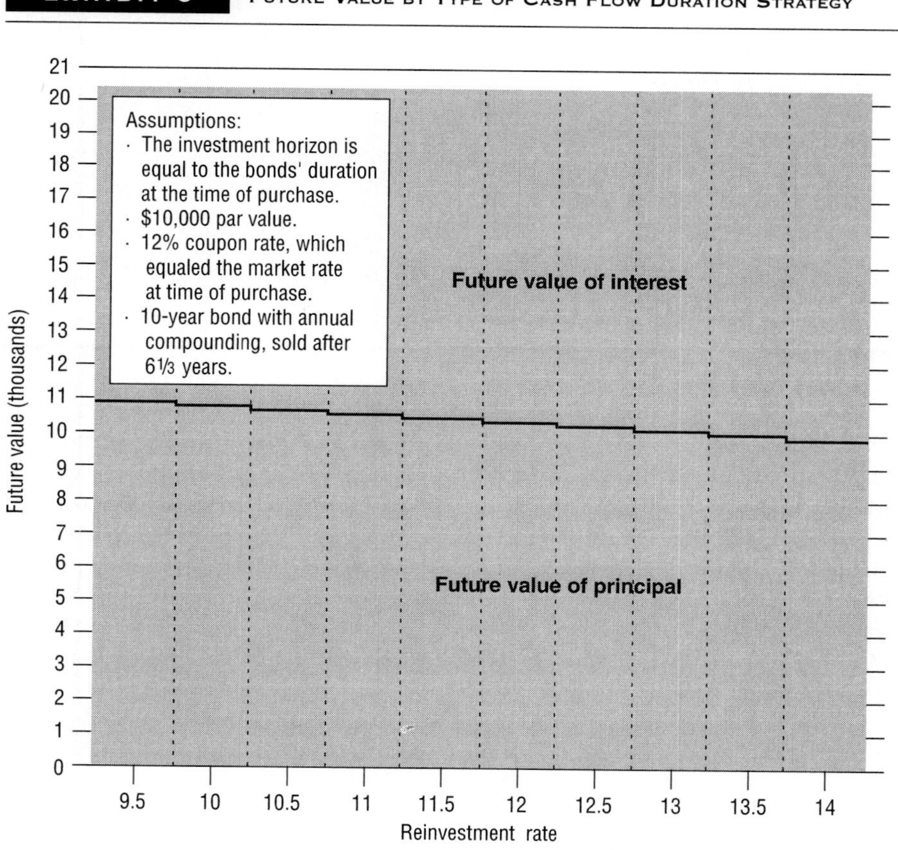

EXHIBIT 6 FUTURE VALUE BY TYPE OF CASH FLOW MATURITY STRATEGY

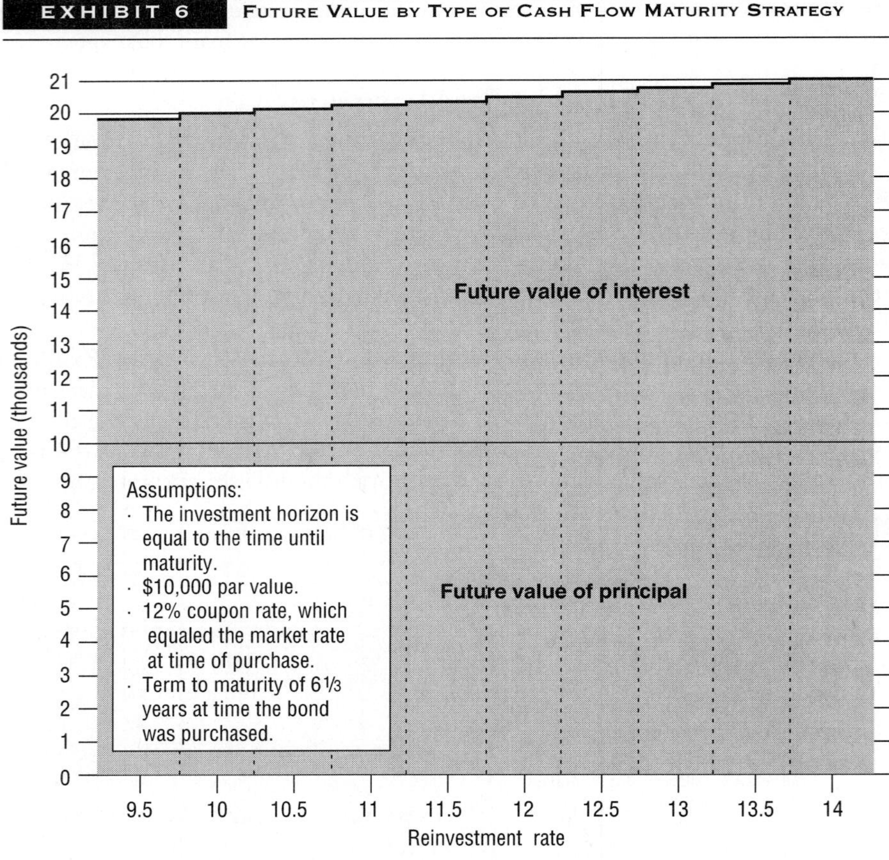

Exhibit 5 illustrates how the immunization strategy locks in the 12% expected yield regardless of interest rate changes. The investment's expected future value is $20,490 (the future valve of a $10,000 investment held for 6⅓ years at 12%). The $20,490 future value is achieved regardless of how interest rates change. It's relatively constant because a market rate change causes an equal and opposite reaction in the price and reinvestment risks. The interest's future value increases as rates increase, but the increase is offset by a decrease in the bond's sales price at the investment horizon's end. The net effect is minimal, and the investment returns the implied 12%.

This offsetting of price and reinvestment risk does not occur if the bond investment is not immunized. Exhibit 6 indicates the future value of a portfolio that has not been immunized. As the exhibit shows, the future value of the principal is constant at par regardless of the direction of interest rates. Reinvestment risk, on the other hand, is still present. With the no price risk to offset the reinvestment risk, the investment's future value is determined by interest rates after the bond purchase.

Immunization also works when there are multiple rate changes if the changes are not extreme. An unlikely scenario exists in which immunization fails to yield the approximate rate implied at purchase. If interest rates fall while the bond is held and increase immediately before sale, the yield on the investment will be lower than anticipated. In this case, the amount earned on reinvested interest is less than the amount expected at purchase (negative reinvestment risk), and the amount received when the bonds are sold is less than par (negative price risk). The opposite is true if interest rates increase while the bonds are held and decrease immediately before sale.

Use of Immunization in Bond Investments

Immunization should be used cautiously. If interest rates are expected to increase, the return on the investment is higher using a maturity strategy than using a duration strategy. This can be seen by comparing exhibits 5 and 6 at 14%. At that rate, the bond investment's future value is greater using the maturity strategy than using the duration strategy. When the maturity strategy is used during periods of rising interest rates, the increase in interest reinvestment earnings is not offset by a decreased amount received at the investment horizon's end. Instead, bond principal is recouped by collecting the par value from the issuing company. The opposite is true during periods of decreasing interest rates.

Predicting interest rate movements over an extended period is very difficult; therefore, the investor's risk attitudes should be considered when choosing a strategy. A conservative investor should use the duration strategy even if interest rates are expected to increase. On the other hand, an investor willing to accept more risk might use the maturity strategy if rates are expected to increase.

Duration also can be used for bond portfolios. To immunize a portfolio, the weighted average duration of all bonds in the portfolio must equal the investment horizon. Interest must be reinvested in bonds so the portfolio's duration equals the investment horizon. This implies an active investment strategy; the portfolio must be monitored and holdings adjusted as the horizon shortens. Quarterly or semiannual adjustments may be necessary, depending on the number of bonds in the portfolio, frequency of interest payments and investment-horizon length.

Means of Diversification

As more investors look to bonds to diversify their investment portfolios, they must consider the bonds' risk and return characteristics before investing. Default risk can be lessened by diversifying the portfolio and purchasing bonds with higher ratings from bond rating agencies much as *Moody's Bond Record.* Interest rate risk can be reduced or eliminated with the duration strategy. While this strategy eliminates most interest rate risk, it may require some management over time as the investment horizon is reduced. Certainly, other factors also should be considered when advising clients about bond investments, but the above strategies will help minimize the long-term risk of bond investing.

Questions

1. Use Exhibit 1 to illustrate the following two principles: (1) If the market interest rate (yield to maturity) equals the coupon rate, the bond trades at par value. (2) If the market interest rate is less than the coupon rate, the bond trades at a premium. (What happens to the bond price if the market interest rate exceeds the coupon rate?)
2. (a) Define interest rate risk, including the two components *reinvestment risk* and *price risk*.

   (b) Use Exhibit 2 to illustrate reinvestment risk.

   (c) Use Exhibit 3 to illustrate that the two components of interest rate risk move in opposite directions.
3. What is the *duration* of a bond?
4. How do you use the concept of duration to immunize an investment in bonds? Explain.
5. Calculate the duration of the following coupon bond:

   Par value = $1,000
   Coupon rate = 10% (payable annually)
   Years to maturity = 2
   Yield to maturity = 10%
6. Calculate the duration of the bond in Question 5 assuming the yield to maturity is 15 percent. Based on your answers to Questions 5 and 6, what is the relationship between duration and yield to maturity of a coupon bond?
7. Calculate the duration of a zero-coupon bond with the following characteristics: Par value = $1,000; years to maturity = 2; yield to maturity = 10%. (*Hint:* The duration of a zero-coupon bond equals its years to maturity.) Based on your answers to Questions 5 and 7, what is the relationship between duration and coupon rate?

Is There Too Much Corporate Debt?

BEN BERNANKE

Borrowing by U.S. corporations has increased dramatically in recent years. The outstanding debt of nonfinancial corporations rose 70 percent between 1983 and 1988, more than two-thirds faster than growth of nominal GNP. Highly leveraged transactions, such as the $25 billion takeover of RJR Nabisco, routinely make the front pages.

Heavy borrowing such as this has raised the issue of whether corporate debt has become excessive. Congress has been considering whether changes should be made in the tax law to try to reduce the rate of corporate debt accumulation. The Federal Reserve has been studying the implications of debt growth for monetary policy and banking system oversight.

In evaluating the debt situation there are many issues to consider, but two questions lie at the heart of the debate. First is the "micro" issue: do high levels of debt increase the efficiency of firms, as some proponents of high leverage have claimed? Then there is the "macro" issue: does increased corporate debt reduce the stability of the country's financial and economic system?

The Micro Issue: Does Debt Promote Efficiency?

The traditional explanation for why corporations use debt as a source of finance is debt's tax advantage: interest payments made by a firm are tax-deductible while dividend payments are not. Offsetting this advantage are the costs of bankruptcy and reorganization that may be incurred should the firm not be able to meet the stipulated interest payments. According to the traditional view, the optimal ratio of debt to equity is the one that just balances these two costs.

More recently, however, financial economists have gone beyond this traditional view to focus on the possibly beneficial effects of debt issuance on managerial performance.[1] This point can be illustrated by a simple example.

At the time of this writing, Ben Bernanke was a professor of economics at Princeton University.

Source: Reprinted from *Business Review*, Federal Reserve Bank of Philadelphia, (Sept./Oct. 1989).

[1] The classic article that introduced this approach is Jensen and Meckling (1976).

A Tale of Two Twins

Suppose that there are two potential entrepreneurs who (like the two characters in a well-known children's magazine) are named Goofus and Gallant.[2] Goofus and Gallant plan to start ice cream stands on opposite sides of town. The necessary equipment for a stand costs $1,000, and since the entrepreneurs each have only $100, they must obtain some outside finance.

Goofus finances his ice cream stand through stock issuance: that is, he finds some friends to put up $900, in exchange for which he promises them 90 percent of the profits. Gallant issues debt instead; he gets a friend to lend him $900, for which Gallant promises to pay $100 in annual interest. Both boys thus have enough capital to get their businesses going.

Things go along well enough at first for both entrepreneurs. But the summer days are hot, and scooping ice cream is hard work. Goofus says to himself, "I've made $100 profit at my stand already this week. If I were to keep working through the weekend, I could make another $100. But I have to share 90 percent with my partners—so that extra $100 really means only $10 for me! I'm not really willing to work the weekend for less than a $25 personal profit, so I think I'll quit and go fishing."

On the other side of town, Gallant is also having a crisis of conscience; he is developing scooper's elbow from serving so much ice cream. He loves to fish as much as Goofus does. Should he quit working? He says to himself, "The $100 I have earned so far is enough to cover the interest payment on my loan. From now on, any profits the ice cream stand earns are mine to keep. If I worked through the weekend, I could earn another $100; that's more than the $25 I would be willing to pay to knock off and go fishing." So Gallant goes back to work.

The two entrepreneurs have faced the same quandary, but have made different decisions. It is important to understand that, in both cases, it is economically efficient to keep the ice cream stand in operation through the weekend, in that the $100 in extra profit that could be earned is greater than the $25 value the proprietor of each stand places on his leisure. Yet, of the two, only Gallant does the "right" thing and keeps working.

Incentives to Do the Right Thing

In the children's magazine, Gallant's decisions to do the right thing stem from his superior moral character. In this example, morality has nothing to do with it; both boys make their decisions based on their calculations of personal gain. The difference between Goofus and Gallant is the way in which they have financed their ventures. By financing with equity, Goofus has created a situation in which his personal rewards are relatively insensitive to the profits of the company; a $100 increase in profits increases his personal return by only $10. This reduces

---

[2] The characters Goofus and Gallant are copyrighted by *Highlights for Children*, and their names are used with permission.

Goofus's incentive to work hard and make decisions that are in the interest of the company. In contrast, once the interest payment is made, Gallant's personal returns fluctuate dollar for dollar with the profits of the company; he thus has a strong incentive to take actions that maximize the company's profits.

Indeed, in this particular example, Gallant would do the right thing (keep working) as long as he was financed at least 60 percent by debt. With 60 percent ($600) in debt, there would be 40 percent ($400) in total equity. Gallant's $100 in original capital would give him 25 percent of that equity, giving him a 25 percent share of the firm's profits. With a 25 percent share, Gallant would be just indifferent between working through the weekend (which nets him an extra .25 x $100 = $25) or going fishing (which is worth $25 to him). With anything above 60 percent debt finance, he would keep working.

Changing the Mode of Financing

We can add another chapter to the story of Goofus and Gallant. At the end of the summer, both boys notice that the debt-financed ice cream stand is more profitable than the equity-financed stand, and that this extra profitability is due entirely to the way in which the stands are financed. This implies that pure profits can be earned by a capital restructuring—a change in the mode of finance—of Goofus's operation. This restructuring can be accomplished if someone takes out a loan and uses the borrowed money to buy back the shares from Goofus's shareholders; this changes the stand's financing from equity to debt. The share buyback is particularly attractive at the current market price for Goofus's company's shares, which—because Goofus is always going fishing—is low. But the buyback would be profitable even if the acquirers had to pay the current stockholders some premium for their shares; the acquirers would simply be sharing with the current shareholders some of the profits expected to be produced by the restructuring.

The capital restructuring of Goofus's stand would work equally well if performed by Goofus, by Gallant, or by someone else.[3] In any case, the swapping of debt for equity is called a *leveraged buyout*, or LBO. If done by Goofus, the current manager of the operation, it could also be called a *management buyout;* if done by Gallant, it would be called a *takeover* (a hostile takeover, if Goofus resisted and tried to hold on to the company). The key point is that, in either case, the leverage of the company (its ratio of debt to equity) would increase, and this would lead to more efficient and profitable operations.

The Recent Explosion of Debt

The parable of Goofus and Gallant illustrates the idea that the financial structure of firms influences the incentives of "insiders" (managers, directors, and large

[3] This assumes, first, that Gallant has time to operate both stands and, second, that Gallant has enough profits from operating his own stand to buy out Goofus's share.

shareholders with some operational interest in the business) and that, in particular, high levels of debt may increase the willingness of insiders to work hard and make profit-maximizing decisions. This incentive-based approach makes a valuable contribution to understanding of a firm's capital structure. But while this theory might explain why firms like to use debt in general, does it explain why the use of debt has increased so much in recent years?

Michael Jensen, a founder and leading proponent of the incentive-based approach to capital structure, argues that it can.[4] Jensen focuses on a recent worsening of what he calls the "free cash flow" problem. Free cash flow is defined as the portion of a corporation's cash flow that it is unable to invest profitably within the firm. Companies in industries that are profitable but no longer have much potential for expansion—the U.S. oil industry, for example—have a lot of free cash flow.

Why is free cash flow a problem? Jensen argues that managers are often tempted to use free cash flow to expand the size of the company, even if the expansion is not profitable. This is because managers feel that their power and job satisfaction are enhanced by a growing company; so given that most managers' compensation is at best weakly tied to the firm's profitability, Jensen argues that managers will find it personally worthwhile to expand even into money-losing operations. In principle, the board of directors and shareholders should be able to block these unprofitable investments; however, in practice, the fact that the management typically has far more information about potential investments than do outside directors and shareholders makes it difficult to second-guess the managers' recommendations.

How More Leverage Can Help

The problem of free cash flow is precisely analogous to the problem in the Goofus and Gallant example. Just as Goofus was willing to sacrifice company profits in order to pursue his personal goals (going fishing), so the company manager with lots of free cash flow may attempt to use that cash to increase his power and perquisites, at the expense of the shareholders. Jensen argues that the solution to the free-cash-flow problem is the same as the solution to the Goofus-Gallant problem: more leverage. For example, suppose that management uses the free cash flow of the company, plus the proceeds of new debt issues, to repurchase stock from the outside shareholders—that is, to do a management buyout. This helps solve the free-cash-flow problem in several ways. First, as in the Goofus and Gallant example, the personal returns of the managers are now much more closely tied to the profits of the firm, which gives them incentives to be more efficient. Second, the re-leveraging process removes the existing free cash from the firm, so that any future investment projects will have to be financed externally; thus, future projects will have to meet the market test of being acceptable to outside bankers or bond purchasers. Finally, the high interest payments implied by re-leveraging impose a

[4] For a summary of Jensen's views, see Jensen (1988). Jensen's article is part of a *Journal of Economic Perspectives* special symposium on takeovers, which provides an excellent and balanced introduction to this subject.

permanent discipline on the managers; in order to meet these payments, they will have to ruthlessly cut money-losing operations, avoid questionable investments, and take other efficiency-promoting actions.

According to Jensen, a substantial increase in free-cash-flow problems—resulting from deregulation, the maturing of some large industries, and other factors—is a major source of the recent debt expansion. Jensen also points to a number of institutional factors that have promoted increased leverage. These include relaxed restrictions on mergers, which have lowered the barriers to corporate takeovers created by the antitrust laws, and increased financial sophistication, such as the greatly expanded operations of takeover specialists like Drexel Burnham Lambert Inc. and the development of the market for "junk bonds."[5] Jensen's diagnosis is not controversial: it's quite plausible that these factors, plus changing norms about what constitutes an "acceptable" level of debt, explain at least part of the trend toward increased corporate debt.[6] However, the implied conclusion—that the debt buildup is beneficial overall to the economy—is considerably more controversial.

Criticisms of the Incentive-Based Rationale for Increased Debt

Jensen and other advocates of the incentive-based approach to capital structure have made a cogent theoretical case for the beneficial effects of debt finance, and many architects of large-scale restructurings have given improved incentives and the promise of greater efficiency as a large part of the rationale for increased leverage. The idea that leverage is beneficial has certainly been embraced by the stock market: even unsubstantiated rumors of a potential LBO have been sufficient to send the stock price of the targeted company soaring, often by 40 percent or more. At a minimum, this indicates that stock market participants *believe* that higher leverage increases profitability. Proponents of restructuring interpret this as evidence that debt is good for the economy.

There are, however, criticisms of this conclusion. First, the fact that the stock market's expectations of company profitability rise when there is a buyout is not proof that profits *will* rise in actuality. It is still too soon to judge whether the increased leverage of the 1980s will lead to a sustained increase in profitability. One might think of looking to historical data for an answer to this question. But buyouts in the 1960s and 1970s were somewhat different in character from more recent restructurings, and, in any case, the profitability evidence on the earlier episodes is mixed.

Even if the higher profits expected by the stock market do materialize, there is contention over where they are likely to come from. The incentive-based theory of capital structure says they will come from improved efficiency. But some

---

[5] Junk bonds, more properly called below-investment-grade or high-yield bonds, have been used in a number of large corporate restructurings. For a discussion of the junk-bond market and the uses of junk bonds in takeovers, see Loeys (1986).

[6] One important piece of evidence in favor of this explanation is that net equity issues have been substantially negative since 1983. This suggests that much of the proceeds of the new debt issues is being used to repurchase outstanding shares. This is what we would expect if corporations are attempting to re-leverage their existing assets, rather than using debt to expand their asset holdings.

opponents have argued that the higher profits will primarily reflect transfers to the shareholders from other claimants on the corporation—its employees, customers, suppliers, bondholders, and the government. For example, Andrei Shleifer and Lawrence Summers in a soon-to-be-published study, present evidence that the premium received by shareholders of Trans World Airlines, when it was taken over, was paid for twice over by the wage concessions wrested from three TWA unions. Customers may be hurt if takeovers are associated with increased monopolization of markets.[7] Bondholders have been big losers in some buyouts, as higher leverage has increased bankruptcy risk and thus reduced the value of outstanding bonds. The government may have lost tax revenue, as companies, by increasing leverage, have increased their interest deductions (although there are offsetting effects here, such as the taxes paid by bought-out shareholders on their capital gains). The perception that much of the profits associated with releveraging and buyouts comes from "squeezing" existing beneficiaries of the corporation explains much of the recent political agitation to limit these activities.[8]

Another possible explanation for the effect of LBOs on stock prices is that the announcement of a buyout provides information about, but does not directly affect, the firm's future prospects. Suppose that the management of a publicly owned pharmaceutical firm has secret information about a revolutionary new drug discovered in its laboratories. This highly profitable new opportunity, being secret, is not reflected in the firm's stock price. The management of this company has a strong incentive to do a buyout, because it knows the stock is currently underpriced relative to the firm's future profits. But if the managers attempt a buyout, this will reveal to the public that the management thinks the stock is underpriced—which will cause the stock price to be bid up. This means that the managers will have to share some of the profits from their inside information with the shareholders. Profits may indeed rise after the buyout— reflecting the introduction of the new drug—but this increase in profits would not be in any way caused by the increase in leverage associated with the buyout. Similar arguments apply if the buyout is initiated by a competitor or someone else who might have better information about the firm than do stock market investors.

The debt buildup can also be criticized from the perspective of incentive-based theories themselves. Two points are worth noting: first, the principal problem that higher leverage is supposed to address is the relatively weak connection between firms' profits and managers' personal returns, which reduces managers' incentives to take profit-maximizing actions. But if this is truly the problem, it could be addressed more directly—without subjecting the company to serious bankruptcy risk—simply by changing managerial

---

[7] McAndrews and Nakamura (1989) present a model in which increased leverage by existing firms can help deter potential competitors from entering the market.

[8] Not much systematic empirical work on the "squeezing" hypothesis has been done to date. In a careful study of 76 companies' management buyouts, Kaplan (1988) found that most of the value gained from the buyout was due to increased operating income and tax benefits, and that the transfers from bondholders were small. However, the study considered only the first two years' experience of each firm after its buyout, and lack of data prevented measurement of the buyout's effects on employees, suppliers, and customers.

compensation schemes to include more profit-based incentives. Robert Vishny and Andrei Shleifer (1988) argue that the approach of tying managers' pay to profits is limited by legal precedents that allow shareholders to sue if managerial compensation is "excessive"; however, if managerial incentives are really the problem, it does seem that more could be done in this direction.

The Downside of Debt Financing

A second point, made by the original Jensen-Meckling (1976) article and many since then, is that increased debt is not the optimal solution to all incentive problems. For example, it has been shown, as a theoretical proposition, that managers of debt-financed firms have an incentive to choose riskier projects over safe ones; this is because firms with fixed-debt obligations enjoy all of the upside potential of high-risk projects but share the downside losses with the debt holders, who are not fully repaid if bad investment outcomes cause the firm to fail.

That high leverage does not always promote efficiency can be seen when highly leveraged firms suffer losses and find themselves in financial distress. When financial problems hit, the need to meet interest payments may force management to take a very short-run perspective, leading them to cut back production and employment, cancel even potentially profitable expansion projects, and sell assets at fire-sale prices. Because the risk of bankruptcy is so great, firms in financial distress cannot make long-term agreements; they lose customers and suppliers who are afraid they cannot count on an ongoing relationship, and they must pay wage premiums to hire workers.

These efficiency losses, plus the direct costs of bankruptcy (such as legal fees), are the potential downside of high leverage. In terms of the ice cream stand, if Gallant does not earn enough to make his interest payment, he may be tempted to skimp on the ice cream or even serve the cracked cones, sacrificing future sales to increase short-run income and avoid bankruptcy. Or he may simply choose to stop working, letting the stand go into default. Maybe a highly leveraged Gallant isn't so gallant after all!

The Macro Issue: Spillovers and Multipliers

Most discussion of corporate debt has focused on the microeconomic efficiency issues. However, the macroeconomic implications of debt are also important. There are several possible (although speculative) scenarios under which high corporate debt could contribute to macroeconomic dislocations.

One scenario is a "liquidity crisis." In 1970, the bankruptcy of the Penn Central railroad, and Penn Central's resulting default on its short-term borrowings, caused a temporary, sharp decrease in new lending in the commercial-paper market. Prompt action by the Federal Reserve stabilized the situation. However, the potential for a similar episode, possibly on a larger scale, exists.

This potential arises from the fact that many firms count on being able to "roll over" their short-term debt (that is, re-borrow) as it comes due. If, for some reason, lenders became worried about bankruptcy risk and refused to roll over maturing debt, then these firms (even though they might be fundamentally solvent) would find themselves illiquid—that is, short of cash to make promised payments.

In most cases, firms would respond to this by taking loans on lines of credit previously negotiated with banks; however, that would spread the illiquidity problem to the banking system, as banks suddenly were subjected to large demands for credit. To ease such a liquidity crisis, the Federal Reserve would have to provide more funds to the financial system, either through the discount window, as it did during the Penn Central episode, or through open-market operations.

Perhaps a more disturbing scenario is a "solvency crisis." Suppose that, for reasons unrelated to financial structure, the economy were to enter a serious recession, leading to falling earnings and (perhaps) rising interest costs. Given high leverage inherited from the past, some firms might find it difficult to service their debt. Firms in financial distress are likely to retrench, cutting back employment, production, and investment. This would reduce total demand, worsening the recession and leading to financial problems in other firms. Thus, the initial recessionary shock could be magnified by high leverage; in the language of traditional Keynesian macroeconomic analysis, the "multiplier" relating the size of the initial disturbance to the size of the resulting recession will have increased.

Distressed Firms Can Have Far-Reaching Effects

The difference between the microeconomic and macroeconomic perspective is that in the macroeconomic approach, we are concerned not only with the effects of financial distress on the distressed firm itself, but with the effects of the distressed firm's actions on other firms. If there are "spillovers" from one firm to another (for example, if the shutdown of a large employer in a town affects the town's economy more generally), then financial distress will increase the multiplier. Higher leverage thus has the potential to increase the vulnerability of the economy to destabilizing shocks. Importantly, the possible effects of spillovers and multipliers will not be taken into account by individual firms when they choose their preferred level of debt.

Are these scenarios likely? Nobody knows for sure, but there are several ways to argue that they are not very likely.

First, it should be pointed out that, despite the rapid increase in debt, corporate debt-to-equity ratios (measured in market-value terms) have not changed much during the 1980s. Indeed, Ben Bernanke and John Campbell (1988), using a sample of 1,400 large U.S. nonfinancial corporations, showed that debt-to-equity ratios in the 1980s remain well below their peaks, which occurred during the 1973-74 recession. The relative stability of the debt-to-equity ratio reflects the bull market in stocks of the 1980s, which allowed stock values to keep up with the high rate of debt issuance. From this perspective, debt burdens have not really increased.

However, even though debt-to-equity ratios have not increased, another measure of debt burden—the ratio of interest payments to total cash flow—has grown significantly. Bernanke and Campbell found this measure of interest burden to be about 50 percent higher in the mid-1980s than in the 1970s; several studies report that this ratio is currently close to its 1981-82 recession high, despite the long expansion that has occurred since the end of 1982.

How do we reconcile the fact that the interest-payments-to-earnings ratios (and debt-to-earnings ratios) have grown while debt-to-equity ratios have not? Mechanically, the answer is that both debt and stock values have grown much faster than earnings. The high ratio of stock prices to current earnings—sometimes called the P/E ratio—implies optimism on the part of investors about future earnings.[9] The stock market can be interpreted as saying that, even though current interest burdens are high, earnings are likely to rise enough in the future for firms to meet their debt obligations.

If we take the stock market's prediction at face value, then, a liquidity crisis or solvency crisis cannot be called a likely event; a reasonable expectation is that the corporate debt will be serviced. This doesn't mean that macroeconomic problems due to debt are not possible, however; it only means that they should be thought of as a sort of worst-case scenario. Nevertheless, good policymaking requires attention to worst-case as well as average outcomes. Indeed, it is during crisis situations in which good policies are most important.

The Likelihood of Macroeconomic Debt Problems

To get an idea of what might happen in a worst-case situation, Bernanke and Campbell (1988) simulated the effects of a recession in their sample of large firms. They asked what would have happened if the changes in cash flow, stock prices, and interest rates that actually occurred in the recessions of 1973-74 and 1981-82 had occurred again in 1986, affecting the very same firms in their sample.

Those two recessions were found to have different effects in the simulations. In the 1973-74 scenario, the stock market declines sharply; the simulation shows that in this type of recession more than 10 percent of the large firms would become technically insolvent, in the sense that the market value of their assets would fall below the market value of their debt.[10] In the 1981-82 scenario the stock market is fairly stable, but cash flow falls and interest rates rise; in this case Bernanke and Campbell found that about 10 percent of their firms would be unable to meet interest obligations without further borrowing. In the terminology introduced above, a 1973-74-type recession would create the potential for a solvency crisis, while a 1981-82-type recession might lead to a liquidity crisis.

---

[9] If the stock market is "efficient," then the price of a share should represent the present discounted value of current earnings and future expected earnings. If the P/E ratio is high, then either interest rates are low (which they currently are not), or future earnings are expected to be high relative to current earnings.

[10] If the value of assets is less than the value of debt, then the debt cannot be repaid; the firm must either eventually go bankrupt or be reorganized.

Overall, then, the high share prices of U.S. corporations—not to mention the willingness of lenders to accept the high leverage of borrowing corporations—suggest that knowledgeable investors consider a macroeconomic debt crisis unlikely. However, unlikely is not the same as impossible; the Bernanke-Campbell simulations suggest that macroeconomic debt problems could be triggered by recessionary shocks of a magnitude that has been experienced twice in the last decade and a half.[11] This risk could possibly be ameliorated in the short run by aggressively expansionary monetary and fiscal policies, but only at the cost of higher inflation and potentially greater instability in the long run.

Has Debt Become Less Risky?

An alternative way to question the possibility of a macroeconomic debt crisis is to argue that, because of changes in the financial environment, a given level of debt poses less risk in 1989 than it would have in, say, 1974. Here is a concrete example: a recent development is the use of what is called "strip financing," in which investors in a firm commit to holding a fixed combination of the firm's debt and equity instruments. The idea is to minimize conflict between debt holders and shareholders (who, under strip financing, are one and the same), thus reducing the potential cost of financial distress and reorganization. Another development, stressed by Jensen, is that financial firms involved in arranging buyouts are in some cases retaining some stake in the management of the LBO firm; thus, the financial firm will have an incentive to assist the reorganization process should the LBO fall into financial trouble.

It is certainly true that the safety of any given level of debt depends on the financial environment. Japanese corporations, for example, have borne much higher levels of debt than their U.S. counterparts without experiencing problems. This works because most Japanese corporate debt is in the form of bank loans, and the large banks take an active role in the management of the firms to which they lend. Should a firm experience difficulties, the bank assists in obtaining new finance or in reorganization; at the same time, the bank is well placed to oversee whatever management or strategy changes the firm must make. These sorts of practices, which contrast with traditional "arm's length" lending in the United States, make high debt burdens safer.

Whether the U.S. financial environment has in fact moved substantially in the Japanese direction is an open question. Oversight of corporate management by the financial firm that arranged the LBO is a step toward the Japanese model; however, it is not clear at this point how widespread this practice is. Working in the other direction is the fact that increasing corporate reliance on below-investment-grade (junk) bonds has come at the expense of corporate use

---

[11] Another quantitative objection to the possibility of a macroeconomic debt crisis is that much of the recent debt buildup has occurred in cyclically insensitive sectors, such as food processing and services (see Roach, 1988). While this is true, it is also true that debt burdens have increased in cyclically sensitive sectors, like durable goods, as well. The simulations reported in the text implicitly take into account any shifting sectoral composition of debt.

of bank loans. Since junk bonds tend to be held by mutual funds, insurance companies, and other institutions not directly involved in the management of the firms to which they lend, the use of junk bonds (in place of bank loans) may strengthen the traditional "arm's length" tendency of U.S. capital markets. This may make negotiated avoidance of bankruptcy more difficult and increase potential bankruptcy costs.

The contention that the risks of leverage have been reduced by institutional changes also raises a theoretical question: according to the incentive-based approach, the whole point of increased leverage is to impose discipline on corporate management. If, because of changes in the financial environment, failure to make contracted interest payments becomes a minor concern, then it would seem that the disciplinary impact of debt on management will be much reduced.

Conclusion

The argument for higher leverage is that it imposes discipline on the managers of the corporation, leading to greater efficiency. Effectively, this greater discipline is achieved by means of a threat: if the firm does not perform up to expectations, it may well suffer insolvency and reorganization. As with the discipline of children, the advantage of a draconian threat is the good behavior it may promote; the disadvantage is that the threat may have to be carried out.

Here is an analogy often used in discussing the costs and benefits of high leverage. Suppose we want people to drive more carefully. One way to do this would be to require every car to have a dagger in the steering wheel, the point aimed directly at the chest of the driver. This would certainly promote more careful driving, since even a fender bender might have ghastly consequences. But suppose there was a sudden worsening in driving conditions—a freak snowstorm, for example—that unexpectedly put even the most careful drivers at risk of accidents. Under these circumstances, the dagger-in-the-wheel policy might well lead to more deaths and injuries than if this "discipline device" had never been used.

In this story, the dagger in the wheel is supposed to represent high corporate leverage—which under normal circumstances promotes profit maximization ("safe driving") by managers. The snowstorm is an economywide recession (or perhaps some other disturbance, like a sharp increase in interest rates). The concern is that high leverage, while possibly a boon in good times, might become a destructive force in bad times.

This trade-off poses a quandary for policymakers. Despite the criticisms and existing uncertainties, few economists would completely dismiss the claim that higher leverage can be used to improve incentives and promote efficiency. Given the importance of improving the performance of U.S. corporations in a competitive international marketplace, it would probably be a severe mistake for the government simply to ban buyouts or limit leverage. On the other hand, pro-debt biases in the tax code, the possibility that higher leverage can help shareholders "squeeze" employees and others, and the possibility of "spillovers" from financial distress all suggest that firms will take on more debt than is good for the economy as a whole.

Three types of policy responses might help the situation. First, the government should take actions to increase the accountability of managers to shareholders (for example, by eliminating legal barriers to paying managers profit-based compensation); this would reduce the need to improve incentives indirectly through high leverage. Second, banking, financial market, and antitrust regulators should carefully scrutinize highly leveraged deals that fall within their purview; it is particularly important that government-insured deposits not be the funding source for risky buyouts, unless the bank's capital is demonstrated to be adequate. Finally, biases in the tax code that favor buyouts and high leverage should be removed.

References

Bernanke, Ben, and John Campbell. "Is There a Corporate Debt Crisis?" Brookings Papers on Economic Activity (1988:1) pp. 83–125.

Jensen, Michael C. "Takeovers: Their Causes and Consequences," *Journal of Economic Perspectives*, vol. 2 (Winter 1988) pp. 21–48.

Jensen, Michael C., and William H. Meckling. "Theory of the Firm: Managerial Behavior, Agency Costs and Ownership Structure," *Journal of Financial Economics*, vol. 3 (1976) pp. 305–60.

Kaplan, Stephen. "Management Buyouts: Efficiency Gains or Value Transfers?" University of Chicago, unpublished (1988).

Loeys, Jan. "Low-Grade Bonds: A Growing Source of Corporate Funding," Federal Reserve Bank of Philadelphia *Business Review* (November/December 1986) pp. 3–12.

McAndrews, James J., and Leonard I. Nakamura. "Entry-Deterring Debt," Federal Reserve Bank of Philadelphia, Working Paper No. 89-15 (1989).

Roach, Stephen. "Living With Corporate Debt," *Economic Perspectives*, Morgan Stanley, November 11, 1988.

Shleifer, Andrei, and Lawrence Summers. "Breach of Trust in Hostile Takeovers," in Alan Auerbach, *Corporate Takeovers: Causes and Consequences*, Chicago: University of Chicago Press (forthcoming).

Vishny, Robert, and Andrei Shleifer. "Value Maximization and the Acquisition Process," *Journal of Economic Perspectives*, vol. 2 (Winter 1988) pp. 7–20.

Questions

1. Describe the trade-off theory of capital structure (the relative mix of debt and equity). Include in your description the roles played by tax deductible interest and bankruptcy costs.
2. Goofus and Gallant invest in ice cream stands, described financially as follows, on opposite sides of town:

	Goofus	Gallant
Total assets	$1,000	$1,000
Personal investment	100	100
Stock issuance	900	0
Debt issuance	0	900
Annual interest expense	0	100
First $100 profit share	10	0
Second $100 profit share	10	100

Goofus and Gallant each acquire $1,000 worth of assets with a personal investment of $100, financing the remainder with equity or debt. Goofus issues stock and must share 90 percent of the profits. Gallant issues debt and must pay $900 in interest. Having earned a $100 profit during the week, they each have the opportunity to work the weekend for an additional $100 profit. Describe the incentive for weekend work assuming that each one values his weekend leisure at $25.

3. What is a corporation's *free cash flow*, and what problem does it potentially present?
4. In what ways does an increase in the debt-equity ratio solve a corporation's problem of free cash flow.
5. A leveraged buyout (LBO) is an acquisition of a company in which investors (often management) borrow heavily using the company's assets as collateral. Upon announcement, an LBO causes the targeted company's stock price to rise, often by 40 percent or more. Despite this benefit, there are criticisms of LBOs. What do the critics say?
6. "... high corporate debt could contribute to macroeconomic dislocations." One scenario is a *liquidity crisis* and the other is a *solvency crisis*. Describe each of these potential macroeconomic problems.
7. Suppose that you head the national highway safety board of a country and wish to increase incentives for safe driving. Furthermore, you are considering two alternative proposals: (a) Place a dagger in the steering wheel, the point aimed at the driver's chest. (b) Place an air bag, which inflates upon impact, in the steering wheel. Which policy would you choose? Explain. In what way does this metaphor (dagger in the steering wheel) relate to financial leverage?

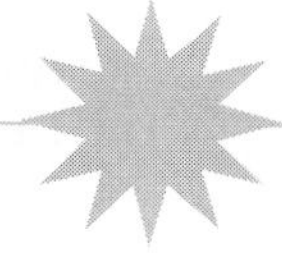

Leverage

MERTON H. MILLER

ABSTRACT

Nobel Memorial Prize Lecture for presentation at the Royal Swedish Academy of Sciences in Stockholm, December 7, 1990. Helpful comments on an earlier draft were made by my colleagues Steven Kaplan and Robert Vishny.

Introduction

Under the terms of Alfred Nobel's will, the Prizes were to be awarded for an "important discovery or invention." Let it be clear from the outset, therefore, that my case must be one of the former, not the latter. Contrary to what you may have read in some press accounts following the announcement of the 1990 Nobel Prizes in Economic Sciences, I am not the co-inventor of the leveraged buyout—the transaction that perhaps more than any other has come to symbolize the supposed financial excesses of the 1980s. Leveraged buyouts (LBOs), in which the younger, active managers of a firm borrowed the funds to buy the controlling shares from a firm's retired founder (or from his estate) were an established feature of the corporate landscape long before Franco Modigliani, the 1985 laureate, and I published our first joint paper on leverage and the cost of capital in 1958. The LBOs of the 1980s differed only in scale, in that they involved publicly-held rather than privately-held corporations and in that the takeovers were often hostile.

That Franco Modigliani and I should be credited with inventing these takeovers is doubly ironic since the central message of our M&M Propositions was that the value of the firm was independent of its capital structure. Subject to one important qualification to be duly noted below, you couldn't hope to enhance shareholder value merely by leveraging up. Investors would not pay a premium

---

At the time of this writing, Merton H. Miller was the Robert R. McCormick Distinguished Service Professor, Graduate School of Business, University of Chicago.

Source: *The Journal of Finance* (June 1991, Vol. XLVI No. 2, pp. 479–488). Reprinted with permission.

for corporate leverage because they could always leverage up their own holdings by borrowing on personal account. Despite this seemingly clear prediction of the M&M analysis, the LBOs of the 1980s were routinely reporting premiums to the shareholders of more than 40 percent, running in some cases as high as 100 percent and all this, mind you, even after the huge fees the deal-making investment bankers were extracting.

The qualification to the M&M value-invariance proposition mentioned earlier concerns the deductibility of interest payments under the unintegrated U.S. corporate income tax. That deductibility can lead, as we showed in our 1963 article, to substantial gains from leveraging under some conditions, and gains of this tax-driven kind have undoubtedly figured both in the rise of corporate debt ratios generally in the 1980s and in some recent LBOs and voluntary restructurings in particular. But after netting out the offsetting tax costs of leveraged capital structures (such as those discussed in my paper "Debt and Taxes" (1977) and its follow-up literature), tax savings alone cannot plausibly account for the observed LBO premiums.

Leveraged Buyouts: Where the Gains Came From

The source of the major gains in value achieved in the LBOs of the 1980s lies, in fact, not in our newly-recognized field of finance at all, but in that older, and long-established field of economics, industrial organization. Perhaps industrial *re*organization might be an apter term. Mikhail Gorbachev, the 1990 Peace Prize Winner, may have popularized the term *perestroika*, but the LBO entrepreneurs of the 1980s actually did it, and on a scale not seen since the early years of this century when so much of what we think of as big business was being put together by the entrepreneurs of consolidation like J. P. Morgan and John D. Rockefeller.

That the LBO entrepreneurs have achieved substantial real efficiency gains by reconcentrating corporate control and redeploying assets has been amply documented in a multitude of academic research studies. (See Kaplan (1989).) But this basically positive view of LBOs and takeovers is still far from universally accepted among the wider public. Some are reacting to the layoffs and factory closings that have sometimes followed hostile takeovers, although far more of both have occurred in our automobile industry which has so far been immune from takeovers. Others worry that these short-run gains may represent merely the improvident sacrifice of opportunities for high, but long deferred future profits—an argument presuming among other things, that the market cannot properly compute discounted present values. Even more fear that the real efficiency gains, if any, will be more than offset by the collateral damage from the financial leveraging used to bring about the restructuring.

The Problems of Corporate Leveraging: Real or Imagined?

These fears will be the main focus of this lecture. The statutes of the Nobel Foundation stipulate that the subject of the Nobel Lecture "should be on or associated with the work for which the prize was awarded," which, in my case means the M&M propositions. Rather than simply reviewing them, however, or discussing the subsequent research they have inspired (a task already undertaken in Miller (1988)) I propose here instead to show how those propositions bear on current concerns about overleveraging—concerns that in some quarters actually border on hysteria. In particular I will argue, first, that the highly visible losses and defaults on junk bonds do not mean that overleveraging did in fact occur; second, paradoxical as it may sound, that increased leveraging by corporations does not imply increased risk for the economy as a whole; third, that the financial distress being suffered by some highly leveraged firms involves mainly private, not social costs; and finally, that the capital markets have built-in controls against overleveraging—controls, moreover, very much in evidence at the moment. Recent efforts by our regulators to override these built-in market mechanisms by destroying the junk bond market and by imposing additional direct controls over leveraged lending by banks will thus have all the unintended consequences normally associated with such regulatory interventions. They will lower efficiency and raise costs (in this case, the cost of capital) to important sectors of our economy.

That the current emphasis on the evils of overleveraging may be misplaced does not mean, of course, that all is well. My message is not: "Relax. Be happy. And, don't worry." Worry we should, in the U.S. at least, but about the serious problems confronting us, such as our seeming inability to bring government spending under rational control or to halt the steady deterioration of our once-vaunted system of public education. Let us not waste our limited worrying capacity on second-order and largely self-correcting problems like financial leveraging.

I hope I will be pardoned for dwelling in what follows almost exclusively on U.S. examples. It's just that a particularly virulent strain of the antileveraged hysteria seems to have struck us first. Perhaps others can learn from our mistakes.

The Private and Social Costs of Corporate Leveraging

The charge that the U.S. became overleveraged in the 1980s will strike some as perhaps too obvious to require any extensive documentation. What could offer more compelling evidence of the overissuance of debt than the defaults of so many junk-bond issuers in late 1989, with news of additional or pending defaults now almost a daily occurrence?

The Junk Bonds as Just Another Risky Security

To argue in this all too natural way, however, is to put too much emphasis on the word "bond" and not enough on the word "junk." Bonds are, indeed, promises to pay. And certainly the issuers of the bonds hoped to keep those promises. But if the firm's cash flow, for reasons competitive or cyclical, fails to cover the commitments, then the promises cannot be kept, or at least not kept in full.

The buyers of the junk bonds, of course, also *hoped* that the promises would be kept. But they clearly weren't counting on it! For all save the most hopelessly gullible, the yields *expected* (in the Markowitz sense of yield outcomes weighted by probability of occurrence) on junk bonds, were below the nominal or promised yields. The high promised yields that might be earned during the good years were understood as compensation for the possible bad years in time and bad bonds in the total junk bond portfolio. The high nominal yields, in short, were essentially risk premiums. And in 1989, for many of the junk bonds issued earlier, the risk happened.

Although the presumption in finance is that defaults represent bad outcomes ex post, rather than systematic misperception of the true ex ante odds, as seems to be the conventional view, that presumption cannot yet be established conclusively. The time series of rates of return on junk bonds is still too short for judging whether those returns are indeed anomalously too low (or perhaps even anomalously too high) relative to accepted asset-pricing models like those of my co-laureate William Sharpe and his successors. Few such anomalous asset classes have so far been identified; and nothing in the nature of high-yield bonds strongly suggests that they will wind up on that short list.

Some may question the fairness of my treating these realized risks on junk bonds as essentially exogenous shocks, like earthquakes or droughts. Surely, they would contend, the very rise of corporate leverage that the junk bonds represent must itself have increased the total risk in the economy. On that point, however, modern finance in general and the M&M propositions in particular offer a different and in many respects, a counter-intuitive perspective.

Does Increased Corporate Leverage Add to Society's Risk?

Imagine that you, as a venerable academic professor of finance are in a dialogue with an equally grizzled corporate treasurer who believes, as most of them probably do, that leveraging *does* increase total risk. "You will surely concede, Professor," he is likely to begin, "that leveraging up the corporate capital structure will make the remaining equity riskier. Right?" "Right," you say. A company with a debt/equity ratio of 1, for example, earning a 20 percent rate of return on its underlying assets and paying 10 percent on its bonds, which, of course, have the first claim on the firm's earnings, will generate an enhanced 30 percent rate of return for its equity holders. Should the earning rate on the underlying assets decline by 25 percent, however, to 15 percent, the rate of return on equity will fall by an even greater extent (33 1/3 percent in this case). That, after all, is why we use the graphic term leverage (or the equally descriptive term gearing that the British seem to prefer). And this greater variability of prospective rates of return to leveraged shareholders means greater risk, in precisely the sense used by my colleagues here, Harry Markowitz and William Sharpe.

That conceded, the corporate treasurer goes on to ask rhetorically: "And, Professor, any debt added to the capital structure must, necessarily, be riskier debt, carrying a lower rating and bearing a higher interest rate than on any debt outstanding before the higher leveraging. Right?" "Right," you again agree, and for exactly the same reason as before. The further a claimant stands from the head of the line at payoff time, the riskier the claim.

Now the treasurer moves in for the kill. "Leveraging raises the risk of the equity and also raises the risk of debt. It must, therefore, raise the total risk. Right?" "Wrong," you say, preparing to play the M&M card. The M&M propositions are the finance equivalents of conservation laws. What gets conserved in this case is the risk of the earning stream generated by the firm's operating assets. Leveraging or deleveraging the firm's capital structure serves merely to partition that risk among the firm's security holders.[1]

To see where the risk goes, consider the following illustrative example. Suppose a firm has 10 security holders of whom 5 hold the firm's bonds and the remaining 5 hold equal shares in the firm's leveraged equity. Suppose further that the interest due on the 5 bonds is covered sufficiently for those bonds to be considered essentially riskless. The entire risk of the firm must thus be borne by the 5 shareholders who will, of course, expect a rate of return on their investments substantially higher than on the assumed riskless bonds. Let 2 of the common stockholders now come to feel that their share of the risks is higher than they want to bear. They ask to exchange their stockholdings for bonds, but they learn that the interest payments on the 2 additional bonds they will get in exchange could not be covered in all possible states of the world. To avoid diluting the claims of the old bondholders, the new bonds must be made junior to the old bonds. Because the new bonds are riskier, the 2 new bondholders will expect a rate of return higher than on the old riskless bonds, but a rate still less, of course, than on their original, and even higher-risk holdings of common stock. The *average* risk and the average expected interest rate of the 7 bondholders taken together has thus risen. At the same time, the risk assumed by the remaining 3 equity holders is also higher (since the 2 shifting stockholders now have taken a prior claim on the firm's earnings) and their expected return must rise as well. Both classes of securities are thus riskier on average, but the *total* risk stays exactly the same as before the 2 stockholders shifted over. The increased risk to the 3 remaining stockholders is exactly offset by decreased risk to the 2 former stockholders who have moved down the priority ladder to become junior bondholders.[2]

Leverage and the Deadweight Costs of Financial Distress

That aggregate risk might be unaffected by modest changes of leverage some might willingly concede, but not when leverage is pushed to the point that

---

[1] In the original M&M paper, that underlying real earning stream was taken as a given, independent of the financing decisions. Subsequent research has identified many possible interactions between the real and the financial sides of the firm, but their effects on risk are not always in the same direction and for present purposes, they can be regarded as of only second-order importance.

[2] Note, incidentally, that this story would have exactly the same conclusions if the 2 defecting common stockholders had opted for preferred stocks rather than junior bonds. Even though accountants classify preferred stocks as equity, preferreds are functionally equivalent to junior debt. Preferred stocks, in fact, were effectively the junk bonds of finance (often with the same bad press) prior to the 1930's when the steep rise in corporate tax rates made them less attractive than tax-deductible, interest-bearing securities of equivalent priority.

bankruptcy becomes a real possibility. The higher the leverage, the greater the likelihood, of course, that just such an unfortunate event will occur.

Actually, however, the M&M conservation of risk continues to hold, subject to some qualifications to be duly noted below, even in the extreme case of default. That result seems paradoxical only because the emotional and psychological overtones of the word bankruptcy give that particular outcome more prominence than it merits on strictly economic grounds. From a bloodless finance perspective, a default signifies merely that the stockholders have now lost their entire stake in the firm. Their option, so to speak, has expired worthless. The creditors now become the new stockholders and the return on their original debt claims becomes whatever of value is left in the firm.

The qualification to the principle of risk conservation noted earlier is that the very process of transferring claims from the debtors to the creditors can itself create risks and deadweight costs over and beyond those involved when the firm was a going concern. Some of these "costs of financial distress," as they have come to be called, may be incurred even before a default occurs. Debtors, like some poets, do not "go gentle into that good night." They struggle to keep their firms alive, even if sometimes the firm would be better off dead by any rational calculation. They are often assisted in those efforts at life-support by a bankruptcy code that materially strengthens their hands in negotiations with the creditors. Sometimes, of course, the reverse can happen and over-rapacious creditors can force liquidation of firms that might otherwise have survived. About all we can safely conclude is that once the case is in bankruptcy court, all sides in these often-protracted negotiations will be assisted by armies of lawyers whose fees further eat away the pool of assets available to satisfy the claims of the creditors. For small firms, the direct costs of the bankruptcy proceedings can easily consume the entire corpus (an apt term), but they are essentially fixed costs and hence represent only a small portion of the recoveries in the larger cases. In the aggregate, of course, direct bankruptcy costs, even if regarded as complete social waste, are minuscule relative to the size of the economy.[3]

The Costs of Financial Distress: Private or Social?

Small as the aggregate deadweight costs of financial distress may be, bankruptcies can certainly be painful personal tragedies. Even so generally unadmired a public figure as Donald Trump has almost become an object of public sympathy as he struggles with his creditors for control over his garish Taj Mahal Casino. But even if he does lose, as seemed probable at the time of this writing, the loss will be his, not society's. The Trump casino and associated buildings will still be there

[3] The deadweight costs of bankruptcy, and of financial distress more generally, may be small in the aggregate, but they do exist. A case can be made, therefore, on standard welfare-economics grounds for eliminating the current tax subsidy to debt implicit in our current unintegrated corporate income tax. Achieving complete neutrality between debt and equity, however, would require elimination of the corporate tax—a step not likely to be undertaken in the foreseeable future.

(perhaps one should add, alas). The only difference will be the sign on the door: Under New Management.[4]

The social consequences of the isolated bankruptcy can be dismissed perhaps, but not, some would argue, bankruptcies that come in clusters. The fear is that the bankruptcy of each overindebted firm will send a shock wave to the firm's equally overindebted suppliers leading in turn to more bankruptcies until eventually the whole economy collapses in a heap. Neither economics generally nor finance in particular, however, offer much support for this notion of a leverage-induced "bankruptcy multiplier" or a contagion effect. Bankrupt firms, as noted earlier, do not vanish from the earth. They often continue operating pretty much as before, though with different ownership and possibly on a reduced scale. Even when they do liquidate and close down, their inventory, furniture and fixtures, employees and their customers flow to other firms elsewhere in the economy. Profitable investment opportunities that one failing firm passes up will be assumed by others, if not always immediately, then later when the economic climate becomes more favorable. Recent research in macro-economics suggests that much of what we used to consider as output irretrievably lost in business cycles is really only output postponed, particularly in the durable goods industries.

To say that the human and capital resources of bankrupt firms will eventually be reemployed, is not to deny, of course, that the personal costs of disemployment merit consideration, particularly when they become widespread. All modern economies take steps to ease the pains of transferring human resources to other and better uses, and perhaps they should do even more. But delaying or preventing the needed movements of resources will also have social costs that can be even higher over the long run as the economies of Eastern Europe are discovering.

The successive waves of bankruptcies in the early 1930s may seem to belie this relatively benign view of bankruptcy as a matter essentially of private costs with no serious externalities, but not really.[5] Contrary to widely-held folk beliefs, bankruptcies did not bring on the Great Depression. The direction of causation runs from depressions to bankruptcies, not the other way around. The collapse of the stock market in 1929 and of the U.S. banking system during 1931–1932 may well have created the appearance of a finance-driven disaster. But that disaster was not just the inevitable bursting of another overleveraged tulip bubble as some have suggested. (Actually recent research has cast doubt on the existence of even the *original* tulip bubble. But that is another story. See Garber (1989).) Responsibility for turning an ordinary downturn into a depression of unprecedented severity lies primarily with the managers of the Federal Reserve System. They failed to carry out their duties as the residual supplier of liquidity to the

---

[4] Actually, according to recent press reports, Trump's creditors have allowed him to keep control, at least temporarily. Should he fail to meet stipulated cash-flow targets, however, the creditors can take over his remaining interests in a so-called "pre-packaged" bankruptcy, that is, one without formal bankruptcy proceedings (and expenses). Further use of this ingenious and efficient method for transferring control can confidently be expected.

[5] True externalities arise, as in the case of air pollution, only when actions by one firm increase the costs of others. A possible analog to pollution for corporate debt might be the shifting to the government and hence to the taxpayers, of the pension costs of failed firms. Once again, however, the aggregate impact is of only second-order significance.

public and to the banking system. The U.S. money supply imploded by 30 percent between 1930 and 1932, dragging the economy and the price level down with it. When that happens even AAA credits get to look like junk bonds.

That such a nightmare scenario might be repeated under present day conditions is always possible, of course, but, until recently at least, most economists would have dismissed it as extremely unlikely. The current chairman of the Federal Reserve Board himself, as well as his staff, are known to have studied the dismal episode of the early 1930's in great depth and to be thoroughly aware of how and why their ill-fated predecessors had blundered. The prompt action by the Federal Reserve Board to support the liquidity of the banking system after the stock market crash of October 19, 1987 (and again after the mini-crash of October 13, 1989) is testimony to the lessons learned. The fear of some at the moment, however, is that both the willingness and the ability of the Federal Reserve to maintain the economy's liquidity and its credit system are being undermined by regulatory overreaction to the S&L crisis—an overreaction that stems in part from underestimating the market's internal controls on overleveraging.

The Self-Correcting Tendencies in Corporate Leveraging

Just what combination of demand shifts and supply shifts triggered the big expansion in leveraged securities in the 1980's will eventually have to be sorted out by future economic historians. The main point to be emphasized here is that whether we are talking automobiles or leveraged equity or high-yield bonds the market's response to changes in tastes (or to changes in production technology) is limited and self-regulating. If the producers of any commodity expand its supply faster than the buyers want, the price will fall and output eventually will shrink. And similarly, in the financial markets. If the public's demand for junk bonds is overestimated by takeover entrepreneurs, the higher interest rates they must offer to junk-bond buyers will eat into the gains from the deals. The process of further leveraging will slow and perhaps even be reversed.

Something very much like this endogenous slowing of leveraging could be discerned in early 1989 even before a sequence of government initiatives (including the criminal indictments of the leading investment bankers and market makers in junk bonds, the forced dumping of junk bond inventories by beleaguered S&L's and the stricter regulations on leveraged lending by commercial banks) combined to undermine the liquidity of the high-yield bond market. The issuance of high-yield bonds not only ground to a halt, but many highly-leveraged firms moved to replace their now high-cost debts with equity.[6]

---

[6] The process of swapping equity for debt (essentially the reverse of the parable in Section 2.2) would have gone even further by now but for an unfortunate feature of U.S. tax law. Swapping equity for debt selling at less than face value creates taxable income from "cancellation of indebtedness." An exception is made for firms in bankruptcy making that option more attractive than otherwise might be for firms whose debts are at a sizeable discount.

Junk Bonds and the S&L Crisis

To point out that the market has powerful endogenous controls against over-leveraging does not mean that who holds the highly leveraged securities is never a matter of concern. Certainly the U.S. Savings and Loan institutions should not have been using government-guaranteed savings deposits to buy high-risk junk bonds. But to focus so much attention on the junk bond losses of a handful of these S&L's is to miss the main point of that whole sorry episode. The current hue and cry over S&L junk bonds serves merely to divert attention from those who expanded the government deposit guarantees and encouraged the S&L's to make investments with higher expected returns, but alas, also with higher risk than their traditional long-term home mortgages.

Some, at the time, defended the enlargement of the government's deposit guarantee as compensation for the otherwise disabling interest rate risks assumed by those undertaking the socially-desirable task of providing fixed rate, long-term mortgages. Quite apart, however, from the presence even then of alternative and less vulnerable ways of supplying mortgage money, the deposit guarantees proved to be, as most finance specialists had predicted at the time, a particularly unfortunate form of subsidy to home ownership. Because the deposit guarantees gave the owners of the S&L's what amounted to put options against the government, they actually encouraged the undertaking of uneconomic long-odds projects, some of which made junk bonds look safe by comparison. The successes went to the owners; the failures, to the insurance fund.

More is at stake, however, than merely assigning proper blame for these failed attempts to overrule the market's judgment that this politically powerful industry was not economically viable. Drawing the wrong moral from the S&L affair can have consequences that extend far beyond the boundaries of this ill-fated industry. The American humorist, Mark Twain, once remarked that a cat, having jumped on a hot stove, will never jump on a stove again, even a cold one. Our commercial bank examiners seem to be following precisely this pattern. Commercial banking may not quite be a cold stove at the moment, but it is, at least, a viable industry. Unlike the S&L's, moreover, it plays a critical role in financing businesses, particularly, but not only, those too small or too little known to support direct access to the public security markets. Heavy-handed restrictions on bank loans by examiners misreading the S&L experience will thus raise the cost of capital to, and hence decrease the use of capital by, this important business sector.[7]

Whether regulatory restrictions of these and related kinds have already gone so far as to produce a "credit crunch" of the kind associated in the past with

[7] Examples of such restrictions are the guidelines, recently promulgated jointly by the Federal Deposit Insurance Corporation, the Comptroller of the Currency and the Federal Reserve Board governing so-called Highly Leveraged Transactions (HLT's). These guidelines have effectively shut off lending for corporate restructuring, whether friendly or hostile. But the rules are so vaguely drawn and so uncertain in their application as to be inhibiting other kinds of loans as well. Bank loans these days often carry provisions calling for automatic interest rate increases of 100 basis points or more if the loans are later classified by the bank examiners as HLT's.

monetary contraction is a subject much being argued at the moment, but one I prefer to leave to the specialists in money and banking. My concerns as a finance specialist are with the longer-run and less directly visible consequences of the current anti-leverage hysteria. This hysteria has already destroyed the liquidity of the market for high-yield bonds. The financial futures markets, currently under heavy attack for their supposed overleveraging are the next possible candidates for extinction, at least in their U.S. habitats.

Many in academic finance have viewed these ill-founded attacks on our financial markets, particularly the newer markets, with some dismay. But they have, for the most part, stood aside from the controversies. Unlike some of the older fields of economics, the focus in finance has not been on issues of public policy. We have emphasized positive economics rather than normative economics, striving for solid empirical research built on foundations of simple, but powerful organizing theories. Now that our field has officially come of age, as it were, perhaps my colleagues in finance can be persuaded to take their noses out of their data bases from time to time and to bring the insights of our field, and especially the public policy insights, to the attention of a wider audience.

References

Garber, Peter, 1989, Tulipmania, *Journal of Political Economy* 97, 535–560.

Kaplan, Steven, N., 1989, The effects of management buyouts on operations and value, *Journal of Financial Economics* 24, 217–254.

Miller, Merton, H., 1977, Debt and taxes, *Journal of Finance* 32, 261–275.

———. 1988, The Modigliani-Miller propositions after thirty years, *Journal of Economic Perspectives* 2, 99–120.

Modigliani, Franco and Merton H. Miller, 1958, The cost of capital, corporation finance and the theory of investment, *American Economic Review* 48, 261–297.

———. 1963, Corporate income taxes and the cost of capital: A correction, *American Economic Review* 53, 433–443.

Questions

1. Modigliani and Miller's 1958 model implies that capital structure is irrelevant, but their 1963 model implies that it is *relevant*. What causes the change from irrelevance to relevance? Explain.
2. What is the source of the major gains in value achieved by leveraged buyouts (LBOs), according to Miller? Explain.
3. Describe Miller's arguments for each of the following four propositions:
   - The highly visible losses and defaults on junk bonds do not mean that overleveraging did in fact occur.
   - Increased leveraging by corporations does not imply increased risk for the economy as a whole.
   - The financial distress being suffered by some highly leveraged firms involves mainly private, not social costs.
   - Capital markets have built-in controls against overleveraging.

4. "Certainly the U.S. Savings and Loan institutions should not have been using government-guaranteed savings deposits to buy high-risk junk bonds." Do you agree with this statement? Why?

Still Searching for Optimal Capital Structure

STEWART C. MYERS

The optimal balance between debt and equity financing has been a central issue in corporate finance ever since Modigliani and Miller (MM) showed in 1958 that capital structure was irrelevant.

Thirty years later the MM analysis is textbook fare, not in itself controversial. Yet in practice it seems that financial leverage matters more than ever. I hardly need document the aggressive use of debt in the 1980s, especially in leveraged buyouts (LBOs), hostile takeovers and restructurings, and the recently renewed appreciation of the comforts of equity.

Of course none of these developments disproves MM's irrelevance theorem, which is just a "no magic in leverage" proof for a taxless, frictionless world. MM's practical message is this: *If* there is an optimal capital structure, it should reflect taxes or some specifically identified market imperfections. Thus managers are often viewed as trading off the tax savings from debt financing against costs of financial distress, specifically the agency costs generated by issuing risky debt and the deadweight costs of possible liquidation or reorganization. I call this the *static tradeoff* theory of optimal capital structure.

My purpose here is to see whether this or competing theories of optimal capital structure can explain actual behavior and recent events in financial markets. I consider the static tradeoff theory, a *pecking order* theory emphasizing problems of asymmetric information, and a preliminary *organizational* theory which drops the assumed objective of shareholder value maximization.

In the end none of these theories is completely satisfactory. However, the exercise of trying to apply them forces us to take the firm's point of view and to think critically about the factors which may govern actual decisions.[1]

At the time of this writing, Stewart C. Myers was the Gordon Y. Billard professor of Finance and the Director of the International Financial Services Research Center at MIT's Sloan School of Management.

Source: From Bank of America *Journal of Applied Corporate Finance*.

[1] This is not a self-contained survey article. I have stated theories intuitively and not attempted to derive them. I have attempted to cite interesting and representative research by others but have nevertheless skipped over many useful empirical and theoretical contributions. For an extensive survey and bibliography, see Ronald Masulis, *The Debt-Equity Choice* (New York: Ballinger Publishing Co., 1988).

The Static Tradeoff Theory

Figure 1 summarizes the static tradeoff theory. The horizontal base line expresses MM's idea that V, the market value of the firm—the aggregate market value of all its outstanding securities—should not depend on leverage when assets, earnings, and future investment opportunities are held constant. But the tax-deductibility of interest payments induces the firm to borrow to the margin where the present value of interest tax shields is just offset by the value loss due to agency costs of debt and the possibility of financial distress.

The static tradeoff theory has several things going for it. First, it avoids "corner solutions" and rationalizes moderate borrowing with a story that makes easy common sense. Most business people immediately agree that borrowing saves taxes and that too much debt can lead to costly trouble.

Second, closer analysis of costs of financial distress gives a testable prediction from the static tradeoff story; since these costs should be most serious for firms with valuable intangible assets and growth opportunities, we should observe that *mature* firms holding mostly *tangible* assets should borrow more, other things constant, than growth or firms which depend heavily on R&D, advertising, etc. Thus we would expect a pharmaceutical company to borrow less than a chemical manufacturer, even if the two firms' business risk (measured by asset beta, for example) are the same. This predicted inverse relationship

FIGURE 1 THE STATIC-TRADEOFF THEORY OF CAPITAL STRUCTURE

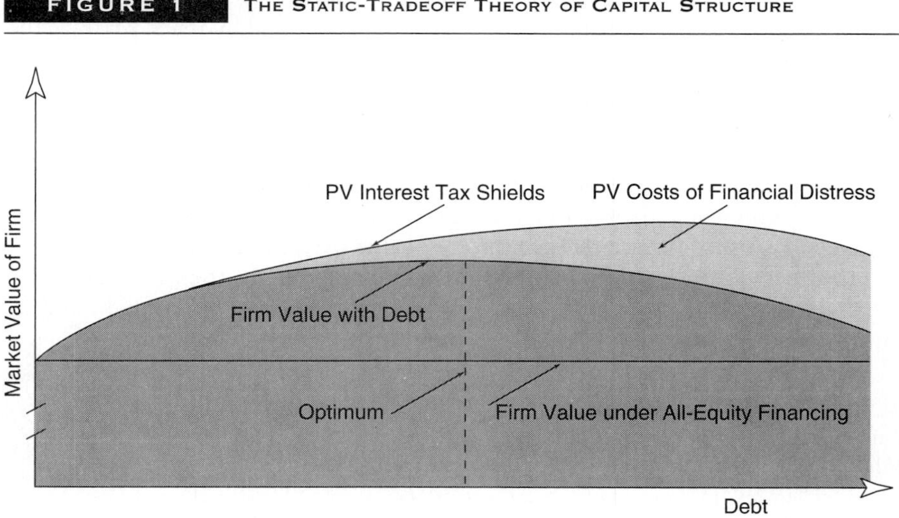

between (proxies for) intangible assets and financial leverage has been confirmed by several studies.[2]

The static tradeoff theory may also seem to draw support from studies of the reaction of stock prices to announcements of security issues, retirements, or exchanges. Clifford Smith's 1986 summary of this research shows that almost all leverage-increasing transactions are good news, and leverage-decreasing transactions bad news.[3] Thus announcements of common stock issues drive down stock price, but repurchases push them up; exchanges of debt for equity securities drive up stock prices, but equity-for-debt exchanges depress them. These impacts are often striking and generally strong enough to bar quibbles about statistical significance; the only exception seems to be debt issue announcements, which on average have no significant effect.[4]

These "event studies" could be interpreted as proving investors' appreciation of the value of interest tax shields, thus confirming the practical importance of the static tradeoff theory's chief motive for borrowing. But on balance this evidence works *against* the theory. First, the competing pecking order theory can explain the same facts as the market's rational response to the issue or retirement of common equity, even if investors are totally indifferent to changes in financial leverage. This point is discussed further in the next section.

Second, the simple static tradeoff theory does not predict what the event studies find. If the theory were true, managers would be diligently seeking optimal capital structure, but find their firms bumped away from the optimum by random events. A couple years of unexpectedly good operating earnings or the unanticipated cash sale of a division might leave a firm below its optimal debt ratio, for example; another firm suffering a string of operating losses might end up too highly levered.

Thus we would expect to observe some firms issuing debt and/or retiring equity to regain the optimal debt ratio—they would move to the right, up the left-hand side of Figure 1. But other firms would be reducing leverage and moving to the left, up the right-hand slope of the figure. The movement should be value-increasing in both cases, and good news if it is news at all.

It's possible, of course, that the leverage-increasing transactions reflect reductions in business risk and increases in target debt ratios. If investors can't observe these changes directly then a debt-for-equity exchange is good news; it demonstrates management's confidence in the level and safety of future earnings.

It is also possible that managers are not value-maximizers and do not attempt to lever up to the optimum. If most firms are sitting comfortably but inefficiently on the left of the upward-sloping value curve in Figure 1, then any increase in

---

[2] See Michael Long and Ileen Malitz in "Investment Patterns and Financial Leverage," in B. Friedman, ed., *Corporate Capital Structure in the United States* (Chicago: University of Chicago Press, 1985). Also, Sheridan Titman and Roberto Wessels find that debt ratios are negatively related to marketing and selling and R&D expenses. These expenses are obvious proxies for intangible assets, although Titman and Wessels interpret them as proxies for "uniqueness." See S. Titman and R. Wessels, "The Determinants of Capital Structure Choice," *Journal of Finance*, vol. 43, no. 1, March 1988, 1–19. See also note 24 below.

[3] Clifford Smith, "Investment Banking and the Capital Acquisition Process," *Journal of Financial Economics*, vol. 15, no. 12, January-February 1986, 3–29.

[4] See L. Shyam-Sunder, "The Stock Price Effect of Risky versus Safe Debt," *Journal of Financial Quantitative Analysis*, vol. 26, no. 4, December 1991, 549–558.

leverage is good news, and any decrease bad news. However, we can't just explain away the event study results without thinking more carefully about how a "managerial" firm would want to arrange its financing. Would it always prefer low debt, for example? This too is left to a later section of the paper.

The most telling evidence against the static tradeoff theory is the strong inverse correlation between profitability and financial leverage. *Within an industry*, the most profitable firms borrow less, the least profitable borrow more. In an extensive study of debt policy in U.S. and Japanese manufacturing corporations, Carl Kester finds that return on assets is the most significant explanatory variable for actual debt ratios. There is other supporting evidence as well.[5]

To repeat: high profits mean low debt. Yet the static tradeoff story would predict just the opposite relationship. Higher profits mean more dollars for debt service and more taxable income to shield. They should mean *higher* target debt ratios.

Could the negative correlation between profitability and leverage reflect delays in firms' adjustment to their optimum debt ratios? For example, a string of unexpectedly high (low) profits could push a firm's actual debt ratio below (above) the target. If transaction costs prevent quick movements back to the optimum, a negative correlation is established—a negative correlation between profitability and *deviations* from target debt ratios.

This explanation is logically O.K. but not credible without some specific theory or evidence on how firms manage capital structures over time. Expositions of the static tradeoff story rarely mention transaction costs;[6] in fact they usually start by accepting MM's Proposition I (the flat base line in Figure 1), which assumes that transaction costs are second order.

None of the evidence noted so far justifies discarding the static tradeoff theory. However, it's foolish not to be skeptical. The theory sounds right to financial economists and business people will give it lip service if asked. It may be a weak guide to average behavior. It is not much help in understanding any given firm's decisions.

---

[5] W.C. Kester, "Capital and Ownership Structure: A Comparison of United States and Japanese Manufacturing Corporations," *Financial Management*, vol. 15, no. 1, Spring 1986, 5-16. J. Baskin gets results similar to Kester's, and cites about a dozen other corroborating studies, in "An Empirical Investigation of the Pecking Order Hypothesis," *Financial Management*, vol. 18, no. 1, Spring 1989, 26-35. Further, Titman and Wessels (1988), cited in note 3, find a significant negative relationship between (an estimate of latent) profitability and market-value debt ratios, but no significant relationship to book ratios. Note, however, that "no significant relationship" does not support the static tradeoff theory, which predicts a positive impact of profitability on book debt ratios.

[6] One exception is the target adjustment models used in empirical studies of capital structure choice. See, for example, A. Jalilvand and R.S. Harris, "Corporate Behavior in Adjusting to Capital Structure and Dividend Targets: An Econometric Study," *Journal of Finance*, vol. 39, no. 1, March 1984, 127-144. In these models, random events change actual capital structures, but transaction costs force firms to work back only gradually towards actual capital structures. Actual capital structures are mean-reverting.

These models work fairly well if one assumes the static tradeoff theory holds and that each firm has a well-defined target debt ratio. Unfortunately, the models work equally well when the firm has no target and follows a pure pecking order strategy. (See S.C. Myers and L. Shyam-Sunder, "Testing Static Tradeoff against Pecking Order Theories of Capital Structure," Working Paper, MIT Sloan School of Management, February 1993.) In other words, the models offer no support for the static tradeoff theory against that competitor.

The Pecking Order Theory

The pecking order theory of capital structure reasons as follows:

1. Dividend policy is "sticky."
2. Firms prefer internal to external financing. However, they seek external financing if necessary to finance positive-NPV real investments.
3. If they do require external financing, they will issue the safest security first—i.e., they will choose debt before equity financing.
4. As the firm seeks more external financing it will work down the pecking order of securities, from safe to risky debt, perhaps to convertibles and other quasi-equity instruments, and finally to equity as a last resort.[7]

In the pecking order theory there is no well-defined target debt ratio. The attraction of interest tax shields and the threat of financial distress are assumed to be second-order. Debt ratios change when there is an imbalance of internal cash flow, net of dividends, and real investment opportunities. Highly profitable firms with limited investment opportunities work down to a low debt ratio. Firms whose investment opportunities outrun internally generated funds are driven to borrow more and more.

This theory gives an immediate explanation for the negative intra-industry correlation between profitability and leverage. Suppose firms generally invest to keep up with industry growth. Then rates of real investment will be similar within an industry. Given sticky dividend payout, the least profitable firm in the industry will have less internal funds for new investment and will end up borrowing more.

The pecking order story is not new. There are longstanding concerns about corporations who rely too much on internal financing to avoid the "discipline of capital markets." Gordon Donaldson, for example, has observed pecking order behavior in careful case studies.[8] But, until Nicholas Majluf's and my papers published in 1984,[9] the preference for internal financing and the aversion to new equity issues was viewed as managerial behavior contrary to shareholders' interests. Our papers showed that managers who act solely in (existing) shareholders' interests will rationally prefer internal finance and will issue the least risky security if forced to seek outside funds.

---

[7] Warrants would be even lower on the pecking order. However, warrants are usually issued in a package with debt—roughly equivalent to a convertible bond.

[8] Gordon Donaldson, *Managing Corporate Wealth: The Operation of a Comprehensive Financial Goals System* (New York: Praeger, 1984).

[9] See S.C. Myers and N.S. Majluf, "Corporate Financing and Investment Decisions When Firms Have Information That Investors Do Not Have." *Journal of Financial Economics*, vol. 13, no. 2, June 1984, 187-221; and S.C. Myers, "The Capital Structure Puzzle," *Journal of Finance*, vol. 39, no. 3, July 1984, 575-592.

The pecking order theory reflects problems created by asymmetric information—a fancy way of saying that managers know more about their firms than outside investors do. How do we know managers have superior information? Well, outside investors clearly think they do because stock prices react to firms' announcements of earnings, major capital expenditures, exchange offers, stock repurchases, etc. The market learns from managers' actions because the managers are believed to have better or earlier information.

Consider the following story:

1. Because managers know more about their firms than outside investors do, they are reluctant to issue stock when they believe their shares are undervalued. They are more likely to issue when their shares are fairly priced or overpriced.
2. Investors understand that managers know more and that they try to "time" issues.
3. Investors therefore interpret the decision to issue as bad news, and firms which issue equity can do so only at a discount.
4. Faced with this discount, firms which have worked down the pecking order and need external equity may end up passing by good investment opportunities (or accepting "excessive" leverage) because shares can't be sold at what managers consider a fair price.

This story has three immediate implications. First, internal equity is better than external equity. (Note that the static tradeoff theory makes no distinction between equity from retained earnings and equity from stock issues.) Because dividends are sticky and debt service predetermined, retention of any excess operating cash flow is more or less automatic and does not convey information to investors.

Second, financial slack is valuable. It relieves managers' fear of passing by a positive-NPV outlay when external equity finance is required, but shares can only be issued at a substantial discount to intrinsic value.

Financial slack means cash, marketable securities, and readily saleable real assets. It also means the capacity to issue (nearly) default-risk free debt. If a new debt issue carries no default risk, potential investors do not have to worry about whether the firm as a whole is over- or undervalued by the market.

Third, debt is better than equity if external financing is required, simply because debt is safer than equity. Asymmetric information drives the firm to issue the safest possible security. This establishes the pecking order.

Why are safer securities better? Not because the manager always wants to issue them. On the contrary, when the market overvalues the firm, the manager would like to issue the most overvalued security: not debt, but equity. (Warrants would be even better.) If the market undervalues the firm, the manager would like to issue debt in order to minimize the bargain handed to investors.

But no intelligent investor would let the manager play this game. Suppose you are a potential buyer of new security issue, either debt or equity. You know the issuer knows more than you do about the securities' true values. You know the issuer will want to offer equity only when it is overvalued—i.e., when the issuer is more pessimistic than you are. Would you ever buy equity if debt were an alternative? If you do the issuer is guaranteed to win and you to lose. Thus you will refuse equity and only accept debt. The firm will be forced to issue debt, regardless of whether the firm is over- or undervalued.

Issuing safer securities minimizes the manager's information advantage. Any attempt to exploit this information advantage more aggressively will fail because investors cannot be forced to buy a security they infer is overvalued. An equity issue becomes feasible in the pecking order only when leverage is already high enough to make additional debt materially expensive, e.g., because of the threat of costs of financial distress. If the manager is known to have a good reason to issue equity rather than debt and is willing to do so in some cases where the equity is actually *under*priced, then purchase of new equity can be a fair game for investors, and issue of new equity becomes feasible despite the manager's information advantage.

In practice the pecking order theory cannot be wholly right. A counterexample is generated every time a firm issues equity when it could have issued investment-grade debt. Nevertheless, the theory immediately explains otherwise puzzling facts, such as the strong negative association between profitability and leverage. It also explains why almost all corporate equity financing has come from retention rather than new issues.[10]

The pecking order model also explains why stock price falls when equity is issued. If the firm acts in the interest of its existing shareholders, the announcement of an equity issue is always bad news.[11] So is an equity-for-debt exchange offer—not because the exchange reduces financial leverage, but because it amounts to a new issue of common stock. The fact that investors pay for the issue with an unusual currency (the issuing firms' previously outstanding debt securities) is irrelevant.

Conversely, a debt-for-equity exchange is good news not because it increases outstanding debt, but because it amounts to a repurchase of equity. If investors believe managers have superior knowledge, then their decision to repurchase signals optimism and pushes stock price up.

Thus the pecking order theory neatly explains why equity issues reduce stock prices, but plain-vanilla debt issues do not. If the probability of default is low, then managers' information advantage is not a major concern to potential buyers of a debt issue. The smaller the managers' advantage, the less information is released by the decision to issue. The pecking order theory would predict a small negative impact when a debt issue is announced (all corporate debt carries some default risk), but for most public issues the effect should be very small and likely to be lost in the noise of the market.

---

[10] See R.A. Brealey and S.C. Myers, *Principles of Corporate Finance*, 4th ed. (New York: McGraw-Hill Book Co., 1991), Table 14-3, p. 326–327.

[11] Majluf and Myers (1984), cited in note 9.

An Organizational Theory of Capital Structure

Both of the theories reviewed so far assume that managers act in their current stockholders' interest. This is a useful convention of modern corporate finance theory but hardly a law of nature.

Witnesses to the market for corporate control in the 1980s have to admit the existence of conflicts between managers and stockholders. Plenty of takeovers, LBOs, and restructurings were undertaken to solve "free cash flow" problems, in which firms with excess cash flow were inclined to waste it rather than paying it out to investors.

Competition tends to punish such waste. We would not expect to find it in toughly competitive industries. But if product market competition doesn't do the job, then competition in the market for corporate control may take its place. U.S. automobile companies were forced to slim down their organizations by their Japanese competitors. However, the Japanese don't pump oil, and so United States oil companies were forced to diet by (actual or threatened) takeovers.

Suppose we accept for sake of argument that there are important divergences between organizations' and investors' interests. What does that say about the role financing decisions play in the market for corporate control? What help does it give us to understand financing decisions made by corporations that are not disciplined by the threat of takeover? In other words, what would a managerial or organizational theory of capital structure look like?

Managerial theories would model capital structure choices in terms of top management's *personal* utility functions, compensation schemes, and opportunities for alternative employment. Perhaps managers' personal risk aversions lead the firm to use too little debt—at least that is a common casual hypothesis.[12] (Ideal compensation schemes could induce value-maximizing financing decisions, eliminating the need for a managerial theory of capital structure.)

Michael Jensen and William Meckling's pathbreaking paper on agency costs stresses managers' natural tendency to extract too many perquisites and analyzes the monitoring, bonding, and contracting undertaken to minimize the net costs of the managers' rational but self-interested behavior.[13, 14] Obviously these costs increase as the managers' personal ownership stake in the firm decreases. This supplies an argument for debt financing and against "public" equity—that

---

[12] Stephen Ross presents a more sophisticated incentive signaling model in which a rational (and possibly risk-neutral) manager sets the mix of debt and equity to his own best advantage, thereby signaling the firm's true value to investors. See S.A. Ross, "The Determination of Financial Structure: The Incentive Signalling Approach," *Bell Journal of Economics and Management Science*, vol. 8, no. 1, Spring 1977, 23–40.

[13] M.C. Jensen and W.H.Meckling, "Theory of the Firm: Managerial Behavior, Agency Costs and Ownership Structure," *Journal of Financial Economics*, vol. 3, no. 4, October 1976, 305–360.

[14] The problem is not that managers get perks but that they would rather have cash. If a manager's contribution justifies a salary of $100,000, there's no inefficiency in giving $80,000 in cash and $20,000 in perks freely chosen by the manager. The problem is that cash payments are much more easily controlled than perks extracted. Given the opportunity, a manager may take perks that he would not buy with his own money. Thus he may end up costing $80,000 in cash and $40,000 in perks but still view his cash-equivalent compensation as $100,000. The $20,000 cost plus the costs of bonding and monitoring to prevent the manager from taking more than $40,000 in perks, is a net drain on the value of the firm.

is, against equity contributed by non- management investors who cannot monitor management effectively.

This agency cost approach is most dramatically expressed in Jensen's free cash flow hypothesis, which starts from the alleged tendency of managers to plow excessive amounts into mature businesses or ill-advised acquisitions. "The problem," Jensen says "is how to motivate managers to disgorge the cash rather than investing it below the cost of capital or wasting it in organizational inefficiencies."[15]

If that's the problem, debt financing is better than equity because it bonds the firm to pay out cash. The ideal debt level would leave the firm with just enough cash in the bank to finance all positive-NPV projects but not a penny left over.[16] Perhaps growth and size are the ultimate perks, but debt can supply the necessary discipline.

This gives a rationale for LBOs, restructurings, and debt-financed takeovers. The "good guys," who are willing to take on debt and disgorge cash, oust the "bad guys" and put their firms on a diet. The good guys stay good because the new management has a substantial equity interest and is more tightly monitored by lenders and the new equity investors.

Unfortunately these ideas are most useful in thinking about the market for corporate control than about capital structure. Suppose we look at other times or places where incumbent management is not threatened by the good guys. Are we reduced to saying that mature firms will (1) invest too much and (2) borrow too little? Why hasn't natural economic selection devised compensation arrangements which lead managers to reach value-maximizing debt levels and disgorge all excess cash?

We can clarify some of these issues by stepping away from managers' personal attributes and incentives, and thinking instead of the firm as a value-maximizing organism.

The Organizational Balance Sheet

Table 1 presents an organizational balance sheet. This has no necessary, direct connection with the firm's books. It is just a way of expressing the identity between the market value of assets and liabilities.

On the left is PVA, the present value of future cash flows from existing assets, plus PVGO, the present value of growth opportunities, less the present value of the government's tax claim, PVTAX. Note that PVGO can be negative if the firm is expected to waste money on negative-NPV capital investments or to overpay for acquisitions.

On the right is D, existing debt; E, equity; plus S, the present value of *organizational surplus*. This surplus reflects the present value of the future costs of

[15] M.C. Jensen, "Agency Costs of Free Cash Flow, Corporate Finance, and Takeovers," *American Economic Review*, vol. 76, no. 2, May 1986, p. 323.

[16] This argument has been formalized and generalized by Rene Stulz in "Managerial Discretion and Optimal Financing Policies," *Journal of Financial Economics*, vol. 26, no. 1 March 1990, 3-27.

TABLE 1 ORGANIZATIONAL BALANCE SHEET*

PV Existing Assets, Pre-Tax	(PVA)	Existing Debt	(D)
PV Growth Opportunities, Pre-Tax	(PVGO)	Employees' Surplus	(S)
PV Future Taxes	(PVTAX)	Existing Equity	(E)
After-Tax Value	(V)	After-Tax Value	(V)

Corporate Wealth = Employees' Surplus + Equity
W = S + E

*All entries at Market Value.

perks, overstaffing, above-market wages, etc. Note that PVA and PVGO arc defined *before* this surplus is subtracted; that is, PVA and PVGO represent the potential values if management maximized total firm value.

Think of organizational surplus as a junior financial claim, a preferred share for example. It is junior because creditors can usually force the firm to go on a diet if debt service is threatened. It is not a true residual claim because many elements of surplus—overstaffing and above-market salaries, for example—tend to be "smoothed" and there are limits to the amount of surplus that can be extracted.[17]

Jack Treynor has suggested that "the financial objective of the corporation is to conserve, and when possible, to enhance the corporation's power to distribute cash," which depends on the net market value of the firm.[18] For a public corporation traded in well-developed capital markets, market value is fungible. Therefore the "power to distribute cash" is proportional to *corporate wealth*. This is the sum of equity and employee surplus, W = E + S.

Gordon Donaldson concluded from his extensive case studies of mature public corporations that "the financial objective that guided the top managers of the companies studied [was] maximization of corporate wealth. Corporate wealth is *that wealth over which management has effective control* and is an assured source of funds."[19]

Of course standard corporate finance theory also assumes the firm maximizes wealth. But it is *shareholders'* wealth. Standard theory says that that dividend policy is irrelevant in perfect, frictionless markets because paying a dollar per share dividend reduces share price by exactly a dollar; shareholders' wealth is

---

[17] There is no simple junior-senior ordering between surplus and equity. In some cases surplus may be the true residual claim. Consider an incorporated consulting company or investment bank, where human capital is the most important asset and employee compensation is heavily weighted towards year-end bonuses. The bonuses may have more variance than dividends paid to shareholders.

[18] J.L. Treynor, "The Financial Objective in the Widely Held Corporation," *Financial Analysts Journal*, March-April 1981, p. 70.

[19] Donaldson (1984), cited in note 8, p. 22; emphasis in original.

unchanged. However, *corporate* wealth declines by a dollar per share. That dollar is no longer under the effective control of management.

Treynor and Donaldson lead us to think of the firm as a coalition. Managers' personal risk aversion is not important because corporate wealth is marketable and risks can be hedged as appropriate with zero-NPV transactions. We are concerned with the behavior of the organization as a whole rather than the personal motives and decisions of a few people at the top of the corporate hierarchy. The coalition maximizes value, and we can work with PVs and NPVs just as in ordinary corporate finance theory.

This may be a powerful simplification, though it is not yet clear whether the objective should be to maximize total corporate wealth (W = E + S) or the net wealth of the organizational coalition (S only). For now we will take Treynor and Donaldson literally and assume the objective is to maximize W.

Investment and Financing Decisions by Firms Seeking to Maximize Corporate Wealth

Consider how several common financial decisions would be analyzed by a firm which maximizes corporate wealth. For simplicity I will assume the organization's decisionmakers have no information advantage over outside investors and also that existing debt is (close to) default-risk free, so there is no temptation to undertake transactions to undercut existing creditors.

Because corporate wealth is measured by market value, rules for ranking capital investments are exactly the same as in standard finance theory. The firm always seeks positive NPV and prefers more NPV to less.

Suppose the firm issues debt to finance additional capital investment projects which happen to have NPV = O.[20] Then there is no change in corporate wealth: the market value of additional real assets are offset by the new debt liability. Thus with debt financing, there is no incentive to overinvest in negative-NPV projects.

However, an issue of debt that replaces equity, holding PVA and PVGO constant, *decreases* corporate wealth. As debt increases, corporate wealth, which is the sum of equity and organizational surplus, must go down.

This could be good news for stockholders. First, PVTAX, the governments claim on the firm could be significantly decreased by interest tax shields on the new debt. Some of the tax savings might be captured in increased surplus, but some would flow through to equity.

Second, the value of organizational surplus would decrease, transferring value to equity. Surplus is similar to a subordinated debt claim, whose market value falls when more senior debt is inserted between the junior debt and the firm's assets.[21]

Thus the organizational theory can explain why debt-for-equity changes are good news for stockholders. (Of course one has to accept that interest tax

---

[20] The present value of interest tax shields on debt supported by the project is included in the project's NPV.

[21] An issue of debt to finance zero-NPV real investment would trigger a similar, but smaller transfer to equity.

shields have significant value and that surplus is an important entry on the organizational balance sheet.) The theory also predicts that firms will not undertake debt-for-equity exchanges except under pressure, say, from threat of a takeover.

An issue of equity that replaces debt would be bad news for investors. The reasoning is just as for a debt-for-equity exchange, with signs of course reversed. But would a new equity issue, or retention of an unanticipated increase in earnings, be bad news if the money is put to a zero-NPV use on the asset side of the balance sheet?

Yes, because employees' surplus increases. Remember that this surplus resembles a junior debt, whose value increases when the firm adds equity-financed assets. Suppose the new equity money is raised by a share issue. Then new equity investors anticipate the value transfer from equity to surplus and mark down the purchase price of the new shares accordingly. The increase in surplus must therefore be extracted from existing equity.

The equity issue may be even worst news if the proceeds are not productively invested. If \$10 million is raised and invested in a project with a value of only \$6 million, existing shareholders lose \$4 million (and also lose whatever the employees gain from appreciation in the value of their junior claim). Other things constant, corporate wealth nevertheless *increases* by \$6 million, and surplus clearly increases, too.

Thus the negative stock market reaction to equity issues is guaranteed if investors fear that marginal investments are negative-NPV. But why should the corporate-wealth-maximizing firm ever accept a negative-NPV project? Why can't it issue equity and buy marketable securities, which presumably have NPV = 0? Then a \$10 million equity issue should add \$10 million to corporate wealth.

This is not an easy question for the organizational theory, but there are some possible answers. First, buying marketable debt securities amounts to lending money. If there is a significant tax advantage to borrowing, there must be a corresponding disadvantage to lending. Thus investment in a Treasury bill should have NPV < 0 after tax. Second, if another company's equity securities are purchased, an additional layer of taxation is created, which should drive NPV negative. This layer of tax is eliminated if the other company is taken over, but takeovers not motivated by real economic gains are also likely to be negative-NPV once transaction costs and takeover premiums are recognized.

Limits to Corporate Wealth

Assume, then, that outlets for investment with zero or positive NPV are limited. That limit defines the maximum scale of a shareholder-value maximizing firm. What limits the scale of a firm that maximizes corporate wealth? It seems that any new equity issue inevitably increases corporate wealth *and* organizational surplus when the proceeds are used to buy real assets. (Corporate wealth and surplus also increase if earnings are retained rather than paid out as dividends.) This is so even if the assets' NPVs are negative, so long as they have any value at all. Why doesn't the firm issue more and more equity, expanding and generating practically unlimited corporate wealth? If corporate wealth is the objective, the firm does not care about the *price* of new shares.

This, too, is not an easy question. One can appeal to the threat of takeover by other firms seeking to maximize *their* corporate wealth by preying on other firms with large employee surpluses or substantial negative-NPV investments. However, takeovers did not appear as a significant threat to large public corporations until relatively recently.[22]

Second, one can also argue that growth firms need to maintain share price to assure access to new equity as needed to finance future real investment. But this does not help explain behavior of mature firms whose internal cash flow outruns positive-NPV opportunities.

A third argument refers to PVGO, the present value of growth opportunities shown in Table 1. A corporation that invests heavily in negative-NPV assets today may lead investors to expect similar future investments. Investors mark PVGO down and eventually set it negative. In extreme cases, where the firm is more or less throwing money away, this year's additions to corporate wealth through PVA could be more than offset by the reduction in corporate wealth from an increasingly negative PVGO.

Corporate wealth is in the end not determined by the corporation but by investors. Only *market* value can be translated into "the power to distribute cash." That depends on what investors are willing to pay. That willingness depends on their assessment of the intelligence of the future operating and investment plans of the firm.

There is a fourth—I think deeper—argument. A large public corporation with management separate from ownership must maintain an adequate market value of equity in order to operate its business efficiently.

The inefficiencies of *not* supporting "adequate" equity value can be seen in an extreme case. Consider a firm that expands assets and corporate wealth at the expense of shareholders so aggressively that the market value of its shares is driven to a small fraction of the firm's potential value. Organizational surplus is then very large; in effect the coalition of employees expropriates most of the potential equity value. I will suppose that this firm is somehow protected from takeover and that internal cash flow more than covers future investment outlays.

In this case organizational surplus must serve as the capital base of the business. There is no equity to support contracts or relationships with suppliers, employees, and customers, or to guarantee the firm's ability to pay its debts.

The present value of organizational surplus could serve as capital if its value were observable. But S is not a traded asset. It can only be valued from scratch, i.e. by valuing the firm's assets and liabilities, then subtracting any debt claims (and the residual market value of equity). For a large firm with many business units, international operations, significant going concern value and other intangible assets, uncertain growth opportunities, and possibly hidden liabilities, this would be a costly and notoriously inaccurate exercise. But absent the exercise it

[22] One can also note the compensation schemes of top management, whose fortunes are tied more closely to equity earnings and stock prices than most of their employees. However, it's not clear why a wealth-maximizing organization would adopt such schemes.

would be imprudent to enter into a contractual or business relationship with such a firm.

The costs and delays that would be imposed on the firm's operations are obvious.[23]

A firm that landed in this box would see two ways out:

1. Eliminate the separation between ownership and control, recreating inside equity investors—perhaps an LBO partnership—with the power and credible incentive to restrict employee surplus. Of course such owners would also prevent the firm from expanding into negative-NPV assets.[24]
2. Make a deal with outside equity investors which limits the size of organizational surplus and reestablishes a significant, objective equity value for the firm. This would also limit negative-NPV expansion.

For all these reasons we see that too aggressive pursuit of corporate wealth at the expense of shareholders does not maximize organizational surplus. The employee coalition therefore seeks, or accepts, an accommodation with shareholders. That leads us to dividend policy.

Dividend policy. Why are shareholders willing to pay anything at all for a mature firm's shares, absent effective voting power or the threat of takeover? The answer is that the firm has somehow bonded itself to distribute cash to shareholders. Obviously the bond is not contractual, as it is with debt, but implicit. This is the reason why firms have fairly well-defined, sticky policies that regulate dividends per share.

A stock issue increases equity value only if this bonded or "promised" future payout increases. Consider the two extreme cases. First suppose a firm issues $10 million in new equity but does not "promise" to pay out any additional future dividends. (Aggregate dividends are maintained but dividends per share drop in proportion to the number of new shares issued.) Then existing shareholders must absorb a $10 million capital loss. In other words, the decision to issue new stock breaks the firm's "promise" to old shareholders. But having just broken that promise, it's not clear where the firm would find any rational *new* shareholders. In other words, an equity issue would probably be infeasible.

At the other extreme the firm could accept an implicit obligation to maintain dividends per share and to pay out additional future dividends with a present value of $10 million. This fully "covers" the newly issued shares, so existing shares maintain their value. Total equity value increases by $10 million.

Corporate wealth also increases by $10 million. However, not much of this goes to employees. The firm has $10 million more assets but has also promised

---

[23] This argument resembles Sheridan Titman's argument that firms with "unique" products and long-term relationships with suppliers and customers should favor conservative debt ratios. S. Titman, "The Effect of Capital Structure on a Firm's Liquidation Decision," *Journal of Financial Economics*, vol. 13, no. 1, March 1984, 137–151.

[24] This may happen automatically. If E falls close to zero, then ownership and control passes to the employee coalition, in which case they should act as inside equity investors.

$10 million to new shareholders. Nothing is left over for organizational surplus, except for the transfer to surplus from existing equity, which occurs because employees now hold better protected junior claims on the firm's assets.

Perhaps this tells us why firms prefer to retain earnings when profits unexpectedly increase. Suppose the firm has "promised" to pay out dividends according to some sticky rule. Then if earnings are higher than anticipated, much of the increase is free for employees to deploy; it has not been promised to shareholders. On the other hand, if there is an unanticipated shortfall, dividends are to some extent protected, and the firm reduces the flow to surplus or turns to outside financing for real investment.

This begins to look like a pecking order. The organizational theory of capital structure may be able to explain why the most profitable firms typically borrow the least. Their higher than "normal" or expected earnings are retained because their contract with shareholders does not require them to be paid out. If real investment opportunities do not increase in proportion to earnings—as is likely for mature firms—and if immediate cash flows to surplus are also sticky, then higher earnings mean greater retention, less reliance on external financing, and presumably a lower debt ratio.

The organizational theory also seems to explain stock market reactions to announcements of security issues, retirements, and exchanges. Overall it is a promising alternative to capital structure theories based on shareholder wealth maximization.

Yet caution is called for. I have not been able to develop the theory fully and formally in this paper. I have not analyzed the implicit contract between the firm and its shareholders or attempted a link-up to the literature on dividend policy. I have compared employees' surplus to a junior debt liability without giving a detailed description of the properties of this claim, and I have implicitly treated organizational surplus as a kind of tax which does not reduce the *potential* value of existing assets and growth opportunities. This is almost certainly oversimplified.

Finally, I have accepted Treynor and Donaldson's suggested objective of maximizing corporate wealth. The discussion above of equity issues and the firms' implicit contract with shareholders suggests that maximizing corporate wealth may not always be in the employees' interest, even if all employees could act as one.

Conclusions

This paper has briefly reviewed three theories—perhaps I should say two theories and one story—of capital structure. I have tried to match them to firms' actual behavior and to judge their ability to explain the two most striking facts about corporate financing.

The first fact is that investors regard almost all leverage-increasing security issues or exchanges as good news, and leverage-decreasing transactions as bad news. The only exception is plain-vanilla debt issues, which apparently are no news at all. The second fact is the strong negative correlation between profitability and financial leverage.

The widely-cited static tradeoff theory, taken literally, explains neither fact. It is at best a weak guide to average behavior.

The pecking order theory, though apparently a minority view, seems to explain both facts.

The organizational theory described in this paper is a first try at restating Jensen's free cash flow theory of the market for corporate control as a general theory of capital structure choice. It may be able to explain the two facts, though its predictions are not as clear and definite as the pecking order model's. A more thorough and formal development of the organizational theory is obviously needed.

The initial plausibility of the organizational theory derives from the financial history of the 1980s, particularly the aggressive use of leverage in LBOs, takeovers, and restructurings. Jensen properly interprets much of this activity as follows: high debt ratios were effective in forcing mature companies on a diet and preventing them from making negative-NPV capital investments or acquisitions. The debt is viewed as a contractual bond which forced overweight companies to distribute cash to investors.

The organizational theory is an extension of this argument, and therefore broadly consistent with it. The static tradeoff theory gives no help with the events of the 1980s unless it is assumed that companies are systematically underleveraged and therefore not maximizing shareholder value. But in that case the static tradeoff theory is no more than an open invitation to develop an organizational theory.

Thus there are really only two contenders in the race to explain capital structure: models such as the pecking order theory which assert asymmetric information as the chief underlying problem, and models which start from the proposition that organizations act in their own interests.

Questions

1. MBI Company's marginal tax rate is 35 percent. MBI pays $10 million of interest expense. How large is the tax shield created by MBI's interest payment? Explain what is meant by *present value of interest tax shields.*
2. Use Figure 1 to describe the static tradeoff theory of corporate capital structure.
3. "The most telling evidence against the static tradeoff theory is the strong inverse correlation between profitability and financial leverage." Explain the meaning of this statement.
4. Asymmetric information exists when corporate managers have information not known by investors. Explain the role played by asymmetric information in understanding why corporate managers would prefer to issue low-risk bonds instead of common stock.
5. Explain why corporate managers might prefer internal financing over external financing.
6. Describe the pecking order theory of corporate capital structure.

7. Sakan Cola Company's common stock trades at $15 per share, but Sakan's managers have reason to believe that it is worth $20 per share. They plan to introduce a profitable new drink called Sakan Orange, which will add $1 million to Sakan's equity value. Introduction of the new drink will require $2 million investment. Sakan has 200,000 shares of common stock currently outstanding, making its aggregate equity value equal to $3 million.
   a. If Sakan issues common stock to finance the new project, how many shares will it need to issue? (Assume zero flotation costs.)
   b. According to management's beliefs, what is the true worth of the new issue of common stock?
   c. If issuing common stock is Sakan's only financing alternative, should it go forward with the investment plan? Explain.
8. Describe the organizational balance sheet displayed in Table 1.
9. Use the organizational theory of capital structure to explain whether shareholder wealth will increase or decrease as a result of each of the following actions: (a) issue debt to replace equity; (b) issue equity to replace debt; (c) issue equity to invest in a zero-NPV project.

PART

III

Capital Budgeting

Panel Discussions on Corporate Investment: Capital Budgeting

SAMUEL C. WEAVER, ROGER L. CASON, AND JOSEPH L. DALEIDEN

Samuel C. Weaver: Welcome to the special session on capital budgeting practices. Our panelists are representatives from companies of varying sizes, but on a relative scale they would all be considered very large companies. We are going to begin with Roger, and then Joe, and I will follow. We have some unique presentations, and I hope we can have a productive exchange with the audience.

Roger L. Cason: Good afternoon. I am Roger Cason and I am in one of the industrial departments of the DuPont Company. I'm going to give a presentation that has very few numbers and absolutely no statistics of any kind. I am going to briefly describe our department and some of our practices so you will know more of my background. Then I want to look at what I view from my position in DuPont as trends, and finally close with a list of what I feel are problems—what I feel we don't do very well and I suspect trouble other companies as well.

I guess DuPont needs no introduction. We are in ninth place in the Fortune 500. I am in the Chemicals and Pigments Department which makes a variety of chemicals, mostly titanium dioxide. We also make freon and a wide variety of other industrial chemicals, most of which are commodities in nature.

Sam sent the three of us a questionnaire to use as a think-piece to help us get a grasp on what we should cover in our discussions. From this, I've listed the company perspective on some of our procedures. Like most other companies of any size, some are fairly formal. The minutia guidance is provided by the Finance Department, while the broad guidance is provided by an organization

At the time of this writing, Samuel C. Weaver worked for Hershey Food Corporation; Roger Cason worked for E.I. DuPont, DeNemours and Co.; and Joe Daleiden worked for Ameritech.

Source: *Financial Management* (Spring 1989, Vol. 18 No. 1, pp. 10–17). Reprinted with permission from *Financial Management;* Samuel C. Weaver; Roger L. Cason, formerly Financial Manager, E. I. DuPont, DeNemours and Co., currently Business and Financial Consultant; and Joseph L. Daleiden, Director—Strategic Planning and Capital Budgeting (retired), Ameritech.

called Corporate Planning, a staff arm of our Executive Committee. Our principal methodology at the moment is Internal Rate of Return. Most of the numbers that get ground out and published are IRR numbers, and our projected cash flows, hurdle rates, and cost of capital all include inflation; in other words, we don't work with so-called real returns.

Our cost of capital is estimated periodically by a variety of methods, all of which lead to about the same answer. We currently have a published rate of 12% internally. In real life, that figure is little used. It is a good first screen for sifting out a lot of really bad ideas, but beyond that our actual capital budgeting process is very much capital-ration driven, and so the typical hurdle rate is unfortunately never published. But we all understand that if a project is not well above 12%, it won't even be considered. The typical hurdle rates are frequently a good bit higher depending upon where the cut occurs on any one year's budget.

Finally, just to mention the one thing several of us were asked to cover at least in passing, when we do a capital lease analysis we do use the long-term cost of debt, which is one of the occasional controversies.

Now, here are what I view as trends within our company. Not too many years ago, appropriation requests tended to be thought of almost in isolation. Someone would bring in an idea and the approving body, normally the Executive Committee, would focus only on that idea and either approve it or not. Now there is a tendency to view the capital budgeting process. Approving a project is just one piece of the overall planning process which works not decision-by-decision but business-by-business. So, business plans will be drawn up to look ahead one, two, five, and ten years into the future for each major business segment, and this plan may or may not involve major capital investment. If it does, the capital investment will be studied and preliminary numbers will be drawn up of the type learned about in a beginning finance class, and then the process will move forward.

The net result is that the business plan has to make sense, and the individual appropriations within the business plan also have to make sense. Obviously, this leads to a process where there is a certain amount of moving back and forth between the business plan and the specific appropriation requests. There is a final authorization step in each project, but this tends to be almost ceremonial. By the time each project is turned in for approval, the decision has already been made, unless some dreadful change has occurred in the environment.

There is a greater emphasis on examining business plans in general rather than individual projects. Money should be concentrated in good businesses (meaning good for us), so even attractive projects in unattractive businesses may not get funded.

Also, we now include capital leases as part of our capital budgeting system along with regular appropriation requests. Unfortunately, operating leases are still a way to beat the capital budgeting system under some circumstances, and we haven't quite found a way to reach out and capture them in a way that is administratively practical.

The last trend I'd like to mention is that we are finally putting more and more emphasis on the fundamentals and less on minutia. We used to have a world-class assortment of minutia on projects that we had to work through. We've gotten rid of all that and now look more at the basics.

What I call my personal list of problems probably looks like that of a lot of others in this room. We really don't do a very good job of dealing with uncertainty when evaluating business plans. The high hurdle rates are one approach, but are not very satisfying intellectually.

Meaningful post audits are a problem for us. We have a post audit system that covers the larger projects—those $2 million or over that were submitted to make money. The results aren't sound for a variety of reasons. One is that superficial answers are accepted. Somebody may say, "This project just barely broke even because the selling price never met our expectations." Selling price is just a surrogate for competitive conditions, market conditions, and so forth, and we haven't really dug in when things go bad to find out what really happened, where our thinking went wrong.

I also think we are still struggling with how to evaluate operating lease situations, and different people in the company have different views on how to do it. I have my way of doing it, and of course I think I'm right, but some of my compatriots have a rather different view and they also think they are right.

We are still learning how to effectively evaluate foreign projects. In the past, we didn't take adequate account of blocked currency and all sorts of other problems that were run into overseas. We used a simplifying set of assumptions. Needless to say, they did not measure up in real life, and we're doing our best now to incorporate real life into our overseas evaluations.

There is also the problem of occasionally letting the desire for functional excellence, which is a buzz word in DuPont at the moment, degenerate into the search for functional perfection, causing an emphasis on minutia and other details that are not very effective.

The last item is not really a capital budgeting problem but is generated by capital budgeting. After a great deal of educating our managers, we finally made them aware of the fact that conceptually there is something called cost of capital, and that this is a cost just like electricity, or labor, or ingredients, or anything else. That cost must be covered. When the managers look over an appropriation request, we'll have this type of discussion with them. They immediately pull out their monthly operating statements, their monthly P&L. They want to know if they're meeting their cost of capital or not. I think that's a valid question and we really don't know how to answer it. We have all these figures, the IRRs and NPVs, which work for a specific decision. Unfortunately, we run businesses year-by-year, and it would be really nice to know if we're meeting our cost of capital in the long range. If any of you are struggling for a research idea I guess that would be my number one choice.

Joseph L. Daleiden: Ameritech is a regional holding company for five Midwest Bell companies and a service company, a system provider company, and a company to provide the information systems to the operating companies. We also own Ameritech Credit, Ameritech Cellular, and Ameritech Publishing company. Our revenues are about $10 billion.*

* This describes Ameritech in 1989 prior to subsequent restructuring.

The most interesting aspect of our company is the huge capital program. We spend $2 billion annually. Now, that would not be a big problem if we could spend it in one lump sum. We could do that if we were like some electric companies who have only one or two major decisions, and thus can really study them. Our problem is that we have maybe one or two decisions a year that might involve an expenditure of $100 or $200 million. When working on those, we have the benefit of all sorts of people studying and researching. However, most of our decisions are much, much smaller. In fact, there might be only ten or twenty decisions in the $10–$20 million range. But we also have hundreds of decisions that are $1 million and thousands of decisions that are $0.5 million or less.

That becomes a problem. How does one devise a set of techniques that cannot be centrally administered in the sense that every decision cannot benefit from an expert study (i.e., the people in the field have to do the studies)? A theoretical model so elegant that no one understands it can't be used. We had to come up with something simple enough that it can be utilized to the best advantage.

We have come up with a system that gives the right tools to the people in the field, enabling them to sift their projects through a group of screens to determine whether or not the project should be approved. The screens are similar to those of any other company—project risk, cost of capital, pay back period, all the elements that go into a project. One of the difficulties is assessing risk, which was not something a utility had to concern itself with in the past.

First, let me just explain why we now want to look at project risk, because there are a lot of people that believe we need not bother because project risk is inherent in a project's cost of capital. Although one project might be riskier than another, on the average it is reflected in the beta and your CAPM model. The problem with this type of thinking is that in the past, most of our projects were those in which we developed a new money-saving technology. We could estimate that very exactly because we knew we were going to save 8 installers or 10 operators by implementing a project.

Now more and more of our projects have to do with revenue generation. So, trying to estimate the possible variance in revenues becomes an integral part of the process. When we first attempted this, it was generally decided that we would accept only those projects that have at least a 20 or 25% return. The trouble with this simplistic criteria is that there could be a case where, if an arbitrary hurdle rate such as 20% is used, and the cash flow is divided by that rate, the resulting present value could be negative and a project with very little risk could be washed out. Again, if it was an expense-saving project that could be estimated very carefully, and we only estimated an 18% return, would we want the project dropped because of this blanket 20% hurdle rate? No. What could happen, though, is we would drop those less risky 18% projects and take on more risky projects that promise a 30 or 40% return, and over time we would push the company into a higher-risk position without ever consciously making that decision.

I don't like the idea of using hurdle rates because they disguise what is really going on. We began looking around to see what other methods we could adopt, and we reviewed what other companies were doing. We decided to ask the people in the field to risk-adjust the cash flows. We told them not to play with the discount rate, not to use a hurdle rate, and not to raise the discount rate arbitrarily. We asked them to just take the cash flows and come up with three estimates—the best case, the worst case, and the most likely. The expected cash flows probably should be broken down between a revenue and an expense. The revenues could be estimated by marketing and the expense by the engineers. Giving us a best case and worse case will pick up any skewness that is inherent in a particular project. Sometimes the people in the field might say they felt very uncomfortable making these estimates. But we all implicitly make these kind of estimates every day. Of course, we are only going to use this technique for certain types of projects. Obviously, there are some projects that we have to undertake because of the service we have to provide as a public utility.

Theories that are being developed today are further and further removed from practical applications. As a practical matter, I think what is most important in improving the estimates and the overall capital budgeting process is tracking estimates. One of our companies institutionalized tracking process. Now we can confront the person in marketing who put his name on the revenue estimates. And we can go back to the engineer who said she was going to cut fifty people out in the work force by doing project *x* and ask her what happened to those fifty people.

When the company announced that it was going to begin tracking, that year's budgets had already been submitted. But the company told every division to take back their submissions and think about the fact that everyone who worked on the project was going to be tracked, and then resubmit the estimates. Seven hundred projects never came back—they just disappeared. Many of the others had much lower estimates.

There are traditional measures that are used in the process of project selection. I'm sure you all know the problems with IRR, and I am not going to discuss them here. But these problems are a concern to us, and so we came up with something that we call the Project Rate of Return (PRR). Basically, the only difference is that cash flows are reinvested at the corporate cost of capital as opposed to the project rate. We are using this to avoid the misleading higher rate of return that occurs when one reinvests at the project rate of return. The problem with PRR is that it doesn't correctly rank projects having different study lengths. Using the PRR as the selection criteria, a project with a higher PRR would always be selected over lower PRR projects even though the latter might provide the returns over a longer period, and may thus produce a higher NPV. But then why not just rank projects based upon their NPVs? The danger is when ranking by NPV, you have to make sure that you don't pick one project with a NPV of say $150 over two projects that have an NPV of say $100 each. Your goal should be to maximize shareowner wealth.

I just showed you why project rate of return does not always work and why NPV doesn't always work. Therefore, we developed a new measure we call the project selection index (PSI). We deliberately use the term 'selection index,' even though the results are returns, because this type of return isn't comparable to the return the bank gives on a bond, and we didn't want to confuse the two. But basically, it is calculated by dividing NPV by the present value of the cash outflows.

There are two interesting differences between this measure and some of my fellow panelists' ideas. First of all, instead of looking at only investment dollars, we consider all cash outflows as coming from the shareowner. Any negative cash flows are potential money that is taken out of the shareowners' pocket. Whether that's called investment or expense seems irrelevant. The fact is, from the shareowners' perspective we're taking money they have or could have. Naturally, the shareholders' want to know what they are getting in return. That is the rationale for evaluating all negative cash flows instead of just investment dollars.

The second difference is that within any capital constraint using the PSI would result in selecting the group of projects which maximize shareowner value.

That is the formulation for our index. We risk adjust the cash flows and then calculate the PSI, which allows us to rank our projects. It does make a difference which method you pick to rank order of projects. The PSI is the one we are putting our money on for the time being. Thank you very much.

Sam Weaver: First of all, let me express my gratitude to the other panelists for their insightful presentations. I would also like to briefly go over what's been discussed up to this point. Roger gave us an excellent overview of a lot of the specific difficulties he encounters at DuPont. Joe gave an excellent presentation. You will see that what Joe was calling project rate of return, I am going to call terminal rate of return. In the literature, it is actually referred to as modified internal rate of return—that is, if you can find literature that discusses it. This is a subject that is very thinly written about.

I'm intending to cover several topics. I'd like to begin with a financial overview to familiarize you with Hershey's capital program background, and then from there how we budget for capital projects, how we evaluate capital projects, how we monitor and control them as they are being undertaken, and then how we perform post completion audits. At Hershey, we really don't do a good job in that area.

To put Hershey into perspective size-wise for you, sales were a little over $2.4 billion in 1987. We're not sure what 1988 is going to look like, because we sold our restaurant business and bought Cadbury USA this summer. We generate about $320 million of operating income and about $150 million of net income. Capital expenditures fluctuates around $100 million.

The financial considerations which I want to discuss are as applicable to capital budgeting as to acquisition or divestiture analysis. Our capital program is a four-phase, four-prong approach. I wanted to highlight to you the approval levels so you know that we are really only involved with projects over $0.5 million. Projects below this level down to $10,000 are the responsibility of each operating division.

We used to use a category system for classifying projects. Projects were classified as profit adding, which generated incremental profit, and profit maintaining. To be honest, after ten years at Hershey I have yet to decipher the distinction between these two projects. Profit maintaining is simply making sure your profits remain constant. Because it is that type of project, you never had to go through an economic rate of return. Likewise, other administrative (such as personal computers, mainframes, new desks, etc.), environmental, and R&D projects were always thought of as necessary.

Now we are looking at a revised system. The three major categories would be conventional capital, new products, and research and development. Essentially, what we are attempting is a move into an era where we can start evaluating all major capital projects over $50,000. Also, we are looking at much lower, realistic hurdle rates that compensate for the risk underlying projects.

When we do annual budgets, we have a menu of projects. We plan to spend $100 million in capital but only about half of the projects will actually be undertaken due to priority adjustments. We can't plan for a number of years because we just don't have solid ideas about what our priorities are going to be next year, let alone five years from now.

Approval at annual budget time is not authorization to go ahead with the project. Each project is individually reviewed. We look at payback period. We also look at net present value, internal rates of return, and something analogous to Joe's project rate of return which I call terminal rate of return or modified internal rate of return. The terminal rate of return or modified internal rate of return, depending on the hurdle rate, reflects the net present value.

There is a tendency in major Fortune 500 firms to not use NPV. Senior management prefers to use rates of return. I can tell you whether a 10% rate of return is good. I know what interest rates are. I know what the cost of capital is. But as we all know, internal rates of return can give you a very erroneous answer. The terminal rate of return will always give an answer consistent with net present value, as long as the reinvestment rate is identical to the discount rate that would have been used for net present value. From a technical point of view, this gives the right answer and in such a way that management can understand it as a rate of return. So it satisfies both constituencies. That is why we began using terminal rate of return.

We have an enormous amount of capital capacity. Unfortunately, we don't have enough projects on the drawing board to utilize all of our capacity. So all I need to do is be consistent with net present value. I am assumming that we do have sources of capital if we really need it. We're not going to take on anything monumental, but we do have the necessary capital for our normal projects. And that concludes our presentations.

Questions

1. The three panelists represent three different companies. For each company, list the evaluation methods (e.g., NPV and IRR) used in capital budgeting.

2. Which of the three companies conduct performance appraisals to evaluate the success or failure of completed or abandoned capital projects?
3. Describe the procedure for approval of capital projects, as reported by the panelists.
4. What is meant by the term *capital rationing*? Which of the three companies engage in capital rationing?
5. Describe the relationship between capital budgeting and strategic planning, as reported by the panelists.

The Hidden Value of Capital Efficiency

Thomas E. Copeland and Kenneth J. Ostrowski

The chief financial officer of a large, regulated company recently noticed a problem. He was seeing increased demand for capital to fund new projects at the same time that his company was suffering from a shortage of internally generated funds. Because conditions in the capital markets were unfavorable, he was not prepared to issue new debt or equity in the necessary amounts to keep the company's capital structure unchanged. So he proposed to raise the hurdle so that fewer projects would be accepted.

A reasonable solution—but somehow the CFO felt uncomfortable. Would raising the hurdle really cut the number of requests? Or would the numbers simply be "cooked" to show higher forecasted returns? The CEO was uncomfortable too. Was this, at best, only a superficial fix that neglected a much deeper problem?

The company's capital budgeting process was fairly standard in its approach. All capital requests above $2 million had to be approved by the CFO's office and had to show an expected 12 percent rate of return. Every year about 200 requests were submitted for review. Despite the formal review process, however, only a few dozen of these actually received careful attention.

Moreover, in most cases the CFO's staff lacked the time and/or expertise to challenge the underlying technical assumptions or design of the proposed projects. The staff were no match for the seasoned engineer who could rattle off technical details and compellingly link just about any project to higher-order issues such as safety, reliability, or customer service.

The CFO had little confidence that the best skills had been applied in finding least-cost options or alternatives to what had been proposed. Rumors from

---

At the time of this writing, Thomas E. Copeland was a principal in McKinsey's New York office. Kenneth Ostrowski was a principal at McKinsey's Cleveland office. We are indebted to many colleagues for providing examples and for helping to push our thinking. We would like to thank, in particular, Joe Avila, Michael Mire, Margot Singer, and Keith Turnipseed.

the field suggested that projects were often gold plated, and external benchmarking confirmed that invested capital levels were well above best practice both within and outside the industry. Field personnel had strong incentives to overengineer because they got into trouble only if there was a shortage of supply to customers. Design engineers were criticized only when something went wrong with a piece of equipment.

In addition, about 60 percent of total expenditure was approved automatically because it fell below the $2 million limit and policy dictated that such projects were not reviewed by the CFO's office at all. They fell into the category of "blanket" spending: small outlays, too numerous to analyze in detail, that were part of routine spending.

Whether the CFO was aware of it or not, capital budgeting at his company was seriously out of control.

Managing Value

Finance textbooks wax eloquent about capital budgeting methodologies as if the use of theoretically correct techniques inevitably results in an optimal allocation of capital. From time to time, academic surveys of CFOs look to see how many of their companies regularly use DCF, IRR, or NPV when evaluating significant investment decisions.[1] But using proper analytic methods does not, and cannot by itself ensure real capital efficiency—the greatest possible enhancement of free cash flows by making sensible reductions in the need for working and/or physical capital.

In other words, capital efficiency is *not* the product only, or even primarily, of methodological choice. It starts, instead, with a marginal understanding of the forces that drive the demand for capital and shape the ways in which capital-dependent projects get defined and implemented at the front lines of an organization. And it rests on a management process that aligns the day-to-day behavior and mindset of the employees who plan and execute such projects with the organization's overall value-creation objectives.

There is nothing magical about a management process focused on value. It simply recognizes that the greatest part of capital spending is controlled by decision makers at the grass roots of an organization. These people have the information required to improve capital efficiency dramatically but—if they are to share it effectively—need top management support in the form of better understanding, more feedback, and, especially, appropriate guidelines and incentives.

The potential impact of improved capital efficiency is enormous. Companies can often cut their capital expenditures by between 10 and 25 percent without any change in revenues or in the quality of services provided to their customers. At the same time, they can often reduce maintenance costs and implementation times (as projects get simplified) and improve interfunctional cooperation (as the new approach gets embedded in general managerial practice). One company, for example, reduced its working capital by $500 million in one year. This

---

[1] *See*, for example, the articles by Klammer and Schall *et al.* listed in "Suggested Reading" at the end of this article.

dramatic improvement had nothing to do with budgeting methodology, but everything to do with developing a value-based approach to capital management throughout the organization.

As well as generating millions of dollars of value for shareholders, improving capital budgeting has a real, direct impact on a company's overall economic health. For example, in 1990, capital spending in electric utilities and telecommunications—two industries where capital budgeting problems often arise—was $110 billion, fully 21 percent of all capital spending in the United States. A disciplined value-based approach typically pares yearly budgets between 10 and 25 percent. That means adopting it in these industries alone could free up tens of billions of dollars a year for investment in new and useful enterprises.

Today, capital efficiency represents such a huge and largely untapped source of value because only limited attention is usually paid to it. And what attention does get paid usually comes from far too high up the chain of command.

Why Does It Matter?

The advantages of improved capital efficiency for unregulated companies are obvious. Those that can do more with less are rewarded by the capital markets. If the same operating cash flows can be achieved by using less working capital or less physical capital, a company's free cash flow increases, which is reflected in a higher market price for its shares. A company that generates a dollar of earnings by spending twenty cents of capital will enjoy a higher share price than a competitor that generates a dollar of earnings by spending fifty cents of capital.

The rationale for capital efficiency at regulated companies, such as utilities and telecoms, is different, especially if the rate of return on their capital base is regulated. Even in this situation, though, capital efficiency has compelling benefits.

First, the regulatory environment is improved: regulators typically benchmark across jurisdictions and reward companies that provide higher-quality service without cost overruns and other inefficiencies. Second, being regulated does not mean that a company can afford to be uncompetitive. Electric utilities, for example, can lose their power contracts with those businesses able to switch to alternative forms of energy, generate power for themselves, or gain access to other electricity supply options such as municipalized service. Telecommunications companies that use their capital inefficiently can lose traffic volume if business customers find it more efficient to build their own systems. Finally, regulated companies that spend capital more efficiently will find that they do not have to go to the capital markets so often.

Exhibit 1 compares Alltel and Rochester Telephone, two regulated telecommunications companies. Between 1987 and 1991, Alltel had lower growth in earnings per share (3.4 percent for Alltel; 10.2 percent for Rochester), but the share price of Alltel grew at 19.3 percent annually, while at Rochester Telephone growth was only 11.2 percent. The difference between them was primarily capital efficiency. Rochester's return on invested capital (ROIC) declined from 14.5 percent to 4.6 percent in the same period, and its ratio of sales to invested capital (capital turns) fell from 0.62 to 0.54. Over the same five years, Alltel's

EXHIBIT 1 COMPARISON OF ALLTEL AND ROCHESTER TELEPHONE

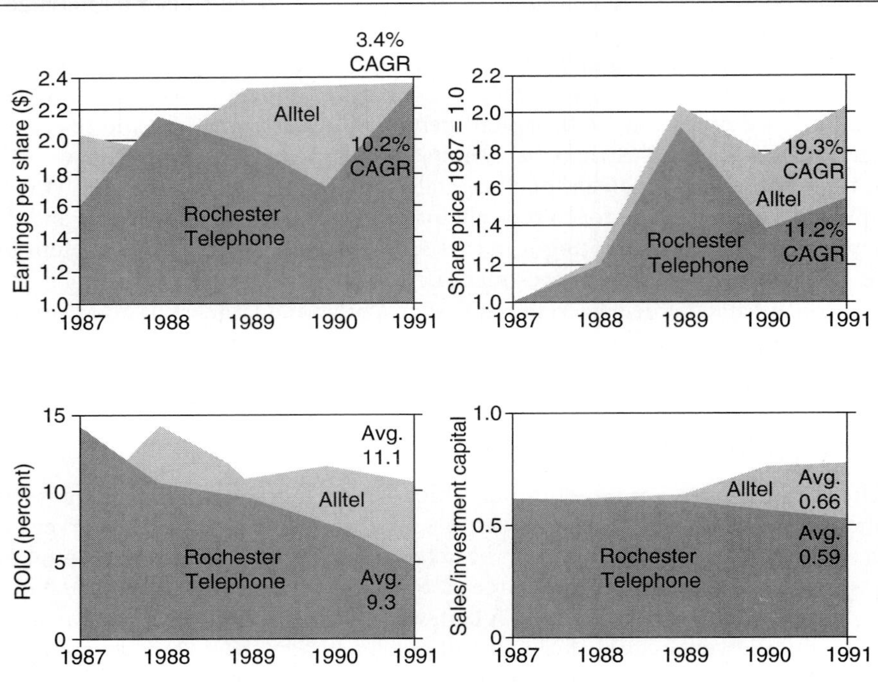

SOURCE: Compustat S & P; McKinsey analysis

ROIC rose from 8.8 percent to 10.4 percent, and its capital turns improved from 0.54 to 0.76. Clearly, the market was responding to capital efficiency as well as to earnings.

Locating Inefficiencies

In general, improvements in capital efficiency result from eliminating non-value-based drivers of demand for capital, promoting creative exploration of lower-cost options, and intensifying attention to day-to-day project execution. Although most CFOs and line managers would agree that additional effort along each of these dimensions will produce incremental benefits, few anticipate the magnitude of savings that can actually be captured. When realization finally dawns, their first reaction—after the initial shock—is to question the motives or intelligence of field personnel. Surely they must have been aware of these inefficiencies?

As the following case examples show, however, most inefficiencies are grounded in "legitimate" past practices, hidden constraints, or misaligned incentives. Left undetected, these subtle influences will continue to deprive companies of significant capital improvement opportunities for years to come.

The Seven Symptoms of Capital Inefficiency

CAPITAL BUDGETING problems often reveal themselves in subtle ways. The presence of one or more of these symptoms should act as a warning that there are capital inefficiencies at work:

Blanket spending. A large portion of the capital budget is spent "automatically" by operating personnel or field engineers via guidelines or procedures that do not require economic justification.

Unintegrated approach. Company budgeting and planning processes treat operating and maintenance spending and capital expenditure as separate rather than integrated uses of company resources.

Myopic planning. It is either "feast or famine" with capital spending, depending on current earnings or cash flow. Alternatively, budgets are set on an annual, incremental basis rather than as part of a multiyear investment program.

"Entitled" spending. An approach to setting annual capital budgets based on expenditure levels in previous years, this is often accompanied by significant year-end spending sprees to "make budgets."

Missed budget targets. There is a skewed bell-shaped curve of project spending results, with many projects over but few under initial spending projections, particularly after adjustments for the scope of work accomplished.

Badly aligned incentives. A *de facto* performance management system admonishes field personnel and engineers for breakdowns and capacity constraints without placing adequate emphasis on prudent risk management or economic efficiency.

No post-audit procedure. There is limited follow-up to assess the magnitude or timing of benefits generated by capital programs.

Focus on Value

Eliminating non-value-based drivers of capital spending requires careful analysis of the root causes and assumptions that lead to capital requests in the first place. Deferral or elimination of projects is often the greatest source of savings, but it is not always readily apparent where the opportunities lie. Take, for example, the determination of how much capacity is required to meet projected demand. Measurement of capacity utilization can be tricky, as an example from a telecommunications company demonstrates.

Exhibit 2 shows a hypothetical cable that is 67 percent used, according to the following "logic": the large cable carries three smaller cables, only one of which is not used. Partial use of a smaller cable counts as full use. Therefore, the large cable is operating at two-thirds capacity. Note, however, that if we turn to the basic unit of transmission, the smallest cables, we see that only 8 out of 33 cables are actually carrying traffic. The real capacity utilization is thus only 24 percent.

EXHIBIT 2 CALCULATING CABLE UTILIZATION

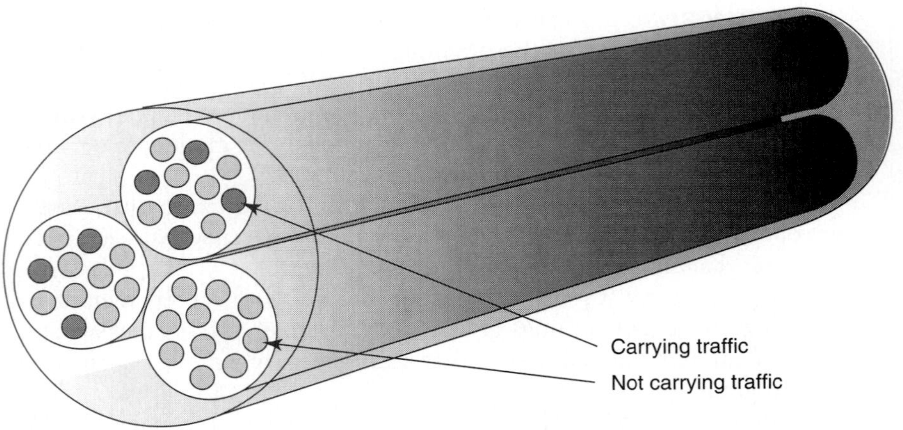

Anomalies like this cannot be easily discovered by the CFO from his or her vantage point at the top of an organization.

In an electric utility system, the proper sizing of transformers is an important element in ensuring adequate capacity. At one company, design engineers were responsible for specifying transformer requirements, though the funding came from operation's capital budget. People barely noticed the engineers unless the transformers became overloaded, causing reliability and quality problems. Then they got yelled at. Consequently, the engineers took the initiative to forecast circuit and customer load patterns in an attempt to assess future capacity requirements.

To protect against unforeseen requirements, they scheduled projects for installation up to two years in advance, and added an extra safety margin of 50 percent to the rated capacity of the equipment, which was already lower than its actual capacity. Sometimes, of course, the projected demand failed to materialize, and the net result was that the utility had a number of transformers in place capable of carrying an overload of about 80 percent. By adding reliability and capital efficiency to the criteria used to select and prioritize projects and by shortening installation lead times in order to improve forecast accuracy, the company was able to reduce its capital expenditure budget by 20 percent.

Opportunities also exist to reduce the appetite for capital consumption by addressing the underlying drivers of "blanket" spending. Anyone who has controlled a blanket budget knows the temptation to underspend during the first three-quarters of the fiscal year, then load up during the fourth quarter. Exhibit 3 illustrates one company's pattern of spending by quarter. The fourth quarter

EXHIBIT 3 Blanket Project Expenditures

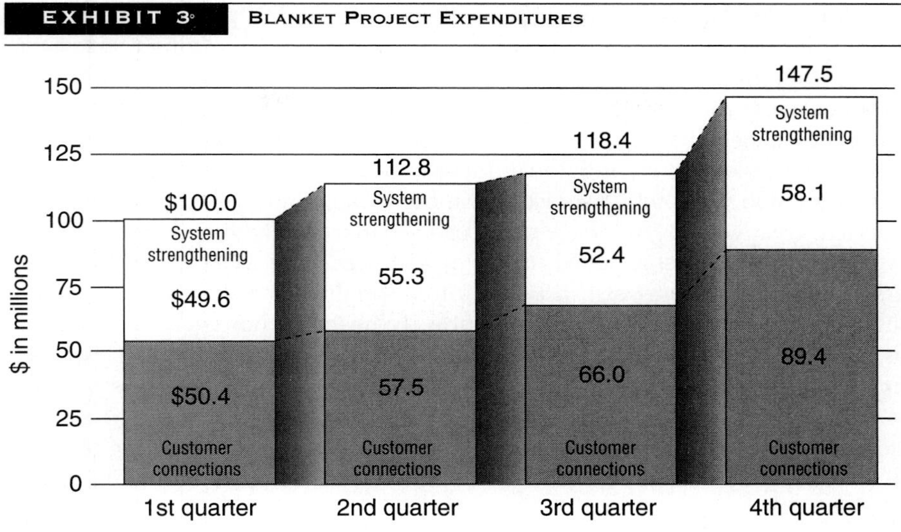

shows levels 25 to 50 percent higher than in each of the previous three. Management had many explanations, but two were particularly compelling and worrisome:

> "If we don't spend it this year, we lose it, and our budget for next year will be lower."
>
> "I'm out of operating budget, but still have room in my capital budget, so I need to find capital jobs to assign my people [read: labor costs] to."

These statements reflect the organizational reality of most capital-spending programs. The result is that projects of lower value are taken on, and work is conducted in less efficient ways—for instance, by expediting materials or working overtime. Thus, actions that attack the attitude of fundamental entitlement in setting annual budgets and that evaluate performance on the basis of demand, productivity, and management of input costs can have dramatic impact in bringing blanket programs under control.

Focus on Costs

Promoting creative exploration of lower-cost options involves examining opportunities for improvement on a "total system," rather than a component basis, and undertaking a value-based review of projects on a line-item basis. Taking a total system view of projects can help identify, upstream or downstream of the proposed fix, lower-cost alternatives that are capable of delivering equal or greater impact.

For example, a company might be about to invest in a project for removing impurities from the downstream phase of a process. By reviewing total system costs, it might discover that there are cheaper options that prevent impurities from entering the system in the first place, perhaps through investment in better maintenance of equipment upstream. Such lower-cost options are, however, often overlooked when individual operating units seek ways to reduce annual operating budgets. But if the distinction between operating and capital funds is relaxed, creative ways to reduce total costs are more likely to be uncovered.

Conducting a value-based review of a project's line-item features is analogous to the "line-item veto" privilege often sought by heads of government in dealings with their respective legislatures. In business, however, the challenge is less to master the politics of the situation than to get the necessary expertise in place to review projects effectively on a disaggregated basis. As one steel company discovered, the payoff for doing so can be significant: involving field personnel in generating, evaluating, and selecting ideas for project simplification led to a 27 percent reduction in the capital required to complete 20 projects (Exhibit 4).

Focus on Execution

Intensifying day-to-day attention to project execution can be a source of improvement for most companies. Frequently, the opportunity manifests itself in the form of chronic budget overruns. These are always a problem, of course, but we have found that overruns in blanket spending are more frequent and add up to a larger overall figure.

EXHIBIT 4 CAPITAL SAVINGS THROUGH PROJECT SIMPLIFICATION

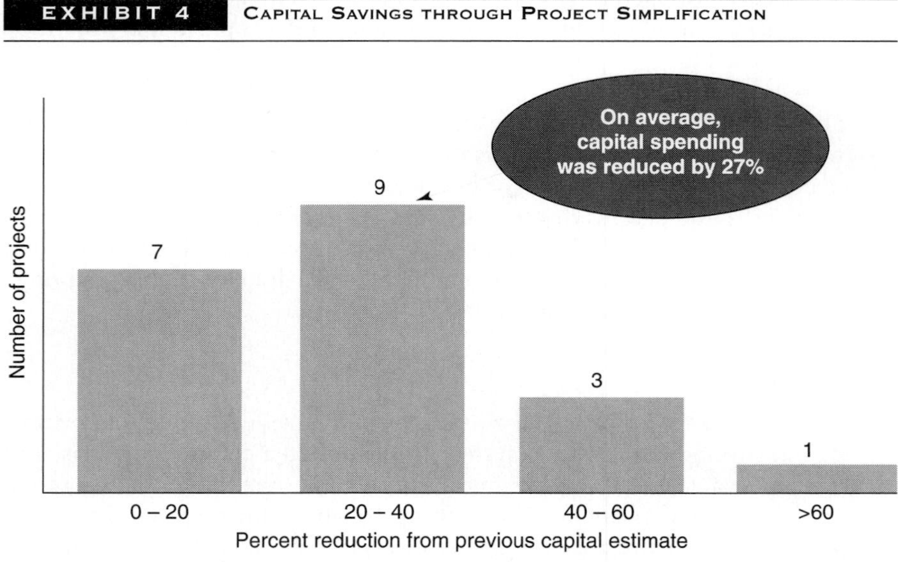

Exhibit 5 shows the evolution of one company's blanket capital spending during the course of a year: actual expenditures ended up 38 percent higher than initially forecast. Nor was there any follow-up audit that held people responsible for overspending. Not surprisingly, interviews with managers indicated that they tended to emphasize timeliness rather than capital efficiency:

"My task is to get the job done by the deadline."

"I don't care what planning says the estimated cost is; I just know I have to get the job done."

"I estimate the cost of a specific task, but I never see what the *actual* cost of doing the job was. Nowhere in the system do we compare estimated and actual job costs other than in aggregate."

Even where jobs do get completed on budget, opportunities for improvement frequently exist. More insightful balancing of cost with time, more accurate reporting of performance to front-line personnel, and more careful removal of barriers to implementation can usually add 5 to 10 percentage points to gains in efficiency already realized.

In some cases, for example, the budget may have been achieved, but the project was not completed on time or in full scope. In others, costs have been transferred between projects to "average out" performance reporting, in the process distorting and obscuring opportunities for leveraging best practices or addressing problem areas. Finally, unless there are explicit rewards for bringing

EXHIBIT 5 BLANKET EXPENDITURES VERSUS BUDGET

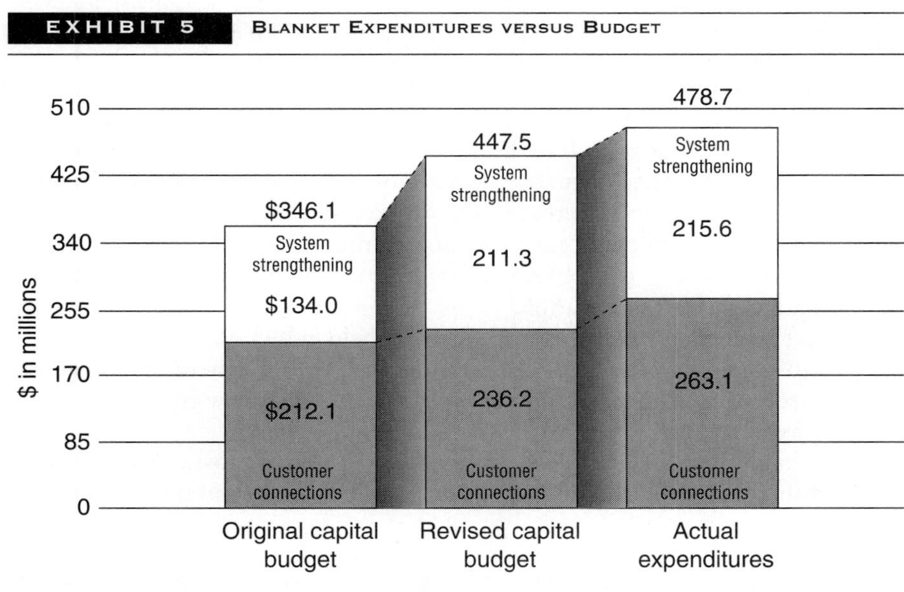

projects in below budget, employees have little incentive for extracting efficiencies from a project that is unlikely to exceed its budget.

Value-Based Management

Disciplined efforts to achieve capital efficiency must, therefore, start with a management commitment to value creation and a managerial process for getting all levels of an organization, particularly the front line, to act in ways consistent with that commitment. Such an orientation is especially important for companies that need to take a long-term view of their business and have relatively high capital intensity. For large projects, the analysis of investment decisions should follow traditional textbook NPV methodology.[2] But for the thousands of smaller decisions that arise from the design of property, plant, and equipment, or from blanket spending, there is need for a consistent but less cumbersome way of thinking. We call this process value-based management.

Detailed net present value calculations do not work here. The scale is all wrong. Value drivers do. Value drivers are the specific, easily tracked metrics—cost per foot of installed cable or pipeline, peak-load transformer utilization, or time to completion of a project—that link micro-level decisions to capital efficiency.

Nurturing and leveraging grassroots awareness of such drivers of value are, thus, essential parts of any process genuinely focused on value creation. At one company, for example, engineers hoarded vital equipment, in violation of policy, as protection against a breakdown in operations. The resulting excess inventory of components amounted to virtually a year's supply. Only when the engineers, together with procurement and stores personnel, were able to establish a guaranteed 24-hour delivery time for replacement parts could this wasteful practice be corrected—and capital efficiency improved.

Similarly, following the destruction of facilities in south central Los Angeles in 1992, PepsiCo experimented with a rapid construction concept and learned how to build a new Taco Bell in 48 hours from start to finish. The company determined that rapid construction was a value driver because its incremental cost was offset by the acceleration of the revenue stream, and because start-to-finish construction time was easy both to communicate and to measure. PepsiCo is now working to implement rapid construction as a key program throughout its whole organization.

Whatever form they take, value drivers can help unlock many hidden sources of improvement in capital efficiency. Exhibit 6 details a general management change process for identifying and tapping these and other types of capital-related improvements.

The value-based management process starts with a diagnosis. Does the company exhibit any of the tell-tale symptoms of inefficient capital management?

---

[2]*See*, for example, the books by Brealey and Myers or Weston and Copeland in "Suggested Reading" at the end of this article.

EXHIBIT 6 A Value-Based Management Process for Improving Capital Efficiency

	Step 1 Assess the situation	Step 2 Develop new process	Step 3 Change mindset	Step 4 Implement new guidelines and incentives	Step 5 Follow through
Bottom-up activities	• Interview decision makers who control blanket spending • Develop database to review project and blanket spending • Review existing performance metrics for validity	• Develop value drivers and operational performance metrics specific to grassroots blanket spending • Revise reporting requirements and process to emphasize value drivers	• Train operating, finance, and engineering managers —Relationship between capital and value —Value drivers • Conduct workshops to find new capital efficiency ideas	• Develop value driver guidelines to control blanket spending • Provide bonuses for improved capital efficiency • Provide indemnification against acceptable failures	• Monitor continual improvement in capital spending value drivers • Retrain people who change jobs and new employees
Top-down activities	• Interview companies that have world-class performance • Estimate magnitude of capital efficiency improvements	• Develop interactive dialogue and review process for reports on capital spending —Project expenditures —Blanket-level spending	• Require analytical rigor for major capital spending decisions • Reinforce importance of capital efficiency • Conduct top-level workshops to generate ideas	• Develop clear linkage between capital spending and overall strategy and objectives • Provide top-level, value-based compensation	• Conduct post-audit reviews of major projects • Reinforce continuation of process
Cross-functional activities	• Assess company's status on the 7 symptoms of capital spending inefficiency	• Develop benchmarking for operational performance whenever possible —Across time —Vis-à-vis other companies	• Train finance and planning staffs • Disseminate results of early wins • Implement interactive dialogue	• Implement careful up-front planning • Provide guidelines for appropriate tradeoffs between capital efficiency and other objectives	• Monitor progress against the 7 symptoms of capital spending inefficiency • Ensure interactive dialogue continues

(See "The Seven Symptoms of Capital Efficiency" on page 179.) How much potential is there for capital efficiency improvements? How valid are the existing performance metrics, such as capacity utilization? How accurate a database is there for reviewing levels of blanket spending? How do decision makers at grass-roots levels actually make blanket spending decisions? What incentives do they have to improve capital efficiency?

Having gained a better understanding of how decisions are actually made, an organization can move to the second step: developing a new process that focuses on grass-roots activity, but with good support from the top as well as across functions on such tasks as developing benchmarks. Bottom-up activities include careful identification of value drivers that can be monitored for continuous improvement, coupled with revised reporting requirements to focus on them. At the top, there must be a review process that centers on a two-way dialogue about both blanket spending and major projects. Its purpose is to make all levels of management smarter about where—and how—value gets created. Senior management needs better to understand the design of projects and the reasoning behind blanket spending; grass-roots managers, the importance of efficient capital spending.

Perhaps the most important part of the VBM process is the third step—changing the mindset of the organization. Workshops should be conducted at the grass-roots level to identify value drivers and brainstorm new capital efficiency ideas. Step 4 then reinforces the change in mindset by revising guidelines and incentives. Incentives are always a thorny issue. It is important, for example, to understand tradeoffs between customer needs and potential equipment failures, then to work toward agreement on guidelines that concentrate on capital efficiency and indemnify field engineers against sporadic equipment breakdowns.

There is always a tendency to slip back into bad habits after an initial capital efficiency program has achieved its first success. The final step, therefore, is follow through. The goal is to have ongoing advances in value-driver performance via continuous improvement programs. Post-audit reviews of major projects enable learning about what went wrong and how to do things better next time. Boosting capital efficiency is a "piano tuner" problem. The task is never finished. But the benefits are clearly worth the continuous application of energy and attention. Value-based management pays.

Suggested Reading

R. Brealey and S. Myers, *Principles of Corporate Finance*, New York, McGraw Hill, 4th edition, 1991.

T. Klammer, "Empirical evidence of the adoption of sophisticated capital budgeting techniques," *Journal of Business*, July 1972, pp. 387–97.

L. Schall, G. Sundem, and W. Geijsbeek, Jr., "Survey and analysis of capital budgeting references," *Journal of Finance*, March 1978, pp. 281–7.

J. F. Weston and T. Copeland, *Managerial Finance*, Fort Worth, Texas, The Dryden Press, 9th edition, 1992.

Questions

1. What is the meaning of the article's title "The Hidden Value of Capital Efficiency"?
2. What are the seven symptoms of capital inefficiency? Describe each one.
3. "In general, improvements in capital efficiency result from eliminating non-value-based drivers of demand for capital, promoting creative exploration of lower-cost options, and intensifying attention to day-to-day project execution." Describe an example of each of these methods for improving capital efficiency.
4. What is a *value driver*, and what is its purpose?
5. Describe the process for improving capital efficiency, as illustrated in Exhibit 6.

Corporate Strategy and the Capital Budgeting Decision

ALAN C. SHAPIRO

The decade 1974 through 1983 was a dismal one for American business in general. It began with the deepest economic decline since the Depression and ended with national recoveries from back-to-back recessions in the early 1980s. Yet throughout these dark years, 13 companies on the Fortune 500 list of the largest U.S. industrial companies were money-making stars, earning consistently high returns. These firms averaged at least a 20 percent return on shareholders' equity (ROE) over this ten-year span. (To gain some perspective, a dollar invested in 1974 at a compound annual rate of 20 percent would have grown to \$6.19 by the end of 1983, a healthy return even after allowing for the effects of inflation.) Moreover, none of these firms' ROE ever dipped below 15 percent during this difficult period.

The 13 were led by a profit superstar, American Home Products, whose ROE not only averaged 29.5 percent during the 1974–83 decade, but also has held above 20 percent for 30 straight years. To appreciate the significance of such a feat, one dollar invested at 20 percent compounded annually would be worth over \$237 at the end of 30 years.

What type of firm can achieve such a remarkable record? Far from being the prototypical high-tech firm or a lucky oil company, American Home Products is the low-profile producer of Anacin, Chef Boy-Ar-Dee pasta products, Brach's candy, and Gulden's mustard, in addition to prescription drugs and nondrug products such as cardiovascular drugs, oral contraceptives, and infant formula.

In general, high technology firms were not well represented among the 13, which included just IBM and two pharmaceutical companies, SmithKline Beckman and Merck. IBM, moreover, with an average ROE of 20.5 percent, ranked only 11th out of the 13, far behind such low-tech firms as Dow Jones (26.3%), Kellogg (24.8%), Deluxe Check Printers (24.1%), and Maytag (23.1%). It was

---

At the time of this writing, Alan C. Shapiro was associate professor of finance at the Graduate School of Management of the University of California at Los Angeles.

Source: From Bank of America *Journal of Applied Corporate Finance*.

even less profitable than a steel company (Worthington Industries—23.9%) and a chemical firm (Nalco Chemical—21.5%).

The demonstrated ability for a firm such as Deluxe Check Printers—a firm on the trailing edge of technology, described as a "buggy whip company threatened with extinction by the 'checkless society'"—consistently to earn such extraordinary returns on invested capital must be due to something more than luck or proficiency at applying sophisticated techniques of investment analysis. That something is the knack for creating positive net present value (NPV) projects, projects with rates of return in excess of the required return. The scarcity of this skill is attested to by the fact that aggregate profits of $68.8 billion for the Fortune 500 in 1983 were, in real terms, 22 percent below the $43.6 billion earned in 1974, a recession year. Keep in mind also that the Fortune 500 have been disciplined savers, re-investing over $300 billion of retained earnings, in their businesses over the ten-year period. This massive reinvestment alone should have produced considerably higher real earnings than 1974's.

This evidence notwithstanding, it is usually taken for granted that positive NPV projects do exist and can be identified using fairly straightforward techniques. Consequently, the emphasis in most capital budgeting analyses is on estimating and discounting future project cash flows. Projects with positive net present values are accepted; those that fail this test are rejected.

It is important to recognize, however, that selecting positive NPV projects in this way is equivalent to picking under-valued securities on the basis of fundamental analysis. The latter can be done with confidence only if there are financial market imperfections that do not allow asset prices to reflect their equilibrium values. Similarly, the existence of economic rents—excess returns that lead to positive net present values—is the result of monopolistic control over product or factor supplies (i.e., "real market imperfections").

It is the thesis of this article that generating projects likely to yield positive excess returns is at least as important as the conventional quantitative investment analysis. This is the essence of corporate strategy: creating and then taking advantage of imperfections in product and factor markets. Thus, an understanding of the strategies followed by successful firms in exploiting and defending those barriers to entry created by product and factor market imperfections is crucial to any systematic evaluation of investment opportunities. For one thing, it provides a qualitative means of identifying, or ranking, ex ante those projects most likely to have positive net present values. This ranking is useful because constraints of time and money limit the number and range of investment opportunities a given firm is likely to consider.

More important, a good understanding of corporate strategy should help uncover new and potentially profitable projects. Only in theory is a firm fortunate enough to be presented, at no effort or expense on its part, with every available investment opportunity. Perhaps the best way to gain this understanding is to study a medley of firms, spanning a number of industries and nations, that have managed to develop and implement a variety of value-creating investment strategies. This is the basic approach taken here.

The first section discusses what happens to economic rents over time, and thus to opportunities for positive NPV projects, in a competitive industry. The

EXHIBIT 1 13 STARS OF THE DECADE 1974–1983

Company	Average ROE 1974–1983	Total return to investors 1974–1983*
American Home Products	29.5%	6.6%
Dow Jones	26.3	29.8
Mitchell Energy	26.0	26.4
SmithKline Beckman	25.4	19.7
Kellogg	24.8	13.3
Deluxe Check Printers	24.1	13.4
Worthington Industries	23.9	41.7
Maytag	23.1	14.5
Merck	21.9	3.8
Nalco Chemical	21.5	11.4
IBM	20.5	11.3
Dover	20.3	26.6
Coca-Cola	20.3	2.9
Median total return to investors for the 13:	13.4%	
Median total return to investors for the Fortune 500:	13.6%	

* Total return to investors as calculated by *Fortune*, April 30, 1984. It includes both price appreciation and dividend yield to an investor and assumes that any proceeds from cash dividends, the sale of rights and warrant offerings, and stock received in spinoffs' were reinvested at the end of the year in which they were received. The return reported is the average annual return compounded over the ten-year period.

Although the 13 have earned extraordinary returns on shareholders' equity capital, Exhibit I shows that returns to the shareholders themselves have been less than earth-shaking. This is consistent with the efficient market hypothesis, the idea that prices of traded securities rapidly reflect all currently available information. Since the high return on equity capital earned by the 13 is not news to investors—these firms have consistently been outstanding performers—investors back in 1974 had already incorporated these expectations in their estimations of firm values. This means that a firm's expected high ROE is already "priced out" or capitalized by the market at a rate that reflects the anticipated riskiness of investing in the company's stock. As a result, investors will earn exceptional returns only if the firm turns out to do even better than expected, something that by definition is not possible to predict in advance. The fact that the 13's median annual total return to investors (stock price appreciation plus reinvested dividends) of 13.4 percent is almost identical to the Fortune 500's median return of 13.6 percent indicates that investor expectations about the relative performances of both groups of firms were subsequently borne out.

This illustrates the key distinction between operating in an efficient financial market and operating in product and factor markets that are less than perfectly competitive. One can expect to consistently earn excess returns only in the latter markets; competition will ensure that excess returns in an efficient market are short-lived. However, it is evident from the generally dismal performance of the Fortune 500 that it is no mean trick to take advantage of those product and factor market imperfections that do exist.

second section considers in more detail the nature of market imperfections that give rise to economic rents and how one can design investments to exploit those imperfections. The third section presents the available evidence on the relationship between various competitive advantages and rates of return on invested capital. The fourth introduces a normative approach to strategic planning and investment analysis. The fifth and final section deals with the rationale and means for domestic firms to evolve into multinational corporations.

Competitive Markets and Excess Returns

A perfectly competitive industry is one characterized by costless entry and exit, undifferentiated products, and increasing marginal costs of production. These undifferentiated products, also known as commodities, are sold exclusively on the basis of price. In such an industry, as every student of microeconomics knows, each firm produces at the point at which price equals marginal cost. Long-run equilibrium exists when price also equals average cost. At this point, total revenue equals total cost for each firm taken individually and for the industry as a whole. This cost includes the required return on the capital used by each firm. Thus, in the long run, the actual return on capital in a competitive industry must equal the required return.

Any excess return quickly attracts new entrants to the market. Their additional capacity and attempts to gain market share lead to a reduction in the industry price and a lowering of returns for all market participants. In the early 1980s, for example, the high returns available in the video-game market, combined with the ease of entry into the business, attracted a host of competitors. This led to a red-ink bath for the industry in 1983, followed by the exit of a number of firms from the industry. Conversely, should the actual return for the industry be below the required return, the opposite happens. The weakest competitors exit the industry, resulting in an increase in the industry price and a boost in the overall return on capital for the remaining firms. This process, which is now taking place in the oil refining business, continues until the actual return once again equals the required return.

The message from this analysis is clear: the run-of-the-mill firm operating in a highly competitive, commodity-type industry is doomed from the start in its search for positive net present value projects. Only firms that can bring to bear on new projects competitive advantages that are difficult to replicate have any assurance of earning excess returns in the long run. These advantages take the form of either being the low-cost producer in the industry or being able to add value to the product—value for which customers are willing to pay a high (relative to cost) price. The latter type of advantage involves the ability to convert a commodity business into one characterized by products differentiated on the basis of service and/or quality. By creating such advantages, a firm can impose barriers to entry by potential competitors, resulting in a less-than-perfectly competitive market and the possibility of positive NPV projects.

Barriers to Entry and Positive Net Present Value Projects

As we have just seen, the ability to discourage new entrants to the market by erecting barriers to entry is the key to earning rates of return that consistently exceed capital costs. If these barriers did not exist, new competitors would enter the market and drive down the rate of return to the required return. High barriers to entry and the threat of a strong reaction from entrenched competitors will reduce the risk of entry and so prolong the opportunity to earn excess returns.

This analysis suggests that successful investments (those with positive NPVs) share a common characteristic: they are investments that involve creating, preserving, and even enhancing competitive advantages that serve as barriers to entry. In line with this conclusion, the successful companies described by Thomas Peters and Robert Waterman in their bestseller, *In Search of Excellence*, were able to define their strengths—marketing, customer contact, new product innovation, low-cost manufacturing, etc.—and then build on them. They have resisted the temptation to move into new businesses that look attractive but require corporate skills they do not have.

A clearer understanding of the potential barriers to competitive entry can help to identify potential value-creating investment opportunities. This section now takes a closer look at the five major sources of barriers to entry—economies of scale, product differentiation, cost disadvantages, access to distribution channels, and government policy—and suggests some lessons for successful investing.[1]

Economies of Scale

Economies of scale exist whenever a given increase in the scale of production, marketing or distribution results in a less-than-proportional increase in cost. The existence of scale economies means that there are *inherent cost advantages in being large*. The more significant these scale economies, therefore, the greater the cost disadvantage faced by a new entrant to the market. Scale economies in marketing, service, research, and production are probably the principal barriers to entry in the mainframe computer industry, as GE, RCA, and Xerox discovered to their sorrow. It is estimated, for example, that IBM spent over $5 billion to develop its innovative System 360, which it brought out in 1963. In natural resource industries, firms such as Alcan, the Canadian aluminum company, and Exxon are able to fend off new market entrants by exploiting economies of scale in production and transportation.

High capital requirements go hand-in-hand with economies of scale. In order to take advantage of scale economies in production, marketing, or new product development, firms must often make enormous up-front investments in plant and equipment, research and development, and advertising. These capital requirements themselves serve as a barrier to entry; the more capital required, the higher the barrier to entry. This is particularly true in industries such as petroleum refining, mineral extraction, and mainframe computers.

---

[1] See, for example, Michael E. Porter, "How Competitive Forces Shape Strategy," *Harvard Business Review*, March-April 1979, pp. 137–145 for a good summary and discussion of these barriers to entry and their implications for corporate strategy.

A potential entrant to a market characterized by scale economies in production will be reluctant to enter unless the market has grown sufficiently to permit the construction and profitable utilization of an economically-sized plant. Otherwise, the new entrant will have to cut price to gain market share, destroying in the process the possibility of abnormal profits. By expanding in line with growth in the market, therefore, entrenched competitors can preempt profitable market entry by new competitors.

Consider, for example, the economics of the cement industry. The low value-to-weight ratio of cement makes the cement business a very regional one; beyond a radius of about 150 to 200 miles from the cement plant, the costs of transport become prohibitive unless cheap water or rail transportation is available. At the same time, the significant economies of scale available in cement production limit the number of plants a given region can support. For instance, suppose that demand in a land-locked region is sufficient to support only one or two modern cement plants. By expanding production and adding substantial new capacity to that already available, a firm can significantly raise the price of market entry by new firms and make plant expansion or replacement by existing competitors look much less attractive. This type of move obviously requires a longer time frame and the willingness to incur potential losses until the market grows larger.

Scale economies are all-important in the grocery retailing business, on the level of the individual stores as well as the city-wide market. Whether a store has $100,000 or $10,000,000 in annual sales, it still needs a manager. In addition, the cost of constructing and outfitting a supermarket doesn't increase in proportion to the number of square feet of selling space. Thus, the ratio of expenses to sales exhibits a significant decline as the volume of sales rises.

Similarly, whether it has 10 percent or 25 percent of a given market, a supermarket chain has to advertise and supply its stores from a warehouse. The higher the share of market, the lower the advertising cost per customer, the faster the warehouse will turn over its inventory, and the more likely its delivery trucks will be used to capacity. These cost efficiencies translate directly into a higher return on capital.

The relationship between the market dominance of a supermarket chain in a given market and its profitability is evident in the relative returns for firms following contrasting expansion strategies. Chains such as Kroger and Winn-Dixie, which have opted for deep market penetration in a limited geographic area (ranking number 1 or 2 in almost all their major markets), have realized returns on equity that far exceed their equity costs. On the other hand, chains such as A&P and National Tea, which expanded nationally by gaining toe-hold positions in numerous, though scattered markets, have consistently earned less than their required returns.

Computer store chains, to take another example, also enjoy significant economies of scale. These show up in the form of lower average costs for advertising, distribution, and training. Even more important, they receive larger discounts on their products from the manufacturers.

LESSON #1: Investments that are structured to fully exploit economies of scale are more likely to be successful than those that are not.

Product Differentiation

Some companies, such as Coca-Cola and Procter & Gamble, take advantage of *enormous advertising expenditures* and *highly developed marketing skills* to differentiate their products and keep out potential competitors wary of the high marketing costs and risks of new product introduction. Others sell expertise and high-quality products and service. For example, Nalco Chemical, a specialty chemical firm, is a problem solver and counselor to its customers while Worthington Industries, which turns semifinished steel into finished steel, has a reputation for quality workmanship that allows it to charge premium prices. As indicated in the introduction to this article, both have been handsomely rewarded for their efforts, with average equity returns exceeding 20 percent annually from 1974 to 1983.

Pharmaceutical companies have traditionally earned high returns by developing unique products that are protected from competition by patents, trademarks, and brand names. Three outstanding examples are SmithKline Beckman's Tagamet, for treating stomach ulcers, and Hoffman-La Roche's tranquilizers, Librium and Valium. American Home Products also owes a great deal of its profitability to several patented drugs.

Similarly, the development of technologically innovative products has led to high profits for firms such as Xerox and Philips (Netherlands). A fat R&D budget, however, is only part of the activity leading to commercially successful innovations. To a great extent, the risks in R&D are commercial, not technical. Firms that make technology pay off are those that closely link their R&D activities with market realities. They always ask what the customer needs. Even if they have strong technology, they do their marketing homework. This requires close contact with customers, as well as careful monitoring of the competition. Studies also indicate that top management involvement is extremely important in those firms that rely heavily and effectively on technology as a competitive weapon. This requires close coordination and communication between technical and business managers.

Failure to heed that message has led to Xerox's inability to replicate its earlier success in the photocopy business. In addition to its revolutionary copier technology, Xerox developed some of the computer industry's most important breakthroughs, including the first personal computer and the first network connecting office machines. But, through a lack of market support, it has consistently failed to convert its research prowess into successful high-tech products.

Service is clearly the key to extraordinary profitability for many firms. The ability to differentiate its computers from others through exceptional service has enabled IBM to dominate the worldwide mainframe computer business with a market share of over 75 percent. Similarly, Caterpillar Tractor has combined dedication to quality with outstanding distribution and after-market support to differentiate its line of construction equipment and so gain a commanding 35 percent share of the world market for earth-moving machinery. American firms, such as the auto companies, that have been somewhat lax in the area of product quality have fallen prey to those Japanese firms for which quality has become a religion.

What may not be obvious from these examples is that it is possible to differentiate anything, even commodity businesses such as fast food, potato chips, theme parks, candy bars, and printing. The answer seems to be quality and service as companies like McDonald's, Disney, Frito-Lay, Mars, and Deluxe Check Printers have demonstrated. Cleanliness and consistency of service are the hallmarks of Disney and McDonald's, with both rating at the top of almost everyone's list as the best mass service providers in the world. Similarly, it is said that Mars' plants are kept so clean one can "eat off the factory floor."

High quality work and dependability have helped Deluxe Check Printers flourish in a world supposedly on the verge of doing without checks. It fills better than 95 percent of orders in two days, and ships 99 percent error free.

Frito-Lay's special edge is a highly motivated 10,000 person sales force dedicated to selling its chips. They guarantee urban supermarkets and rural mom and pop stores alike a 99.5 percent chance of a daily call. Although they get only a small weekly salary, the sales people receive a 10 percent commission on all the Lay's, Doritos, and Tostitos they sell. So they hustle, setting up displays, helping the manager in any way possible, all the while angling for that extra foot of shelf space or preferred position that can mean additional sales income. There are also tremendous side benefits to close contact with the market. Frito can get a market test rolling in ten days and respond to a new competitive intrusion in 48 hours.

A similar level of service is provided by Sysco, a $2 billion firm in the business of wholesaling food to restaurants and other institutional businesses. It is a very mundane, low-margin business—one where low cost is seemingly all that matters. Yet, behind its slogan, "Don't sell food, sell peace of mind," Sysco earns margins and a return on capital that is the envy of the industry. Even in that business, a large number of customers will pay a little more for personalized service. And in a low-margin business, a little more goes a long way.

Sysco's secret was to put together a force of over 2,000 "marketing associates" who assure customers that "98 percent of items will be delivered on time." They also provide much more, going to extraordinary lengths to produce a needed item for a restaurateur at a moment's notice. Chairman John Baugh summed it up as follows:

The typical food service company picks a case of frozen french fries out of the warehouse and drops it on the restaurant's back porch. Where is the skill in that? Where is the creativity? Service isn't a free lunch. The price tag (and cost) is higher; but even at the lower end of the market, most customers (not all, to be sure) will pay some additional freight for useful service.[2]

Other firms have made their owners wealthy by understanding that they too are *selling solutions to their customers' problems*, not hardware or consumables.

---

[2] Quoted in *Forbes*, October 11, 1982, p. 58.

John Patterson, the founder of National Cash Register, used to tell salesmen: "Don't talk machines, talk the prospect's business." Thomas Watson, the founder of IBM, patterned his sales strategy on that admonition. Thus, while other companies were talking technical specifications, his salesmen were marketing solutions to understood problems, such as making sure the payroll checks came out on time.

These days, Rolm Corp., a leader in the crowded market for office communications systems, is taking a page out of IBM's book. It has built up a service force of over 3,400 employees whose main job is to reassure customers mystified by the complexities of modern technology, while selling them more equipment. The common strategic vision and approaches of the two firms may help explain why IBM, when it decided to enter the telecommunications business, did so by acquiring Rolm (in 1984) rather than another firm.

The contrast between the approaches followed by IBM and DEC is particularly revealing. DEC has developed excellent narrow-purpose minicomputers, trusting that application solutions can be developed by others to justify advanced technology. That simple strategy—selling machines on their merits to scientists and engineers—worked spectacularly for two decades, turning DEC into the world's second-largest computer company. One consequence of that strategy, however, is that DEC never needed to and never did develop the kind of marketing orientation IBM is noted for.

The advent of the personal computer, which can perform many of the functions of a minicomputer at a fraction of the cost, has underscored the shortcomings inherent in DEC's product-rather than market-oriented strategy. As its traditional business has stagnated, DEC has attempted to reposition itself to compete in the nimble new world of personal computers. But it has failed thus far to adapt marketing and sales strategies to the new, less technically sophisticated customers it has tried to attract.

The results are painfully obvious. On October 18, 1983, DEC's stock nosedived 21 points after it announced that quarterly earnings would be 75 percent lower than the year before. Thus far at least, IBM, and its strategy of utilizing proven technology to market solutions to known problems, has prevailed in the marketplace.

LESSON #2: Investments designed to create a position at the high end of anything, including the high end of the low end, differentiated by a quality or service edge, will generally be profitable.

Cost Disadvantages

Entrenched companies often have cost advantages that are unavailable to potential entrants, independent of economies of scale. Sony and Texas Instruments, for example, take advantage of the *learning curve* to reduce costs and drive out actual and potential competitors. This concept is based on the old adage that you improve with practice. With greater production experience, costs can be expected to decrease because of more efficient use of labor and capital, improved plant layout and production methods, product redesign and standardization, and the substitution of less expensive materials and practices. This cost decline creates a barrier to entry because new competitors, lacking experience face higher unit costs than established companies. By achieving market leadership, usually by price cutting, and thereby accumulating experience faster, this entry barrier can be most effectively exploited.

Proprietary technology, protected by legally enforceable patents, provides another cost advantage to established companies. This is the avenue taken by many of the premiere companies in the world, including 3M, West Germany's Siemens, Japan's Hitachi, and Sweden's L.M. Ericsson.

Monopoly control of low-cost raw materials is another cost advantage open to entrenched firms. This was the advantage held for so many years by Aramco (Arabian-American Oil Company), the consortium of oil companies that until the early 1980s had exclusive access to low-cost Saudi Arabian oil.

McDonald's has developed yet another advantage vis-a-vis potential competitors; it has already acquired, at a relatively low cost, many of the best fast-food restaurant locations. Favorable locations are also important to supermarkets and department stores.

A major cost advantage enjoyed by IBM's personal computer is the fact that software programs are produced first for it since it has a commanding share of the market. Only later—if at all—are these programs, which now number in the thousands, rewritten for other brands. Companies that don't develop IBM look-alikes must either write their own software, pay to have existing software modified for their machines, or wait until the software houses get around to rewriting their programs.

Sometimes, however, new entrants enjoy a cost advantage over existing competitors. This is especially true in industries undergoing deregulation, such as the airlines and trucking. In both of these industries, regulation long insulated firms from the rigors of competition and fare wars. Protected as they were, carriers had little incentive to clamp down on costs. And still they were quite profitable. The excess returns provided by the regulatory barrier to entry were divided in effect between the firms's stockholders and their unionized employees.

Deregulation has exposed these firms to new competitors not saddled with outmoded work rules and high-cost employees. For example, new low-cost competitors in the airline industry, such as People's Express and Southwest Airlines, have much lower wages (about half of what big airlines pay) and more flexible work rules (which, for example, permit pilots to load baggage and flight attendants to man reservations phones).

One firm that managed to stay ahead of the game is Northwest Airlines. For years, Northwest has been run as if competition were fierce, while still making the most of the protections of regulations. It gained a reputation for fighting labor-union demands and hammered away to increase productivity. As a result, Northwest's overhead costs are only about 2 percent of total costs, compared with about 5 percent for major competitors. Similarly, its labor costs are about two-thirds the industry average. Consequently, it is the most efficient of the major airlines, which has greatly enhanced its competitive position.

LESSON #3: Investments aimed at achieving the lowest delivered cost position in the industry, coupled with a pricing policy to expand market share, are likely to succeed, especially if the cost reductions are proprietary.

Access to Distribution Channels

Gaining distribution and shelf space for their products is a major hurdle that newcomers to an industry must overcome. Most retailers of personal computers, for example, limit their inventory to around five lines. Currently, over 200 manufacturers are competing for this very limited amount of shelf space. Moreover, the concentration of retail outlets among chains means that new computer makers have even fewer avenues to the consumer. This presents new manufacturers with a Catch-22: you don't get shelf space until you are a proven winner, but you can't sell until you get shelf space.

Conversely, well-developed, better yet unique, distribution channels are a major source of competitive advantage for firms such as Avon, Tupperware, Procter & Gamble, and IBM. Avon, for example, markets its products directly to the consumer on a house-to-house basis through an international network of 900,000 independent sales representatives. Using direct sales has enabled Avon to reduce both its advertising expenditures and the amount of money it has tied up in the business. Potential competitors face the daunting task of organizing, financing, and motivating an equivalent sales force. Thus, its independent representatives are the entry barrier that allows Avon consistently to earn exceptional profit margins in a highly competitive industry. Similarly, the sales forces of Frito-Lay, Sysco, and IBM help those firms distribute their products and raise the entry barrier in three very diverse businesses.

Conversely, the lack of a significant marketing presence in the U.S. is perhaps the greatest hindrance to Japanese drug makers attempting to expand their presence in the U.S. Marketing drugs in the U.S. requires considerable political skill in maneuvering through the U.S. regulatory process, as well as rapport with American researchers and doctors. This latter requirement means that pharmaceutical firms must develop extensive sales forces to maintain close contact with their customers. There are economies of scale here: the cost of developing such a sales force is the same, whether it sells one product or one hundred. Thus, only firms with extensive product lines can afford a large sales force, raising a major entry barrier to Japanese drug firms trying to go it alone in the U.S.

One way the Japanese drug firms have found to get around this entry barrier is to form joint ventures with American drug firms, in which the Japanese supply the patents and the American firms provide the distribution network. Such licensing arrangements are a common means of entering markets requiring strong distribution capabilities. Union Carbide, for example, follows a strategy of using high R&D expenditures to generate a diversified and innovative line of new products. Since each new product line requires a different marketing strategy and distribution network, firms like Union Carbide are more willing to trade their technology for royalty payments and equity in a joint venture with companies already in the industry.

LESSON #4: Investments devoted to gaining better product distribution often lead to higher profitability.

Government Policy

We have already seen in the case of the airline, trucking, and pharmaceutical industries that government regulations can limit, or even foreclose, entry to potential competitors. Other government policies that raise partial or absolute barriers to entry include import restrictions, environmental controls, and licensing requirements. For example, American quotas on Japanese cars have limited the ability of companies such as Mitsubishi and Mazda to expand their sales in the U.S., leading to a higher return on investment for American car companies. Similarly, environmental regulations that restrict the development of new quarries have greatly benefited those firms, such as Vulcan Materials, that already had operating quarries. The effects of licensing restrictions on the taxi business in New York City are reflected in the high price of a medallion (giving one the right to operate a cab there), which in turn reflects the higher fares that the absence of competition has resulted in.

A change in government regulations can greatly affect the value of current and prospective investments in an industry. For example, the Motor Carrier Act of 1935 set up a large barrier to entry into the business as it allowed the Interstate Commerce Commission to reject applicants to the industry. The Act also allowed the truckers themselves to determine their rates collectively, typically on the basis of average operating efficiency. Thus carriers with below-average operating costs were able to sustain above-average levels of profitability. It is scarcely surprising, then, that the major trucking companies pulled out all the stops in lobbying against deregulation. As expected, the onset of trucking deregulation, which greatly reduced the entry barrier, has led to lower profits for trucking companies and a significant drop in their stock prices.

LESSON #5: Investments in projects protected from competition by government regulation can lead to extraordinary profitability. However, what the government gives, the government can take away.

Investment Strategies and Financial Returns: Some Evidence

Ultimately, the viability of a value-creating strategy can only be assessed by examining the empirical evidence. Theory and intuition tell us that companies which follow strategies geared towards creating and preserving competitive advantages should earn higher returns on their investments than those which do not. And so they do.

William K. Hall studied eight major domestic U.S. industries and the diverse strategies followed by member firms.[3] The period selected for this study was

---

[3] William K. Hall, "Survival Strategies in a Hostile Environment," *Harvard Business Review*, September-October 1980, pp. 75–85.

1975–1979, a time of slow economic growth and high inflation. These were especially hard times for the eight basic industries in Hall's study. They all faced significant cost increases that they were unable to offset fully through price increases. In addition, companies in each of these industries were forced by regulatory agencies to make major investments to comply with a variety of health, environmental, safety, and product performance standards. To compound their problems, competition from abroad grew stronger during this period. Foreign competitors achieved high market shares in three of the industries (steel, tire and rubber, and automotive); moderate shares in two others (heavy-duty trucks and construction and materials handling equipment); and entry positions in the other three (major home appliances, beer, and cigarettes).

The net result of these adverse trends is that profitability in the eight basic industries has generally fallen to or below the average for manufacturers in the United States. According to Table 1, the average return on equity for these eight industries was 12.9 percent, substantially below the 15.1 percent median return for the Fortune 1000. A number of firms in these industries have gone bankrupt, are in financial distress, or have exited their industry.

Yet this tells only part of the story. As Table 1 also shows, some companies survived, indeed prospered, in this same hostile environment. They did this by developing business strategies geared towards achieving one or both of the following competitive positions within their respective industries and then single-mindedly tailoring their investments to attain these positions:

1. Become the lowest total delivered cost producer in the industry, while maintaining an acceptable service/quality combination relative to competition.

TABLE 1 Return on Equity in Eight Basic Industries: 1975–1979*

Industry	Return on Equity	Leading Firm	Return on Equity
Steel	7.1%	Inland Steel	10.9%
Tire and rubber	7.4	Goodyear	9.2
Heavy-duty trucks	15.4	Paccar	22.8
Construction and materials handling eq.	15.4	Caterpillar	23.5
Automotive	15.4	General Motors	19.8
Major home appliances	10.1	Maytag	27.2
Beer	14.1	G. Heilman Brewing	25.8
Cigarettes	18.2	Philip Morris	22.7
Average—eight industries	**12.9**	**Average—leading companies**	**20.2**
Median—Fortune 1000	**15.1**		

*From William K. Hall, "Survival Strategies in a Hostile Environment."

2. Develop the highest product/service/quality differentiated position within the industry, while maintaining an acceptable delivered cost structure.

Table 2 provides a rough categorization of the strategies employed by the two top-performing companies in each of the eight industries studied. In most cases, the industry profit leaders chose to occupy only one of the two competitive positions. Perhaps this is because the sources and skills necessary to achieve a low-cost position are incompatible with those needed to attain a strongly differentiated position.

At least three of the 16 leaders, however, combined elements of both strategies with spectacular success. Caterpillar has combined lowest-cost manufacturing with outstanding distribution and after-sales service to move well ahead of its domestic and foreign competitors in profitability. Similarly, the U.S. cigarette division of Philip Morris has become the industry profit leader by combining the lowest-cost manufacturing facilities in the world with high-visibility brands, supported by high-cost promotion. Finally, Daimler Benz employs elements of both strategies, but in different business segments. It has the lowest cost position in heavy-duty trucks in Western Europe, along with its exceptionally high-quality, feature-differentiated line of Mercedes Benz cars.

Other examples of the benefits of attaining the low-cost position in an industry or picking and exploiting specialized niches in the market abound. For example, the low-cost route to creating positive NPV investments has been successfully pursued in, of all places, the American steel industry. The strategy has involved building up-to-date mini-mills employing non-union workers who earn substantially less than members of the United Steelworkers Union. Minimills melt scrap, which is cheaper in the U.S. than anywhere else, and their modern plant and equipment and simplified work practices greatly reduce their need

TABLE 2 COMPETITIVE STRATEGIES EMPLOYED BY LEADERS IN EIGHT BASIC INDUSTRIES*

Industry	Low Cost Leader	Meaningful Differentiation	Both Employed Simultaneously
Steel	Inland Steel	National	—
Tire and rubber	Goodyear	Michelin (French)	—
Heavy-duty trucks	Ford, Daimler Benz (German)	—	—
Construction and materials handling equipment	—	John Deere	Caterpillar
Automotive	General Motors	Daimler Benz	—
Major home appliances	Whirlpool	Maytag	—
Beer	Miller	G. Heilman Brewing	—
Cigarettes	R.J. Reynolds	—	Philip Morris

*From William K. Hall, "Survival Strategies in a Hostile Environment."

for labor. Chapparal Steel of Midlothian, Texas, a big—and profitable—mini-mill, has pared its labor costs to a mere $29 on a ton of structural steel. This compares with average labor costs of $75 a ton at big integrated U.S. plants.

The chief disadvantage is that their steelmaking capabilities are limited. They can't, for example, make the industry's bread-and-butter item: flat-rolled steel. But in the product areas where mini-mills do compete—rod, bar, and small beams and shapes—big producers have all but surrendered. So, too, have foreign mills. In just two years, Nucor Corp's mini-mill in Plymouth, Utah, cut the Japanese share of California's rod and bar market from 50 to 10 percent.

Taking a different tack, Armstrong Rubber Co. has specialized in grabbing small market segments overlooked by its rivals. Today, Armstrong ranks second in industrial tires and second or third in both the replacement market for all-season radials and in tires for farm equipment and off-road recreational vehicles. Its niche-picking strategy relies heavily on the design and production innovations arising from its large investments in research and development.

A number of chemical firms, including Hercules, Monsanto, Dow, and Belgium's Solvay, have attempted to lessen their dependence on the production of commodity chemicals and plastics by investing heavily in highly profitable specialty products for such industries as electronics and defense. These specialty chemicals are typically sold in smaller quantities but at higher prices than traditional bulk commodity chemicals. Perhaps the most successful chemical "niche-picker" is Denmark's Novo Industri—one of the world's largest producers of enzymes and insulin, and a pioneer in genetic engineering techniques. Novo's continued success is largely due to its ability to find and exploit small but profitable market niches. For instance, industry analysts credit Novo's success at selling enzymes in Japan to the company's ability to outdo even Japanese purity standards and to concentrate on small specialty markets that Japan's chemical giants can't be bothered with. In fact, most of Novo's markets appear too small for giant chemical firms such as Germany's Hoechst or Du Pont to pursue.

James River Corp. has combined cost cutting with product differentiation to achieve spectacular growth and profits in the paper-goods industry, an industry where many companies are struggling to hold their own. Typically, James River buys other companies' cast-off paper mills and remakes them in its own image. It abandons all or most of the commodity-grade paper operations. It refurbishes old equipment, and supplements it with new machinery to produce specialty products (automobile and coffee filters, airline ticket paper, peel-off strips for Band-Aids, and cereal-box liners) that are aimed at specific markets and provide higher profits with less competition. At the same time, James River cuts costs by extracting wage concessions from workers and dismissing most executives. It also raises the productivity of those employees who stay by allowing many of them to join the company's lucrative *profit-sharing* programs. James River's success in following this two-pronged strategy is reflected in its 1983 net income of $55.1 million, 332 times larger than its 1970 earnings of $166,000.

Designing an Investment Strategy

Although a strong competitive edge in technology or marketing skills may enable a firm to earn excess returns, these barriers to entry will eventually erode, leaving the firm susceptible to increased competition. Existing firms are entering new industries and there are growing numbers of firms from a greater variety of countries, leading to new, well-financed competitors able to meet the high marketing costs and enormous capital outlays necessary for entry. Caterpillar Tractor, for example, faces a continuing threat from low-cost foreign competitors, especially Japan's Komatsu, which is second in worldwide sales. To stay on top, therefore, a firm's strategy must be constantly evolving, seeking out new opportunities and fending off new competitors.

Xerox clearly illustrates the problems associated with losing a competitive edge. For many years, Xerox was the king of the copier market, protected by its patents on xerography, with sales and earnings growing over 20 percent annually. The loss of its patent protection has brought forth numerous well-heeled competitors, including IBM, 3M, Kodak, and the Japanese, resulting in eroding profits and diminished growth prospects. Xerox has tried to transfer its original competitive advantage in technology to new products designed for the so-called office of the future. However, its difficulties in closely coordinating its R&D and marketing efforts have led to a series of serious, self-confessed blunders in acquisitions, market planning, and product development. For example, as mentioned earlier, the basic technology for the personal computer was developed by Xerox's Palo Alto Research Center in the early 1970s, but it remained for Apple Computer and IBM to capitalize on this revolutionary product.

More recently, Xerox's 1982 acquisition of Crum & Forster, a property and casualty insurance company, has called into question the company's strategy. It is unclear how Xerox, for whom high technology has been the chief competitive advantage, can earn excess returns in a business in which it has no experience. As we have already seen, firms that stick to their knitting are more likely to succeed than those that don't.

Common sense tells us that, in order to achieve excess returns over time, the distinctive competitive advantage held by the firm must be difficult or costly to replicate. If it is easily replicated, it will not take long for actual or potential competitors to apply the same concept, process, or organizational structure to their operations. The competitive advantage of experience, for example, will evaporate unless a firm can keep the tangible benefits of its experience proprietary and force its competitors to go through the same learning process. Once a firm loses its competitive advantage, its profits will erode to a point where it can no longer earn excess returns. For this reason, the firm's competitive advantage has to be constantly monitored and maintained so as to ensure the existence of an effective barrier to entry into the market. Should these barriers to entry break down, the firm must react quickly either to reconstruct them or build new ones.

Caterpillar has reacted to Komatsu's challenge by attempting to slash its costs, closing plants, shifting productions overseas, forcing union and nonunion workers alike to take pay cuts, eliminating many positions, and pressuring its suppliers to cut prices and speed deliveries. To get lower prices, the company is shopping around for hungrier suppliers, including foreign companies. This is reflected in its philosophy of worldwide sourcing, as described by its director of purchasing: "We're trying to become international in buying as well as selling. We expect our plants, regardless of where they're located, to look on a worldwide basis for sources of supply."[4] For example, German and Japanese companies now supply crankshafts once made exclusively in the U.S.

One important source of extra profit is the quickness of management to recognize and use information about new, lower-cost production opportunities. The excess profits, however, are temporary, lasting only until competitors discover these opportunities for themselves. For example, purchasing the latest equipment will provide a temporary cost advantage, but this advantage will disappear as soon as competitors buy the equipment for their own plants. Only if the equipment is proprietary will the firm be able to maintain its cost advantage. Along the same line, many American electronics and textile firms shifted production facilities to Taiwan, Hong Kong, and other Asian locations to take advantage of lower labor costs there. However, as more firms took advantage of this cost reduction opportunity, competition in the consumer electronics and textiles markets in the U.S. intensified, causing domestic prices to drop and excess profits to dissipate. In fact, firms in competitive industries must continually seize new non-proprietary cost reduction opportunities, not to earn excess returns but simply to make normal profits, or just survive.

Similarly, marketing-oriented firms can earn excess returns by being among the first to recognize and exploit new marketing opportunities. For example, Crown Cork & Seal, the Philadelphia-based bottle-top maker and can maker, reacted to slowing growth in its U.S. business by expanding overseas. It set up subsidiaries in such countries as Thailand, Malaysia, Ethiopia, Zambia, Peru, Ecuador, Brazil, and Argentina. In so doing, as it turns out, they guessed correctly that in those developing, urbanizing societies, people would eventually switch from home-grown produce to food in cans and drinks in bottles.

Profitable markets, however, have a habit of eventually attracting competition. Thus, to be assured of having a continued supply of value-creating investments on hand, the firm must institutionalize its strategy of cost reduction and/or product differentiation. Successful companies seem to do this by creating a corporate culture—a set of shared values, norms, and beliefs—that has as one of its elements an obsession with some facet of their performance in the marketplace. McDonald's has an obsessive concern for quality control, IBM for customer service, and 3M for innovation. Forrest Mars set the tone for his company by going into a rage if he found an improperly wrapped candy bar leaving the plant. In order to maintain its low-cost position in the structural steel market, Chapparal Steel has teams of workers and foremen scour the world in search of the latest production machinery and methods.

Conversely, AT&T's manufacturing orientation, which focused on producing durable products with few options, was well-suited to the regulated environment in which it operated throughout most of its existence. But such an

---

[4] As quoted in the *Wall Street Journal* (August 10, 1971), p. 1.

inward-looking orientation is likely to be a significant barrier to the company's ability to compete against the likes of IBM and other market-oriented, high-tech companies that react quickly to consumer demand. Prior to the breakup of AT&T, the manufacturers at Western Electric, AT&T's manufacturing arm, freely decided which products to make and when. They controlled the factories, supplying telephones to a captive market of Bell companies. AT&T was essentially an order taker, no more needing a sales force than any other utility does. There were no competitors forcing quicker market reaction nor any marketers challenging manufacturers' decisions.

Although AT&T claims that it is now "market-driven," evidence abounds that the company's older, entrenched manufacturing mentality is still dominant. Unless AT&T can change its corporate culture—a difficult and demanding task for any company, much less for a giant set in its ways—and marry manufacturing and marketing, it will have a difficult time competing with firms such as IBM in the office automation and computer businesses it has set its sights on.

The basic insight here is that sustained success in investing is not so much a matter of building new plants as of seeking out lower-cost production processes embodied in these plants, coming up with the right products for these plants to produce, and adding the service and quality features that differentiate these products in the marketplace. In other words, it comes down to people and how they are organized and motivated. The cost and difficulty of creating a corporate culture that adds value to capital investments is the ultimate barrier to entry; unlike the latest equipment, money alone can't buy it.

In the words of Maurice R. (Hank) Greenberg, president of American Insurance Group (A.I.G.), a worldwide network of insurance companies that has enjoyed spectacular success by pioneering in territory relatively unpopulated by competitors, "You can't imitate our global operation. It's just incapable of being reproduced. Domestically, we have some imitators for pieces of our business, but not the entire business. And in any event, you can only imitate what we've done. You can't imitate what we're thinking. You can't copy what we're going to do tomorrow."[5]

Corporate Strategy and Foreign Investment

Most of the firms we have discussed are multinational corporations (MNCs) with worldwide operations. For many of these MNCs, becoming multinational was the end result of an apparently haphazard process of overseas expansion. But, as international operations become a more important source of profit and as domestic and foreign competitors become more aggressive, it is apparent that domestic survival for many firms is increasingly dependent on their success overseas. To ensure this success, multinationals must develop global strategies that will enable them to maintain their competitive edge both at home and abroad.

---

[5] Wyndham Robertson, "Nobody Tops A.I.G. in Intricacy—or Daring," *Fortune*, May 22, 1978, p. 99.

Overseas Expansion and Survival

It is evident that if one's competitors gain access to lower-cost sources of production abroad, following them overseas may be a prerequisite for domestic survival. One strategy often followed by firms for whom cost is the key consideration, such as Chapparal Steel, is to develop a global scanning capability to seek out lower-cost production sites or production technologies worldwide.

Economies of Scale

A somewhat less obvious factor motivating foreign investment is the effect of economies of scale. We have already seen that in a competitive market, prices will be forced close to marginal costs of production. Hence, firms in industries characterized by high fixed costs relative to variable costs must engage in volume selling just to break even.

A new term has arisen to describe the size necessary in certain industries to compete effectively in the global marketplace: *world scale.* These large volumes may be forthcoming only if firms expand overseas. For example, companies manufacturing products such as mainframe computers that require huge R&D expenditures often need a larger customer base than that provided by even a market as large as the United States in order to recapture their investment in knowledge. Similarly, firms in capital-intensive industries with significant economies of scale in production may also be forced to sell overseas in order to spread their overhead over a higher volume of sales.

To take an extreme case, L.M. Ericsson, the highly successful Swedish manufacturer of telecommunications equipment, is forced to think internationally when designing new products since its domestic market is too small to absorb the enormous R&D expenditures involved and to reap the full benefit of production scale economies. Thus, when Ericsson developed its revolutionary AXE digital switching system, it geared its design to achieve global market penetration.

Many firms have found that a local market presence is necessary in order to continue selling overseas. For example, a local presence has helped Data General adapt the design of its U.S. computers and software to the Japanese market, giving the company a competitive edge over other U.S. companies selling computers in Japan. Data General has also adopted some Japanese manufacturing techniques and quality-control procedures that will improve its competitive position worldwide.

More firms are preparing for global competition. For example, although Black & Decker has a 50 percent market share worldwide in power tools, new competitors like the Japanese are forcing the company to change its manufacturing and marketing operations. Black & Decker's new strategy is based on a marketing concept known as "globalization," which holds that the world is becoming more homogenized and that distinctions between markets are disappearing. By selling standardized products worldwide, a firm can take advantage of economies of scale, thereby lowering costs and taking business from MNCs that customize products for individual markets. Until recently, the latter strategy of customization was the one that Black & Decker followed: the Italian subsidiary made tools for Italians, the British subsidiary tools for Britons.

By contrast, Japanese power-tool makers such as Makita Electric Works don't care that Germans prefer high-powered, heavy-duty drills and that Americans want everything lighter. Instead, Makita's strategy, which has been quite successful, is based on the notion that if you make a good drill at a low price, it will sell from Brooklyn to Baden-Baden. In response, Black & Decker recently unveiled 50 new power tools, each standardized for world production. It plans to standardize future products as well, making only minimal concessions, which require only minor modifications, to cultural differences.

Knowledge Seeking

Some firms enter foreign markets for the purpose of gaining information and experience that is expected to prove useful elsewhere. For instance, Beecham, an English firm, deliberately set out to learn from its U.S. operations how to be more competitive, first in the area of consumer products and later in pharmaceuticals. This knowledge proved highly valuable in competing with American and other firms in its European markets. Unilever, the Anglo-Dutch corporation, learned to adapt to world markets, with impressive results, the marketing skills it acquired in the U.S. through its American affiliate Lever Bros.

In industries characterized by rapid product innovation and technical breakthroughs by foreign competitors, it pays constantly to track overseas developments. The Japanese excel in this. Japanese firms systematically and effectively collect information on foreign innovation and disseminate it within their own research and development, marketing, and production groups. The analysis of new foreign products as soon as they reach the market is an especially long-lived Japanese technique. One of the jobs of Japanese researchers is to tear down a new foreign computer and analyze how it works as a base on which to develop a product of their own that will outperform the original. In a bit of a switch, as pointed out above, Data General's Japanese operation is giving the company a close look at Japanese technology, enabling it quickly to pick up and transfer back to the United States new information on Japanese innovations in the areas of computer design and manufacturing. Similarly, Ford Motor Co. has used its European operations as an important source of design and engineering ideas and management talent.

Designing a Global Expansion Strategy

The ability to pursue systematically policies and investments congruent with worldwide survival and growth depends on four interrelated elements.

1. The first, and the key to the development of a successful global strategy, is to understand and then capitalize on those factors that

have led to success in the past. In order for domestic firms to become global competitors, therefore, the sources of their domestic advantage must be transferable abroad. A competitive advantage predicated on government regulation, such as import restrictions, clearly doesn't fit in this category.

2. Second, this global approach to investment planning necessitates a systematic evaluation of individual entry strategies in foreign markets, a comparison of the alternatives, and selection of the optimal mode of entry.
3. The third important element is a continual audit of the effectiveness of current entry modes. As knowledge about a foreign market increases, for example, or sales potential grows, the optimal market penetration strategy will likely change.
4. Fourth, top management must be committed to becoming and/or staying a multinational corporation. Westinghouse demonstrated its commitment to international business by creating a new position of President-international and endowing its occupant with a seat on the company's powerful management committee. A truly globally oriented firm —one that asks, "Where in the *world* should we develop, produce, and sell our products and services?"—also requires an intelligence system capable of systematically scanning the world and understanding it, along with people who are experienced in international business and know how to use the information generated by the system.

Summary and Conclusions

We have seen that rates of return in competitive industries are driven down to their required returns. Excess profits quickly attract new entrants to the market, lowering returns until actual and required returns are again equal. Thus, the run-of-the-mill firm operating in a highly competitive market will be unable consistently to find positive net present value investments—ones which earn excess returns relative to their required returns. The key to generating a continual flow of positive NPV projects, therefore, is to erect and maintain barriers to entry against competitors. This involves either building defenses against potential competitors or finding positions in the industry where competition is the weakest.

The firm basically has two strategic options in its quest for competitive advantage: it can seek lower costs than its competitors or it can differentiate its product in a number of ways, including high advertising expenditures, product innovation, high product quality, and first-rate service.

Each of these options involves a number of specific investment decisions: construction of efficient-scale facilities and vigorous pursuit of cost reduction through accumulated experience, in the case of cost leadership; if product differentiation is the main goal, the focus is on advertising, R&D, quality control, customer-service facilities, distribution networks and the like. The more an investment widens a firm's competitive advantage and reduces the chances of successful replication by competitors, the greater the likelihood that investment will be successful.

Despite our understanding of the subject matter, it is difficult to give a set of rules to follow in developing profitable investment strategies. If it were possible to do so, competitors would follow them and dissipate any excess returns. One must be creative and quick to recognize new opportunities. Nevertheless, without dictating what should be done in every specific circumstance, there are some basic lessons we have learned from economic theory and the experiences of successful firms. The basic lessons are these:

1. Invest in projects that take advantage of your competitive edge. The corollary is, stick to doing one or two things and doing them well; don't get involved in businesses you are unfamiliar with.
2. Invest in developing, maintaining, and enhancing your competitive advantages.
3. Develop a global scanning capability. Don't be blindsided by new competitors or lower-cost production techniques or locations.
4. Pick market niches where there is little competition. Be prepared to abandon markets where competitors are catching up and apply your competitive advantages to new products or markets.

Assuming that a firm does have the necessary resources to be successful internationally, it must carefully plan for the transfer of these resources overseas. For example, it must consider how it can best utilize its marketing expertise, innovative technology, or production skills to penetrate a specific foreign market. Where a particular strategy calls for resources the firm lacks, such as an overseas distribution network, corporate management must first decide how and at what costs these resources can be acquired. It must then decide whether (and how) to acquire the resources or change its strategy.

Questions

1. The Coca-Cola Company earned an average annual return on shareholder equity of 20.3 percent during 1974–1983. During this same period, shareholders averaged only 2.9 percent annually on their investment in Coca-Cola's common stock. Explain why the shareholders earned only 2.9 percent annually while the company earned 20.3 percent annually.
2. Describe the characteristics of a perfectly competitive market. Why is it useful to understand these characteristics, even though perfectly competitive markets do not exist?
3. "... a firm can impose barriers to entry by potential competitors resulting in a less-than-perfectly competitive market and the possibility of positive NPV projects." Interpret the preceding statement. What kind of barriers to entry can a firm impose?

4. IBM is more profitable in the mainframe computer business than GE, RCA, and Xerox. Kroger and Winn-Dixie are more profitable supermarkets than A&P and National Tea. What factors account, in part, for these differences in profitability?
5. Briefly describe the strategic advantages of the following companies: (a) Coca-Cola, (b) Nalco Chemical, (c) Frito-Lay, (d) McDonald's, (e) Southwest Airlines, (f) Avon, (g) Vulcan Materials, and (h) Daimler Benz.
6. What basic strategies in capital budgeting does the author recommend?

Uncovering the Hidden Value in High-Risk Investments

David J. Sharp

While U.S. policy makers voice concern over their country's decline in international competitiveness, unprecedented changes are taking place in Europe. The economic consolidation of Western Europe and the movement from centrally planned to market-based economies in Eastern Europe provide some of the greatest investment opportunities today. But they also present some of the greatest business risks. This article suggests ways to enhance the investment appraisal process for very high-risk environments, such as those in Europe.

The U.S. decline, generally to the benefit of Pacific Rim countries, has been attributed, among other things, to western-trained managers' aversion to risk. However, their unwillingness to take risks is less a consequence of differences in national cultures and risk preferences than of a flawed institutional process for capital investment decision making. Control systems in western firms typically require a formal, quantitative, multistage procedure for project evaluation that involves a proposal, review, and reconsideration by higher management. Projects are accepted or rejected on the basis of some form of net-present-value (NPV) criterion. But NPV's effectiveness for investment appraisal is limited; the present value of an investment's cash flows excludes the valuable *options* embedded within the investment.[1] These options give the company the ability to take advantage of certain opportunities later. For projects with long-term strategic consequences, the options are frequently the most valuable part of the investment. Since NPV

At the time of this writing, David J. Sharp was an assistant professor of accounting at Boston College. I acknowledge with thanks the valuable research assistance of Michael Pollitt, comments of several colleagues at the Carroll School of Management, and research funding from Boston College.

Source: Reprinted from "Uncovering the Hidden Value in High-Risk Investments," by David J. Sharp, *Sloan Management Review*, Summer 1991, pp. 69–74, by permission of publisher.

[1] See R.A. Brealey and S.C. Myers, *Corporate Finance*, 3rd ed. (New York: McGraw Hill, 1988), pp. 495–514.

calculations understate value, a selection process driven by NPV will reject some potentially profitable projects.

The threat to competitiveness lies not in the possibility that managers will select investments that turn out to be unprofitable, but that they will *fail* to undertake very risky, but strategically vital, ones. If they follow control system requirements, they will reject projects that may be strategically important because the NPV analysis excludes options. If they follow their instinct and experience, they must override the formal, quantitative NPV analysis with the nebulous justification that the project must be undertaken "for strategic reasons." But top management will blame any subsequent problems with the project on their decision to defy the system, and a postaudit will reveal no data and analysis to justify their choice. Control systems penalize managers for accepting a venture that turns out to be unsuccessful, not for failing to undertake an investment that would have been very profitable.

Current financial theory supports the acceptance of a risky project in spite of its negative NPV, as do writers who recognize that discounted cash flow (DCF) analyses are often misused and fail to include the value of real options—for example, in justifying new manufacturing systems.[2] However, because only the simplest real options can be valued with any precision, it is hardly surprising that control systems rarely include them in formal quantitative analyses. To make matters worse, the option value actually *increases* with uncertainty and project duration; omitting options in the evaluation process is most harmful for high-risk, long-term projects.

Managers need a *practical*, *formal* procedure to support their intuition to accept highly uncertain and apparently unprofitable but strategically important projects. Without it, control systems will encourage them to err on the side of caution and reject investments that fail to meet NPV criteria, even though they make good business sense. This article is a step toward filling this void in the managerial decision-making tool kit. It adds a stage to the appraisal process in which managers identify, analyze, and approximately value the options embedded in high-risk investments, without recourse to complex option valuation formulas.

Understanding the nature and value of embedded options provides several benefits. First, by more precisely identifying the project's strategic value, managers can make more informed, and therefore better, investment decisions. Specifically, they can argue more soundly for valuable, risky projects that might otherwise be rejected, and better identify priorities among competing investments. Second, managers can identify the right tool for the decision-making job. The NPV is the wrong criterion for a proposed investment with significant options. Finally, option analysis can also help in the timing of decisions; it permits managers to distinguish between investments that are better made before

---

[2] See S.C. Myers, "Financial Theory and Financial Strategy," *Interfaces*, January-February 1984, pp. 126–137. J. Meredith and M. Hill, "Justifying New Manufacturing Systems: A Managerial Approach," *Sloan Management Review*, Summer 1987, pp. 49–61. R.S. Kaplan, "Must CIM Be Justified by Faith Alone?" *Harvard Business Review*, March-April 1986, pp. 87–95; and W.C. Kester, "Today's Options for Tomorrow's Growth," *Harvard Business Review*, March-April 1984, pp. 153–160.

environmental uncertainty is resolved (those with significant options) and those that should be deferred.

I illustrate these guidelines with a topical problem: planning for the creation of the single European market and responding to Eastern Europe's massive political and economic restructuring. However, the proposal has wide applicability since these kinds of uncertainties are typical, not unusual, and certainly not limited to Europe.

Investment Uncertainties in a New Europe

A single European market, with no barriers to the flow of goods, services, capital, and labor, is fast approaching, though few expect the process to be anywhere near completed by 1992. Much uncertainty, deriving from both government and industry, remains. We still don't know the relationship between Eastern European countries and the EC, and the role of reunified Germany, not to mention another half dozen or so potential new members. We also can't predict how individual EC member governments will protect their own industries. To the extent that policy makers place the interest of European competitiveness over local constituent pressures, the EC could become the greatest competitive force in the world. But if member governments continue their nationalistic agendas, they will never realize this potential. The unprecedented spate of mergers and strategic alliances among European firms also adds to the uncertainty. These aggressive firms, fired with a renewed enthusiasm for global battle, are changing the face of European competition.

Add to this uncertainty the political and economic changes in Eastern Europe. Its markets opening up to the West, and demand is great, but currencies are unconvertible. These countries no longer see foreign investment as a capitalist threat, yet property rights laws are unclear at best. And at the back of many minds lurks a nagging question: "What might happen in the Soviet Union?"

It is in this context of unprecedented change that an option analysis approach to investing has the most value.

A Decision-Making Process

My framework rests on two notions: that well-informed, experienced managerial judgment is an excellent, practical substitute for exact option valuation; and that managerial judgments must be embedded in a formal decision-making process. If managers can identify options, and if they understand the circumstances under which they would exercise them, then their estimate of the options' value is likely to be at least as good as a formal calculation using the "exact" Black-Scholes formula or its derivatives. The fact is that the precision of option value calculation is illusory; except for the simplest of options, calculation requires heroic assumptions and estimates.[3]

---

[3] Brealey and Myers (1988), p. 509.

An option is, in this context, *the ability, but not the obligation, to take advantage of opportunities available at a later date that would not have been possible without the earlier investment.* Unlike cash flows, whose value may be positive or negative, option values can never be less than zero, because they can always be abandoned. Embedded options can therefore only add to the value of an investment. Options are only valuable under uncertainty: if the future is perfectly predictable, they are worthless.

Figures 1 and 2 illustrate how cash flow and option value vary with project duration and environmental uncertainty. Figure 1 illustrates a short-term project, such as the investment required to retool an auto assembly line for a new model year. Its short duration and finite nature mean that it contains few options. A low-risk environment (no likelihood of oil shocks or rapid technological innovation) provides fewer options than a high-risk environment. For example, the manufacturer may want the option to install a smaller, more efficient engine, or a larger, more powerful one, as demand warrants. The ability to change engine size at some later date is more valuable when the future price of oil is uncertain.

Figure 2 illustrates a project with a large option component, such as an investment in a new product and market. Even in a fairly predictable environment, such as a mature technology, a new product introduction opens up several possibilities; over time, the company could modify the product, or find new uses and customers, based on its experience with the first investment. However, in an uncertain environment, such as one involving rapidly changing technology, the opportunities for finding new markets and developing improved products are even greater. The options' value could even exceed the expected cash flows from the initial product, as the high uncertainty bar shows.

FIGURE 1 SHORT-TERM PROJECT

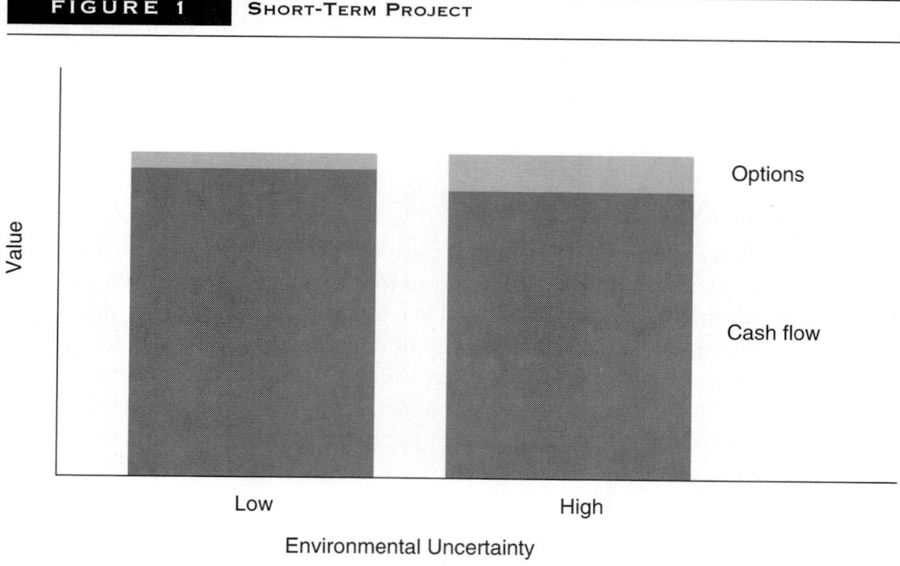

FIGURE 2 LONG-TERM PROJECT

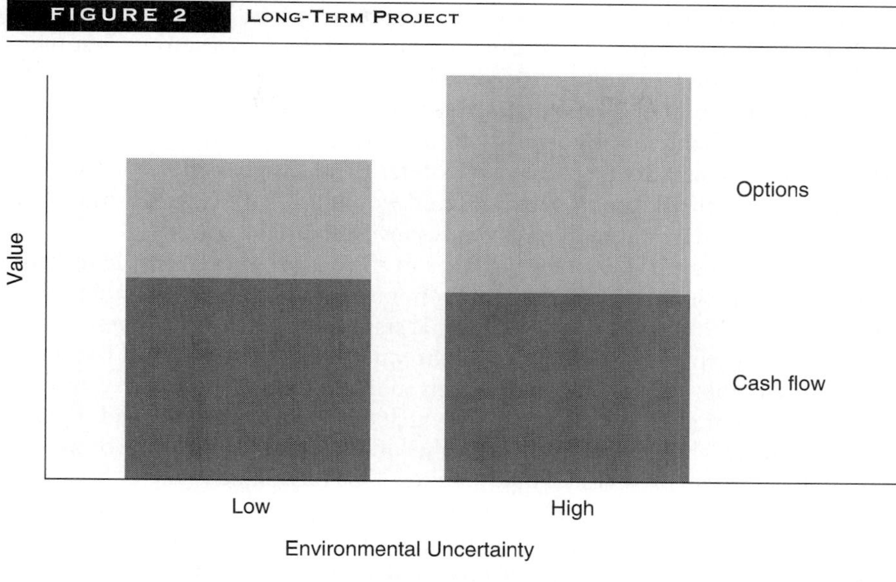

Because the European environment is very uncertain, and because many of the ventures currently under consideration there are open-ended, strategic investments, the options embedded in most of them have significant value. The NPV of their cash flows alone therefore seriously understates their total value, and managers who use NPV as the sole criterion will reject strategically important investments. The proposed procedure for identifying options could therefore be very useful.

Real options are of two types. The first are *incremental* in nature: they provide the firm with opportunities down the line to undertake profitable incremental investments. The example noted above—learning the characteristics of a new market that are transferrable to other markets—is typical of this type. In general, projects that create organizational learning that is applicable to subsequent similar investments contain incremental options. Virtually all investments contain options of this type; indeed, the ability to diffuse expertise across activities is at the core of economies of scope.

The second type is generated by *flexibility.*[4] Whereas incremental options require additional investment, flexibility options make use of investments already in place. If a project's cost structure can be changed fairly easily, such as by moving production if costs become expensive, then it contains a valuable flexibility option. A typical example is creating capacity in excess of immediate requirements at a second plant location, which allows managers to source from the alternative location, when production is interrupted.

---

[4] See B. Kogut, "Designing Global Strategies: Profiting from Operational Flexibility," *Sloan Management Review*, Fall 1985, pp. 27–38.

Most investments are an inseparable combination of both cash flows and options. For example, the introduction of a domestic product into its first overseas market not only creates value from the new cash flows, but also enables the firm to learn something about what makes it successful overseas. The firm therefore has the subsequent opportunity to introduce the product to other countries, if the prospects are favorable, or to defer the decision if they are not. This opportunity is valuable in its own right and would not have existed without the knowledge gained from the initial overseas investment.

The key to better investment choices in risky environments is the identification and valuation of the option components. In the absence of usable valuation methods, I propose a simple additional stage—consisting of three steps—in the investment appraisal process, after the valuation of cash flows. First, managers identify the options embedded in given investment. Second, they evaluate the environment and circumstances in which each might be exercised. Finally, managers judge whether the aggregate value of the options sufficiently outweighs any shortfall in the project's cash flow value. This technique is useful because it identifies more precisely *what* managers have to take into consideration over and above a project's cash flows (its options) and provides a simple binary decision criterion—are the options worth more than the shortfall in NPV?

Managers must not use these steps merely to justify weak proposals. They must subject the options identified in this stage to the same critical review process as they do the cash flows.

An Action Checklist

The following checklist elaborates on the procedure outlined above.

Identify Options

Consider the potential *incremental options* that might allow you to generate cash flows in addition to those explicitly included in the proposal. An important source of these options is *learning*. When a firm acquires and masters a new production technology or enters a new product or geographic market, the organization and its members gain new knowledge; they learn. They will likely be able to apply that learning elsewhere. New production or distribution technologies likewise require an organization to learn their effective use. They provide an opportunity to use that knowledge in previously unanticipated applications.

For example, Digital Equipment Corporation recently announced a joint venture in Hungary, after a ten-year enforced absence. While serving former customers will provide some revenue, most of the investment's value lies in the opportunity to participate in as yet unknown demand in areas such as telecommunications, which will arise from rebuilding of the country's infrastructure. Digital has the product range but needs to understand current demand. Likewise, service firms such as Price Waterhouse, which is already in Budapest and

Moscow and has plans for Warsaw and Prague, have established offices in Eastern Europe not in order to meet demand from existing clients, but to be in a position to serve unknown future needs.

Next, consider the *flexibility options* that might be created by capacity in excess of immediate requirements. Multiple sourcing is the obvious example; it provides management with not merely additional capacity but also with a sourcing *choice*. If the plants are physically separated, they almost certainly have different operating costs, which means that one of them will always be more attractive at any given time. An investment in general-purpose rather than specialized equipment buys a flexibility option. Valuable flexibility options can easily be built into a project through the choice of appropriate asset capacity and specificity.

Ford Motor Company recently announced plans for an automotive audio component manufacturing plant in Portugal. Since it already has similar plants in Brazil and Canada, the additional capacity will provide the option to locate worldwide production at the lowest cost site. If the Portuguese escudo were to depreciate significantly in real terms (or the Brazilian cruzado or Canadian dollar were to appreciate), the Portuguese plant would become more cost competitive. To the extent that the three plants are flexible, production can be moved from one plant to another as costs change. The Portuguese plant also provides some insurance against output interruptions from the other two plants.

Analyze Environmental Uncertainty

Options are only valuable in an uncertain environment. Uncertainty creates firm-specific opportunities: investments in which learning can be exploited and flexibility exercised.

Incremental options exist where future investment possibilities are more uncertain than usual. For instance, in Europe critical governmental decisions on procurement regulations and technical standards have yet to be made. European competitors are building strategic alliances through mergers and joint ventures. Any decision to invest now with an eye toward future investment opportunities must take these uncertainties into account.

The majority of recent foreign investments in Europe are motivated by incremental options—future opportunities, not current profitability. Investments provide the "foot in the door" without which future prospects are seriously jeopardized. Non-European firms fear that if they cannot be classified as European by 1992, the EC may be closed to them. AT&T's link with the Italian telecommunications company Italtel provided AT&T with exactly this status, as well as the opportunity to share in a $30 billion modernization of Italy's telephone system. In Eastern Europe, immediate business prospects are virtually nonexistent, but the long-term outlook is very promising. Digital admitted as much for their joint venture in Hungary.

Flexibility options are rarely the primary motivation for investments, but they are nevertheless valuable. Ford's investment in Portugal provides an option on real exchange rates. Its value increases with the variability of exchange rates, the degree of uncertainty in the two existing plants' output, and the flexibility of the production systems of all three plants. The history of the escudo's variability in real terms and prospects of unplanned shutdowns in existing plants could provide some indication of environmental uncertainty.

Value Project Options

First, compile a list of the options provided by the project together with the specific environment uncertainty under which exercising each option would be valuable. Then, make a subjective, but well-informed, assessment of the value of each. The simplest valuation process is to consider each option and ask, "How much would we be willing to pay now for this future flexibility or opportunity?" Or, for choices that could be made either now or later, "How much would we be willing to pay to defer this choice to a later date of our own choosing?" Unfortunately, the theory of option pricing rarely offer a simple answer. Instead, managers should recognize that their experience and wisdom are the best tools for judging the value of opportunities and flexibility.

However, some simple guidelines are available.[5] First, the value of options *increases with uncertainty*. When the environment is predictable, options have no value because all decisions can be made at the time of investment. However, when environmental uncertainty is high, the value of options is much greater. It follows paradoxically that investment decisions that primarily involve option acquisition—such as establishing a European presence without committing to a particular product line—should be undertaken *before* the uncertainty is resolved.

Similarly, flexibility options are most valuable when uncertainty is highest. Ford's ability to shift production is worth most when real exchange rates are very volatile but worth little if the European Monetary System can stabilize the escudo against the Brazilian cruzado and Canadian dollar in real terms. Kogut and Kulatilaka have simulated the value of options of this type for typical values of real exchange rate volatility.[6] Assuming that switching costs 2.5 percent of mean quarterly profits, they find that flexibility adds 5 percent to a project's expected annual return when the standard deviation of the real exchange rate is 5 percent per quarter, and 17 percent when the volatility is 20 percent per quarter. If a currency is 50 percent under- or overvalued at the time of investment, returns are reduced by about two percentage points.

Second, all other things equal, value *increases with the duration* of the option. For flexibility options, the longer the plants are expected to operate, the greater the value of flexibility. It is a square-root relationship; quadrupling the duration

---

[5] For the calculation of the value of simple incremental options, see: Brealey and Myers (1988), p. 503; for simple flexibility options, see: L. Trigeorgis and S.P. Mason, "Valuing Managerial Flexibility," *Midland Corporate Finance Journal*, Spring 1987, pp. 14–21.

[6] B. Kogut and N. Kulatilaka, "Multinational Flexibility and the Theory of Foreign Direct Investment" (Philadelphia: The Reginald H. Jones Center, The Wharton School, University of Pennsylvania, Working Paper No. 88-10, 1988).

doubles the option's value. But other things are rarely equal, especially for incremental options. Delaying the exercise of an incremental option increases the likelihood that a competitor will preempt its exercise. The life of an incremental option is finite, no longer than the time it takes the firm's fastest competitor to catch up.

Third, it is possible to place limits on option value. The lower bound is zero. The upper bound is the NPV of the most profitable alternative. In the case of an incremental option critical to the firm's survival, the value is very high; failing to acquire that option could cost the value of the firm.

Armed with a list of options and an estimate of their value, managers can make better-informed decisions on risky investments. While it is a simple matter to total the value of all the options and add it to the value of the cash flows, in practice it is sufficient to decide only whether their aggregate value exceeds the shortfall in the cash flow value.

Conclusion

Avoiding risk is a recipe for missing vital opportunities, which leads to competitive decline. Formal investment appraisal procedures invariably omit an important component of value, namely embedded options. Because option value is greatest for long-term, high-risk investments, and because many decisions critical to a company's competitiveness are of this type, a formal procedure to guide managers' attempts to value the option component of investments is a useful decision-making tool. The foregoing enhancement to the investment appraisal process provides a simple means to identify options and value them approximately, without resorting to complex calculations. It provides criteria by which managers can identify an investment's nebulous "strategic value." It forces managers to think through their responses to uncertainty in an organized way. This leads to improved project design. For example, managers may discover that, with minimal additional cost, they can build more flexibility into a project, enhancing its value even further. This procedure also permits a planned corporate response to uncertainty, rather than a merely reactive response. Most important, a formal decision-making process can justify high-risk, competitiveness-enhancing investments that would be rejected under the overly narrow criterion of project appraisal systems using only NPV.

Questions

1. What is "the hidden value in high-risk investments?"
2. An *option* may be defined as a contract that gives the holder the right, but not the obligation, to buy or sell an asset at a stated price during a specified period of time. What is a call option? A put option?
3. "To make matters worse, the option value actually *increases* with uncertainty…" To illustrate, consider a 3-month call option (on common stock) with a $50 exercise price. If the price of the underlying stock is also $50 and there is no chance for it to

change, then the value of the option is zero. In contrast, if there is 50 percent probability of the stock trading for either $25 or $100 before the option expires, then the option has value. A $25 stock price causes the option to be worth zero, but a $100 stock price causes it to be worth $50. Based on the probabilities, what is the expected value of the option? (*Note*: Unlike the stockholder, the owner of the call option benefits from a volatile stock price.)

4. The management of ABC Motors decides to open a plant in Poland even though the project has a negative net present value. Management views the investment as having strategic value. Describe the embedded option (also called a real option) associated with this "foot-in-the-door" strategy.
5. Midsouth Electric plans to construct a new electric power plant. A coal-fired plant costs about the same as an oil-fired plant, but a flexible plant that burns either coal or oil costs 30 percent more. Because of the uncertainty surrounding the future price of coal and of oil, management chooses the flexible plant. Describe the embedded option associated with the flexible plant.
6. Describe the real option in each of the following cases:

    - Management postpones the plant expansion for a new product even though it has a positive net present value. The delay will help management learn more about demand for the product.
    - Valero Company owns and runs a copper mine that has low fixed costs but high variable costs. When copper prices fall unexpectedly, management temporarily shuts down the mining operation.
    - Diamond Shamrock's oil refinery transforms crude oil into gasoline, jet fuel, heating oil, and other products. Management alters the product mix depending on the relative prices of the products.

7. "The key to better investment choices in risky environments is the identification and valuation of the option components. In the absence of usable valuation methods, I propose a simple additional stage—consisting of three steps—in the investment appraisal process, after the valuation of cash flows." Describe the author's proposal.

Finance Theory and Financial Strategy

STEWART C. MYERS

Despite its major advances, finance theory has had scant impact on strategic planning. Strategic planning needs finance and should learn to apply finance theory correctly. However, finance theory must be extended in order to reconcile financial and strategic analysis.

Strategic planning is many things, but it surely includes the process of deciding how to commit the firm's resources across lines of business. The financial side of strategic planning allocates a particular resource, capital.

Finance theory has made major advances in understanding how capital markets work and how risky real and financial assets are valued. Tools derived from finance theory, particularly discounted cash-flow analysis, are widely used. Yet finance theory has had scant impact on strategic planning.

I attempt here to explain the gap between finance theory and strategic planning. Three explanations are offered:

1. Finance theory and traditional approaches to strategic planning may be kept apart by differences in language and "culture."
2. Discounted cash flow analysis may have been misused, and consequently not accepted, in strategic applications.
3. Discounted cash flow analysis may fail in strategic applications even if it is properly applied.

Each of these explanations is partly true. I do not claim that the three, taken together, add up to the whole truth. Nevertheless, I will describe both the problems encountered in applying finance theory to strategic planning, and the potential payoffs if the theory can be extended and properly applied.

At the time of this writing, Stewart C. Myers was affiliated with the Sloan School of Management at the Massachusetts Institute of Technology.

Source: MIT Sloan School of Management.

The first task is to explain what is meant by "finance theory" and the gap between it and strategic planning.

The Relevant Theory

The financial concepts most relevant to strategic planning are those dealing with firms' capital investment decisions, and they are sketched here at the minimum level of detail necessary to define "finance theory."

Think of each investment project as a mini-firm, all-equity financed. Suppose its stock could be actively traded. If we know what the mini-firm's stock would sell for, we know its present value, and therefore the project's present value. We calculate the net present value (NPV) by subtracting the required investment.

In other words, we calculate each project's present value to investors who have free access to capital markets. We should therefore use the valuation model which best explains the prices of similar securities. However, the theory is usually boiled down to a single model, discounted cash flow (DCF):

$$PV = \sum_{t=1}^{T} \frac{C_t}{(1+r)^t}$$

where

PV = present (market) value;

C_t = forecasted incremental cash flow after corporate taxes—strictly speaking the mean of the distribution of possible $\tilde{C}_t$s;

T = project life (C_T includes any salvage value);

r = the opportunity cost of capital, defined as the equilibrium expected rate of return on securities equivalent in risk to the project being valued.

NPV equals *PV* less the cash outlay required at $t = 0$.

Since present values add, the value of the firm should equal the sum of the values of all its mini-firms. If the DCF formula works for each project separately, it should work for any collection of projects, a line of business, or the firm as a whole. A firm or line of business consists of intangible as well as tangible assets, and growth opportunities as well as assets-in-place. Intangible assets and growth opportunities are clearly reflected in stock prices, and in principle can also be valued in capital budgeting. Projects bringing intangible assets or growth opportunities to the firm have correspondingly higher *NPV*s. I will discuss whether DCF formulas can capture this extra value later.

The opportunity cost of capital varies from project to project, depending on risk. In principle, each project has its own cost of capital. In practice, firms simplify by grouping similar projects in risk classes, and use the same cost of capital for all projects in a class.

The opportunity cost of capital for a line of business, or for the firm, is a value-weighted average of the opportunity costs of capital for the projects it comprises.

The opportunity cost of capital depends on the use of funds, not on the source. In most cases, financing has a second-order impact on value: You can make much more money through smart investment decisions than smart financing decisions. The advantage, if any, of departing from all-equity financing is typically adjusted for through a somewhat lowered discount rate.

Finance theory stresses cash flow and the expected return on competing assets. The firm's investment opportunities compete with securities stockholders can buy. Investors willingly invest, or reinvest, cash in the firm only if it can do better, risk considered, than the investors can do on their own.

Finance theory thus stresses fundamentals. It should not be deflected by accounting allocations, except as they affect cash taxes. For example, suppose a positive-*NPV* project sharply reduces book earnings in its early stages. Finance theory would recommend forging ahead, trusting investors to see through the accounting bias to the project's true value. Empirical evidence indicates that investors do see through accounting biases; they do not just look naively at last quarter's or last year's EPS. (If they did, all stocks would sell at the same price-earnings ratio.)

All these concepts are generally accepted by financial economists. The concepts are broadly consistent with an up-to-date understanding of how capital markets work. Moreover, they seem to be accepted by firms, at least in part: any time a firm sets a hurdle rate based on capital market evidence, and uses a DCF formula, it must implicitly rely on the logic I have sketched. So the issue here is not whether managers accept finance theory for capital budgeting (and for other financial purposes). It is why they do not use the theory in strategic planning.

The Gap between Finance Theory and Strategic Planning

I have resisted referring to strategic planning as "capital budgeting on a grand scale," because capital budgeting in practice is a bottom-up process. The aim is to find and undertake specific assets or projects that are worth more than they cost.

Picking valuable pieces does not insure maximum value for the whole. Piecemeal, bottom-up capital budgeting is not strategic planning.

Capital budgeting techniques, however, ought to work for the whole as well as the parts. A strategic commitment of capital to a line of business is an investment project. If management does invest, they must believe the value of the firm increases by more than the amount of capital committed—otherwise they are throwing money away. In other words, there is an implicit estimate of net present value.

This would seem to invite the application of finance theory, which explains how real and financial assets are valued. The theory should have direct application not only to capital budgeting, but also to the financial side of strategic planning.

Of course it has been applied to some extent. Moreover, strategic planning seems to be becoming more financially sophisticated. Financial concepts are stressed in several recent books on corporate strategy [Fruhan 1979; Salter and Weinhold 1979; and Bierman 1980]. Consulting firms have developed the concepts' strategic implications [Alberts 1983].

Nevertheless, I believe it is fair to say that most strategic planners are not guided by the tools of modern finance. Strategic and financial analyses are not reconciled, even when the analyses are of the same major project. When low net present value projects are nurtured "for strategic reasons," the strategic analysis overrides measures of financial value. Conversely, projects with apparently high net present values are passed by if they don't fit in with the firm's strategic objectives. When financial and strategic analyses give conflicting answers, the conflict is treated as a fact of life, not as an anomaly demanding reconciliation.

In many firms, strategic analysis is partly or largely directed to variables finance theory says are irrelevant. This is another symptom of the gap, for example:

1. Many managers worry about a strategic decision's impact on book rate of return or earnings per share. If they are convinced the plan adds to the firm's value, its impact on accounting figures should be irrelevant.
2. Some managers pursue diversification to reduce risk—risk as they see it. Investors see a firm's risk differently. In capital markets, diversification is cheap and easy. Investors who want to diversify do so on their own. Corporate diversification is redundant; the market will not pay extra for it.

If the market were willing to pay extra for diversification, closed-end funds would sell at premiums over net asset value, and conglomerate firms would be worth more to investors than their components separately traded. Closed-end funds actually sell at discounts, not premiums. Conglomerates appear to sell at discounts too, although it is hard to prove it, since the firm's components are not traded separately.

Much of the literature of strategic planning seems extremely naive from a financial point of view. Sometimes capital markets are ignored. Sometimes firms are essentially viewed as having a fixed stock of capital, so that "cash cows" are needed to finance investment in rapidly growing lines of business. (The firms that pioneered in strategic planning actually had easy access to capital markets, as do almost all public companies.) Firms may not like the price they pay for capital, but that price is the opportunity cost of capital, the proper standard for new investment by the firm.

The practical conflicts between finance and strategy are part of what lies behind the recent criticism of U.S. firms for allegedly concentrating on quick payoffs at the expense of value. U.S. executives, especially M.B.A.s, are said to rely too much on purely financial analysis, and too little on building technology, products, markets, and production efficiency. The financial world is not the real world, the argument goes; managers succumb to the glamour of high finance. They give time and talent to mergers, spinoffs, unusual securities, and complex financing packages when they should be out on the factory floor. They pump up current earnings per share at the expense of long-run values.

Much of this criticism is not directed against finance theory, but at habits of financial analysis that financial economists are attempting to reform. Finance theory of course concentrates on the financial world—that is, capital markets. However, it fundamentally disagrees with the implicit assumption of the critics, who say that the financial world is not the real world, and that financial analysis diverts attention from, and sometimes actively undermines, real long-run values. The professors and textbooks actually say that financial values rest on real values and that most value is created on the left-hand side of the balance sheet, not on the right.

Finance theory, however, is under attack too. Some feel that any quantitative approach is inevitably short-sighted. Hayes and Garvin, for example, have blamed discounted cash flow for a significant part of this country's industrial difficulties. Much of their criticism seems directed to misapplications of discounted cash flow, some of which I discuss later. But they also believe the underlying theory is wanting; they say that "beyond all else, capital investment represents an act of faith" [Hayes and Garvin 1982, p. 79]. This statement offends most card-carrying financial economists.

I do not know whether "gap" fully describes all of the problems noted, or hinted at, in the discussion so far. In some quarters, finance theory is effectively ignored in strategic planning. In others, it is seen as being in conflict, or working at cross-purposes, with other forms of strategic analysis. The problem is to explain why.

Two Cultures and One Problem

Finance theory and strategic planning could be viewed as two cultures looking at the same problem. Perhaps only differences in language and approach make the two appear incompatible. If so, the gap between them might be bridged by better communication and a determined effort to reconcile them.

Think of what can go wrong with standard discounted cash flow analyses of a series of major projects:

1. Even careful analyses are subject to random error. There is a 50 percent probability of a positive *NPV* for a truly border-line project.
2. Firms have to guard against these errors dominating project choice.
3. Smart managers apply the following check. They know that all projects have zero *NPV* in long-run competitive equilibrium. Therefore, a positive *NPV* must be explained by a short-run deviation from equilibrium or by some permanent competitive advantage. If neither explanation applies, the positive *NPV* is suspect. Conversely, a negative *NPV* is suspect if a competitive advantage or short-run deviation from equilibrium favors the project.

In other words, smart managers do not accept positive (or negative) *NPVs* unless they can explain them.

Strategic planning may serve to implement this check. Strategic analyses look for market opportunities—deviations from equilibrium—and try to identify the firm's competitive advantages.

Turn the logic of the example around. We can regard strategic analysis, which does not explicitly compute *NPV*s as showing absolute faith in Adam Smith's invisible hand. If a firm, looking at a line of business, finds a favorable deviation from long-run equilibrium, or if it identifies a competitive advantage, then (efficient) investment in that line must offer profits exceeding the opportunity cost of capital. No need to calculate the investment's *NPV*: the manager knows in advance that *NPV* is positive.

The trouble is that strategic analyses are also subject to random error. Mistakes are also made in identifying areas of competitive advantage or out-of-equilibrium markets. We would expect strategic analysts to calculate *NPV*s explicitly, at least as a check; strategic analysis and financial analysis ought to be explicitly reconciled. Few firms attempt this. This suggests the gap between strategic planning and finance theory is more than just "two cultures and one problem."

The next step is to ask why reconciliation is so difficult.

Misuse of Finance Theory

The gap between strategic and financial analysis may reflect misapplication of finance theory. Some firms do not try to use theory to analyze strategic investments. Some firms try but make mistakes.

I have already noted that in many firms capital investment analysis is partly or largely directed to variables finance theory says are irrelevant. Managers worry about projects' book rates of return or impacts on book earnings per share. They worry about payback, even for projects that clearly have positive *NPV*s. They try to reduce risk through diversification.

Departing from theoretically correct valuation procedures often sacrifices the long-run health of the firm for the short, and makes capital investment choices arbitrary or unpredictable. Over time, these sacrifices appear as disappointing growth, eroding market share, loss of technological leadership, and so forth.

The non-financial approach taken in many strategic analyses may be an attempt to overcome the short horizons and arbitrariness of financial analysis as it is often misapplied. It may be an attempt to get back to fundamentals. Remember, however: finance theory never left the fundamentals. Discounted cash flow should not in principle bias the firm against long-lived projects, or be swayed by arbitrary allocations.

However, the typical mistakes made in applying DCF do create a bias against long-lived projects. I will note a few common mistakes.

Ranking on Internal Rate of Return

Competing projects are often ranked on internal rate of return rather than *NPV*. It is easier to earn a high rate of return if project life is short and investment is small. Long-lived, capital-intensive projects tend to be put down the list even if their net present value is substantial.

The internal rate of return does measure bang per buck on a DCF basis. Firms may favor it because they think they have only a limited number of bucks. However, most firms big enough to do formal strategic planning have free access to capital markets. They may not like the price, but they can get the money. The limits on capital expenditures are more often set inside the firm, in order to control an organization too eager to spend money. Even when a firm does have a strictly limited pool of capital, it should not use the internal rate of return to rank projects. It should use *NPV* per dollar invested, or linear programming techniques when capital is rationed in more than one period [Brealey and Myers 1981, pp. 101–107].

Inconsistent Treatment of Inflation

A surprising number of firms treat inflation inconsistently in DCF calculations. High nominal discount rates are used but cash flows are not fully adjusted for future inflation. Thus accelerating inflation makes projects—especially long-lived ones—look less attractive even if their real value is unaffected.

Unrealistically High Rates

Some firms use unrealistically high discount rates, even after proper adjustment for inflation. This may reflect ignorance of what normal returns in capital markets really are. In addition:

1. Premiums are tacked on for risks that can easily be diversified away in stockholders' portfolios.
2. Rates are raised to offset the optimistic biases of managers sponsoring projects. This adjustment works only if the bias increases geometrically with the forecast period. If it does not, long-lived projects are penalized.
3. Some projects are unusually risky at inception, but only of normal-risk once the start-up is successfully passed. It is easy to classify this type of project as "high-risk," and to add a start-up risk premium to the discount rate for all future cash flows. The risk premium should be applied to the startup period only. If it is applied after the startup period, safe, short-lived projects are artificially favored.

Discounted cash flow analysis is also subject to a difficult organizational problem. Capital budgeting is usually a bottom-up process. Proposals originate in the organization's midriff, and have to survive the trip to the top, getting approval at every stage. In the process political alliances form, and cash flow forecasts are bent to meet known standards. Answers—not necessarily the right ones—are worked out for anticipated challenges. Most projects that get to the top seem to meet profitability standards set by management.

According to Brealey and Myers's Second Law, "The proportion of proposed projects having positive NPV is independent of top management's estimate of the opportunity cost of capital" [Brealey and Myers 1981, p. 238].

Suppose the errors and biases of the capital budgeting process make it extremely difficult for top management to verify the true cash flows, risks and present value of capital investment proposals. That would explain why firms do not try to reconcile the results of capital budgeting and strategic analyses. However, it does not explain why strategic planners do not calculate their own *NPV*s.

We must ask whether those in top management—the managers who make strategic decisions—understand finance theory well enough to use DCF analysis effectively. Although they certainly understand the arithmetic of the calculation, they may not understand the logic of the method deeply enough to trust it or to use it without mistakes.

They may also not be familiar enough with how capital markets work to use capital market data effectively. The widespread use of unrealistically high discount rates is probably a symptom of this.

Finally, many managers distrust the stock market. Its volatility makes them nervous, despite the fact that the volatility is the natural result of a rational market. It may be easier to underestimate the sophistication of the stock market than to accept its verdict on how well the firm is doing.

Finance Theory May Have Missed the Boat

Now consider a firm that understands finance theory, applies DCF analysis correctly, and has overcome the human and organizational problems that bias cash flows and discount rates. Carefully estimated net present values for strategic investments should help significantly. However, would they fully grasp and describe the firm's strategic choices? Perhaps not.

There are gaps in finance theory as it is usually applied. These gaps are not necessarily intrinsic to finance theory generally. They may be filled by new approaches to valuation. However, if they are, the firm will have to use something more than a straightforward discounted cash flow method.

An intelligent application of discounted cash flow will encounter four chief problems:

1. Estimating the discount rate,
2. Estimating the project's future cash flows,
3. Estimating the project's impact on the firm's other assets' cash flows, that is through the cross-sectional links between projects, and
4. Estimating the project's impact on the firm's future investment opportunities. These are the time series links between projects.

The first three problems, difficult as they are, are not as serious for financial strategy as the fourth. However, I will review all four.

Estimating the Opportunity Cost of Capital

The opportunity cost of capital will always be difficult to measure, since it is an expected rate of return. We cannot commission the Gallup Poll to extract probability distributions from the minds of investors. However, we have extensive evidence on past average rates of return in capital markets [Ibbotson and Sinquefield 1982] and the corporate sector [Holland and Myers 1979]. No long-run trends in "normal" rates of return are evident. Reasonable, ballpark cost of capital estimates can be obtained if obvious traps (for example, improper adjustments for risk or inflation) are avoided. In my opinion, estimating cash flows properly is more important than fine-tuning the discount rate.

Forecasting Cash Flow

It's impossible to forecast most projects' actual cash flows accurately. DCF calculations do not call for accurate forecasts, however, but for accurate assessments of the mean of possible outcomes.

Operating managers can often make reasonable subjective forecasts of the operating variables they are responsible for—operating costs, market growth, market share, and so forth—at least for the future that they are actually worrying about. It is difficult for them to translate this knowledge into a cash flow forecast for, say, year seven. There are several reasons for this difficulty. First, the operating manager is asked to look into a far future he is not used to thinking about. Second, he is asked to express his forecast in accounting rather than operating variables. Third, incorporating forecasts of macroeconomic variables is difficult. As a result, long-run forecasts often end up as mechanical extrapolations of short-run trends. It is easy to overlook the long-run pressures of competition, inflation, and technical change.

It should be possible to provide a better framework for forecasting operating variables and translating them into cash flows and present value—a framework that makes it easier for the operating manager to apply his practical knowledge, and that explicitly incorporates information about macroeconomic trends. There is, however, no way around it: forecasting is intrinsically difficult, especially when your boss is watching you do it.

Estimating Cross-Sectional Relationships between Cash Flows

Tracing "cross-sectional" relationships between project cash flows is also intrinsically difficult. The problem may be made more difficult by inappropriate project definitions or boundaries for lines of businesses. Defining business units properly is one of the tricks of successful strategic planning.

However, these inescapable problems in estimating profitability standards, future cash returns, and cross-sectional interactions are faced by strategic planners even if they use no financial theory. They do not reveal a flaw in existing theory. Any theory or approach encounters them. Therefore, they do not explain the gap between finance theory and strategic planning.

The Links between Today's Investments and Tomorrow's Opportunities

The fourth problem—the link between today's investments and tomorrow's opportunities—is much more difficult.

Suppose a firm invests in a negative-*NPV* project in order to establish a foothold in an attractive market. Thus a valuable second-stage investment is used to justify the immediate project. The second-stage must depend on the first: if the firm could take the second project without having taken the first, then the future opportunity should have no impact on the immediate decision. However, if tomorrow's opportunities depend on today's decisions, there is a time-series link between projects.

At first glance, this may appear to be just another forecasting problem. Why not estimate cash flows for both stages, and use discounted cash flow to calculate the *NPV* for the two stages taken together?

You would not get the right answer. The second stage is an option, and conventional discounted cash flow does not value options properly. The second stage is an option because the firm is not committed to undertake it. It will go ahead if the first stage works and the market is still attractive. If the first stage fails, or if the market sours, the firm can stop after Stage 1 and cut its losses. Investing in Stage 1 purchases an intangible asset: a call option on Stage 2. If the option's present value offsets the first stage's negative *NPV*, the first stage is justified.

The Limits of Discounted Cash Flow

The limits of DCF need further explanation. Think first of its application to four types of securities:

1. DCF is standard for valuing bonds, preferred stocks and other fixed-income securities.
2. DCF is sensible, and widely used, for valuing relatively safe stocks paying regular dividends.
3. DCF is not as helpful in valuing companies with significant growth opportunities. The DCF model can be stretched to say that Apple Computer's stock price equals the present value of the dividends the firm may eventually pay. It is more helpful to think of Apple's price, P_0, as:

$$P_0 = \frac{EPS}{r} + PVGO,$$

where

EPS	=	normalized current earnings
r	=	the opportunity cost of capital
$PVGO$	=	the net present value of future growth opportunities.

Note that *PVGO* is the present value of a portfolio of options—the firm's options to invest in second-stage, third-stage, or even later projects.

4. DCF is never used for traded calls or puts. Finance theory supplies option valuation formulas that work, but the option formulas look nothing like DCF.

Think of the corporate analogs to these securities:

1. There are few problems in using DCF to value safe flows, for example, flows from financial leases.
2. DCF is readily applied to "cash cows"—relatively safe businesses held for the cash they generate, rather than for strategic value. It also works for "engineering investments," such as machine replacements, where the main benefit is reduced cost in a clearly defined activity.
3. DCF is less helpful in valuing businesses with substantial growth opportunities or intangible assets. In other words, it is not the whole answer when options account for a large fraction of a business' value.
4. DCF is no help at all for pure research and development. The value of R&D is almost all option value. Intangible assets' value is usually option value.

The theory of option valuation has been worked out in detail for securities—not only puts and calls, but warrants, convertibles, bond call options, and so forth. The solution techniques should be applicable to the real options held by firms. Several preliminary applications have already been worked out, for example:

1. Calculations of the value of a federal lease for offshore exploration for oil or gas. Here the option value comes from the lessee's right to delay the decisions to drill and develop, and to make these decisions after observing the extent of reserves and the future level of oil prices [Paddock, Siegel, and Smith 1983].
2. Calculating an asset's abandonment or salvage value: an active second-hand market increases an asset's value, other things equal. The second-hand market gives the asset owner a put option which increases the value of the option to bail out of a poorly performing project [Myers and Majd 1983].

The option "contract" in each of these cases is fairly clear: a series of calls in the first case and a put in the second. However, these real options last longer and are more complex than traded calls and puts. The terms of real options have to be extracted from the economics of the problem at hand. Realistic descriptions usually lead to a complex implied "contract," requiring numerical methods for valuation.

Nevertheless, option pricing methods hold great promise for strategic analysis. The time-series links between projects are the most important part of financial strategy. A mixture of DCF and option valuation models can, in principle, describe these links and give a better understanding of how they work. It may also be possible to estimate the value of particular strategic options, thus eliminating one reason for the gap between finance theory and strategic planning.

Lessons for Corporate Strategy

The task of strategic analysis is more than laying out a plan or plans. When time-series links between projects are important, it's better to think of strategy as managing the firm's portfolio of real options [Kestler 1982]. The process of financial planning may be thought of as:

1. Acquiring options, either by investing directly in R&D, product design, cost or quality improvements, and so forth, or as a by-product of direct capital investment (for example, investing in a Stage 1 project with negative *NPV* in order to open the door for Stage 2).
2. Abandoning options that are too far "out of the money" to pay to keep.
3. Exercising valuable options at the right time—that is, buying the cash producing assets that ultimately produce positive net present value.

There is also a lesson for current applications of finance theory to strategic issues. Several new approaches to financial strategy use a simple, traditional DCF model of the firm [For example, Fruhan 1979, Ch. 2]. These approaches are likely to be more useful for cash cows than for growth businesses with substantial risk and intangible assets.

The option value of growth and intangibles is not ignored by good managers even when conventional financial techniques miss them. These values may be brought in as "strategic factors," dressed in non-financial clothes. Dealing with the time-series links between capital investments, and with the option value these links create, is often left to strategic planners. But new developments in finance theory promise to help.

Bridging the Gap

We can summarize by asking how the present gap between finance theory and strategic planning might be bridged.

Strategic planning needs finance. Present value calculations are needed as a check on strategic analysis and vice versa. However, the standard discounted cash flow techniques will tend to understate the option value attached to growing profitable lines of business. Corporate finance theory requires extension to deal with real options. Therefore, to bridge the gap we on the financial side need to:

1. Apply existing finance theory correctly.
2. Extend the theory. I believe the most promising line of research is to try to use option pricing theory to model the time-series interactions between investments.

Both sides could make a conscious effort to reconcile financial and strategic analysis. Although complete reconciliation will rarely be possible, the attempt should uncover hidden assumptions and bring a generally deeper understanding of strategic choices. The gap may remain, but with better analysis on either side of it.

References

Alberts, W.A. and McTaggart, James M. 1984, "Value based strategic investment planning," *Interfaces*, Vol. 14, No. 1 (January-February), pp. 138–151.

Bierman, H. 1980, *Strategic Financial Planning*, The Free Press, New York.

Brealey, R.A. and Myers, S.C. 1981, *Principles of Corporate Finance*, McGraw-Hill Book Company, New York.

Foster, G. 1978, *Financial Statement Analysis*, Prentice-Hall, Inc., Englewood Cliffs, New Jersey.

Fruhan, W.E., Jr., 1979, *Financial Strategy: Studies in the Creation, Transfer and Destruction of Shareholder Value*, Richard D. Irwin, Inc., Homewood, Illinois.

Hayes, R.H. and Garvin, D.A. 1982, "Managing as if tomorrow mattered," *Harvard Business Review*, Vol. 60, No. 3 (May-June), pp. 70–79.

Holland, D. M. and Myers, S. C. 1979, "Trends in corporate profitability and capital costs," in R. Lindsay, ed., *The Nation's Capital Needs: Three Studies*, Committee on Economic Development, Washington, DC.

Ibbotson, R.G. and Sinquefield, R.A. 1982, *Stocks, Bonds, Bills and Inflation: The Past and the Future*, Financial Analysts Research Foundation, Charlottesville, Virginia.

Myers, S.C. and Majd, S. 1983, "Applying option pricing theory to the abandonment value problem," Sloan School of Management, MIT, Working Paper.

Paddock, J.L.; Siegel, D.; and Smith, J.L. 1983, "Option valuation of claims on physical assets: the case of offshore petroleum leases," Working Paper, MIT Energy Laboratory, Cambridge, Massachusetts.

Salter, M.S. and Weinhold, W.A. 1979, *Diversification Through Acquisition*, The Free Press, New York.

Questions

1. "The opportunity cost of capital depends on the use of funds, not on the source." Explain the meaning of this statement.
2. The objective of capital budgeting is to invest in projects that are worth more than they cost. Explain how net present value relates to this objective.
3. Why do capital projects have net present values of zero in long-run competitive equilibrium? Do capital projects necessarily have net present values of zero in short-run competitive equilibrium? Explain.

4. Explain why net present value, properly used, will not bias a company against long-lived capital projects.
5. According to the author, what are some possible misuses of finance theory in capital budgeting?
6. Define a call option and a put option.
7. Financial analysts who properly apply discounted cash flow in capital budgeting may still encounter problems in estimating: (a) the discount rate, (b) future cash flows from the project, (c) the impact of the project on cash flows of other company projects, and (d) the impact of the project on the company's future investment opportunities. Describe why an analyst might experience difficulty in estimating each of these four variables.

PART
IV

Managing Working Capital

Innovations in Short-Term Financial Management

WILLIAM L. SARTORIS AND NED C. HILL

People used to call short-term financial management "working capital management." This term focused attention on the accounting definition of working capital, current assets, and current liabilities. More recently, "short-term financial management" has been used to focus attention on all decisions of an organization that affect cash flows in the short term—usually less than a year.

The cash flows for most organizations can be thought of in three ways: "permanent" cash inflows, primarily collections resulting from sales; internal cash flows; and "permanent" cash outflows, primarily payments to vendors and employees. The cash inflows and outflows are usually consequences of operating decisions. Internal cash flows consist either of cash being moved within the firm or "temporary" cash flows, such as an investment in a marketable security or a takedown under a line of credit. Some internal cash flows may involve external agents, but the intent is that the cash flow will be reversed at some future time. Internal cash flows usually are between a liquidity reserve, in the form of available cash or marketable securities, and backup liquidity, in the form of credit arrangements or access to additional credit.

Although the treasury manager—perhaps called cash manager, assistant treasurer, or treasurer—has direct responsibility for managing the short-term cash flows, the operating activities that generate the cash flows are frequently controlled by others in the organization. The players and the impact of their decisions on the timing and amount of cash flows are illustrated in Figure 1. For example, in the selling activities of a firm, credit and marketing managers have a major influence on the sequence of orders and the timing and form of payment. For buying activities, purchasing and payables managers determine when the

---

At the time of this writing, William L. Sartoris was an associate professor of finance at the Indiana University School of Business and Ned C. Hill was the Joel C. Peterson Professor of Business Administration at Brigham Young University, Provo, UT.

Source: Reprinted from *Business Horizons*, November–December 1989, Copyright 1989 by the Foundation for the School of Business at Indiana University. Used with permission.

FIGURE 1 Individual Responsibilities on the Cashflow Timeline

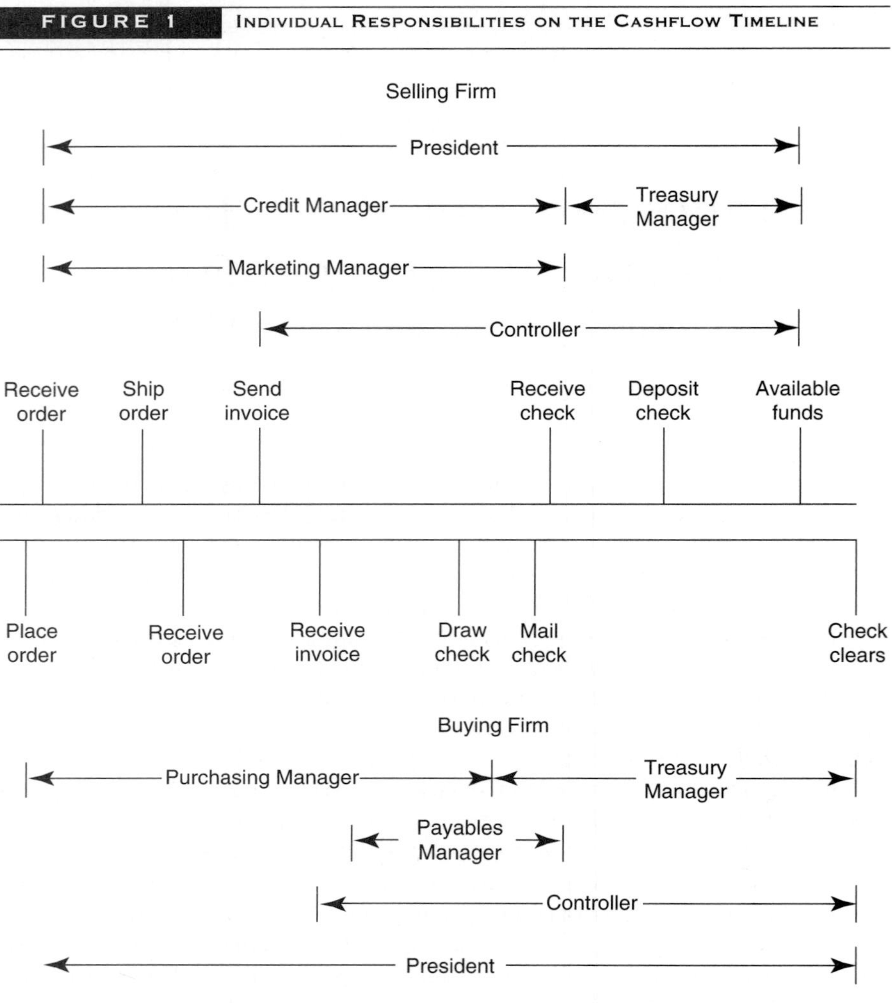

cash outflow is initiated. The treasury manager's role historically has been limited to designing the collection or disbursement system, to manage the flow of cash after the payment is initiated, and arranging for financing.

One problem of having many people involved in the decision process is a lack of coordination. Separation by physical location and by position on the organization chart frequently results in suboptimal, segmented decisions. Changes in competition, technology, and institutional arrangements have both increased the need for streamlined organizations and altered the way business is conducted. In many organizations the treasury manager is in a good position to perform an integrative role for short-term decisions. Because he has responsibility for both the collection and payment systems, the treasury manager knows both the selling and the buying side of the firm. Additionally, the treasury manager needs to identify the impacts and coordinate the activities of other players to prepare accurate short-term budgets and cash forecasts and to provide financing.

Over the last few years several financial and technological changes have begun to alter the role of the treasury manager. Below we discuss three of these developments: changes in economic conditions and the payments system; new investment and risk-management vehicles; and the development of electronic data interchange (EDI).

Changing Economic Conditions and Payment Systems in the Early 1980s

Much of the focus on short-term finance during the late 1970s and early 1980s was on cash management issues. Interest rates were at historically high levels. The payment system was hampered by inefficient physical movement of paper through the mail and the check-clearing systems. At an interest rate of 20 percent, speeding collection (or slowing payment) on $1 million by one day was worth approximately $550. Cash management efforts were understandably concentrated on optimizing the value of float.

Corporations learned to use the system to their advantage. One tactic was to expand the use of lockboxes. A lockbox is essentially a post office box, frequently with a unique zip code, to which a particular company's incoming checks are directed. The checks are collected by a bank as often as 20 times a day so they can be processed and quickly entered into the clearing system. The lockboxes are geographically located to minimize a check's mail time and availability time (the time until a deposited check's funds become available). High interest rates made multiple lockbox locations economical.

Remote disbursing to extend the time until a written check is presented for payment was another aggressive technique used. Checks drawn on banks in small towns in Washington, Montana, North Carolina, or even Guam were not uncommon. One aggressive midwestern grocery chain wrote checks one day prior to the due date and express mailed them to New Orleans to be mailed individually from a branch post office. The checks were drawn on a bank in a small town in South Carolina. While the extra mail time delay was a direct cost to the receiving firm, the extra clearing delay to the bank in South Carolina was borne by the banking system or the Federal Reserve.

Changes in the Paper System

Several changes in the payment system shifted the focus of collection and disbursement systems:

- The Monetary Control Act of 1980 required the Federal Reserve to reduce the float in the check-clearing system or charge for it;

- Revisions in the Fed Interdistrict Transportation System and improvements in the U.S. Postal Service took much of the slack out of the systems;
- Banks developed better cost-accounting systems to assess the cost of services more accurately;
- Banks unbundled charges for their services. Previously, banks relied on customer relationships and large, investable demand-deposit balances to provide acceptable overall profits from accounts. As corporate treasurers increased their purchases of "loss leaders" from banks, banks moved to charge the full cost for each service used. The net effect of these changes was reduced float, reduced value of float, and increased cost of services; and
- Public reaction to attempts to create inefficiencies in the systems, most notably by E.F. Hutton, raised questions about the ethics, if not the legality, of some practices.

Cash Management Reaction

The diminished role of float and increased service costs shifted the focus to more effective and efficient management of the cash flow systems. Treasurers realized that information availability and administrative cost savings are just as valuable as float savings. The new objective is to balance float costs, transaction costs, and the timing and accuracy of cash flow information.

Companies have decreased the number of lockboxes in their collection systems, reducing the administrative costs of obtaining information while increasing its accuracy. Costs of moving funds from lockbox banks to the headquarters bank have also been reduced.

Disbursement systems have been changed from remote disbursing, where the objective is to increase float, to controlled disbursing, where the objective is to improve timeliness and accuracy of cash flow information. With controlled disbursing, the disbursing bank notifies the company by mid-morning of checks being paid on that day. The treasurer arranges for a balance in the account needed to cover the checks and invests the rest while the money market is active and good rates are still available. Banks operate controlled disbursing in one of two ways: if the bank is part of a multibank holding company, the checks may be drawn on an affiliate bank that receives only one early morning presentment of checks from the Fed. Otherwise, the bank receives an electronic transmission from the Fed by mid-morning of the dollar amount of the checks to be presented later in the day.

Electronic Payments

While the above developments in collection and disbursement systems have increased the efficiency of the paper-based system, an even more important change has occurred. The revolution in computer and communications technology has made it feasible to replace wood fibers with electrons as a medium for storing value and transporting information. Fedwire, the wire transfer system operated by the Federal Reserve, has been available for many years to transfer money for same-day settlement. However, high transaction costs restrict its use to large dollar amounts. For example, in 1986 wire transactions constituted only 0.11 percent of the number of transactions in the United States but handled 78.5 percent of the dollar amount. The development of the automated clearing house (ACH) system made electronic transfers for next-day settlement feasible for small transactions.

Direct Deposit

One of the most widespread uses of ACH payments is for the direct deposit of consumer payments. A major factor in the early acceptance of direct deposits was the decision to make Social Security payments by ACH. Although the primary motivation was to reduce fraud and theft involved with mailed checks, cost savings were also achieved. The cost of producing a check for the Social Security system is estimated to be 26 cents, versus 3 cents for an electronic payment. More than 230 million Social Security payments of more than $90 billion are now made by electronic funds transfer each year. With ACH the float from employees who are slow in depositing checks is lost, but many organizations see the benefits, such as employees not taking time from work to deposit checks, as outweighing the lost float.

Corporate Payments

The other primary use of the ACH system by corporations has been for internal movement of cash. Efficient monitoring and use of cash requires that it be moved from the point of first deposit in the firm's banking system to the headquarters (concentration) bank. For example, a retail firm with many locations likely has many local deposit banks, each of which receives relatively small deposits. Both the amount of cash to be moved and the number of locations makes wires prohibitively expensive when compared to the ACH system.

Several factors have hindered rapid acceptance of direct corporate-to-corporate payments by ACH:

- Electronic payment results in the loss of float to the paying firm. Firms are happy to receive electronic payments from customers, but do not like to initiate them to suppliers;
- An electronic payment system adds fixed costs; and, because not everyone can or will use electronic payments, it is necessary to maintain a dual (paper and electronic) payment system;
- It is difficult to convey payment information, such as invoice numbers, in a form that can be understood by vendors with different systems.

> With a paper check a copy of the invoice with a notation that part of the shipment was damaged can be stapled to the check. However, it is somewhat more difficult to attach the invoice to the pulses of electrons representing the payment in an electronic system.

These obstacles are being overcome. The loss in float value can be shared by buyer and seller through negotiated payment terms. The decreased uncertainty of the timing of the cash flow is of value to both, and the dual system problem may be temporary for many companies if they can convince their suppliers (at least the critical ones) to accept electronic payments. The third impediment is being overcome by the use of EDI and standard formats. Although the solutions to all three of these impediments are closely linked, we will present an example of how two organizations have addressed the first two issues and leave the third until we discuss EDI.

The GM Payments System

General Motors has developed an electronic payment system for their suppliers with the goal of converting all suppliers to electronic payments and eliminating paper checks. GM averaged 3.6 days of disbursement float with checks. Under the electronic payment system, it has moved the payment date back three days, thus retaining three days of float and passing 0.6 days on to suppliers. In addition, it has reduced the uncertainty of the timing of the payments by specifying up to a year in advance the exact date on which the electronic transfers will be made.

Vendor Express

The federal government is also playing a major role in the move toward electronic payment of vendors. A program called Vendor Express, which uses both EDI and electronic payments, is being implemented. The short-term goal is to convert all Treasury payments and one-half of the non-Treasury payments, a total of 77 million vendor payments, to Vendor Express instead of paper. The savings in check-preparation fees alone are estimated to be over $20 million per year.

The Impact on Short-Term Finance

As the move toward electronic payments accelerates, we can expect to see some major changes in the treasury function. The most obvious change will be the virtual elimination of unintentional or unknown delays in the payment system. "The payment is stuck on the satellite" just does not have the same ring as "The check is in the mail." The geographic location of banks used for making or receiving payments will be unimportant. A payment to a supplier's bank in Chicago will be received just as quickly from Detroit as from San Diego. Firms thus will have less need for multiple banking relationships. Banks will have to improve their information systems to be able to send and receive electronic information accompanying the payment. Banks that do not make this investment in systems capability will likely find themselves relegated to being almost strictly retail, consumer-oriented banks. The move over the last few years toward consolidation in the banking industry may likely be accelerated by the shift to electronic payments. Finally, for electronic payments to be acceptable to both buyer and seller, payment may have to be negotiated. Buyers and sellers will find it much easier to view one another as trading partners, not adversaries.

Developments in Investments

In addition to managing the cash flows resulting from operating decisions, the treasury manager is responsible for maintaining the firm's liquidity. One of the primary sources of liquidity is the portfolio of marketable securities. A short-term portfolio's primary goal is to ensure the safety of the principal while earning a return on excess cash. If the firm has an unexpected need for cash before the security matures, it must be able to sell that security in the secondary market without loss of value. One way to achieve this goal is to invest only in very safe, short-term instruments, such as T-bills. However, this requires a sacrifice of another desirable characteristic—return. Investment for a longer term usually results in a higher return, but at a cost of price (or interest rate) risk if the security must be sold. Two different types of instruments exist to help the treasury manager increase yield and control the level of risk: adjustable-rate securities and hedging instruments, such as financial futures and options.

Adjustable-Rate Securities

Several different versions of preferred stock offer price protection against rising interest rates as well as a tax advantage. The price protection is from an adjustment in the dividend rate at periodic intervals. The tax advantage is from a partial dividend tax exclusion to a corporation. Currently 70 percent of the dividend on a stock held by a corporation for more than 46 days is nontaxable. Thus, a firm with a 34 percent tax rate purchasing a preferred stock yielding 6 percent would have an after-tax yield of 5.4 percent. To achieve the same after-tax yield on a fully taxable security, the before-tax yield would have to be 8.2 percent.

Adjustable-Rate Preferred Stock

Adjustable-rate preferred stock (ARPS) was developed to give investors a variable-rate investment vehicle. The dividend is adjusted at periodic intervals, usually quarterly. The rate is based on a set spread from a base rate, such as the three-month T-bill rate or the 10-year or 20-year Treasury bond rate. However, there are two types of risks in ARPS. If the credit rating of the issuing firm deteriorates, the increase in risk premium could cause the price to fall. Also, changes in the shape of the yield curve may change the relationship between short and long rates and cause the prices to vary.

Convertible Adjustable Preferred Stock

Convertible adjustable preferred stock (CAPS) is adjustable-rate preferred stock that can be converted into common stock. It was created to overcome problems with capital erosion that might occur with ARPS. Since the conversion value increases with the price of the common stock, there is a potential capital gain. However, if CAPS is purchased at a price above par, there is the potential for a capital loss if the price of the common falls.

Money Market Preferred Stock

Money market preferred stock (MMPS), also called auction-rate preferred stock, was created to offer a money market-type instrument with a variable rate that should always trade at par. The dividend rate is set by a Dutch auction every 49 days. The winning rate is the lowest rate that will cause all intended shares to be sold. There is a liquidity risk if the auction fails (not enough bids are received to sell all shares). In this case the rate is set based on a commercial paper composite rate. Thus, an investor wishing to sell at the auction might be forced to hold the security until the next auction or sell it at a higher rate (lower price).

Hedging Instruments

Hedging a marketable security is a way of "selling" the interest risk to someone else. A hedge is created through an additional instrument whose price will move opposite to that of the security. For example, a rise in interest rates would cause the price to fall and a loss to be incurred if the security had to be sold. By appropriately buying or selling an instrument whose value would rise on an increase in interest rates, the manager would be able to offset the price risk on the security. A manager typically will not try to hedge the entire portfolio of marketable securities. The portion of the portfolio chosen to be hedged would depend on the uncertainty about changes in interest rates and how much price risk the firm can afford to take.

Financial Futures

A financial futures contract is an obligation to either make or take delivery of a specified financial instrument. Financial futures contracts on T-bills and Eurodollar time deposits are most commonly used for short-term hedging. Both contracts are for 90-day instruments; thus their prices will depend on anticipated changes in three-month interest rates. Since financial futures are an obligation, not an option, gains and losses are symmetric. That is, if a rise in rates causes the price to fall, a drop in rates will cause the price to rise. The treasury manager that sold a T-bill futures contract (agreed to make delivery of a 90-day T-bill on the delivery date) would offset losses on the portfolio as interest rates increase, but would also offset gains on the portfolio as rates decrease.

A futures contract is really just a promise to make or take delivery at a future date. To ensure that the promise is upheld, the holder of a futures contract must establish a margin account and mark to market on a daily basis. Any gains on the contract are credited to the margin account and can be withdrawn. Any losses on the contract are deducted from the margin account. If the margin account balance falls below some specified level, additional funds must be deposited in the margin count. Obviously, a futures contract is not a hedging instrument that can be purchased (sold) and forgotten. It is necessary to monitor the futures position actively and continuously.

In determining the number of contracts needed, the manager needs to calculate the hedge ratio, which is a function of the amount of the security to be hedged and the remaining maturity of the security. Because the hedge ratio will change over time, the hedge ratio may call for a non-integer number of contracts; because the interest on the hedged security may not be perfectly correlated with the interest rate on the futures contract, it may not be possible to establish a perfect hedge where all price risk is eliminated. The manager may be forced to live with an imperfect hedge and still absorb some price risk.

Options

Unlike futures contracts, which are obligations, options can be allowed to expire by the buyer without exercising them. Two types of options are used: a call option, which entitles the buyer to purchase a security at a specified price; and a put option, which entitles the buyer to sell a security at a set price. Since the option will only be exercised if it results in a gain, the profit function is not symmetrical. Numerous strategies have been developed by investment advisory firms for using combinations of put and call options. They all attempt to maximize dividend or interest income while reducing the risk of capital loss.

Electronic Data Interchange

As we saw from the timeline in Figure 1, much of short-term financial management is related to operating decisions. Many of these operating aspects involve the flow of documents along the timeline. Accounts receivable, for example, measure the time delay between the date on an invoice and the date a payment is received and credited to a customer's account. A recent survey showed that almost 80 percent of the documents transacted between firms use paper as the medium to carry the information. EDI replaces paper documents with electronic communications. The impact on short-term financial management can be significant.

Electronic messaging involves moving data electronically between two points. The various forms of electronic messaging may be arrayed along a continuum (see Figure 2). EDI is the movement of business data electronically between or within firms in a structured, computer-processible data format. This format permits data to be transferred from a computer-supported business application in one location to a computer-supported business application in another

FIGURE 2 ELECTRONIC MESSAGING

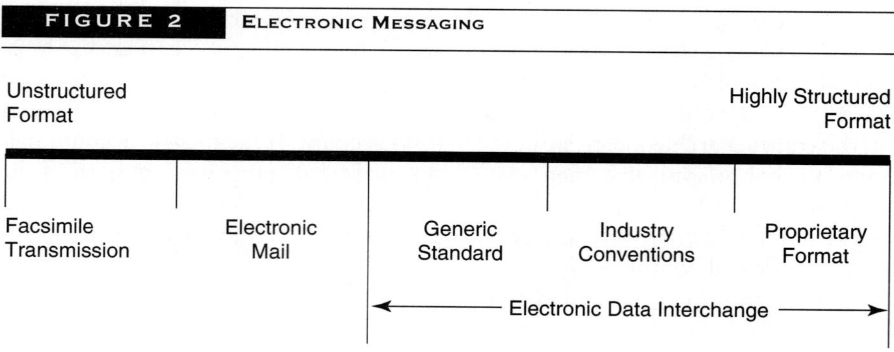

Electronic data interchange includes generic standards (ANSI X-12, USC, WINS) as well as more narrowly defined industry standards and very specific proprietary formats.

location without rekeying. EDI is not facsimile transmission or electronic mail. Facsimile transmission represents the transfer of totally unstructured data. Anything from photographs to purchase orders may be sent by this means. Although time delays are avoided, the receiver of a facsimile transmission is not able to enter the image directly into a business application. Electronic mail also moves business data electronically but generally uses a free format rather than a structured format. Since the sender may choose any format, it is difficult to design an application program that directly accepts electronic mail input without significant manual editing.

Electronic payments is a subset of EDI that not only transfers payment information between two partners but also requires a financial institution to arrange for the transfer of value. The ACH system and Fedwire discussed earlier are examples of electronic payments.

The Impact of EDI on Short-Term Financial Management

EDI has become an important issue today for several reasons. The intense competitive environment in the worldwide economy has caused many firms to reexamine the current paper-based transaction system and its attendant inefficiencies. Also, a number of large firms are moving rapidly to implement EDI and are sending the message that trading partners should be prepared to use EDI or face the loss of relationships. Finally, the infrastructure is now largely in place to make EDI a reality.

Inefficiencies in the Paper-Based Information System

In the perspective defined above, problems that may be solved by EDI are discussed below.

Time Delays

With a paper-based transaction system, delays along the timeline are caused primarily by two factors: the transportation delay caused by the system required to move paper documents between parties, or the manual processing delay caused by the keying and rekeying of information along the timeline. Many of the documents produced are based on information that has already been keyed once. Figure 3 illustrates a simplified transaction showing the keying steps for two trading partners. Time for keying and transportation results in ordering delays, billing delays, payment delays, poor customer service and poor management information.

Labor Costs

In a paper-based system, manual processing is required for data keying, document storage, retrieval and matching, envelope stuffing, and other tasks. Automated equipment can help, but labor costs for document processing are still significant.

Errors

Because the same information is keyed several times, paper-based systems are error prone. The A.D. Little study of the grocery industry in 1980 estimated that more than 3 percent of all invoices between wholesaler and distributor contained errors. These errors could be largely eliminated with EDI.

Inventory

Because of delays and uncertainties in paper processing, inventories may be higher than they need be. In a manufacturing firm, it may be nearly impossible to

FIGURE 3 DATA FLOWS BETWEEN BUSINESS APPLICATIONS (PAPER TRANSACTION SYSTEM)

Step 1. Buyer identifies that inventory needs to be purchased. A purchase order is typed (keyed) and sent in the mail to the seller.

Step 2. Seller keys purchase order into order entry system and fills order.

Step 3. Seller prints out filled order and keys it into the invoicing system.

Step 4. Seller prepares invoice and mails to buyer. Keying may be involved in producing envelope and/or invoice.

Step 5. Buyer keys invoice data into accounts payable system.

Step 6. Buyer keys data from purchasing application into accounts payable application to insure that goods invoiced were actually received.

Step 7. Buyer enters approved invoices into check payment application and checks are prepared and sent.

Step 8. Seller receives check and keys data into accounts receivable application giving buyer credit for payment.

achieve a just-in-time inventory system with the delays inherent in the paper-based processing system.

Uncertainty

Uncertainty exists in three areas. Transportation and keying delays mean that timing is uncertain; once a transaction is sent, the sender does not know when the transaction will be received nor when it will be processed. The sender does not know whether the transaction is received nor whether the firm agrees with what was sent. And it is difficult to tell when a paper check will clear back to the disbursing bank.

Problems in a Paper-Based System Solved by EDI

Labor costs relative to other factors of production have increased at a higher rate, and labor costs in the U.S. are higher than labor costs in many other countries. On the other hand, the cost of computers and communications equipment has gone down over the past few years. Hence, to save on the costs of production, firms are turning to the use of computerized processes to reduce labor costs. Electronic data interchange is one way to reduce the labor costs involved with the processing of paper documents.

A typical EDI transaction would follow the sequences illustrated in Figure 4. Information for a purchase order is keyed into the system, producing an electronic purchase order. Most of the information is only keyed once, since the same information is the basis for all remaining documents. The electronic purchase order is sent either directly to the seller or through an electronic

FIGURE 4 DATA FLOWS BETWEEN BUSINESS APPLICATIONS (EDI SYSTEM)

Step 1. Buyer identifies that inventory needs to be purchased. A purchase order is keyed and sent electronically to the seller.

Step 2. Seller's computer translates purchase order into order entry system and fills order.

Step 3. Seller's computer transfers data electronically (bridges) into invoicing system.

Step 4. Seller's computer translates invoice data into electronic format and sends through network to buyer.

Step 5. Buyer receives invoice data and translates into accounts payable system.

Step 6. Buyer bridges data from purchasing application into accounts payable application and does a computer match to ensure that goods invoiced were actually received.

Step 7. Buyer bridges approved invoices into electronic payment application and sends payment electronically to seller's bank. Remittance information sent electronically to seller directly or through the bank.

Step 8. Seller receives remittance information and translates it into accounts receivable application giving buyer credit for payment.

mailbox provided by a communications network. The seller receives the electronic purchase order and translates the data into the form needed by the seller's order-entry application. An electronic acknowledgment is sent back to the buyer indicating that a transmission has been received. This is called a "functional acknowledgement." It is also possible for the seller to read the purchase order and send the buyer a purchase order acknowledgment reporting on the availability of items in the order.

The seller's order entry system then generates internal instructions to the warehouse, plant, or service center regarding the filling of the order. The order entry application may also feed into the invoicing application so an electronic invoice can be prepared. The remaining steps are similar. The translation process formats data so it can be sent to or received from a trading partner. The bridging process couples two separate applications.

The results of EDI implementation can be dramatic. Time delays are greatly reduced. Mail and processing delays are eliminated. Timing uncertainty is eliminated in some cases and reduced in others, enabling the treasury manager to more accurately forecast cash flows. Immediate acknowledgements provided through an EDI system mean that the buyer knows that a purchase order was received, enhancing the relationship between buyer and seller. A content acknowledgment provides the buyer with fast feedback on whether the order will be filled, lessening the need for safety stock. One-time keying means that labor costs can be reduced. Because data is always in computer-readable form, matching, filing, retrieving, sorting, reporting, and auditing can be accomplished with fewer people and at much faster rates. Paper and mail costs can be reduced. Payment can be processed through the settlement system the day after initiation.

A Supporting Infrastructure for EDI Implementation

Talk of a paperless society been an unfulfilled prophecy. The primary reason for the slow movement to an electronic transaction-processing environment has been the lack of a cost-effective infrastructure. Recently, however, this infrastructure has been rapidly developing. It includes four primary elements: accepted formatting standards for most business documents, off-the-shelf software for translating internally stored data into standard formats, communication networks and internetworking communication standards, and low-cost computer hardware. These four developments have lowered the barriers to EDI implementation.

National Standards

To send documents to each other electronically, firms must agree on a data format and technical environment. In the early days of EDI, large firms announced a proprietary format and communication interface and either encouraged or mandated trading partner participation. K-Mart, for example, developed a proprietary purchasing system for sending electronic purchase orders to its suppliers. Firms wanting to sell to K-Mart agreed to adopt those conventions.

Proprietary data formats and technical requirements work well enough when a firm deals with only a small number of partners. But suppose the K-Mart supplier also wants to supply Sears, which has a different data format. The supplier would have to install a second system to comply with the Sears format. Suppose the supplier also wants to sell to Service Merchandise, which has yet another format. A third system would be needed for the Service Merchandise format.

It should be clear that widespread implementation of EDI could not proceed without the development of widely accepted data format and communication standards. If K-Mart, Sears, and Service Merchandise agree to use a common standard, then the supplier who wants to sell to all three needs to maintain only one system to read electronic purchase orders from them all.

Transportation Data Coordinating Committee

The development of widely accepted standards has been formally under way since the formation of the Transportation Data Coordinating Committee (TDCC) in 1968. This nonprofit organization set out to establish standards for communications between and within railroads, ocean carriers, air carriers, and motor carriers. The first TDCC standard was published in 1975. TDCC has subsequently broadened its reach to serve as administrator for several different industry groups. Each industry served has a standards committee made up of industry representatives. The standards committees determine new standards, modify existing ones, and pass the information on to the TDCC for publication and distribution.

ANSI X12 Committee

In 1978 the Credit Research Foundation and TDCC formed the BUSAP (for Business Applications) Committee, which subsequently received a charter from the American National Standards Institute (ANSI) as the ANSI X12 Committee. The committee's charge is to develop standards acceptable across industry groups. Since 1983 the ANSI X12 Committee has published standards for more than 20 documents, including the purchase order, remittance advice, invoice, and request for quote. Work is going forward to define EDI formats for an additional 100 documents.

Parallel efforts in standards development have been proceeding in Europe, leading to the development of the EDIFACT standards (EDI for Administration, Commerce and Trade). The EDIFACT committee worked out a common data dictionary and syntax rules so that standards development in different industries and countries can begin with the same building blocks.

Translation Software

EDI translation software performs three functions. The file-conversion software takes data stored in the firm's business application and reformats it for input into the formatting software. The formatting software translates this input into the desired EDI standard format. The communication software then dials the trading partner or communication network and sends (or receives) the EDI formatted data to (or from) another party's computer using acceptable protocols.

Over the past five years, a number of software firms have developed off-the-shelf translation packages, available at initial costs ranging from $800 to $3,000 (plus annual maintenance fees), that support EDI translation on a microcomputer. Mini and mainframe software costs range from $10,000 to $30,000 plus annual maintenance. Most EDI software is table driven, meaning that by changing input tables, the software can produce any desired transaction set.

Value-Added Networks

When firms first began using EDI, most communications were directly between trading partners. In recent years, a service has been developed that solves some of the problems of direct communication.

Direct computer-to-computer communications with a trading partner requires that both firms use similar communication protocols, have the same transmission speed, have phone lines available at the same time, and have compatible computer hardware. If these conditions are not met, communication becomes difficult if not impossible.

Value-added networks (VANs) can provide several services relating to EDI. Mailboxing permits one trading partner to send transactions sets to the other's mailbox for storage. When the other trading partner is ready, it will retrieve the transactions sets. This solves the problem of finding a time when both partners can communicate. Protocol conversion means that one partner can use a communication package with one transmission protocol and communicate with the other partner that uses another protocol. Some VANs offer standards conversion, meaning that a transaction set could be received in a proprietary format and then translated into an X12 format before being sent to a trading partner. Some VANs also provide implementation assistance in the form of consulting, software, and training of trading partners. All VANs permit line-speed conversion so messages may be received and sent at whatever line speed the user requires.

Inexpensive Computer Hardware

It is clear to anyone who monitors the prices of microcomputer systems that the unit costs of computer power have decreased significantly over time. Costs for a microcomputer system capable of running most EDI translation packages are in the neighborhood of $4,000 to $6,000. Machines are now faster and have more memory. This increase in power, coupled with the decrease in cost, has made EDI quite accessible to even very small firms.

Because of the many benefits of electronic communications over paper documents, EDI will have a significant impact on short-term financial management. EDI affects virtually every organizational segment of the timeline. A few of the direct consequences of EDI implementation on short-term finance are discussed below.

Redefinition of Managerial Responsibilities

Each management position responsible for a segment of the cash flow timeline could see a dramatic change in roles. Cash managers, for example, who traditionally have focused on "float management" associated with paper-based processing, will see dramatic changes in their function in the firm. Much of their traditional role could be eliminated. The treasury manager will have more time to spend coordinating the activities that affect short-term finance and investigating better investment opportunities.

Service Products Supporting Short-Term Finance

Many of the service products provided by banks and other third parties to support the short-term finance function could become obsolete or diminished in importance.

More Certainty in Cash Flows

As information flows electronically rather than by mail, the payment date can be determined with more certainty. This means that the borrowing and investing function of the firm will rely less on uncertain forecasts and overnight investment/borrowing.

Credit Term Changes

Current credit terms, like "2/10, net 30," have been used since Civil War days and are based on an assumption of paper/mail/manual processing. Electronic communications and payment changes the underlying assumption and should therefore permit changed credit terms. Some firms currently implementing EDI and electronic payment are renegotiating payment terms with their partners.

Just-in-Time Inventory Management

EDI permits the implementation of low or no inventory levels.

Although the paperless world may not be immediately around the corner, as so many have predicted for years, the movement is solidly in that direction. The technological infrastructure—standards, software, value added networks, and inexpensive computer hardware—is in place. The need is unquestionably present. Several industry leaders have already committed themselves to making

EDI happen. It is only a matter of time before EDI becomes the standard model of corporate information exchange.

References

Earl Bass, "The Language of EDI," *FORUM: The Journal of Electronic Data Interchange,* Vol. 1, 1989, pp. 114–119.

Charles Coffee, Dennis Kordyak, and Michael Serlin, "Electronic Data Interchange (EDI): Uncle Sam as Your Trading Partner," NCCMA Ninth Annual Conference, Dallas, Texas, October 23, 1988.

Daniel M. Ferguson, Ned C. Hill, and Steven F. Maier, "The State of U.S. EDI: 1988," *FORUM: The Journal of Electronic Data Exchange,* Vol. 1, 1989, pp. 21–29.

R.H. Harvey, "Electronic Corporate Trade Payments, A Business Strategy: GM-EDS Electronic Payment System," EFT/EDI Conference, Chicago, Illinois, May 16, 1988.

Ned C. Hill and Daniel M. Ferguson, "Cash Flow Timeline Management: The Next Frontier of Cash Management," *Journal of Cash Management,* May-June 1985, pp. 12–22.

Ned C. Hill and Daniel M. Ferguson, "Negotiating Payment Terms in An Electronic Environment," *Advances in Working Capital Management,* (New York: JAI Press, 1988), pp. 99–114.

I.G. Kawaller, "How and Why to Hedge a Short-term Portfolio," *Journal of Cash Management,* January-February 1985, pp. 26–30.

M.K. Perkins, "Investment Opportunity Alternatives for a Short-term Portfolio," *Journal of Cash Management,* March-April 1986, pp. 32–45.

Questions

1. Identify several different examples of decisions in short-term financial management.
2. "Although the treasury manager—perhaps called cash manager, assistant treasurer, or treasurer—has direct responsibility for managing the short-term cash flows, the operating activities that generate the cash flows are frequently controlled by others in the organization." Use Figure 1 to explain the individual responsibilities within the selling firm and within the buying firm.
3. At an interest rate of 5 percent, speeding collection (or slowing payment) on $10 million by one day is worth how many dollars?
4. Define the terms *lockbox* and *remote disbursing.*
5. Compare and contrast corporate use of the Fedwire with the ACH (automated clearing house) system.
6. Some treasury managers invest temporarily excess cash in adjustable rate preferred stock (ARPS). What are the benefits of this type of investment to the company?
7. Define the terms *financial futures* and *options.*
8. Compare and contrast the data flows of a traditional paper transaction system (Figure 3) with the electronic data interchange (EDI) system (Figure 4).
9. What are the advantages of EDI relative to the traditional paper transaction system?

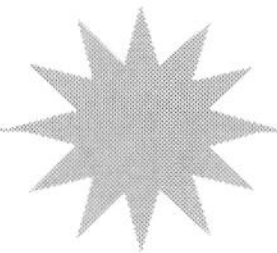

Commercial Paper

THOMAS K. HAHN

Commercial paper is a short-term unsecured promissory note issued by corporations and foreign governments. For many large, creditworthy issuers, commercial paper is a low-cost alternative to bank loans. Issuers are able to efficiently raise large amounts of funds quickly and without expensive Securities and Exchange Commission (SEC) registration by selling paper, either directly or through independent dealers, to a large and varied pool of institutional buyers. Investors in commercial paper earn competitive, market-determined yields in notes whose maturity and amounts can be tailored to their specific needs.

Because of the advantages of commercial paper for both investors and issuers, commercial paper has become one of America's most important debt markets. Commercial paper outstanding grew at an annual rate of 14 percent from 1970 to 1991. Figure 1 shows commercial paper outstanding, which totaled \$528 billion at the end of 1991.

This article describes some of the important features of the commercial paper market. The first section reviews the characteristics of commercial paper. The second section describes the major participants in the market, including the issuers, investors, and dealers. The third section discusses the risks faced by investors in the commercial paper market along with the mechanisms that are used to control these risks. The fourth section discusses some recent innovations, including asset-backed commercial paper, the use of swaps in commercial paper financing strategies, and the international commercial paper markets.

At the time of this writing, Thomas K. Hahn was a consultant with TKH Associates.
The author would like to thank Timothy Look, Bob LaRoche, Jerome Fons, and Mitchell Post for comments.

Source: Thomas K. Hahn, author. Reprinted with permission from Federal Reserve Bank of Richmond and *Economic Quarterly*. Opinions expressed herein are those of the author and not necessarily those of the Federal Reserve Bank of Richmond or the Federal Reserve System.

FIGURE 1 COMMERCIAL PAPER OUTSTANDING

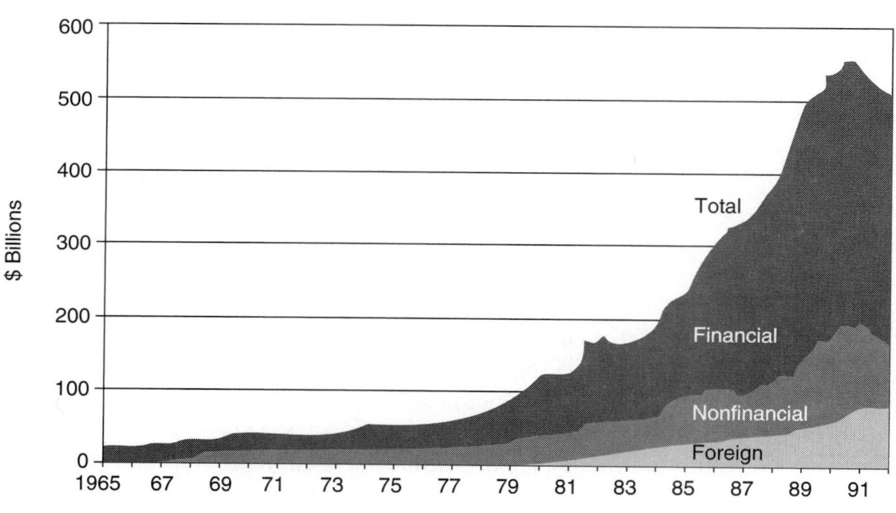

SOURCE: Board of Governors of the Federal Reserve System.

Characteristics of Commercial Paper

The Securities Act of 1933 requires that securities offered to the public be registered with the Securities and Exchange Commission. Registration requires extensive public disclosure, including issuing a prospectus on the offering, and is a time-consuming and expensive process.[1] Most commercial paper is issued under Section 3(a)(3) of the 1933 Act which exempts from registration requirements short-term securities as long as they have certain characteristics.[2] The exemption requirements have been a factor shaping the characteristics of the commercial paper market.

One requirement for exemption is that the maturity of commercial paper must be less than 270 days. In practice, most commercial paper has a maturity of between 5 and 45 days, with 30–35 days being the average maturity. Many issuers continuously roll over their commercial paper, financing a more-or-less constant amount of their assets using commercial paper. Continuous rollover of notes does not violate the nine-month maturity limit as long as the rollover is not automatic but is at the discretion of the issuer and the dealer. Many issuers will adjust the maturity of commercial paper to suit the requirements of an investor.

---

[1] Registration for short-term securities is especially expensive because the registration fee is a percent of the face amount at each offering. Thirty-day registered notes, rolled over monthly for one year, would cost 12 times as much as a one-time issuance of an equal amount of one-year notes.

[2] Some commercial paper is issued under one of the two other exemptions to the Securities Act. Commercial paper which is guaranteed by a bank through a letter of credit is exempt under Section 3(a)(2) regardless of whether or not the issue is also exempt under Section 3(a)(3). Commercial paper sold through private placements is exempt under Section 4(2). See Felix (1987) for more information on the legal aspects of commercial paper issuance.

A second requirement for exemption is that notes must be of a type not ordinarily purchased by the general public. In practice, the denomination of commercial paper is large: minimum denominations are usually $100,000, although face amounts as low as $10,000 are available from some issuers. Because most investors are institutions, typical face amounts are in multiples of $1 million. Issuers will usually sell an investor the specific amount of commercial paper needed.

A third requirement for exemption is that proceeds from commercial paper issues be used to finance "current transactions," which include the funding of operating expenses and the funding of current assets such as receivables and inventories. Proceeds cannot be used to finance fixed assets, such as plant and equipment, on a permanent basis. The SEC has generally interpreted the current transaction requirement broadly, approving a variety of short-term uses for commercial paper proceeds. Proceeds are not traced directly from issue to use, so firms are required to show only that they have a sufficient "current transaction" capacity to justify the size of the commercial paper program (for example, a particular level of receivables or inventory).[3] Firms are allowed to finance construction as long as the commercial paper financing is temporary and to be paid off shortly after completion of construction with long-term funding through a bond issue, bank loan, or internally generated cash flow.[4]

Like Treasury bills, commercial paper is typically a discount security: the investor purchases notes at less than face value and receives the face value at maturity. The difference between the purchase price and the face value, called the discount, is the interest received on the investment. Occasionally, investors request that paper be issued as an interest-bearing note. The investor pays the face value and, at maturity, receives the face value and accrued interest. All commercial paper interest rates are quoted on a discount basis.[5]

Until the 1980s, most commercial paper was issued in physical form in which the obligation of the issuer to pay the face amount at maturity is recorded by printed certificates that are issued to the investor in exchange for funds. The certificates are held, usually by a safekeeping agent hired by the investor, until presented for payment at maturity. The exchanges of funds for commercial paper first at issuance and then at redemption, called "settling" of the transaction, occur in one day. On the day the commercial paper is issued and sold, the investor receives and pays for the notes and the issuer receives the proceeds. On the day of maturity, the investor presents the notes and receives payment. Commercial banks, in their role as issuing, paying, and clearing agents, facilitate the settling

---

[3] Some SEC interpretations of the current transaction requirement have been established in "no-action" letters. "No-action" letters, issued by the staff of the SEC at the request of issuers, confirm that the staff will not request any legal action concerning an unregistered issue. See Felix (1987, p. 39).

[4] Past SEC interpretations of Section 3(a)(3) exemptions have also required that commercial paper be of "prime quality" and be discountable at a Federal Reserve Bank (Release No. 33-4412). The discounting requirement was dropped in 1980. An increased amount of commercial paper in the later 1980s was issued without prime ratings.

[5] The Federal Reserve publishes in its H.15 statistical release daily interest rates for dealer-offered and directly placed commercial paper of one-month, three-month and six-month maturities. All rates are based on paper with relatively low default risk. Commercial paper rates of various maturities for select finance issuers and a dealer composite rate are also published daily in *The Wall Street Journal.*

of commercial paper by carrying out the exchanges between issuer, investor, and dealer required to transfer commercial paper for funds.

An increasing amount of commercial paper is being issued in book-entry form in which the physical commercial paper certificates are replaced by entries in computerized accounts. Book-entry systems will eventually completely replace the physical printing and delivery of notes. The Depository Trust Company (DTC), a clearing cooperative operated by member banks, began plans in September 1990 to convert most commercial paper transactions to book-entry form.[6] By May 1992, more than 40 percent of commercial paper was issued through the DTC in book-entry form.

The advantages of a paperless system are significant. The fees and costs associated with the book-entry system will, in the long run, be significantly less than under the physical delivery system. The expense of delivering and verifying certificates and the risks of messengers failing to deliver certificates on time will be eliminated. The problem of daylight overdrafts, which arise from nonsynchronous issuing and redeeming of commercial paper, will be reduced since all transactions between an issuing agent and a paying agent will be settled with a single end-of-day wire transaction.

Market Participants

Issuers and Uses of Commercial Paper

Commercial paper is issued by a wide variety of domestic and foreign firms, including financial companies, banks, and industrial firms. Table 1 shows examples of the largest commercial paper issuers. Figure 2 shows outstanding commercial paper by type of issuer.

TABLE 1 COMMERCIAL PAPER OUTSTANDING BY MAJOR ISSUER (BILLIONS OF DOLLARS)

Category	Major Issuer	Average Amount Outstanding	Dealer
Finance	General Electric Capital (subsidiary of GE)	$36.9	Direct, Multiple
Auto Finance	General Motors Acceptance (subsidiary of GM)	$23.6	Direct
Investment Banking	Merrill Lynch	$ 7.5	Dealer is subsidiary
Commercial Banking	J.P. Morgan	$ 4.4	Multiple
Industrial	PepsiCo	$ 3.4	Multiple
Foreign	Hanson Finance	$ 3.5	Multiple
Asset-Backed	Corporate Asset Funding	$ 5.3	Goldman Sachs

Note: Quarterly Average Commercial Paper is for the first quarter of 1992, except GE, GMAC, and PepsiCo, which are for the fourth quarter of 1991.
SOURCE: *Moody's Global Short Term Record,* June 1992.

[6] See The Depository Trust Company (1990).

FIGURE 2 COMMERCIAL PAPER OUTSTANDING BY ISSUER TYPE END OF 1991 TOTAL $528.1 BILLION (BILLIONS OF DOLLARS)

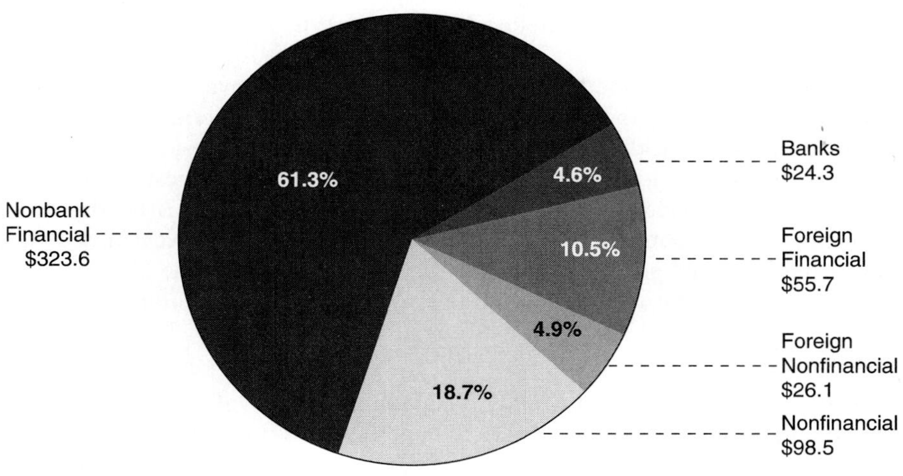

SOURCE: Board of Governors of the Federal Reserve System.

The biggest issuers in the financial firm category in Figure 2 are finance companies. Finance companies provide consumers with home loans, retail automobile loans, and unsecured personal loans. They provide businesses with a variety of short- and medium-term loans including secured loans to finance purchases of equipment for resale. Some finance companies are wholly owned subsidiaries of industrial firms that provide financing for purchases of the parent firm's products. For example, a major activity of General Motors Acceptance Corporation (GMAC) is the financing of purchases and leases of General Motor's vehicles by dealers and consumers. The three largest issuers—GMAC, General Electric Capital, and Ford Motor Credit—accounted for more than 20 percent of the total nonbank financial paper outstanding at the end of 1991.

The financial issuer category also includes insurance firms and securities firms. Insurance companies issue commercial paper to finance premium receivables and operating expenses. Securities firms issue commercial paper as a low-cost alternative to other short-term borrowings such as repurchase agreements and bank loans, and they use commercial paper proceeds to finance a variety of security broker and investment banking activities.

Commercial bank holding companies issue commercial paper to finance operating expenses and various nonbank activities. Bank holding companies have recently decreased their commercial paper issues following declines in the perceived creditworthiness of many major domestic bank issuers.

More than 500 nonfinancial firms also issue commercial paper. Nonfinancial issuers include public utilities, industrial and service companies. Industrial and service companies use commercial paper to finance working capital (accounts receivable and inventory) on a permanent or seasonal basis, to fund operating expenses, and to finance, on a temporary basis, construction projects. Public utilities also use commercial paper to fund nuclear fuels and construction. Figure 3 shows that commercial paper as a percent of commercial paper and bank loans for nonfinancial firms rose from just 2 percent in 1966 to over 15 percent at the end of 1991.

The domestic commercial paper issuers discussed above include U.S. subsidiaries of foreign companies. Foreign corporations and governments also issue commercial paper in the U.S. without use of a domestic subsidiary and these foreign issues have gained increased acceptance by U.S. investors. Foreign financial firms, including banks and bank holding companies, issue almost 70 percent of foreign commercial paper (Federal Reserve Bank of New York 1992). Industrial firms and governments issue the remainder. Japan, the United Kingdom, and France are among the countries with a significant number of issuers.

Investors

Money market mutual funds (MMFs) and commercial bank trust departments are the major investors in commercial paper. MMFs hold about one-third of the outstanding commercial paper, while bank trust departments hold between 15 and 25 percent.[7] Other important investors, holding between 5 and 15 percent, are nonfinancial corporations, life insurance companies, and private and

FIGURE 3 COMMERCIAL PAPER AS A PERCENT OF COMMERCIAL PAPER AND BANK LOANS, NONFINANCIAL FIRMS

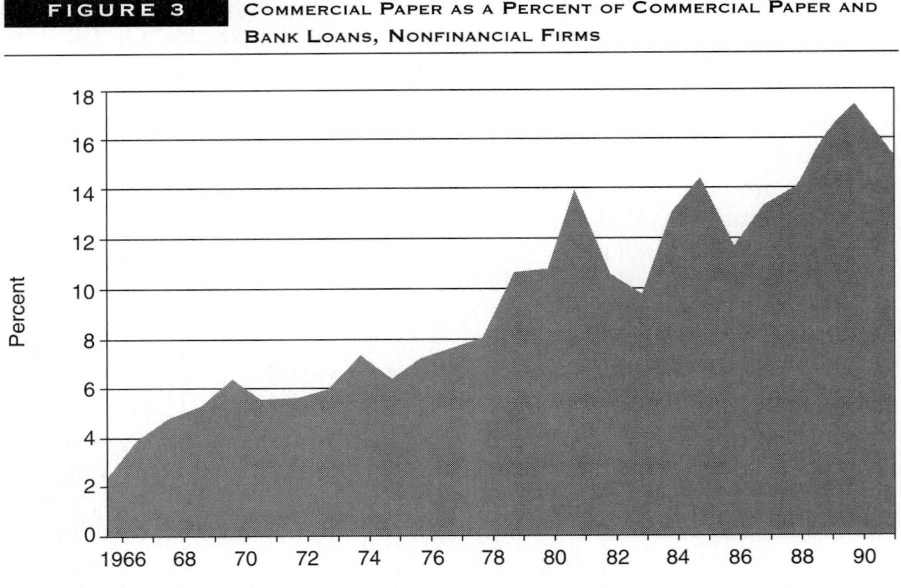

SOURCE: Board of Governors of the Federal Reserve System.

[7] Precise data on holdings of commercial paper by investor type, except by MMFs, are not available. Some estimates are provided in Board of Governors of the Federal Reserve System (1992, p. 52), Stigum (1990, p. 1027), and Felix (1987, p. 13).

government pension funds. Other mutual funds, securities dealers, and banks also hold small amounts of commercial paper. Individuals hold little commercial paper directly because of the large minimum denominations, but they are large indirect investors in commercial paper through MMFs and trusts.

There have been major shifts in ownership of commercial paper during the post-World War II period. Prior to World War II, the most important investors in commercial paper were banks, which used commercial paper as a reserve asset and to diversify their securities portfolios. In the fifties and sixties, industrial firms began to hold commercial paper as an alternative to bank deposits, which had regulated interest rates that at times were significantly below the market-determined rates on commercial paper. Historically high and variable interest rates during the 1970s led households and businesses to hold more of their funds in short-term assets and to transfer funds from bank deposits with regulated interest rates to assets like MMF shares with market-determined rates. At the same time, many large businesses found that they could borrow in the commercial paper market at less expense than they could borrow from banks. MMFs demanded the short-term, large-denomination, relatively safe, and high-yield characteristics offered by commercial paper and hence absorbed a major portion of new commercial paper issues. Table 2 shows that both the commercial paper market and MMFs have experienced very rapid growth since 1975. By the end of 1991, MMFs held 36 percent of the commercial paper outstanding and commercial paper composed 42 percent of their total assets.

Placement and Role of the Dealer

Most firms place their paper through dealers who, acting as principals, purchase commercial paper from issuers and resell it to the public. Most dealers are subsidiaries of investment banks or commercial bank holding companies. A select group of very large, active issuers, called direct issuers, employ their own sales forces to distribute their paper. There are approximately 125 direct issuers, most of which are finance companies or bank holding companies. These issuers sell significant amounts of commercial paper on a continuous basis.

TABLE 2 MONEY MARKET MUTUAL FUNDS AND COMMERCIAL PAPER

End of	MMF Assets ($ billions)	Commercial Paper Outstanding ($ billions)	MMF Holdings of CP ($ billions)	CP as Percent of MMF Assets	Percent of CP Held by MMFs
1975	3.7	47.7	0.4	11	1
1980	74.5	121.6	25.0	33	21
1985	207.5	293.9	87.6	42	30
1990	414.8	557.8	199.1	48	36
1991	449.7	528.1	187.6	42	36

Note: MMFs exclude tax-exempt funds.
SOURCE: Board of Governors of the Federal Reserve System.

When an issuer places its commercial paper through a dealer, the issuer decides how much paper it will issue at each maturity. The dealer is the issuer's contact with investors and provides the issuer with relevant information on market conditions and investor demand. Dealers generally immediately resell commercial paper purchased from issuers and do not hold significant amounts of commercial paper in inventory. Dealers will temporarily hold commercial paper in inventory as a service to issuers, such as to meet an immediate need for a significant amount of funds at a particular maturity.

The difference between what the dealer pays the issuer for commercial paper and what he sells it for, the "dealer spread," is around 10 basis points on an annual basis. A large commercial paper program with $500 million in paper outstanding for one year would cost the issuer $500,000 in dealer fees.

Because independent dealers are relatively inexpensive, only large and well-recognized issuers distribute their own commercial paper. Direct issuers are typically committed to borrowing $1 billion or more in the commercial paper market on a continuous basis (Felix 1987, p. 20). Partly as a result of the decline in dealer spreads over the last ten years, the percentage of total commercial paper issued directly fell from almost 55 percent in 1980 to just 35 percent at the end of 1991. An additional factor in the growth of dealer-placed commercial paper has been the entry into the market of smaller issuers who do not have borrowing needs large enough to justify a direct sales force.

Competition among dealers significantly increased in the late 1980s after the entrance into the market of bank dealers, which are subsidiaries of bank holding companies. Prior to the mid-1980s, commercial banks mainly acted as agents who placed commercial paper without underwriting and who carried out the physical transactions required in commercial paper programs, including the issuing and safekeeping of notes and the paying of investors at maturity. Bank dealers entered the market after legal restrictions on underwriting by bank holding companies were relaxed, and the increased competition led to declines in profit margins and the exit from the market of some major investment bank dealers. Salomon Brothers closed its dealership and Paine Webber sold its dealership to CitiCorp. Goldman Sachs, another important dealer, responded to increased competition by rescinding its longstanding requirement that it be the sole dealer for an issuer's commercial paper. Issuers have increased their use of multiple dealers for large commercial paper programs, frequently including a bank dealer in their team of dealers.

The largest commercial paper dealers are still the investment banks, including Merrill Lynch, Goldman Sachs, and Shearson Lehman. Commercial bank holding companies with large commercial paper dealer subsidiaries include Bankers Trust, CitiCorp, BankAmerica, and J.P. Morgan. Some foreign investment and commercial bank holding companies have also become significant dealers.

The secondary market in commercial paper is small. Partly the lack of a secondary market reflects the heterogeneous characteristics of commercial paper, which makes it difficult to assemble blocks of paper large enough to facilitate secondary trading. Partly it reflects the short maturity of the paper: investors know how long they want to invest cash and, barring some unforeseen cash need, hold commercial paper to maturity. Dealers will sometimes purchase paper from issuers or investors, hold the paper in inventory and subsequently trade it. Bids for commercial paper of the largest issuers are available through brokers.

Some direct issuers offer master note agreements which allow investors, usually bank trust departments, to lend funds on demand on a daily basis at a rate tied to the commercial paper rate. Each day the issuer tells the investor the rate on the master note and the investor tells the issuer how much it will deposit that day. At the end of 1991, approximately 10 percent of GMAC's short-term notes outstanding were master notes sold to bank trust departments (GMAC 1992, p. 13).

Risk in the Commercial Paper Market

Ratings

Since 1970, when the Penn Central Transportation Co. defaulted with $82 million of commercial paper outstanding, almost all commercial paper has carried ratings from one or more rating agency. Currently, the four major rating agencies are Moody's, Standard & Poor's, Duff & Phelps, and Fitch. An issuer's commercial paper rating is an independent "assessment of the likelihood of timely payment of [short-term] debt" (Standard & Poor's 1991, p. iii). Table 3 lists the four rating agencies, the rating scales they publish, and the approximate number of commercial paper ratings issued at the end of 1990. The ratings are relative, allowing the investor to compare the risks across issues. For example Standard & Poor's gives an A-1 rating to issues that it believes have a "strong" degree of safety for timely repayment of debt, an A-2 rating to issues that it believes have a degree of safety that is "satisfactory," and an A-3 rating to issues

TABLE 3 RATING AGENCIES AND COMMERCIAL PAPER RATINGS

	Higher A/Prime	Lower A/Prime	Speculative Below Prime	Defaulted	Approx. # of CP Ratings	Major Publication Listing CP Ratings
Moody's	P-1	P-2, P-3	NP	NP	2,000	Moody's Global Short-Term Market Record
Standard & Poor's	A-1+, A-1	A-2, A-3	B, C	D	2,000	S&P Commercial Paper Ratings Guide
Duff & Phelps	Duff 1+, Duff 1, Duff 1-	Duff 2, Duff 3	Duff 4	Duff 5	175	Short-Term Ratings and Research Guide
Fitch	F-1+, F-1	F-2, F-3	F-5	D	125	Fitch Ratings
Range of Likely S&P Long-Term Bond Rating	AAA, AA, A	A, BBB	BB, B, CCC, CC, C			

that it believes have a degree of safety that is "adequate." Below these three categories are the speculative grades in which the capacity for repayment is small relative to the higher-rated issues. Finally, a D rating indicates the issuer has defaulted on its commercial paper. Almost all issuers carry one of the two highest Prime or A ratings.

Issuers hire the rating agencies to rate their short-term debt and pay the agencies an annual fee ranging from $10,000 to $29,000 per year. For an additional fee the agencies will also rate other liabilities of the issuer, including their long-term bonds. The ratings are provided to the public, generally by subscription, either through publications, computer databases, or over the phone. Major announcements by the rating agencies are also reported on news wire services. Table 3 lists each agency's major publication in which commercial paper ratings appear.

Rating agencies rely on a wide variety of information in assessing the default risk of an issuer. The analysis is largely based on the firm's historical and projected operating results and its financial structure. Relevant characteristics include size (both absolute and compared to competitors), profitability (including the level and variation of profits), and leverage. Table 4 shows the means of selected historical characteristics of a sample of publicly traded nonfinancial issuers by commercial paper rating category. The table shows that higher-rated issuers are on average more profitable than lower-rated issuers and, with some exceptions, larger. Additionally, higher-rated issuers rely less heavily on debt financing than lower-rated issuers and have stronger interest-coverage and debt-coverage ratios.[8] In addition to evaluating the firm's operating results and financial structure, rating agencies also evaluate more subjective criteria like quality of

TABLE 4 Characteristics of Industrial Commercial Paper Issuers by Rating, Three-Year Averages

Standard & Poor's Commercial Paper Rating	Number of Companies	Assets (millions)	Interest Coverage	Debt Coverage	Leverage	Profitability
A-1+	91	$4,547	8x	.7x	27%	18%
A-1	102	$2,924	5x	.5x	35%	16%
A-2	97	$1,866	4x	.4x	36%	14%
A-3	9	$5,252	2x	.2x	52%	10%

Notes: Sample consists of nonfinancial commercial paper issuers required to file with the SEC.
Interest coverage is defined as the ratio of income available for interest to interest expense. Income available for interest is defined as pre-tax income less special income plus interest expense.
Debt coverage is defined as the ratio of cash flow to short- and long-term debt. Cash flow is income plus preferred dividends plus deferred taxes.
Leverage is defined as the ratio of total debt to invested capital. Invested capital is the sum of short- and long-term debt, minority interest, preferred and common equity, and deferred taxes.
Profitability is defined as the ratio of income available for interest to invested capital.
SOURCE: Standard & Poor's Compustat Services.

[8] Because ratings depend on historical operating results, researchers have had some success in predicting ratings based on accounting data. See, for example, Peavy and Edgar (1983).

management and industry characteristics. The same factors influence the issuer's short-term and long-term debt rating so there is generally a close correspondence between the commercial paper rating and the bond rating.

Ratings are crucially important in the commercial paper market. Ratings are useful as an independent evaluation of credit risk that summarizes available public information and reduces the duplication of analysis in a market with many investors (Wakeman 1981). Ratings are also used to guide investments in commercial paper. Some investors, either by regulation or choice, restrict their holdings to high-quality paper and the measure of quality used for these investment decisions is the rating. For example, regulations of MMFs limit their holdings of commercial paper rated less than A1-P1. Other market participants, including dealers and clearing agencies, also generally require issuers to maintain a certain quality. Again, credit quality is measured by the rating.

Backup Liquidity

Commercial paper issuers maintain access to funds that can be used to pay off all or some of their maturing commercial paper and other short-term debt. These funds are either in the form of their own cash reserves or bank lines of credit. Rating agencies require evidence of short-term liquidity and will not issue a commercial paper rating without it. The highest-rated issuers can maintain liquidity backup of as little as 50 percent of commercial paper outstanding, but firms with less than a high A1-P1 rating generally have to maintain 100 percent backup.

Most commercial paper issuers maintain backup liquidity through bank lines of credit available in a variety of forms. Standard credit lines allow borrowing under a 90-day note. Swing lines provide funds on a day-to-day basis, allowing issuers to cover a shortfall in proceeds from paper issuance on a particular day. Increasingly, backup lines of credit are being structured as more secure multiyear revolver agreements in which a bank or syndicate of banks commit to loan funds to a firm on demand at a floating base rate that is tied to the prime rate, LIBOR rate, or Certificate of Deposit rate. The spread over the base rate is negotiated at the time the agreement is made and can either be fixed or dependent on the bond rating of the borrower at the time the loan is drawn down. The length of the revolver commitment varies, but the trend in revolvers has been towards shorter terms, typically around three years. As compensation for the revolver commitment, the firm pays various fees to the bank. The facility fee is a percentage of the credit line and is paid whether or not the line is activated. The commitment fee is a percentage of the unused credit line. This type of fee has become less common in recent years. A usage fee is sometimes charged if the credit line is heavily used.

Backup lines of credit are intended to provide funds to retire maturing commercial paper when an event prevents an issuer from rolling over the paper. Such an event may be specific to an issuer: an industrial accident, sudden liability exposure, or other adverse business conditions that investors perceive as significantly weakening the credit strength of the issuer. Or the event may be a general development affecting the commercial paper market. For instance, a major issuer might default, as Penn Central did in 1970, and make it prohibitively expensive for some issuers to roll over new paper, or a natural disaster such as a hurricane may interrupt the normal function of the market.

Backup lines of credit will generally not be useful for a firm whose operating and financial condition has deteriorated to the point where it is about to default on its short-term liabilities. Credit agreements frequently contain "material adverse change" clauses which allow banks to cancel credit lines if the financial condition of a firm significantly changes. Indeed, the recent history of commercial paper defaults has shown that as an issuer's financial condition deteriorates and its commercial paper cannot be rolled over, backup lines of credit are usually canceled before they can be used to pay off maturing commercial paper.

General factors affecting the commercial paper market may also result in the disruption of backup lines of credit. Standard & Poor's has emphasized this point in an evaluation of the benefits to investors of backup credit lines: "A general disruption of commercial paper markets would be a highly volatile scenario, under which most bank lines would represent unreliable claims on whatever cash would be made available through the banking system to support the market" (Samson and Bachmann 1990, p. 23). Part of the risk assumed by commercial paper investors is the possibility of this highly volatile scenario.

Credit Enhancements

While backup lines of credit are needed to obtain a commercial paper rating, they will not raise the rating above the underlying creditworthiness of the issuer. Issuers can significantly increase the rating of their paper, however, by using one of a variety of credit enhancements which lower default risk by arranging for an alternative party to retire the commercial paper if the issuer cannot. These credit enhancements differ from backup lines of credit in that they provide a guarantee of support which cannot be withdrawn. Some smaller and riskier firms, which normally would find the commercial paper market unreceptive, access the commercial paper market using these enhancements.

Some large firms with strong credit ratings raise the ratings of smaller and less creditworthy subsidiaries by supporting their commercial paper with outright guarantees or with less secure "keepwell" agreements which describe the commitment the parent makes to assist the subsidiary to maintain a certain creditworthiness (Moody's, July 1992). Since parent companies may have incentives to prevent default by their subsidiaries, the affiliation of a subsidiary with a strong parent can raise the credit rating of the subsidiary issuer.

Firms also raise their credit ratings by purchasing indemnity bonds from insurance companies or standby letters of credit sold by commercial banks. Both of these enhancements provide assurance that the supporting entity will retire maturing commercial paper if the issuer cannot. With a letter of credit, for example, the issuer pays a fee to the bank, attaches the letter of credit to the commercial paper and effectively rents the bank's rating. The attention of the rating agency and investors shift from the issuer to the supporting bank. The issue will generally receive the same rating as the bank's own commercial paper and offer an interest rate close to the bank's paper. Since relatively few U.S. banks have A1-P1 ratings, highly rated foreign banks are the primary sellers of commercial paper letters of credit. At the end of the first quarter of 1992, approximately 6 percent of commercial paper was fully backed by a credit enhancement, primarily bank letters of credit, issued by a third party unaffiliated with the issuer (Federal Reserve Bank of New York 1992).

Slovin et al. (1988) show that the announcement of a commercial paper program with a credit enhancement[9] has been associated with a significant increase in the value of the issuer's equity, but the announcement of a commercial paper program with no credit enhancement has no impact on firm value. This evidence suggests that by issuing a letter of credit and certifying the creditworthiness of the issuer, the commercial bank provides new information to the capital markets. These results provide support for the hypothesis that banks generate information relevant for assessing credit risk that the securities markets do not have. Banks supply this information to the capital market through commercial paper programs supported by letters of credit.

Default History and Yields

Commercial paper pays a market-determined interest rate that is closely related to other market interest rates like the rate on large certificates of deposit. Because commercial paper has default risk, its yield is higher than the yield on Treasury bills. From 1967 through 1991, the spread of the one-month commercial paper rate over the one-month Treasury bill rate averaged 117 basis points.

Default risk also creates a differential between the rates on different quality grades of commercial paper. Figure 4 shows the spread between the yield on commercial paper rated A1-P1 and the yield on paper rated A2-P2. This spread averaged 52 basis points from 1974 through 1991. Default risk as measured by the quality spread shows some variation over time, rising during recessions and falling during expansions.

Historically, the commercial paper market has been remarkably free of default. As shown in Table 5, in the 20-year period from 1969 through 1988 there were only two major defaults. The low default rates in the commercial paper market largely reflect the tastes of commercial paper investors. As shown in Table 4, investors typically prefer commercial paper issued by large firms with long track records, conservative financing strategies, and stable profitability. Most investors will not buy paper from small, unknown, highly leveraged issuers unless the paper has credit enhancements attached. Moreover, rating services will not assign a prime rating to these issues and most dealers will not distribute the paper.

---

[9] The credit enhancements examined were standby letters of credit and, for programs outside the United States, note issuance facilities.

FIGURE 4 SPREAD BETWEEN THE RATES ON PRIME- AND MEDIUM-GRADE COMMMERCIAL PAPER

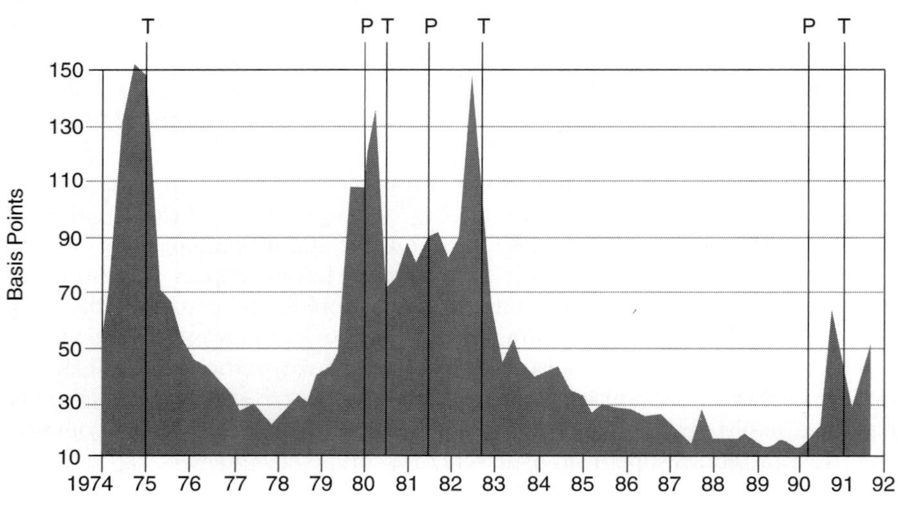

SOURCE: Board of Governors of the Federal Reserve System.

TABLE 5 MAJOR DEFAULTS IN THE U.S. COMMERCIAL PAPER MARKET

Issuer	Date of Default	Amount Outstanding at Default ($ millions)	Original Rating of Longest Outstanding Defaulting CP: Moody's	S&P
Penn Central	6/21/70	82.0	NR	NR
Manville Corp.	8/26/82	15.2	P-2	A-2
Integrated Resources	6/15/89	213.0	NR	A-2
Colorado Ute Electric	8/17/89	19.0	P-1	A-1
Equitable Lomas Leasing	9/12/89	53.0	P-3	A-3
Mortgage & Realty Trust	3/15/90	166.9	NR	A-2
Washington Bancorp	5/11/90	36.7	NR	NR
Stotler Group	7/25/90	0.75	NR	NR
Columbia Gas	6/12/91	268.0	P-2	A-2

SOURCE: Fons and Kimball (1992), *Wall Street Journal, Dow Jones News Wire, Business Week,* Standard & Poor's.

Even a major issuer can find the commercial paper market unreceptive if its financial condition is perceived by the market to have weakened. Fons and Kimball (1992) estimate that issuers who defaulted on long-term debt withdrew from the commercial paper market an average of almost three years prior to default. As ratings declined, these issuers significantly decreased their commercial paper borrowings. Fons and Kimball (1992) take this "orderly exit" mechanism as evidence that investors in the commercial paper market are "unreceptive to lower-quality paper." Crabbe and Post (January 1992) document the orderly exit mechanism using a sample of bank holding company issuers during 1986 to 1990. For issuers which experienced Moody's commercial paper rating downgrades, commercial paper outstanding declined on average by 12.2 percent in the ten weeks prior to the rating change and 15.7 percent in the first four weeks after the change.

The number of commercial paper defaults rose to seven in 1989 to 1991, but even in this period the default rate was low. Fons and Kimball (1992) estimate the dollar amount of defaults over this period as a percentage of the total volume issued.[10] They find that the default rate for the United States was only 0.0040 percent in 1989–91, which means that "an investor purchasing U.S.-issued commercial paper ... throughout the 1989–1991 period experienced, on average, interruption in promised payments of roughly [40/100] of a penny for every $100 invested" (p. 13).

The rise in defaults in the 1989 to 1990 period may have partially reflected an increased tolerance for riskier paper in the later part of the 1980s. Unrated commercial paper grew significantly in the late 1980s to $5 billion in January 1990. Over the same period, the spread between the yields on A1-P1 paper and A2-P2 paper was unusually low (averaging less than 30 basis points). These developments were reversed in the early 1990s following the rise in commercial paper defaults, the deterioration in economic conditions, and the bankruptcy of Drexel Burnham, a major dealer and promoter of unrated commercial paper. By early 1991, unrated paper outstanding had fallen to below $1 billion and the A1-A2 spread had risen to almost 50 basis points, its highest level since 1982.

The commercial paper defaults in 1989 and 1990 had a significant impact on the demand for lower-rated paper by money market mutual funds. Several MMFs were major holders of defaulted paper of Integrated Resources and Mortgage & Realty Trust.[11] Following these defaults, some MMFs began to voluntarily restrict their commercial paper holdings to A1-P1 issues. Then in June 1991, SEC regulations became effective that limited MMFs to investing no more than one percent of their assets in any single A2-P2 issuer and no more than 5 percent of assets in A2-P2 paper. Previously, there had been no restriction on MMF total holding of A2-P2 paper, and MMFs had held approximately 10 percent of their assets in A2-P2 paper at the end of 1990. Crabbe and Post (May 1992) find that by the end of 1991, MMFs had reduced their holdings of A2-P2 commercial paper to almost zero. Along with the 1989 and 1990 defaults, they point to the June 1991 regulations as an important factor influencing MMF investment choices.

Innovations

Asset-Backed Commercial Paper

A relatively new innovation in the commercial paper market is the backing of commercial paper with assets. The risk of most commercial paper depends on the entire

---

[10] Fons and Kimball (1992) estimate the total volume of commercial paper issuance as average outstanding commercial paper times (365/average maturity). Average maturity is estimated at 30 days.

[11] Value Line's MMF, for example, held 3.5 percent of its portfolio in $22.6 million of Integrated's paper. Value Line protected the fund's investors, absorbing the loss at an after-tax cost of $7.5 million.

firm's operating and financial risk. With asset-backed paper, the paper's risk is instead tied directly to the creditworthiness of specific financial assets, usually some form of receivable. Asset-backed paper is one way smaller, riskier firms can access the commercial paper market. The advantages of asset-backed securities have led large, lower-risk commercial paper issuers to also participate in asset-backed commercial paper programs. Asset-backed programs have grown rapidly since the first program in 1983. Standard & Poor's has rated more than 60 asset-backed issues (Kavanagh et al. 1992, p. 109) with an estimated $40 billion outstanding.

Asset-backed commercial paper is issued by a company, called a special purpose entity, which purchases receivables from one firm or a group of firms and finances the purchase with funds raised in the commercial paper market. The sole business activity of the special company is the purchase and finance of the receivables so the risk of the company and the commercial paper it issues is isolated from the risk of the firm or firms which originated the receivables.

The trade receivables and credit card receivables that are typically used in asset-backed programs have a predictable cash flow and default rate so the risk of the assets can be estimated. Asset-backed paper programs are structured so that the amount of receivables exceeds the outstanding paper. In addition to this over-collaterization, credit enhancements are used, including guarantees by the firm selling the receivables, bank letters of credit, or surety bonds. As with all commercial paper issues, rating agencies require backup liquidity.

The combining of similar receivables from a group of companies into a pool large enough to justify a commercial paper program allows small firms to participate in asset-backed programs and serves to diversify some of the receivables' default risk. Typically, the financing firm which pools the receivables is managed by a commercial bank which purchases assets from its corporate clients.

Swaps

A factor in the growth of the commercial paper market during the 1980s has been the rapid growth in the market for interest rate swaps. Interest rate swaps are one of a variety of relatively new instruments that have significantly increased the financing options of commercial paper issuers. Swaps provide issuers with flexibility to rapidly restructure their liabilities, to raise funds at reduced costs, and to hedge risks arising from short-term financing programs.

Interest rate swaps are agreements between two parties to exchange interest rate payments over some specified time period on a certain amount of unexchanged principal. To appreciate the role of swaps it is necessary to understand that there are two interest rate risks associated with commercial paper borrowing. First, the firm faces market interest rate risk: the risk that the rate it pays on commercial paper will rise because the level of market interest rates increases. A change in the risk-free rate, such as the Treasury bill rate, will cause a corresponding change in all commercial paper and borrowing rates. Second, the firm faces idiosyncratic interest rate risk: the risk that commercial paper investors will demand a higher rate because they perceive the firm's credit risk to have increased. With idiosyncratic risk, the rate on its commercial paper can rise without an increase in the risk-free rate or in other commercial paper rates.

A commercial paper issuer can eliminate market interest rate risk by entering into a swap and agreeing to exchange a fixed interest rate payment for a variable interest rate. For example, in the swap the firm may pay a fixed interest rate that is some spread over the multi-year Treasury bond rate and receive the floating six-month LIBOR rate. If the commercial paper rate rises because of a general rise in the market interest rate, the firm's increased interest payment on its commercial paper is offset by the increased payment it receives from the swap. This swap allows the firm to transform its short-term, variable-rate commercial paper financing into a fixed-rate liability that hedges market interest rate risks in the same manner as long-term fixed-rate, noncallable debt. Note that the firm still bears the risk of idiosyncratic changes in its commercial paper rate. If its own commercial paper rate rises while other rates, including the LIBOR rate, do not rise, the cost of borrowing in the commercial paper market will rise without a corresponding increase in the payment from the swap.

Alternatively, the firm can fix the cost of its idiosyncratic risk by borrowing in the long-term market at a fixed rate and entering into a swap in which it pays a floating rate and receives a fixed rate. The swap effectively converts the long-term fixed-rate liability into a floating-rate liability that is similar to commercial paper. The firm now faces the risk of a general change in the level on interest rates, just like a financing strategy of issuing commercial paper, but has fixed the cost of its idiosyncratic risk by borrowing long-term in the bond market at a fixed-rate.

One important and unresolved issue is what the advantage of swaps are relative to alterative financing strategies. For example, why would a firm issue short-term debt and swap the flexible rate into a long-term rate instead of issuing long-term debt? Researchers have advanced a variety of hypotheses to explain the rapid growth of the interest rate swap market, but no real consensus has been reached. Many explanations view swaps as a way for firms to exploit differences in the premium for credit risk at different maturities and in different markets. For example, one firm may find it can issue commercial paper at a rate close to the average for similarly rated issuers but pays a significantly higher spread in the long-term fixed-rate market. If the firm prefers fixed-rate financing, a commercial paper program combined with a swap may provide cheaper financing than issuing fixed-rate debt. But it is uncertain what causes these borrowing differentials.[12]

The two interest rate swaps discussed above are the most basic examples of a wide variety of available swaps. The examples are constructed to highlight some important aspects of interest rate swaps, but it is not known how many of these swaps are currently being used in conjunction with commercial paper programs.[13] Some commercial paper programs involve international debt issues in conjunction with both interest rate and currency swaps.

---

[12] Some suggested reasons include market inefficiencies and differences in agency costs and bankruptcy costs across various forms of debt. Wall and Pringle (1988) provide a review of the uses and motivations for interest rate swaps.

[13] Einzig & Lange (1990) discuss some examples of interest rates swaps used in practice.

Foreign Commercial Paper Markets

While the U.S. market is by far the largest, a variety of foreign commercial paper markets began operating in the 1980s and early 1990s. Table 6 lists the international markets and shows estimates of paper outstanding at the end of 1990. Even though the U.S. commercial paper market continued to grow in the later 1980s, its share of the worldwide commercial paper market fell from almost 90 percent in 1986 to less than 65 percent in 1990. The Japanese market, which began in 1987, is the largest commercial paper market outside the United States. In Europe, the French, Spanish, and Swedish commercial paper markets are well established and the German market has shown rapid growth since it began in 1991.[14]

Some U.S. firms simultaneously maintain a commercial paper program in the United States and issue dollar-denominated commercial paper abroad in the Euro commercial paper market. The Euro commercial paper market developed from note issuance and revolving underwriting facilities of the late 1970s in which firms issued tradable notes with the characteristics of commercial paper in conjunction with a loan agreement in which a bank or bank syndicate agreed to purchase the notes if the issuer was unable to place them with investors. In the early 1980s, higher-quality issuers began issuing notes without the backup facilities. The Euro commercial paper market grew rapidly from 1985 to 1990. By the middle of 1992, outstanding Euro commercial paper totaled $87 billion. U.S. financial and industrial firms are important issuers, either directly or through their foreign subsidiaries. Approximately 75 percent of Euro commercial paper is denominated in U.S. dollars while the remainder is denominated in

TABLE 6 International Commercial Paper Markets Amounts Outstanding, End of 1990 (Billions of U.S. dollars)

United States	557.8
Japan	117.3
France	31.0
Canada	26.8
Sweden	22.3
Spain	20.0*
Australia	10.9
United Kingdom	9.1
Finland	8.3
Norway	2.6
Netherlands	2.0
Euro-CP	70.4
Total	878.5

*Estimate
SOURCE: Bank for International Settlements.

[14] Bank of International Settlements (1991) reviews the international commercial paper markets. Also see Euromoney (1992) for a review of the European money markets.

European currency units, Italian liras, and Japanese yen. Issuers commonly issue Euro commercial paper in dollars and use swaps or foreign exchange transactions to convert their borrowings to another currency. The foreign markets, including the Euro commercial paper market, provide issuers flexibility in raising short-term funds, allowing them to diversify their investor base, to establish presence in the international credit markets, and to obtain the lowest cost of funds.

While the Euro commercial paper market has similarities to the U.S. market, there are some important differences. The maturity of Euro commercial paper has been longer than in the United States, typically between 60 to 180 days, and, partly reflecting the longer maturities, there is an active secondary market. There is some evidence that the credit quality of the typical issuer in the Euro commercial paper market is not as high as in the U.S. market. Both Standard & Poor's and Moody's rate Euro commercial paper programs, but ratings have not been as crucial in the Euro market as they have been in the U.S. market. U.S. firms with less than A1-P1 ratings have found that the Euro market has been more receptive than the domestic market to commercial paper issues with no credit enhancements attached. Higher default rates abroad reflect the less stringent credit standards. Fons and Kimball (1992) estimate that the amount of defaults as a percent of the total volume of commercial paper issued in the non-U.S. markets (including the Euro commercial paper market) in 1989 to 1991 was 0.0242 percent, which was significantly greater than the 0.0040 percent in the U.S. market. In 1989, the four Euro commercial paper defaults affected almost 1 percent of the market.

The Growing Importance of Commercial Paper

The rapid growth of commercial paper shown in Figure 1 reflects the advantages of financing and investing using the capital markets rather than the banking system. To a significant extent, the advantage of commercial paper issuance is cost: high-quality issuers have generally found borrowing in the commercial paper to be cheaper than bank loans. The cost of commercial paper programs, including the cost of distribution, agent fees, rating fees, and fees for backup credit lines, are small, amounting to perhaps 15 basis points in a large program. A highly rated bank borrows at a cost of funds comparable to other commercial paper issuers, and it must add a spread when lending to cover the expenses and capital cost of its operations and to cover any reserve requirements. Riskier firms are willing to pay this spread because the bank adds value by generating information about the creditworthiness of the borrower which enables it to lend at less cost than the commercial paper market. A large creditworthy issuer will generally find it cheaper to bypass the bank and raise funds directly in the credit market.

The growth of the commercial paper market can be viewed as part of a wider trend towards corporate financing using securities rather than bank loans. Other aspects of this trend, commonly referred to as asset securitization, include the rapid growth of the bond and junk bond markets and the market for asset-backed securities. The pace of asset securitization increased sharply in the 1980s. New security technology, including the development of risk management tools like swaps and interest rate caps, became widespread. At the same time, established markets expanded to include new issuers. Smaller, riskier firms increased their issuance of long-term bonds and entered the commercial paper market with asset-backed paper and letter of credit programs. Commercial paper is likely to remain a significant source of financing for domestic and foreign firms and a relatively safe short-term security for investors.

References

Bank for International Settlements. *International Banking and Financial Market Developments.* Basle, Switzerland, August 1991.

Board of Governors of the Federal Reserve System. *Flow of Funds Accounts, Financial Assets and Liabilities, First Quarter 1992.* Washington: Board of Governors, 1992.

Crabbe, Leland, and Mitchell A. Post. "The Effect of a Rating Change on Commercial Paper Outstandings." Washington: Board of Governors of the Federal Reserve System, January 1992.

———. "The Effect of SEC Amendments to Rule 2A-7 on the Commercial Paper Market." Washington: Board of Governors of the Federal Reserve System, May 1992.

The Depository Trust Company. Final Plan for a Commercial Paper Program. Memorandum, April 1990.

Einzig, Robert, and Bruce Lange. "Swaps at TransAmerica: Analysis and Applications," *Journal of Applied Corporate Finance*, vol. 2 (Winter 1990), pp. 48–58.

"1992 Guide to European Domestic Money Markets," published with Euromoney, September 1992.

Federal Reserve Bank of New York. Press Release No. 1932, Market Reports Division, May 13, 1992.

Felix, Richard, ed. *Commercial Paper.* London: Euromoney Publications, 1987.

Fons, Jerome S., and Andrew E. Kimball. "Defaults and Orderly Exits of Commercial Paper Issuers," *Moody's Special Report*, Moody's Investor Service, February 1992.

General Motors Acceptance Corporation. *1991 Annual Report.* Detroit, Michigan: 1992.

Kakutani, Masaru, M. Douglas Watson, Jr., and Donald E. Noe. "Analytical Framework Involving the Rating of Debt Instruments Supported by 'Keepwell' Agreements," *Moody's Special Comment*, Moody's Investors Service, July 1992.

Kavanagh, Barbara, Thomas R. Boemio, and Gerald A. Edwards, Jr. "Asset-Backed Commercial Paper Programs," *Federal Reserve Bulletin*, vol. 78 (February 1992), pp. 107–16.

Peavy, John W., and S. Michael Edgar. "A Multiple Discriminant Analysis of BHC Commercial Paper Ratings," *Journal of Banking and Finance*, vol. 7 (1983), pp. 161–73.

Samson, Solomon B. and Mark Bachmann. "Paper Backup Policies Revisited," *Standard & Poor's Creditweek*, September 10, 1990, pp. 23–24.

Slovin, Myron B., Marie E. Sushka, and Carl D. Hudson. "Corporate Commercial Paper, Note Issuance Facilities, and Shareholder Wealth," *Journal of International Money and Finance*, vol. 7 (1988), pp. 289–302.

Standard & Poor's Corporation. *Commercial Paper Ratings Guide.* April 1991.

Stigum, Marcia. *The Money Market.* Homewood, Ill.: Dow Jones-Irwin, 1990.

Wakeman, L. Macdonald. "The Real Function of Bond Rating Agencies," *Chase Financial Quarterly*, vol. 1 (Fall 1981), pp. 19–25.

Wall, Larry D., and John J. Pringle. "Interest Rate Swaps: A Review of the Issues," Federal Reserve Bank of Atlanta *Economic Review*, November/December 1988, pp. 22–40.

Questions

1. Commercial paper has been defined traditionally as short-term, unsecured promissory notes issued by large corporations. In what way(s) has some recently issued paper broken with tradition?
2. "The Securities Act of 1933 requires that securities offered to the public be registered with the Securities and Exchange Commission." Under what conditions is commercial paper exempt from SEC registration?
3. Describe the major issuers of commercial paper. Provide evidence supporting your answer.
4. Describe the major purchasers of commercial paper. Provide evidence supporting your answer.
5. Companies issue commercial paper in two ways: direct placement and dealer placement. Compare and contrast these two methods.
6. Issuers hire rating agencies to rate their commercial paper and pay the agencies an annual fee ranging from $10,000 to $29,000.
   a. Why do issuers pay agencies to rate their commercial paper?
   b. Having received a sizable fee from the issuer, will the rating agency be biased in favor of the issuer?
   c. Describe the ratings provided by the four major rating agencies.
   d. What information do rating agencies use in the assignment of ratings?
7. In what way does a line of credit at a bank provide backup liquidity for a commercial paper issue?
8. "While backup lines of credit are needed to obtain a commercial paper rating, they will not raise the rating above the underlying creditworthiness of the issuer." In what ways can issuers increase the rating of their commercial paper?
9. In your opinion, does the historical record of default in the commercial paper market inspire confidence? Provide evidence supporting your answer.
10. Describe the challenge presented by commercial paper to U.S. commercial banks.

What You Should Know about Repos

Daniel L. Kovlak

A repurchase (repo) agreement is an agreement in which an investor (buyer-lender) transfers cash to a broker-dealer or a financial institution (seller-borrower). The broker-dealer or financial institution transfers securities to the entity and promises to later repay the cash plus interest in exchange for the same securities. (This description is from the viewpoint of a savings and loan association or a state or local government; banks and broker-dealers call this agreement a "reverse repurchase agreement.")

There are several types of repo agreements. If the same securities are returned, the agreements are sometimes referred to as "vanilla" or "plain vanilla" agreements because there is nothing complicated about these transactions. In "dollar repurchase agreements," different securities are returned. There are two types of dollar repo agreements: fixed coupon repo agreements in which different securities are returned but with the same stated interest rate and with maturities similar to the securities transferred, and yield maintenance agreements in which different securities are returned that provide the seller-borrower with a yield as specified in the agreement.

This article focuses on those agreements in which the same securities are returned. An example of such a repo transaction on the trade date is shown in Figure 1. The transaction at maturity is shown in Figure 2.

The terms of repo agreements also vary. "Overnight repo agreements" mature in one day. "Term repo agreements" are those that mature in more than one day. "Open repo agreements" have no specific maturity; both parties have the right to close the transaction at any time. "Repo agreements to maturity" are those that mature on the same day as the underlying securities.

At the time of this writing, Daniel L. Kovlak was a practice fellow from Peat, Marwick, Mitchell & Co. at the Governmental Accounting Standards Board (GASB) in Stamford, CT.

Source: Reprinted from *Management Accounting.* Copyright by Institute of Management Accountants, Montvale, NJ, May 1986.

FIGURE 1 REPURCHASE-REVERSE REPURCHASE AGREEMENT USING FULL COUPON TREASURY SECURITIES AS COLLATERAL

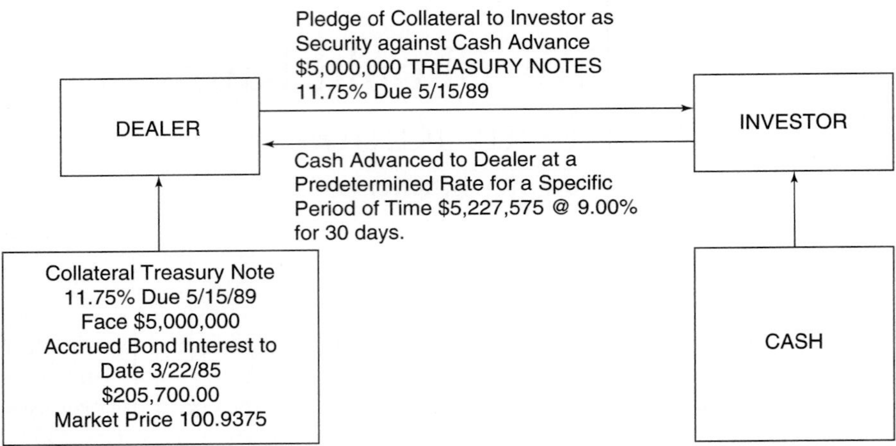

$$\text{Face value} \times \left(\begin{array}{c}\text{Market} \\ \text{price}\end{array} - \begin{array}{c}\text{Initial} \\ \text{margin}\end{array} \right) + \begin{array}{c}\text{Accrued} \\ \text{bond} \\ \text{interest}\end{array} = \begin{array}{l}\text{Agreed upon value} \\ \text{of collateral}\end{array}$$

$$\$5{,}000{,}000 \times (1.009375 - 0.005 \text{ price points}) + \$205{,}700.00 = \$5{,}227{,}575$$

(1) Trade date/settlement date dealer delivers collateral to investor on a delivery versus payment basis with payment equal to the agreed value of the collateral for repurchase.

(2) During the life of the Repurchase-Reverse Repurchase agreement there may be fluctuations in collateral value due to market price movements and interest payments on the underlying security. These variations and interest paydowns must be monitored on a daily basis by both sides to insure proper collateralization levels and maintenance of initial margin levels.

Investors invest in repos because they want to obtain a better yield on their temporary idle cash. In a repurchase agreement, when the investor transfers money to the seller-borrower, the investor receives as collateral government securities or government agency securities (such as GNMA, FNMA, and so forth). In most cases, the market value of those securities is in excess of the amount of cash transferred. This excess is called a "haircut" and protects the buyer-lender against fluctuations in the market value of the underlying securities. At the end of the repo agreement term, the buyer-lender returns the securities in exchange for the original amount of the agreement plus interest.

FIGURE 2 AT MATURITY*

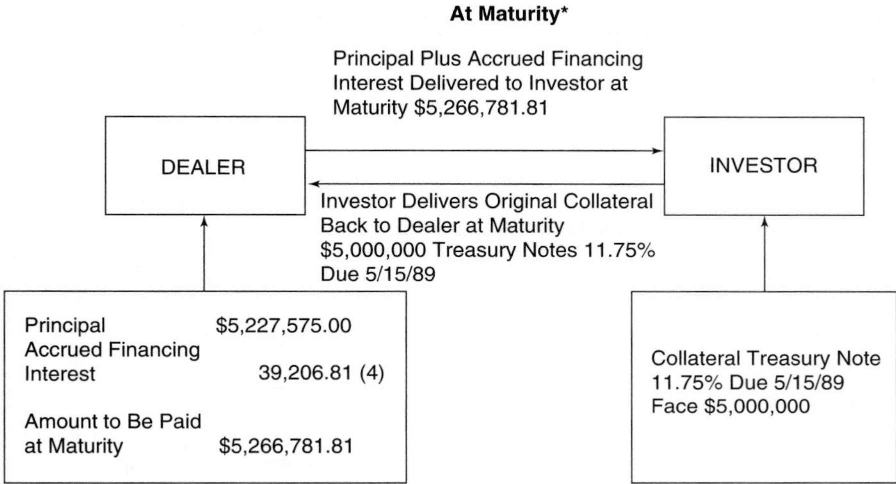

(3) At maturity the investor delivers the collateral back to the dealer on a delivery versus payment basis. At maturity the repurchase price includes the initial principal advanced, plus the sum of the daily financing accrual at the predetermined rate.

(4)	Principal	×	Rate	×	Number of days/360	=	Accrued interest
	$5,227,575	×	0.09	×	30/360	=	$39,206.81

*These examples do not contemplate the repurchase-reverse repurchase agreement crossing a coupon payment date, which would require use of various collateralization procedures.

Repo Environment: $300 Billion Market

In the book *The Money Market* published in 1983, Marcia Stigum estimates that between $150 and $160 billion of overnight repo agreement transactions occur each day. In addition, there are approximately $200 to $300 billion of term repo agreements outstanding. These numbers are probably significantly higher now because the U.S. government's debt has increased significantly since 1983, and U.S. government debt is financed through treasury bills, bonds, and notes. Government securities usually are the underlying securities, or collateral, for repo agreements, which is why investors think repo agreements are so safe.

There are 36 primary government securities dealers and approximately 200 secondary dealers. Primary dealers are permitted to make direct bids on new Treasury offerings. They submit daily reports of market activity and positions and monthly financial statements to the Federal Reserve Bank of New York and are subject to its informal oversight. Secondary dealers cannot bid on new offerings and are largely unregulated. Certain secondary dealers, including banks

TABLE 1 PAST DISASTERS INVOLVING REPOS

Dealers	Date	Total Losses in Millions	Major Industries
Bevill, Bresler & Schulman	April 1985	$240	Savings & Loan Associations
ESM	March 1985	$300	State & Local Governments Savings & Loan Associations*
Lion Capital	May 1984	$89	69 Municipalities (60 N.Y. State School Districts)
RTD Securities	May 1984	$5	8 Municipalities (7 N.Y. State School Districts)
Lombard-Wall	August 1982	$55	N.Y. State Dormitory Authority
Drysdale	May 1982	$160	Banking (Chase)
		$849	

*Led to the closing of the 71 S&Ls in Ohio for several days in March 1985.

and Securities & Exchange Commission broker-dealers, may be regulated by federal bank regulators or the SEC. Most secondary dealers, however, are unregulated. Because of this fact and because of a lack of investor awareness of the risks, there have been a number of losses in recent years (Table 1).

The most recent loss occurred in April 1985 when Bevill, Bresler and Schulman, a small government securities dealer in New Jersey, failed. Losses in that case have been estimated to be as high as $240 million. Those losses were incurred mostly by savings and loan associations and banks.

In March 1985, ESM Government Securities also went bankrupt, leaving its investors with losses of up to $300 million. In this case, local governments, in addition to savings and loan associations, were the losers. Home State Savings and Loan in Cincinnati, Ohio, had over $150 million invested with ESM, which led to a run on the savings and loan associations in Ohio. As a result, 71 savings and loan associations in Ohio were closed until they could prove they qualified for federal insurance. Municipalities that had repos with ESM included Toledo, Ohio ($19 million); Beaumont, Texas ($20 million); and Pompano Beach, Florida ($12 million).

How do these losses occur? In both situations, these losses resulted from the fact that the buyer-lender in the repo agreement did not take delivery of the securities underlying the agreement. If the investors had taken delivery of the securities, either physically or through an independent third party, they could have sold those securities and recovered the amount of their investments. However, if broker-dealers are requested to deliver securities in a repo agreement, most lower the interest rate for the repo agreement. Many investors, therefore, do not take possession of the securities because they naturally want to realize the highest rate.

Because delivery was not required, some government securities dealers were entering into several repurchase agreement transactions and were using the same securities as collateral for each of the transactions. In that case, some of the repo agreement transactions were not collateralized.

What Are the Risks?

The two major risks associated with repo agreements are credit risk and market risk. Credit risk is the risk that the other party to the transaction will not fulfill its obligation. This risk can be associated with the dealer of the repo agreement or with a third party holding the underlying securities (collateral). Credit risk exposure can be affected by a large concentration of investments with any one dealer.

Market risk is the risk that the market value of the underlying securities will decline. Market risk is affected by the length to maturity of the repo agreement, the extent that the underlying securities exceed the amounts invested, and the frequency at which the amount of collateral is adjusted for changing market values.

There are several ways an investor can minimize risks. An investor should always know the dealer. An investor can obtain information about the dealer by reviewing its credit rating and the latest financial statements. Regardless of the personal relationships that exist between the investor and a dealer, a financial review should be performed periodically. Lavish offices, impressive yachts, or expensive entertainment flaunted by dealers often can mislead investors.

Dealers offering excessively high interest rates also should be avoided. There is usually a good reason why a dealer is offering higher rates than other dealers. In many cases, it is because he really needs the business. As with other investments, the rate of return is related to the risks involved.

The best way investors in repo agreements can avoid significant losses and minimize credit risk is to take physical possession of the securities or have them delivered to an independent third party (custodian). The investor should never permit the dealer or the dealer's agent to hold the underlying securities. Those securities need to be accessible to the investor in the event of a dealer failure.

Another precaution the investor should take to minimize market risk, is to "mark-to-market." This phrase means that the market value of the underlying securities should be checked periodically to determine that it is in excess of the amount of the repo agreement. If the market value of the underlying securities falls below the value of the investment, the investor should insist on receiving more securities or a return of cash.

Written agreements also limit risk when entering into repo agreements. A written agreement can be drafted for each repo transaction or a master agreement can be written that covers all repo transactions with that dealer. These agreements should clearly establish the rights of each of the parties to the transactions. Moreover, investors should also enter into agreements with the custodian holding the underlying securities. Custodial agreements should specify the custodian's responsibilities which include: disbursing cash for repo agreements only when the underlying securities are delivered; obtaining additional securities or a return of cash if the required margin on a repo agreement is not maintained because of market fluctuations; holding the securities separately from all other securities of the custodian; and reporting periodically to the investor on the market value of underlying securities.

What Is Being Done to Protect Investors?

A number of organizations have taken steps to protect investors and prevent losses in repo transactions. The American Institute of CPAs issued its "Report of The Special Task Force on Audits of Repurchase Securities Transactions" in June 1985. This report describes the risks associated with repo agreements and the audit implications of these transactions. The AICPA also has drafted a Statement of Position (SOP) that will soon be issued by its Savings and Loan Association Committee to supplement the Savings and Loan Association Audit Guide. The draft SOP requires certain disclosures of repo agreement and reverse repurchase agreement transactions.

The Governmental Accounting Standards Board (GASB) issued an exposure draft of a statement of "Accounting and Financial Reporting for Deposits with Financial Institutions, Investments (including Repurchase Agreements), and Reverse Repurchase Agreements" in June 1985. The GASB believes the risks associated with repo agreements also exist for deposits with financial institutions when the deposits are in excess of insured amounts and collateral has not been received for those amounts. The proposed statement would require disclosure of legal or contractual provisions for deposits and investments, including repurchase agreements, and reverse repurchase agreements. In addition, certain disclosures would be required as of the balance sheet date. The purpose of these disclosures is to help financial statement users to assess the risks the governmental entity is taking with its investments.

In January 1986, the Securities & Exchange Commission issued "Disclosure Amendment to Regulation S-X regarding Repurchase and Reverse Repurchase Agreements." The Federal Reserve Bank is in the process of holding a number of educational programs to educate the public about repurchase agreements, their risks, and safeguards against those risks. They have issued a brochure, "It's 8:00 a.m. … Do You Know Where Your Collateral Is?"

In September 1985, the Government Securities Act of 1985 was passed by the U.S. House of Representatives. The bill would create a nine-member Government Securities Rule-making Board, a self-regulatory organization composed of industry and investor representatives under the supervision of the Federal Reserve Board. The new board would set minimum capital standards requirements and adopt bookkeeping, reporting, and other rules for all government securities dealers, including the approximately 200 currently unregulated dealers. In addition to this bill, the Senate has two other proposals that deal with this matter.

In January 1986, the U.S. Treasury and the Federal Reserve Board agreed to allow state and local governments to establish accounts with the Federal Reserve Banks for safekeeping of government securities. This agreement will allow governments to provide for better safekeeping and third-party verification of the securities underlying their repo agreements.

Many people believe that there has been an overreaction to recent failures of government securities dealers. They believe that because these failures have been well publicized, most investors are aware of the risks involved in repo agreements and will protect themselves against future failures. This argument is challenged by critics who point out that even though the failures of 1982 and 1984 were well publicized, the 1985 losses still occurred! In light of this experience it is hard to believe that without some action, other failures will not occur.

To help protect against these types of losses, corporate treasurers, investment officers of savings and loan associations, state and local governments, and other organizations need to be fully aware of the risks involved in repo agreements. Users of financial statements cannot assess the risks of these types of organizations without reviewing and understanding financial statement disclosures about those risks. Finally, it would seem that more regulation of the government securities industry is needed to guard against inadequately capitalized or unscrupulous dealers.

Questions

1. Describe a typical repurchase agreement.
2. Repurchase (repo) agreements are classified in the following ways: (a) reverse agreements, (b) plain vanilla agreements, (c) dollar agreements, (d) overnight agreements, (e) term agreements, (f) open agreements, and (g) agreements to maturity. Briefly describe each of these agreements.
3. What risks are faced by an investor in repos?
4. What can an investor in repos do to reduce the risk?

Evaluating the Risk in Negotiable CDs

JOHN T. ZIETLOW

For corporate treasurers investing less than \$1 million, there are essentially four major investments to choose from: certificates of deposit (CDs) issued by major banks, commercial paper of bank holding companies and corporations, other time deposits of banks and U.S. Government (mainly Treasury) securities [5]. This makes investment analysis of banks' short-term securities imperative.

The present analysis focuses on CDs and suggests how the corporate treasurer investing up to \$1 million can best evaluate the risk and risk-return tradeoffs of these securities. The treasurer able to invest \$1 million has the added advantage of being able to liquidate the position before maturity, if the bank is one of the *top twenty* whose CDs actively trade on the national secondary market. The treasurer does not necessarily forfeit liquidity on lesser denominations, however, as the company can use the CD as collateral for a bank loan in the event of a cash shortfall.

This article examines the difficulty of risk evaluation, followed by a listing of risk evaluation approaches, an elaboration of a ratings-based approach and some cautions and actionable guidelines.

Analyzing the Risk and Return of Negotiable CDs

Accurate return (yield) data are easily available. The treasurer can get, via phone or facsimile transmission, individual bank yield quotes—that may be directly negotiated for newly issued CDs (*primary market rates*), particularly on larger denominations. Secondary market comparative quotes are also readily available.

At the time of this writing, John T. Zietlow was an associate professor of finance at Indiana State University. Sian Chye Lim assisted in the research of this article, and Marilyn Prout of Standard & Poor's provided the ratings data used in the statistical models.

These might come from trading desks at banks, brokers and dealers or from a third-party online reporting system such as Telerate or the National CD Network. National CD Network's *Qwick-Rate* service focuses on the $100,000 "jumbo" CDs of 1,000-1,200 institutions on a daily basis, and up to 3,500 institutions monthly. The treasurer can compare realized yields with reported data from a third-party service, such as Bank Rate Monitor.

Risk evaluation and risk-return analysis are problematic, however. The financial analysis of a bank by an outsider is complex, since the quality of assets is difficult to assess. This *asymmetric information* problem is compounded by the substantial off-balance sheet exposure of banks, which, for large banks, amounts to triple the total assets.[1] Most corporate treasurers would be ill-equipped to incorporate such information into a default risk measure.

In addition, there is no clearly superior way to evaluate the risk-return tradeoffs appropriate for different issuers. What yields are appropriate for money-center banks versus super-regionals? Foreign issuers of Eurodollar deposits versus Yankee CDs? Thrifts versus banks or a Southwest versus a conservatively managed Midwest region bank? Risk premiums might be based on an issuer's loan loss exposure, default risk or another dimension of security risk, such as secondary market selling risk. However, it is a guessing game estimating what yield spread would be appropriate to compensate for default risk or selling risk in any case.

Given the difficulties associated with making the risk assessment, one might wonder if it is really necessary. After all, the FDIC guarantees principal up to $100,000, some $1 million CDs are *brokered* sums of ten different banks' $100,000 amounts, and the Federal Government seems to have protected large depositors in the past. Closer inspection suggests reasons for concern, however:

- The $100,000 deposit guarantee is minimal on a $1 million negotiable CD.
- Brokered $100,000 CDs are essentially a retail (not wholesale) product,[2] because $100,000 denominations are generally not negotiable.
- FDIC handling of the MCORP disposition suggests that uninsured deposits will not always be covered, and pending federal legislation leans further away from *de facto* coverage of uninsured deposits.
- Premiums on traded CDs are not insured, leaving the treasurer especially vulnerable on zero coupon CDs, which might have large premiums.[3]
- A preliminary study of perceived soundness of the Government guarantor, now exclusively the FDIC, predicts that its deteriorating condition may lead to a greater yield for CDs relative to Treasury bills.

---

[1] For extended discussions, see Lewis and Davis [6], p. 153, and Arshadi [1].

[2] See Stigum and Branch [7], p. 107.

[3] "Yield Lure Can Lead Investors Into Turbulent Waters," *Wall Street Journal*, October 24, 1989, p. C1.

Even if the treasurer *does* have some basis for evaluation, perhaps through experience in the markets, he or she may lack the time, information, analytical tools or expertise for the sophisticated evaluation demanded. A more objective, in-depth risk assessment should be extremely valuable.

Approaches to Risk Evaluation

There are two logical approaches to objective CD risk assessment: judgmental evaluation of yield premiums and use of third-party credit ratings. Each of these will be considered here, with relevant considerations and cautions offered for the short-term investor.

Measuring Risk from Yield Premiums

One approach is to assess risk based on yield premiums. For example, one might infer that the roughly 20-50 basis point yield spread between Eurodollar CDs and domestic CDs of the same issuer is due to greater risk, in that the $100,000 federal guarantee is absent. One might also compare a bank's CD rate with an identical term T-bill, implicitly assuming that the yield difference is due to default risk differences. Although early studies could not detect higher yields for riskier banks, more recent studies have all found higher yields offered by riskier banks.[4] Exhibit 1 illustrates this approach with a yield comparison of large

EXHIBIT 1 YIELD SPREADS: 1986–1989
THREE-MONTH TREASURY BILLS, CDs

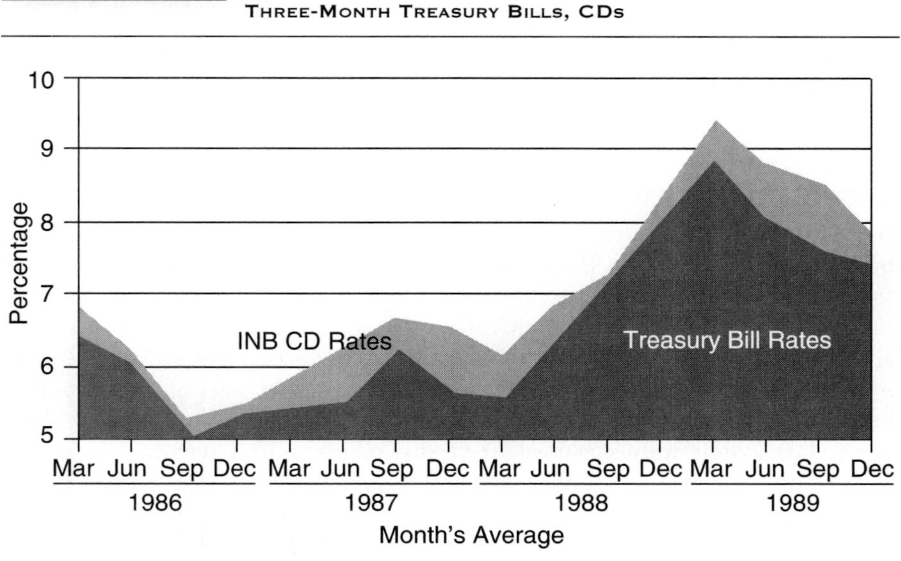

SOURCE: CD rates from INB National Bank, Indpls.

[4] See Table 3, pp. 14–15, of Gilbert [3].

denomination CD rates offered by INB National Bank (formerly Indiana National Bank) with bond-equivalent yields on T-bills for the same periods.

Such yield comparisons are inadequate for risk evaluation purposes, however. First, yield premiums are constantly changing. As money market rates move up, bank CD yields at times noticeably lag T-bill rates. Second, there are important risk factors, other than default or marketability risk, that influence yield spreads:

- The supply and demand of loanable funds in a banks' *relevant market*
- The negative *halo effect* of the concentration of problem banks in a bank's geographic area (e.g., the *Texas* premium)
- Current money market conditions (especially in the federal funds and commercial paper markets which impact CD yields differently at various points in time).

Even more problematic is the counter-intuitive historical evidence. This evidence indicates that this CD-Treasury bill *default* premium is highest for one-month CDs (despite their excellent liquidity) and declines with maturity (apparently due to the Treasury's dominant role in the bill market). The evidence also maintains that longer-maturity expected premiums are lower during recessions than during good times [2]. The treasurer would have to analyze instrument average premiums (CDs vs Treasury bills, CDs vs commercial paper, CDs vs Dutch Auction Rate Preferred Stock, CDs vs term repos, etc.) as well as issuer-characteristic premiums (money center vs regional banks, for example), which would be very hard to segregate from the yield figures. In summary, using yield premiums to infer default risk accurately is tremendously difficult.

Getting Help from the Specialist

A number of agencies currently rate banks for performance and creditworthiness: Standard & Poor's, Keefe Bankwatch,[5] Moody's and Duff & Phelps are four of the most important. The corporate treasurer must consider whether the expense of a separate CD rating is worthwhile. In fact, one consultant and textbook author recommends using a bank's bond ratings for CD evaluation.[6] These bond ratings are pretty widely available, and might already be part of the treasurer's information data base because of their relevance for corporate financing decisions. These debt ratings *do* measure creditworthiness and default risk, but the treasurer must consider whether they adequately incorporate liquidity factors a other financial data that would also impinge on bank creditworthiness and CD safety. This is an empirical question addressed later in this study. Alternatively,

[5] Formerly part of Keefe, Bruyette and Woods, the Bankwatch agency is now a subsidiary of International Thomson, Ltd., and is now officially Thomson Bankwatch, Inc. The Keefe name is temporarily being used to provide continuity for marketing purposes.

[6] Hampton & Wagner [4], p. 177.

one can use the specific "CD Safety Rankings," illustrated in Exhibit 2 by Standard & Poor's (S&P) ratings, which were first published in 1985.

The first rater to rate CDs (Keefe Bankwatch rates overall creditworthiness and performance, not any specific bank liability) with a multi-class system, S&P specifically rates bank CD creditworthiness because many large corporate and institutional investors are only partly covered by the $100,000 FDIC guarantee, and smaller investors would be inconvenienced in the event of bank failure. CD ratings are based on the following:

- Fundamental credit analysis of portfolio quality, liquidity, earnings and profitability and capital adequacy
- Subjective factors, such as management depth and quality, risk profile, business aggressiveness and regulatory sponsorship and support.

Regarding the regulatory support, S&P suggests that it will weight financial strength heavily in ranking a weak bank, regardless of S & P's perception of regulatory support. Moody's, by contrast attempts to *predict* regulatory support for uninsured depositors. Exhibit 2 gives an abbreviated listing (long-term CDs only, with an original maturity of one year or more) of the possible ratings. It is

EXHIBIT 2 STANDARD & POOR'S CERTIFICATE OF DEPOSIT RATINGS

Long-term rating categories (grades)

Investment grades

AAA	Overwhelming repayment capacity, highest grade.
AA	Very high degree of safety and repayment capacity, differing by only a small degree from AAA.
A	Somewhat more likely to experience effects of economic conditions.
BBB	Satisfactory safety and repayment capacity, but more vulnerability to unfavorable economy or changing circumstances.

Speculative grades

BB	Less near-term chance of default than other two grades of speculative CDs, but major ongoing uncertainties or vulnerability to bad economic or financial conditions, posing threat to ability to pay interest, repay principal on timely basis.
B	Still have capacity to pay interest and repay principal but greater chance of default than BB. Likely that adverse business, financial or economic conditions will *impair capacity* to continue to make those payments at some future time.
CCC	*Currently identifiable* vulnerability to default and show dependency on continued favorable conditions to maintain payments. Adverse developments would make payments unlikely.

SOURCE: S&P's Bank Book, 1989, Volume 1.

noteworthy that rating downgrades have significantly exceeded rating upgrades during the 1980's.

Confidence in the ability of raters to capture key financial data requires an understanding of what data are most important in determining ratings assignments. To provide further insight into what goes into a bank's CD rating, S&P's initial (1985) CD ratings are modeled based on COMPUSTAT bank data and using several multi-variate statistical techniques.[7] The financial variables and ratios best able to classify banks into the assigned ratings were statistically selected from among those listed in Appendix 3. Taken jointly, and judged by the ability to mirror assigned ratings most closely, the best set of classification variables is: net income, equity reserves, debt ratio, price-to-book ratio and equity. Classification accuracy was 74.4 percent, with 61 out of 82 banks ranked accurately. (The model chi-square value was 83.26, statistically significant at the .0001 level;[8] complete classification results are presented in Appendix 1.)

The size effect (where larger implies safer) is found to be important in classifying banks based on the creditworthiness of their CDs. Size is associated with the rating, whether measured by sales revenue, total assets or equity, with equity performing the best—presumably because it also gives some indication of the institution's capital cushion. Primary capital, return on assets and liquidity indicators all perform poorly in terms of their classification ability, either on an absolute or incremental basis. The most difficult distinction to model is that between the safest and the moderately safe banks—with the worst performance for the model coming in the safest class. The data used for classification are computed as five-year averages, but separate analyses not reported here done on one-year averages, with lead times of from one to four years or in the same year of the rating (1985), did not result in significantly worse prediction accuracy. The price-to-book variable is the only variable that is relatively more important in those analyses.

CD Ratings vs Bond Ratings

With the widespread public availability of banks' bond ratings, the treasurer might wonder if these would encompass all the risk information impounded in the CD ratings. Put another way, is there marginal information in the CD ratings to justify the expense ($2,000, in the case of S&P)? Furthermore, ratings announcements are made public to the wire services within ten minutes of any public action and are printed in S&P's *Credit Week* publication.[9]

---

[7] S & P originally had only four rating classes, which enabled a reasonable study to be conducted with the 82 bank holding companies for which data were available. Original results of the classification models, using multi-nominal logit, discriminant analysis and rank-transformation discriminant analysis, are reported in Zietlow [8]. The results reported here are based on the rank-transformation fits; by using ranks instead of raw values, one need not be concerned with violation of the multivariate normality assumption that plagues standard (parametric) discriminant analysis.

[8] Although not part of the best model, both ROE and the par value of bonds were incrementally helpful when substituted for several of the five predictor variables in the fitted model.

[9] Rating services offer other benefits as well. For example, S&P provides: monthly updated ratings for banks, bank holding companies, thrifts and brokerages; seminars; facsimile service on global developments not normally picked up by wire services; and analysts on call to answer questions on specific banks.

The evidence is that the only other rating that would substitute effectively for the short-term CD rating is the bank's CP rating. One approach, documented in Appendix 2, uses an appropriate association measure to find out if CD ratings can be predicted by bond or other bank security ratings, both for short-term and long-term CDs. For short-term CDs (maturity up to one year), knowing the senior debt rating is only moderately helpful in predicting the CD rating (d = .544; if d = 0 the items are independent; and if d = 1 there is perfect correlation). As these are the CDs most likely to appeal to the treasurer with a short-term investment horizon, this deficiency in bond ratings seriously reduces their value for CD risk assessment. Two related aspects of CD ratings reported elsewhere [9] indicate that:

- When one uses numerous financial variables and ratios to classify banks into assigned CD ratings, then also includes the bank's bond rating in the predictor set, the original combination of predictor variables retains both its statistical significance and its ability to help pinpoint bank creditworthiness
- Computing the association between CD ratings and various financial variables and ratios, then recomputing that relationship when controlling for the bank's bond ratings, only partly eliminates the original association.

In other words, there is added value to an investor's assessing a bank's risk (and the risk-return tradeoff) with available CD ratings. A further ramification is that overall bank performance ratings, as opposed to security-specific ratings, might not be entirely adequate for the CD investor. The present concern is: How can the treasurer use the creditworthiness ratings to make the risk-return tradeoff in marketable securities investment decisions?

Using the Ratings in CD Risk Evaluation

There are two basic ways to incorporate the information in CD ratings into the investment process: generating an *approved list* and developing performance benchmarks against which to evaluate realized returns.

Generating the Approved List

The *approved list* specifies which banks will be considered for future CD investments and what maximum amount can be invested in the CDs of each. Ratings provide an intuitive and easily implemented means of setting a dollar limit for a certain institution. While yields are segmented largely on size alone, the ratings are also a function of other variables—giving the treasurer *value added* in the risk assessment. Ratings are especially valuable for considering issuers of Yankee CDs, which are issued by foreign banks.

A joint approach could be used here: $10 million per top-rated institution, $5 million for institutions ranked in the second class and no investment in any lower class. Or one might invest in only the shortest maturities of lower-rated issuers.

Developing Performance Benchmarks

One benchmark, useful in selecting CDs as investments as well as evaluating realized returns from CDs recently held, is to compute *risk-adjusted* yield premiums. This simply involves subtracting T-bill rates from a bank's quoted CD rate and assessing the difference *in light of the bank's CD rating*. A novel approach to investment *vehicle selection* is: Assuming the approved list has already been generated, the treasurer might switch from T-bills to listed CDs whenever the CD yields exceed those of T-bills by a certain number of basis points, with the exact spread depending on the issuing institution's rating class. For example, INB's top-rated CDs might have been bought in June and December 1987 and September 1989, when yield spreads exceeded 50 basis points (refer to Exhibit 1). Should INB's rating drop one class, the treasurer might shy away from its CDs until the yield spread exceeded 65 or 70 basis points.

Another benchmark useful for portfolio evaluation is the average yield of similarly rated banks for the most recent investment period. The treasurer can determine if appropriate *risk-based* yields were obtained.

Guidelines and Cautions

In making short-term investment decisions, the treasurer should use CD ratings to assess risk. Yield premiums and debt ratings are shown to be inadequate for the identification of default risk. The treasurer with access to commercial paper ratings might use these, as they do proxy well for the CD ratings, at least for the S & P ratings profiled here (see Appendix 2). The S & P ratings have an added advantage: that of splitting out long-term and short-term maturities. This ensures that the treasurer wishing to invest in three-month negotiable CDs has security-specific information to use.

Some important concluding cautions:

- Most banks are rated in the top one or two classes.
- Bank ratings have different meanings, depending on which provider is doing the rating.
- Ratings measure default risk exclusively and give no insight into marketability risk.

Ratings Distribution

While ratings give an *absolute* evaluation, it is important to keep a sense of the *relative* rankings. For example, the 1989 distribution of 31 banks rated by Duff & Phelps indicates that roughly seven of ten banks are rated in the top two categories, and none fall into the lowest (fifth) rating category. In every year since 1982, Duff & Phelps has lowered more ratings than it has raised, so this pattern may be changing.

Ratings Agency Differences

Three of the major ratings agencies, S & P, Moody's and Duff & Phelps, rate CDs and other specific securities; Keefe Bankwatch rates the *institution's* overall performance and creditworthiness. Moody's, perhaps more than the other raters, attempts to discern regulatory and legislative trends, such as the likelihood of covering uninsured depositors in the event of a bank failure. Bankwatch offers immediate notification of rating changes, which might be advantageous for treasurers not committed to a *buy-and-hold* strategy. Each rater has a unique approach and analytical routine, and it makes sense for a treasurer to evaluate each to determine if the information and fees are best suited to his or her needs.

Marketability Risk

Finally, the treasurer must still worry about the *marketability* risk being borne, as we have focused here on *default* risk by using ratings designed to capture a bank's creditworthiness. For the buyer of $1 million, highly marketable CDs, this may not vary across domestic issuers. For the buyer of smaller denominations or of Yankee or Eurodollar CDs, the marketability consideration takes on greater importance and should be studied carefully.

References

[1] Arshadi, N., "Capital Structure, Agency Theory, and Banks," *Financial Review*, February 1989, pp. 31–52.

[2] Farna, E.F., "Term Premiums and Default Premiums in Money Markets," *Journal of Financial Economics*, September 1986, pp. 175–196.

[3] Gilbert, R.A., "Market Discipline of Bank Risk: Theory and Evidence," *Federal Reserve Bank of St. Louis Review*. January/February 1990, pp. 3–18.

[4] Hampton, J.J., and Wagner, C.L., *Working Capital Management*, New York, John Wiley & Sons, 1989.

[5] Kallberg, J.G., and Parkinson K., *Current Asset Mangement: Cash, Credit, and Inventory*. New York, John Wiley & Sons, 1984, p. 87.

[6] Lewis, M.K., and Davis K.T., *Domestic and International Banking*, Cambridge, MA, The MIT Press, 1987.

[7] Stigum, M.L., and Branch, R.O., *Managing Bank Assets and Liabilities: Strategies for Risk Control and Profit*, Homewood, IL, Dow Jones-Irwin, 1983.

[8] Zietlow, J.T., "Certificates of Deposit Safety Rankings: Analysis of Determinants," *Proceedings, Academy of Financial Services Annual Meeting*, October 1988.

[9] Zietlow, J.T., "Bank CD and Bond Ratings: Correspondence and Classification Analysis," Paper Presentation, Financial Management Association, October 1989.

Questions

1. What is a negotiable CD?
2. Identify the various sources of information on negotiable CD yields.

3. "There are two logical approaches to objective CD risk assessment: judgmental evaluation of yield premiums and use of third-party credit ratings." Describe each of these approaches.
4. What are the factors used by Standard & Poor's to rate CDs?
5. What financial variables are found by the author to be related to S&P's CD ratings? How accurate are these variables in classifying CDs according to S&P's ratings? (See Appendix 1.)
6. Are agency ratings of a bank's senior debt, subordinated debt, preferred stock, and commercial paper good substitutes for the rating on the bank's CDs? Explain.

Appendix 1: Classification Results for CD Ratings

S&Ps assigned rank	**Number of banks classified by model into rank:**			
	Riskiest (3)	Moderate (2)	Safest (1)	Total
Riskiest	12[c]	5	0	17
	(71%)	(29%)	(0%)	(100%)
Moderate	3	28[c]	6	37
	(8%)	(76%)	(16%)	(100%)
Safest	0	7	21[c]	28
	(0%)	(25%)	(75%)	(100%)
Total	15	40	27	82

Notes: Superscript c denotes correct classifications.
Percentages in cells are of row totals.

Appendix 2: Predicting CD Ratings from other Ratings*

All securities rated by S&P (1989; n = 113)

Other rating for bank	**Predicting short-term certificates**	**Predicting long-term certificates**
Sr. debt	.544	.882
Sub. debt	.793	.663
Pref. stock	.506	.803
Commercial Paper	.936	.696

*__Interpretation:__ The larger the association, the more useful it is to know a bank's debt, preferred stock or commercial paper rating to predict the CD rating. This would imply that the first rating would proxy well for the CD (predicted) rating, making the CD rating largely redundant.

Appendix 3: Variable Definitions

Level Variables

ASSETS	=	Total assets
AVGEQTY	=	Average equity
BOOKVAL	=	Year-end book value
AVGLOAN	=	Average loans (gross)
TIMEDEP	=	Total tune deposits (other than savings)
AVGBORR	=	Average borrowings
LTDEBT	=	Long-term debt not classified as capital
BADDEBT	=	Reserve(s) for bad debt losses on loans
CAPNOTE	=	Capital notes and debentures
PREFSTK	=	Preferred stock - par value
NETOPER	=	Net current operating earnings
CURRCHGS	=	Net credit or charge to reserve for bad debts from loan recoveries or charge-offs
NETINC	=	Net income
SLSTOT	=	Total revenue

Ratio Variables

OPERRAT	=	Net operating income / total assets
SVCRAT	=	(Capital notes + pref. stock + L-T debt)/total assets
DEBT	=	Debt/total assets
CASH	=	Cash/debt
COVG	=	Coverage of fixed charges
PRPAR	=	Price of stock / par value of bonds
PRBK	=	Price of stock / book value of stock
OPPROF	=	Operating profit margin
ROA	=	Return on assets
WCSLS	=	Working capital / total revenue
SLSNW	=	Total revenue / net worth
SUBOR	=	Subordinated capital / total assets
ISSUE	=	Amount of debt issued / total assets
ROE	=	Return-on-equity
NONPER	=	Non-performing assets / total assets
PRIMCAP	=	Primary capital / total assets
EQRESV	=	Total equity reserves / total assets
TEMPIN	=	Temporary investments / total assets
PURFDS	=	Purchased funds / total assets
NWTA	=	Net worth / total assets
TEXPREV	=	Total expenses / total revenue

Qualitative Variables

GEOG = Geographical region of primary operations, where coding is:

1 = Money center - NYC
2 = Money center - Outside NYC
3 = Regional - Eastern
4 = Regional - Southeastern
5 = Regional - Midwestern
6 = Regional - Southwestern
7 = Regional - West Coast

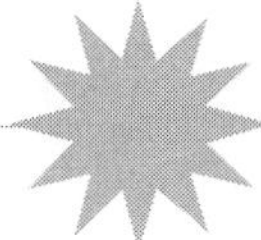

On the Significance of Trade Credit Limits

WILLIAM BERANEK AND
FREDERICK C. SCHERR

A credit limit is the maximum credit a lender will provide a borrower at one time. Little is known about lenders' motives for establishing these limits or the policies that govern them. The single survey focusing on credit limits is Besley and Osteryoung's [1], who found: (1) a majority of firms use credit limits, (2) the primary rationale is to control exposure to risk, and (3) subjective judgment is the predominant limit-setting method.

Credit limits represent firms' responses to problems in developing and monitoring selling relationships. Studying credit limits shows how firms perceive their credit policy problems and how they attempt to resolve them. This paper reports results of an exploratory survey of practice in using trade (commercial) credit limits. The main research question is: why are credit limits used?

Section I discusses the questionnaire design, the sampling procedure, and results regarding the prevalence of limits, methods of making credit decisions, and the relationship between credit limit policies, the seller's industry, and the seller's size. Section II presents our major research results and relates the survey to justifications from the finance literature for using credit limits. Section III discusses implications for practice and teaching.

At the time of this writing, William Beranek was a professor of finance at the University of Georgia, Athens, GA, and Frederick C. Scherr was an associate professor of finance at West Virginia University, Morgantown, WV.

Source: *Financial Practice and Education* (Fall/Winter 1991, pp. 39–44). Reprinted with permission from *Financial Practice and Education*, William Beranek, and Frederick C. Sherr, now a professor of finance, College of Business and Economics, West Virginia University.

Questionnaire Design and Sample Characteristics

Questionnaire and Sampling Procedure

We mailed a 16-item questionnaire (available from the authors) to all Fortune 500 firms in 1988.[1, 2] We asked respondents to indicate the *one most appropriate* answer to most of the questions, though the alternative answers were not always mutually exclusive.[3] We requested that the questionnaire be filled out by the manager of corporate credit (if credit policy were uniform among the firm's units) or by the credit manager of the unit of the firm having the largest sales volume (if credit policies were not uniform). One hundred and seventy responses were received, a response rate of 35.0 percent.

We also asked each respondent to report the firm's industry, sales (in dollars), identity, and number of customers. The dollar sales figure acts as a proxy for firm size.[4] Respondents were asked to indicate the industries in which their firms did the greatest sales volumes. There were 28 possible choices, based on two and three digit SIC codes. Six industry groups were used in our analysis: (1) Agriculture, Food, and Tobacco, (2) Extractive, (3) Chemicals and Petroleum, (4) Manufacturers of Nondurables, (5) Manufacturers of Durables and Construction, and (6) Wholesale and Retail.[5]

Exhibit 1 displays the distribution of responses by industry group and firm size. The distribution was skewed toward lower sales volume. (68 percent of respondents reported sales of less than $2 billion.)

Pervasiveness of Credit Limits

Even firms that use credit limits do not necessarily apply them to all customers. To shed light on practice, managers were asked to report the percentage of their customers to whom credit limits are assigned. Exhibit 2 shows the markedly skewed frequency distribution.[6] Slightly over 58 percent of respondents reported

---

[1] The sample population consists of very large firms. This is consistent with much prior survey research on corporate financial practice [5, 7], but may reduce generalizability of the results if practices of large firms differ from those of smaller firms. Because of this potential bias, the results presented here should be regarded as applicable only to large firms.

[2] The design of any survey instrument requires compromises. To increase the response rate, the survey was kept brief and limited to information readily at hand. This restricted both the scope and depth of the issues that could be addressed. Questions were phrased in language which was a compromise between precision and intelligibility. (For discussion of such issues in financial surveys, see Singhvi [11].) A leading researcher in the use of financial policy questionnaires provided advice regarding questionnaire design. The questionnaire was also pretested on a group of credit managers, and their evaluations were used to revise the questionnaire before mailing.

[3] This approach was used in the interests of simplicity. Credit managers may use a variety of strategies, some more frequently than others. Rather than ask the percent of the cases in which each strategy is used, which requires a relatively complicated response, we asked that the most appropriate policy (and, by implication, the most frequently used policy) be indicated. This approach tends to under-represent policies used less frequently.

[4] Sales volume was chosen over asset size because (1) the latter is based on historical cost, and (2) many respondents, representing divisions of larger entities, would have difficulty reporting asset data.

[5] This six-industry grouping is used to portray the pattern of responses and later as a basis for statistical comparison of credit limit policy among industries. Groups were formed based on homogeneity of business line and on sample sizes required for these statistical tests.

[6] Not all respondents answered all questions, so the number of responses in this and other exhibits will not total 170. The statistical tests presented later relate responses on one question to those on another and require responses to both questions, with commensurate reductions in sample size.

EXHIBIT 1 NUMBER OF RESPONDENTS BY INDUSTRY GROUP AND SALES VOLUME

Sales Volume	Industry Group*							
	(1)	(2)	(3)	(4)	(5)	(6)	(7)	Margin Totals
No Response for Sales Volume	0	1	0	1	1	1	0	4
Sales < $500M	3	6	0	8	7	1	3	27
$500M - 999M	5	3	9	8	12	2	3	42
$1B - $1.999B	8	6	8	7	8	4	3	44
$2B - $4.999B	3	6	6	10	8	0	0	33
> $4.999B	1	3	8	2	4	0	2	20
Margin Totals	20	25	31	36	40	7	11	170

*Identities of numbered columns are as follows:

(1) Agriculture, Foods and Tobacco
(2) Extractive
(3) Chemicals and Petroleum
(4) Manufacturers of Nondurables
(5) Manufacturers of Durables and Construction
(6) Wholesale and Retail
(7) No Response

EXHIBIT 2 PERCENT OF CUSTOMERS ASSIGNED CREDIT LIMITS

Percent of Customers Assigned Limits	Number	Percent	Cumulative Percent
0 - 10	18	11.11	11.11
11 - 20	1	0.62	11.73
21 - 30	3	1.85	13.58
31 - 40	1	0.62	14.20
41 - 50	9	5.56	19.76
51 - 60	1	0.62	20.38
61 - 70	7	4.32	24.70
71 - 80	13	8.02	32.72
81 - 90	15	9.26	41.98
91 - 100	94	58.02	100.00
TOTALS	162	100.00	

assigning limits to over 90 percent of their customers, while 80.2 percent indicated using them on over 50 percent. However, some firms use limits far less frequently: 11 percent reported applying them to 10 percent or fewer of their customers.[7]

To crosscheck the pervasiveness of credit limits, firms were asked to indicate their primary method of making credit decisions. Choices were: (1) the credit-limit approach, (2) the cut-off method, or (3) a combination of the two, in which some customers are assigned limits while others are subjected to the cut-off approach.[8] Responses were consistent with our prior results on percentages of customers with assigned credit limits. Most firms (62.3 percent) reported that establishing credit limits is their primary approach to credit granting. Only 7.1 percent of firms favor the cut-off method, while 30.6 percent use a combination of the two approaches.

Credit Limit Policy, Seller's Industry, and Seller's Size

The finance literature suggests several reasons why credit limit policy may be related to characteristics of the credit-granting firm, such as size and industry. Lewellen, McConnell, and Scott [8] suggest that trade credit exists because the relatively larger sellers have better access to financial markets than the relatively smaller buyers and use trade credit to pass along borrowing capacity to smaller firms. Emery [3] suggests that sellers may use trade credit policy to smooth production; if this is so, credit policy should vary across industries as demand uncertainty, and thus the need for such smoothing, does.

To test for these relationships, we related responses on the survey's 10 questions regarding credit limits and credit investigation policy to: (1) the seller's size as measured by sales volume and (2) the seller's industry group among those identified in Exhibit 1. Analysis of variance (ANOVA) was used to test for differences in seller sales volume among credit policy responses; chi-square was used to relate industry and policy responses. Of the 20 tests performed, only three indicated statistically significant relationships (two for size, both at the .10 level, and one for industry, at the .05 level). That is about the number of significant associations that would be expected by chance. Consequently, we conclude that there is no substantive correlation between size or industry and credit policy.

Why Are Credit Limits Used?

The finance literature reveals three generic explanations for the use of credit limits: (1) increase in the probability of default as receivable size increases, (2) type of risks that the selling firm faces in conjunction with credit decisions, and (3) the

---

[7] Statistical tests were performed relating this and other credit policies to the seller's size, industry, average sales per customer, and four measures of seller financial risk. Results will be discussed later in the paper.

[8] In credit parlance, the "cut-off approach" to the credit granting decision involves comparing the applicant's credit worthiness to a set of predetermined credit standards. These credit standards may be set judgmentally by the credit manager or the firm, or they may be derived from a credit-scoring model. If the applicant is sufficiently credit worthy, unlimited ("open") credit is granted, otherwise no credit is granted. This is functionally equivalent to assigning credit limits with only infinite or zero values.

relationship between credit limits and credit investigation expenses. The following subsections present our results regarding each of these explanations.

Credit Limits and Default Probability

Most survey participants (92.7 percent) said that credit limits are used for risk control, a result similar to that found by Besley and Osteryoung. One of our major goals was to find out what type of risk is referenced in such responses, and much of the questionnaire was devoted to it.

One hypothesis posits that the greater the amount of credit extended, the higher the probability of default/delinquency [2, 9, 12]; this proposition is consistent with, but not equivalent to, adverse selection as an explanation for credit rationing in banking [13]. Credit limits may be a response to that perceived relationship.

To test the two hypotheses that credit managers perceive a positive relationship between default/delinquency probability and sales volume and that such a relationship is reflected in credit limit policy, survey participants were asked to indicate the assumption on which they base credit policy. The majority (55.5 percent) indicated that they base credit policy on the assumption that default/delinquency risk *does not* increase with credit granted, but a substantial fraction (26.8 percent) believe that it *does*. Further, of those who did not take either position (the remaining 17.7 percent), many indicated that the relationship and consequent policy depends on the characteristics of the customer: the probability of default or delinquency is believed to increase with the amount of credit granted for some customers but remain fixed for others.[9] Thus, although a majority does not support the perception, there remains a significant minority which does.

Credit Limits and Risk Control

Our review of the finance literature identified four other potential explanations for credit in terms of risk or uncertainty. These are not necessarily mutually exclusive.

1. Credit limits hedge uncertainty with respect to the likelihood of default or delinquency [6].
2. Since default of a major customer can increase the probability of the seller's default in a domino effect, credit limits reduce that risk by limiting receivables from such customers [10].

---

[9] There was no statistically significant association between these interesting responses and the seller's size, industry, average sales per customer, or any of our measures of the seller's financial risk. One possible explanation is that the majority of the sellers in our sample trade principally with buyers that have such a low probability of default and that this probability increases so slowly with amount purchased that any changes in default probability are imperceptible. However, if this were true it would be expected that these responses would vary by industry, since the proportion of such buyers is likely to vary by industry, and no such association was found.

3. Granting credit to a buyer with a higher beta than that of the seller increases the seller's asset beta, thus increasing the required return on all the seller's assets [2].
4. Credit limits are really a manifestation of agency problems in monitoring the performance of credit managers, and not actually "risk control" at all. Because it is difficult to base evaluation criteria for credit managers on the risk-adjusted value of their decisions, credit managers may be judged instead by the dollar amount of bad debt from the accounts they manage. As a result, they may limit sales to risky customers even when such sales would be of advantage to the firm.

The first three of these rationales lead to optimal values for credit limits based on shareholder wealth maximization; procedures to determine these optimal limits are given in the respective references. In the fourth rationale, credit limits result from managers' conflicting objectives to grant credit and to limit bad debt. The resulting credit limits will depend on the relative strengths of the two incentives within a firm.

Respondents were asked to choose their best perceptions of the types of risk their limits were intended to control.[10] Exhibit 3 presents responses and the actual text of the four alternatives, in the order presented above.

EXHIBIT 3 TYPE OF RISK CONTROLLED BY CREDIT LIMITS

Type of Risk, as formulated in questionnaire choices.	Number of Responses	Percent of Responses
Credit limits are used to hedge uncertainty with respect to the chance of delinquency or default. We never quite know how likely or unlikely a customer is to become delinquent or; to default, and so we use credit limits to hedge our decisions.	37	24.3%
We can make fairly certain estimates of the chance of delinquency and default, but recognize that granting credit to risky customers increases the risk of collection of our receivables. We don't want an excessive portion of our receivables to come from any one customer.	23	15.1%
Granting credit is just like investing in another firm. Some of our customers are in more risky businesses than we are; by limiting receivables from them, we reduce our own risk.	47	30.9%
By setting credit limits to reduce the amount owed by each customer, we reduce the risk of bad credit.	17	11.2%
Other	28	18.5%
Totals	**152**	**100.0%**

[10] The differences between these risk concepts are subtle; reducing them to choices which could be understood without paragraphs of explanation or reference to original articles was a major challenge in questionnaire construction.

Responses differed widely. The lack of consensus may be due to: (1) a true diversity of behavior, (2) difficulties in questionnaire construction leading to misunderstanding of the risk concepts described, or (3) control of a primary risk that is not captured by the alternatives described.

Finally, if credit limit policy is intended to control risk, such policies should vary with the risk of the seller, so that sellers who have higher operating, financial, or similar risks use stronger risk controls. (This potential tradeoff between credit risk and other risks is similar to that between operating and financial risk discussed in the finance literature [4]). We asked respondents, at their option, to identify themselves; 109 (64 percent of respondents) did so. Using publicly available data on these 109, four measures of the seller's risk (the seller's current ratio, ratio of long-term debt to common equity, average operating income for the last five years divided by the standard deviation of this income, and the latest beta as measured by Value Line) were computed. No significant patterns of association were found between these four risk measures and credit policy. (Details are available from the authors.)

Credit Limits and Credit Investigation Costs

A major task of credit management is to control credit investigation expenses. Mehta [9] shows that since such costs increase with the amount of information gathered, the optimal quantity of information collected will depend upon amount owed, profit margin, information costs, and default and/or delinquency probabilities. Credit limits can be set at the maximum credit grantable upon prior investigation without triggering additional investigation costs. We found both direct and indirect evidence to support the hypothesis that firms use credit limits in this way.

Direct Evidence

Firms implementing Mehta's procedure for credit limits would be expected to use the limits as triggers for further investigation. We asked firms what action they take when the limit is violated. Of those responding, 65.1 percent indicated that violation induced additional investigation, but only 1.8 percent said the order would be automatically rejected. Of the remaining 33.1 percent, many indicated that the customer is asked to pay outstanding invoices so that the amount owing after the sale does not exceed the limit. Thus the majority of firms use limits as investigation triggers; a minority impose limits absolutely.

Indirect Evidence

We also found considerable indirect evidence that firms use credit limits as investigation triggers. The indirect evidence comes from two sources: (1) responses to other survey questions, and (2) statistically significant associations between average sales per customer and survey responses.

The first indirect evidence comes from sellers' policies on informing buyers about their credit limits. Both costs and benefits are associated with revealing the credit limit to a customer. Some buyers may be disappointed at the limit's level and look for new suppliers. On the other hand, revealing a relatively low limit may allow the seller to bargain for additional credit-related information from the customer. If limits are absolute rather than triggers, it is generally in the interests of both parties to reveal them so that customers are spared the embarrassment of having orders rejected.

Exhibit 4 reveals how often customers are advised of their credit limits. If credit limits serve as triggers for obtaining additional credit information rather than as absolute receivable limits (as they would be if, for example, they were used to control for increases in default probability), most firms would not generally reveal them. Since the "Seldom" and "Sometimes" categories capture a majority of responses (69.8 percent), the idea that credit limits are internal triggers receives indirect support.

A second piece of indirect evidence comes from responses regarding the negotiability of revealed limits. If sellers reveal the limit as a strategy to bargain with customers for information, then the customer should be advised that the limit is negotiable and thus subject to revision upward if the customer provides more information. We asked firms that reveal limits whether they inform the customer that the limit is flexible. Of those responding (see Exhibit 5), 85.4 percent indicated that they advise customers that the limit is flexible, again supporting the hypothesis that limits are information-related.

The relationship between average sales per customer and the credit limit policy also constitutes indirect evidence. If firms use credit limits to control

EXHIBIT 4 FREQUENCY OF ADVISING CUSTOMERS OF CREDIT LIMIT

Frequency	Number of Responses	Percent of Responses	Cumulative Percent
Never	10	5.9	5.9
Seldom	55	32.5	38.4
Sometimes	63	37.3	75.7
Frequently	18	10.7	86.4
Always	19	11.2	97.6
Other	4	2.4	100.0
Totals	**169**	**100.0**	

EXHIBIT 5 NEGOTIABILITY OF CREDIT LIMITS

Degree of Negotiability	Number of Responses	Percent of Responses
Credit limit is flexible.	135	85.4
Credit limit is binding.	6	03.8
Other or multiple responses	17	10.8
Totals	**158**	**100.0**

credit investigation expenses, then the credit limit policy should vary among firms according to average sales per customer; the larger the average sales, the larger the average receivable balance given the seller's terms of sale, and consequently the greater the optimal credit investigation expenditures. Several significant associations among these factors were found.

An ANOVA test showed that firms which follow a policy of collecting a predetermined amount of credit information, rather than varying the amount of information collected with receivable size, had significantly higher sales per customer than did firms who collected more information when orders were larger (significant at 0.10; results appear in Exhibit 6). This finding is consistent with optimal credit investigation policy; the larger the average sales per customer, the more likely it is that the optimal credit investigation is relatively complete, in which case a predetermined (and presumably large) amount of information is collected and no additional investigation is required.

Another ANOVA test showed that firms using primarily the cut-off approach in making credit decisions had significantly higher average sales per customer than did firms using the credit-limit approach or both cut-off and credit-limit approaches (significant at .01). There was also a negative Pearson correlation of -.280 (significant at .01 using a t test) between average sales per customer and the percent of customers assigned credit limits.[11] Both these relationships support the use of limits as investigation triggers. If firms gather more information when the customer's receivable is larger, firms who sell larger volumes to each customer are more likely to have performed a relatively complete credit investigation. Upon full investigation, some buyers will be found to be very credit-worthy and be assigned unlimited credit, while others will be found

EXHIBIT 6 POLICY MOST FREQUENTLY USED TO DETERMINE AMOUNT OF INFORMATION GATHERED

Policy	**Number of Responses**	**Percent of Responses**	**Average Yearly Sales per Customer Thousands)**
Predetermined amount gathered for all applicants	48	28.6	$1,206.4
More information collected if receivables may be large	98	58.3	395.4
Other or multiple responses	22	13.1	1,549.7
Totals	**168**	**100.0**	

[11] We also asked firms the frequency with which customers' credit limits are reviewed, a process which may or may not entail out-of-pocket costs. Review policy was found to be significantly associated with average sales per customer. Data on this question are not presented here because of space limitations.

unworthy of any credit at all. Both these types of buyers are appropriately dealt with by the cutoff approach. Thus, firms with larger per-customer sales are more likely to use cut-offs and will assign credit limits to a smaller proportion of their customers.

Summary and Implications

Like Besley and Osteryoung [1], we found that most firms use credit limits, and that most assign these limits to a majority of customers. Like them, we found that the rationale given for the use of the limits was "risk control."

But risk control is too general a concept to advance development of practice or teaching. A major objective of our research was to clarify the concept as it applies to the practice of credit granting. Our results provide several insights.

Although most respondents do not assume that the probability of default and/or delinquency increases with the amount owed, there remain a significant minority that base credit limit policy on this perception. Though credit managers indicate they use credit limits to control risk, we were not able to find a common conception of what type of risk was being controlled, nor did we find evidence that the seller's credit limit policy was associated with its risk characteristics.

We found strong support, however, for the idea that a major function of credit limits is to control credit investigation expenses. Most credit managers report that violation of an existing credit limit triggers additional investigation expenditure. Several aspects of credit limit policy vary significantly with sales per customer, and these variations agree with what would be expected if limits were used as investigation controls. This is "risk control" in the sense that credit investigation produces information regarding a buyer's ability to pay.

Our results have some implications for practice and teaching in credit management. In practice, if credit limits are used as investigation triggers, quantitative approaches which are based on shareholder wealth maximization may result in better decisions than the subjective heuristics currently in use, even if these heuristics follow optimal investigation in principle. In particular, the direct application of the procedures for optimal credit investigation given by Mehta [9] in a decision-tree format and by Stowe [14] in an integer programming format can be applied to yield not only the appropriate credit investigation for a given order size, but also the maximum order size which triggers additional investigation. Maximum order size is a wealth-maximizing credit limit for credit investigation purposes.

From a teaching perspective, these models of credit investigation should be introduced to students as methods of setting credit limits.

References

1. S. Besley and J.S. Osteryoung, "Survey of Current Practices in Establishing Trade-Credit Limits," *Financial Review* (February 1985), pp. 70–81.

2. T.E. Copeland and N.T. Khoury, "A Theory of Credit Extensions with Default Risk and Systematic Risk," *Engineering Economist* (Fall 1970), pp. 35–52.

3. G. Emery, "An Optimal Financial Response to Variable Demand," *Journal of Financial and Quantitative Analysis* (June 1987), pp. 209–225.

4. M.G. Ferri and W.H. Jones, "Determinants of Financial Structure: A New Methodological Approach," *Journal of Finance* (June 1979), pp. 631–644.

5. L.J. Gitman and C.E. Maxwell. "Financial Activities of Major U.S. Firms: Survey and Analysis of Fortune's 1000," *Financial Management* (Winter 1985), pp. 57–65.

6. D.M. Jaffee and T. Russell, "Imperfect Information, Uncertainty and Credit Rationing," *Quarterly Journal of Economics* (November 1976), pp. 651–666.

7. R.R. Kamath, S. Khaksari, H.H. Meir and J. Winklepeck, "Management of Excess Cash: Practices and Developments," *Financial Management* (Autumn 1985), pp. 70–77.

8. W. Lewellen, J. McConnell and J. Scott, "Capital Market Influences on Trade Credit Policies," *Journal of Financial Research* (Fall 1980), pp. 105–113.

9. D. Mehta, "The Formulation of Credit Policy Models," *Management Science* (October 1968), pp. B-30 to B-50.

10. F.C. Scherr, "Credit-Granting Decisions Under Risk," *Engineering Economist*, forthcoming.

11. S. Singhvi, "One Financial Executive's Responses to Surveys," *Financial Management* (Winter 1981), pp. 82–83.

12. V. Srinivasan and Y.H. Kim. "Designing Expert Financial Systems: A Case Study of Corporate Credit Management," *Financial Management* (Autumn 1988), pp. 33–43.

13. J. Stiglitz and A. Weiss, "Credit Rationing in Markets with Imperfect Information," *American Economic Review* (June 1981), pp. 393–410.

14. J.D. Stowe, "An Integer Programming Solution for the Optimal Investigation/Credit Granting Sequence," *Financial Management* (Summer 1985), pp. 66–77.

Questions

1. Describe the evidence indicating that companies normally impose credit limits on their customers.
2. What types of risk are potentially controlled by imposing credit limits?
3. In what way do credit limits help the credit manager to control credit investigation expenses?
4. Answer the following true-false questions based on the survey results reported by the authors:

   T F When customers violate their credit limits, most companies reject further orders from those customers.

   T F Selling companies almost always inform their customers about their credit limits.

   T F Most credit limits are negotiable.

T F Most companies collect a predetermined amount of credit information, rather than varying the amount of information collected according to receivable size.

5. Suppose that you overhear the following exchange in the credit department of a manufacturer:

Salesperson:	"If we don't give Alley Company the $100,000 credit line it wants, we will lose them as a customer!"
Credit Manager:	"But Alley has only a $25,000 line with us."
Salesperson:	"I know, I know. We should increase the line."
Credit Manager:	"I don't know. It worries me."

What factors should be considered in the decision to increase Alley Company's credit limit?

Factoring Accounts Receivable

EDWARD J. FARRAGHER

In many firms, managers who are marketing or production oriented often give insufficient attention to accounts receivable. This can cause a slowdown in cash receipts and/or abnormal credit loses. Fortunately, such firms can eliminate delayed collections and credit loss by factoring their accounts receivable. This article provides survey evidence of the characteristics of factoring and proposes a methodology for separate evaluation of its credit management and financing services. It is intended to help treasury managers broaden their perspective as suggested by Hill and Ferguson [3].

Credit Administration Services

Factoring is a credit management service whereby a client firm sells its accounts receivable to a factor who guarantees the amount and timing of the cash due. Factors generally do not deal with clients on an emergency basis but rather establish ongoing relationships with minimum annual factoring requirements. The survey data indicate that the respondents favor a minimum annual accounts receivable factoring volume of $750,000 to $1,000,000 per year. At present, factoring activity mainly includes textile-related products with some expansion into the furniture, sporting goods and toy industries (Exhibit 1).

As owner of the accounts receivable, a factor typically assumes all credit management responsibilities—analysis, accounting, collection and bad-debt loss exposure. Additionally, a factor may provide cash advances to clients. The respondent's perceptions of the relative importance to clients of each of these services is indicated in Exhibit 2.

At the time of this writing, Edward J. Farragher was affiliated with DePaul University.

EXHIBIT 1 INVOLVEMENT IN VARIOUS INDUSTRIES

Industry	Average Level of Involvement*	Growing Involvement Yes	Growing Involvement No
Manufacturing:			
Finished Apparel	6.38	18	3
Textile Mill Products	5.71	14	7
Furniture/Fixtures	3.00	11	10
Plastic	2.05	3	18
Food	1.81	4	17
Electrical	1.67	4	17
Toys	1.62	4	17
Shoes	1.57	3	18
Lumber/Wood	1.57	3	18
Scientific Instruments	1.52	4	17
Wholesaling:			
Sporting/Toys	2.71	11	10
Furniture/Furnishings	2.67	8	13
Apparel	2.33	4	17
Electrical	1.62	3	18
Hardware/Plumbing	1.57	2	19
Lumber/Construction Materials	1.43	4	17
Auto Parts	1.43	3	18
Paper/Paper Products	1.29	3	18

*On a scale of one (Rarely Involved) to seven (Heavily Involved).
Note: Questionnaires were sent to all 33 members of the National Commercial Finance Association, the trade association of the accounts receivable factoring industry; 21 usable responses were received. The data show that the respondents were high level and, hopefully, well-informed managers.

EXHIBIT 2 RELATIVE IMPORTANCE OF SERVICES PROVIDED TO THEIR CUSTOMERS

Service	Relative Importance*
Credit Analysis	6.48
Bad-Debt Loss Exposure	6.33
Cash Advance	5.52
Collection	5.29
Accounting	4.81

*On a scale of one (Not Important) to seven (Very Important).

A factor usually assumes a client's credit exposure by purchasing approved accounts receivable without recourse. The factor expects to provide faster, better and lower cost credit analyses because it has in-depth, up-to-date credit files; full-time, experienced credit managers; and, through computerization, significant economies of scale. The factor only assumes losses due to nonpayment for financial reasons. The client bears any losses due to product disputes. Because a factor is larger and more diversified than its clients, it is able to assume more credit exposure. This allows clients to handle a greater volume of business and to sell to borderline credit risk customers. A client also benefits from the improved consistency/quality of receivables cash flow. Late payments are eliminated because the factor guarantees the amount and timing of payment, and planning is improved because uncertainty in accounts receivable collection is no longer a problem.

Most factoring is on a notification basis whereby a client's customers are notified that a factor has purchased the receivables and are instructed to pay the factor. Factors prefer this method because it provides direct interaction with a client's customers, thus easing their ability to obtain the up-to-date information essential for accurate credit analysis. Additionally, it provides a factor with direct control over collection of accounts receivable. Another client benefit is that the factor becomes the collection agency and assumes the risk of being viewed negatively when a customer is paying late. There is less animosity between a client and its customers because the client can disavow late payment collection practices by blaming a third party—the factor. In turn, the factor can be more determined in its collection activities since it is not overly concerned about a client's customer complaints.

In return for its credit management services, a factor receives a percentage of the face value of the receivable. The survey indicated that the fee ranges from .35% to 4.0%, with an average of 1.03%. It is a negotiated rate dependent upon the:

- Stability of the client's product line
- Financial quality of client's customers
- Client's annual credit sales volume
- Average dollar amount per invoice
- Number of separate customers of client
- Length of client's credit terms.

The more stable a client's product line and the higher financial quality of its customers, the lower the fee because a factor assumes less risk. The higher a client's credit sales volume and the larger the average dollar amount per invoice, the greater are a factor's economies of scale and, thus, the lower the fee. The fewer customers a client has, the lower the fee because the factor is required to gather credit information and prepare analysis for fewer firms. The longer a client's payment period, the greater is the factor's credit exposure, resulting in a higher fee. Exhibit 3 indicates the relative importance factors assign to each of these items.

When deciding whether to factor, a firm should compare, on a present value basis, its in-house credit costs with the cost of factoring. This involves an extensive

EXHIBIT 3 RELATIVE IMPORTANCE IN FEE DETERMINATION

Factor Fee Determinants	Relative Importance*
Financial Stability of Client's Customers	6.14
Client's Annual Factoring Volume	6.05
Average Dollar Amount per Invoice	5.71
Number of Repeat Customers per Invoice	4.90
Client's Credit Period	4.57
Financial Stability of Client	4.48

*On a scale of one (Not Important) to seven (Very Important).

accounting effort to identify all costs that can be eliminated by factoring. An illustration of the in-house credit management versus the factoring decision process is provided in Appendix A.

Financing Services

A factor typically does not pay a client immediately upon purchase of accounts receivable. The payment date depends on the type of factoring: maturity or discount. *Maturity factoring* (illustrated in Appendix A) involves cash payment on either the actual or average due date of the accounts receivable. Maturity factoring provides only credit management and bad-debt loss protection, not cash advances. *Discount factor* provides credit management, bad-debt loss protection and the option of taking cash advances. The survey indicates that approximately 55% of factoring volume is on a discount basis, 36% on a maturity basis and 9% is customized to a client's wishes. Whether a firm using discount factoring should take cash advances depends on the effective annual rate of interest for factor-provided financing vis-a-vis the effective cost of alternative financing sources. Appendix B provides an illustration of the amount and time of cash flows with discount factoring.

Summary

For many firms, factoring provides a means for obtaining credit management and short-term financing. A firm must perform a cash flow analysis of in-house versus factoring credit management costs when deciding whether to use maturity factoring and must compare the effective annual cost of cash advances with the cost of alternative sources of financing when deciding whether to take cash advances. The successful cash manager must be aware of the distinct credit management and cash advance services a factor can provide and must work together with the credit manager in jointly determining whether to use the services of a factor. A thorough awareness of nontraditional cash management functions, such as factoring, should provide significant potential for broadening the scope of cash management to include the entire cash flow timeline.

References

1. Boldin, Robert J. and Patti D. Feeney, "The Increased Importance of Factoring," *Financial Executive*, April 1981, pp. 19–21.
2. Boldin, Robert J. and Susan J. Mulholland, "A Banker's Primer on Factoring," *The Bankers Magazine*, January-February 1981, pp. 73–77.
3. Hill, Ned C. and Daniel M. Ferguson, "Cash Flow Timeline Management: The Next Frontier of Cash Management," *Journal of Cash Management*, May/June 1985, pp. 12–22.
4. Moore, Carroll G., "Factoring; A Unique and Important Form of Financing and Service," *The Business Lawyer*, Vol. XIV, No. 3.
5. National Commercial Finance Conference, *Special Bulletin No. 62: Impact of Factoring Costs on Procedures and Rates*, New York (1974).
6. ———, *Special Bulletin No. 84: Seminar on Atypical Factoring Arrangements*, New York (1979).
7. ———, *Special Bulletin No. 93: Factoring: Past, Present and Future*, New York (1980).

Questions

1. Define *factoring* and identify the services typically provided by factors. Distinguish between maturity factoring and discount factoring.
2. Which manufacturers commonly use factoring?
3. In a factoring arrangement, who bears the risk of customers not paying because of bankruptcy? Because of product disputes?
4. Factors charge a fee for credit management services usually within the range of 0.35 percent to 4.0 percent. What would cause the factor's fee to be in the high end of this range?
5. Tres Faux Wholesalers' monthly credit sales are $2 million. Credit terms are 2/10, net 60, and 20 percent of receivables are paid on the 10th. Because of financial difficulties experienced by its customers, Tres Faux's bad-debt expense averages 0.5 percent of monthly credit sales. Credit department costs are 2 percent of monthly credit sales and are paid on the 30th. Tres Faux has never experienced customer disputes over the quality of its products. Fechere Factoring offers to buy Tres Faux's accounts receivable on a maturity basis for a 2 percent fee. Tres Faux uses a 10 percent discount rate for the analysis of its receivables. Based on present value analysis, should Tres Faux factor its receivables? Show calculations supporting your answer. (See Appendices.)

Appendix A

A manufacturing firm sells $1,000,000 per month on credit with terms of 2/10; Net 60. Historically, 20% of the accounts receivable are discounted and paid on the 10th, the bad-debt loss rate is 1%, and credit department costs, 2% of the face amount of accounts receivable, are paid on the 30th. It is expected that 5% of the accounts will be disputed and not paid until the 120th day after sale. A factor offers to buy all of the manufacturer's accounts receivable on a maturity basis charging a 1 ½% fee. The factor will make a cash settlement on the net date (60th) less a 5% holdback for non-payment due to product quality disputes. It is expected that all such disputes will be settled and the factor will release the holdback on the 120th day. The manufacturer has a 10% opportunity rate of return. The following present value analysis of the incremental cash flows indicates that the manufacturing firm should factor its accounts receivable.

Day		
10th	Discounted Payments	
	Collect $1,000,000 × 20% =	$200,000
	Discounts $200,000 × 2% =	($4,000)
30th	Credit Department Costs	
60th	Collection of Balance less Disputed Payments	
	$800,000 − (5%)($1,000,000)	
	Payment from Factor $1,000,000 less:	
	$15,000 Factor fee	
	$4,000 Discount	
	$50,000 Holdback	
120th	Collection of Disputed Accounts less Bad Debt Loss	
	$50,000 − (1%)($1,000,000)	
	Factor Releases Holdback	

Cash without Factoring	Cash with Factor	Incremental Cash due to Factoring	10% Discount Rate	Present Values
196,000		(196,000)	.9973	(195,470)
(20,000)		20,000	.9918	19,835
750,000	931,000	181,000	.9837	178,050
40,000	50,000	10,000	.9675	9,675
Present Value Advantage to Factoring				$12,090

Appendix B

It was decided (Appendix A) that the manufacturer should factor it accounts receivable. Now the question becomes should it take cash advances from the factor. The factor will charge 17% simple interest with a 90% client availability allowance. The client availability allowance indicates the maximum amount of client equity which the factor will advance. It depends upon the client's financial character, the likelihood of excessive product quality disputes and the liquidation value of the factored accounts receivable. The client equity is equal to the face value of the factored accounts receivable less potential early payment discounts, the factor fee and the product quality holdback. Assuming the manufacturer takes the maximum cash advance, the amount and timing of the cash flows are as follows:

Factored Accounts Receivable	$1,000,000
Less: Potential Early Payment Discounts	(4,000)
Factor Fee	(15,000)
Product Quality Dispute Holdback	(50,000)
Client Equity	$931,000
Availability Allowance	× 90%
Maximum Cash Advance	$837,900

Cash Advance Outstanding	**Interest Rate**	**Days**	**Interest Expense**
$837,900	17%	10	$3,900
$641,900*	17%	50	$14,950
		Total Interest	$18,850

(* $837,900 Cash Advance less $196,000 early payments)

Whether or not the manufacturer should take the factor's cash advance would depend on its annual percentage cost of 17% as compared to the availability and cost of alternative sources of short-term financing.

	Amount	Cash Received	Date Cash Received
Factored Accounts Receivable	$1,000,000		
Less: Factor Fee	(15,000)		
Early Payment Discounts	(4,000)		
Interest Expense	(18,850)		
Gross to Manufacturer	$962,150		
Less: Cash Advance	(837,900)	$837,900	1st
Net to Manufacturer	$124,250		
Less: Product Quality Holdback	(50,000)		
Cash to Manufacturer	$74,250	$74,250	60th
Release of Product Quality Holdback		$50,000	120th
Total Cash Received		$962,150	

Will Just-in-Time Inventory Techniques Dampen Recessions?

DONALD P. MORGAN

In the past, fluctuations in inventories have been an important factor in business cycles, particularly in recessions. Indeed, one prominent analyst went so far as to assert: "Recessions *are* inventory swings" (Blinder). Recent signs, however, suggest the role of inventories in recessions may be diminishing. While recessions in the past were often foreshadowed by a rising inventory-sales ratio, the current recession was not. In fact, the inventory-sales ratio has declined noticeably since the last recession ended in 1982.

This unusual behavior in the inventory-sales ratio may be due to inventory management techniques adopted by some U.S. firms in the 1980s. With these techniques, firms reduce and control their inventories by producing just in time to sell. Many analysts claim these techniques—if prevalent and successful—may reduce the inventory swings that aggravated past recessions. This recession and future recessions may be milder as a result.

This article concludes that just-in-time techniques will dampen recessions. The first section of the article reviews the role of inventories in past recessions and considers signs this role may be changing. The second section discusses how firms reduce their inventories with just-in-time techniques and where such techniques are being applied. The third section presents evidence just-in-time techniques are affecting aggregate inventory behavior. The final section explores how recessions will be dampened by these techniques.

Inventories and Business Fluctuations

Inventories figure in business fluctuations in part because inventory investment—the change in the level of inventories—is a component of GNP.[1] In fact,

---

At the time of this writing, Donald P. Morgan was an economist at the Federal Reserve Bank of Kansas City.

Source: *Economic Review*, Federal Reserve Bank of Kansas City.

[1] Only inventory investment is counted because GNP is intended to measure goods produced in the current quarter. The total stock of inventories is not counted because it includes goods produced in previous quarters.

fluctuations in inventory investment play a disproportionate role in GNP fluctuations. While the level of inventory investment represents only about 1 percent of the level of GNP, changes in inventory investment from one quarter to the next usually account for about half of the corresponding changes in GNP.

The Role of Inventories in Recessions

Sharp drops in inventory investment have been especially important in recessions. During the 1973–75 recession, for example, inventory investment declined by $78.1 billion from the onset of the recession—the business cycle peak—to the end of the recession—the business cycle trough. During the same period, GNP declined $120.1 billion. Thus, about 65 percent of the decline in GNP was attributed to the decline in inventory investment. The prominent role of inventory investment in the 1973–75 recession was not unusual: on average over postwar recessions, declines in inventory investment accounted for about 80 percent of the decline in GNP.

The reason firms reduce inventories in recessions relates to the reason firms hold inventories in the first place. Businesses have historically held two or three months' worth of sales in inventory to protect against production halts or a sudden increase in sales. But of course sales decline during recessions, so firms' desired inventory stock falls proportionately. To reduce inventories, firms must then reduce inventory investment by scaling back their production.

The sharp drop in inventory investment during recessions occurs because firms have, typically failed to cut production promptly when sales decline. Instead, firms have maintained production for a time after sales declined, perhaps because firms expected sales to rebound quickly. In the meantime, however, inventories accumulated. By the time firms recognized a recession was underway and that sales would remain slow indefinitely, their warehouses were crowded with unwanted inventories. Firms were then forced to cut inventory investment dramatically to balance their inventories with the lower sales rate.

This inventory cycle of rising and then sharply falling inventory investment amplifies recessions. If firms cut production promptly when sales decline, they could prevent unwanted inventories from accumulating. In turn, firms would not need to eventually cut production so sharply, and the recession would be milder.

Evidence the Inventory Cycle May Diminish

The onset of an inventory cycle is usually signaled by a rise in the ratio of inventory to sales. This ratio measures the number of months' worth of sales held as inventories. For example, a firm with $3 million of inventories in stock and sales of $1 million per month would have an inventory-sales ratio of three months ($3 million divided by $1 million/month).

The inventory-sales ratio typically rises late in the expansion after sales fall and firms allow inventories to accumulate.[2] Only after firms finally cut produc-

---

[2] Because inventories are increasing due to a decline in sales, the rise in the inventory-sales ratio late in the expansion reflects unintended accumulation of inventories. In contrast, the rise in the inventory-sales ratio that sometimes occurs in the middle of expansions reflects intended accumulation of inventories in anticipation of faster sales (Dornbusch and Fischer).

tion during the recession does the inventory-sales ratio itself begin falling. This behavior of the inventory-sales ratio is evident in Chart 1. The vertical bands in the chart denote recessions: the first vertical line in a band corresponds to a peak in business activity, and the second vertical line corresponds to a trough.[3]

In the 1981–82 recession, for example, the inventory-sales ratio began rising in the spring of 1981, before the peak in business activity in July. The inventory-sales ratio did not begin declining until near the trough, as firms cut production sufficiently to actually reduce their inventories.

The behavior in the inventory-sales ratio since the 1981–82 recession suggests the role of the inventory cycle may be diminishing. After beginning a sharp decline in 1982, the ratio reached an all-time low in 1988.[4] Moreover, the ratio merely leveled off rather than rising perceptibly as the current recession began in late 1990. As a result, firms may not need to reduce inventory investment as sharply as in past recessions. If not, the current recession will be milder. And if the inventory-sales ratio remains low, the role of inventories in recessions may be permanently diminished.

CHART 1 AGGREGATE INVENTORY-SALES RATIO

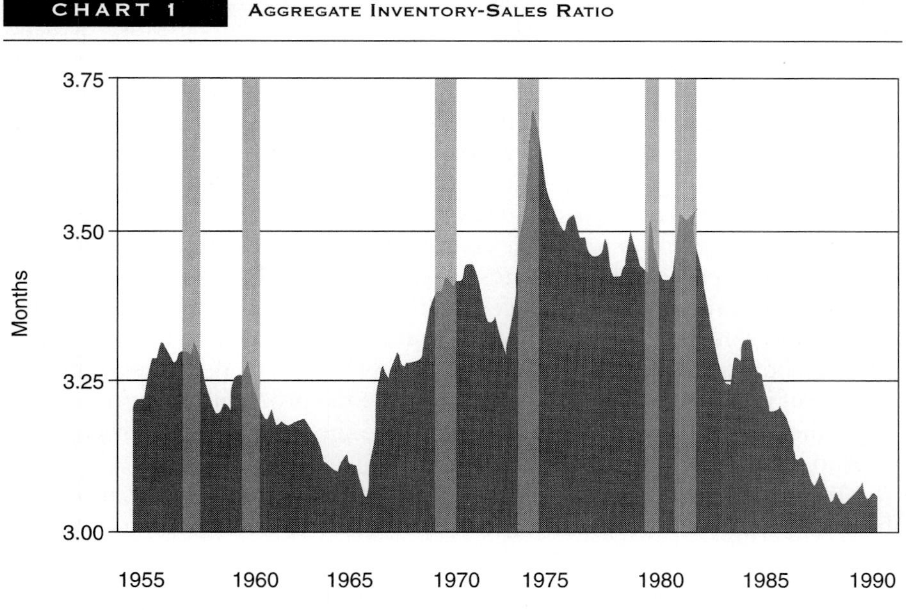

SOURCE: Board of Governors of the Federal Reserve System.

Note: Vertical bands indicate recessions.

---

[3] The dates of the peaks and troughs indicated in Chart 1 are determined by the National Bureau of Economic Research. These dates do not necessarily correspond to peaks and troughs in GNP.

[4] One might date the decline in the ratio back to 1975. However, this is an illusion created by the rise and fall in the inventory-sales ratio during the 1973–75 recession. Ignoring that spike, the ratio was trendless from 1976 to 1982 and began declining thereafter. The ratio declined from 3.5395 months in 1982:Q2 to 3.0379 months in 1988:Q2 and then leveled off at 3.0498 months in 1990:Q2. Before this decline, the nadir of the inventory-sales ratio was 3.0535 months in 1965:2.

The New Inventory Techniques

Many analysts attribute the low inventory-sales ratio to inventory reduction techniques increasingly adopted by U.S. firms in the 1980s. With these techniques, firms reduce their inventories by purchasing just in time (JIT) to produce and producing just in time to sell. JIT was most widely adopted in the U.S. manufacturing sector in the 1980s, particularly in the automotive and computer industries.

Why Do Firms Use JIT to Reduce Inventories?

Firms prefer to reduce inventories because holding inventories is costly. Firms incur interest costs in holding inventories because firms could have held interest-bearing assets instead. Inventories also entail costs in the form of insurance, obsolescence, depreciation, pilfering, storage, and handling. Taken together, these various costs average close to 10 percent of the value of the inventory stock per year (Blinder and Maccini). Such high costs are a powerful incentive to reduce inventories.

But inventories are also beneficial to firms. Inventories of materials and supplies used in producing finished goods protect against various problems such as late deliveries or defects. Inventories of finished goods ensure that a firm can satisfy demand in the event of a sudden increase in sales or a production halt. In addition, inventories help firms hedge against inflation. Rapid inflation in the late 1970s and early 1980s motivated firms to stock up on inventories early—before prices rose.

Firms determine their ideal level of inventories by trading off the costs and benefits of inventories. The ideal level of inventories fell after 1983 because the costs of holding inventories rose and the benefits fell. Adding to the cost side were the record-high interest rates in the early 1980s. At the same time, the declining inflation rate after 1982 reduced one of the benefits of holding inventories.

Even if interest rates were to fall or inflation to rise, firms would be expected to hold lower inventories than before adopting JIT. According to just-in-time thinking, holding inventories against such problems as late deliveries or defects is a cost of inventories—not a benefit—because the problems are never solved. Thus, the just-in-time approach is to eliminate the problem, thereby enabling firms to lower inventories permanently (Hay).

Another important factor motivating U.S. firms to reduce inventories in the 1980s was fierce competition from Japanese firms. Many analysts attribute the success of Japanese firms in U.S. markets in part to JIT (Celley and others; Kim and Schniederjans). The use of JIT reduced Japanese firms' inventory costs, which in turn helped Japanese firms undersell U.S. firms. In response to this challenge, U.S. firms sent representatives to Japan to learn how to reduce inventories with just-in-time techniques.[5]

---

[5] The case of Harley Davidson is illustrative. As Raia (1987) tells the story, the maker of rough-running motorcycles (known affectionately as hogs) was driven to the verge of bankruptcy in the early 1980s by its JIT practicing Japanese competitors. In response, Harley Davidson did as many companies do: it lobbied for and received temporary trade barriers to protect it from foreign competition. During the respite, however, Harley Davidson adopted JIT and then asked Congress to lift the trade barriers. So rare is the latter act that President Reagan himself flew to the company's headquarters in York, Pennsylvania, to commemorate the occasion.

How Do Firms Lower Inventories with JIT?

Firms practicing JIT reduce inventories at all stages by purchasing just in time to produce and producing just in time to sell. These practices represent a drastic departure from traditional purchasing and production practices in the United States. Accordingly, firms adopting JIT must confront the problems the traditional practices were designed to accommodate.

To reduce inventories of materials and supplies, firms are changing their purchasing practices under JIT.[6] Traditional practices called for infrequent orders of large lots of materials and supplies, well in advance of when needed for production. Such practices were intended to minimize ordering and transportation costs and to allow time for late deliveries and inspection of goods upon arrival.

In contrast, just-in-time purchasing calls for frequent orders of small lots of material and supplies, just in time to produce. Upon delivery, materials and supplies are whisked directly onto the assembly line. For example, Hewlett-Packard orders materials and supplies in lots of just a few hours' worth of production, several times a day (Raia 1990).

Just-in-time purchasing requires rapid delivery by suppliers. To speed delivery, suppliers are encouraged to locate near the buyer. For example, suppliers of General Motors' Buick division are all located within one shift (eight hours) of the manufacturing plant (Raia 1987). In addition, many suppliers are switching from trains to trucks as their primary delivery mode. Trucks are more economical than are trains when delivering small lots. Trucks are also more flexible, permitting delivery on shorter notice and permitting delivery directly to the assembly line to eliminate unnecessary handling.

To reduce inventories of finished goods, manufacturing firms are also changing their production practices under JIT. Traditional manufacturing practices called for production of large batches of goods, which were then stored as inventories until inspected and sold. These practices were intended to minimize the costs of setting up for a production run and to ensure an adequate supply of the finished goods in case of defects, strikes, or a surge in demand.

JIT entails frequent production runs of small batches. Ideally, manufacturers should produce goods continuously at roughly the same rate the goods are sold. That way, if sales decline, production declines in step to prevent inventories from accumulating. To provide for an increase in sales, on the other hand, manufacturers must maintain excess production capacity to avoid missing sales.

JIT also requires firms to reduce the time needed to set up for production of a particular good, in order to respond quickly to new orders. Setup times are being reduced in several ways. Manufacturers are installing more flexible machinery that can be quickly switched between production of different goods. For example, automobile makers are installing computer-aided machinery that is

---

[6] Unless other sources are indicated, the following comparison between traditional inventory practices and JIT practices is from Hay, and Mecimore and Weeks.

quickly reprogrammed to produce a variety of different components.[7] And instead of bolting machines to the floor, manufacturers are using quick-release clamps so machines can be moved quickly between stations where different goods are produced.

Just-in-time purchasing and production both require improved quality control since firms hold smaller inventories against defects. To improve quality, manufacturers and their suppliers are using computer programs to control quality. These programs monitor the dimensions of goods produced and automatically halt production if the dimensions exceed the desired specification. In addition, the technique of ordering and producing in small lots improves quality because defects are detected sooner.

Where Was JIT Adopted in the 1980s?

A strategy resembling JIT was practiced in the wholesale and retail trade sectors well before 1980 (Ackerman). While this strategy went under a different name—postponement—the principle was the same: postpone ordering as long as possible in order to minimize inventories (Kim and Schniederjans). Grocery store managers, for example, have long lived by this strategy because their stock in trade is perishable. If purchased too soon, food will rot in the warehouse before it is sold.

Under intense competition from Japanese firms, U.S. manufacturing firms began adopting just-in-time techniques in the 1980s (Mecimore and Weeks).[8] Within the manufacturing sector, adoption of JIT has been most visible at large companies in the automotive industry and the computer and office equipment industry—industries facing the fiercest competition from Japan. The Big Three of the auto industry—Ford, General Motors, and Chrysler—all began practicing JIT to some extent in the early 1980s. In the computing and office equipment industry, Hewlett-Packard, IBM, NCR, and Xerox also adopted just-in-time techniques in the early part of the decade (Zipkin; Im and Lee).

Beyond the few examples just noted, how many other manufacturing firms adopted JIT in the 1980s? Short of asking each and every firm, this question cannot be answered with certainty. Surveys suggest, however, that a sizable number of manufacturing firms have embraced just-in-time practices.[9] For example, the

---

[7] While some firms use computers in practicing JIT, computers are not essential. All that is needed is some signal that inventories are low and more should be produced or purchased. Many firms just use empty containers as a signal while others use red and green lights. On the other hand, computer production techniques do not necessarily reduce inventories unless combined with the JIT principle of ordering just in time to produce and producing just in time to purchase (Sauers; Kim and Lee). For a description of computer production techniques, see Johnson.

[8] Toyota developed JIT in the 1950s and 1960s, followed by other Japanese firms in the 1970s. Analysts have discussed many reasons JIT was practiced by Japanese manufacturers before their U.S. counterparts. One important reason is the closer physical and business relationship between Japanese firms and their suppliers. For example, they are physically closer (because Japan is smaller) and this fact expedites delivery. Another reason is that strikes are rarer in Japan, which reduces the need for inventories. In a pinch, however, U.S. manufacturers realized the superior highway system here might offset the greater distances suppliers must travel. And to the extent better roads were not enough, U.S. firms began relocating suppliers nearby. Finally, the decline in union membership in the United States facilitated JIT by, among other things, reducing the threat of strikes.

[9] In a survey conducted by the accounting firm Price Waterhouse, 37 percent of 210 manufacturing executives indicated their firms had applied JIT to some extent (Moscal).

percentage of firms ordering materials and supplies just in time increased dramatically beginning around 1980 (Chart 2, Panel A).[10] On average, from 1956 to 1980 only about 5 percent of manufacturing firms were ordering JIT. By 1990 about 15 percent were doing so.

While the fraction of firms ordering JIT tripled in the 1980s, 15 percent is still a small share. As a practical matter, not all firms can completely eliminate

CHART 2 JUST-IN-TIME PURCHASING

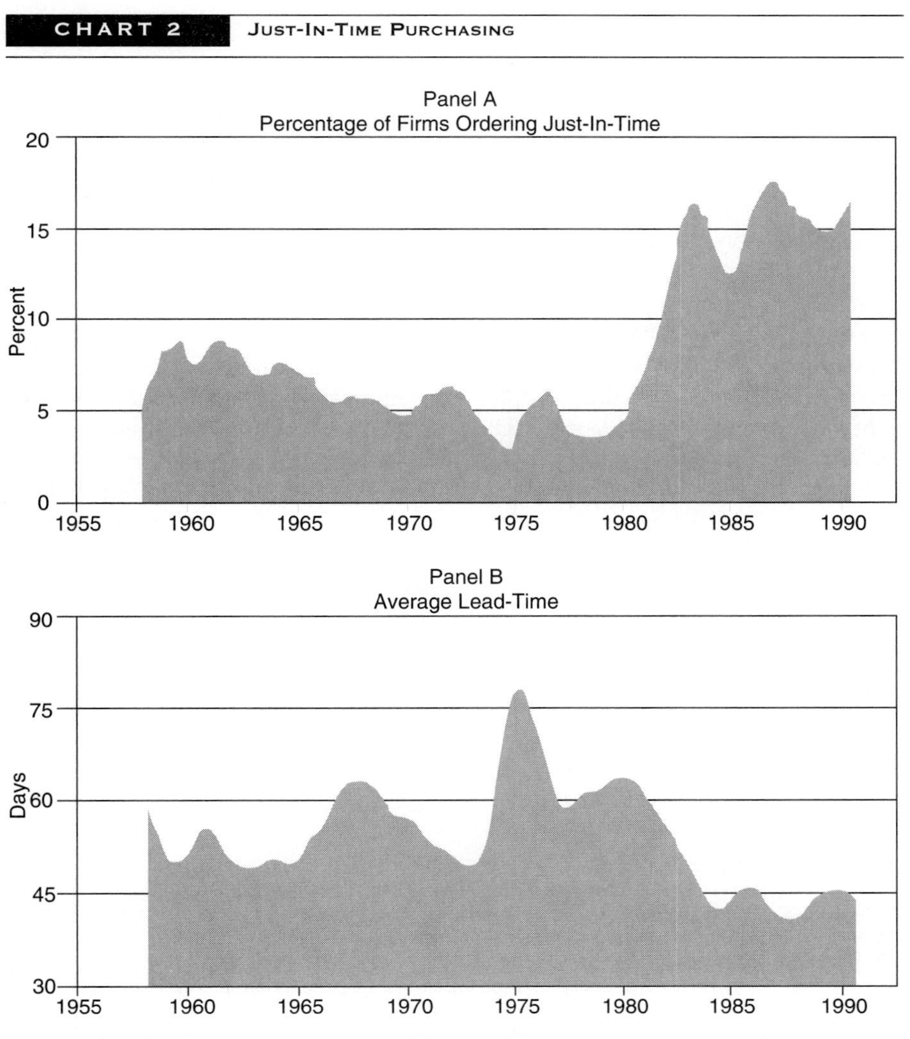

SOURCE: National Association of Purchasing Managers.

[10] These data are from a monthly survey of 250 purchasing managers of manufacturing companies in all industries, across the country. They represent the percentage of managers indicating they were ordering "hand to mouth," which is interpreted here as "just in time." The data were smoothed slightly to highlight the trend.

inventories of materials and supplies by ordering just in time to produce. Many firms, however, appear to be at least reducing inventories by gradually reducing the lead time between ordering and production (Chart 2, Panel B).[11] The average lead time across manufacturing firms has fallen substantially since 1980. After cycling upward from 1960 to 1980, the average lead time was more than 60 days in 1980. Lead times then headed down after 1980. By 1990 the average lead time was only about 45 days.[12]

JIT Reduces Aggregate Inventories

Skeptics assert that firms practicing JIT reduce their inventories by pushing them onto suppliers who may not be practicing JIT. If so, then JIT may amount to *just inventory transfers* at the aggregate level. Evidence against this possibility is the dramatic decline in inventory sales in the sector and industries where JIT was most widely applied in the 1980s.

Is JIT Just Redistributing Inventories?

Individual firms practicing JIT typically report substantial reductions in inventories. Hewlett-Packard, for example, reduced inventories by more than 50 percent after adopting just-in-time practices. General Motors used just-in-time techniques to reduce inventory costs from $8 billion to $2 billion (Johnson).

Are such firms just shunting their inventories onto their suppliers?[13] One survey found JIT was more prevalent among large firms than among the smaller companies that supply them.[14] A supplier not practicing JIT may hold larger inventories against the possibility of an unexpected, rush order from a JIT buyer. Suppliers may also inspect goods themselves and hold larger inventories against defects. If such practices are widespread, then JIT may merely be redistributing inventories from one firm to another.

Just-in-time buyers have an incentive not to force inventories onto suppliers because suppliers eventually pass their higher inventory costs back to the buyers. Suppliers can do so because they usually operate under long-term contracts that allow them to raise their prices when their costs increase (Hall).

---

[11] The data are actually a weighted average: lead-time multiplied by the percentage of firms reporting that lead time. The lead times used in the National Association of Purchasing Managers survey are 30 days, 60 days, 90 days, and 180 days or more. These data were also smoothed slightly to highlight the trend.

[12] The reduction in lead times would suggest that suppliers' delivery performance was improving. Surprisingly, the percentage of buyers reporting late deliveries was trendless in the 1980s (National Association of Purchasing Managers). Given the reduced lead times, however, the absence of deterioration can be taken as evidence of improvement. Further evidence of improvement is the fact late deliveries did not increase in the last stages of the expansion as in the past.

[13] For example, Raia (1987) noted a newspaper item suggesting the Detroit warehouse business was being revived by auto industry suppliers needing space to store larger inventories. The alleged revival came after the warehouse district was first decimated when automakers themselves reduced inventories after adopting JIT. While this report was speculative, the possibility that JIT may just redistribute inventories is real (Hall).

[14] The survey found more than two-thirds (67 of 97) of small supplier companies were delivering to their customers on a just-in-time basis; fewer than half of the suppliers, however, had adopted JIT internally (Sheridan).

Just-in-time buyers try to prevent shifting inventories onto suppliers with several measures. First, buyers often provide suppliers with forecasts of purchasing orders. Armed with a forecast, suppliers can time production of material and supplies so they are ready when the actual order arrives. Second, buyers can encourage suppliers to adopt genuine quality improvement programs. By improving quality, suppliers need not inspect each good before shipping and can hold smaller inventories against defects (Lorinez).

Most important, buyers can encourage suppliers to adopt just-in-time techniques themselves. Many automobile manufacturers, for example, weigh a prospective supplier's commitment to JIT before awarding a long-term contract to the supplier (Raia 1987). Suppliers practicing JIT can be relied on to purchase and produce materials and supplies just in time to fill the buyers' orders. In turn, buyers can order just in time to produce the final good. In this manner, inventories are reduced all the way down the production chain—from the smallest producer of materials and supplies to the largest producer of the final good.

Evidence JIT Is Reducing Inventories

Is there evidence JIT is reducing inventories? If JIT were merely redistributing inventories across companies, the aggregate inventory-sales ratio would not be expected to decline. But, as already noted, the ratio declined markedly after 1982.[15] Of course, some factor other than JIT may be reducing inventories. However, two pieces of evidence link the decline in inventories to JIT. First, the decline in the aggregate inventory-sales ratio stemmed entirely from the sector where JIT was newly applied in the 1980s—manufacturing (Chart 3). Second, the decline in the manufacturing sector inventory-sales ratio was most dramatic in the industries where JIT was most visibly adopted—the computing and office equipment industry and the motor vehicle industry (Chart 4). This evidence suggests the adoption of just-in-time techniques by U.S. manufacturing firms in the 1980s has, in fact, reduced aggregate inventories. Smaller aggregate inventories imply lower inventory costs and a stronger competitive position for U.S. firms. From a broader perspective, the use of just-in-time techniques implies a more stable U.S. economy.

Implications of JIT for the Economy

Inventory cycles have historically played a destabilizing role in the economy. By helping firms reduce and control their inventories, JIT can be expected to reduce

[15] The monthly disaggregated data in Chart 3 are available only back to 1967. The inventory-sales ratios differ from quarterly inventory-sales ratios shown in Chart 1 because two series use different sales figures. The Commerce Department survey from which these data obtain includes a sample of smaller companies (U.S. Department of Commerce).

CHART 3 INVENTORY-SALES RATIO BY SECTOR

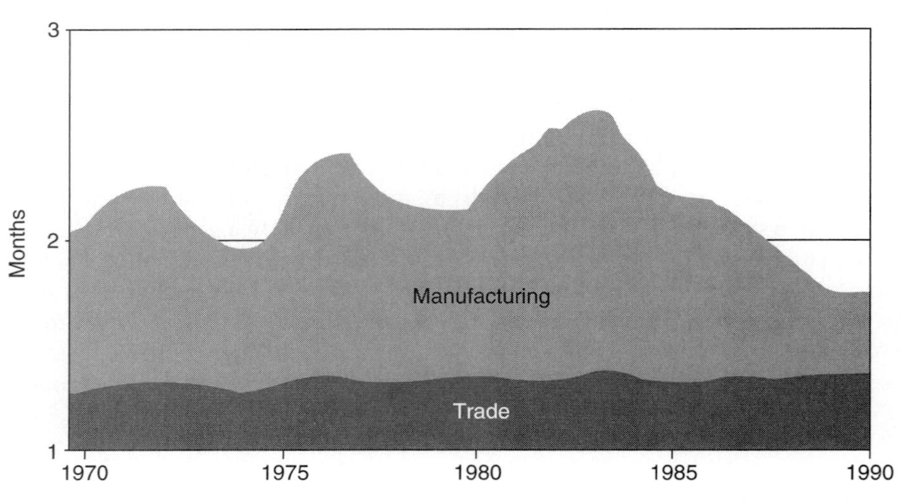

SOURCE: Board of Governors of the Federal Reserve System.

CHART 4 INVENTORY-SALES RATIO—SELECTED MANUFACTURING INDUSTRIES

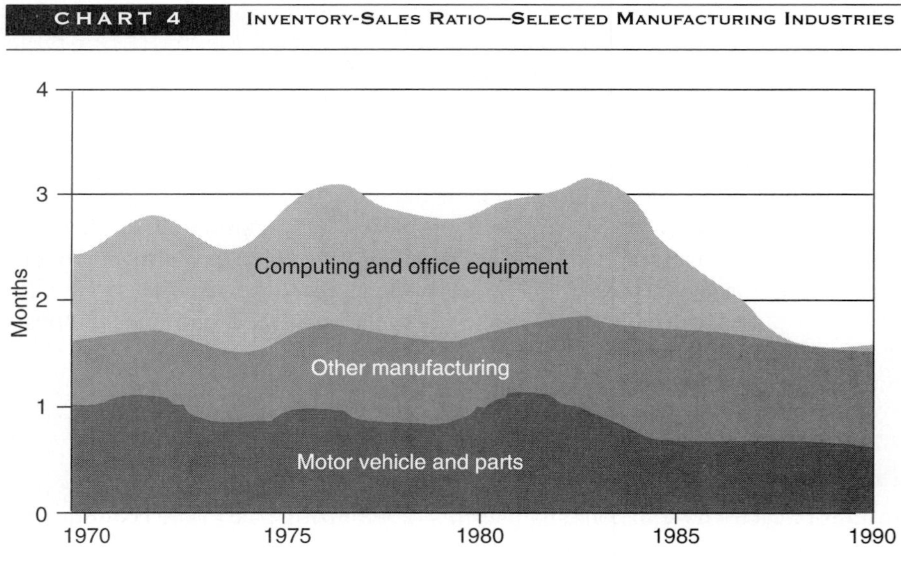

SOURCE: Board of Governors of the Federal Reserve System.

inventory cycles. Reduced inventory cycles in turn will dampen, but not eliminate, recessions.

JIT Can Dampen Recessions

In the past, large swings in inventories have amplified the effect of a change in business sales on output. That is, the decline in production (the recession) following a decline in sales has been both deeper and longer because of large inventory cycles. The large inventory cycles of the past resulted because firms' desired ratio of inventory to sales was high and because firms were slow to adjust production to maintain the desired ratio (Dornbusch and Fischer).

An example helps illustrate how these factors influence the characteristics of a recession. Suppose sales decline for an indefinite period because government spending declines. The depth of the ensuing recession depends on how deeply firms cut production, which in turn depends on how much firms must reduce inventories. If firms' desired ratio of inventory to sales is high, the decline in sales causes a large decline in firms' desired inventory stock. And if firms do not cut production promptly after sales decline, inventories will increase instead of decrease. Under these conditions, firms' warehouses soon swell with undesired inventories. As a result, production must eventually decline considerably more than the original decline in sales in order to eliminate the unwanted inventories. In this way, the inventory cycle deepens the recession.

The inventory cycle may also prolong the recession. Because of the buildup of unwanted inventories, firms may need to postpone increasing production even after sales increase. If so, the inventory cycle delays the recovery, or prolongs the recession.[16]

JIT diminishes inventory cycles for two reasons. First, firms' desired inventory-sales ratio is lower under JIT. Thus, a given decline in sales causes a smaller decline in desired inventories. For example, if firms' desired inventory–sales ratio declines from three months to two months under JIT, then a decline in sales of $1 billion would reduce desired inventories by only $2 billion instead of $3 billion. Second, because firms reduce production sooner after sales fall under JIT, fewer unwanted inventories accumulate. Therefore, a smaller cut in inventories is needed when firms finally cut production.

By diminishing inventory cycles, JIT dampens the effect of a decline in business sales on output, making the recession shallower and shorter. Production falls by less because firms wish to reduce inventories by less after sales decline. And firms need less time to eliminate unwanted inventories because they are smaller to start with. Thus, firms can increase production sooner after sales increase.

While the above discussion is merely hypothetical, there is real-world evidence suggesting JIT stabilizes output by stabilizing inventory investment. One researcher compared the variability of production and sales from 1957 to 1986 in seven industrial countries (West).[17] In the United States, production was about 30 percent more variable than sales. In general, he discovered production was

---

[16] In fact, JIT can also smooth output by dampening the effect of an increase in sales. When sales increase, firms with high desired inventory-sales ratios will increase their inventory investment more than will firms with low desired inventory-sales ratios. Thus, the change in production resulting from the increase in sales will be smaller under JIT. This point is ignored here, in part, because changes in inventory investment figure less in expansions than in recessions (Maccini).

[17] The countries were Canada, France, Italy, Japan, United Kingdom, United States, and West Germany.

more variable than sales in all but one country: Japan. In Japan—where JIT was most prevalent—production and sales were about equally variable.[18]

The Power of JIT Is Limited

While JIT may dampen recession by stabilizing inventory investment, JIT cannot eliminate recessions. Indeed, there is no evidence that fluctuations in inventory investment actually cause recessions (Blinder and Maccini). Most analysts think recessions result from other types of shocks to the economy, such as higher oil prices or reduced government spending. The inventory cycle following a shock only influences the depth and length of the recession caused by the shock. JIT may dampen a recession, but the recession may occur nevertheless.

Nor can JIT be relied on to prevent deep and long recessions. These characteristics of a recession depend on both the shock and the condition of the economy when the shock occurs. Hence, a severe recession could still result from a persistent shock to a weak economy. For example, a sustained increase in the price of oil in an economy laboring under a heavy debt burden could cause a severe recession. The most one can say is that the recession might have been even worse without JIT.

Saying so, however, invites a question: Will just-in-time techniques make the current recession milder? The answer depends on how prevalent the techniques are today. Unfortunately, evidence on that point is only suggestive. One small survey suggests reason for hope. In 1988, only 25 percent of the firms surveyed had just-in-time programs in place. Fully half of the firms, however, expected to be practicing JIT by 1990.[19] If the results of this survey are representative, then the new inventory techniques may be ... just in time.

References

Blinder, Alan S. 1981. "Retail Inventory Behavior and Business Fluctuations," *Brookings Papers on Economic Activity*, 2.

———, and Louis J. Maccini. 1991. "The Resurgence of Inventory Research: What Have We Learned?" *Journal of Economic Perspectives*, Winter.

Celley and others. 1986. "Implementation of JIT in the United States," *Journal of Purchasing & Materials Management*, Winter.

Dornbusch, Rudiger, and Stanley Fischer. 1984. *Macroeconomics*, 3d ed. New York: McGraw Hill.

---

[18] Closer to home, the 1980 recession in the United States illustrates how reduced inventory cycles dampen recessions. Inventory investment fell only $1.8 billion during the recession itself, contributing only about 2 percent of the decline in GNP during the recession. This fact may help explain why the 1980 recession was much briefer and shallower than average (Blinder). But, of course, the small inventory cycle in 1980 was not likely due to JIT because U.S. firms were just beginning to adopt JIT at that time. Indeed, Blinder rejects the possibility that improved inventory control techniques explained the behavior of inventories in that episode and concludes instead that businesses were forewarned of recession in time to cut inventory investment early.

[19] The accounting firm Touche Ross conducted this survey of 200 manufacturers and distributors (*Traffic Management*).

Hall, Ernest H., Jr. 1984. "Just-In-Time Management: A Critical Assessment," *The Academy of Management Executive*, vol. 3.

Hay, Edward J. 1988. *The Just-In-Time Breakthrough.* New York: John Wiley and Sons.

Im, Jin H., and Sony M. Lee. 1989. "Implementation of Just-In- Time Systems in U.S. Manufacturing," *International Journal of Operations and Production Management*, vol. 9.

Johnson, Alicia. 1986. "MRP? MRPII? OPT? CIM? FMS? JIT? Is Any System Letter Perfect?" *Management Review*, no. 9.

Kim, Gyu Chan, and Sang M. Lee. 1989. "Impact of Computer Technology on the Implementation of Just-In-Time Production Systems," *Production and Inventory Management Journal.*

———, and Marc J. Schniederjans. 1990. "An Evaluation of Computer Integrated Just-In-Time Production Systems," *Production and Inventory Management Journal*, First Quarter.

Lorinez, James A. 1985. "Suppliers Question Approaches to JIT," *Purchasing World*, March.

Maccini, Louis J. 1987. "Inventories," *New Palgrave Dictionary of Economics.* London: Macmillan.

Mecimore, Charles D., and James K. Weeks. 1987. *Techniques in Inventory Management and Control.* Montvale, N.J.: National Association of Accountants.

Moscal, Brian S. 1989. "Just In (the Wrong) Time," *Industry Week*, August 15.

National Association of Purchasing Managers. Various issues. *Report on Business.*

Raia, Ernest. 1990. "JIT Delivery: Redefining 'On-Time,'" *Journal of Purchasing and Materials Management*, September 3.

———. 1987. "Just-In-Time USA: Journey to World Class," *Journal of Purchasing and Materials Management*, September 24.

Traffic Management. 1988. "JIT ... Not Just a Buzzword Anymore," September, pp. 42–49.

Sauers, Dale G. 1986. "Analyzing Inventory Systems," *Management Accounting*, May.

Sheridan, John H. 1989. "Ignoring the Real Promises of JIT?" *Industry Week*, March 6, pp. 44–45.

U.S. Department of Commerce. 1989. "Current Industrial Report Series." December 14.

West, Kenneth D. 1988. "Evidence from Seven Countries on Whether Inventories Smooth Aggregate Output," National Bureau of Economic Research working paper no. 2664, July.

Zipkin, Paul H. 1991. "Does Manufacturing Need a JIT Revolution?" *Harvard Business Review*, January-February.

Questions

1. Suppose a company's inventory-sales ratio is 2, meaning that it holds 2 months worth of sales in inventory—perhaps to protect against production halts or sudden increases in sales. Approximately what is the company's inventory turnover ratio?

2. Past recessions were often foreshadowed by rising inventory-sales ratios. Explain the behavior of the aggregate inventory-sales ratio during the 1973–1975 recession. (See Chart 1.)
3. Describe the benefits and the costs of holding inventories.
4. "Inventory is evil, and we sought to eradicate it," says Norman Garrity, who oversees several factories owned by Corning Inc. "If you understand what causes inventory, you get to the root causes of a lot of manufacturing problems." Interpret Mr. Garrity's philosophy of inventory management.
5. "Firms practicing JIT reduce inventories at all stages by purchasing just in time to produce and producing just in time to sell." Describe the just-in-time (JIT) system of inventory management as applied to purchasing and to production.
6. Why did Japanese companies, according to some analysts, adopt JIT systems prior to their adoption by U.S. companies?
7. Do JIT companies reduce their inventories by pushing them onto suppliers that do not employ JIT practices? Explain.
8. In what way does the adoption of JIT systems by U.S. companies dampen recessions?

A Study of the Information Needs of Commercial Loan Officers

ROBERT S. KEMP, JR., AND GEORGE A. OVERSTREET, JR.

The study discussed in this article first examines the information needs of commercial lenders; specifically, the study seeks to find what information they would like to get from companies' annual reports. Second, this study looks at the decision criteria used by lenders as implied by the information they use. Using a questionnaire, this work extends and updates previous work on the information needs of users of financial statements.

Background

The American Accounting Association's *Statement on Accounting Theory and Theory Acceptance* states, "The primary objective of accounting is to provide financial information about the economic affairs of an entity to interested parties for use in making decisions. This objective statement is a premise which most people seem to find acceptable, subject to slight variations." This goal clearly acknowledges that information is a means for making decisions. The emphasis on decision making gives the decision maker the shared authority in determining what information should be provided.

The needs of lenders have frequently been eclipsed by the attention and emphasis given investors. This is due in part to the Securities and Exchange Commission's (SEC's) aggressive pursuit of its duties to protect small investors. Bankers have information needs which they share with other user groups, including equity investors, but they also have unique needs. The need to understand the reporting entity's economic health is shared by most users of financial information; however, how economic health is measured and judged differs with particular users.

At the time of this writing, Robert S. Kemp, Jr. and George A. Overstreet, Jr., were associate professors of commerce at the McIntire School of Commerce, University of Virginia, Charlottesville.

The Commercial Lending Decision

Commercial lenders, like all providers of capital, attempt to measure and judge economic health by determining value first and then judging whether such value is adequate. The value of an item is the present value of the benefits which the owner expects to receive from owning the item and, as such, is a function of the magnitude, risk, and timing of the expected benefits.

Value of the Loan

In the lending decision, the banker must decide whether a loan is justified and whether, if the loan is made, it will maintain its value. The value of the loan is a function of the amount, risk, and timing of the loan payments (that is, the benefits of the loan to the bank).

The information needs of bankers thus center on these items. Ultimately, what the banker must decide is whether the bank can expect to be repaid, when that repayment will occur, and whether there is sufficient security if the loan is not repaid.

Understanding Accounting Definitions

Therefore, the banker must first understand the borrower's current earnings/cash-generating process, including details on the borrower's operations, assets, and financing. Second, the banker must understand how the earnings/cash-generating process might change in the future. Third, like all users of information, the banker must understand the accounting definitions and the accounting processes and procedures that generate the information.

The Accounting Dilemma of Information Choice

The accounting profession needs to provide bankers with the proper information if they are to perform their function efficiently and effectively. This is easier said than done given the infinite amount of information required to describe operations and assets completely and given the competing needs of other users of financial information.

Previous Attempts

This dilemma is not new. Attempts to construct a normative theory of accounting information are numerous.[1] All came to the conclusion that decision usefulness is the appropriate criterion for choosing what information to report. Putting this criterion into operation proves difficult.

Currently, financial accounting reporting is put into operation with a framework of general-purpose financial statements. With these statements serving as the norm, no one specific user group can be targeted. This standard attempts to

---

[1] A few attempts at constructing a normative theory of accounting information include: Sanders, T.H., H.R. Hatfield, and U. Moore, *A Statement of Accounting Principles*, American Institute of Certified Public Accountants, New York, 1938; May, G.O., *Financial Accounting*, The Macmillan Co., 1943; and Paton, W.A. and A.C. Littleton, *An Introduction to Corporate Accounting Standards*, Monograph No. 3, American Accounting Association, 1940.

provide the user of the information with both the accountant's estimate and information on how that estimate was derived. Communicating the process of estimation is important, for it permits the user to adjust the accountant's estimate to reflect the user's perspective.

Challenge to Meet Information Needs

The need for a standard of general-purpose financial statements is not a justification for neglecting the needs for specific user groups. Rather, it serves to underscore the depth of the challenge to meet those needs. The Financial Accounting Standards Board clearly recognizes bankers, along with investors and other users, as a primary group to be served by accounting information.

The attempts to determine the information needs of varying users are numerous, varied, and dated. The most current study dates back to 1974 and dealt with investors. No work has been conducted and published examining the needs of bankers in the past 20 years.

Research Design

This study uses a research design similar to that used by S.L. Buzby in 1974. A questionnaire was administered to 100 commercial bankers; 77 observations were usable.[2] Participants were selected randomly from bankers throughout the U.S. with the final sample containing bankers from 29 states. All bankers were responsible for commercial lending decisions and were college educated. Participant ages ranged from 24 to 56, averaging 34; years of banking experience ranged from 1 to 27, averaging 14; and years of commercial lending experience ranged from 1 to 24, averaging 7. The number of accounts managed ranged from 10 to 1,400, averaging 134.

Each banker was asked to evaluate 48 pieces of information on a scale of 0 to 4, where 4 indicated high importance and 0 indicated low importance. The 48 pieces of information dealt with the current earnings/cash-generating process, how the earnings/cash-generating process will change in the future, and the nature of the information and how it is defined. Information selected for inclusion in the questionnaire came from previous studies and interviews with commercial bankers. Figure 1 is a list of the selected pieces of information.

Research Results

The relative frequency, mean response, standard deviation, and rank per piece of information are listed in Figure 2. A score of 3 or 4 indicated a high importance; 23 pieces of information had a mean score of 3 or above. Only 11 pieces had a mean below 2.5.

Most Important Information

The most important information appears to be long-term debt (F_{42}), sources and uses of funds-working capital (F_{45}), sources and uses of funds-cash (F_{44}), cost of

---

[2] Due to participants omitting data, 23 observations were not usable.

FIGURE 1 INFORMATION EXAMINED

Informational Piece	
F_1	Information on company directors, such as their names and major outside affiliations.
F_2	Information on management, such as names, ages, and functional responsibilities.
F_3	Information on the existence or nonexistence of board committees such as independent audit committees, nominating committees, and compensation committees.
F_4	Information on management remuneration such as salary, option plans, and perquisites.
F_5	Forecasts of next year's earnings per share.
F_6	Planned R&D expenditures in the next year for R&D and new product development.
F_7	Plans for the next year for entry into new markets.
F_8	Allowance for doubtful accounts.
F_9	Breakdown of inventories into raw materials, goods in process, and finished goods.
F_{10}	Method used to determine the cost of inventories, for example, lower of cost or market.
F_{11}	Description of major plants and warehouses including location, function, and size.
F_{12}	Description of major products produced including an indication of those products that are new.
F_{13}	Information about the firm's stock option plan.
F_{14}	Dollar value of the firm's order backlog.
F_{15}	Breakdown of tangible assets into a form such as land, equipment, and buildings.
F_{16}	Indication of the original cost, accumulated depreciation, and the current amount of depreciation charged to income for tangible assets.
F_{17}	Specification of the method used to compute depreciation.
F_{18}	Current market value of marketable securities.
F_{19}	Dollar value of the firm's capital expenditures.
F_{20}	Current value information as regards cost of goods sold; depreciation expense; and plant, property, and equipment.
F_{21}	Information about consolidated and unconsolidated subsidiaries such as percentage ownership, dividends received, equity in undistributed earnings, and summary financial statements.
F_{22}	Pertinent information about investments in firms not qualifying as subsidiaries such as cost and market value of the investment, percentage ownership, dividends received and equity in undistributed earnings.
F_{23}	Information about the leasing of assets.
F_{24}	Information pertaining to the company's employee pension plan.
F_{25}	Budgeted capital expenditures for the coming year.
F_{26}	Discussion of the major factors which will influence next year's results to include an indication of the firm's relationship to its industry and the economy.
F_{27}	Management analysis of the historical relationships of general economic ratios and industry ratios.

FIGURE 1 INFORMATION EXAMINED (CONTINUED)

F_{28}	Historical summary of important operating data.
F_{29}	Measure of the physical level of output such as the percentage of plant capacity utilized.
F_{30}	Number of employees.
F_{31}	Indication of employee morale such as the rate of absenteeism and turnover.
F_{32}	Information on the effects of changing of prices, such as pertinent price indices or supplementary price level adjusted statements.
F_{33}	Information about current R&D expenditures.
F_{34}	Number of stockholders.
F_{35}	Maintenance and repair expenditures.
F_{37}	Breakdown of operating earnings by major product line and customer classes.
F_{38}	Indication of sales revenue and net income attributable to foreign operations.
F_{39}	Statement of company objectives and dividend policy.
F_{40}	Information regarding nonaudit services provided by the firm's independent auditor such as type of service and amount of fee.
F_{41}	Information on business combinations such as the accounting method used to record the combination, prices paid, method of payment, and accounting treatment of goodwill.
F_{42}	Schedule of interest and principal due on long-term debt in future years.
F_{43}	Information pertaining to changes in accounting methods.
F_{44}	Statement of sources and uses of cash funds.
F_{45}	Statement of sources and uses of working capital funds.
F_{46}	Reconciliation of the calculation of primary and fully diluted earnings per share.
F_{47}	Information on deferred taxes, for example, reconciliation of the amount charged to income and amount actually paid.
F_{48}	Social and environmental information.

inventories (F_{10}), and allowance for doubtful accounts (F_8). What appears to dominate the commercial lender's perspective is the current debt position of the borrower and the flow of funds to meet these obligations. The nature and character of the borrower's liquidity, cost of inventories, and allowance for doubtful accounts are also important to the lender. The quality of inventories and receivables can be a collateral or risk issue but, more important, affects the firm's cash flow through realization and collection of sales.

Other Important Factors

The next five pieces of information, in rank of importance, are change in accounting method (F_{43}), consolidation information (F_{21}), marketable securities (F_{18}), depreciation (F_{16}), and breakdown of inventories (F_9). Besides the liquidity element of marketable securities, it appears that lenders are concerned with the methodology of the financial statements. The subjective process of selecting and changing accounting procedures (for example, depreciation) is at the heart of the accounting dilemma. It appears lenders consider this information important as they struggle to understand a borrower's true economic status. The fourth- and fifth-ranked pieces of information, cost of inventories and allowance for doubtful accounts, further support this finding.

FIGURE 2 SAMPLE MEANS, STANDARD DEVIATIONS, D. STATISTICS, AND RANKING OF INFORMATION

	Information Piece	Relative Frequency 0	1	2	3	4	Mean	Standard Deviation	Rank
	Year's Results								
F_{42}	Long-term debt	0.0	0.0	5.2	10.4	84.4	3.792	0.522	1
F_{45}	Sources and uses of working capital funds	1.3	0.0	5.2	7.8	85.7	3.766	0.667	2
F_{44}	Sources and uses of cash funds	1.3	2.6	2.6	7.8	85.7	3.740	0.750	3
F_{10}	Cost of inventories	1.3	2.6	2.6	13.0	80.5	3.688	0.765	4
F_8	Allowance for doubtful accounts	1.3	0.0	3.9	18.2	76.6	3.688	0.674	5
F_{43}	Changes in accounting method	1.3	2.6	3.9	13.0	79.2	3.662	0.788	6
F_{21}	Consolidated and unconsolidated	1.3	2.6	1.3	19.5	75.3	3.649	0.757	7
F_{18}	Marketable securities	1.3	0.0	5.2	23.4	70.1	3.610	0.710	8
F_{16}	Depreciation	1.3	2.6	5.2	18.2	72.7	3.584	0.817	9
F_9	Breakdown of inventories	1.3	3.9	3.9	18.2	72.7	3.571	0.850	10
F_{19}	Capital expenditures	2.6	0.0	5.2	26.0	66.2	3.532	0.821	11
F_{15}	Tangible assets	2.6	1.3	7.8	18.2	70.1	3.519	0.898	12
F_{17}	Method used to compute depreciation	1.2	1.3	10.5	20.8	66.2	3.494	0.837	13
F_{20}	Current value information as regards cost of goods sold, etc.	1.3	3.9	3.9	33.8	57.1	3.416	0.848	14
F_{22}	Information about investments	3.9	0.0	11.7	36.4	48.0	3.247	0.948	15
F_{47}	Deferred taxes	0.0	3.9	15.6	32.5	48.1	3.247	0.861	16
F_{23}	Information about leasing	1.3	1.3	13.0	45.4	39.0	3.195	0.812	17
F_{28}	Historical summary	2.6	3.9	14.2	33.8	45.5	3.156	0.988	18
F_{36}	Breakdown of sales revenue	2.6	3.9	14.2	36.4	42.9	3.130	0.978	19
F_{38}	Foreign operations	1.3	3.8	18.2	33.8	42.9	3.130	0.937	20
F_{41}	Business combinations	2.6	9.1	14.3	22.1	51.9	3.117	1.124	21

FIGURE 2 SAMPLE MEANS, STANDARD DEVIATIONS, D. STATISTICS, AND RANKING OF INFORMATION (CONTINUED)

	Information Piece	Relative Frequency 0	1	2	3	4	Mean	Standard Deviation	Rank
F_2	Management, names, ages, and functional responsibilities	5.2	2.6	14.3	29.9	48.0	3.052	1.134	22
F_{37}	Breakdown of operating earnings	1.3	7.8	16.9	33.7	40.3	3.026	1.076	23
F_{26}	Factors which will influence next year's results	3.9	5.1	221	39.0	29.9	2.883	0.973	24
F_{25}	Budgeted capital expenditures	2.6	6.5	26.0	31.1	33.8	2.870	1.043	25
F_{39}	Company objectives and dividend policy	0.0	7.8	28.6	35.0	28.6	2.844	0.933	26
F_7	New markets	3.9	6.5	24.6	32.5	32.5	2.831	1.081	27
F_4	Management remuneration	3.9	6.5	23.3	41.6	24.7	2.766	1.025	28
F_6	Planned R&D expenditures	3.9	2.6	33.8	33.8	25.9	2.753	1.002	29
F_{24}	Employee pension plan	2.6	2.6	33.8	40.3	20.7	2.740	0.909	30
F_{12}	Description of major products	3.9	9.1	22.1	41.6	23.3	2.714	1.050	31
F_{33}	Current R&D expenditures	2.6	6.5	33.8	33.8	23.3	2.688	0.990	32
F_{14}	Firm's order backlog	2.6	7.8	28.6	41.6	19.2	2.675	0.966	33
F_{46}	Primary and fully diluted earnings per share	2.6	14.3	26.0	27.3	29.6	2.675	1.129	34
F_{27}	Management analysis of the historical relationships	2.6	9.1	28.6	39.0	20.7	2.662	0.995	35
F_{29}	Physical level of output	3.9	6.5	27.3	44.2	18.1	2.662	0.982	36
F_5	Forecasts of next year's earnings per share	5.2	10.4	27.3	33.8	23.3	2.597	1.015	37
F_1	Company directors	6.5	14.3	32.5	16.9	29.8	2.494	1.242	38
F_{35}	Maintenance and repair expenditures	2.6	15.6	40.3	18.2	23.3	2.442	1.094	39
F_{11}	Description of major plants (1)	3.9	13.0	35.1	31.2	16.8	2.442	1.045	40

FIGURE 2 SAMPLE MEANS, STANDARD DEVIATIONS, D. STATISTICS, AND RANKING OF INFORMATION (CONTINUED)

F_{34}	Number of stockholders (1)	6.5	15.6	33.8	23.4	20.7	2.364	1.169	41
F_{30}	Number of employees	7.8	13.0	35.1	28.6	15.5	2.312	1.127	42
F_{13}	Stock option plan (1)	5.2	20.8	37.7	24.7	11.6	2.169	1.056	43
F_{32}	Effects of changing prices (1)	13.0	20.8	31.2	20.8	14.2	2.026	1.235	44
F_{48}	Social and environmental information (1)	16.9	20.8	27.3	18.2	16.8	1.974	1.328	45
F_3	Board committees (1)	14.3	19.5	42.9	15.6	7.7	1.831	1.105	46
F_{40}	Nonaudit services provided by firm's independent auditor	22.1	33.8	24.7	13.0	6.4	1.481	1.165	47
F_{31}	Employee morale	32.5	32.5	26.0	9.0	0.0	1.117	0.973	48

(1) When statistically tested, it could not be conclusively inferred (99% confidence interval) that the results for this piece of information were not random.

Least Important Information

The least important pieces of information, passing the randomness test, are employee morale (F_{31}), nonaudit auditor services (F_{40}), number of employees (F_{30}), description of major plants (F_{11}), maintenance and repair expenditures (F_{35}), and company directors (F_1). Intangible factors which affect the value-generating process of the borrower indirectly appear less important than some of the more tangible, direct factors such as inventories. Although these intangible items affect a firm's performance, they are often difficult to interpret in loan decisions.

The Information Needed by Bankers

The most and least important pieces of information which bankers seek appear well-founded in banking theory and practice. Of note, however, is the difference between investors and bankers. The results of this study, which used bankers, and studies such as Gyan Chandra's in 1975 and S.L. Buzby's in 1974, which used investors, demonstrated both similar and dissimilar information needs. Comparing the results noted in Figure 2 with Chandra's work, only three pieces of information ranked in the top ten by bankers are ranked in the top ten by investors, that is, sources and uses of funds (F_{45}, F_{44}) and consolidated and unconsolidated data (F_{21}). In comparison to Buzby's results, only four pieces of information ranked in the top ten by bankers are ranked in the top ten by investors, that is, sources and uses of funds (F_{45}, F_{44}), cost of inventories (F_{10}), and change in accounting method (F_{43}).

One of the dominant forces driving a firm's stock value is earnings per share. No other factor theoretically is more important in normal stock valuation. Chandra finds that investors rank earnings per share the most important item among the 39 factors rated. Buzby finds investors rank earnings per share 10th among the 38 pieces of financial information rated.

To commercial lenders, earnings are viewed as a residual which only indirectly affect the loan decision. This relative difference in views is demonstrated by the low rank (number 34) for primary and fully diluted earnings per share (F_{46}). In sharp contrast, bankers rank sources and uses of funds working capital (F_{45}) number two, whereas Chandra and Buzby find investors rank this piece of information number nine and seven, respectively.

Another interesting comparison regards the importance of present versus future financial information. Bankers and investors share a common interest in a company's future; however, stock value is predicated on future financial performance while loan value is more predicated on current financial welfare. The SEC Advisory Committee in 1977 surveyed investors and found that business outlook information was extremely useful and of more importance than information about present operations. Bankers ranked pieces of information about the future relatively low. Bankers ranked factors which will influence next year's results (F_{26}) number 24, budgeted capital expenditures (F_{25}) number 25, planned research and development (R&D) expenditures (F_6) number 29, and forecasts of next year's earnings per share (F_5) number 37.

Lending Criteria of Bankers

As noted earlier, the lending decision is based on first understanding the earnings/cash-generating process, including the details of the borrower's operations, assets, and financing. Looking down the ranks in Figure 2, the information needed to acquire this understanding ranks very high, for example, sources and uses of funds (F_{45}, F_{44}) ranking second and third, respectively. Clearly, lenders seek to understand the present and past before they proceed to estimating the future.

Concern with Future Cash Generating

Lenders are also concerned with potential changes in the earnings/cash-generating process. It is puzzling that information about such future factors was not ranked as high as expected. Factors affecting next year's results (F_{26}) ranked 24th, budgeted capital expenditures (F_{25}) ranked 25th, planned R&D expenditures (F_6) ranked 29th, order backlog (F_{14}) ranked 34th, earnings per share forecasts (F_5) ranked 37th.

This result may be a function of the accounting profession's preoccupation with the past and present, and, hence, the nature of the data. Perhaps lenders seek to understand the future through nonaccounting information. Certainly, the data from this study suggest a short-run flavor to the commercial lender's orientation.

Definitions and Procedures

Lenders also seek an understanding of the definitions and procedures underlying accounting information. Ranking of this sort of information varied. Changes in accounting methods (F_{43}) ranked 6th while depreciation methodology (F_{17}) ranked 13th. Clearly, this information is valued and affects the lender's perceptions and, thus, decisions.

Summary and Conclusions

Using the decision-usefulness criterion, this study examines the information needs of commercial lenders, who have a definite hierarchy of information needs. As expected, the nature of their orientation centers on a borrower's ability to repay a loan and the sources of repayment. For example, commercial lenders ranked long-term debt, sources and uses of funds, and various methodological items highly. Information about intangible items such as employee morale and auditor-provided nonaudit services were rated low. Commercial lenders also had relatively little interest in management forecasts, budgets, and expenditure plans.

The findings of this study highlight the fact that bankers do not have the same information needs as other users of financial information. Given the importance of the commercial loan decision, it is important that the accounting profession better understand and meet lenders' particular information needs.

In addition, commercial lenders primarily use accounting information to evaluate the present and past operations of the borrower. Accounting information tends to be less important in evaluating the borrower's future. This may indicate a problem with the accounting professions' orientation or the loan underwriting process. Certainly, further study is warranted.

Bibliography

American Accounting Association. Committee to Prepare a Statement of Basic Accounting Theory. *A Statement of Basic Accounting Theory (ASOBAT)*. Evanston, Ill.: American Accounting Association, 1966.

American Institute of Certified Public Accountants. Study Group on the Objectives of Financial Statements. *Objectives of Financial Statements*. New York: American Institute of Certified Public Accountants, 1973.

Beaver, W.H. "The Information Content of Annual Earning Announcements." *Journal of Accounting Research* 6, Supplement 1968, pp. 67–92.

Beaver, W.H. and R.E. Dukes. "Interperiod Tax Allocation, Earnings Expectations, and the Behavior of Security Prices." *The Accounting Review* 47, April 1972, pp. 320–32.

Beaver, W.H., P. Kettler, and M. Scholes. "The Association Between Market Determined and Accounting Determined Risk Measures." *The Accounting Review* 45, Oct. 1970, pp. 654–82.

Buzby, S.L. "Selected Items of Information and Their Disclosure in Annual Reports." *The Accounting Review* 49, July 1974, p. 423.

Carpenter, C.G., A.J. Francia, and R.H. Strawser. "Perception of Financial Reporting Practices: An Empirical Study." *MSU Business Topics*, pp. 56–62.

Cert, A.R. *Corporate Reporting and Investment Decisions.* The University of California Press, 1961.

Chandra, Gyan. "Information Needs of Security Analysts." *The Journal of Accountancy*, Dec. 1975, pp. 65–70.

Copeland, R.M. and W. Fredericks. "Extent of Disclosure." *Journal of Accounting Research*, Spring 1968, pp. 106–13.

Financial Accounting Standards Board, *Objectives of Financial Reporting by Business Enterprises.* Stamford, Conn.: Financial Accounting Standards Board, 1978.

May, G.O. *Financial Accounting.* New York: The Macmillan Co., 1943.

Moonitz, M. *The Basic Postulates of Accounting.* Accounting Research Study No. 1. New York: American Institute of Certified Public Accountants, 1961.

Paton, W.A. and A.C. Littleton. *An Introduction to Corporate Accounting Standards.* Monograph No. 3. Evanston, Ill.: American Accounting Association, 1940.

Sanders, T.H., H.R. Hatfield, and U. Moore. *A Statement of Accounting Principles.* New York: American Institute of Certified Public Accountants, 1938.

Singhvi, S.S. and H.B. Desai. "An Empirical Analysis of the Quality of Corporate Financial Disclosure." *The Accounting Review* 46, Jan. 1971, pp. 129–38.

U.S. Securities and Exchange Commission, Advisory Committee on Corporate Disclosure. *Report of the Advisory Committee on Corporate Disclosure to the Securities and Exchange Commission.* Volumes 1 and 2, Nov. 3, 1977. Washington, D.C.: U.S. Government Printing Office, 1977.

Questions

1. The value of an asset (e.g., a share of common stock or a bank loan) is a function of what three fundamental variables? Explain the relationship between value and each of the variables.
2. Who are the various groups of people who use a company's financial statements as information for decision making? Identify the primary concerns of each group.
3. Based on the survey results, answer the following questions on commercial loan officer opinions:
   a. What are the ten most important pieces of information for a loan decision? What are the loan officers' apparent concerns reflected in this information?
   b. What are several of the least important pieces of information? Do these results appear reasonable? Explain.
4. Compare and contrast the information needs of commercial loan officers and investors.

5. "Lenders are also concerned with potential changes in the earnings/cash-generating process. It is puzzling that information about such future factors was not ranked as high as expected." To which pieces of information does this quotation refer? Why do the authors find these results puzzling?

Lessons on Lending and Borrowing in Hard Times

LEONARD I. NAKAMURA

Problem loans and highly leveraged transactions have brought home a truth about lending that is easily forgotten in good times: loans sometimes fail, with sad consequences for both borrower and lender. Many existing loans have soured, causing lenders to tighten credit terms on new lending. Meanwhile, borrowers have complained—and policymakers have openly worried—that lenders are refusing sound loans.

New theories about lending and about loan contracts emphasize the difficulties lenders face in ensuring repayment of their loans. According to these theories, the collateral for a loan is not just a back-up source of repayment if the borrower defaults; collateral is also crucial for inducing payments from borrowers who can make them.

Cash-strapped borrowers, when their businesses sour, will often try to put off lenders and keep paying their employees, suppliers, and landlords. In response, lenders will threaten to seize collateral and declare loans in default to ensure they get their fair share of a distressed borrower's cash flows.

This threat is a blunt instrument that often harms the lender as much as the borrower. After all, the value of the borrower's collateral, particularly during a recession, may be insufficient to repay the loan. But there are other considerations, as well. A foreclosure causes valuable resources to be lost that would not be lost otherwise. Management may lose partial control over the firm because of bankruptcy rules, or spend too much time in court, struggling against creditors and other claimants, and too little time running the business. Customer relationships inevitably worsen as customers begin looking for alternative suppliers. And ultimately, if an otherwise viable borrower is liquidated, valuable relationships between management, employees, and customers are lost.

At the time of this writing, Leonard I. Nakamura was a senior economist in the Banking and Financial Market Section of the Research Department, Federal Reserve Bank of Philadelphia.

Source: Reprinted from *Business Review*, Federal Reserve Bank of Philadelphia, (July/Aug. 1991).

If a borrower's business is fundamentally sound, its longer-term profitability ought to be the best source to repay the loan. But if the lender forces the borrower out of business, this source of funds is lost.

The Dilemma of Foreclosure

In the tale of the goose that laid the golden eggs, the owner foolishly tried to get the goose's prized eggs more quickly by killing it. Lenders are not so unwise; still, they might have to threaten foreclosure as a way to force borrowers to repay. When lenders must carry out their threats, they kill the golden goose—and this is the dilemma of foreclosure.

Unfortunately, standard economic theory had assumed away this dilemma, maintaining that the interests of borrowers and lenders could always be aligned through loan agreements. Consequently, economists believed that inefficiencies associated with loan default were small and that liquidation decisions were always sound. After all, wasn't it true that only firms having no value as going concerns were liquidated?

More recent theories offer less optimistic conclusions about lending. They show that firms having value as going concerns may well be liquidated and that inefficiencies associated with loan default can have important consequences for aggregate economic activity. In particular, the implication is that some loans that would ordinarily be made in good times would not be made in uncertain times. These newer theories are more realistic about the potential for conflicts between borrower and lender; accordingly, they are useful guides—to all parties—for anticipating, and thereby lessening, the pain associated with hard economic times.

Two theories in particular have emphasized the importance, and difficulty, of maintaining the borrower's incentive to repay. The idea is disarmingly simple: if given a choice of how much to repay, a borrower who wishes to maximize profits will always choose to repay the smallest amount. One theory, originated by Robert Townsend,[1] underscores the lender's ignorance, relative to the borrower, of the borrower's net worth. The other theory, originated by Oliver Hart and John Moore,[2] emphasizes the borrower's control over cash flows (the revenues that flow to the borrower from sales of products and services).

Townsend: Loan Contracts Reduce Information Costs

Townsend's model stresses the cost to investors of obtaining financial information about borrowers. Before granting a loan, outside financial investors must first obtain detailed information about the firms seeking finance. This informa-

---

[1] Robert M. Townsend, "Optimal Contracts and Competitive Markets With Costly State Verification," *Journal of Economic Theory* 21 (1979) pp. 265–93.

[2] Oliver Hart and John Moore, "Default and Renegotiation: A Dynamic Model of Debt," MIT Working Paper (August 1989).

tion extends to the firm's products and services, the customer base, marketing data, advertising plans, management, alternative financial resources, plant and equipment, labor resources and costs—in short, a detailed financial analysis and forecast. And until the financing is actually in hand, the firm has a strong incentive to provide investors with satisfactory information.

But once the investment is made, the investors may not be well positioned to keep informed about a firm's net worth. Information gathering is a costly procedure, requiring, at a minimum, an audit of current assets and liabilities, an explanation of variances between planned income and expenses and the results achieved, and an evaluation of future profit prospects.

The loan contract, according to Townsend, minimizes this informational cost by specifying a fixed dollar amount that the borrower agrees to pay; as long as repayment is made, no further financial investigation is required. If the borrower fails to repay, however, the lender investigates the borrowing firm, learns of its net worth, and seizes its assets up to the value of the debt plus the cost of the investigation. A solvent borrower will have a strong incentive to repay, as long as the costly investigation following default makes a solvent borrower worse off. The loan contract thus minimizes the cost of post-investment financial investigation while preserving the incentive to repay.[3]

The Defaulting Borrower Pays a Penalty

In practice, a borrower who fails to make timely repayments faces the threat of loan foreclosure and seizure of collateral. (See the box on p. 350 for a discussion of collateral.) Although the borrowing firm can partially protect itself by seeking bankruptcy protection, its business and plans become subject to legal restrictions and scrutiny by the lender. Such constraints, not to mention the loss of reputation and goodwill that bankruptcy may entail, can hurt the firm. The key consequence of default, as required by Townsend's theory, is that the borrower pays a penalty:[4] a loss of asset value. The penalty can be imposed on borrowers through various methods—loan workouts, liquidation, takeover of the firm by an outside administrator acting on behalf of creditors, or seizure and selling of collateral. (The practical steps on the road to liquidation are briefly defined in the second box.)

Let's take, as an example, an investment in a fictitious computer chip manufacturer, Custom Chip. Custom Chip's value is only partially its factory and inventory of materials and chips; much of its value is its new *ideas* for chips. Only an expert in the computer chip business can know how much Custom

---

[3] Townsend's model can best be understood by comparing the loan contract with a venture-capital contract, whereby the investor expects to receive a share of the venture's net worth. This financing contract repays the investor an amount depending on the firm's net worth; if the investor is ignorant of the firm's position, the owner, in an effort to minimize the repayment, will likely claim that the firm has low net worth. As a result, this type of contract requires the investor to always know the firm's net worth—which is costly information to obtain–and is likely only when the investor takes a large stake in the firm and the venture shows potential for substantial returns. Venture capitalists invest relatively large stakes in small start-ups and follow them closely.

[4] For a precise specification of how the losses of collateral associated with liquidation relate to the optimal debt contract, see Jeffrey M. Lacker, "Collateralized Debt as the Optimal Contract," Federal Reserve Bank of Richmond Working Paper 90–3 (March 1990).

Chip's value increased—or decreased—in a given period. One way to find out might be to auction off Custom Chip's patents, its chip-design department, and its manufacturing plant (as would happen in a liquidation). But doing that would destroy the firm.

Are You Sure It's Collateral?

Collateral may be any asset of the borrower. Physical assets would be land, plant, equipment, and inventory. Financial assets would include receivables (customers' promises to pay) and financial securities (stocks and bonds).

However, collateral is of value only to the extent that the lender can actually claim, seize, and dispose of it in the event of default. For most borrowers, collateral is property that is a functional part of the business, and its value varies with the business's ups and down. Then there are other important assets—customer goodwill and other future profit opportunities, for example—that are intangible and cannot be used as collateral because the lender cannot seize and sell them.

Establishing a clear claim to collateral is not always easy. Lenders must follow procedures, set forth in the Uniform Commercial Code, to ensure that their claim is valid. In essence, this requires clearly identifying the collateral, making sure that no one else has a prior claim to it, and making public the lender's claim. This process is called securing and perfecting collateral. If not crucial to the borrower's business, the collateral may actually be held by the lender. However, very often the collateral is integral to the borrower's business and cannot conveniently be held by the lender.

Numerous anecdotes attest to the problems that can arise with collateral. In one instance, the collateral was salad oil, held in vats. When default occurred, the vats turned out to contain water with a thin film of oil on top. In another instance, collateral was mineral rights and a car. But the borrower, it turned out, had never bought the mineral rights, and when the lender came to collect the car, he found that it had already been sold.

A cattle rancher pledged five steers as collateral for a loan, but none of the steers was specifically identified as such. Just before the rancher defaulted, five steers left the herd and, caught in a lightning storm, sought shelter under a tree. The tree was struck by lightning and the five steers died. The rancher was able to argue successfully that the bank's claim was to the five dead steers.

Collateral often deteriorates in value when the firm's lines of business deteriorate. When oil prices slumped in 1986, drilling rigs fell in value. When retail sales slumped in 1990, the value of unsold merchandise declined along with them. If a firm's sales falter because its customers are in financial straits, the firm's receivables will turn out to have little value.

If Custom Chip owes its lender $2 million, then as long as the firm's true value is greater than $2 million, the owners will have a strong incentive to repay the debt rather than risk having the firm thrust into bankruptcy. The threat of foreclosure enforces the loan repayment and means that the lender need not pay computer consultants to analyze Custom Chip's value. However, if Custom Chip cannot or will not repay the $2 million, the lender may have to declare a default and thrust Custom Chip into bankruptcy.

The high cost of default is most obvious when the lender seizes collateral. The collateral is then no longer available to the borrower, who was actively using it, and it goes to a lender, for whom it has no direct use. The borrower loses by not having use of the collateral, which is often necessary to doing business. In addition, the lender incurs costs in seizing, storing, and selling the collateral. And as the lender has no special expertise with the collateral, its value may deteriorate further while in the lender's possession.

Lender Must Carry Out the Threat

In Townsend's model, the story ends there. Once default occurs, the lender must carry through the threat of foreclosure and seize the collateral. Thus, Townsend's theory predicts that costly bankruptcies will arise from the existence of debt contracts—and that firms having more value as going concerns than in liquidation may be liquidated solely because they cannot pay their debts. If lenders chose instead to renegotiate the terms of the loan, then borrowers would lose their incentive to repay. Unfortunately, by foreclosing on borrowers who are potentially viable, the lenders may lose their best source of repayment: the borrower's value as an ongoing business.

A partial parallel for the lender's dilemma can be found in the famous Bible story about King Solomon. The wise king was able to discern which of two women claiming to be a baby's mother was telling the truth when he threatened to cut the child in two. Similarly, the lender must threaten to destroy the firm in order to learn the owners' true assessment of its worth. In both cases, the threat must be made in order to learn information. King Solomon, at least, had the advantage of knowing that his threat was only a threat. But in Townsend's model, the lender may discover that the firm cannot repay and that the threat will have to be carried out. And so, a temporary cash shortage can result in business failure when the lender cannot verify that the borrower's problems are indeed temporary.

Hart and Moore: Collateral Makes Renegotiation Possible

A more recent model, by Hart and Moore, explores loan renegotiation as an alternative to liquidating the firm. But unlike Townsend's model, this one assumes that investors have no difficulty maintaining good information about borrowers—only trouble controlling them contractually.

Hart and Moore assume that investors and entrepreneurs begin with the same information and that they always learn new information simultaneously. However, entrepreneurs control cash flows and can always divert them from investors by, say, using cash to pay workers and suppliers instead.

The only commitment entrepreneurs can make is collateral—and lenders can seize collateral if fixed payments are not made. This collateral, however, is worth more when left in the hands of the entrepreneur. And if collateral falls in value, as often happens in recessions, the lenders' ability to collect payment decreases.

This theory rests on the idea that the variety of possible events that can affect a business is simply too large and complex to be captured in a contract. Moreover, as contract provisions become more complicated, both writing and interpreting the contract become increasingly expensive. Lenders thus keep financial contracts in a form as simple as possible in order to enforce them at low cost. This allows them control over specific types of collateral, but not over details about cash flows.

The Road to Liquidation: Some Terminology

Bankruptcy - A debtor is afforded relief from its debt under the provisions of the Bankruptcy Code either through a liquidation (Chapter 7 of the Code) or rehabilitation (Chapter 11 for commercial enterprises and Chapter 13 for individuals). In a liquidation proceeding, the assets are collected and distributed by a trustee. In a bankruptcy, lenders cannot seize assets or attempt to collect payments; secured lenders are entitled, eventually, to payments equal in value to their collateral, but unsecured lenders often receive little. Rehabilitation and emergence from bankruptcy proceedings typically involve the consent of creditors and equity holders.

Collateral - Any property of the borrower that secures the debt to a lender. In the event of default, a lender may seize the borrower's collateral; in bankruptcy proceedings, a secured lender has first claim to proceeds from collateral.

Default - A borrower's violation of the loan's terms. Failure to make timely payments or to fulfill other terms, such as providing timely and accurate financial data, constitutes a default. The lender's response—foreclosure of the loan—typically includes the right to demand full loan repayment and the right to seize any collateral specified in the loan contract.

Loan workout - A business plan by which a borrower tries to resolve a problem loan. The business plan is typically an agreement arrived at by the lender and the borrower in an effort to avoid bankruptcy proceedings. Renegotiation of loan payments is often a part of a loan workout.

Liquidation - The collection and disposal of a borrower's assets.

Renegotiation - Resetting the terms of a loan contract, typically involving a delay of payments and often a reduction in interest or principal.

By Hart and Moore's reasoning, the owner of Custom Chip will repay the loan as long as the manufacturing plant and inventory of computer chips (as distinct from anticipated future profits) remain valuable. However, if the plant and inventory fall in value, the owner can divert cash and ideas to start up a new firm, defaulting on the original loan, even if current cash flows would suffice to repay it.

Threat of Loss Enforces Repayment

Another example of the role collateral plays in enforcing payment can be found in the mortgage market. Consider Robin House, who is buying a $200,000 house with a 10 percent down payment of $20,000; her debt is therefore $180,000. Initially, the value of the collateral—the house—exceeds the value of the debt by $20,000. The threatened loss of home easily enforces Robin's mortgage payments. But suppose the housing market deteriorates and the home falls in value to $150,000. If Robin values her credit reputation (including assets the mortgage lender might be able to seize) at only $20,000, she has an economic incentive to default on the mortgage: her debt exceeds the value of the collateral plus bankruptcy cost. She may refuse to make mortgage payments even though she can afford them.

Borrowers who lose their incentive to repay when their collateral falls in value frequently do default. It is also true that when borrowers are unable to repay, their collateral is often low in value—and both situations occur for the same reason: a weak economic environment. Consider inventory as collateral. When a firm fails, its inventory will consist of those goods it could not sell at close to the original price. Loans that are overcollateralized when made may be severely undercollateralized when foreclosed on. Yet, this does not mean that the collateral serves no purpose; indeed, it helps ensure repayment during periods in which the borrower *can* repay.

While lenders would prefer collateral with an unshakable value, it is extremely hard to find. Indeed, it is not always easy to put the proper value on collateral in the first place. Collateral may not be as difficult to evaluate as the value of an ongoing concern, but it still may not be straightforward. (See the box on difficulties in determining how much the home underlying a mortgage is worth.)

Collateral Is Key to Renegotiation

In Hart and Moore's model, lenders can renegotiate a loan instead of seizing collateral. In a renegotiation, lenders may allow payments to be stretched out or even reduced so as to avoid the losses from seizing collateral. But since only collateral can enforce repayment, the lender will be willing to do this only if the borrower can offer immediate cash and future collateral that are at least as good as what the lender can gain through immediate seizure. If future collateral is inadequate, the lender will foreclose and a viable firm may be lost. Thus, renegotiation only partially solves the dilemma.

Who Assumes the Risk in Offers to Pay Closing Costs?

Real estate ads sometimes include the come-on "Seller will pay closing costs." This practice creates the innocent appearance of a generous home seller helping the prospective buyer who otherwise would have trouble making the down payment on the house. But is this practice innocent from the perspective of the mortgage lender? No, because the seller is really being generous with the lender's money.

An offer to pay closing costs actually inflates the house's selling price. To see this, consider a house priced by its owner at $100,000 but whose true market value has fallen to $92,000. In method 1, the standard method, the owner straightforwardly lowers the price by $8,000, to $92,000. In method 2, the owner offers to pay the borrower $8,000 up front by paying the buyer's closing costs.

	Method 1	Method 2
House price	$92,000	$100,000
Down payment	$9,200	$10,000
Mortgage loan	$82,800	$90,000
Closing costs	$8,000	$8,000
Buyer puts up	$17,200	$10,000
Seller gets	$92,000	$92,000

The only difference in the bottom line is that the lender has loaned $7,200 more to the borrower; in both cases, the seller winds up with exactly the same amount of money. But suppose the house falls in value by 10 percent, to $82,800. In the first case, the lender is fully protected, and the borrower has no incentive to default on the mortgage. But in the second case, the lender is likely to take a substantial loss if the borrower defaults on the mortgage—and now the borrower may have an incentive to default because the collateral that the borrower loses is less than the debt the borrower would otherwise have to pay.

Suppose Custom Chip is unable to repay a loan during a period in which profit margins decline because of a recession in the computer industry. The lender has two options. One, it could seize the plant and its inventory of chips. Or two, it could renegotiate—permit Custom Chip to stay in business, accept an incomplete payment of the loan, accept the owner's beach condo, say, for additional collateral, and agree to a partial write-down of the remaining debt. However, if Custom Chip cannot come up with some combination of current cash and future collateral that is more valuable than existing collateral, the lender will go with the first option and seize the collateral. So, in this case, although Custom Chip might have a good chance of substantial future earnings, it is unable to realize them because it cannot promise the lender an adequate share of future earnings.

Renegotiations preserve the firm's value. And loans that make renegotiation more possible by preserving repayment incentives are attractive to borrowers as well as lenders. In renegotiation, loans in which borrowers have uncommitted resources to offer the lender are preferable to loans in which borrowers have no negotiating room. In the Custom Chip example, the fact that the owner's beach condo can be put up as collateral helps keep the firm alive. If the owner lacked this resource, renegotiation would be less attractive to the lender.

In 1989, Michael Jensen[5] argued that highly leveraged transactions would not result in bankruptcies because lenders would always be better off renegotiating. In retrospect, Jensen's argument appears incorrect. One reason may be that, in many highly leveraged transactions, the borrowers had very little cash margin, or extra collateral, with which to renegotiate.

Lending during a Recession

Lenders' most difficult decisions are made during recessions. For the prospective borrower, access to additional financing may be crucial to survival. But for the lender, recession financing is treacherous. In recessions, the probability of bad economic outcomes is higher than at other times, and inefficient, costly bankruptcies and liquidation are more likely.

Unless lenders have established procedures for commanding cash flows from troubled borrowers, they will be unable to lend profitably during recessions, when cash flows become more questionable. Collateral is crucial—both as an ultimate source of repayment and as a threat to command repayment. But in recessions, collateral—unfortunately—becomes less reliable.

Loan Contracts Are Less Efficient in Recessions

According to both of the models just discussed, firms with going-concern value may be shut down if loan repayments cannot be made. This is more likely to occur during recessions, when demand falls and cash flows dry up. As a consequence, loan contracts are more likely to lead to inefficiency during bad times than in good times, since bankruptcies and liquidations are more likely. Thus, the practice of making fewer loans in a weak economy is consistent with these theories.

Several other points about lending during a recession fall out of these models:

1. *More collateral will be required to further ensure repayment, although this makes borrowing more difficult.* During a recession, the increased risk that collateral will fall in value means that lenders will need larger amounts of it to maintain the

---

[5] Michael Jensen, "Is Leverage an Invitation to Bankruptcy? On the Contrary—It Keeps Shaky Firms Out of Court," *Wall Street Journal*, February 1, 1989.

borrower's incentive to repay. Inevitably, more potential borrowers will find that they lack the collateral necessary for the loan they're seeking.

2. *More documentation will be presented, and past lender-borrower relationships will be more important.* Lenders should attempt to know more about borrowers during recessions because default is more likely—and more expensive—when lenders are relatively ignorant. This makes it doubly hard on borrowers whose normal lenders themselves become cash constrained; for borrowers to exchange a lender who knows them well for one who does not will be expensive, if not impossible. Detailed and accurate record-keeping may make the difference in whether new financing is obtained.

3. *Noncredit terms on loans will tighten.* Tightening noncredit terms for borrowers may make it harder for them to qualify for loans, but at least lenders will be able to continue making profitable loans in hard times. For example, in a weak real estate market, lenders should require higher down payments on mortgages and be particularly wary of techniques home sellers may use to foist greater risk on the lender.

In addition, lenders may demand more *covenants* to their loan. Loan covenants are legal conditions added to the loan contract that permit the lenders to declare loans in default. Some covenants constrain managerial discretion; others specify standards of continued creditworthiness. Covenants increase the lender's ability to seize collateral while it retains much of its value.

Renegotiation in Recession

Hart and Moore's model also has implications for what borrowers and lenders can expect from loan renegotiations during a recession. The lender's purpose in renegotiating a loan is to achieve new combinations of cash and collateral that leave the lender better off than under the previous agreement.[6] For example, a lender will write down an unsecured loan, forgiving part of the debt to obtain collateral and immediate cash under a new agreement.

Conversely, borrowers should realize that in times of a weak economy, failure to repay a loan is likelier to have serious consequences—collateral may be seized, for example. In assessing their possibilities for a successful renegotiation, borrowers should review those assets that may be used for cash and collateral.

Lenders are best off pushing for low-risk operation of the firm. A debt-burdened borrower has a strong incentive to divert funds at the lender's expense.[7] To counter this, the lender will—in what is called a "loan workout"—actively negotiate the borrower's business plan to maximize the probability of receiving cash

---

[6] This article assumes that a firm's lenders are acting in concert. A natural tension between lenders often emerges in loan renegotiations, and the presence of many independent lenders may complicate renegotiation outside the framework of bankruptcy court. A lender acting independently should be cautious about infringing on the right of other lenders; indeed, obtaining a preference over other lenders can be reversed if bankruptcy actually occurs. Worse yet, if the borrower is viewed as being in a lender's control, that lender may become liable to other lenders for the borrower's debts.

[7] See Leonard I. Nakamura, "Loan Workouts and Commercial Bank Information: Why Banks Are Special," Federal Reserve Bank of Philadelphia Working Paper 89-11 (February 1989).

flows. In the loan workout, the lender should push to err on the side of safety and carefully monitor the borrower's expenses and receipts to see whether the borrower is adhering to plan. (A bank that handles a borrower's transactions is often well positioned to conduct a loan workout because it can best observe the borrower's behavior.) Cutting costs to conserve cash should almost always be part of a workout plan. A borrower who must give up something during renegotiation is less likely to default frivolously.

Both parties to the renegotiation should recognize the fundamental importance of good information. A strong relationship between lender and borrower and full, open communication are crucial to sound loan renegotiations. In a renegotiation, lenders often demand more information than in the initial loan process. Borrowers should recognize that, lacking good information, lenders ought not to make concessions in a renegotiation.

A final but crucial point following from the logic of Hart and Moore's model is one more pertinent to planning for the next recession than surviving the current one. When embarking on a relationship with a lender, borrowers too often care only about the short term, believing that all will be fine if only the lender grants the loan request. But borrowers ought to be forward-thinking, too, and ask themselves whether the lender will be helpful in hard times or force them to turn elsewhere when loan funds tighten generally. Just as lenders must look for sound borrowers, so should borrowers seek out sound lenders.

Conclusion

Recent theories on lending and the loan contract build on the idea that borrowers may lack adequate incentives to repay lenders. One conclusion they share is that loan defaults can have important economic consequences and lead to the failure of otherwise viable businesses. Another conclusion is that noncredit terms of loans can be expected to tighten in recessions.

In a downturn, credit terms to new borrowers normally tighten. The models attribute this tightening to the inherent conflicts that intensify between lender and borrower during recessions. Consequently, lending becomes less efficient and is more likely to lead to foreclosures and real economic losses. By tightening up lending practices, lenders may be able to increase their confidence in repayment and perhaps avoid being excessively conservative in hard times. And by anticipating potential credit problems, borrowers may be better able to minimize them.

Tighter credit terms are unpleasant for the borrower and may reduce the borrower's activity from the original plan. But they may be crucial for borrowing to continue in a tough economic environment.

Questions

1. What are the two roles of collateral in bank lending?
2. Failure to meet loan covenants triggers default and legally empowers the lender to demand repayment of the entire loan, which may force the borrower into

bankruptcy? In many cases, however, the lender stops short of "pulling the trigger." What accounts for this apparently generous behavior of lenders?

3. In the event of default, what are the alternatives short of bankruptcy available to the borrower and the lender?
4. *Loan A* and *Loan B* are essentially identical in all respects except that *Loan A* requires monthly payments and *Loan B* requires semiannual payments. What is the informational advantage of *Loan A* to the lender?
5. Honest Charlie is a used-car dealer specializing in cars 7 to 10 years old. Mr. Charlie actually changed his name from Anthony to Honest because he likes to emphasize his honest deals. "Honest car deals" is Mr. Charlie's slogan. He floor-plans cars for his east-side lot and his west-side lot.

   Honest Charlie's banker is Wally Peeps, vice president of Valley National Bank. Mr. Peeps visits Mr. Charlie at his east-side lot to check the inventory of cars against the trust receipts the bank holds. The bank has 30 trust receipts and Mr. Peeps counts 30 cars. After Mr. Peeps finishes the count, Mr. Charlie coaxes him to go to Edna's Diner for lunch. Mr. Charlie says, "Wally, you can check the west-side lot after lunch." Mr. Peeps agrees, and they go to lunch. Mr. Peeps later counts 23 cars at the west-side lot as indicated by trust receipts.

   Comment critically on the diligence of Mr. Peep's field inspection. If Mr. Charlie were crooked, what sleight of hand might he have used on Mr. Peeps?
6. Explain why work-in-process inventory and supplies are usually ineligible to serve as collateral for bank loans.
7. "Lenders' most difficult decisions are made during recessions... recession financing is treacherous." What can bankers do to lessen the risk of lending during recessions?

PART

V

Analyzing and Planning Financial Performance

WILLIAM L. STONE
Financial Statement Analysis—A Two-Minute Drill

BARRY E. MILLER
Mastering Cause-and-Effect Ratio Analysis

RAVINDRA KAMATH
How Useful Are Common Liquidity Measures?

BENTON E. GUP, WILLIAM D. SAMSON, MICHAEL T. DUGAN, MYUNG J. KIM, AND THAWATCHAI JITTRAPANUN
An Analysis of Patterns from the Statement of Cash Flows

CLAIRE STARRY AND NICK MCGAUGHEY
Growth Industries: Another Look

GEORGE W. KESTER
How Much Growth Can Borrowers Sustain?

GEORGE W. KESTER
Why Borrowers Become Profit Rich and Cash Poor

Financial Statement Analysis—A Two-Minute Drill

WILLIAM L. STONE

Commercial loan officers often face the situation where they would like to make a quick appraisal of a financial statement. Some loan requests, for example, can be declined in short order because the financial statements reflect a weak condition. However, loan officers must have the skill to focus on those factors that would reveal that further discussion is fruitless. More important, they should be able to develop several pertinent questions regarding the problem areas of a company's operation as revealed by a brief analysis of the financial statements.

It is not uncommon for a loan applicant to present a loan officer with two or three years of financial statements in support of an application being presented orally. The loan officer does not have the luxury of analyzing the statements thoroughly while the applicant patiently sits in silence. The applicant, of course, is anxious and apprehensive about laying out the company's financial history to the banker. Most applicants can tolerate a minute or two of idleness while the loan officer reviews the statements. The limit, however, is about two minutes.

Within that two-minute period, the loan officer should be able to make an analysis that is thorough enough to reveal the company's problem areas on which the subsequent questioning should focus. This article will explain how those two minutes can be spent most efficiently so that the loan officer will have a clear picture of the company's financial strengths and weaknesses.

Cautions

Several cautions, while obvious, require emphasis before proceeding. First, the two-minute drill that is presented here should not be taken as a substitute for a thorough analysis of the credit once the applicant has left the bank. Loan officers

At the time of this writing, William L. Stone was a vice president at Bank of the West, San Jose, CA.

Source: Copyright 1983 by Robert Morris Associates. Reprinted with permission from *The Journal of Commercial Lending*, November 1983.

should not permit themselves to fall into the trap of thinking that they have completely analyzed the financial statements once they have completed the two-minute drill.

Second, the analysis suggested here does not concern itself with nonfinancial factors such as management quality, market, products, prospects, the economy, and a myriad of other factors that are crucial to the success of every business. This system of analysis relates only to relationships of figures on the financial statements.

Third, since speed is of the essence in this analysis, rough rounding off is recommended. For example, $93,439 may be appropriately rounded off to $90,000 or even $100,000. Further, it is not important that the classification of assets and liabilities as current or noncurrent be carefully scrutinized. If, for instance, the statement shows prepaid assets of $18,713 as a current asset and it is your bank's practice to treat prepaid assets as noncurrent, it is not important, unless the amount is unusually large, that the current assets as shown on the statement be adjusted for the purposes of this analysis. One could argue that accuracy will suffer at the expense of speed, but as will be seen, we will work with estimates as indications of problem areas.

Fourth, there appears to be, in the writer's experience, some differences throughout the country about standards of liquidity, leverage, and profitability. Readers should establish their own standards if those suggested here are significantly different from their own. Keep in mind, however, that the standards presented here lend themselves to the computations.

Six Standards for Comparison

Three ratios—current, debt-to-worth, and net profit margin—and three turnovers—receivables, inventory, and payables—form the basis of the two minute drill. These six relationships (turnovers are often referred to as ratios, but in the strictest sense, they are not ratios) were selected for several reasons. First, they are important indicators of a specific aspect of a company's financial condition. Second, taken together, they are indicative of the three important areas for credit purposes: liquidity, leverage, and profitability. Third, we can establish a standard that is easy to compute and understand against which a company's performance can be measured.

It is the third factor that is essential to this system of analysis. Loan officers often hedge on the subject of an acceptable or unsatisfactory figure for a given ratio with the comment that "every business is different." While it is true that every business is different, it is also true that the performance of a wide range of companies can be compared to a series of standards in an effort to establish a line of inquiry for the loan officer. The point, of course, is that management may have an entirely reasonable explanation for the company's performance being substantially different from the standard. If, though, the loan officer did not have the standard as a means of comparison, the difference in the company's operation might not have been revealed.

It is, then, the thesis of this article that by comparing the company's three ratios and three turnovers to the standards explained here, we will determine quickly what areas of the company's operation require further inquiry. The advantage of the system of analysis suggested here is that after studying the statements for less than two minutes, loan officers will be able to ask some pertinent questions about the business in the initial interview, even if they have never seen the applicant or the statements before.

Refer to Table1 for a summary balance sheet and profit and loss statement for Wobbly Widgets, Inc., which will be used as the statement to be analyzed. Each of the ratios and turnovers will be discussed. First, the standard for each will be established. Second, the fastest method for mentally computing the ratio or turnover will be explained. Since the use of even a small, hand calculator might intimidate the applicant, it is recommended that the loan officer develop the skill to make the computations mentally. After some practice, the calculations suggested here can be made faster mentally than by using a calculator.

TABLE 1 WOBBLY WIDGETS, INC.

Balance Sheet
December 31, 1982

Assets		**Liabilities and Net Worth**	
Cash	$ 18.3	Accounts Payable	$ 87.8
Accounts Receivable	248.6	Notes Payable	32.0
Inventory	77.4	Current Portion Term Debt	22.6
Prepaid Assets	10.0	Accrued Liabilities	13.7
Current Assets	354.3	Current Liabilities	156.1
Fixed Assets (net)	210.0	Term Debt	110.0
Total Assets	$564.3	Total Liabilities	266.1
		Net Worth	298.2
		Total Liabilities and Net Worth	$564.3

Profit and Loss Statement
for the Twelve-Month Period Ended December 31, 1982

Sales	$1,314.6
Cost of Goods Sold	739.2
Gross Profit	575.4
Operating Expenses	448.1
Operating Profit	127.3
Income Taxes	53.6
Net Income	$ 73.7

Current Ratio

The generally accepted standard for the current ratio—current assets divided by current liabilities—is 2.0. In practice, a current ratio of 2.0 appears to be more of a goal, or comfort figure, than a minimally accepted standard, but it does serve as a good figure to use as a standard.

To compute the current ratio mentally, it is best to look first at current liabilities, round it off, and double that figure. For Wobbly Widgets, current liabilities rounded off is 160. Twice 160 is 320. If current assets were 320, the current ratio would be 2.0. Current assets, though, total 354.3. An estimate of the current ratio is 2.1. If current assets were between 160.0 and 320.0, the current ratio would be between 1.0 and 2.0. The lending officer must estimate the current ratio, but it is important to recognize that the precise calculation is simply irrelevant. Rather, we wish to estimate the current ratio (and all of the other ratios presented here) as an indication of whether or not there is a problem in the company's financial health. Once you have estimated the current ratio, jot it down (see Table 2) and go on to the next ratio, keeping in mind that a current ratio of 2.1 indicates a satisfactory position.

Notice that we looked at current liabilities before current assets. The rationale for this approach is that it is easier to double a number than it is to divide it by two. If we looked at current assets first, we would have to divide it by two, mentally, to establish a point of reference. Certainly, we could use that approach, but since our overriding objective is to make the analysis quickly, we should pick the easiest type of computation. In this case, multiplying is easier than dividing.

Debt-to-Worth Ratio

As with the current ratio, the standard for the debt-to-worth ratio is 2.0. However, of the six relationships we will study, this one will cause the greatest disagreement about the standard. Some banks will probably not entertain the application of a company whose ratio is as high as 2.0, whereas other banks consider 4.0 an acceptable figure.

First, look at total liabilities. On most CPA-prepared statements, a total liabilities figure is not shown, so the first step is to add up current liabilities and noncurrent liabilities. Second, is total liabilities more than or less than net worth (compute and use tangible net worth if there is a significant amount of intangible assets)? If total liabilities and net worth are approximately the same, determine whether the ratio should be .9 or 1.1, jot it down, and go on to the next ratio. If total liabilities are significantly more than net worth, round off the net worth figure and double it. What, then, is the relationship between total liabilities and two times net worth? The process is one of narrowing down total liabilities to an approximate multiple of net worth.

In the case of Wobbly Widgets, net worth is slightly more than total liabilities, so the approximate ratio is .9. If total liabilities were 512.0, for example, we would estimate debt to worth at 1.7 (500 ÷ 300), indicating that total liabilities were somewhat less than twice net worth. Again, jot down the estimated debt-to-worth figure and go on to the next ratio.

Net Profit Margin

The generally accepted average for net profit margin—net profit divided by net sales—is 5%, which will serve as a good standard for our purposes. The computation of the net profit margin is the most difficult relationship to compute mentally. The first step is to round off net sales. In the case of Wobbly Widgets, we should use 1,300 as the sales figure. The next step is to move the decimal point two places to the left, or 13 in this case. If net profit were 13, then the net profit margin would be 1%. In our case, net profit is significantly more than 13. Two approaches are possible at this point. The first one is to move the decimal point on the sales figure one place to the left, or 130, which represents 10% net profit, and compare it to the actual figure. A second approach is to divide 13 into 70. In Wobbly's case, 13 cannot be easily divided into 70 mentally, so we should return to the first approach. We observe that the actual figure 70 is well below the 10% figure of 130. Half of 130, or 10% of sales, is 65, which would represent 5% of sales. Since our net profit figure is 70, net profit is approximately 6% of sales. The actual net profit margin (73.7 divided by 1314.6) is 5.61%, which makes our 6% estimate correct for our purposes.

Again, the mental computation of the net profit margin is the most difficult of the six relationships discussed here. It is the writer's experience that the computation is often intimidating to many people, particularly those who do not feel proficient at math. In this case, however, the concept is not difficult; it is the mechanics that cause the difficulty. Once the concept is understood, practice is all it takes to make a reasonably accurate and quick estimate of the net profit margin.

Accounts Receivable Turnover

The accounts receivable turnover compares accounts receivable to sales. Generally it is assumed that all sales are on a credit basis. If loan officers have information to the contrary, they should adjust the sales figure accordingly to reflect only credit sales. There are several ways to compute the accounts receivable turnover. The computation used here will be accounts receivable divided by sales times the number of days in the period covered by the profit and loss statement. For annual statements, 360 days is used as the number of days in a year. The other turnovers are computed in the same manner. The resulting answer is expressed in days and is intended to represent the average amount of time that each dollar of receivables (and inventory and payables) stays on the books.

From time to time, significant variances occur in these accounts in a given company and within industries. Furthermore, it must be remembered that the figure shown on the balance sheet may or may not be representative of the average level of receivables (or inventory or payables) during the year. These possible distortions notwithstanding, we can establish our standard for all three turnovers as 36 days. As a practical matter, 36 days would generally indicate a very favorable turnover, which should be considered when comparing the actual figures to our standard.

Since the computation of the turnovers is a two-step process, mental computation would be very difficult. We can, however, simplify the process. First, round off the sales figure and move the decimal one place to the left. The resulting number, 130 in Wobbly's case, represents 10% of sales. Since annual sales, 1,300 for Wobbly, represents 360 days of sales, receivables of 130 would represent 36 days of sales. Second, compare the 10% of sales figure (130) to accounts receivable. Wobbly's accounts receivable are 248.6, or almost twice as much as the 10% figure. Therefore, accounts receivable are remaining on the books for an average of slightly less than the 72 days. The writer recommends rounding off turnovers to multiples of five days. In this case, if Wobbly's accounts receivable were 125.0, 35 days would be a reasonable estimate. If they were 300.0, 80 days—slightly more than twice 36 days—would be a reasonable estimate.

Inventory Turnover

As noted above, the computation of the inventory turnover is similar to the accounts receivable turnover. The only difference is that inventory is compared to cost of goods sold. The computation is otherwise the same. First, round off cost of sales and move the decimal one place to the left. The resulting number, 74 in Wobbly's case, represents 10% of the cost of sales. Disregarding seasonal factors, the first 74 of cost of sales expense should be incurred in the first 10%, or 36 days, of the year. If, then, Wobbly's inventory were 74, we could conclude that the company had inventory on hand 36 days.

Such a conclusion presumes one additional factor. The inventory (and accounts payable) turnover should compare inventory (and accounts payable) to purchases. In a number of cases, however, the purchases figure is not available. In other cases, it can only be found in a supplemental schedule or in the footnotes. Further, over the period of a year, the difference between purchases and cost of sales does not generally vary significantly. As a result, most analysts use the cost of sales when computing inventory and accounts payable turnovers. For our purpose, the accuracy achieved in using the purchases figure will usually not justify the time required to find that figure.

In the case of Wobbly, inventory is slightly more than 10% of cost of sales, so we can estimate Wobbly's inventory turnover to be 40 days. If inventory were 150, we would estimate the turnover to be 50 days. The key element of the computation is to compare 10% of the annual cost of sales to the actual inventory figure, remembering that 10% of the annual cost of sales represents 36 days.

Accounts Payable Turnover

To estimate the accounts payable turnover, compare the same 10% of the annual cost of sales figure to actual accounts payable and estimate the turnover. If, for example, the accounts payable figure were 74, we would conclude that on the average, accounts payable are paid when they are 36 days old. In Wobbly's case, accounts payable total 88, so we would estimate the turnover to be 45 days.

TABLE 2 SAMPLE WORKSHEET

	1980	1981	1982
CR			2.1
D/W			0.9
NPM			5%
AR T/O			70
INV T/O			40
AP T/O			45

Analysis

The writer suggests that loan officers have a simple worksheet available that looks like Table 2.

A quick glance at Table 2 reveals that the company's financial condition for 1982 is pretty much in line except for the accounts receivable. The trap into which many loan officers fall is to stop once a chart such as Table 2, or a spread sheet, is completed. On the contrary, no analysis has been accomplished yet. The numbers do not have any meaning until the loan officer understands what the numbers mean. What, for instance, do the numbers in Table 2 indicate about the company's liquidity, leverage, and profitability? What problems—and therefore what areas of further inquiry—are indicated by the figures in Tables 1 and 2?

It should occur to readers that unless they go through an exercise such as the two-minute drill, they will have difficulty knowing what line of inquiry to pursue. The two-minute drill gives the loan officer the opportunity to focus on those areas of apparent weakness. An important side benefit is that the applicant realizes right away that the loan officer "understands" the applicant's business because he can ask direct, pertinent questions after only a brief review of the statements, for example, "What is your difficulty in collecting the money owed to you?" "Do you have a lot of obsolete inventory?" "Are you being pressured by your trade creditors to bring your payables current?"

Conclusion

It is worth emphasizing again the cautions that appear near the beginning of this article. Briefly, the two-minute drill is not intended to be a substitute for a thorough analysis of a credit. Rather, it provides quick estimates of several important financial relationships that can serve as a basis for inquiries in the early stages of the application process.

Initially, the shortcuts presented here might appear to be too complex to be of any value. They are not. *Every* loan officer should be able to develop the skill to complete the two-minute drill for a single statement in less than two minutes. Once loan officers have developed that skill, they will conduct more effective and productive initial interviews and will increase their own level of self-confidence in dealing with applicants. Try it. It will work.

Questions

1. Use the financial data for Wobbly Widgets, Inc. to calculate the following ratios: (a) current ratio, (b) debt-equity ratio, (c) after-tax profit margin, (d) average collection period, (e) days' sales in inventory, and (f) average payables period. (Note: These financial ratios are the same as those suggested by the author; the names used here reflect common usage among analysts.)
2. According to the author, what values for the financial ratios in Question 1 should be used in the "Two-Minute Drill?"
3. BFM Company's balance sheet for the year ending December 31, 19X9, is as follows:

Cash	$ 14,000	Accounts payable	$ 70,000
Receivables	130,000	Other current	35,000
Inventory	150,000	Current liabilities	$105,000
Current assets	$294,000	Long-term debt	160,000
Fixed assets (net)	300,000	Total debt	$265,000
Total assets	$594,000	Common equity	329,000
		Total claims	$594,000

BFM's sales for the year were $1,100,000; cost of goods sold equaled $800,000; and earnings after taxes were $50,000. Use the "Two-Minute Drill" to assess BFM's financial strengths and weaknesses. Note: (a) Do not use a calculator or formal calculations; make mental calculations only. (b) Time yourself; try to do the exercise in two minutes!

4. Nike Inc.'s financial statements are provided below. Your task is to use the "Two-Minute Drill" to assess Nike's financial strengths and weaknesses.

Balance Sheet, May 31, 19X1
(in Thousands of Dollars)

Cash and equivalents	$ 119,804	Accounts payable	$ 165,912
Accounts receivable	521,588	Notes payable	300,364
Inventory	586,594	Other current liabilities	162,196
Other current assets	52,274		
		Total current liabilities	$ 628,472
Total current assets	$1,280,260	Long-term liabilities	46,869
Noncurrent assets	428,170	Shareholder equity	1,033,089
Total assets	$1,708,430	Total claims	$1,708,430

Income Statement
Year Ended May 31, 19X1
(in Thousands of Dollars)

Net sales	$3,003,610
Less cost of goods sold	1,850,530
Gross profit	$1,153,080
Less operating expenses	664,018
EBIT	$ 489,062
Less interest expense	27,316
Earnings before taxes	$ 461,746
Less taxes	174,700
Earnings after taxes	$ 287,046

Mastering Cause-and-Effect Ratio Analysis

BARRY E. MILLER

Financial statement analysis is a logical method of assessing business risk. It is, however, far more than the mechanical application of a universal formula to obtain a "yes" or "no" assessment of creditworthiness or determine the dollar amount of a credit limit.

A particularly versatile technique, cause-and-effect ratio analysis, enables credit decision-makers to investigate each customer's financial condition at the level of detail required by specific circumstances, particularly the size of the specific order under consideration or the customer's future sales potential.

Developed by Donald E. Miller (former chairman of NACM's Credit Interchange Board of Governors) nearly 30 years ago and refined continually since that time, cause-and-effect ratio analysis has proven highly valuable in both corporate planning and credit management. It is a step-by-step method that facilitates rapid processing of most credit requests and also enables in-depth understanding of the financial structure, trends, strengths, and weaknesses of major customers whose credit needs call for more extensive analysis.

Four Ratios Are Used in Most Cases

Cause-and-effect ratio analysis employs a total of 16 key financial relationships for in-depth analysis of operating performance and financial structure. However, only four of these ratios require attention in the credit analysis of most customers:

- current assets to current liabilities (the current ratio), which measures a company's ability to cover its obligations due during the next year by means of cash plus other assets that are expected to flow through the cash cycle within that 12-month period;

At the time of this writing, Barry E. Miller was a financial management consultant in Reading, PA.

Source: "Mastering Cause-and-Effect Ratio Analysis," Barry E. Miller, *Business Credit Magazine*, Feb. 1993 pp. 24–27, National Association of Credit Management (Columbia, MD).

- cash and short-term investments plus accounts receivable to current liabilities (the quick ratio or acid-test ratio), which measures a company's ability to cover its current obligations without the need to convert inventory to cash, thus recognizing the possibility that inventory may not be salable at its stated value, particularly in the event of liquidation;
- total liabilities to net worth (the debt-to-worth ratio or debt-to-equity ratio), which measures a company's amount of funds from creditors versus the investment of owners, thereby revealing the pressure of total business debt relative to owners' equity (net worth); and,
- net profit to net sales (the return-on-sales ratio), which measures a company's ability to generate adequate profit on its average sales dollar and indicates vulnerability to potential price-cutting competition.

The first two financial measures are calculated in the usual ratio form: one number (for example, the sum of cash and short-term investments plus accounts receivable) divided by a second number (such as current liabilities). Although the debt-to-worth ratio is most frequently calculated in the same manner, some publications display this measure as a percentage. Like all measures of expenses and profitability, the return-on-sales ratio is consistently calculated as a percentage (by multiplying the ratio by 100).

Short-term trade creditors appropriately consider a customer's financial structure and performance from a defensive standpoint before examining the customer's long-term potential for sales growth. Customarily in an unsecured position, trade creditors feel the greatest negative impact of business reversals. Consequently, the four credit screening ratios, which together indicate the probability of a change in a company's present payment pattern and measure loss exposure, deserve particular attention from credit analysts.

The basic reasoning is straightforward. If current liabilities are well covered by current assets (as shown by the current ratio)—particularly by means of cash and short-term investments plus accounts receivable (as shown by the quick ratio)—a customer should be able to meet obligations in a consistent manner, provided that the return-on-sales ratio is satisfactory.

Taking into account the possibility of an unexpected reversal of business fortune, the credit analyst should also evaluate the debt-to-worth ratio, which shows the claims of creditors in relation to the stake of owners in the business. In addition to indicating the extent of creditor pressure, the current ratio and the debt-to-worth ratio also show the proportionate shrinkage of assets that could occur before working capital and net worth would be entirely depleted (see Table One.)

Beware of Comparing Apples to Oranges

Credit analysts have long sought specific numerical standards that will provide reasonable assurance of a customer's timely payment and will indicate protection against an eventual bad-debt loss if the company should experience operating difficulties or major asset writedowns. As a practical matter, however, such standards cannot be uniformly applied to all lines of business because each manufacturing, wholesaling, retailing, and service sector has its own financial characteristics.

TABLE ONE CURRENT RATIO AND DEBT-TO-WORTH RATIO AS MEASURES OF POSSIBLE ASSET SHRINKAGE

Current Assets to Current Liabilities (Current Ratio)	Current Assets: % of Shrinkage Before Working Capital Reduced to Zero	Total Liabilities To Net Worth (Debt-to-Worth Ratio)	Total Assets: % of Shrinkage Before New Worth Reduced to Zero
2.00x	50.0%	1.00x	50.0%
1.90	47.4	1.10	47.6
1.80	44.4	1.25	44.4
1.70	41.2	1.40	41.7
1.60	37.5	1.67	37.5
1.50	33.3	2.00	33.3
1.40	28.6	2.50	28.6
1.30	23.1	3.33	23.1
1.20	16.7	5.00	16.7
1.10	9.1	10.00	9.1

In manufacturing, for example, the *1992 Annual Statement Studies* published by Robert Morris Associates revealed that the median current ratio was only 1.0 for processors of frozen fruits, fruit juices, and vegetables, 1.2 in logging and in motor vehicles and passenger car bodies, and 1.3 in eight other sectors ranging from dairy products to periodical publishing and printing.

On the other hand, the median current ratio for manufacturers of instruments for measuring electricity and electrical signals was 2.4, while manufacturers of telephone and telegraph apparatus reported a 2.5 median and companies in the brick and structural clay tile sector topped the list at 2.8.

Among bakers, the range of the middle half of responses ("mid-range") for the current ratio, as displayed in the *1992 Annual Statement Studies,* was 0.9 (relatively unfavorable) to 1.8 (comparatively favorable for that industry sector). During the same year, the mid-range for manufacturers of electrical measuring instruments was 1.6 to 3.7, showing that the current ratio for the least favorable one-fourth of companies in this manufacturing sector was similar to that of the most favorable one-fourth of bakeries.

A company's financial statement must be evaluated in relation to the competitive conditions prevailing in its specific industry sector. The application of a single credit rating formula to all companies in a broad classification, such as manufacturing, would systematically exclude a large proportion of potential customers in some business lines, yet also lead to automatic acceptance of companies with competitive weaknesses in other industry sectors.

With rare exceptions, an established company that shows all of its four screening ratios—the current ratio, the quick ratio, the debt-to-worth ratio and the return-on-sales ratio—among the most favorable three-fourths of values reported for its industry sector is unlikely to experience a rapid deterioration in its ability to meet trade obligations. If a company's present payment record is marginal or unacceptable, satisfactory ratios will probably not reverse that negative pattern in the near future.

A poor credit history is often an accurate indication of future payment performance regardless of the company's financial strength. On the other hand, the absence of any clearly unfavorable signals from the credit screening ratios indicates that a company with an adequate to excellent payment record is not a prime candidate for difficulty in the near term.

Even within lines of business having relatively weak financial characteristics, a company that demonstrates stronger screening ratios than 25 percent of the other firms in the industry will ordinarily possess a reasonable degree of safety from competitive pressures. Unless special knowledge reveals that many processors of dairy products are likely to go sour or that many periodical printers are about to fold up, the satisfactory performers in those industries should not be automatically rejected or restricted.

What If the Ratios Don't Look Good?

By means of the initial ratio screening process, a large proportion of potential and existing customers will be quickly recognized as having no immediate financial problems. But what is the next step in evaluation when one or more of a company's four credit screening ratios is found to be among the lowest 25 percent in the industry sector? If only a single key financial measure is classified among the unfavorable one-fourth of values, the underlying cause or causes can be readily determined by referring to TableTwo. However, if more than one of the four credit screening ratios falls within the unfavorable zone both Table Two and Table Three should be used to analyze the company's fundamental financial structure.

When the amount of the credit request (or the salesperson's projection of future credit requirements) demonstrates the need for thorough analysis of financial capacity, Tables Two and Three should be completed—even if all four of the credit screening ratios are within the upper 75 percent of ratio values for the appropriate comparison group.

Identification of important multi-year trends by means of cause-and-effect ratio analysis is particularly important in a thorough evaluation of operating performance and financial structure. If all four of the credit screening ratios have become more favorable or remained stable during the past two or three years, further trend investigation may not be required. However, significant deterioration of even one key screening measure during that times calls for an investigation of the underlying causes. Once again, Tables Two and Three will be helpful in focusing on the specific causal factors for each ratio.

Look at Several Consecutive Statements

Examination of financial statements for several consecutive years will reveal the stability of reported profit. In a single fiscal year, profit can be enhanced by speeding up production during the last quarter, offering temporary price concessions to boost sales and gain marginal net revenue, deferring management compensation, and even delaying recognition of invoices for vendor services. These actions, however, can rarely be continued indefinitely, and the reverse effects will usually appear in the next year's financial statement.

The degree of confidence that should be placed in a financial statement depends on the nature of the accountant's role in preparation and on the character of management. Information about significant accounting changes,

TABLE TWO ANALYSIS OF UNFAVORABLE CREDIT SCREENING RATIOS

When only one of the four credit screening ratios is within the unfavorable one-fourth of ratio values in the appropriate comparison group, this table will enable quick identification of the specific cause or causes that require evaluation.

When more than one of the four ratios are classified as unfavorable, this table should be used in conjunction with Table Three.

- **Low current ratio (current assets to current liabilities)**
  Possible causes of unfavorable rating (evaluate both):
  - Slow collection of customer invoices: **high (unfavorable) collection period of accounts receivable**, indicating need to evaluate the creditworthiness of the customer's customers.
  - Insufficient working capital: **high (unfavorable) net sales to working capital**, indicating a significant weakness that requires further analysis.
- **Low quick ratio (cash and short-term investments plus accounts receivable to current liabilities)**
  Cause of unfavorable rating:
  - Sluggish inventory turnover/throughput: **low (unfavorable) cost of sales to inventory,** indicating need to determine whether the problem is excess raw material, slow movement of work-in-process, or a build-up of unsold finished goods and to determine whether inventory is produced in response to firm contracts (and, if so, whether inventory has value in event of contract cancellation) or made to stock (and, if so, whether/why the unsold amount is high).
    Note: When both the **current ratio** and the **quick ratio** are unfavorable, low **cost of sales to inventory** may be the underlying cause of each condition.
- **High debt-to-worth ratio (total liabilities to net worth)**
  Possible causes of unfavorable rating (evaluate both):
  - Substandard asset utilization: **low (unfavorable) net sales to total assets,** a fundamental weakness that requires further evaluation.
  - Inadequate owners' equity (original investment plus retained earnings): **high (unfavorable) net sales to net worth**, a fundamental weakness that can be corrected only by increasing net worth more rapidly than sales volume is expanded or by reducing net sales.
- **Low return on sales ratio (net profit to net sales)**, a fundamental weakness that indicates a need to determine whether the cause is a decrease in sales volume (as a result of price competition or a decline in unit sales), an increase in expenses (cost of sales, operating expenses, and/or net non-operating expenses), or both.

  If this ratio is low or reveals a loss, the credit analyst is advised to check two financial measures that indicate the possibility of an unfavorable change in bank relations (which could result in a sudden slowdown in the company's payments to trade creditors):
  - **Earnings before interest and taxes to interest expense (the times-interest-earned ratio)**, which shows the margin of safety (or proportionate shortfall) in covering interest payments from profit last year.
  - **After-tax net profit plus depreciation to current maturities of long-term debt (the cash-flow-to-current-maturities ratio)**, which compares the company's net cash flow generated last year with the amount of long-term debt due within the following 12 months, primarily reflecting the balance between depreciation and principal reduction as well as highlighting any balloon payments that must be met within 12 months.

  These are not causal ratios (and are not included within the usual cause-and-effect method). However, because of their importance to bankers, they should be evaluated whenever the profit-on-sales ratio is within the lower quartile or discloses a loss.

TABLE THREE CAUSES OF UNFAVORABLE FINANCIAL CONDITION

Operating performance and financial structure represented by the four credit screening ratios in Table Two are determined by five fundamental factors, the causal ratios:

- **High (unfavorable) collection period of accounts receivable,** which causes:
  - **Lower (unfavorable) current ratio** [even when working capital is sufficient relative to sales volume] by increasing current liabilities
  - **Lower (unfavorable) quick ratio** [assuming no change in inventory] by increasing current liabilities [However, **quick ratio** will become **higher (favorable)** if accounts receivable are substituted for inventory.]
  - **Higher (unfavorable) debt-to-worth ratio** by increasing total liabilities
  - **Lower (unfavorable) profit-on-sales ratio** whenever related interest costs, administrative costs, and bad debts offset profit from marginal accounts
- **Low (unfavorable) cost of sales to inventory, which causes:**
  - **Lower (unfavorable) current ratio** [even when working capital is sufficient relative to sales volume] by increasing current liabilities
  - **Lower (unfavorable) quick ratio** [particularly when inventory is substituted for accounts receivable or cash] by increasing current liabilities
  - **Higher (unfavorable) debt-to-worth ratio** by increasing total liabilities
  - **Lower (unfavorable) profit-on-sales ratio** whenever related interest costs, storage costs, and inventory writeoffs offset profit from longer work-in-process time, broader inventory or safety stock
- **Low (unfavorable) net sales to fixed assets, which causes:**
  - **Lower (unfavorable) current ratio** by drawing funds away from working capital
  - **Lower (unfavorable) quick ratio** by drawing funds away from working capital
  - **Higher (unfavorable) debt-to-worth ratio** by increasing total liabilities
  - **Lower (unfavorable) profit-on-sales ratio** whenever related interest costs, maintenance costs and depreciation offset profit from additional capacity
    Note: A high (unfavorable) level of other non-current (miscellaneous) assets has the same effect on financial structure as a high level of fixed assets
- **High (unfavorable) net sales to net worth,** which causes:
  - **Lower (unfavorable) current ratio** by providing less working capital to support sales volume
  - **Lower (unfavorable) quick ratio** by providing less working capital to support sales volume
  - **Higher (unfavorable) debt-to-worth ratio** by providing less owners' equity in relation to sales volume, resulting in higher debt to support total assets
  - **Lower (unfavorable) profit-on-sales ratio** whenever interest-bearing liabilities are substituted for net worth [However, return on equity (net profit to net worth) may be increased by the multiplier effect of greater net sales to net worth, even at a lower profit-on-sales ratio.]
- **Low long-term liabilities to total non-current assets,** which causes:
  - **Lower (unfavorable) current ratio** by providing less working capital to support sales volume
  - **Lower (unfavorable) quick ratio** by providing less working capital to support sales volume

  The effect on the debt-to-worth ratio is neutral if long-term liabilities are reduced by increasing current liabilities by the same amount over time.

TABLE THREE CAUSES OF UNFAVORABLE FINANCIAL CONDITION (CONTINUED)

The effect on the profit-on-sales ratio may be favorable if non-interest-bearing current liabilities (particularly trade credit) is substituted for long-term liabilities or may be unfavorable if the interest rate on short-term bank credit is higher than the long-term rate.

In cause-and-effect ratio analysis, the profit-on-sales ratio is ordinarily considered a causal measure because it exerts a major influence on the other key financial ratios by increasing (or decreasing) net worth through retained earnings (or through operating losses or asset writeoffs). From a credit analysis standpoint, however, the profit-on-sales ratio is most effectively evaluated by considering the impact of asset management, owners' reinvestment policy, and the balance between current and long-term liabilities, as represented by the ratios in this table.

pledged assets, refinancing, an irregular principal repayment schedule, debt subordinations, leases, insurance proceeds, lawsuits, and contingent liabilities can all have a major bearing on interpretation of financial statement data. Because customers' operating performance and financial structure are constantly changing, the most recent financial statement should be sought at least once each year.

Adjust Strategies to Your Company

Cause-and-effect ratio analysis of your own company's financial statement can serve as the basis for refining sales and credit policy. Suppose, for example, your comparative analysis reveals a low (unfavorable) current ratio and a low (unfavorable) quick ratio, coupled with a low (favorable) debt-to-worth ratio, for your own company. Unless liquidity is improved by shifting a portion of current debt to long-term status, this finding would suggest placing relatively greater emphasis on customers' prompt payment records and favorable liquidity measures (the current ratio and the quick ratio) in making future credit evaluations.

Sales and credit decision-makers in a company with the opposite characteristics—high liquidity, but relatively heavy debt in relation to equity due to a relatively large investment in fixed assets—would likely benefit from directing greater efforts to obtain and accommodate slow paying, but financially solid, customers.

For credit professionals who employ a numerical rating scheme that establishes a specific dollar limit for each customer, the insights provided by cause-and-effect ratio analysis can assist in refining the weight assigned to each key measure in the formula. In addition, by initially focusing on the four screening ratios, the cause-and-effect ratio approach can be used to simplify the rating procedure for most customers, since more extensive analysis is ordinarily required in only a comparatively small number of cases.

Analysis Is Both Art and Science

Successful credit analysis is as much an art as it is a science. Just as great works cannot be painted "by the numbers," outstanding credit management goes beyond mechanical calculation of financial data. True credit professionals consider all aspects of business performance, particularly management skills and character traits, when evaluating significant customers and fully address the fundamental credit principle, "know your customer." They make skillful use of financial statement analysis to simplify routine credit evaluations—and to gain greater insight into customers capabilities when making the difficult decisions that distinguish top performers in the credit profession.

Questions

1. "Cause-and-effect ratio analysis employs a total of 16 key financial relationships for in-depth analysis of operating performance and financial structure. However, only four of these ratios require attention in the credit analysis of most customers."
   a. Identify and define each of these four ratios.
   b. Interpret the financial meaning of each ratio.
2. Use Table Two to identify and explain the possible causes of: (1) a low current ratio, (2) a low quick ratio, (3) a high debt-equity ratio, and (4) a low return on sales ratio (after-tax profit margin).
3. Use Table Three to identify and explain the impact of the five causal ratios on the four credit screening ratios.
4. One rule of thumb states that a company's current ratio should be 2.0, and another states that a company's quick ratio should be 1.0.
   a. Prove that these two rules of thumb, taken together, imply that inventories should equal current liabilities.
   b. How valid is the rule of thumb for the current ratio as applied to the following industries: periodical publishing and printing versus manufacturers of telephone and telegraph apparatus. Explain and state your assumptions.
5. Three companies—Loliq, Medliq, and Hiliq—are similar in most respects, but they have differing current ratios:

Loliq	Medliq	Hiliq
$CR = \frac{\$50}{\$100} = 0.5$	$CR = \frac{\$100}{\$100} = 1.0$	$CR = \frac{\$200}{\$100} = 2.0$

   a. What happens to their current ratios when each company uses $25 to pay accounts payable? What mathematical principles do these cases illustrate?
   b. Are the companies more or less liquid after they make the $25 payment? What are your assumptions in answering this question?
6. Trumpet Company's balance sheet for the year ending July 31, 19X4, is as follows:

Cash	$ 10,000	Current liabilities	$ 50,000
Marketable securities	50,000	Long-term debt	100,000
Accounts receivable	100,000	Total liabilities	$150,000

Inventory	140,000	Owner equity	350,000
Fixed assets	200,000	Total claims	$500,000
Total assets	$ 500,000		

Trumpet Company's sales for the year were $2,000,000; cost of goods sold equaled $1,400,000; and earnings after taxes were $30,000.

a. Calculate the four credit screening ratios for the company.

b. Calculate the five causal ratios for the company.

c. As a credit manager for a supplier, would you grant credit to Trumpet Company? Explain.

How Useful Are Common Liquidity Measures?

RAVINDRA KAMATH

The measurement and evaluation of corporate liquidity are important for diverse corporate activities. Textbooks in corporation finance devote several chapters to working capital management, analysis of financial statements and related issues. Commercial bank management texts deal with the same issues in regard to the bank lending process. Most of these textbooks suggest the use of current ratio and quick ratio to gain an insight into a firm's liquidity condition, while noting the limitations of these ratios in assessing liquidity.

More recently, some textbooks have suggested supplementing the traditional liquidity ratios with computation of a cash conversion cycle to evaluate a firm's performance better with respect to liquidity. However, Richards and Laughlin [6] note the possibility of getting conflicting signals regarding liquidity with the conventional ratios and the cash conversion cycle.

The objective of this paper is four-fold:

- To compare and contrast the information content of the conventional liquidity ratios with that of the cash conversion cycle
- To ascertain if the net trade cycle can serve as a good approximation to the cash conversion cycle
- To evaluate if, within the framework of cross-sectional industry analysis, the traditional ratios in fact give rise to results contradictory to those provided by the cash conversion cycle
- To ascertain the relationships between these liquidity measures and a measure of firm profitability.

At the time of this writing, Ravindra Kamath was a professor of finance at Cleveland State University.

Data from ninety firms in six retail industries over a fifteen-year period are used to meet these objectives.

Background

The most commonly employed measures of corporate liquidity are the *current* ratio and *quick* ratio. However, their ability to do an adequate job is questioned by many authors (e.g., Emery [3]). Essentially, because of their static nature, these ratios cannot be counted on to measure or estimate adequately the pattern and the sizes of future cash flows, which in reality determine the extent to which a firm is liquid. In addition, their embedded notion of margin of safety relies on a liquidation concept rather than a going-concern concept. Based on these and similar arguments, Bernstein [1] has pointed out that, "There is no direct or established relationship between balances of working capital items and the pattern that future cash flows are likely to assume."

While the quick ratio offers a more stringent gauge of corporate liquidity than the current ratio, the total omission of inventories as a potential source of current funds poses a separate problem for the analyst.

In a 1974 paper, Gitman [4] presents a simplified approach to estimating the minimum cash balance requirement of a firm. The cornerstone is the calculation of a total cash cycle from which the cash turnover and liquidity requirements could be computed. The total cash cycle is defined by Gitman as the number of days from the time the firm pays for its purchases of raw materials to the time the firm collects for the sale of its finished product. Gitman and Sachdeva [5] later refined Gitmam's original framework.

Richards and Laughlin [6] suggest the use of a cash conversion cycle for evaluating corporate liquidity to supplement the traditional current and quick ratios. According to them, "An examination of conventional, static balance sheet liquidity ratios indicates the inherent potential for misinterpreting a firm's relative liquidity position." To support their arguments, they provide an example of Martin Marietta Corporation for the 1975–1978 period. Within the context of that example, they contend that the normal interpretation of current ratio would have given a wrong indication (worsening) of liquidity problems and the quick ratio would have failed to give any clear signals.

Bernstein [1] recommends the use of net trade cycle, a measure similar to the cash conversion cycle, to measure liquidity on a flow concept. According to Bernstein, the net trade cycle concept increases uniformity and simplicity of calculation since it uses net sales instead of cost of goods sold and purchases to compute the average age of inventory and average age of accounts payable.

Two other liquidity measures that have recently surfaced are Emery's Lambda [3] and a net liquid balance measure by Shulman and Cox [7]. These measures along with the other four are briefly described in the Appendix.

To understand the crux of the arguments better, we rely on data from firms in retail industries. The retail industry was chosen for two reasons. First, since the analysis was to include the quick ratio, the sample industry had to belong to a group for which the quick ratio is a highly recommended ratio for measuring liquidity. Second, this is an industry for which annual purchases can be easily approximated even when such data are not directly available from the publicly available information. To approximate credit purchases, the following equation is used:

$$\text{Purchases} = \text{Ending inventory} + \text{costs of goods sold} - \text{beginning inventory}.$$

The data needed were obtained from COMPUSTAT tapes. Ninety firms from six industries are included in the analysis.

Findings

The liquidity measures of retail grocery stores, the industry with the largest number of firms, are examined first. Exhibit 1 gives the industry averages along with the standard deviations and the smallest and the largest values for the respective cash conversion cycles, current ratios and quick ratios for 1970–1984. Also included are the means and standard deviations of net trade cycles.

Below are the liquidity measures of five firms from the retail grocery industry for 1971:

Firm	A	B	C	D	E
Current ratio	1.84	1.39	1.57	1.86	1.82
Quick ratio	0.64	0.64	0.66	0.66	0.69
Cash Conversion Cycle	19.1	2.8	34.2	82.0	13.1

Based on a comparison of quick ratios, the five firms appear to exhibit the same level of liquidity, all below the industry average of 0.89. A comparison of current ratio shows that while all five firms are less liquid than an average firm in their industry, firms B and C are farther away from the industry average than the other three. Relying on the current and the quick ratios would lead one to conclude that firm B is the least liquid of the five firms. However, a look at the cash conversion cycle indicates that this firm was able to operate with a proportionately much shorter collection period, and/or a faster inventory turnover, while possibly obtaining much of its short-term financing from suppliers. In fact, it was the only firm in this industry to have its accounts payable equal to its inventory. This partially explains the low current ratio. It is also interesting to note the range of cash conversion cycles compared to that of the two ratios for these firms. The quick ratio comparison shows an equal degree of protection (or lack of it) for the suppliers of short-term credit to these firms. Yet, the cash conversion cycles indicate drastically different levels of efficiency with respect to strategies for obtaining short-term financing.

EXHIBIT 1 LIQUIDITY MEASURES OF RETAIL GROCERY INDUSTRY, 1970–1984

	Cash conversion cycle				Net trade cycle		Current ratio				Quick ratio			
Year	Mean	Smallest	Largest	Standard deviation	Mean	Standard deviation	Mean	Smallest	Largest	Standard deviation	Mean	Smallest	Largest	Standard deviation
1970	26.7	6.2	143.8	28.0	22.7	23.7	1.98	1.31	3.26	0.57	0.88	0.31	2.56	0.54
1971	28.6	2.8	115.3	25.0	24.7	22.9	2.03	1.35	4.33	0.72	0.89	0.33	3.44	0.66
1972	25.5	6.8	76.5	16.6	21.8	14.6	2.02	1.02	3.63	0.69	0.85	0.30	2.21	0.51
1973	24.1	-1.2	56.4	13.2	20.2	11.5	1.92	1.14	3.56	0.57	0.71	0.22	1.87	0.43
1974	23.9	4.0	56.1	11.8	19.8	10.0	1.80	1.18	3.77	0.54	0.62	0.21	2.11	0.40
1975	21.7	-2.9	52.7	12.1	18.3	10.3	1.78	1.20	3.88	0.54	0.63	0.24	2.60	0.46
1976	21.7	2.7	50.2	11.2	18.1	9.5	1.80	1.23	4.16	0.57	0.65	0.21	2.75	0.48
1977	20.5	-0.5	50.7	12.2	17.1	10.3	1.75	1.20	3.93	0.54	0.64	0.24	2.65	0.45
1978	21.3	0.2	53.7	12.5	17.7	10.3	1.66	0.88	3.47	0.51	0.63	0.13	2.26	0.41
1979	20.2	-4.7	60.4	13.0	16.7	10.7	1.62	1.01	3.57	0.51	0.61	0.21	2.24	0.42
1980	18.5	-3.0	71.3	14.8	15.5	12.4	1.57	1.09	3.92	0.53	0.62	0.22	2.67	0.46
1981	16.8	-2.8	64.6	14.2	14.2	11.8	1.56	1.01	3.83	0.51	0.64	0.18	2.73	0.49
1982	17.8	1.1	54.7	12.8	15.0	10.7	1.63	1.06	4.37	0.63	0.73	0.20	3.20	0.59
1983	20.9	-0.6	63.8	15.4	17.1	12.4	1.64	0.92	4.38	0.65	0.70	0.20	3.21	0.60
1984	15.4	-2.5	38.9	9.9	13.2	8.4	1.61	0.91	5.06	0.87	0.77	0.19	3.88	0.84

To carry this discussion one step further, additional information is provided for firms A and D:

	Firm A*			Firm D*		
	CR	**QR**	**CCC**	**CR**	**QR**	**CCC**
1971	1.84	0.64	19.1	1.86	0.66	82.0
1972	1.73	0.58	20.8	1.61	0.83	76.5
1973	1.47	0.41	16.7	2.01	0.80	42.6
1974	1.30	0.30	18.8	1.80	0.65	41.7
1975	1.50	0.38	18.0	1.85	0.74	37.0

* CR, QR and CCC stand for current ratio, quick ratio, and cash conversion cycles, respectively.

A casual glance at the trend of traditional liquidity ratios of these two firms indicates that while firm D has been able to maintain its liquidity, firm A became less liquid. A careful examination of complete data (not presented here) reveals that firm D was able to increase its sales by 86.5 percent over the 1971–1975 period while increasing its inventory by just 7.8 percent and accounts receivable by 11.57 percent. The other three parameters, namely the costs of goods sold, purchases and accounts payable increased by 85.3, 91.1 and 90.1 percent, respectively. Thus, it appears that firm D made a determined effort to reduce its relative investment in inventory and accounts receivable and was rather successful at it while not altering its average age of accounts payable of 27 days. This successful effort is reflected in the reduction of its cash conversion cycle from 82 days to 37 days. The very fact that the current ratio in 1975 was very close to its 1971 level suggests that the current assets and current liabilities must have increased at the same rate, and indeed they did. Since the inventories and accounts receivables grew at less than 12 percent over this period while the accounts payable grew at 90.1 percent, the rate of growth of current assets and current liabilities can be equal if and only if some other short-term assets grew at a phenomenal rate or the short-term financing, other than accounts payable, shrank. It was the latter that occurred, since the firm's need to finance its inventory and accounts receivable had been reduced significantly. Thus, even for trend analysis, a careful examination of the cash conversion cycle can provide additional useful information beyond that provided by the traditional ratios.

Firm A, meanwhile, increased its net sales by 171.6 percent accompanied by a 170.8 increase in cost of sales and a 166.2 percent increase in purchases. However, unlike firm D, A's sales increase was accomplished with an increase of 157.4, 68.3 and 141.2 percent in inventory, accounts receivable and accounts payable, respectively. While holding down accounts receivable was helpful, because of the large proportion of inventory in the current assets (75.3 percent), the increase in inventory had a severe, undesirable impact on the quick ratio. The current ratio was adversely affected because a portion of the inventory had to be financed with other forms of short-term financing. A small improvement in A's cash conversion cycle can be explained by increases in inventory and accounts receivable at rates lower than those of cost of goods sold and sales, along with less reliance on trade supplier financing. In this case, the cash conversion cycle, by itself, does not give a clear picture of liquidity condition since a sizable amount of short-term financing came from non-trade sources. Thus, an analysis that includes all three measures would be an appropriate one.

Exhibit 1 shows that the average cash conversion cycle in the retail grocery industry has declined gradually from 28.6 days in 1971 to 15.4 days in 1984, with a few exceptions. This improvement appears to be largely from firms that had unusually large cash cycles compared to the industry average, as partially evidenced by decreases in the largest cash cycles as well as in the standard deviation.

The gradual decrease in the cash conversion cycle from 1971 to 1984 is paralleled by a similar decrease in the average current ratio. Thus, while the average cash conversion cycle figures tend to indicate an improvement in working capital management, the comparable figures of current and quick ratios tend to indicate less protection for short-term credit suppliers. Indeed, when the industry average cash conversion cycle decreased from 28.6 to 21.7 days between 1971 and 1975, the industry average current ratio dropped from 2.03 to 1.78. While the quick ratio also shows a similar trend, the strength of this relationship seems to be lower.

Cash Conversion Cycles and Net Trade Cycles

Net trade cycle provides information similar to that provided by the cash conversion cycle. Instead of computing number of days purchases in accounts payable and number of days of costs of goods sold in inventory, the net trade cycle calculates number of days of sales in both. This results in some distortion.

Indeed, in an example of firms A and D in the previous section, it was noticed that the percentage increases in net sales, cost of goods sold and purchases were more or less identical. If this is generally true for all firms over a period of years, the cash conversion cycle and the net trade cycle would be positively correlated and they would produce similar rankings of firms within any industry. In an empirical test of this, the results generally show the coefficients with the expected signs with significance at the 99 percent level.[1] Thus, neither hypothesis can be rejected.

Cash Conversion Cycles and the Current Ratios

Based on the views expressed by Richards and Laughlin [6] and based on the observations of Exhibit 1, one can argue that whenever a firm attempts to

[1] This hypothesis was empirically tested for firms in each of the six industries, over the fifteen-year period. First the Pearson's product moment correlation coefficients between the two measures were calculated. Then the Spearman's and Kendall's rank correlations were computed, based on the rankings of the firms provided by the two measures.

reduce its cash conversion cycle by shortening either its average age of inventory or its collection period and/or by lengthening its average age of accounts payable, its current ratio also tends to fall. However, this line of reasoning has its drawbacks. First, a reduction in the average collection period would mean a reduction in accounts receivable and, hence, a reduction in the numerator of the current ratio. However, if the reduction in accounts receivable also results in a reduced need of financing, the current ratio may or may not decrease, depending on the size of the reduction in the short-term financing requirement. A similar argument applies when one tries to reduce the cash conversion cycle by reducing the average age of inventory. Second, an effort to reduce the cash cycle by relying more on financing from trade suppliers may not reduce the current ratio if the increased financing from trade suppliers simply replaces other forms of short-term financing. Accordingly, the arguments of Richards and Laughlin may not be as convincing as they at first appear.

To test the validity of their arguments, it is hypothesized that the cash conversion cycles and current ratios are positively correlated. It is additionally hypothesized that the rankings of firms within an industry based on cash conversion cycles and the current ratios would be negatively correlated.

Our data produced correlation coefficients with the expected positive sign, though only on 22 occasions are they seen to be statistically significant, out of a total of 90 coefficients. Therefore, the first hypothesis would have to be rejected. The rank correlations are generally found with the expected negative sign; however, out of a total 180 only 62 of these coefficients are statistically significant. For the largest of the six industries with 28 firms, 29 of the 30 rank correlation coefficients are statistically significant with the hypothesized sign. Thus, while the second hypothesis would have to be rejected for five of the six industries, it cannot be rejected for the retail grocery industry.

Cash Conversion Cycles and the Quick Ratios

Richards and Laughlin felt that the quick ratios would echo the current ratios with respect to changes in the cash conversion cycles. However, in their example of Martin Marietta Corporation, they found a "mixed behavior pattern." Following the arguments in the previous section, any reduction in the cash conversion cycle brought on by increasing the inventory turnover would not affect the quick ratio. Moreover, since the inventories generally represent the largest component of the current assets, on an *a priori* basis, one would not expect any consistent relationship between the quick ratios and the cash conversion cycles.

Accordingly, it is hypothesized that the correlation coefficient between the two measures would not be significantly different from zero. It is also hypothesized that the rankings of the firms within any industry according to these two measures would not show any consistent pattern. For our sample industries, we could not reject either hypothesis. In other words, within the framework of cross-sectional industry analysis, quick ratios do not seem to give rise to results contradictory to those provided by the cash conversion cycles.

Liquidity Measures and Profitability

While maintaining an adequate level of liquidity has numerous benefits, ranging from being able to take cash discounts to reducing the probability of technical insolvency, these benefits are not free. Conceptually, it is easy to understand that the benefits from maintaining liquidity are obtained by paying a price through reduced profitability. For example, the cost of warehousing and storage of inventory, insurance, spoilage, etc., would be expected to reduce operating profits. A similar pattern exists with respect to investigation costs, collection costs and bad debt costs of accounts receivable.

In Exhibit 2, the correlation coefficients between the profitability measure and each of the four liquidity measures are tabulated. The expected sign for the coefficients is negative. The current ratios and the quick ratios are not related to the profitability with the expected sign. That, unfortunately, is equivalent to saying that one can increase liquidity without hurting the profitability of a firm. The correlation coefficients between the cash conversion cycles and the operating profit measures show the expected sign in 14 out of the 15 years, even though

EXHIBIT 2 RELATIONSHIPS BETWEEN OPERATING PROFITS ON TOTAL ASSETS AND LIQUIDITY MEASURES OF RETAILERS

	Correlation coefficients between operating profits/total assets and:			
Year (sample size)	**Cash conversion cycle**	**Net trade cycle**	**Current ratio**	**Quick ratio**
1970(79)	-0.193*	-0.245**	0.153	-0.006
1971(84)	-0.135	-0.184*	0.186*	0.053
1972(88)	-0.073	-0.111	0.236**	0.208*
1973(90)	-0.028	-0.084	0.207*	0.139
1974(92)	-0.147	-0.193*	0.170	0.138
1975(94)	-0.003	-0.064	0.194*	0.163
1976(94)	-0.105	-0.144	0.266***	0.156
1977(94)	-0.187*	-0.255**	0.167	0.168
1978(94)	-0.255**	-0.265***	0.137	0.183*
1979(93)	-0.141	-0.174*	0.155	0.164
1980(91)	-0.174*	-0.225**	0.235**	0.079
1981(93)	-0.170	-0.199*	0.336***	0.171
1982(92)	-0.217**	-0.249**	-0.079	0.032
1983(86)	0.046	-0.051	0.300***	0.171
1984(78)	-0.017	-0.092	0.041	0.006

*, **, *** denote significance at 90, 95, and 99 percent, respectively.

it is statistically significant in only four years. The results are much better in case of the net trade cycle measure of liquidity. Not only is the relationship inverse in every year, as would be expected, but it is also significant in nine years for the sample at hand.

Summary

This paper attempted to compare the information content of the current ratio and quick ratio with that of the cash conversion cycle. The results cited for a few individual firms from the retail grocery industry and the broader industry analysis indicated that, although each measure can provide useful information, it can also provide misleading clues regarding a firm's liquidity management. However, when all three measures are used simultaneously, much insight into a firm's liquidity condition as well as its efficiency of working capital management can be obtained.

It was found that the net trade cycle would provide the same basic information as the cash conversion cycle in spite of the distortion caused by the former measure. The results of rank correlations indicated that the rankings of firms within an industry by these two measures would be similar.

The six industry analysis failed to support the Richards/Laughlin view [6] that the cash conversion cycle and the traditional liquidity ratios would be positively correlated. To test if the traditional measures of liquidity would produce rankings of firms within an industry opposite those produced by cash conversion cycle criteria, rank correlation coefficients were examined. With one exception, the findings did not indicate an existence of such a relationship. Within the "retail grocery" industry, the rank correlation coefficients between the current ratio and cash conversion cycle rankings were found to be statistically significant with a negative sign.

The traditional measures of liquidity, the current ratio and the quick ratio, were not found to exhibit the inverse relationship with an operating profit measure. The cash conversion and net trade cycle, however, were found to be negatively correlated with the profitability measure, indicating the expected relationship between the benefits and costs of maintaining liquidity.

While all the conclusions in this paper were made with respect to the retail firms, given the underlying rationale, there is no reason to expect that contrary results would be obtained in other industries.

References

1. Bernstein, L.A. *Financial Statement Analysis: Theory, Application, and Interpretation*, 3rd edition, Homewood Ill., Richard D. Irwin, Inc., 1983.
2. Brick, J.R. *Commercial Banking: Text and Readings*, Haslett, Mich., Systems Publications, Inc., 1984.
3. Emery, G.W. "Measuring Short-term Liquidity," *Journal of Cash Management*, (July/August 1984), pp. 25–32.

4. Gitman, L.J. "Estimating Corporate Liquidity Requirements: A Simplified Approach," *The Financial Review*, (1974), pp. 79–88.
5. Gitman, L.J. and K. S. Sachdeva, "A Framework for Estimating and Analyzing the Required Working Capital Investment," *Review of Business and Economic Research*, (Spring 1982), pp. 35–44.
6. Richards, V.D. and E.J. Laughlin, "A Cash Conversion Cycle Approach to Liquidity Analysis," *Financial Management*, (Spring 1980), pp. 32–38.
7. Shulman, J.M. and R.A.K. Cox, "An Integrative Approach to Working Capital Management," *Journal of Cash Management*, (November/December 1985), pp. 64–67.

Appendix: Six Measures of Liquidity

1. Current ratio $= \dfrac{\text{current assets}}{\text{current liabilities}}$

2. Quick ratio $= \dfrac{\text{current assets} - \text{inventory}}{\text{current liabilities}}$

3. Cash conversion cycle
   = average age of inventory + average age of accounts receivable
   − average age of accounts payable

$$= \frac{\text{inventory} \times 365}{\text{cost of goods sold}} + \frac{\text{net accounts receivable} \times 365}{\text{net sales}} - \frac{\text{accounts payable} \times 365}{\text{purchases}}$$

4. Net trade cycle

$$= \frac{\text{inventory} \times 365}{\text{net sales}} + \frac{\text{accounts receivable} \times 365}{\text{net sales}} - \frac{\text{accounts payable} \times 365}{\text{net sales}}$$

5. Net liquid balance by Shulman and Cox
   = cash + marketable securities − all liquid financial obligations including short-term notes payable and the current portion of long-term debt.

6. Emery's Lambda

$$= \frac{\text{initial liquid reserve} + \text{total anticipated net cash flow during the analysis horizon}}{\text{uncertainty about net cash flow during the analysis horizon}}$$

The larger the value of Lambda, the more liquid is the firm.

Questions

1. Chock Full O'Nuts (CFON) generated sales of $270,169 during 19X1, with cost of goods sold equal to $193,329. CFON's balance sheet at the end of the sales year is provided below:

Assets		**Liabilities and Equity**	
Cash and equivalents	$ 1,861	Accounts payable	$ 9,570
Accounts receivable	26,672	Accrued expenses	9,904
Inventories	34,098	Short-term debt	2,143
Other current assets	3,934	Total current liabilities	$ 21,617
Total current assets	$ 66,565	Long-term liabilities	109,762
		Common stock	38,662
Net fixed assets	49,181	Retained earnings	21,430
Other noncurrent assets	75,725	Total claims	$191,471
Total assets	$191,471		

   a. Calculate CFON's current ratio, quick ratio, cash conversion cycle, and net trade cycle. (Assume that cost of goods sold equals purchases.)
   b. What is the meaning of the term *cash conversion cycle?*
   c. Is CFON a highly liquid company? Explain.

2. Below are liquidity measures for five retail grocery store companies:

	A	B	C	D	E
Current ratio	1.8	1.4	1.6	1.9	1.8
Quick ratio	0.6	0.6	0.7	0.7	0.7
Cash conversion cycle	19	3	34	82	13

   a. Which is the most liquid company? Explain.
   b. Which is the least liquid company? Explain.

3. Describe the trends in liquidity measures shown in Exhibit 1.
4. Explain the trade-off between a company's liquidity level and its expected profitability.
5. Is it possible for a highly liquid company to also be highly profitable? Explain.
6. What empirical relationship between company liquidity and profitability does the author find? (See Exhibit 2.)

An Analysis of Patterns from the Statement of Cash Flows

Benton E. Gup, William D. Samson, Michael T. Dugan, Myung J. Kim, and Thawatchai Jittrapanun

In 1987, the Financial Accounting Standards Board (FASB) issued its Statement No. 95, in which the Statement of Cash Flows (SCF) became a required part of the financial statement package. The primary objective of the SCF is to provide investors and creditors with information about a firm's cash receipts and disbursements during the period. In the mandated SCF format, cash-related transactions are classified as either cash flows from operating activities, cash flows from investing activities, or cash flows from financing activities. The signs (positive or negative) of the firm's net cash flows from its operating, investing, and financing activities appearing in its SCF constitute a cash flow pattern. As will be discussed later in the paper, there are eight possible cash flow patterns.

The SCF provides information about a firm's cash flows that is intended to complement the information appearing in the accrual-basis income statement and balance sheet. The SCF also indicates why and how the cash amount changed: what generated cash and how cash was used. Finally, under the indirect approach, the SCF "reconciles" net income to operating cash flow, indicating the differences between accrual-based net income and cash flow from operating activities.

The SCF replaced the Statement of Changes in Financial Position (SCFP), which had been required since 1971. Accountants and users often had criticized the stated objectives of the SCFP as too broad and not achievable in a single financial statement (Gup and Dugan [3]). The SCFP also was criticized for permitting considerable flexibility in its form, content, and terminology, in particular the range of alternatives allowed to define "funds." The SCFP could be based

---

At the time of this writing, Benton E. Gup was the Robert Hunt Cochrane/Alabama Banker Association Chair of Banking, William D. Samson was a professor of accounting, Michael T. Dugan was an associate professor of economics, Myung J. Kim was an assistant professor of economics, and Thawatchai Jittrapanun was a graduate research assistant, all at the University of Alabama, Tuscaloosa, AL.

Source: *Financial Practice and Education* (Fall 1993, pp. 73–79). Reprinted with permission.

on cash flow, working capital flow or some intermediate definition, which impaired comparability across firms.

Since the SCF replaced the SCFP, the former's usefulness and limitations have been scrutinized. Despite the FASB Statement 95 requirements, variations in the presentation and format of the SCF persist. Indeed, the alternatives of reporting net cash flow from operating activities by either the "direct" or the "indirect" method are just one example of such variation. Another, as noted by Gentry, Newbold, and Whitford [2], is the lack of standardization of cash flow components. Though such variations may limit the usefulness of the SCF, they perhaps exist partly because FASB Statement 95 encouraged experimentation to help discover the most useful presentation and format.

Among the empirical studies using the SCF, Weaver and Marshall [4] derived ratios for 111 electric utility companies over a five year period and then tested the ratios against bond ratings and other indicators of financial risk. They found the cash flow information useful, but their tests were not robust. Also, Board and Day [1] examined the association between stock market returns and cash flow measures in the United Kingdom. While the cash flow measures they considered are not the same as those appearing in the SCF, it is instructive to know that Board and Day found those measures provided little useful information in explaining abnormal stock returns.

Since these earlier studies examining the usefulness of ratios constructed from cash flow information have met with limited results, this paper examines the SCF information from a different perspective. We describe the eight possible cash flow patterns from the SCF, and then we analyze selected financial characteristics of firms within each pattern. While we take a "naive" approach by considering the signs, either positive or negative, of cash flow amounts within each pattern, this approach is but one step in understanding the usefulness of the Statement of Cash Flows. Obviously, the magnitudes and the relative magnitudes of the cash flow amounts, as well as their composition within each pattern, change from period to period, and may prove to be more useful and informative.

This paper should be helpful to financial statement users in at least two ways. First, information about the cash flow patterns provides the user with another way of analyzing a firm's economic condition, complementing other tools such as ratio analysis. Additionally, determining the profile of financial characteristics typical of the firms in each cash flow pattern may enable the user to gain insights simply by identifying a firm's particular cash flow pattern. Such insights may help in deciding what other financial information should be examined and what other analyses should be performed.

The paper is organized as follows. The following section describes the eight possible cash flow patterns, and the next section provides an empirical analysis of selected financial characteristics of firms in each pattern. The last section addresses the limitations inherent in the pattern approach and offers some suggestions for future research. Concluding remarks are contained in the final section.

Description of Eight Cash Flow Patterns

As well as describing each pattern, we provide our *ex ante* expectations about how these cash flow patterns are likely to relate to the firm's economic condition. These expectations about the economic condition of firms in each pattern are compared with data in the second section of the paper.

As noted previously, the SCF provides information about cash flows from operating, investing, and financing activities. Not considering magnitudes, there are eight possible patterns of inflows (positive, +) and outflows (negative, -) of the three activities:

	Cash Flows from		
Patterns	**Operating**	**Investing**	**Financing**
Pattern Number 1	+	+	+
Pattern Number 2	+	-	-
Pattern Number 3	+	+	-
Pattern Number 4	+	-	+
Pattern Number 5	-	+	+
Pattern Number 6	-	-	+
Pattern Number 7	-	+	-
Pattern Number 8	-	-	-

The only significance to the order of the patterns is that we consider positive cash flows from operating activities first (Patterns One through Four), and negative cash flows from operating activities next (Patterns Five through Eight). Cash flows from operating activities are amounts generated internally that are available for acquiring assets, paying liabilities, and paying cash dividends. Stated otherwise, expected cash flows produced from operating activities are the basis for asset expansion (investment activities) and for inflows from financing. Cash flow generated by operations provides the bulk of the cash to repay investors and creditors (financing activities).

In the first pattern (+,+,+), the firm has positive cash flow from all three activities. In other words, the firm is generating a positive net cash flow from operating activities, and also selling its long-term assets (e.g., depreciable assets, long-term investments, etc.), and raising additional debt and/or equity capital. Pattern One is unusual in that the firm is accumulating cash from all three activities. We expect the pattern to be transitory as well, for the cash "treasure chest" is likely to be used in the near future to finance a stock repurchase, to repay long-term debt principal, to purchase a large investment such as a subsidiary, or to expand operating facilities.

In the second patten (+,-,-), the firm is generating enough positive operating cash flow to invest in long-term assets and to reduce its debt or pay dividends. This pattern reflects a mature successful firm. We believe that Pattern Two should be relatively common. The firm can use its operating cash flow to finance internally a modest expansion, or at least the replacement of existing depreciated assets. Any excess operating cash flow can be used to service debt payments or even to pay dividends or repurchase shares of the firm. Using cash to reduce equity and/or long-term debt suggests that the firm no longer needs to raise capital externally. A large expansion of capacity or investment in other long-lived assets would not seem warranted given the apparently limited opportunity for returns on such investments. Such firms are likely to have reached the stage of maturity where they are returning some of the investors' capital.

In Pattern Three (+,+,-), the operating and investing cash flows are positive, while financing cash flow is negative. The positive operating cash flow and the proceeds from the sale of long-term assets are used to repay debtholders and/or shareholders. We believe Pattern Three, like Pattern One, is unusual. In this case, the cash flow from operations is coupled with the sale of long-term assets to reduce long-term debt and/or pay owners. The pattern is unusual because firms' investing activities typically produce outflows rather than inflows (i.e. buying or replacing long-term assets); inflows do arise, however, from the sale of long-term assets after LBOs. In Pattern Three, plant and equipment, subsidiaries and divisions, or investments in stocks and bonds are being sold, perhaps to make up for any shortfall in operating cash inflow so that investors and long-term creditors can be paid. Obviously, selling off income-generating assets in this way cannot continue without the corporation being liquidated. If this pattern persists, it suggests a firm with few profitable investing alternatives, since it is contracting both operating capacity and investment assets.

In the fourth pattern (+,-,+), we expect that the firm's operating cash flow is not sufficient to support its investing activities. As a result, a portion of the investing outflow is financed by the proceeds from the issuance of new debt or equity. We believe that this pattern reflects a growing firm. The firm with Pattern Four requires new investment in long-term assets, such as plant and equipment, in order to expand its revenue-generating ability. Given this growth scenario, the cash outflow for acquiring new investment assets cannot be financed entirely from operating cash flow. The shortfall requires debt or equity financing. Because there is a net cash inflow from issuing debt or equity, investors apparently believe that the firm can earn enough return from the new investments to ensure repayment.

Pattern Five (-,+,+) also appears unusual: a firm with a net outflow of cash from operating activities may make up that deficit by selling long-term assets and also by issuing debt or equity capital. Lenders or shareholders would probably not put more cash into this business unless they thought that the negative cash flow from operations was temporary. However, the shrinkage in long-term assets suggests reduced growth potential for the firm, relative to any growth in the firm's recent past. This scenario indeed raises the question of why investors and creditors are providing more capital.

In the sixth pattern (-,-,+), even though the firm has a negative operating cash flow, it is investing in long-term assets. The two negative cash flows (operating and investing) are financed, at least in part, by issuing additional debt or equity. Pattern Six suggests that the negative operating cash flow is temporary, perhaps because a young, fast-growing company is expanding such components of working capital as receivables and inventory, or paying off current liabilities, to support rapidly increasing sales. Because investors are lending money in exchange for debt instruments or are buying the firm's newly issued shares, they must believe that the operating cash flow is only temporarily negative, and that the firm has investment opportunities that will generate significant cash inflows.

In Pattern Seven (-,+,-), the firm has a deficit in operating cash flow and is shrinking by distributing cash to shareholders and/or repaying debtholders. Pattern Seven suggests that the firm may be showing losses on its income statement that are contributing to a net operating cash outflow. At the same time, creditors (or possibly the shareholders) are being repaid. The sale of the long-lived assets generates the cash to pay for the operating and investing outflows. Such a pattern is unlikely to persist for many periods without causing the liquidation of the firm.

In the eighth and last pattern (-,-,-), all activities have negative cash flows. This situation can occur only when previously accumulated cash balances are being consumed to offset negative cash flows. Like Patterns One, Five, and Seven, Pattern Eight is unusual, with cash flowing out for operating, investing and financing activities. In this case, the company is acquiring new long-lived assets at the same time it is paying off creditors (and perhaps owners). Along with these two outflows, the operating activities also are consuming cash. Needless to say, the firm's cash reserves will be stretched to the limit if this pattern persists.

The following section of the paper analyzes selected financial characteristics of firms in each of the eight patterns, to determine how closely the data fit the expectations described above.

Empirical Analysis

Analysis of a sample of firms drawn from the COMPUSTAT file identified the cash flow patterns most frequently observed in each. Examination of the sample firms then determined whether the expectations about firm condition that we attributed to the eight patterns are consistent with the firms' actual financial characteristics.

Exhibit 1 presents selected average financial statistics for the 1989 cash flow patterns of 1,745 of the 2,000 largest firms included in COMPUSTAT. (For the other 255 firms, cash flow data were not available.) Even when cash flow data were available, other data may be missing for one or more years. Therefore, the sample size varies across measures. The data used in this study indicate the percentage of firms in each cash flow pattern, and include mean measures of the financial characteristics of size, financial leverage, growth, and profitability. The definitions of the financial indicators used are presented in Appendix A. These indicators are not intended to be collectively exhaustive.

Because of extreme values and large standard deviations of the variables, the mean data may be misleading in some cases. To address this problem, we truncated the extreme values of the returns on equity (ROE). The criterion was to truncate ROEs above 100 percent and below minus 100 percent. Since the ROEs were truncated, we used the same firms to compute the internal growth

EXHIBIT 1 SELECTED AVERAGE STATISTICS FOR CASH FLOW PATTERNS*

Variables		Cash Flow Patterns (Operating, Investing, Financing)								
		One	Two	Three	Four	Five	Six	Seven	Eight	
		+++	+--	++-	+-+	-++	--+	-+-	---	
Distributions of 1,745 Firms		0.40	45.67	7.39	34.90	0.86	7.34	2.41	1.03	
Number of Firms in Each Pattern		7	797	129	609	15	128	42	18	
	Range (Min-Max)									N
Asset Size ($Mill)	[129-160,893]	761	3111	1619	2100	560	1986	965	1968	1745
Asset Growth/5 Years	[-27.93-172.76%]	-0.63	10.97	8.99	20.76	11.15	20.43	15.39	5.56	1327
Internal Growth Rate	[-195.55-277.07%]	-5.61	7.24	6.25	5.36	5.47	-2.64	1.53	11.82	1657
Dividend Growth Rate (5 Years)	[-36.9-203.6%]	-8.70	10.02	9.10	5.94	1.52	2.63	3.31	4.27	1032
Debt-To-Asset Ratio	[0-185.03%]	17.18	28.78	44.53	37.21	40.50	43.43	47.91	44.23	1745
Return on Assets	[-38.40-53.00%]	-1.81	6.01	2.50	3.83	-2.33	-0.94	-1.16	-0.65	1657

*Data are for 1989.

rate and return on assets.[1] We used return on assets as our measure of profitability.[2] The statistical relationships among the means appear in Exhibit 2.

The data in Exhibit 1, consistent to a degree with our expectations, show that almost 46 percent of the firms have cash flow Pattern Two (+,-,-): a firm using cash flow from operating activities to acquire long-term assets and to reduce debts and/or pay cash dividends to equity investors. Such firms may be characterized as stable, mature and successful. Firms with this cash flow pattern are the largest firms in terms of total assets, and they grew at a moderate average rate of 10.97 percent per year over the last five years. Their debt-to-total assets ratio (28.78%) is low relative to that of the other firms. The debt-to-total assets ratio, rather than debt-to-equity, is used here to measure financial leverage, because some restructured firms have negative shareholders' equity. Firms in Pattern Two are the most profitable as shown by their return on assets (ROA), and they have the highest cash dividend growth rates.

The second largest group of firms, almost 35 percent of the sample, has cash flow Pattern Four (+,-,+): a firm using cash from operations and from additional debt or equity financing to expand. Thus, such a pattern indicates potential growth. As would be expected, firms with this pattern are somewhat smaller firms than those with Pattern Two. Their assets have grown at a rapid rate (20.76%), depending heavily on the use of debt and/or equity capital, as well as internally generated cash.

EXHIBIT 2 STATISTICAL SIGNIFICANCE OF DIFFERENCES BETWEEN THE MEANS OF EACH VARIABLE IN CASH FLOW PATTERN TWO AND THOSE IN OTHER CASH FLOW PATTERNS

		Cash Flow Patterns (operating, investing, financing)							
Variables		One +++	Two +--	Three ++-	Four +-+	Five -++	Six --+	Seven -+-	Eight ---
Asset Size	$	S	-	S	S	S	N	S	N
Asset Growth/5 Years	%	N	-	N	S	N	S	N	N
Internal Growth Rate	%	N	-	N	N	N	S	N	N
Dividend Growth Rate/5 Years	%	N	-	N	S	S	S	S	S
Debt-To-Asset Ratio	%	N	-	S	S	N	S	S	N
Return on Assets	%	N	-	S	S	S	S	S	S

S = Statistically significant @5%
N = Not statistically significant @5% using a t-statistic of equal means

[1] Though ROE served as the basis for data truncation, the ROE results are not reported here; they are available from the authors on request.
[2] Some firms that had been restructured had negative stockholders' equity and negative incomes, resulting in different signs for ROE and ROA. Therefore, we use ROA as the profitability measure.

Slightly more than 7 percent of the firms have cash flow Pattern Three (+,+,-): a firm using cash from operations and from sales of fixed assets to reduce its debts and/or equity. This is the pattern one would expect from a successful restructuring. Not all firms with this pattern, however, have undergone restructuring. Cash flow from operating activities is positive despite large interest costs, yet not apparently large enough to pay all debts as they mature without the sale of long-term assets. On average, firms with this pattern are about half the size of the firms in Pattern Two, possibly because they have been selling assets to pay their debts. They have modest rates of growth and are highly leveraged.

Another 7 percent of the firms have cash flow Pattern Six (-,-,+): firms with shortfalls in cash flows from operating activities and from acquiring fixed assets financed by debt or equity. Consistent with our expectations, the data suggest that these are growth firms, using relatively high levels of debt and equity to finance their growth in anticipation of positive operating cash flows in the future.

The remaining 5 percent of the firms have cash flow patterns One, Five, Seven, or Eight. In Pattern One (+,+,+), a firm is using cash generated from operations, the sale of assets, and debt and/or equity financing to increase its cash position and liquidity. As indicated in Exhibit 1, firms with this cash flow pattern are relatively small and have negative rates of growth. They have the lowest debt-to-asset ratios and, despite the positive cash flow from operating activities, are not on average profitable.

Pattern Five (-,+,+) comprises firms whose negative cash flows from operations are being offset by proceeds from the sale of fixed assets and from borrowings. As shown in Exhibit 1, the borrowing and retention of cash provide moderate growth and mixed measures of profitability.

Pattern Seven (-,+,-) indicates a firm that finances operating cash flow shortages and payments of debt or dividends through the sale of fixed assets. As expected, firms in this category are not profitable (negative ROA). Given that firms in this pattern have the highest debt levels of all the patterns, they appear to have used debt to expand their assets, expecting profits and cash flows that were not realized. Thus, these firms are now selling long-term assets to meet their maturing debt obligations and operating shortfalls.

Firms showing Pattern Eight (-,-,-) clearly are in financial trouble. These firms are using their cash reserves to finance shortfalls in operations and pay long-term creditors and/or investors. As expected given their apparent financial woes, firms in this pattern have low asset growth and high debt-to-asset ratios, and on average they do not have profitable ROAs.

Exhibit 2 compares selected financial characteristics of firms with cash flow Pattern Two with those of firms with other cash flow patterns. The statistical significance is measured by a t-test. In Exhibit 2, the letter "S" signifies that the mean financial characteristic for firms with cash flow Pattern Two was statistically significantly different at the 5 percent confidence level from the mean financial characteristic of firms with other cash flow patterns. The letter "N" indicates that the means were not statistically significantly different at the 5 percent level. The small sample sizes for cash flow Patterns One, Five, and Eight reduce the power of t-tests involving those patterns, and therefore our ability to find significance in those circumstances is limited.

The results of the statistical tests show that the mean Return on Assets (ROA) for the firms in Pattern Two was significantly higher than for firms in all other cash flow patterns except Pattern One. Consistent with our expectations, firms in Pattern Two are generating such a high level of operating income and cash flow that they can pay off debtholders and shareholders as well as invest in property, plant, and equipment. This pattern identifies highly profitable operations as well as expectations of future profitability from the firm's investments.

The tests also reveal that the mean debt-to-asset ratio for firms in Pattern Two was significantly smaller than for firms in Patterns Three, Four, Six, and Seven. Consistent with our expectations about firms in Pattern Two, such firms' profitability and operating cash flow enable them to pay off debtholders, and at the same time expand their long-term assets without new debt financing.

Finally, the mean growth rate of assets for the firms in Pattern Two was significantly smaller than for firms with cash flow Patterns Four and Six. As is consistent with our expectations, firms in Patterns Four and Six are fast-growing firms, and require infusions of financing (debt and equity) to expand in order to generate positive operating income and cash flow. We believe that investors provide such infusions because they expect high growth and future profitability from those firms. The firms themselves must also believe in their potential profitability, to embark on large expansion of their long-term assets. By contrast, firms in Pattern Two are not growing as rapidly; they reflect their maturity by limiting new investments in long-term assets since they expect lower profitability, and by using excess operating cash flow to pay off debtholders and shareholders.

Limitations and Future Research

This approach to analyzing the Statement of Cash Flows, using patterns that reflect only the FASB-mandated rules for the classification of cash flows, may have limited usefulness for determining firms' underlying economic conditions. We considered only the sign of the net cash flow from each of the three major groupings (operating, investing, financing) of the SCF. Potentially useful information could be obtained by also considering the magnitudes of net cash flow associated with each grouping, as well as the relative amounts across groupings and changes in the signs and magnitudes of the amounts over time.

Potentially useful information could also be obtained by considering the details of the cash inflows and outflows within each grouping. For example, consider the added information that indicates a financing outflow to shareholders (for dividend or repurchase) paid for by issuing debt. Conceivably these two financing flows could offset exactly so that the net flow is zero; yet users of the SCF might find it very useful to learn that the dividend was debt-financed. The pattern-based approach obscures such information, which can be discerned clearly on the current FASB-mandated SCF.

Despite its inherent limitations, we believe that our pattern-based approach is a good "first pass" at analysis and is helpful by establishing which financial characteristics are likely to be exhibited by a firm with a given pattern. Richness and depth of analysis may come from considering magnitudes, relative magnitudes, and details within a pattern, as well as longitudinal changes in the patterns.

We believe that future research that considers these issues would refine the approach to predicting a firm's economic condition.

The second limitation of our pattern-based approach comes from the way in which the SCF reports information. Cash flows are classified as operating, investing or financing according to procedures appearing in FASB Statement 95. It may be argued that some cash flows could be classified more usefully and appropriately.

Specifically, we believe that the FASB-mandated classifications impose accrual-based classification concepts and definitions on cash flow transactions. Therefore, starting with net income, firms using the indirect approach to calculate net cash flow from operating activities add back non-cash expenses such as depreciation and amortization. For most capital-intensive businesses, depreciation is a major item; it is the allocated cost that represents the using up of property, plant, and equipment in operations. Arguably, the consumption of equipment might be considered a reduction of the equipment purchased, when reporting the net increase in investment. As the SCF currently is structured, a steel firm, for example, might have depreciation of $100,000,000 and a purchase of new plant and equipment of $1,000. If this were the only change in long-term assets (no plant or equipment is sold), the net cash flow from investing activities is negative. Therefore, in our pattern analysis this company would be considered as "expanding," when in reality it is consuming property plant and equipment and is shrinking its capacity. This suggests that both pattern analysis and the SCF itself could mislead users who focus only on the investing category.

Exhibit 3 shows the frequency count percentage of the sample firms with positive cash flows and negative cash flows for operating, investing, and financing groupings. Not surprisingly, given the SCF format and classification requirements, 88.36% of the firms have a positive net operating cash flow, and 88.94% have a negative net cash flow for investment. Thus, the add-back to net income of such items as depreciation expense will make it likely that even companies with significant losses will still report a positive operating cash flow. The proportion of firms with net cash outflow for investing is overwhelmingly larger than that of firms with net cash inflow from investing. This result is not surprising given the likelihood that firms are purchasing at least a few long-lived assets to replace

EXHIBIT 3 PERCENTAGES OF OBSERVED PATTERNS

	Positive(+)/Negative(-)
Cash Flow from Operations (One, Two, Three, Four) vs. (Five, Six, Seven, Eight)	88.36%/11.64%
Cash Flow from Investing (One, Three, Five, Seven) vs. (Two, Four, Six, Eight)	11.06%/88.94%
Cash Flow from Financing (One, Four, Five, Six) vs. (Two, Three, Seven, Eight)	43.5%/56.50%

those consumed in operations (as well as additional long-lived assets), and that the proceeds from the sale of long-lived assets are usually minor compared to their cost. Indeed, we believe that the FASB-mandated classification of depreciation on the SCF results in an artifact: the net outflow for investing overstates the number of firms actually expanding their long-lived assets.

As another example of FASB rules, Statement 95 requires that cash inflows of interest and dividends be classified as cash flows from operating activities. In reality, these cash inflows arise from the firm's investment in the debt and equity securities of other corporations (i.e., they are an investing activity). Thus, pattern analysis may not reflect reality if a positive net operating cash flow results from cash inflows of interest and dividends. Furthermore, the net cash flow for investment also may not reflect reality, since this amount might otherwise be positive instead of appearing as a negative amount on the statement.

Similarly, Statement No. 95 requires that interest payments on debt be classified as an operating cash outflow; yet in reality, they relate directly to debt financing (i.e., a financing activity). Again, the pattern analysis may not reflect reality if a significant component of operating cash flow is interest payment. At the extreme, a negative net cash flow from operations may otherwise be positive if the interest payment is reclassified as a cash outflow to a financing activity. Similarly, the sign of the financing flow would change from a positive to a negative in such a reclassification.

Finally, pattern-based analysis may incorrectly categorize a firm with significant non-cash transactions, since the FASB does not require that such non-cash transactions be disclosed in the body of the SCF. This exclusion from SCF disclosure may not affect our analysis if the transaction is a pure non-cash financing exchange (i.e., conversion of debt into equity), or alternatively a pure investing exchange (long-term assets exchanged for other long-term assets). However, our patterns may be affected if a non-cash financing/investing transaction, such as an exchange of a long-term note payable for acquisition of a building, has occurred. The numbers provided in the body of the SCF allow neither the non-cash inflow from financing nor the non-cash outflow for investing to be reflected in our patterns. Thus, including the effect of these non-cash transactions in analyzing the SCF patterns would produce a clearer picture of a firm's economic condition and behavior (contracting/expanding, etc.).

In summary, the problems we have examined here that limit the usefulness of the SCF point toward future research—a study comparing the classifications as the FASB currently mandates them with our proposed alternative classifications, to determine which approach provides more useful information. Future studies should also consider magnitudes of the net amounts of cash flows from operating, investing and financing groupings, and longitudinal changes in the patterns, as well as details within each grouping.

Conclusion

The format of the Statement of Cash Flows (SCF) dictated by FASB No. 95 provides a reasonably consistent basis for analyzing cash flows from operating, investing, and financing activities. One approach to the analysis of the SCF uses cash flow patterns based on the signs (positive or negative) of the firm's net cash flows from its operating, investing, and financing activities. There an eight possible patterns of these cash flows. Almost 46 percent of the 1,745 firms examined had cash flow pattern two (+,-,-). This pattern suggests mature, successful firms. Another 35 percent had cash flow pattern four (+,-,+), which is characteristic of growth firms. Slightly more than 7 percent had cash flow pattern three (+,+,-), which is associated with restructuring. Accordingly, the classification of firms by cash flow patterns provides another useful way of investigating a firm's economic condition. The insights gained by this analysis of the SCF also suggest an agenda for future research, as discussed in the prior section. As additional SCF data become available, changes in cash flow patterns and long-term trends may be examined.

References

1. J.L.G. Board and J.F.S. Day, "The Information Content of Cash Flow Figures," *Accounting and Business Research* (Winter 1989), pp. 3–11.
2. J.A. Gentry, P. Newbold, and D.T. Whitford, "Profiles of Cash Flow Components," *Financial Analysts Journal* (July–August 1990), pp. 41–48.
3. B.E. Gup and M.T. Dugan, "Cash Flow: The Tip of an Iceberg," *Business Horizons* (November/December 1988), pp. 47–50.
4. C.G.K. Weaver and S.B. Marshall, "Cash Flow Statements and Risk Evaluation," *Public Utilities Fortnightly* (February 15, 1990), pp. 16–20.

Appendix

Asset Size =	Total Assets (AT).
Asset Growth/5 years =	Compound growth rate of total assets for 5 years. $((AT_{1989}/AT_{1984})^{1/5} - 1) \times 100$
Internal Growth Rate =	ROE(1 − DVPOR/100) ROE = Return on Equity DVPOR = Dividend Payout Ratio: cash dividends on common stock divided by income before extraordinary items.
Dividend Growth Rate/5 years =	Compound growth rate of cash dividends for 5 years (CDV5).
Debt-To-Assets =	Total Debt (DT) divided by total assets (AT), then multiplied by 100. DT is the sum of long-term debt and debt in current liabilities.

ROA = Return on total assets. Income before extraordinary items divided by AT, then multiplied by 100.

ROE = Return on equity. Income before extraordinary items divided by common equity, then multiplied by 100.

These definitions are based on Standard and Poor's Compustat Services, Inc., COMPUSTAT PC PLUS.

Questions

1. The first equation below describes a company's balance sheet. Each succeeding equation is a modification of the one preceding it:

$$\text{Assets} = \text{Liabilities} + \text{Shareholder equity}$$

$$\text{Changes in assets} = \text{Changes in liabilities} + \text{Changes in shareholder equity}$$

$$\text{Changes in cash} + \text{Changes in assets other than cash} = \text{Changes in liabilities} + \text{Changes in shareholder equity}$$

$$\text{Changes in cash} = \text{Changes in liabilities} + \text{Changes in shareholder equity} - \text{Changes in assets other than cash}$$

$$\text{Increases in cash} = \text{Increases in liabilities} + \text{Increases in shareholder equity} + \text{Decreases in assets other than cash}$$

   a. Write the equation for *Decreases in cash*.

   b. Why is an understanding of the preceding equations important in the construction of a statement of cash flows?

   c. Suppose that over the past year a company's assets other than cash decreased \$1,000, shareholder equity increased \$2,000, and liabilities decreased \$3,000. What is the net effect of these changes on the company's cash balance? Explain.

2. A statement of cash flows classifies company activities into three categories: operating activities, investing activities, and financing activities. Place each of the following items into the proper category:

   - Proceeds from long-term debt issuance.
   - Acquisition of plant and equipment.
   - Increase in inventories.
   - Payment of dividends.
   - Earnings after taxes.

- Depreciation.
- Decrease in accounts receivable.
- Investment in another company.
- Payment of dividends.
- Issuance of common stock.

3. Identify the impact (increase or decrease) on cash of each item in Question 2.
4. Approximately 80 percent of the sample companies exhibit one or the other of the following patterns of cash flow:

Describe the financial characteristics of the companies exhibiting each pattern.

		Cash Flows from	
Patterns	**Operating**	**Investing**	**Financing**
Pattern Number 2	+	-	-
Pattern Number 4	+	-	+

5. Approximately 15 percent of the sample companies exhibit one or the other of the following patterns of cash flow:

Describe the financial characteristics of the companies exhibiting each pattern.

		Cash Flows from	
Patterns	**Operating**	**Investing**	**Financing**
Pattern Number 3	+	+	-
Pattern Number 6	-	-	+

6. Approximately 5 percent of the sample companies exhibit one or the other of the following patterns of cash flow:

Describe the financial characteristics of the companies exhibiting each pattern.

		Cash Flows from	
Patterns	**Operating**	**Investing**	**Financing**
Pattern Number 1	+	+	+
Pattern Number 5	-	+	+
Pattern Number 7	-	+	-
Pattern Number 8	-	-	-

7. The authors provide arguments for alternative classifications of the following cash-related transactions: (1) depreciation, (2) interest and dividends earned, and (3) interest payments. Compare and contrast the authors' alternative classifications with those mandated by FASB Statement 95.

Growth Industries: Another Look

CLAIRE STARRY AND NICK MCGAUGHEY

Because an industry's life cycle may include a stage of very rapid growth, many industries pass through a time when they are "growth industries." Rapid growth is often transitory; some of the top-growing industries today may quickly become slow-growing in a few years. Others may mature into large industries with stable but average growth. No industry has been able to maintain consistent high growth over an extended period of time.

Over the past decade, the authors have evaluated growth industries to understand patterns of growth and identify ways to predict future growth industries. This article updates a previous study published in *Business Horizons* (Starry and McGaughey 1988) by evaluating the fastest growing industries during the late 1980s and early 1990s and the ways that economic, technological, and international considerations will affect these and other growth industries through the remainder of the 1990s.

We define growth industries as industries that achieve exceptionally high rates of growth in sales volume over a five-year period. Although this assumption is somewhat arbitrary, we believe it helps to isolate industries that are rapidly growing—not just for a few months or a year, but over a longer period of time. Choosing a longer period—say, 10 to 20 years—would mask some of the interesting growth dynamics that occur because of regulation, technology, international trade, and other competitive factors. Because we use data published in *Forbes*, we will use its definition of industry, which excludes many of the smaller and emerging companies. Our statistical and quantitative analyses of industry performance are based on past performance. That is, we examine the growth industries of the past to gain insights into potential future growth industries.

At the time of this writing, Claire Starry was the president of IDS Economics in Menlo Park, CA, and Nick McGaughey was a managing director at APPLIED Information also in Menlo Park.

Source: Reprinted from *Business Horizons*, July–August 1993.

TABLE 1 THE FASTEST GROWING INDUSTRIES BY TIME PERIOD, 1982–1991

Industry	5-Year ROE	12-Month ROE	5-Year Sales	12-Month Sales	5-Year EPS	12-Month EPS
1987–1991						
Software	26.6	10.2	47.2	13.9	NM	-29.5
Retail, consumer electronics	14.1	11.6	33.1	15.7	NM	-30.0
Broadcasting and cable	DEF	DEF	29.1	8.0	NM	D-D
Environmental and waste	18.7	12.4	25.8	24.2	21.5	9.8
Retail, home improvement	11.9	7.8	25.3	11.8	NM	-26.1
Health care services	17.6	16.5	21.2	17.5	11.6	25.3
Movies	18.3	3.9	21.0	5.1	14.9	-89.1
Air freight	12.3	13.0	20.5	7.6	16.4	5.1
Retail, specialty	15.7	11.1	19.8	9.3	8.2	-5.2
Airlines	7.3	DEF	18.3	9.7	NM	P-D
1982–1986						
Health care services	24.7	11.4	32.5	19.2	24.4	-10.8
Recreational vehicles	18.5	8.5	28.0	-2.8	20.5	-24.8
Thrift institutions	15.8	17.9	23.8	9.5	NM	27.4
Brokerage houses	19.4	18.5	23.5	17.9	-5.9	11.3
Retailers—miscellaneous	18.8	14.7	22.0	12.9	17.9	2.3
Retail, consumer electronics	33.4	7.2	21.6	-4.1	NM	-33.9
Retailers—catalog showroom	10.0	DEF	20.1	-1.8	-14.3	P-D
Retailers—convenience stores	16.3	10.8	19.3	-0.7	11.3	-18.9
Life and health insurance	13.1	14.3	17.3	12.9	10.1	54.2
Retailers—apparel	18.3	13.9	15.2	10.2	10.8	19.9

Note: All figures are percentages.
D-D: deficit-to-deficit; P-D: profit-to-deficit; DEF:deficit; NM: not meaningful
SOURCE: *Forbes*, January 6, 1992 and January 12, 1987.

What Causes Growth?

Industry growth comes from a variety of sources. Examining growth industries over the past decade leads to several conclusions about causes of growth. Table 1 lists the ten fastest growing industries based on sales in two recent five-year periods, starting in 1982 and ending in 1991.

New Products and Technologies

It is clear the information age has come to fruition. The fastest growing industries include software (sales have increased 47 percent per year over this five-year period), consumer electronics, and broadcasting and cable television. The retailing industry has benefited as well: consumer electronics retailing is one of the top growth industries.

Changes in Regulations

Changing regulations have helped spur growth industries. Effects on industry growth patterns generally depend on the length of time the regulation is in effect or the time taken to complete its implementation successfully. Environmental regulations (for example, the Clean Air Act Amendments of 1990) have turned environmental and waste management into a growth industry.

Health care remains a growth industry, although it has fallen from first place during 1982–1986 to sixth place during 1987–1992. Much of the growth in health care comes through insurance and other means to reduce its cost to consumers below actual costs. If consumers begin paying a greater share of the health care dollar directly, some growth may be abated. Regulation of the industry may make additional changes to its structure and growth.

Changes in Preferences

As demographics change, so do consumer spending patterns. Because consumer spending makes up about two-thirds of final demand in the United States, consumer preferences exercise significant influence on industry growth. Home improvement, a cyclical phenomenon that arises during recessions, has recently demonstrated strong growth.

The desire and need to travel has boosted airline sales. Air travel increases proportionately faster than income; this should continue to be a growth area. Growth should be especially strong in international markets serving emerging countries. However, airline performance is highly cyclical; there will be good and bad periods that follow business cycles.

Changes in Business

Some industries grow because of changes in the way companies operate. In today's environment of corporate downsizing and corporate reengineering, many functions that were done internally are now being outsourced.

Industrial services are growing, perhaps because many companies are focusing on their business competencies and relying more on outside services than internal employees—for functions from payroll to janitorial services, logistics to maintenance.

Changes in World Markets

The United States is increasingly becoming integrated with world markets. This has intensified competition faced by U.S. companies in domestic markets and caused decline in some industries. However, ties to world markets have contributed to growth in other industries.

International trade, globalization of business, and just-in-time manufacturing techniques have helped keep the air freight industry sales expanding. The oil crises of the 1970s caused growth in petroleum products (because of price increases rather than volume increases), as well as leading to strong performances in mining and drilling activities and equipment.

How Long Can an Industry Be a Growth Industry?

Industries spurred by major changes in technologies that have widespread applications will tend to be on the list for a considerable period of time. Software exemplifies this phenomenon. Health care represents another industry that shows long-term growth. Growth has been supported by several factors, including the spread of health insurance, the aging population, new technologies, and greater concern for prolonging life. At least one of these trends, health insurance, may now be reversing itself. Government regulation of the health industry and a cost-conscious marketplace likely will have a negative impact on its growth.

Consumer preference changes also have a long-term effect on industry growth. As Americans become more affluent, and new technologies help to reduce production and distribution costs, many product and service areas enjoy a major growth spurt while the area's penetration rate grows from near zero to a long-term equilibrium. Consumer electronics supports this statement: most households now own one or more VCRs, and the percentage of households with computers and video games continues to grow.

It is noteworthy that a major shift has occurred in growth industries over the years covered in this study. For example, only two of the 1987–1991 growth industries overlap those of 1982–1986—health care and consumer electronics.

What Has Happened to Past Growth Industries?

Growth industries over the past two decades reflect changing economic conditions. In the mid-1970s, energy was the growth area, in response to a series of oil price shocks. Oil, gasoline, coal, electricity, and the equipment to support mining and exploration dominated the list of growth industries. Because energy problems continued into the early 1980s, many of these industries remained on the list; some, such as coal, were replaced with new growth industries.

Financial institutions boomed in the 1980s, with growth promoted by deregulation, leveraged buyouts, and heavy real estate investments. Health care and computers also made strong gains, but for different reasons. Expanding insurance coverage and government programs made health care more accessible to more people; new technologies promoted computer industry growth.

Consumer electronics, software, and health care dominate the list throughout the 1980s and into the 1990s. However, banking and financial industries now plagued by problems created by excessive growth and expansion during the 1980s have dropped off the list of growth industries. Specialty retailers remain, but the specialties change from period to period. Catalog sales provided the growth for retail markets a decade ago; now home improvement is strong, though indications are that sales are also dropping there.

Many industries fall on financial hard times after rapid growth, as did oil and gas exploration and financial industries. Still other growth industries seem to be momentary aberrations of market conditions that make a mature industry's sales grow rapidly and probably not too profitably (airlines and broadcasting are recent examples).

Are Growth Industries Profitable?

Which industries were profitable in 1987–1991? Table 2 lists the ten most profitable industries in terms of five-year return on equity. Of the ten industries listed in Table 1, only two (software and environmental and waste management) are among the most profitable. Established industries, such as pharmaceutical, tobacco, beverages, and specialty chemicals, are consistently among the most profitable, because companies in these industries are able to earn high returns on investment without relying on rapid industry growth.

Growth and profitability are not necessarily linked. However, some rapidly growing yet maturing industries, such as software, are able to maintain industry profitability. Can these industries remain profitable as sales begin to level off? Some will, others will not.

Are Growth Companies Always in Growth Industries?

Correlation exists between rapidly growing companies and rapidly growing industries. The ten fastest growing companies during 1987–1991 based on five-year sales growth are listed in Table 3. Three were in computers, one was in environmental consulting and management, and two were in distribution. Other fast growing companies were in apparel, business services, telecommunications, and life insurance.

TABLE 2 THE TEN MOST PROFITABLE INDUSTRIES, 1987–1991

Industry	5-Year ROE	12-Month ROE	5-Year Sales	12-Month Sales	5-Year EPS	12-Month EPS
Software	26.6	10.2	47.2	13.9	NM	-29.5
Drugs	22.3	29.2	11.4	12.4	16.2	19.0
Tobacco	20.6	14.8	14.1	16.1	14.9	16.3
Insurance, brokerage	20.5	18.1	10.3	7.7	8.1	-3.9
Apparel and shoes	20.1	13.7	14.0	7.8	14.1	12.0
Food processors	19.4	17.1	10.0	5.3	14.6	8.9
Environmental and waste	18.7	12.4	25.8	24.2	21.5	9.8
Chemicals, specialized	18.6	15.5	12.7	4.6	13.9	-0.4
Retail, apparel	18.4	13.8	16.2	9.2	2.0	-0.5
Electrical equipment	18.4	14.2	8.9	1.7	9.4	-37.1

Note: All figures are percentages.
NM: not meaningful
SOURCE: *Forbes*, January 6, 1992.

TABLE 3 THE TEN FASTEST GROWING COMPANIES, 1987–1991

Company	Industry	5-Year ROE	12-Month ROE	5-Year Sales	12-Month Sales	5-Year EPS	12-Month EPS
Vishay Intertech	Peripherals	18.5	13.3	653.4	2.2	21.0	-3.0
Office Depot	Specialty retail	11.8	7.5	162.1	108.0	NM	-16.7
Intelligent Electronics	Electronics	33.2	26.4	137.5	26.4	111.0	33.3
LA Gear	Apparel	61.3	DEF	136.2	-17.3	106.1	P-D
Conner Peripherals	Peripherals	47.8	20.6	132.0	39.8	80.8	7.9
First Financial Mgt.	Business services	15.5	14.2	102.2	22.2	43.9	23.7
McCaw Cellular	Telecommunications	DEF	DEF	89.1	44.4	NM	P-D
Oracle	Software	26.0	5.9	82.9	9.6	NM	-54.5
Conseco	Life insurance	43.1	53.6	82.1	68.7	65.6	191.6
ICF International	Environmental	29.3	DEF	81.5	25.9	8634.0	P-D

Note: All figures are precentages.
P-D: profit-to-deficit; DEF: deficit; NM: not meaningful
SOURCE: *Forbes*, January 6, 1992.

It is far easier for a company to grow rapidly if it is in an industry that is growing rapidly. Demand for a company's products in growing industries increases and competition for market share is less intense than in mature industries.

Are Profitable Companies Always in Profitable Industries?

Some correlation also exists between highly profitable companies and profitable industries (as measured by return on equity). Table 4 lists the ten most profitable companies based on five-year return on equity.

Many of these are in the top profitable industries (see Table 2). Specialty chemical and drug companies are especially prevalent among the list of profitable companies. Some very profitable companies, however, do not belong to especially profitable industries. An example is King World Products in broadcasting.

Profitable industries generally erect barriers to entry that prevent profits from eroding through widespread competition. Most of these industries are large or require heavy capital or research investments. Some growth industries can be very profitable in their early stages, but the entry of large numbers of new competitors quickly lowers average profits.

Can Companies Sustain Growth and Profitability?

Although industries appear unable to sustain rapid growth over prolonged periods, individual companies can. Table 5 shows the fastest growing and most profitable companies over the ten-year period covered in this article. Only one company (American Home Products) is listed in both time periods evaluated. The others were not able to adapt their business model. This list was composed from the 25 fastest growing companies and 25 most profitable companies during 1982–1986 and 1987–1991.

Why is difficult for companies to perform so well for long periods, especially when many of the most profitable performers are very large, established companies, such as Lockheed or General Mills? Growth on a percentage basis is harder to maintain as a company becomes large, so percentage growth rates naturally fall. Perhaps very high profitability, when everything goes right for several years, tends to be an aberration; problems will eventually emerge that reduce profitability.

What Industries Are Likely to Be the Best Performers in the 1990s?

A few industries have been identified as probable high performers in this decade. The spread of communications and information processing will help keep some of today's growth industries on top for the next five to seven years. Although the recent recession has taken a toll on computer and information industries, they still show signs of above-average to high growth. Computer hardware is

TABLE 4 THE TEN MOST PROFITABLE COMPANIES, 1987–1991

Company	Industry	5-Year ROE	12-Month ROE	5-Year Sales	12-Month Sales	5-Year EPS	12-Month EPS
Holly Corp.	Energy	68.3	49.1	8.9	11.6	NM	-51.0
Pulitzer Publishing	Publishing	66.0	16.3	7.8	-3.0	7.1	-56.3
King World Products	Broadcasting	65.7	61.5	26.3	4.9	40.7	10.7
Vigoro	Specialty chemicals	61.5	44.4	15.9	4.7	31.5	44.5
LA Gear	Apparel	61.3	DEF	136.2	-17.3	106.1	P-D
American Home Products	Drugs	60.6	49.7	5.2	1.0	NM	10.0
Sterling Chemicals	Specialty chemicals	59.9	34.0	NM	7.3	-20.3	-37.4
Georgia Gulf	Specialty chemicals	59.8	NE	13.4	-6.5	38.5	-54.7
Pamida Holdings	Discount retail	56.7	DEF	7.0	4.4	NM	P-D
General Mills	Food processing	52.3	42.6	8.8	9.6	24.2	21.7

Note: All figures are percentages.
P-D: profit-to-deficit; DEF: deficit; NE: negative equity; NM: not meaningful
SOURCE: *Forbes*, January 6, 1992.

TABLE 5 TOP COMPANY PERFORMERS BY TIME PERIOD, 1982–1991

Company	Industry	Qualified by ROE/Growth	1982–86	1987–91
Lockheed	Aerospace	ROE	X	
LA Gear	Apparel	Both		X
Liz Claiborne	Apparel	Both	X	
Nike	Apparel	Both	X	
Emerson Radio	Appliances	Growth	X	
ConAgra	Branded foods	Both	X	
King World Products	Broadcasting	ROE		X
First Financial Management	Business services	Growth		X
Georgia Gulf	Chemicals (specialty)	ROE		X
Sterling Chemicals	Chemicals (specialty)	ROE		X
Vigoro	Chemcials (specialty)	ROE		X
Apple Computer	Computers	Both	X	
Intergraph	Computers	Both	X	
SCI Systems	Computers	Growth	X	
Conner Peripherals	Computers/peripherals	Growth		X
Vishay Intertech	Computers/peripherals	Growth		X
Pamida Holdings	Discount retail	ROE		X
American Home Products	Drugs	ROE	X	X
Intelligent Electronics	Electronics	Growth		X
Tandy	Electronics	ROE	X	
Holly Corp.	Energy	ROE		X
ICF International	Environment	Growth		X
General Mills	Food processing	ROE		X
James River of VA	Forest products	Growth	X	
Conseco	Insurance (life/health)	Growth		X
Pulitzer Publishing	Publishing	ROE		X
Oracle	Software	Growth		X
Office Depot	Specialty retail	Growth		X
McCaw Cellular	Telecommunications	Growth		X
TIE/Communications	Telecommunications	Growth	X	
Coleco Industries	Toys/electronics	Both	X	
Hasbro	Toys/electronics	Growth	X	

Both = Top ROE and sales growth company
SOURCE: *Forbes*, January 6, 1992 and January 12, 1987.

likely to face tough competition and a slower growing market. Peripherals, including local area networks and international communications systems, should benefit from expanding applications.

Biotechnology may become a growth industry in the next five years. Commercial applications are becoming viable in health care and agriculture. New materials, such as composites, are evolving and finding more applications in the automotive and aerospace industries, among others.

Environmental management should continue to do well, especially as laws and regulations force governments, industries, and households to clean up.

Companies involved in hazardous material and waste removal will be in demand as more and more sites come under scrutiny.

Urban transportation faces many rough challenges in the 1990s. Highway congestion forces new construction and new alternatives (an increase in transit systems after many years of neglect), and the Clean Air Act Amendments of 1990 require significant reductions in emissions. To meet these reductions, oil companies and auto and truck manufacturers are developing new technologies to lower emissions.

Health care continues to be a growth industry, despite efforts to control costs. An aging population and new technologies that prolong life will add to health care expenditures, while cutbacks in funding from private and public entities may limit growth.

While outsourcing is not a specific industry, it is becoming prevalent in many industries and is covering many new areas. These new areas go beyond data processing, including order fulfillment, state tax reporting, and financial management. Responding to outsourcing should be a growing and profitable activity in the 1990s for companies able to maintain a low-cost position.

What Can Your Company Learn from Growth Industries?

Although growth is an important business consideration, the above analysis indicates that growth may be costly in terms of profitability and other similar measures of performance. Growth requires a commitment to change through technology or carefully identifying trends that will affect industry performance over the next few years.

Perhaps even more important than trying to become part of a growth industry is the ability of a company to position itself within its industry and structure its internal operations and management to become a top performer. The definition of "top performer" may be different in various companies, but some of the techniques for moving into this position are common across companies and industries.

How Can Companies Build and Defend Industry Leadership?

No firm is immune to the forces of marketplace competition. Nearly every industry has undergone dramatic shifts in competitive position over the past decade.

New competitors have demonstrated that clarity of purpose, along with an ability to engage every employee in the quest for competitive advantage, may be more critical to building long-term leadership than initial resource positions. Likewise, established firms fighting to maintain leadership have learned that long-held orthodoxies may be more dangerous than well-financed competitors.

Yet in the 1990s the battle will be not over incremental advantages in well-defined businesses. The struggle will be to create fundamentally new businesses, many of which are unimaginable at present. Recovering lost ground is not similar to staking out new industry territory. Firms that can do no more than imitate the existing advantages of faster moving competitors will surrender tomorrow's opportunities.

Pace-setting competitors are easily recognized. They exhibit many characteristics, including extraordinary depth of business knowledge and commitment, a focus on profitable gains in market share, relentless investing to support their goals, formalized total quality and customer satisfaction programs, a knowledge of the competition based on benchmarking, effective employee communications and involvement, and an operations strategy that competes on process and product and service designs.

Key trends are changing the rules for selling in nearly all industries. New information technologies are transforming the manner by which sellers sell and buyers buy. As a result, traditional strategies are steadily becoming less productive and cost-effective.

Increasing customer and user sophistication is changing the nature of typical customer-vendor relationships. Customers are demanding responsive, consultative value-added partnerships while eschewing conventional, transactional relationships. Buyers are reducing the number of approved vendors while demanding longer-lived contracts, shorter order cycles, more responsive service, and even *price* reductions.

The competitive environment is becoming increasingly more fluid in response to productivity pressures, new global competitors, and evolving corporate strategies. In turn, these changes will require increased flexibility in customer acquisition and retention.

Changing business strategies are forcing organizations to refocus resources dynamically, set new priorities, sell new products and services, and meet the demands of unfamiliar industries as boundaries become fuzzy. Evolving margin erosion is forcing organizations to focus their ever scarcer resources on more selectively chosen, high-potential industry segments.

Few firms become industry leaders by accident. Equally, there is no way to plan a five-to-seven-year campaign for industry leadership based on growth or profitability. Senior management must focus organizational attention on long-term leadership goals. Even in a world of impatient investors and increasing turbulence, consistency in vision and direction is a prerequisite for achieving industry leadership.

Launching a product or service may represent only the final mile of a skill-building marathon lasting many years. Today, there should be a race to build the capabilities that will form the basis of new business creation and product advantage in the future. Few firms are organized to win this long-term race. What is needed is an ability to conceive of the firm as a portfolio of capabilities and businesses.

The pace of change in many industries is so rapid today that industry boundaries and market segments are in a state of almost permanent stress. This represents an enormous threat to firms that are unable to challenge long-held assumptions about industry structure and business definition. This also provides an enormous opportunity to firms that can proactively reshape industry boundaries to their own advantage. Research has shown that fast-growth companies are superior at business definition (McGaughey 1993).

While top management spends a great deal of time on the task of resource allocation, it does not spend enough time determining how to achieve the maximum competitive impact from limited resources. It is the capacity for resource leverage that ultimately determines industry winners and losers. Strategy is not about making bigger bets than competitors, but about accomplishing more with less.

References

N. McGaughey. "Fast-Growing Companies: An Enabling Practices Study," manuscript submitted for publication, 1993.

C. Starry and N. McGaughey, "Growth Industries: Here Today, Gone Tomorrow," *Business Horizons*, July–August 1988, pp. 69–74.

Questions

1. Identify the five causes of growth in sales, as noted by the authors, and the industries benefiting from each.
2. "As Americans become more affluent, and new technologies help to reduce production and distribution costs, many product and service areas enjoy a major growth spurt while the area's penetration rate grows from near zero to a long-run equilibrium." Explain this statement.
3. Are industries with high growth rates also those with high levels of profitability? What evidence supports your answer?
4. Are companies with high growth rates from industries with high growth rates? What evidence supports your answer?
5. Are companies with high levels of profitability from industries with high levels of profitability? What evidence supports your answer?
6. In your opinion, which of the top company performers listed in Table 5 are likely to perform well in the 1990s? Explain.
7. What are some corporate strategies for building and defending a company's position in the marketplace?

How Much Growth Can Borrowers Sustain?

George W. Kester

The situation in which a borrower requests additional financing occurs all too frequently in commercial lending. It occurs for several reasons. One reason is improperly structured loans. The borrower has obtained loans in the form of 90-day notes to finance the permanent increases in working capital associated with sales growth.[1] Another reason is that even if a borrower's working capital is financed through long-term borrowings, continued growth in sales requires additional investments in working capital, thereby necessitating more loans.

Eventually, the need for additional loans creates a potentially dangerous situation of too much debt and too little equity. Either additional equity must be obtained or the borrower will have to reduce his or her rate of expansion to a level that can be sustained without an increase in financial leverage. Indeed, the bankruptcy courts are filled with cases of companies that have overreached themselves financially and expanded themselves right out of business.

My article addresses this problem by describing a method for evaluating how much growth a borrower can sustain. Such analysis is important for both borrowers and lenders since it determines the level of sales growth that is consistent with the realities of the company and the financial marketplace.

Sustainable Growth Rate

The sustainable growth rate (SGR) of a firm is the maximum rate of growth in sales that can be achieved, given the firm's profitability, asset utilization, and desired dividend payout and debt ratios. If actual sales growth exceeds the SGR, something must give. The firm must become more profitable, utilize its assets

---

At the time of this writing, George W. Kester was an associate professor of finance at Bucknell University, Lewisburg, PA.

[1] See George W. Kester and Thomas W. Bixler, "Why 90-Day Working Capital Loans Are Not Repaid on Time," *The Journal of Commercial Bank Lending*, August 1990, for a discussion of permanent and temporary working capital.

more efficiently, or reduce its dividend payout. Otherwise, the firm is faced with the choice of controlling (reducing) its sales expansion or obtaining additional external financing, either in the form of additional equity or debt exceeding the desired maximum debt ratio. The latter, of course, could lead to a problem loan situation.

To estimate a firm's SGR, a simple model is described based on the assumption that the future is the same as the past with respect to the firm's profitability and earnings retention ratio.

A Simple Model

In its simplest form, a firm's SGR is calculated by multiplying its return on equity by RR, its earnings retention ratio. This is shown in Equation 1.[2]

$$\text{SGR} = \frac{\text{Net Profit}}{\text{Beginning Equity}} \times \text{RR}$$

Equation 1

It is important to note that the firm's most recent year's net profit should be divided by its beginning equity—the equity balance at the beginning of the period over which the net profit was earned.

An Expanded Model

It is more instructive and analytically useful to expand Equation 1 to reflect the components of a firm's return on equity: asset turnover, profit margin, and financial leverage. See Equation 2.

$$\text{SGR} = \left[\left(\frac{\text{Sales}}{\text{Beginning Assets}}\right)\right] \left[\left(\frac{\text{Net Profit}}{\text{Sales}}\right)\right] \left[\left(1 + \frac{\text{Debt}}{\text{Equity}}\right)\right] \text{RR}$$

Equation 2

As an estimate of future sales growth, Equation 2 implicitly assumes that the firm's asset utilization, as measured by its sales-to-beginning-assets ratio, and its profit margin, as measured by its profit-to-sales ratio, will remain constant in the future. It is also assumed that the firm's leverage multiplier, as measured by 1 plus its debt-to-equity ratio, and its earnings retention ratio will remain constant in the future. It is also assumed that no new issues of equity are expected.

---

[2] This model is derived from a more elaborate model developed by Robert C. Higgins, "How Much Growth Can a Firm Afford?" *Financial Management*, Fall 1977. Also see Robert C. Higgins, "Sustainable Growth Under Inflation," *Financial Management*, Autumn 1981, and Dana J. Johnson, "The Behavior of Financial Structure and Sustainable Growth in an Inflationary Environment," *Financial Management*, Autumn 1981.

Based on these assumptions, Equations 1 and 2 calculate the maximum growth rate in sales that a firm can achieve in the future.

An Example

To illustrate the usefulness and application of the SGR concept, suppose that a company's abbreviated income statement and balance sheet data are as shown in Table 1. Based on these data, Table 2 shows the variables used to calculate the company's SGR.

With these data and variables, the sustainable growth rate using Equation 2 is 10%.[3]

$$SGR = \left[\left(\frac{\text{Sales}}{\text{Beginning Assets}}\right)\right]\left[\left(\frac{\text{Net Profit}}{\text{Sales}}\right)\right]\left[\left(1+\frac{\text{Debt}}{\text{Equity}}\right)\right] RR$$

$$SGR = [(1.33)\ (0.10)\ (1+0.50)]\ 0.50 = 10\%$$

TABLE 1 BALANCE SHEET AND INCOME STATEMENT DATA

	Year 1	Year 2
Total Assets	$3,000	$3,300
Total Liabilities	$1,000	$1,100
Stockholders' Equity	2,000	2,200
Total	$3,000	$3,300
Sales		$4,000
Net Profit		$400
Dividends		$200

TABLE 2 VARIABLES FOR SUSTAINABLE GROWTH RATE CALCULATION

Asset Utilization	
Sales/Beginning Assets = $4,000/$3,000 =	1.33
Profit Margin	
Net Profit/Sales = $400/$4,000 =	0.10
Financial Leverage	
Debt/Equity = $1,000/$2,000 =	0.50
Earnings Retention Ratio (RR)	
(1 - Dividend Payout) = (1 - $200/$400) =	0.50

[3] The same results also can be obtained by using Equation 1:

$$SGR = \frac{\text{Net Profit}}{\text{Beginning Equity}} \times RR \qquad SGR = \frac{\$400}{\$2{,}000} \times 0.50 = 10\%$$

Given the company's asset utilization, profit margin, financial leverage, and earnings retention ratio, the maximum sustainable rate of sales growth that the company can achieve is 10% per year. The result of sales growth of 10% in year 3 is shown in Table 3.

This example is based on the assumption that the company's current asset utilization, profit margin, financial leverage, and earnings retention ratio will remain constant in the future. Of course, this may not necessarily be the case. Equation 2 also can be used to evaluate the effects of changes in one or more of the input variables to the SGR model.

For example, assume that due to economies of scale (operating leverage), the company believes that its profit margin will increase to 12% in the future. Also, assume that its asset utilization is expected to improve, with the sales-to-assets ratio increasing to 1.50. If these improvements can indeed be achieved, holding financial leverage and the earnings retention ratio constant, the company's SGR will increase to 13.5%:

$$\text{SGR} = [(1.50)\,(0.12)\,(1 + 0.50)] \times 0.50 = 13.5\%$$

Let's assume, however, that due to expected demand for the company's products, management expects sales growth to be 25%, which exceeds its SGR of 13.5%. In this case, the company is faced with the choice of accepting a lower rate of sales growth, increasing the earnings retention ratio (reducing dividend payout), or obtaining additional external financing. Assume that management is willing to reduce dividends from 50 to 30% of net profit, increasing the earnings retention ratio to 70%. This will increase the SGR to 18.9%, which is still lower than the expected sales growth of 25%:

$$\text{SGR} = [(1.50)(0.12)(1 + 0.50)] \times 0.70 = 18.9\%$$

TABLE 3 **RESULT OF 10% SALES GROWTH IN YEAR 3**

Sales:	
Year 2 Sales × (1 + SGR) = $4,000 × (1.10) =	$4,400
Net Profit:	
Sales × Profit Margin = $4,400 × 0.10 =	$440
Earnings Retained:	
Net Profit × Earnings Retention Ratio = $440 × 0.50 =	$220
Assets:	
Year 2 Assets × (1 + SGR) = $3,300 × 1.10 =	$3,630
Shareholders' Equity:	
Year 2 Equity + Earnings Retained = $2,200 + $220 =	$2,420
Liabilities:	
Equity × (Debt/Equity Ratio) = $2,420 × 0.50 =	$1,210
Total Debt & Equity	$3,630
Asset Utilization:	
Sales/Year 2 Assets = $4,400/$3,300	1.33

This leaves only two alternatives: Accept a lower growth rate in sales or obtain additional financing. If management is unwilling to accept a lower rate of sales growth and if additional equity is not feasible or desirable, the only alternative left to the firm is to overextend itself by obtaining debt exceeding its desired maximum debt-to-equity ratio, which may be unacceptable to the company's management or lenders. How much must the debt-to-equity ratio increase to support the expected sales growth rate of 25%?

Solving for Other Variables

To answer this question, Equation 2 can be rearranged to solve for the required debt-to-equity ratio needed to achieve a target SGR, assuming no changes in the firm's asset utilization, profit margin, and earnings retention ratio (Equation 3).

$$\text{Required Debt-to-Equity Ratio} = \left[\frac{\text{Target SGR}}{\left(\frac{\text{Sales}}{\text{Beginning Assets}}\right)\left(\frac{\text{Net Profit}}{\text{Sales}}\right)\text{RR}}\right] - 1$$

Equation 3

Continuing my example, the company's debt-to-equity ratio must increase from 0.50 to 0.98 in order for the company to achieve the expanded sales growth rate of 25%:

$$\text{Required Debt-to-Equity Ratio} = \left[\frac{0.25}{(1.50)\,(0.12)\,(0.70)}\right] - 1 = 0.98$$

This can be shown by recalculating the company's SGR using Equation 2:

$$\text{SGR} = [(1.50)\,(0.12)\,(1 + 0.98)\,] \times 0.70 = 25\%$$

Of course, a debt-to-equity ratio of 0.98 may not be acceptable to either the company's management or its lenders, in which case other alternatives must be explored. These alternatives include the often hard-to-swallow prospect that the expected sales growth simply cannot be achieved.

Equation 2 also can be rearranged to solve for the other variables in the SGR model, given a target SGR. Equation 4 calculates the asset utilization needed to achieve a target SGR, assuming no changes in the other variables.

$$\text{Required Asset Utilization} = \frac{\text{Target SGR}}{\left[\left(\frac{\text{Net Profit}}{\text{Sales}}\right)\left(1 + \frac{\text{Debt}}{\text{Equity}}\right)\right]\text{RR}}$$

Equation 4

Equation 5 calculates the profit margin required to achieve a target SGR, assuming no changes in the other variables.

Required Profit Margin =

$$\frac{\text{Target SGR}}{\left[\left(\frac{\text{Sales}}{\text{Beginning Assets}}\right)\left(1 + \frac{\text{Debt}}{\text{Equity}}\right)\right] \text{RR}}$$

Equation 5

And, finally, Equation 6 calculates the earnings retention ratio required to achieve the target SGR, assuming no changes in the other variables.

Required Earnings Retention Ratio =

$$\frac{\text{Target SGR}}{\left[\left(\frac{\text{Sales}}{\text{Beginning Assets}}\right)\left(\frac{\text{Net Profit}}{\text{Sales}}\right)\left(1 + \frac{\text{Debt}}{\text{Equity}}\right)\right]}$$

Equation 6

Returning to my example, assume that the required debt-to-equity ratio of 0.98 is indeed unacceptable. What level of earnings must be retained for the company to achieve the expected sales growth rate of 25%, assuming the debt-to-equity ratio remains at its current level of 0.50? The earnings retention ratio in Equation 6 must be increased to 92.6%.

Required Earnings Retention Ratio =

$$\frac{0.25}{[(1.50)(0.12)(1 + 0.50)]} = 0.926$$

This can also be shown by recalculating the company's SGR using Equation 2:

$$\text{SGR} = [(1.50)(0.12)(1 + 0.50)] \times 0.926 = 25\%$$

A Graphic Presentation

Extending the well-known Du Pont chart method of breaking a ratio into its various components, the illustration on page 425 shows a graphic depiction of the SGR model reflected in Equation 2. This chart demonstrates the effects that various policies and decisions are likely to have on a firm's SGR.

For example, the effects of improving asset turnover can easily be traced through the chart to the likely impact on SGR, thus highlighting the importance of effective cash, receivables, and inventory management and the efficient

Sustainable Growth Rate

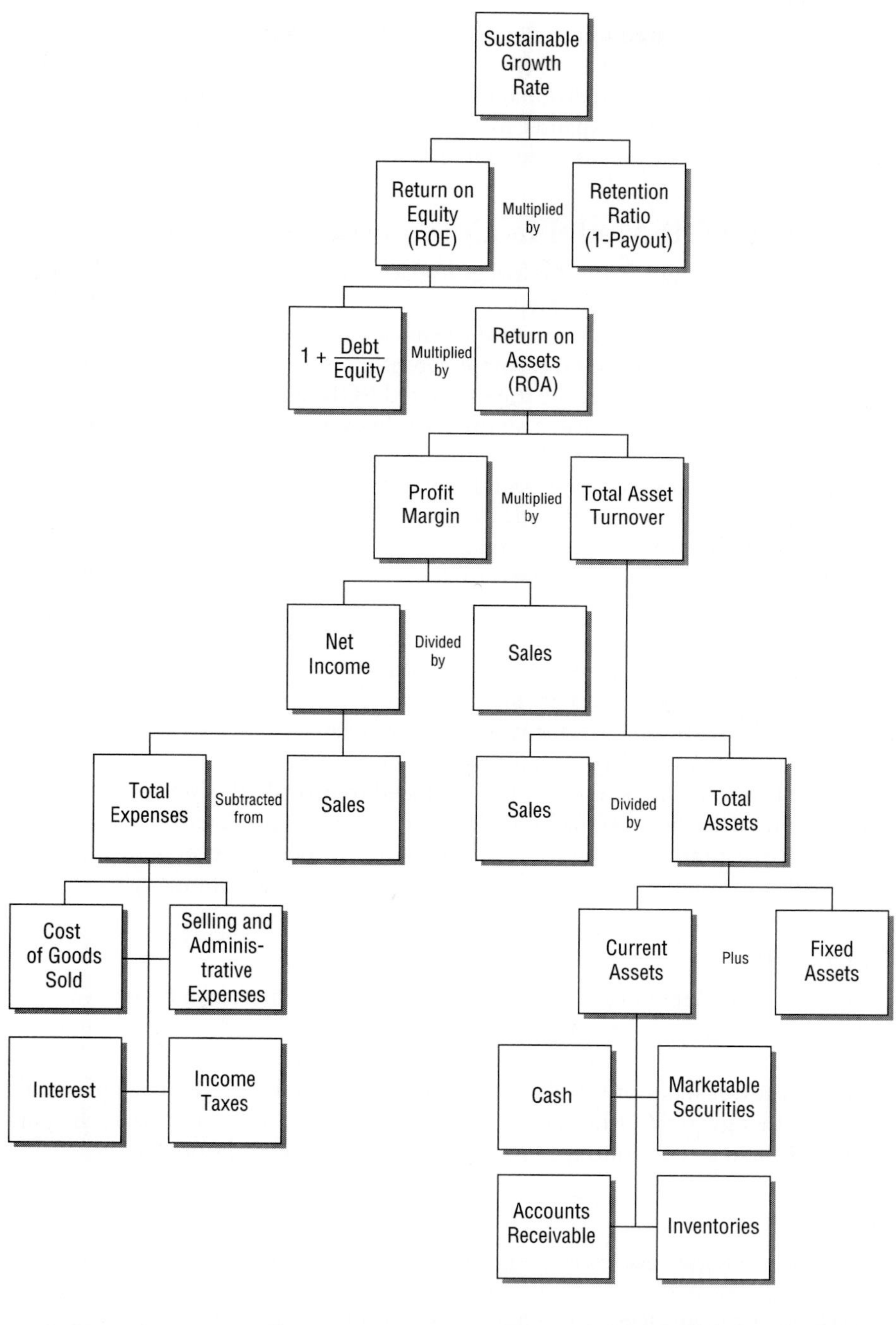

utilization of fixed assets. Similarly, the effect of a change in the dividend payout ratio or improved profitability through greater expense control can be traced through the chart.

It should be pointed out, however, that changes in one variable may affect one or more variables included in the model. For example, tighter control of receivables may result in additional expenses as well as a decline in sales. Or an increase in fixed assets to expand capacity, which initially reduces asset turnover, may increase a firm's expected sales and profits.

Using the SGR Model in Commercial Lending

As should be apparent from the foregoing straightforward examples, the SGR model is simple to use and provides an estimate of the level of sales growth a borrower can achieve, given his or her current or expected asset utilization, profitability, financial leverage, and earnings retention ratio. To the extent that actual or planned sales growth exceeds the estimated SGR, a potential problem loan is in the making. At a minimum, a significant divergence between expected sales growth and the estimated SGR should serve as a warning signal to lenders, prompting further investigation and discussions with the borrower.

Using the SGR model provides a convenient means for checking the consistency of the borrower's growth plans. Borrowers often desire the best of all worlds: high sales growth, low levels of debt, and high dividends. As is often the case, however, these objectives may be inconsistent with each other. And it is certainly better to recognize these inconsistencies before the fact rather than after.

Also, as illustrated, the SGR model and its variations provide a convenient method of performing sensitivity analysis on the key variables that affect a company's sales growth. What improvements are necessary in the company's asset utilization or profitability to achieve the desired or expected level of sales growth? How much must dividends be reduced to provide the internal resources needed to finance the growth? What level of debt is required, and is it acceptable to the borrower and its lenders? Can the expected or desired level of sales growth be realistically attained, given the constraints placed on the company?

Conclusion

In short, the SGR model can be a valuable tool for commercial lenders in assessing their borrower's ability to plan for and manage growth in a financially sound manner. Lenders must be comfortable that their borrowers understand that a business cannot just continue to expand without making adequate plans for financing that growth. Otherwise, borrowers and lenders are faced with the perpetual problem of continuous requests for renewals and additional loans.

Questions

1. "... even if a borrower's working capital is financed through long-term borrowings, continued growth in sales requires additional investments in working capital, thereby necessitating more loans." Explain the meaning of this statement.

2. An alternative to the debt-equity ratio is the equity multiplier—total assets divided by equity. Show the mathematical relationship between the equity multiplier and the debt-equity ratio.

3. The extended Du Pont model expresses return on equity (ROE) in terms of total asset turnover (TATO), profit margin (PM), and equity multiplier (EM; or one plus the debt-equity ratio):

$$\text{ROE} = \text{TATO} \times \text{PM} \times \text{EM}$$

Show that this equation holds true.

4. Templeton University currently has a $100 million endowment fund invested in common stock on which the fund manager expects to earn 12 percent per year. The endowment fund contributes 6 percent of the endowment each year for payment of University expenses. For example, the fund's contribution will be $6 million at the end of next year.

   a. Complete the following table describing the expected contribution and endowment value for each of the next three years (in millions):

(1) Year	(2) **Beginning Balance**	(2) x 12% = (3) **Dollar Return**	(2) + (3) = (4) **Ending Balance**	(5) **Cash Contribution**	(4) - (5) = (6) **Remaining Investment**
1	$100	$12	$112	$6	$106
2	106	______	______	______	______
3	______	______	______	______	______

   b. In view of the annual cash contribution to T.U., what is the annual growth rate of the endowment fund expected by the manager? Explain.

   c. Calculate the endowment fund's expected sustainable growth rate (SGR) as indicated by Equation 1. (*Hint:* The rate should be the same as that calculated in Part *b.*)

5. Stonewell Manufacturing Inc.'s (SMI) abbreviated balance sheet data and income statement are provided below:

	19X7	**19X8**
Total assets	$ 4,500	$ 5,040
Total liabilities	2,250	2,520
Stockholders' equity	2,250	2,520
Total	$ 4,500	$ 5,040
Sales		$ 9,000
Net income		450
Dividends		180

   a. Calculate SMI's sustainable growth rate (SGR) using Equation 2. Explain the meaning of your answer.

   b. Assume that sales grow at the rate calculated in Part *a*. Now calculate the following items for 19X9: sales, net income, earnings retained, total assets, stockholders' equity, and total liabilities. Also calculate total asset turnover based on 19X9 sales and 19X8 total assets. (*Hint:* You should get 2.0, the same answer as that for the preceding year.)

c. Suppose SMI's CEO wants to achieve an SGR of 30 percent and is willing to cut dividends to zero but is unwilling to issue additional stock. Holding other variables constant, calculate the required debt-equity ratio necessary to achieve the CEO's objective. (Check your answer using Equation 2.)

d. Suppose SMI's CEO is unwilling to increase the debt-equity ratio and to issue additional stock but is willing to cut dividends to zero. Holding other variables constant, calculate the required profit margin to achieve an SGR of 30 percent. (Check your answer using Equation 2.)

e. Return to the original conditions in Part *a* and summarize qualitatively the ways to increase SGR. (No calculations are necessary.)

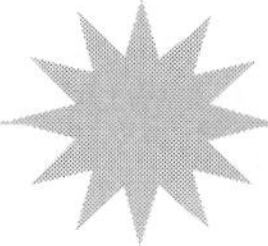

Why Borrowers Become Profit Rich and Cash Poor

George W. Kester

Why do borrowers become profit rich and cash poor? After all, doesn't sales growth mean more profits, which means more cash? Not necessarily. This may be an accurate statement for service firms that operate on a cash basis. However, for manufacturing, retail, and wholesale firms, the additional net working capital required to support sales growth often exceeds profits. This results in a continuing need for cash until sales growth slows down or levels out. Indeed, from the viewpoint of cash flow, an optimistic sales forecast is often a pessimistic cash flow forecast.

This normal consequence of growth needs to be understood and anticipated by both borrowers and lenders. Commercial loan workout departments (as well as bankruptcy courts) are filled with cases of borrowers who have underestimated their financing requirements and expanded themselves into severe financial problems.

My article demonstrates why firms become profit rich and cash poor and how a firm can become *less* cash poor through effective management of cash, accounts receivable, inventory, and accounts payable.

Application of Methodology

How a company becomes profit rich and cash poor can be illustrated with a relatively straightforward example. Assume that a new firm, Blue Ridge Bicycle Company (BRBC), has been organized to manufacture and market specialty all-terrain fitness bicycles. The forecasted sales and profits for BRBC for 1993 to 1999 are shown in Figure 1.

As reflected in Figure 1 data, the firm's profit margin is expected to benefit from economics of scale, increasing from 5% in 1993 to 8% by 1998 and 1999, when sales growth is expected to level out.

At the time of this writing, George W. Kester was an associate professor of finance at Bucknell University, Lewisburg, PA.

FIGURE 1 FORECASTED SALES AND PROFITS ($000S)

Year	Sales $	Sales Growth %	Profit Margin %	Profit $
1993	500		5	25
1994	1,000	100	5	50
1995	1,500	50	6	90
1996	2,000	33	6	120
1997	2,500	25	7	175
1998	2,750	10	8	220
1999	2,750	0	8	220

To focus on the relationships of sales growth, profits, and net working capital, let's ignore depreciation and fixed-asset expenditures. Assume that the firm will maintain an average cash balance of 2.8% sales and an average accounts receivable balance of 35 days sales (9.7% of sales). Suppose further that the firm's average inventory balance will be 75 days cost of goods sold (20.8% of cost of goods sold). Assuming that cost of goods sold will be 80% of sales, inventory will be 16.7% of sales. Also, suppose that the firm's average accounts payable balance will be 30 days purchases (8.3% of purchases). Assuming that purchases will be 50% of sales, accounts payable will be 4.2% of sales. As shown in Figure 2, the firm's investment in net working capital will be 25% of sales.

Expressing net working capital as a percent of sales provides a convenient way to estimate the net working capital required to support different sales levels. For example, in 1993, BRBC's sales are forecasted to be $500,000. Therefore, the dollar investment in net working capital will be $125,000 ($500,000 ×0.25). In 1994, sales are expected to increase to $ 1 million. The corresponding investment in net working capital will therefore increase to $250,000 ($1 million × 0.25).

To the extent that profit in 1994 is insufficient to finance the $125,000 increase in net working capital (and other investments associated with the 100% sales growth), the firm has to obtain external financing, either as debt or equity. In other words, the firm will become profit rich and cash poor!

The forecasted sales, profits, and net working capital requirements of BRBC for the seven-year period of 1993 to 1999 are shown in Figure 3. Included are the differences between forecasted profits and the investments in net working capital required to support each year's sales growth.

For each of the years 1993 to 1996, profits are insufficient to finance the investments (change) in net working capital. On a cumulative basis, the investments in net working capital exceed profits until 1999, the last forecasted year. All else remaining constant, the differences shown in Figure 3, when negative, represent the amounts of financing required to support BRBC's forecasted sales growth.

The required financing, which is also shown in Figure 4, reaches a peak of $215,000 in 1996. If it is obtained in the form of loans, repayment cannot

FIGURE 2 NET WORKING CAPITAL REQUIREMENTS

	Percent of Sales
Cash	2.8
Accounts Receivable	9.7
Inventory	16.7
Current Assets	29.2
Less: Accounts Payable	(4.2)
Net Working Capital	25.0

FIGURE 3 FORECASTED SALES, PROFITS, AND NET WORKING CAPITAL ($000s)

	1993	1994	1995	1996	1997	1998	1999
Sales	500	1,000	1,500	2,000	2,500	2,750	2,750
Net Working Capital @25%	125	250	375	500	625	688	688
Profit	25	50	90	120	175	220	220
– Change in Net Working Capital	125	125	125	125	125	63	0
Difference	-100	-75	-35	-5	50	157	220
Cumulative Difference	-100	-175	-210	-215	-165	-8	212

FIGURE 4 REQUIRED FINANCING

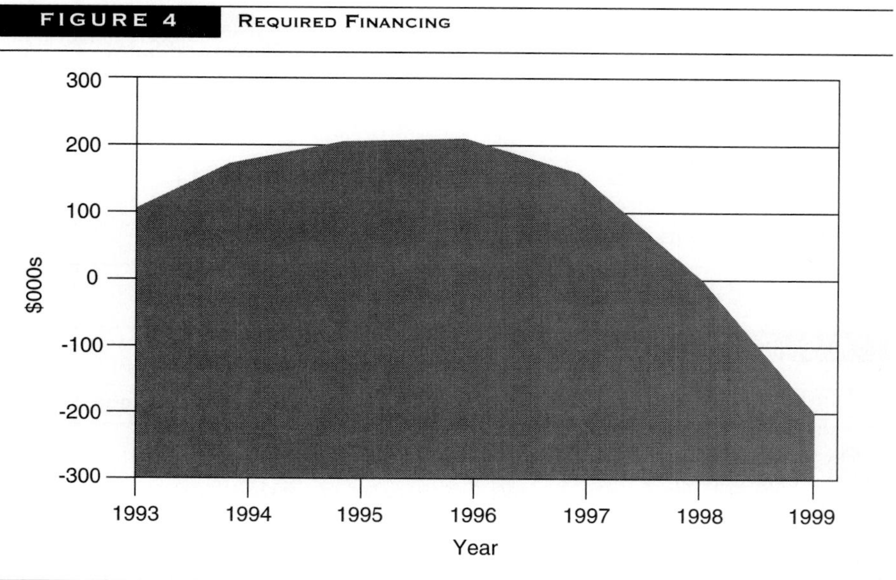

begin until 1997, when profits begin to exceed the investment in net working capital. Sales are not forecasted to increase during 1999; hence, there is no additional investment in net working capital. The firm has reached the status of a cash cow.

It should be clear from the data presented in Figures 3 and 4 that until sales and net working capital growth slow down or level out, loan repayment cannot be reasonably expected. Unfortunately, many lenders prefer to see periodic payments of principal (in addition to interest) on a regular basis for long-term financing. This is counterproductive to the objective of working capital financing since loan repayments drain the borrower's cash at the very time when the borrower desperately needs it.

Importance of Effective Working Capital Management

This methodology provides a convenient framework for using sensitivity analysis to illustrate the importance of effective working capital management. In the preceding example, 25% of every sales dollar is invested in net working capital. What if management's forecast of the average collection period of 35 days sales (9.7% of sales) turns out to be optimistic? For example, what if the average accounts receivable balance turns out to be 42 days sales (11.7% of sales)? As shown in Figure 5, net working capital would increase to 27% of sales, and, as shown in Figures 6 and 7, BRBC's financing requirements would increase from $215,000 to $255,000. The firm would be profit rich and *more* cash poor!

FIGURE 5 NET WORKING CAPITAL REQUIREMENTS: ACCOUNTS RECEIVABLE = 42 DAYS SALES

	Percent of Sales
Cash	2.8
Accounts Receivable	11.7
Inventory	16.7
Current Assets	31.2
Less: Accounts Payable	(4.2)
Net Working Capital	27.0

FIGURE 6 FORECASTED SALES, PROFITS, AND NET WORKING CAPITAL ($000S): ACCOUNTS RECEIVABLE = 42 DAYS SALES

	1993	1994	1995	1996	1997	1998	1999
Sales	500	1,000	1,500	2,000	2,500	2,750	2,750
Net Working Capital @27%	135	270	405	540	675	742	742
Profit	25	50	90	120	175	220	220
– Change in Net Working Capital	135	135	135	135	135	67	0
Difference	-110	-85	-45	-15	40	153	220
Cumulative Difference	-110	-195	-240	-255	-215	-62	158

REQUIRED FINANCING

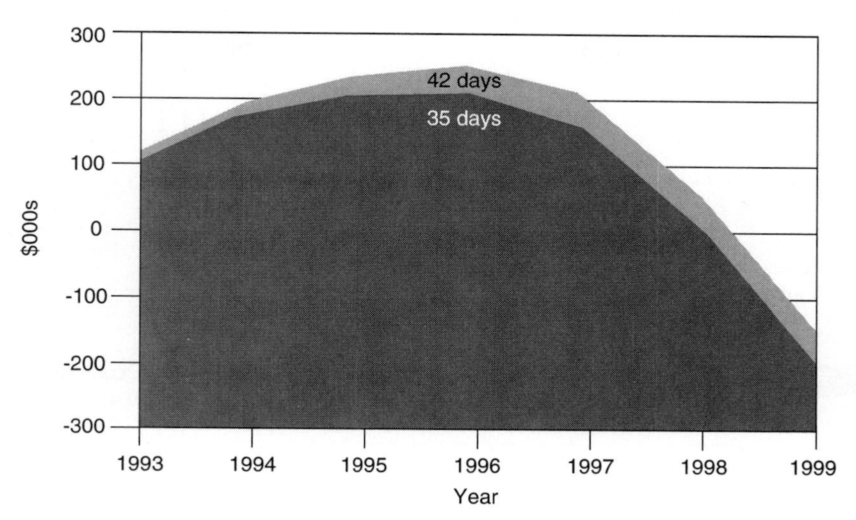

Becoming Profit Rich and Less *Cash Poor*

How can a firm become profit rich and *less* cash poor? As suggested by our example, the firm can reduce its sales growth, increase its profit margin, or reduce its net working capital investment in relation to sales. To again focus on net working capital, suppose that management is unwilling to reduce the firm's sales growth and is unable to increase its profit margin significantly. This leaves a reduction in net working capital as the last option.

A firm's net working capital can be reduced through more effective cash, accounts receivable, and inventory management, or through greater reliance on ("stretching") trade credit. To illustrate, what if BRBC were able to reduce its accounts receivable collection period from the originally assumed 35 days sales to 25 days sales (from 9.7% to 6.9% of sales). This would reduce the firm's net working capital from the originally assumed 25% of sales to 22.2% of sales and, as shown in Figure 8, the peak financing requirement to $168,000.

In addition to the reduction in accounts receivable, suppose BRBC is able to reduce inventory from 75 days to 60 days cost of goods sold (from 16.7% to 13.3% of sales, assuming again that cost of goods sold is 80% of sales). This would further reduce the firm's net working capital to 18.8% of sales, and as shown in Figure 9, the peak financing requirement to $117,000.

And, finally, suppose that accounts payable is stretched from 30 days to 40 days purchases (from 4.2% to 5.6% of sales, assuming purchases are 50% of sales). This increased reliance on trade credit would further reduce the firm's net working capital to 17.4% of sales and, as shown in Figure 10, the peak financing requirement would drop from $117,000 to $99,000.

FIGURE 8 FORECASTED SALES, PROFITS, AND NET WORKING CAPITAL ($000s): ACCOUNTS RECEIVABLE = 25 DAYS SALES

	1993	1994	1995	1996	1997	1998	1999
Sales	500	1,000	1,500	2,000	2,500	2,750	2,750
Net Working Capital @22.2%	111	222	333	444	555	610	610
Profit	25	50	90	120	175	220	220
– Change in Net Working Capital	111	111	111	111	111	55	0
Difference	-86	-61	-21	9	64	165	220
Cumulative Difference	-86	-147	-168	-159	-95	70	290

FIGURE 9 FORECASTED SALES, PROFITS, AND NET WORKING CAPITAL ($000s): ACCOUNTS RECEIVABLE = 25 DAYS SALES; INVENTORIES = 60 DAYS COST OF GOODS SOLD

	1993	1994	1995	1996	1997	1998	1999
Sales	500	1,000	1,500	2,000	2,500	2,750	2,750
Net Working Capital @18.8%	94	188	282	376	470	517	517
Profit	25	50	90	120	175	220	220
– Change in Net Working Capital	94	94	94	94	94	47	0
Difference	-69	-44	-4	26	81	173	220
Cumulative Difference	-69	-113	-117	-91	-10	163	383

FIGURE 10 FORECASTED SALES, PROFITS, AND NET WORKING CAPITAL ($000s): ACCOUNTS RECEIVABLE = 25 DAYS SALES; INVENTORIES = 60 DAYS COST OF GOODS SOLD; ACCOUNTS PAYABLE = 40 DAYS PURCHASES

	1993	1994	1995	1996	1997	1998	1999
Sales	500	1,000	1,500	2,000	2,500	2,750	2,750
Net Working Capital @17.4%	87	174	261	348	435	478	478
Profit	25	50	90	120	175	220	220
– Change in Net Working Capital	87	87	87	87	87	43	0
Difference	-62	-37	3	33	88	177	220
Cumulative Difference	-62	-99	-96	-63	25	202	422

The cumulative effects of each of these changes on BRBC's required financing is shown graphically in Figure 11. Even with these more optimistic assumptions regarding accounts receivable and inventory, along with increased reliance

FIGURE 11 REQUIRED FINANCING

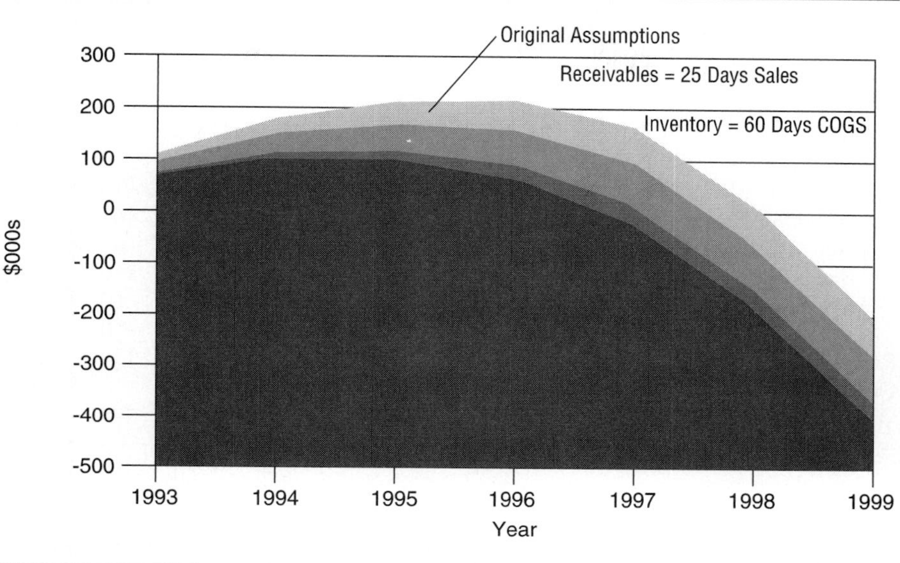

on trade credit, the firm will still be profit rich and cash poor, albeit less so than under the original assumptions.

Expanded Example

So far our example has focused on the relationships among sales growth, profits, and net working capital. Depreciation and other noncash charges, fixed-asset expenditures, repayment of existing debt, dividends, and other changes in cash flow have been ignored. However, our example easily can be expanded to reflect a more complete picture of BRBC's financing requirements.

To illustrate, Figure 12 shows an expanded analysis of the firm's cash flow based on the original assumptions regarding net working capital along with assumed amounts for depreciation, fixed-asset expenditures, debt repayment, and dividends. The excess cash flow, when negative, represents BRBC's need for external financing. The required financing reaches a peak of $730,000 in 1996. Again, if obtained in the form of loans, repayment cannot begin until 1997, when BRBC's excess cash flow is forecasted to turn positive.

Conclusion

How can a firm avoid becoming profit rich and cash poor? From the foregoing example, the solution is obvious. Maintain as little cash as possible, do not sell on credit, manufacture (or purchase) only to order, stretch trade credit to the limit, and, by all means, avoid sales growth.

FIGURE 12 REQUIRED FINANCING: EXPANDED ANALYSIS ($000S)

	1993	1994	1995	1996	1997	1998	1999
Sales	500	1,000	1,500	2,000	2,500	2,750	2,750
Net Working Capital @25%	125	250	375	500	625	688	688
Profit	25	50	90	120	175	220	220
+ Depreciation	50	50	50	75	75	75	75
– Change in Net Working Capital	125	125	125	125	125	63	0
– Fixed-Asset Expenditures	0	0	0	500	0	0	0
– Debt Repayment	60	60	60	60	60	60	60
– Dividends	0	0	0	0	0	0	0
Excess Cash Flow	-110	-85	-45	-490	65	172	235
Cumulative Excess Cash Flow	-110	-195	-240	-730	-665	-493	-258

Unfortunately, this solution is neither feasible nor desirable for most firms. The fact is that the net working capital requirements of most manufacturers, retailers, and wholesalers are such that sales growth often results in cash shortages. The more rapid the sales growth, the more severe the problem.[1] As a result, borrowers and lenders are faced with continuous requests for renewals and additional loans.

Understanding how a firm can become profit rich and cash poor can lead to more appropriate loan structuring. Detailed financial projections are needed to estimate the amount and timing of the borrower's financing requirements and subsequent repayment ability. Such an analysis of rapidly growing firms reveals the borrower's inability to make principal payments during the growth period and indicates that a revolving credit arrangement would be an appropriate loan structure. And it is certainly better to recognize this before the fact rather than after. At the very least, continuous requests for renewals and additional loans will not come as total surprises.

Questions

1. "Why do borrowers become profit rich and cash poor? After all, doesn't sales growth mean more profits, which means more cash?" Explain.
2. Show that each of the following relationships is true (assume 1 year = 360 days):
   a. An average accounts receivable balance of 35 days sales is equivalent to 9.7 percent of annual sales.

[1] George W. Kester, "How Much Growth Can Borrowers Sustain?" *The Journal of Commercial Bank Lending*, June 1991, pp. 53–60, provides a detailed discussion of the maximum rate of growth in sales that can be achieved, given a firm's profitability, asset utilization, divided payout, and financial leverage.

b. An average inventory balance of 75 days cost of goods sold is equivalent to 20.8 percent of annual cost of goods sold.

c. If cost of goods sold equals 80 percent of sales, then the inventory balance in Part *b* is 16.7 percent (rounded up) of annual sales.

d. An average accounts payable balance of 30 days purchases is equivalent to 8.3 percent of annual purchases.

e. If the purchases in Part *d* equal 50 percent of annual sales, then accounts payable is 4.2 percent of annual sales.

3. Explain the derivation of the numbers in Figure 3 and their managerial implication.
4. Compare and contrast Figure 6 with Figure 8. What is the managerial implication of the two Figures?
5. Compare and contrast Figure 9 with Figure 10. What is the managerial implication of the two Figures?
6. Rework Figure 3 using the following assumptions:
   - Average cash balance = 2.0 percent of sales.
   - Accounts receivable = 25 days sales.
   - Inventories = 45 days cost of goods sold.
   - Accounts payable = 40 days purchases.

   What is the managerial implication of the reworked Figure?

PART
VI

Institutional Features of Long-Term Financing

Corporate Securities

Dividend Policy

The Truth about Junk Bonds

SEAN BECKETTI

Junk bonds have been a common element in some of the country's worst financial wrecks this year. The Campeau retailing conglomerate collapsed in January under a heavy debt burden, much of it junk bonds. First Executive Corporation, one of the nation's largest insurance companies, announced a fourth-quarter 1989 loss of $859 million on its junk bond holdings. And Drexel, Burnham, Lambert, the investment bank responsible for the growth of the junk bond market, filed for bankruptcy in February 1990.

These corporate casualties are only the most recent of the problems blamed on junk bonds. For years, some critics have claimed junk bonds are responsible for a host of broader financial market ills. According to these critics, junk bonds fueled the merger mania of the 1980s, caused the rapid growth in the level of corporate debt in recent years, and more generally increased financial market volatility.

If these serious charges are accurate, it may be time for laws or regulations to restrict the use of junk bonds. But if the charges are not accurate, restricting the use of junk bonds would unnecessarily increase the cost of funds for many businesses.

The truth is that the evidence does not support these extreme charges against junk bonds. To be sure, there may be other concerns about junk bonds, such as whether junk bonds are suitable investments for banks and thrifts. This article does not address concerns such as these. Instead, the article examines whether junk bonds should be blamed for the rise in corporate mergers, corporate debt, and financial market volatility. The first section of the article defines junk bonds. The second section explains why some critics make these accusations against junk bonds, and the third section shows why these charges are not well-founded.

What Are Junk Bonds?

A corporation can obtain funds in many ways. It can raise funds by retaining earnings, issuing equity, or floating debt. If it chooses to take on debt, the corporation faces further choices. For short-term finance, it can issue commercial

---

At the time of this writing, Sean Becketti was a senior economist at the Federal Reserve Bank of Kansas City.

Source: *Economic Review*, Federal Reserve Bank of Kansas City.

paper or take out bank loans. For intermediate and long-term finance, it can take out bank loans, mortgage property, privately place bonds, or issue marketable corporate bonds. If the corporation chooses to issue marketable bonds, the bonds might be junk bonds.

Junk bonds are corporate bonds with low ratings from a major ratings service. Bond ratings are letter grades that indicate the rating services' opinions of the likelihood of a default. High-rated bonds are called investment-grade bonds, low-rated bonds are called speculative-grade bonds or, less formally, junk bonds.

A bond may receive a low rating for a number of reasons. If the financial condition or business outlook of the company is poor, bonds are rated speculative-grade. Bonds also are rated speculative-grade if the issuing company already has large amounts of debt outstanding. Some bonds are rated speculative-grade because they are subordinated to other debt—that is, their legal claim on the firm's assets in the event of default stands behind the other claims, so-called senior debt.

Junk bonds are traded in a dealer market rather than being listed on an exchange. A small group of investment banks makes a market in these securities; that is, they stand ready to buy or sell junk bonds.[1] Participating investment banks typically make a market in the issues they underwrite and in a limited number of relatively heavily traded issues considered "good credits."

Institutional investors hold the largest share of junk bonds. At the end of 1988, insurance companies, money managers, mutual funds, and pension funds held three-quarters of the face value of the outstanding junk bonds (SEC 1990, p. 22). Individual investors held only 5 percent of the outstanding bonds.

Why Are Junk Bonds Criticized?

Junk bonds have been blamed for three financial market ills in recent years: the merger boom, the rise in corporate debt, and the increase in financial market volatility. Critics connect junk bonds with these developments because they occurred simultaneously during the 1980s.

The market for junk bonds was revitalized in the late 1970s and the 1980s after decades of inactivity.[2] In 1977, the investment banking firm of Drexel, Burnham, Lambert began underwriting original-issue junk bonds. From 1977 through 1981, new issues never exceeded $1.5 billion (Chart 1). Then, starting in 1982, junk bond issues enjoyed five years of explosive growth. New issues peaked in 1986 and receded slightly in the last few years to between $25 billion and $30 billion a year. The face value of outstanding junk bonds is currently in the neighborhood of $200 billion, up almost twentyfold over ten years ago.[3]

---

[1] A small number of junk bonds, including some RJR Nabisco issues, are listed on the New York Stock Exchange (SEC 1990, p. 1).

[2] Junk bonds are just low-rated bonds, and low-rated bonds have always been a component of debt markets. In fact, in the 1920s and 1930s, junk bonds accounted for about 17 percent of new issues of corporate bonds on average (Hickman 1958, p. 153). However, the high default rates of the 1930s soured investors on junk bonds, and the market languished until the late 1970s.

[3] The SEC estimates that $204 billion par value registered securities were outstanding as of September 30, 1989. There are no reliable estimates of the market value of these securities (SEC 1990, p. 1). Altman (1987) gives estimates of the value of outstanding junk bonds for earlier years.

CHART 1 NEW ISSUES OF JUNK BONDS

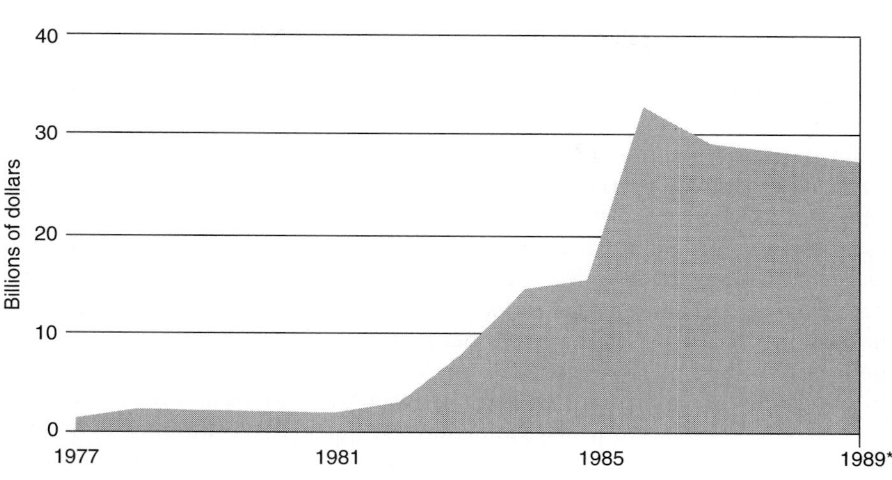

*Annualized estimate from data for the first nine months of 1989.
SOURCES: Perry and Taggart, Jr. 1990 (1977–80); SEC 1990 (1981–89).

As the junk bond market flourished during the last decade, mergers, corporate debt, and financial market volatility also grew. From the end of 1979 through the end of 1989, the value of U.S. mergers grew more than 300 percent.[4] Corporate debt grew over 270 percent.[5] Volatility in U.S. bond markets reached an all-time high in the 1980s. In addition, notable episodes of financial market volatility were the stock market collapses of October 1987 and October 1989.

More than mere coincidence, however, is needed to blame the financial market ills of the 1980s on the growth of the junk bond market. The decade of the 1980s saw the rise of many financial market innovations besides junk bonds—financial futures, program trading, portfolio insurance, and asset-backed securities to name just a few.[6] Why single out junk bonds as the cause of the merger boom, the growth in corporate debt, and financial market volatility?

Some observers suggest that junk bonds caused both the merger boom and the growth in corporate debt by extending credit too freely. According to this argument, corporations unable to borrow in traditional debt markets obtained

[4] This figure is from the database maintained by *Mergers & Acquisitions* magazine. This database tracks mergers of domestic firms with at least $1 million in assets. The value of each merger is recorded as the estimated value of all forms of consideration paid—cash, stocks, bonds, options, etc.—for the acquired company.

[5] There are many ways to measure the increase in corporate indebtedness in the 1980s. Two thorough examinations of this issue are Bernanke and Campbell 1988 and Faust 1990.

[6] Links have been suggested between financial market problems and some of these innovations. For example, program trading and portfolio insurance have been blamed for financial market volatility. However, none of these innovations has been connected with all three financial market developments.

funds by issuing junk bonds. Some potential acquirers found it easy to float junk bonds to raise the funds for their corporate takeovers. Similarly, some corporate borrowers took advantage of lower credit standards in the junk bond market to go on a debt "binge."[7]

Observers also suggest that the unusual volatility and unpredictability of junk bonds led to higher financial market volatility. This argument is related to the previous one. If, as some critics believe, junk bonds are the result of declining credit standards, then the market for junk bonds is prone to collapse. Investors may initially enjoy high returns, but the borrowers' failure to generate enough earnings to redeem the bonds leads inevitably to defaults. The prospect of these defaults causes frequent shifts in investor portfolios, from junk bonds to safer assets and back again, as investor confidence in junk bonds ebbs and flows with every change in the financial news. These shifts into and out of junk bonds increase the volatility of returns in other markets, such as the market for investment-grade corporate bonds and the market for equities.[8]

These arguments about the links between junk bonds and other financial market developments imply that junk bonds are qualitatively different from other securities and forms of debt. No one claims that such conventional securities as investment-grade bonds or equity extend funds too freely. Nor are these conventional forms of finance accused of causing excessive financial market volatility. Thus, if junk bonds are responsible for the growth in corporate debt, the merger boom, and the increase in financial market volatility, they must have some special characteristic that sets their behavior very much apart from that of other forms of finance.

The Truth about Junk Bonds

This section disputes the idea that junk bonds have special characteristics—the key assumption behind the charges against junk bonds. The section then discusses specific flaws in each of the claims and draws the following conclusions: First, junk bonds played a relatively small role in financing the merger boom of the 1980s. Second, junk bonds are too small a part of the debt market to account for the growth in corporate debt. Third, the timing of the growth in junk bond issues is not closely related to financial market volatility.

---

[7] A number of observers make these or similar claims. For examples on the connections between junk bonds and the merger boom, see the comments of Gail I. Hessol, Managing Director for Standard & Poor's, a major securities rating service (Hessol 1988 and *Wall Street Journal* 1990).

To the extent junk bonds caused the merger boom, they also contributed to the growth in corporate debt, since a part of the growth in debt represents the financing of mergers (Clark and Malabre 1988).

[8] Hessol (1988) testified both to the current and prospective risk of junk bonds. In addition, if junk bonds caused the merger boom and the growth of corporate debt, then junk bonds may also have indirectly increased financial market volatility, because some analysts believe that both the merger boom and higher debt affected financial market performance. This point was made in a speech by Rand Araskog, the chairman of ITT Corporation (Clark and Malabre 1988). More recently, some market participants attributed the stock market disruptions of October 1989 to the collapse of the United Airlines buyout.

Junk Bonds Are Similar to Conventional Investments

Junk bonds are similar to other, familiar investments with respect to the four principal characteristics of investments: risk, return, liquidity, and control over corporate management.[9] When measuring investments along each of these four dimensions, junk bonds lie between such conventional investments as equities, investment-grade bonds, bank loans, and private placements.[10]

Junk bonds are *riskier* than investment-grade bonds but less risky than equities. Altman (1988) finds that the junk bond default rate, a key component of risk, was 2.2 percent for the years 1970 through 1986, compared with just 0.2 percent for all publicly issued corporate bonds.[11] A more comprehensive measure of risk is the standard deviation of returns. Perry and Taggart (1990) find the standard deviation of monthly returns of junk bonds is greater than that of investment-grade bonds but less than that of equities and of the capital market as a whole.

Junk bond *returns* lie between those of investment-grade bonds and equities. Blume and Keim (1990) find that from January 1977 through December 1988 average monthly junk bond returns were 0.89 percent, higher than the 0.71 percent earned by investment-grade bonds and lower than the 1.14 percent earned by stocks. Perry and Taggart examined the relative performance of various portfolios in the quarters just preceding, during, and just after the seven post-World War II recessions. They found, again, that junk bond returns were intermediate between those of investment-grade bonds and equities.[12]

Junk bonds are more *liquid* than bank loans and private placements but less liquid than equities. Loan contracts and private placements typically contain customized clauses protecting the rights of the investors and restricting the actions of the borrowers. These clauses reduce the marketability of loans and private placements by increasing the cost to third parties of analyzing and valuing the debts and by increasing the frequency of renegotiation. Junk bonds, in contrast, are relatively standardized securities with an established secondary market. Even issues in default have a limited secondary market allowing investors to cut their losses and avoid protracted bankruptcy proceedings.[13] Recent disruptions in the junk bond market, however, are a reminder that the junk bond secondary market is neither as developed nor as liquid as the secondary market for equities.

---

[9] The similarity of junk bonds to conventional investments does *not* imply that junk bonds are appropriate investments for all investors. For example, junk bonds may not be appropriate for banks and thrifts, just as some other conventional investments—equities, for example—are considered inappropriate investments for banks and thrifts.

[10] Private placements are essentially loans made by non-banks, typically such institutional investors as insurance companies. They may take the form of either loan contracts or bonds. However, if they are bonds, they are not offered for sale on the public market. Private placements are underwritten by commercial and investment banks.

[11] Junk bonds are, of course, expected to have a higher default rate than investment-grade bonds. That is why they are rated lower than investment-grade bonds. A number of studies attempt to quantify the default risk of junk bonds. Most report annual default rates in the 1 to 3 percent range. Asquith, Mullins, and Wolff (1989) find much higher annual default rates, in the 3 to 9 percent range.

[12] Some observers argue that changes in the nature of junk bond issues make historical evidence on the risk and return of junk bonds an unreliable guide to their future behavior. If these observers are correct, junk bonds could be much riskier and could earn lower returns in the future.

[13] Altman (1989) reports that, on average, junk bonds sell for slightly less than 40 percent of face value at the end of the month in which default takes place.

Junk bonds offer investors more *control over corporate management* than investment-grade bonds but less control than bank loans, private placements, and equities. Some junk bonds contain "equity kickers," that is, options or conversion privileges that let investors obtain an equity share in the borrowing firm. These features give investors the option to participate in the management of the firm.[14] In addition, some junk bonds are sold in strip financing deals, where both bonds and stocks are sold in fixed proportions to investors. In this case, bond holders have voting rights in the management of the firm.[15]

Since junk bonds are not markedly different from other securities, it is hard to understand why they should have any special ability to trigger corporate borrowing sprees. Junk bonds may have cost or tax advantages that allow for some marginal increase in debt. But these advantages are not likely to induce bondholders to invest in junk bonds more recklessly than they do in other debt instruments that are not materially different from junk bonds. Indeed, the bulk of junk bonds are purchased by the same institutional investors who purchase the bulk of private placements, investors who presumably apply the same credit standards to both types of investment.

Again, because junk bonds are similar to traditional financial instruments, it is doubtful they have any special ability to disrupt financial markets. As in any new financial market, the junk bond market may endure brief periods of somewhat greater volatility than average as the market matures and as investors learn how to analyze the investment characteristics of junk bonds. This extra volatility in the junk bond market may be transmitted to other markets as investors adjust their holdings of junk bonds and other securities. However, the fundamental investment characteristics of junk bonds are similar to those of other well-understood securities, such as equities and investment-grade bonds. All of these markets endure episodes of turbulence: the junk bond market does not stand alone in this regard.

In sum, the similarity of junk bonds to conventional financial instruments casts doubt on claims that junk bonds are responsible for the financial market ills of the 1980s. Furthermore, there are specific reasons why junk bonds should not be blamed for these events.

Junk Bonds and the Merger Boom of the 1980s

The junk bond market is too small to have caused the 1980s merger boom. Although a large fraction of the junk bonds issued in the late 1980s were used to

---

[14] Equity kickers also allow investors to share in any unexpectedly high profits the firm might earn. This characteristic stands in contrast to traditional bonds where returns are limited to the coupons explicitly offered by the bond. These features not only increase the expected return to bondholders but also serve as a form of call protection since borrowers are more likely to call bonds when profits increase.

[15] Some observers argue that strip financing, along with other forms of junk bond finance, is chosen to reduce the double taxation of corporate dividends while retaining an equity relationship with investors. In other words, according to this view, junk bonds in strip financing function as though they were common stock. The interest paid on the junk bonds is tax deductible to the corporation, in contrast to any dividends paid. Since bondholders and stockholders are the same entities, the net tax burden can be decreased by paying out earnings as coupon payments on the junk bonds rather than as dividends on the common shares.

finance corporate takeovers, junk bonds accounted for only a small share of merger finance.[16] Even if all junk bonds issued had been used to finance mergers, junk bonds would have accounted for less than 8 percent of the value of U.S. mergers each year. Because not all junk bonds are used to finance mergers, this ratio is a generous upper bound on the junk bond share of merger finance. Moreover, a General Accounting Office study (1988) found that the bulk of the initial financing for tender offers came not from junk bonds but from bank loans. Thus, junk bonds appear to have played a minor role in financing mergers in the 1980s.

Some critics argue that junk bonds were the catalyst for many mergers and, in this way, caused the merger boom despite their small share in merger finance. It is true that junk bonds played a prominent role in several well-publicized mergers, and it is likely that the availability of junk bonds made a few more mergers possible than would have been the case without junk bonds. However, there are many ways to finance a merger. If junk bonds had not been available, mergers that made economic sense would probably have found other forms of finance. Indeed, previous merger booms have occurred without the aid of junk bonds. For example, during the merger wave of the late 1960s—the most recent merger wave prior to the current one and by some measures as significant as the wave of the 1980s—there was no market for original-issue junk bonds. This lack of junk bond financing in no way restrained the 1960s merger wave.

In fact, the merger boom of the 1980s may have helped establish the junk bond market rather than the other way around. The surge in new issues of junk bonds in the late 1980s coincided with the peak in the merger boom. Some part of the demand for debt generated by the merger boom may have increased interest in junk bonds and other innovative debt instruments.

Junk Bonds and Corporate Debt

There is a striking coincidence in the growth of corporate debt and the revitalization of the junk bond market. However, the growth in outstanding junk bonds in the 1980s is not large enough to account directly for the growth in corporate debt. Junk bonds outstanding increased $189 billion from the end of 1979 to the end of 1989. Over the same period, corporate debt increased $1,322 billion. Thus, junk bonds accounted for only 14 percent of the growth in corporate debt.

Furthermore, it is difficult to say that junk bonds were more responsible for the growth in total corporate debt than any another component. During the 1980s, investment-grade bonds increased more than 100 percent, bank loans grew more than 150 percent, and commercial paper outstanding increased more than 300 percent (Board of Governors of the Federal Reserve System 1990, pp. 35–36). These three forms of debt account for two-thirds of the growth in corporate debt. Clearly, all of these forms of debt played a part in the growth.

[16] Drexel, Burnham, Lambert estimated that all forms of acquisition financing accounted for 79 percent of junk bond issues in 1987 and 83 percent in 1988. First Boston found that acquisition financing accounted for 76 percent of junk bond issues in 1989 (SEC 1990, p. 20).

Indeed, it is possible that the growth in corporate debt contributed to the growth of the junk bond market, rather than the other way around. A prominent trend in financial markets in the 1980s was the move toward securitization of debt, that is, a move away from intermediated, nonmarketable forms of debt, such as bank loans, and toward marketable securities, such as corporate bonds.[17] Many of the financial innovations of the 1980s came to popularity as part of this trend. Junk bonds may be just another reflection of the securitization phenomenon.

Junk Bonds and Financial Market Volatility

Financial markets in the late 1980s endured some difficult times—particularly the stock market collapse of October 1987. Some observers claim the growth of the junk bond market increased financial market volatility.

One problem with this claim is the lack of an apparent relationship between the growth of the junk bond market and stock market volatility. Chart 2 shows

CHART 2 JUNK BOND ISSUES AND STOCK MARKET VOLATILITY

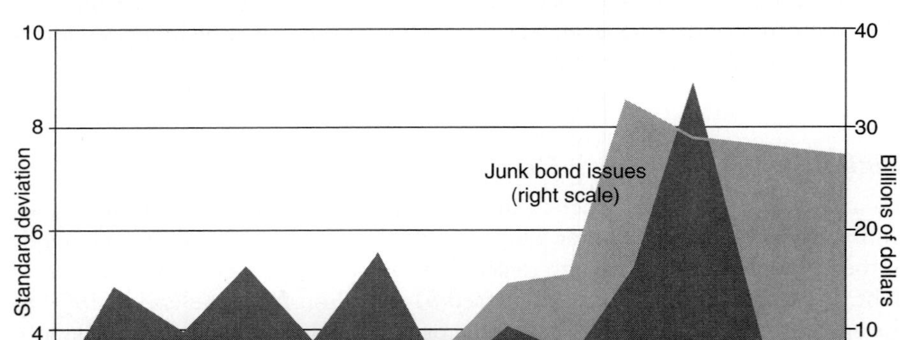

Note: In this chart, volatility is measured by the annual standard deviation of monthly stock returns of the Standard & Poor's index of 500 stocks.
SOURCES: See chart 1 (junk bond issues); Center for Research in Security Prices (stock market volatility).

---

[17] All forms of corporate debt grew in the 1980s. However, bank loans grew more slowly than bonds, causing them to lose market share to corporate bonds.

new issues of junk bonds and stock market volatility from 1981 through 1989.[18] Junk bond issues grew rapidly through 1986 and then leveled off. Stock market volatility was very high in 1987, thanks to the October market collapse, but was unexceptional otherwise.[19] If there were a connection between stock market volatility and the growth of the junk bond market, stock volatility would be high throughout the late 1980s instead of just in 1987.

Furthermore, the growth of the junk bond market and volatility in high-grade corporate bond returns are inversely related. Chart 3 shows new issues of junk bonds again, but this time with the volatility of the Salomon Brothers index of long-term, high-grade corporate bonds.[20] Bond market volatility began the 1980s at record levels and was lower thereafter. If there were a connection

CHART 3 JUNK BOND ISSUES AND BOND MARKET VOLATILITY

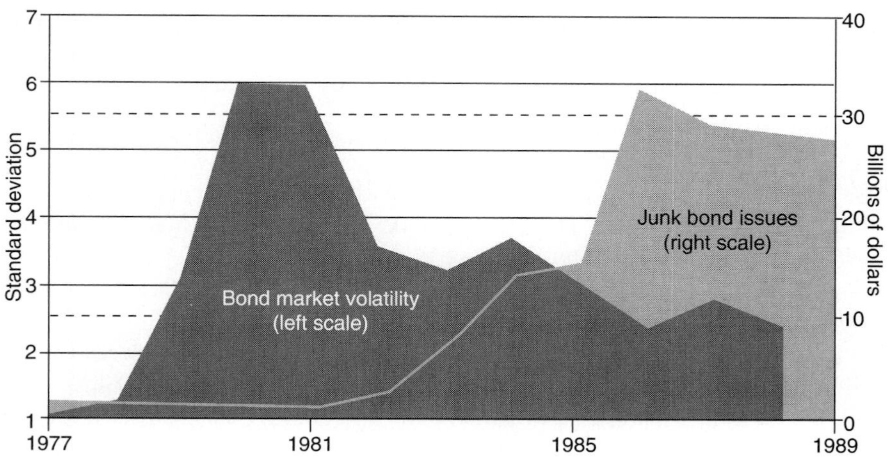

Note: In this chart, volatility is measured by the standard deviation of monthly returns of the Salomon Brothers' Long-Term High-Grade Corporate Bonds Index.
SOURCES: See chart 2.

[18] New issues of junk bonds are compared with the annual standard deviation of monthly returns to see if the growth of the junk bond market increased financial market volatility generally. It might be the case that very short-lived disruptions in the junk bond market caused similarly brief disruptions in other financial markets. That is not the kind of volatility considered here.

The rate of new issues is used to measure the size of the junk bond market in this chart. Essentially the same picture would be produced by using the value of outstanding junk bonds to measure the size of the market.

[19] For the post-World War II period, the annual standard deviation of monthly stock returns averaged 3.9 percent. Excluding 1987, the annual standard deviation of monthly stock returns in the 1980s was again 3.9 percent.

[20] The Salomon Brothers index includes AAA and AA corporate bonds with maturities of ten years or more. These data end in 1988. In the post-World War II era, the annual standard deviation of this index averaged 1.8 percent. In the 1980s, the annual standard deviation averaged 3.7 percent.

between bond market volatility and the growth of the junk bond market, bond volatility would have risen rather than fallen in the late 1980s.[21]

Conclusion

For years, critics have blamed junk bonds for a variety of financial market ills. The merger boom of the 1980s, the rise in corporate debt, and financial market volatility in the 1980s are all traced, by some observers, to junk bonds.

The truth is that the evidence does not support these charges against junk bonds. The key premise in the case against junk bonds—the belief that junk bonds have special properties that upset financial markets—is questionable. While the junk bond market grew at the same time that financial market problems surfaced, this circumstantial link turns out to be unpersuasive. The junk bond market has accounted for only a small part of the merger boom and of the growth in corporate debt, and the growth in the junk bond market is not closely associated with the trends in financial market volatility. Of course, there may be other concerns over junk bonds; for example, it may be inappropriate for banks and thrifts to hold junk bonds. Nevertheless, the three charges against junk bonds examined in this article are not supported by the evidence.

References

Altman, Edward I., ed. 1987. "The Anatomy of the High-Yield Bond Market," *Financial Analysts Journal*, July/August.

———. 1988. "Analyzing Risks and Returns in the High-Yield Bond Market," *Financial Markets and Portfolio Management.*

———. 1989. "The 'Junk Bond' Default Rate Debate," Working Paper 539, Salomon Brothers Center for the Study of Financial Institutions, New York University, November.

Asquith, P., D. Mullins, and E. Wolff. 1989. "Original Issue High Yield Bonds: Aging Analyses of Defaults, Exchanges, and Calls," *Journal of Finance.* September.

Bernanke, Ben S., and John Y. Campbell. 1988. "Is There a Corporate Debt Crisis?" *Brookings Papers on Economic Activity.*

Blume, Marshall E., and Donald B. Keim. 1990. "Risk and Return Characteristics of Lower-Grade Bonds, 1977–1987," in Edward I. Altman, ed., *The High-Yield Debt Market: Investment Performance and Economic Impact.* Homewood, Ill.: Dow Jones-Irwin.

Board of Governors of the Federal Reserve System. 1990. Balance Sheets for the U.S. Economy 1945–89.

---

[21] Although bond market volatility fell during the 1980s, it remained above its post-World War II average throughout the decade. Some observers maintain that increased corporate leverage in the 1980s, that is, higher ratios of corporate debt to equity, is responsible for this generally higher bond market volatility. Even if this claim is correct, all forms of corporate debt grew in the 1980s, and there is no reason to single out junk bonds as the sole or most important debt component responsible for increased volatility.

Clark, Jr., Lindley H., and Alfred Malabre, Jr. 1988. "Takeover Trend Helps Push Corporate Debt and Defaults Upward," *Wall Street Journal.* March 15.

Faust, Jon. 1990. "Will Higher Corporate Debt Worsen Future Recessions?" *Economic Review*, Federal Reserve Bank of Kansas City, March/April.

General Accounting Office. 1988. *Financial Markets: Issuers, Purchasers, and Purposes of High Yield, Non-investment Grade Bonds.* Washington: Government Printing Office. February.

Hessol, Gail. 1988. *United States General Accounting Office Hearing on High Yield Bonds*, comments in appendix. General Accounting Office. May, p. 177.

Hickman, W. Braddock. 1958. *Corporate Bond Quality and Investor Experience.* Princeton, N.J.: Princeton University Press.

Perry, Kevin J., and Robert A. Taggart, Jr. 1990. "Development of the Junk Bond Market and Its Role in Portfolio Management and Corporate Finance," in Edward I. Altman, ed., *The High-Yield Debt Market: Investment Performance and Economic Impact.* Homewood, Ill.: Dow Jones-Irwin.

U.S. Securities and Exchange Commission. 1990. *Recent Developments in the High Yield Market.* Staff report, March.

Wall Street Journal. 1990. "Reactions to Milken: Villain or Victim?" April 25.

Questions

1. What are junk bonds?
2. Moody's Investors Service, a bond rating agency, uses the following symbols to rate corporate bonds: Aaa, Aa, A, Baa, Ba, B, Caa, Ca, and C. What do these symbols mean?
3. Why are junk bonds criticized? Explain.
4. "Junk bonds are similar to other, familiar investments with respect to the four principal characteristics of investments: risk, return, liquidity, and control over corporate management." Evaluate junk bonds relative to other investments based on these four principal characteristics.
5. Provide arguments against each of the following propositions:
   a. Junk bonds caused the merger boom in the 1980s.
   b. Junk bonds are responsible for the rise in total corporate debt during the 1980s.
   c. Junk bonds increased financial market volatility during the 1980s.
6. In your opinion, should the Securities and Exchange Commission restrict the issuance of junk bonds? Explain.

Bond Market Innovations and Financial Intermediation

DONALD J. SMITH AND ROBERT A. TAGGART, JR.

For many years the bond market was the realm of blue chip issuers and conservative investors. Its sedate pace suited those whose primary objectives were steady income and preservation of capital.

The upheaval began gradually. Increased market volatility in the late 1960s and 1970s led to growing awareness of interest rate and currency risk. This in turn sparked a demand for new types of market instruments, new strategies for managing risk, and new ways to exploit interest rate differentials across markets.

In the 1980s, the flow of innovation has become a flood. New instruments have proliferated in a bewildering variety. Financial engineering allows the uncoupling of investor demand from the instruments that issuers want to supply and has fundamentally altered the structure of financial intermediation. Bond markets have become truly global in scope, with trading occurring around the clock and around the world.

This article will describe the common characteristics of these bond market innovations and the underlying forces that have caused the recent wave of change. It first analyzes the general determinants of bond market demand and supply. It then describes some of the major innovations of the 1970s and 1980s, explaining how they represent a pattern of accelerating response to changing market conditions.

Bond Market Demand and Supply

A bond or any other financial instrument can be viewed as a package of characteristics such as return, risk, and liquidity. Investors, of course, prefer high returns, low risk and high liquidity, but issuers will not be able to produce that package at reasonable cost. Hence, tradeoffs will be determined by supply and demand.

At the time of this writing, Donald J. Smith was an associate professor of finance and Robert A. Taggart, Jr. was a professor of finance, both at Boston College.

Source: Reprinted from *Business Horizons*, November–December 1989. Copyright 1989 by the Foundation for the School of Business at Indiana State University. Used with permission.

On the demand side, these tradeoffs are influenced by the distribution of investable wealth, tax rules, regulatory restrictions, and perceptions of the relative importance of various risk categories. In the 1980s, for example, Japanese financial institutions have accumulated an increased share of the world's total investable wealth. It is not surprising, then, that the tax and regulatory rules facing these institutions have affected the form of bond market instruments.

Changing perceptions of risk have influenced investors' views of bonds in both the 1970s and 1980s. Credit risk was once thought to be the most important category of bond risk, but investors have now become more keenly aware of interest rate and currency risk. The corporate restructuring wave of the 1980s has also given rise to "event risk," that of a sudden decline in credit quality resulting from a takeover, divestiture, or recapitalization.

Increased sensitivity to these risks has in turn spurred a demand for securities with protective features. Examples include floating-rate notes, zero-coupon bonds, and put bonds. New investment strategies designed to tailor the overall risk of a portfolio more precisely, such as immunization and hedging strategies using futures and swaps, have also been developed. Finally, the market volatility generating these risks has increased the demand for liquidity, thus enhancing the appeal of public securities markets. Investors have discovered that risk-management strategies require a liquid portfolio.

On the supply side, bond issuers face a set of cost conditions for providing financial services. They will try to issue securities that minimize the cost of providing a given financial services package. These costs include both the explicit costs of executing transactions and the implicit costs of bearing financial risk, and they are affected by available technology, tax and regulatory rules, and the issuer's ability to offset various forms of risk.

For example, the relative costs of issuing debt in the public and private markets have been affected by Securities and Exchange Commission Rule 415, which makes it faster and easier for large companies to bring a public issue to market. Advances in communications and information processing technology have helped allow continuous and flexible access to debt markets.

Tax considerations have clear effects on the costs of servicing bond issues and can thus influence their design. A primary motivation for the introduction of zero-coupon and other original issue discount bonds in 1981 was the advantageous way that issuers could deduct the discount amortization from annual tax payments.

An issuer's ability to bear particular risks will influence the degree of risk protection offered to investors. Commercial banks have been frequent issuers of floating-rate notes, since their interest rate risk is hedged by the tendency of their revenues to vary directly with interest rates. Producers of commodities, such as silver or oil, have been natural issuers of commodity-backed bonds, whose ultimate payoff is indexed to a specified commodity price level.

The demand and supply sides of the bond market can be joined in two ways. They can meet directly when the issuers supply bonds with characteristics ultimate investors desire. This has been the traditional sphere of the public bond markets. Alternatively, they can meet indirectly through a financial intermediary.

The intermediary purchases the issuer's debt security and in turn issues a claim on itself having characteristics that are more highly valued by the ultimate investors. This has been the traditional role of commercial banks, which purchase debt securities from businesses (make loans to them) and issue more liquid, less risky deposits to investors.

One of the most important developments is the way in which traditional methods for joining the two sides of the market have been completely transformed. The increasingly global scope of bond markets has afforded more opportunities to issue securities tailored to particular investor tastes, tax rules, or regulatory restrictions. Formerly, the issuer may not have been willing to bear the specialized risks such securities entail. Beginning in the 1970s and increasingly in the 1980s, however, markets have developed for reallocating these risks. The swaps market, for example, allows issuers to offer securities in either fixed or floating-rate form in any currency and then swap the associated profile of interest rate and currency risk for another, more desired profile.

Traditional patterns of intermediation have also changed radically. Investment bankers now play a more overt role in financial intermediation by buying market securities and repackaging them for sale to investors (stripped Treasury bonds or collateralized mortgage obligations, for example). These activities have impinged on the traditional business of commercial banks, who have been forced in turn to define new roles for themselves, such as the market-maker role many large commercial banks have assumed in the swaps market.

Bond Market Innovations of the 1970s

World financial markets faced several new sources of upheaval in the 1970s. Inflation rates grew higher and more volatile. Interest rates went through the same changes. In addition, the demise of the Bretton Woods Agreement in 1971 introduced a new element of volatility to world exchange rates.

Motivated largely by these new sources of risk, a number of innovations either were introduced or first became prominent in the 1970s. Six of these will be addressed here: floating-rate notes, Eurobonds, the early stages of the junk bond market, mortgage pass-through securities, parallel loans, and financial futures contracts.

Floating-rate notes are debt instruments on which the coupon rate is periodically reset to bring it into line with some easily observed market rate. For example, the contract formula might call for the coupon rate to be reset every quarter to equal the prevailing 91-day U.S. Treasury bill rate plus 2 percent. Such instruments had been issued elsewhere, but they did not enter U.S. bond markets until 1973, and they did not attract widespread attention until Citicorp's $850 million issue in 1974. The impetus for the innovation was the sudden volatility of U.S. inflation and interest rates, which imposed losses on holders of long-term, fixed-rate bonds. Long-term investors, aware of the need to protect themselves against increases in interest rates, wanted an instrument whose coupon rate would automatically adjust with the market. At the same time, banks and finance companies were natural issuers of such securities; their assets were primarily short-term or even floating-rate loans, so their revenues afforded a built-in hedge against floating-rate liabilities. Government regulation provided a further incentive for innovation, since U.S. commercial banks were still subject to interest rate ceilings on deposits. By issuing floating-rate notes instead of certificates of deposit, banks could pay market rates yet still offer investors a relatively safe and liquid investment. In this case, a new source of variability gave rise to natural clienteles of both investors and issuers, and floating-rate notes allowed the two sides to be brought together.

Another security that attained its first real prominence in the 1970s was the Eurobond, a bond issued outside the regulatory confines of any particular market. Its currency denomination may or may not be the same as the domestic market of the issuer. For example, a U.S. corporation can issue Euroyen or Eurodollar bonds in London, and neither issue will be subject to U.S. securities regulation. Although the first Eurobond was issued in 1957, the market remained relatively small until the mid-1970s, when several forces combined to fuel its rapid growth. For corporations in the U.S. and elsewhere, volatile inflation caused sharper fluctuations in the availability of internal funds. Since they were forced to tap the external funds markets more frequently during a time of relatively high interest rates, corporate treasurers looked for new ways to economize on both interest and issue costs. One way to reduce interest costs is to seek an untapped clientele of investors who place special value on your securities. Since conditions in other countries had created a demand outside the U.S. for dollar-denominated securities, large and well-recognized U.S. companies sought to lure foreign investors. Securities issued in the U.S. to these investors could not be easily sold, however. Since the late 1960s, the federal government had imposed a 30 percent withholding tax on interest paid to foreign holders of domestically issued securities. It was natural to turn to the Eurobond market, where no such tax existed and where bonds could be issued in bearer form to preserve investor anonymity. In addition, issuers in this market did not face the SEC's costly and time-consuming registration and disclosure requirements. Aided by these advantages, annual Eurobond issues grew from $2.1 billion in 1974 to $24 billion in 1980. In this case, a more urgent need to economize on the costs of raising funds helped spur the trend toward global integration of securities markets.

Although its spectacular growth phase did not occur until the mid-1980s, the junk bond market should be mentioned in this same context. Junk bonds (or "high-yield" bonds, as their promoters prefer to call them), are publicly issued bonds that are either rated below investment grade by the rating agencies or unrated altogether. Junk bonds have long existed. They accounted for 17 percent of total bond issue proceeds to U.S. corporations during the years 1909–43. In the wake of the Great Depression, however, the new issue market dried up and became dormant. It was not until 1977 that it revived. The same emphasis on economy and flexibility that was important in the Eurobond market's growth provided an impetus for this revival. Lower-grade issuers formerly confined to negotiated loans from commercial banks, finance companies, or insurance companies discovered they could economize by going directly to the public market.

And public issues typically contained fewer restrictive covenants than negotiated loans. The move to the public markets also illustrated the growing competition among different types of financial institutions during the 1970s. Drexel Burnham Lambert, the investment banking firm credited with reviving the junk bond market, was able to win business away from commercial banks and others by taking debt contracts that would formerly have been held as bank loans and selling them in a public market. Thus the growth of the junk bond market can be seen as part of the more general "securitization" phenomenon, in which non-marketable credit instruments that intermediaries would once have held privately become publicly traded securities.

For securitization to work, of course, public investors must demand the securities. Several factors interacted to create the demand for junk bonds. First, investors discovered during the 1970s that high credit quality would not protect them from inflation and interest rate fluctuations. Junk bonds were attractive on this score because of their high yields. In addition, their higher default risk causes junk bond values to fluctuate more with their issuers' asset values. Consequently, junk bonds are relatively less susceptible to pure interest rate risk than are investment grade bonds. Finally, the ability of Drexel Burnham and other securities firms to make relatively liquid markets in junk bonds greatly enhanced their appeal to investors.

Securitization manifested itself in a different form in the development of mortgage pass-through securities. The first Government National Mortgage Association (GNMA, or "Ginnie Mae") pass-throughs appeared in 1970. These securities are backed by portfolios, or pools, of government-insured home mortgages, all of them bearing the same contract interest rate. Monthly payments of principal and interest are passed through proportionately to holders of the securities at an interest rate 50 basis points below the contract rate. The securities are issued directly by mortgage originators, such as mortgage banks, commercial banks or thrift institutions, but timely payment of the scheduled interest and principal is guaranteed by GNMA. A fee of six basis points is paid to GNMA for providing this guarantee; the remaining 44 basis points of the difference between the contract rate and the pass-through rate goes to the issuer as a servicing fee.

In this case, securitization is helped by the standardized features of the pass-throughs. The U.S. home mortgage market had been quite segmented. Lenders were hindered in their attempts to exploit regional interest rate differentials by the difficulty of evaluating the credit quality of home mortgages far removed from their own territory. The government guarantee and restrictions on the mortgages eligible for the pool made pass-throughs far more homogeneous than the typical direct mortgage investment. This homogeneity in turn allowed the growth of secondary trading, making pass-throughs more liquid. Pass-throughs helped to satisfy investors' increased demand for real estate-related securities. Thus, the mortgage market was opened to a broader spectrum of investors and national integration of the market was furthered.

In addition to new instruments and broader markets for existing instruments, the volatility of the 1970s also gave rise to new risk-management strategies. One such strategy, the parallel loan, was the precursor of the booming 1980s market in interest rate and currency swaps. Parallel loans were designed primarily to circumvent exchange controls and their attendant exchange rate risk. Suppose, for example, that Company A does business in Country B and faces a stream of future receipts denominated in B's currency. Because of exchange restrictions, Company A will not be able to freely convert these receipts into its own currency and thus will be exposed to future exchange rate risk. If Company B, operating in Country A, faces the analogous situation, however, the two companies can eliminate exchange risk through a parallel loan. Company A lends Company B an amount denominated in A's currency. Simultaneously, Company B lends Company A an amount denominated in B's currency. Since the initial loan amounts are equivalent, no money changes hands at the outset. In the future, B repays its loan with its A-denominated receipts and A repays its loan with its B-denominated receipts. The two companies have effectively swapped their future receipts, thus fixing them in their own currencies and insulating themselves against future exchange rate risk.

In this instance, the increased importance of exchange rate risk, in combination with regulatory restrictions, gave rise to an innovative strategy. But that strategy had the same limitation as barter: each party needed a counterparty with exactly offsetting needs. Because of this limitation, and because the loan agreement exposed each party to default risk, even as it protected against exchange rate risk, parallel loans remained a small and specialized feature of financial market activity throughout the 1970s.

Financial futures markets, which also began in the 1970s, addressed exactly this type of weakness by allowing parties to interact anonymously through an exchange clearinghouse mechanism. A financial futures contract is an agreement that sets the terms on which a financial instrument will be bought or sold on a specified future date. Unlike a forward contract, it is traded on an organized futures exchange, and buyers and sellers strike their bargains with the exchange clearinghouse, not with each other. The exchange sets rules about contract terms, thus ensuring the degree of standardization needed to promote anonymous auction trading. Furthermore, the contracts are "marked to market" each day by the exchange. That is, parties on both sides of the market have their accounts debited or credited by the amount of daily price movements, and they must maintain sufficient "margin" in their accounts to protect the exchange from default by either side.

The first financial futures contracts in the U.S. were for currencies traded on the International Monetary Market in Chicago. These were soon followed by contracts on GNMA pass-throughs and U.S. Treasury bills and bonds. Their popularity was attributable to the increased volatility of both exchange rates and interest rates in the 1970s, as they afforded new opportunities for both investors and bond issuers to either hedge or speculate on market fluctuations. But, although these contracts were conducive to high-volume trading and liquid markets, their marking-to-market feature was cumbersome to large corporate and institutional users. In addition, the heavy volume needed to justify the market's operation meant trading was confined to a limited number of instruments and future dates. Thus, an opportunity remained for a risk-management mechanism that was somewhere between the highly specialized parallel loan and the highly standardized futures contract.

To summarize, the major bond market innovations of the 1970s offered new ways to deal with interest rate and currency risk in an environment of uncertain inflation. Liquidity and flexibility are important in such an environment. Therefore, several of the innovations were aimed at tapping the advantages afforded by public markets. In addition, some of the innovations exhibited the trends toward globalization and securitization that would become hallmarks of bond markets in the 1980s.

Innovations of the 1980s

An important feature of financial markets in the 1980s has been the continuation and further evolution of trends that began in the 1970s. This includes the natural growth of existing markets and instruments in the face of increased demand, their adaptation to new uses, and their alteration to address perceived problems.

Financial futures trading, for example, has mushroomed, both in the U.S. and abroad. Available contracts now cover not only traded securities, but also market indexes. The junk bond market has continued its tremendous growth: by the end of 1988, the amount outstanding exceeded $180 billion, more than 20 percent of the total public corporate bond market. This growth was fueled, in part, by the realization that the flexibility and rapid access to capital afforded by junk bonds were ideally suited to leveraged buyouts, takeovers, and other corporate restructuring.

Market instruments have undergone continuous tinkering in an attempt to meet the needs of investors and issuers more efficiently. Although floating-rate notes protect investors against interest rate risk, for example, they do not protect against credit risk. A bond whose coupon rate is set at a fixed spread over the Treasury bill rate will still decline in value if the issuer's credit quality deteriorates. Hence, there have been some issues of "puttable" or "extendable" bonds. These are floating-rate bonds that give the investor the option to periodically put (resell) the bonds to the issuer at par. As long as the issuer can honor this option, then, the extent to which the bonds' value can fall below par will be limited. In a similar vein, "reset" bonds call for the interest rate to be periodically reset by the underwriter to a level that will allow the bonds to trade at par.

Other variations in contract design call for adjustments to interest or principal payments that are geared to some index other than market interest rates. Examples include commodity price levels, such as oil, gold, and silver; general price levels, such as the Consumer Price Index; and even business activity levels, such as New York Stock Exchange trading volume. The motivation for such wrinkles is to better match investors' desires to protect against price risk with the issuers' own ability to hedge these risks.

The market for any security type will always be limited if the desires of investors and issuers must be precisely matched. In our opinion, then, the most significant financial innovations of the 1980s have been those that allow an uncoupling of investor and issuer desires. This has been accomplished through a radical change in the role of investment bankers and in patterns of financial intermediation. We will illustrate this development by considering, in some detail, three of its primary manifestations: zero-coupon bonds, collateralized mortgage obligations, and the use of specialized securities in combination with swaps to exploit market niches around the world.

Zero-Coupon Bonds

A zero-coupon bond, which promises a single payment on a specified future date, is the most basic security imaginable. Indeed, any conventional bond, with its stream of coupon and principal payments, can be considered a series of zero-coupon bonds. Because of its intermediate payments, a conventional bond returns cash to the purchaser more quickly than does a zero-coupon bond of identical maturity. This implies that the conventional bond has a shorter duration, which means that its value is less sensitive to changes in market yields than is the identical-maturity zero. On the other hand, the zero-coupon bond allows the investor to lock in the stated yield to maturity: since there are no coupons, no assumption need be made about the rates at which intermediate payments will be reinvested.

Despite their simplicity, zeros were virtually unheard of until the 1980s, even though there have never been any legal or regulatory restrictions against issuing or investing in them. The absence of zeros is perhaps as important to understanding innovation as is their introduction.

In theory, there should be ready buyers for zeros as long as there is some difference of opinion on future interest rates. Some short-term speculators might like the long-duration aspect of zeros, since their prices will rise faster than those of conventional bonds in the event of a decline in rates. Likewise, some long-term, buy-and-hold investors might like the absence of coupon reinvestment risk and the ability to lock in the promised yield to maturity. In particular, the passive investment strategy known as immunization is easier and less costly to implement with zeros than with coupon bonds. But this latent demand for zeros was not really sparked until the cyclical peak in interest rates in 1982. Persistent inflation kept upward pressure on market rates throughout the late 1970s. In that environment investors were interested in shortening, not lengthening, the average maturity of their portfolios. Floating-rate notes, which protect against interest rate increases, were more likely to attract investor attention than zero-coupon bonds.

In addition, there was virtually no natural supply of zero-coupon securities before 1980. Since most investment projects generate a stream of revenues, few corporate or governmental funding needs call for single, lump-sum payments at specific future dates. A corporate borrower issuing zero-coupon debt would also have to convince skeptical investors that the lack of coupons was not a sign of financial weakness.

The impetus for the rise of the zero-coupon bond market in the 1980s came from corporate tax strategy rather than from interest rate risk management. According to IRS rules prevailing at the time, the issuer of an original issue discount (O.I.D.) bond[1] had to amortize the discount on a straight-line basis over the lifetime of the bond. The amortized amount is treated as interest expense by the issuer and interest income by the investor, so the issuer has a tax write-off and the investor has a tax obligation even though no cash is exchanged. The use of straight-line rather than compound-interest amortization on the O.I.D. bond allowed the corporate issuer to have a tax-deductible expense larger than the true financial expense, lowering its effective cost of funds. That tax treatment did not suddenly become available in 1980, but the value of the net tax advantage to corporate issuers was attractive only in periods of high interest rates. Thus there was a large volume of corporate zero-coupon issues in 1981 and early 1982.

The initial demand for zeros was also influenced by taxes. In a number of countries, most notably Japan and the United Kingdom, the increase in value as the zero approaches maturity was treated as a capital gain rather than an accrual of interest. In Japan such capital gains were untaxed, and thus zeros had a substantial appeal to taxable investors.

The Tax Equity and Fiscal Responsibility Act of 1982 removed the tax advantage for U.S. corporations issuing zeros. Any O.I.D. debt issued after July 2, 1982 had to use compound-interest amortization. That might have spelled the end of the zero-coupon market, but the dramatic decline in interest rates in mid-1982 spurred additional demand for zeros that had been absent in previous years. The demand was focused, however, on Treasury zeros, which are not sullied by credit risk considerations.

Treasury-backed zero-coupon bonds are a prototype of the financial engineering activities that have burgeoned in the 1980s. There was substantial demand for long-term Treasury zeros, but limited supply. A market in stripping and selling coupons from bearer Treasury bonds existed, but this market was small and illiquid because of the necessity for physically handling small-denomination coupon certificates. Then, in August of 1982, Merrill Lynch introduced TIGRs (Treasury Investment Growth Receipts), and other investment banks soon followed with their own versions—for example, Salomon Bros.' CAT (Certificates of Accrual on Treasury Securities) or Lehman Bros' LIONs (Lehman Investment Opportunity Notes).

TIGRs and CATS are remarkably simple in design, as illustrated in Figure 1. The investment bank buys conventional Treasury bonds and places them in a single-purpose dedicated trust. The trust, which is managed by a custodian commercial bank, issues the zero-coupon securities. The coupon and principal cash flows from the conventional bonds are used to pay the principal on the derivative zeros at their maturity dates. The investment bank profits by purchasing the coupon Treasuries for less than the total sale price of the zeros. In the declining interest rate environment of late 1982 and 1983, buyers were willing to pay extra for a long-duration zero with no credit risk. The investment bank operates as a

[1] An O.I.D. bond is one in which the issue price is less than 100 minus 0.25 times the number of years to maturity. For example, if the price of a 10-year bond is less than 97.5 percent of the face value at issuance, it is considered O.I.D. for tax purposes.

FIGURE 1 TREASURY-BACKED ZEROS

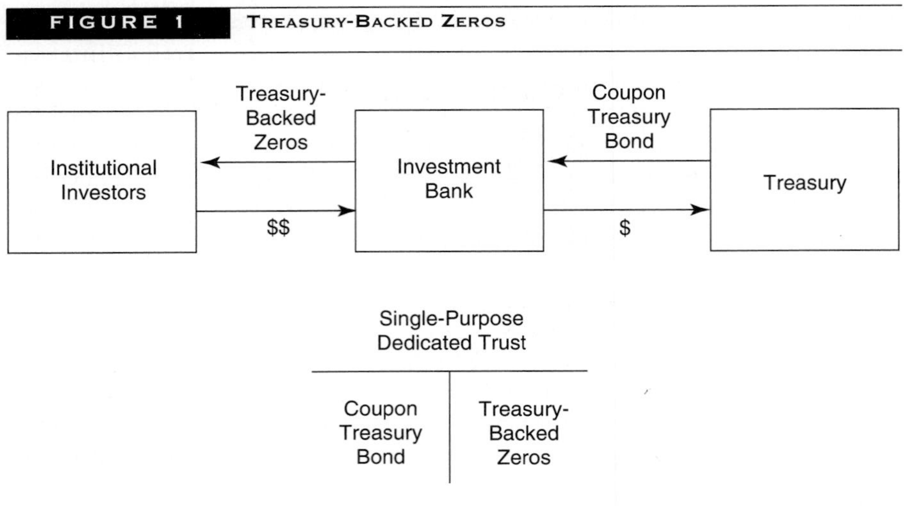

traditional financial intermediary, a role usually taken by a commercial bank or mutual fund. One security's characteristics are transformed by the intermediation process to supply the market with a security it prefers to hold.

Given the investment banks' profit from creating zeros via coupon stripping, one might wonder why the Treasury did not, itself, immediately issue zero-coupon debt (other than nonmarketable Series EE Savings Bonds). However, the Treasury has never sought the role of financial innovator. Because of its large scale, it intentionally seeks to be predictable with respect to the timing, amount, and type of its debt issues. The Treasury auctions its bills, notes, and bonds at scheduled offerings in announced quantities so the private sector can work around its dominating presence. Nevertheless, the unprecedented size and carrying cost of the national debt in the 1980s has forced the Treasury to respond to market pressures and design its securities with (increasingly overseas) investors in mind.

The Treasury finally addressed the overwhelming success of the financially engineered zero-coupon market by introducing its STRIPS (Separate Trading of Registered Interest and Principal of Securities) program in February 1985. Any financial institution having access to the Federal Reserve's book entry system can participate by buying specially designated Treasury notes or bonds and converting them to STRIPS. This effectively requires separate registered owners for each of the cash flows and allows the individual coupon and principal payments to be sold as zero-coupon instruments. The program eliminates the need for the custodian bank and dedicated trust in the CATS or TIGRs framework. STRIPS now have such an established place in the Treasury market that their prices and yields are quoted in the *Wall Street Journal* alongside the traditional bonds, notes, and bills.

Collateralized Mortgage Obligations

The broad decline in market interest rates after mid-1982 also induced issuers of callable debt to exercise their prepayment options and refinance at the lower prevailing rates. This especially hurt investors in mortgage securities. Whereas corporate bonds usually have a call protection period and are callable at some premium over par value, mortgages can be paid off at any time, often without a prepayment penalty.

Investors in GNMA pass-throughs found out about prepayment risk in the early 1980s. Prepayment risk, of course, had always been present, but in the rising interest rate environment of the 1970s voluntary refinancings of mortgages were rare. In fact, some creative real estate financing strategies were designed to pass on an existing, low-rate mortgage to the home buyer. GNMAs seemed to institutional investors to offer a low-risk way to pick up some extra basis points relative to Treasury securities, especially since the default risk was viewed to be equivalent. But unexpected prepayments meant that realized returns fell short of expectations, as more funds had to be reinvested sooner at lower rates.

Investment banks soon recognized the market demand for a mortgage-backed security that had less prepayment risk than the traditional GNMA pass-through. Each investor in a GNMA pass-through owns a share of the underlying mortgage pool and receives all payments, including principal prepayments, on a pro rata basis. Therefore, all shares of the GNMA mortgage pool have the same maturity and prepayment risk. The idea behind collateralized mortgage obligations (CMOs), which were introduced in 1983, is to redistribute the timing and amount of interest and principal cash flows across the investor base. This provides a range of expected maturities and redistributes the prepayment risk.

To create a CMO, an investment bank first buys a pool of GNMAs, say \$100 million of 30-year pass-throughs with a 10 percent coupon rate (GNMA 10s). Then, following the TIGRs and CATS prototype, the GNMAs are placed in a single-purpose, dedicated trust that issues various classes of CMOs. Like Treasury-backed zeros, the CMOs are derivative securities: the funds to pay the interest and principal on the CMOs are derived from the cash receipts on the underlying GNMAs. This process is pictured in Figure 2.

The CMO structure has turned out to be a remarkably flexible way to transform GNMA cash flows. The first CMOs divided up the principal payments according to time, basically letting the various classes "queue up" for receipt of principal. For example, the CMO could have two \$50 million classes, A and B. Class A receives all scheduled and unscheduled principal paid on the underlying GNMAs while Class B receives only interest. Class B has "prepayment protection" until Class A is fully paid off. In technical terms, the structure divided a 30-year GNMA with a duration of, say, 12 years into two smaller pieces with durations of, say, 6 and 18 years. Typically, these CMOs have three or more classes, sometimes with different coupon rates and often including a zero-coupon class.

The investment bank profits when the CMOs are sold for more than the purchase price of the GNMAs, so the key for the intermediary is to identify

FIGURE 2 COLLATERALIZED MORTGAGE OBLIGATIONS (CMOs)

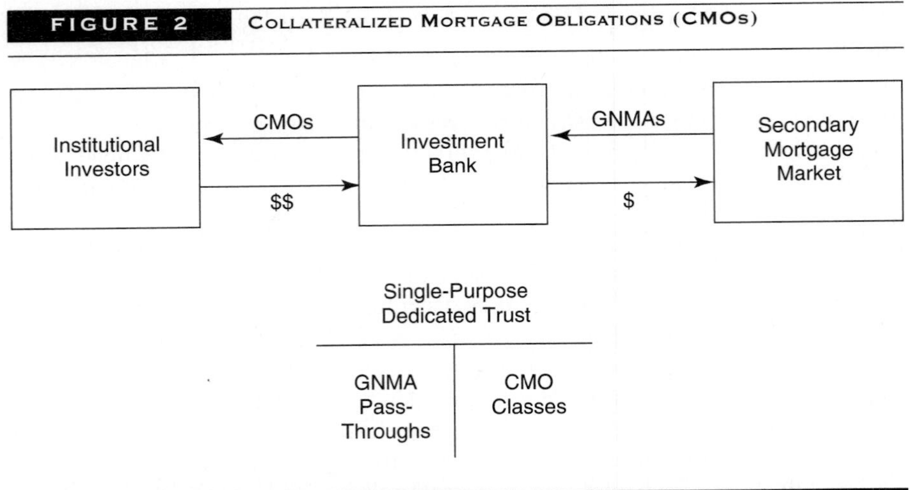

investor market segments that have different hedging needs or different views on future market conditions. The basic CMO structure creates a "mortgage yield curve" and allows investors to specialize in particular maturity ranges. Thrift institutions were drawn to the "fast-pay" classes to match their relatively short-term deposits. Pension funds and insurance companies were drawn to the "slow-pay" classes to match their long-term liabilities. The 1980s trend toward global integration of financial markets has created many other opportunities to serve specialized market segments; CMOs have afforded a pliable device for realizing these opportunities.

Another relatively simple CMO structure divides the underlying GNMAs into "high coupon" and "low coupon" classes. For example, the pool of GNMA 10s could be divided into two $50 million classes, one with a 12 percent coupon rate priced at a premium, and the other with an 8 percent coupon rate priced at a discount. These classes will perform differently depending on whether prepayments are faster or slower than originally expected. Investors with different views on future market rates will prefer one class over another.

An extreme version of this type of innovative structure is the "interest only/principal only" (IO/PO) CMO. The GNMA 10s again could be divided into two classes, one that receives all of the interest payments, and the other that receives all of the principal. Each class would have a principal of $100 million (a "notional" principal in the case of the IO) and would be priced at a discount. These classes turn out to be extremely sensitive to changes in market interest rates. If rates plummet and mortgage refinancings soar, the PO class would jump in value, since cash flows are received much sooner than expected. The IO class would decline in value, since future interest receipts disappear altogether as principal is prepaid. The organizer of the CMO is, of course, unconcerned about this interest rate risk as long as the separate pieces can be fully sold at prices that exceed the purchase price of the GNMAs.

CMOs can also be used to create a floating-rate class, even though the underlying securities are fixed-rate mortgages. This requires creation of another innovative security, an inverse floating-rate note ("bull floater"), whose coupon rate goes up when market rates fall. Such a security would experience a large increase in value when market rates decline and hence would be attractive to investors who are bullish on bonds. Creation of these two classes is possible as long as the combined interest payments to the CMO classes never exceed those on the underlying GNMAs.

Floating-rate CMOs proved to be very popular after their introduction in 1986 and are credited with supplanting the unsecured floating-rate note in the Eurodollar market. The main reason is that the CMO offers much lower credit risk than the typical corporate obligation, since the underlying GNMAs are insured. This structure also deals with prepayment risk in a novel way. As long as the floating-rate class trade at or close to par value, principal prepayment is of little consequence since funds can be reinvested in equivalent securities.

The basic CMO structure has also been adapted to other types of credit instruments, such as auto loans and credit card receivables. Because of its flexibility in parceling out cash flow streams, it can securitize virtually any type of loan agreement.

Specialized Securities with Swaps

Currency swaps evolved from parallel loans to address the problem of default risk. If one of the parties to a parallel loan defaults, the other cannot easily suspend its own obligation since there are separate loan agreements. A currency swap is, in principle, merely an exchange of the principal and coupon cash flows on bonds of equal value but denominated in different currencies. The coupons can be either fixed or floating rate. In the swap agreement, performance of one party depends on the continued performance of the other; if one side defaults, the other can suspend its payments.

The interest rate swap market developed in the 1980s from currency swaps. An interest rate swap is an exchange of coupon cash flows on bonds of equal value. For example, one coupon stream might represent fixed-rate payments, while the other might represent floating-rate payments. Since the bonds are denominated in the same currency, an exchange of principal is unnecessary.

A swap can be viewed as a series of forward contracts, since it sets the terms on which cash will change hands on specified future dates. However, the agreement is made without the margin accounts and daily marking-to-market procedures that characterize exchange-traded futures contracts. Swaps, therefore, are more flexible but less liquid than futures contracts, and have greater default risk than futures.

Interest rate and currency swaps are key factors in integrating worldwide capital markets. They provide an efficient tool to transform the nature of liabilities—

a firm can issue in the market and currency where it is most advantageous and then convert that debt to the desired currency or coupon pattern via swap agreements. This continuous search for arbitrage opportunities brings rates into alignment, making the markets more efficient.

Swaps can be used to lower funding costs by identifying investors with specialized needs and designing innovative securities for them. If a security's cash flow stream does not meet the issuer's needs, it can simply be swapped. For example, suppose that a firm can issue an inverse floating-rate note at 21 percent minus the London Interbank Offer Rate (LIBOR) in the Eurodollar market. It can then enter an interest rate swap with a commercial bank to receive a fixed rate of 10 percent and pay a floating rate of LIBOR. The financially engineered package, as exhibited in Figure 3, results in fixed-rate funding at approximately 11 percent. A firm would do this if the cost of funds, including the default risk it bears on the swap, is lower than its alternative fixed rate cost. This might occur in the case of the inverse floater if some pocket of investors is particularly bullish on bonds expects LIBOR to fall.

In the 1980s, a large number of innovative securities have been aimed at Japanese institutional investors. The increasing pool of accumulated savings in Japan has been an attractive target for the security issues of governments and corporations around the world. It is only natural, then, that new debt instruments and markets have been developed to address the unique needs of Japanese investors, especially the large life insurance companies. Two particular regulations facing these institutions have affected the design of debt instruments: first, they face a limit on the percentage of foreign (non-yen-denominated) assets they can hold; second, they are required to pay dividends only from coupon interest income and not from capital gains.

FIGURE 3 SWAP-DRIVEN INVERSE FLOATING RATE NOTE

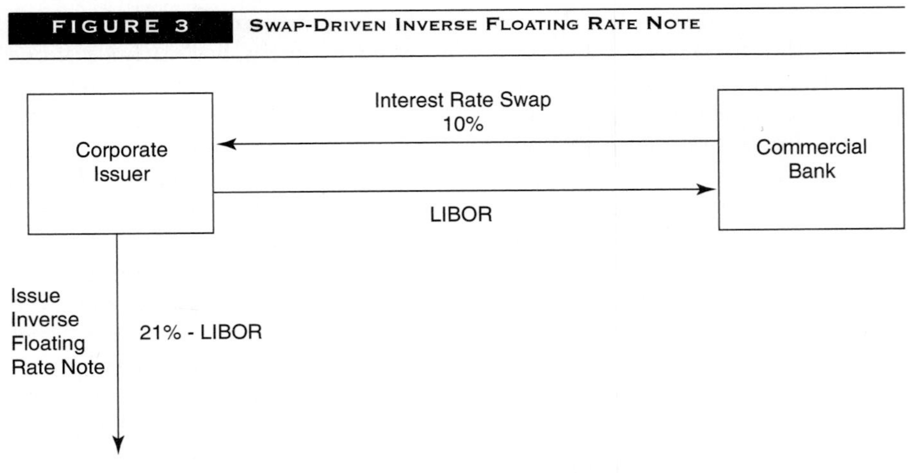

Dual-currency bonds are a classic example of a security that comes from investor demand and not issuer supply. These bonds pay coupon interest in one currency and principal in another. The usual pattern has been coupons in a relatively low-interest currency, such as the Swiss franc or Japanese yen, and principal in a high-interest currency, such as the U.S. dollar. A dollar/yen dual currency bond deals with the regulatory constraints on Japanese life insurers in a clever manner. First, the Japanese Ministry of Finance has ruled that such a bond is "primarily yen-denominated" and so does not fall within the foreign asset constraint. Second, since the U.S. dollar is expected to depreciate against the yen, such a bond must bear a higher coupon rate than a straight yen bond. The increased interest income in turn helps the Japanese life insurance companies pay dividends and essentially represents a tradeoff between the (desirable) coupon and (less desirable) principal components of total return.

The corporate issuer, on the other hand, is unlikely to have a project generating that unique stream of yen and dollar cash flows. Thus, the corporate issuer would not have found it attractive to issue a dual-currency bond prior to the development of the swaps market. Now, however, a currency swap can be used to hedge the issuer's yen exposure, since it sets the terms on which dollars will be exchanged for yen on future coupon dates.

Japanese institutional investors' appetite for high coupon debt also led to the development of "weak currency" capital markets such as the Australian dollar and New Zealand dollar. In 1987, U.S. corporations issued more than $1 billion in Eurobonds denominated in these two currencies. This represented approximately 5 percent of their total Euromarket borrowing in that year; U.S. corporate borrowing in those currencies had been negligible as recently as 1984. The globalization of capital markets in the 1980s has enabled corporate borrowers to issue debt in any currency, whether or not they have matching income streams. Currency swaps have been the vehicle for this capability: the firm can always swap for the desired liability. Hence, a large percentage of Eurobond issues in both the traditional and newly integrated currencies have been accompanied by swaps. Tokyo has been the ultimate destination of much of these debt issues, in part because of the perceived need for global diversification and in part because of the need for high coupon income.

The New Structure of Financial Intermediation

The pace of financial innovation in recent years has been breathtaking. Sparked by technological advances, changing risk-management needs, taxes and regulation, and a changing distribution of the world's investable wealth, new instruments and strategies have poured forth in seemingly endless variety. The bond markets have become truly global in scope. In our view, however, the outcome of bond market innovation in the 1980s can best be summarized by examining the changes it has brought about in the structure of financial intermediation.

A financial intermediary—a commercial bank, thrift institution, credit union, mutual fund, or pension fund—sells securities to ultimate lenders, using the proceeds to buy other securities from ultimate borrowers. The key element is that securities held as assets differ from those held as liabilities along one or more dimensions, such as maturity, default risk, denomination, and marketability. The intermediation process serves to transform the securities and allows borrowers and lenders to transact with financial instruments that meet their particular needs. In its most classic form, large-denomination, individually risky, nonmarketable business loans are transformed by commercial banks into small-denomination, low-risk, highly liquid consumer deposits.

In this type of intermediation, the bank purchases debt claims for which there is little or no organized market. During the 1980s, however, investment bankers have found new ways to bring formerly nonmarketable credit instruments within the scope of organized securities markets. With junk bonds they have done so simply by acting as market makers and providing liquidity. In other cases, the investment banks have served as true financial intermediaries.

Traditionally this was not the case. Investment banks underwrote new issues or developed secondary markets in existing securities, but did not transform the securities they purchased. This has changed in the 1980s as the very nature of investment banking has changed. Investment bank intermediation, as in the creation of Treasury-backed zeros and CMOs or the combining of securities issues with swaps, differs from traditional intermediation in several ways. In commercial banking, the transactions are on the balance sheet and are primarily designed to meet the needs of the domestic retail depositor. Intermediation for an investment bank is aimed at exploiting some unmet, perhaps short-lived, market demand. The transactions are primarily off the balance sheet (via single-purpose dedicated trusts or swap agreements) and are aimed at the needs of the global institutional investor.

Investment banks have been drawn to this activity in part because their own traditional business has shifted its emphasis. Starting with the advent of shelf registration in 1982, investment banking has increasingly been based more on the ability to execute transactions than on customer relationships. The day of the long-standing, almost inviolate, connection between corporation and investment banker has passed. Instead, corporations now seek out the least-cost bidder to provide them with financial services.

One result of this has been an emphasis on innovation as a means to increase market share. The investment bank that is first to develop (and name) a new type of security or strategy can win new business that in previous days would have been tied by customer relationships to other firms. Others will naturally imitate the innovation, but the originator has a head start. In this environment, investment banks have sought to establish reputations for creativity and expertise in financial engineering. They have increasingly hired professionals with advanced technical training to staff their new-product research departments.

As a result of this emphasis on innovation, an institutional investor can now hold securities no primary borrower would consider issuing. Some innovative instruments, such as an IO/PO mortgage-backed security, would be virtually impossible, perhaps even illegal, to issue directly. Others, such as an inverse floater, would test the limits of project finance. However, the newfound ability to transform cash flows with respect to timing and amount—types of intermediation far beyond the classic role of a commercial bank—irrevocably breaks any necessary link between ultimate borrower and ultimate investor.

Commercial banks, of course, have not sat idly by while investment banks chipped away at their business. They, too, have adapted to a more transactions-based environment by increasingly separating and repackaging different facets of their traditional intermediation function. Even when they choose not to hold the loans on their balance sheets, for example, commercial banks and thrift institutions still earn fee income by originating and servicing the mortgages underlying various types of mortgage-backed securities. Commercial banks have also separated the credit analysis component of their traditional business in a variety of innovative ways. When a company goes directly to the public debt markets, a bank can support the issue with a letter of credit. Many large, money center banks have assumed a market-making role in the swap market. They serve as the direct counterparty in swap agreements and then manage their interest rate and currency risk exposure by entering into offsetting agreements with other parties. However, since they do not set up the same system of margin accounts and marking-to-market that characterizes futures exchanges, this role in turn requires that banks assess the credit-worthiness of any party with whom it has made a swap agreement. In capacities such as these, then, the banks act as facilitators of market transactions rather than as true financial intermediaries.

Whether the pace of bond market innovation will be as rapid in the 1990s remains to be seen. It will depend on changes in risk perceptions, tax laws and regulations, and technological advances. Whatever these changes may be, however, the innovations of the 1980s have fundamentally changed the way that market participants conceive of the process of financial intermediation.

References

Keith C. Brown and Donald J. Smith, "Recent Innovations in Interest Rate Risk Management and the Reintermediation of Commercial Banking," *Financial Management*, Winter 1988, pp. 45–58.

Ian Cooper, "Innovations: New Market Instruments," *Oxford Review of Economic Policy*, Winter 1986, pp. 1–17.

John D. Finnerty, "Financial Engineering in Corporate Finance: An Overview," *Financial Management*, Winter 1988, pp. 14–33.

Richard M. Levich, "Financial Innovations in International Financial Markets," National Bureau of Economic Research Working Paper No. 2227, June 1987, Cambridge Mass.

Merton H. Miller, "Financial Innovation: The Last Twenty Years and the Next," *Journal of Financial and Quantitative Analysis*, December, 1986, pp. 459–471.

Kevin J. Perry and Robert A. Taggart, Jr., "The Growing Role of Junk Bonds in Corporate Finance," *Continental Bank Journal of Applied Corporate Finance*, Spring 1988, pp. 37–45.

Donald J Smith, "The Pricing of Bull and Bear Floating-Rate Notes: An Application of Financial Engineering," *Financial Management*, Winter 1988, pp. 72–81.

Marcia Stigum and Frank L. Fabozzi, *The Dow Jones-Irwin Guide to Bond and Money Market Investments* (Homewood, Ill.: Dow Jones-Irwin, 1987).

Dimitri Vittas, "The New Market Menagerie," *The Banker*, June 1986, pp. 16–27.

Questions

1. a. Identify the factors that influence the demand for bonds.
   b. Identify the factors that influence the supply of bonds.
   c. Describe the two ways for joining the demand and supply sides of the bond market.
2. Why is a commercial bank referred to as a financial intermediary?
3. Six major innovations in the bond market during the 1970s are as follows: floating-rate notes, Eurobonds, junk bonds, mortgage pass-through securities, parallel loans, and financial futures contracts. Describe each of these innovations and the stimuli that brought it forth.
4. Auto loans (called CARS—certificates of automobile receivables), credit card loans (called CARDS—certificates of amortizing revolving debts), and other receivables have been securitized. Describe the process of securitization.
5. "The market for any security type will always be limited if the desires of investors and issuers must be precisely matched. In our opinion, then, the most significant financial innovations of the 1980s have been those that allow an uncoupling of investor and issuer desires." Explain this statement.
6. What are zero-coupon bonds, TIGRs, CATs, LIONs, and STRIPs? Describe the role of the investment bank in the creation of TIGRs and CATs.
7. Suppose a financial institution converts the following Treasury bond into STRIPs: a two-year Treasury bond with a par value of $1,000 and a coupon rate of 7 percent, payable semiannually. How many zero-coupon bonds can be formed from stripping this T-bond? Explain.
8. What is meant by the *prepayment risk* of GNMA pass-throughs?
9. What are collateralized mortgage obligations (CMOs)? Describe the role of the investment bank in the creation of CMOs.
10. What is a currency swap? An interest rate swap?
11. Describe the swap-driven inverse floating rate note portrayed in Figure 3.
12. "Dual-currency bonds are a classic example of a security that comes from investor demand and not issuer supply." Explain this statement.

Financing with Preferred Stock

Arthur L. Houston, Jr., and Carol Olson Houston

Significant changes occurred in the market for preferred stock during the 1980s. The most apparent change was the number of new types of preferred stock. These innovations, including various types of adjustable rate and auction rate preferred stock, have received considerable attention in the business and academic press (see, for example, Alderson, Brown, and Lummer [1], Finnerty [12], and Winger et al. [25]). However, because of fundamental economic developments during the 1980s, there is good reason to believe that the changes go far beyond the innovations in preferred stock instruments. The 1980s witnessed a highly active merger market and turbulence and regulatory change in the financial services industry that is unprecedented since the Great Depression. Also important are the recent downturn in capital expenditures by the utility industry and changes in the tax laws. Taken together, these factors have produced major shifts in the pattern of industry issuances of preferred stock.

The theory of preferred stock—how preferred stock fits into the capital structure framework—has also undergone considerable development in the past few years. Fooladi and Roberts [13] integrate preferred stock into Miller's [18] "Debt and Taxes" framework. Because preferred stock is a tax-advantaged investment for corporate investors, positive amounts of preferred stock will be both supplied and demanded in a Miller equilibrium. Elmer [10] integrates the Miller equilibrium model with the tax shield uncertainty model of DeAngelo and Masulis [9]. He demonstrates how preferred stock interacts with nondebt tax shields to influence a firm's optimal capital structure, showing that low preferred stock yields effectively enable low tax rate firms to sell excess tax shields. In this way, firms can effectively achieve tax advantages similar to debt financing regardless of their present and expected tax rates. Both studies provide the testable implication that lightly taxed firms are more likely to issue preferred

At the time of this writing, Arthur L. Houston, Jr. was an assistant professor of finance and Carol Olson Houston was an assistant professor of accountancy, both at San Diego State University, San Diego, CA.

Source: *Financial Management* (Autumn 1990, Vol. 19 No. 1, pp. 42–54). Reprinted with permission from *Financial Management;* Arthur L. Houston, Jr., associate professor of finance and Carol Olson Houston, associate professor of accountancy, both at San Diego State University.

stock than heavily taxed firms. In a related paper, Trigeorgis [23] provides empirical evidence, within subsectors of the public utility industry, that lower average effective tax rates are associated with higher proportions of preferred stock issuances.

There are two main goals here. One is to obtain evidence to substantiate the expectation of major changes on the supply side of the preferred market. The second is to empirically test the two implications of the tax hypothesis: *(i)* that firms issuing preferred stock have lower-than-average tax rates and *(ii)* that firms investing in preferred stock have higher-than-average tax rates. The first goal, along with part *(i)* of the second goal, is achieved through an analysis of the annual reports of 643 firms which together made 892 issues of preferred stock from 1981–1987. Part *(ii)* of the second goal is achieved by analyzing the annual reports of 117 firms which held preferred stock as short-term (current) investment during the same period. The annual report data were obtained from the National Automated Accounting Research System (NAARS) database, and were supplemented by the responses from a survey of a random sample of the preferred stock issuers identified in NAARS.

The results show that, in sharp contrast to previous periods, industrial firms rather than utilities issued the majority of preferred stock during the 1980s. Of the 892 issues in the sample, 60% were issued by industrials, 30% by the financials, and only 10% by the utilities. There is strong support for the tax hypothesis, but not for some common generalizations about preferred stock found in the literature. For example, financials do not primarily issue variable dividend preferred stock, and the majority of convertible preferred stock issues are not used to finance mergers.

Major Economic Developments Affecting the Market for Preferred Stock

Developments in the Financial Services Industry

The 1980s were a period of intense change in the financial services industry, both in the thrift and commercial-banking sectors. The problems plaguing the industry have led to a number of regulatory changes and to the passage in August 1989 of the Financial Institutions Reform, Recovery, and Enforcement Act (FIRREA). A number of these regulatory changes, enacted both before and after the passage of FIRREA, have important implications for capital structure choice.

Of major significance is a change made to Federal Home Loan Bank Board (FHLBB) regulations in 1984 which permits thrifts to transfer up to 30% of their assets to wholly owned financial subsidiaries for the purpose of collateralizing the issuance of securities, typically preferred stock. Once transferred, such assets may not be attached to satisfy obligations of the parent firm, as the subsidiary is a separate legal entity. Consequently, preferred stock issued against these assets, if sufficiently over-collateralized, can receive the highest ratings from the rating agencies regardless of the rating of the parent thrift. Additionally, thrifts can use existing net operating losses (NOLs) to shield subsidiaries' earnings from taxes.

The end result is a comparatively low-cost source of funds. By the end of 1987 thrifts had issued over $4 billion of preferred stock through these subsidiaries.[1]

Additionally, capital definitions and policies were reformulated in 1981. As a result, perpetual preferred stock (either fixed or variable dividend) now qualifies as primary capital for determining capital adequacy ratios. (See Cooper and Fraser [7] and Nagle and Petersen [19].) Also, in response to FIRREA, the Office of Thrift Supervision (OTS) has issued tough, new capital standards for thrifts which include:

(i) Tangible capital of 1.5%, consisting of common and preferred stock, retained earnings, and purchased mortgage-servicing rights;

(ii) Core capital of 3%, consisting of tangible capital plus supervisory goodwill; and

(iii) Risk-based capital, consisting of 6.4% of the value of risk-weighted assets (risk weights are applied to a thrift institution's assets according to the assets' inherent riskiness).

Similar capital standards are being implemented for commercial banks.

Finally, a recently implemented set of regulations requires insured institutions to replace Regulatory Accounting Principles (RAP) with Generally Accepted Accounting Principles (GAAP). The transition to GAAP reduces the proportion of capital that qualifies as regulatory capital for many financial institutions. Previously authorized categories of "regulatory capital," including appraised equity, unamortized gains and losses, and certain other items, will be phased out. The resulting reduction in capital can be quite substantial. For the largest financials, both thrifts and commercial banks, it is not unusual for capital recognized under RAP to exceed that recognized under GAAP by a factor of more than two to one (see Berger [2]).

As a result of all these changes, financial institutions are in a capital-building mode.[2] Financials made increased use of the capital markets during the 1980s, and this trend is expected to continue for the foreseeable future. Thus, financials are likely to have substantially increased their participation in the supply of preferred stock to the capital markets.

Developments in the Utility Industry

Earlier studies have shown the utility industry to be the dominant supplier of preferred stock prior to 1980. During the first half of the 1980s, however, the utilities had lower growth in nominal capital expenditures than their prior historical average, and since 1986 the industry has experienced a downturn in capital

---

[1] See "News Report," *Journal of Accountancy* (January 1988), p. 14.

[2] Capital ratios can be increased either by increasing capital or by shrinking the asset base. Many financials are undoubtedly doing both in order to comply with the new capital standards.

expenditures.[3] Consequently, relative to the other industry groups, a reduction is expected in the utility industry's use of preferred stock during the 1980s.

Developments in the Merger Market

The prolonged and active merger market of the 1980s is also likely to have influenced industry patterns of preferred stock usage. The sheer magnitude of this market is striking: prior to 1981 there were no billion-dollar hostile tender offers. In 1984 alone there were 18 takeovers with announced prices exceeding $1 billion, including SOCAL's $13.4 billion purchase of Gulf Oil, Beatrice Companies' $2.5 billion takeover of Esmark, and Kohlberg Kravis Roberts & Co.'s subsequent acquisition of Beatrice for $4.9 billion in a leveraged buyout.

Preferred stock has been used by both target firms and acquiring firms. A number of potential target firms have used preferred stock issues as an anti-takeover device to decrease their attractiveness. A simple but effective defensive measure is to privately place in friendly hands an issue of preferred which has voting rights in the event of a takeover attempt. Other more elaborate devices include a convertible preferred stock dividend plan in which preferred stock is issued as a dividend to the firm's existing stockholders. The preferred stock has redemption and conversion features, triggered by a takeover, which allow stockholders to continue to participate as equity owners in the postacquisition firm. Additionally, there may be a "fair price" provision under which the preferred typically converts into postacquisition equity with a market value equal to not less than the price paid by the acquirer for the target firm's stock during the 12 months preceding the consummation of the takeover.

Acquisitions are often made by paying the selling shareholders cash and securities. Preferred stock has long been popular for this purpose, in part because of various tax advantages to both parties. Tax advantages to selling shareholders have generally become more restrictive over the years although, surprisingly, properly structured issues of preferred stock may still be tax-free to selling shareholders—see, for example, Walter and Strasen [24]. Two recent innovations, exchangeable preferred and payment-in-kind (PIK) preferred, have become popular with acquiring firms. Preferred stock which is exchangeable into debt permits the acquiring firm to reap the tax advantages of preferred stock (over debt) during the low tax rate years immediately following the acquisition, and to cost-effectively exchange the preferred stock for debentures when tax rates (and debt capacity) subsequently increase. PIK preferred stock gives acquirers the option of issuing additional shares of preferred stock in lieu of dividends during the years of lean cash flow immediately following a takeover. PIK preferred has typically been used in conjunction with junk bonds to effect highly leveraged takeovers and buyouts.

Casual observation leads one to believe that takeovers involving the issuance of substantial amounts of securities have been concentrated predominantly

[3] See various issues, the *Utility Investment Report,* published by The Conference Board, Inc.

among industrial firms, and secondarily among the financials. While the market for failed financial institutions has been quite active, subsidies from regulatory agencies and special tax benefits may have somewhat lessened the need for additional external financing in these acquisitions. Thus, given the size of the merger market during the 1980s, one would expect to see an increase in the participation of the industrials and financials the preferred market, all other things equal.

Implications for the Pattern of Preferred Stock Issuances

In summary, a number of economic developments during the 1980s have in all likelihood led to major changes on the supply side of the market for preferred stock. Taken together, the clear implication of these developments is that industrials and financials are likely to have greatly increased the proportion of preferred stock they supply to the market relative to the utilities. Evidence in support of this prediction is provided in the sections which follow.

Descriptive Statistics

The Data

A sample of 892 issues of preferred stock was identified in the NAARS database. The data were collected from the financial reports of 643 firms which reported issuing preferred stock during fiscal years 1981–1987 (period ending June 1988). The NAARS database was selected for three reasons. First, because it contains the complete text of corporate annual reports, including footnotes, NAARS has a richness of detail other databases lack. Second, NAARS contains the population of greatest interest—over 4,200 of the more heavily capitalized, publicly traded companies including those traded on the New York and American Stock Exchanges and those over-the-counter companies which the Federal Reserve has put on margin. Finally, in contrast to the SEC data and other sources such as the Corporate Financing Directory of the Investment Dealer's Digest, which only list public, cash offerings of preferred stock, data in NAARS includes both cash and exchange offerings, and both public offerings and private placements.

Recent Trends in the Use of Preferred Stock by Type

The sample has been partitioned into four mutually exclusive categories. In order of priority, the preferred stock categories are *(i)* variable dividend, *(ii)* convertible, *(iii)* redeemable/exchangeable, and *(iv)* perpetual. For example, a preferred stock issue which has both a variable dividend and is convertible is reported here as a variable dividend. A fixed dividend issue which is described by its issuer as both convertible and redeemable is included as convertible. Thus, all variable dividend preferreds have been grouped together in one category. In the following sections, convertible, redeemable/exchangeable, and perpetual are sometimes referred to collectively as fixed dividend preferred. To maintain consistency with previous studies, the empirical results are reported in terms of issues of preferred stock.

Recent trends in the issuances of the various types of preferred stock based on the NAARS database are shown in Exhibit 1. From 1982–1985, variable dividend preferred consisted primarily of adjustable-rate preferred stock. The decline in the amount of variable dividend preferred issued in 1984 and 1985 from its initial peak in 1983 is generally attributed to investor disappointment in the price-volatility experienced with adjustable-rate preferred over this period. The upturn in variable dividend preferred issuances in 1986 was primarily due to the introduction of auction rate preferred, which has substantially lower price volatility. Interestingly, the substantial amount of variable dividend preferred stock supplied to the market since 1982 has not appeared to detract from the steadily increasing use of fixed dividend preferred stock over this period.

Industry Usage of Preferred Stock

Exhibit 2 summarizes industry participation on the supply side of the market for preferred stock over the 1981–1987 period, by category of preferred stock. Firms issuing preferred stock have been partitioned into three industry groups: industrials, financials, and utilities. This industry classification is identical to Moody's except that communication, transportation, and real estate firms have been included with the industrials.[4] Exhibit 2 illustrates several interesting points. The primary importance of the industrials, which issued 60% of the total sample of preferred stock over this period, is quite evident. Of the 533

EXHIBIT 1 ANNUAL ISSUES OF PREFERRED STOCK[a]

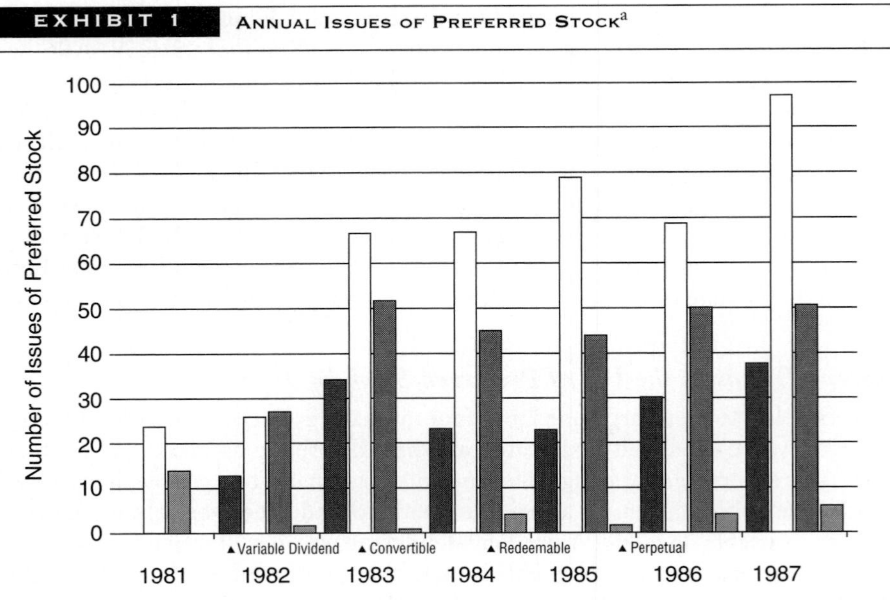

SOURCE: NAARS.

[a]Encompasses all issuances for fiscal years 1981–1987 (period ending June 1988) for a total of 892 issues.

[4] Communication, transportation, and real estate firms account for 2%, 5%, and 3% of total issues, respectively.

EXHIBIT 2 INDUSTRY STATISTICS FOR 892 ISSUES OF PREFERRED STOCK BETWEEN 1981–1987 BY TYPE OF PREFERRED STOCK

	Variable Dividend		Convertible		Straight Redeemable		Straight Perpetual		Total Sample	
	Issues	%	Issues	%	Issues	%	Issues	%	Issues	%
Industrials	33	20	328	76	161	57	11	58	533	60
Financials	109	68	93	22	54	19	8	42	264	30
Utilities	19	12	10	2	66	24	0	0	95	10
Total	161	100	431	100	281	100	19	100	892	100
Percent of Total Sample	18		48		32		2		100	

total issuances by industrials, 62% were convertible, 30% were straight (nonconvertible) redeemable, 6% were variable dividend, and 2% were perpetual. The preference demonstrated by the industrials for convertible preferred is consistent with the findings of previous studies; see Linn and Pinegar [14], Marr and Thompson [15], Melicher [16], and Pinches [20].

Financials ranked second in total issues of preferred stock with 30% of the total. While the financials supplied most of the variable dividend preferred (68%), they issued less variable dividend preferred than fixed dividend. Of the total issuances by financials, 41% were variable dividend and 59% were fixed dividend preferred stock.

To underscore the continuing interest of financial institutions in fixed dividend preferred, contrast these results with those of Linn and Pinegar [14] who, using data from the period 1962–1984, found that 52% of the preferred stock issued by financials was adjustable-rate preferred. Since no adjustable-rate preferred was issued prior to 1982, the number of "variable dividend" preferred issues during 1982–1984 outweighed all of the fixed dividend preferred issued by the financials during the years 1962–1984. In contrast, in this sample the various types of variable dividend preferred account for only 41% of the issues of preferred stock financials during the seven-year period 1981–1987. Thus, it can be concluded that the sharp increase in the participation of the financials during the 1980s has been primarily attributable to an increase in the number of issues of fixed dividend preferred, and only secondarily attributable to the introduction of variable dividend preferred.

The relatively low participation by the utility industry, 10% of total issues, stands in sharp contrast to previous decades in which the utility industry dominated this market. Of the total issuances by utilities, 71% were straight redeemable, 11% were convertible, and 18% were variable dividend. These results are consistent with previous findings that utilities primarily issue nonconvertible preferred stock, such as Linn and Pinegar [14], Marr and Thompson [15], and Pinches [20].

The analysis to this point substantiates the prediction of major changes from historical patterns of industry behavior. First, industrials and financials dominated the supply side of the market during the 1980s. Moreover, utilities did not issue most of the straight fixed-rate preferred and financials did not generally issue variable dividend preferred.[5] In the sample, utilities issued only 22% of the straight fixed-rate preferreds, and only 41% of total issuances by financials were adjustable-rate (variable dividend) preferred.

These major changes in industry behavior raise a further important question. Have there been concomitant changes in the corporate purposes for which firms issued preferred stock in the 1980s? Because publicly available data do not provide evidence relating to this question, it was collected via a survey instrument.

Survey of Preferred Stock Issuers

Design

In June 1988, questionnaires were mailed to the highest ranking financial officer in each of 200 firms, randomly selected from the NAARS population. The

[5] See Bildersee [3], Brealey and Myers [4], and Linn and Pinegar [14].

questionnaire included: *(i)* a listing of the types of preferred stock issued since 1980; *(ii)* statements designed to profile the uses to which the funds were put; and *(iii)* the title of the respondent and the name of the firm. In July 1988, a second request was sent to all firms which had not responded to the first questionnaire. A total of 99 usable responses were received, resulting in a response rate of 49%.

Exhibit 3 presents a comparison of the NAARS population, the target sample, and the respondent firms. Overall, the random sample portrays approximately the same characteristics as the NAARS population relating to industry participation measured by number of firms, number of issues, and dollar amounts of issues. A response bias exists to the extent that financials are overrepresented and industrials are underrepresented relative to all three measures.

Survey Results

Survey participants were asked to indicate how they used the proceeds from the issuance of preferred stock. Preselected responses included two broad categories: *(i)* acquisition of assets (long-term assets, mergers or acquisitions, and working capital); and *(ii)* restructuring of the balance sheet (reduction of long-term debt, reduction of short-term debt, repurchase of common, and redemption of preferred). Analysis of responses is based on the number of issuances instead of the number of respondent firms.

EXHIBIT 3 INDUSTRY COMPOSITION AND AMOUNTS OF PREFERRED STOCK (ALL TYPES COMBINED) ISSUED BY THE NAARS POPULATION, THE SURVEY TARGET SAMPLE, AND THE SAMPLE OF SURVEY RESPONDENTS

	Number of Firms		Number of Issues		Dollar Amount (in millions)	
			Panel A. NAARS Population[a]			
Utilities	61	10%	95	10%	$5,803.9	12%
Financials	182	28%	264	30%	18,831.0	40%
Industrials	400	62%	533	60%	22,750.6	48%
Total	643	100%	892	100%	47,385.5	100%
			Panel B. Survey Target Sample[b]			
Utilities	12	6%	23	7%	1,170.8	5%
Financials	71	35%	118	36%	8,586.4	37%
Industrials	117	59%	188	57%	13,199.2	58%
Total	200	100%	329	100%	22,956.4	100%
			Panel C. Survey Response Sample[c]			
Utilities	7	7%	12	7%	473.8	5%
Financials	45	45%	75	45%	6,392.2	66%
Industrials	47	48%	78	48%	2,765.4	29%
Total	99	100%	165	100%	9,631.4	100%

[a] Companies in the NAARS database issuing preferred stock from 1981–1987.
[b] The 200 firms randomly selected from the NAARS population.
[c] The firms in the target sample providing usable responses.

Exhibit 4 provides industry summaries of the uses of all types of preferred taken together. From Exhibit 4 it can be noted that the majority of firms in each industry issued preferred stock to acquire assets. Firms acquire assets either to expand the asset base, to replace worn-out assets, or both. In all likelihood, the financing of capital expenditure leads, on average, to an expansion of the asset base. In the case of industrials, Mikkelson and Partch [17] find empirical evidence that financings of capital expenditures, on average, lead to a large relative change in total assets. In the case of financials, preferred stock often qualifies as regulatory capital and, within regulatory limitations, can substitute for common stock. Normally, the primary reason for increasing regulatory capital would be to expand the asset base.[6] It appears, therefore, that for each industry group the majority of preferred stock financings are used to support corporate growth.

The utilities showed a strong tendency to use preferred either for acquiring long-term assets (43%) or for reducing long-term debt (39%). None of the utilities responding to the survey had used preferred for the purpose of mergers or acquisitions.

Financials and industrials made similar use of preferred stock in two ways. First, neither made significant use of funds to repurchase common stock or

EXHIBIT 4 USES OF FUNDS BY SURVEY RESPONDENTS, BY INDUSTRY (% OF TOTAL ISSUES)

	Industrials (45)[a]	Utilities (7)	Financials (43)	Total (95)
Acquisition of Assets				
Long-term assets	12	43	26	22
Mergers or acquisitions	37	0	39	35
Working capital	17	9	24	20
Subtotal	66	52	89	77
Financial Restructuring				
Reduce short-term debt	10	0	1	4
Reduce long-term debt	25	39	6	16
Repurchase common	0	0	3	2
Redeem preferred	0	9	1	1
Subtotal	35	48	11	23
Total	101[b]	100	100	100

[a] Number of firms providing useable responses in parentheses.
[b] Exceeds 100% due to rounding.

[6] We provided space for respondents to indicate any use of funds other than those we preselected. We are indebted to a number of respondents from financial institutions who wrote in "the acquisition of regulatory capital" as their use of funds. We did not provide this as a preselected response because we were primarily interested in the ultimate use of funds, which in the case of regulatory capital would normally be to increase the asset base. Of course, in the current situation where increases in required capital ratios are being phased in, the acquisition of capital might be necessary to simply maintain the existing asset base. We appreciate the fact that for most financial institutions the only reason the funds were used for the ultimate purpose of increasing (or maintaining) the asset base was because preferred stock qualified as regulatory capital. This implies that any increased restrictions on the qualification of preferred stock as regulatory capital could have the effect of reducing its use by financial institutions.

redeem previously issued preferred stock. Second, the most prevalent use of funds for both groups was to facilitate mergers and acquisitions (37% for industrials and 39% for financials). There were, however, two major differences in the way financials and industrials made use of preferred stock. First, industrials were more than three times as likely as financials to use funds for restructuring the balance sheet (35% versus 11%). Specifically, industrials used over four times as many issues for reducing long-term debt (25% versus 6%), and ten times as many issues for reducing short-term debt (10% versus 1%). A potential explanation is that long-term debt is simply more prevalent in the balance sheets of industrials. Financial intermediaries generally favor the use of short-term liabilities such as deposits and central bank borrowings over the use of long-term debt. Moreover, preferred stock of most types would generally not be viewed as a reasonable substitute for deposits or central bank borrowings.

Concurrent with the use of a lower percentage of preferred for restructuring activities, financials used a higher percentage of issues (89% versus 66%) to acquire assets (including mergers and acquisitions). For industrials, the restructuring activity was overwhelmingly in the direction of reducing leverage; that is, preferred stock was used to reduce debt rather than to repurchase common.

Exhibit 5 is similar to Exhibit 4 except that uses of funds are shown for the various types of preferred stock, with all industries taken together. Aggregated totals for Exhibit 5 differ slightly from the industry totals in Exhibit 4 because a small number of firms reported multiple issues of preferred and multiple uses for the proceeds, but did not provide sufficient information to separate the specific uses to which each type of preferred was put. Exhibit 5 partitions variable dividend preferred into auction rate and adjustable rate in order to identify any dissimilarity in usage with differences in duration. There are some interesting variations in usage. For example, the predominant use of convertible, straight redeemable, and adjustable rate preferred was to facilitate mergers and acquisitions, whereas the predominant use of straight perpetual preferred was to acquire long-term assets. Of greatest interest, however, is the fact that there is no single use to which the majority of preferred stock proceeds were applied. This is true both for each type of preferred stock and for all types taken together. It is interesting to note that preferred stock was used by the survey respondents to finance the entire spectrum of corporate activities. The most popular use, to facilitate mergers and acquisitions, accounts for only 36% of the total usage of preferred funds. As a whole, there is little support for another common generalization—that convertible preferred stock is issued primarily to finance mergers (see, for example, Brealey and Meyers [4], Brigham and Gapenski [5], Melicher [16], and Pinches [20]). Exhibit 5 shows that only 31% of the convertible preferred was used for that purpose, in spite of the fact that this was a period of intense activity in the merger market.

The Tax Hypothesis of Preferred Stock Issuance

Background

Puzzlement about why firms issue preferred stock is often expressed in terms of traditional arguments which focus exclusively on the issuing firm. In terms of

EXHIBIT 5 Uses of Funds by Survey Respondents, by Type of Preferred (in %)

	Convertible (48)[a]	Redeemable (22)	Perpetual (11)	Adjustable (24)	Auction (6)	Total (111)
Acquisition of Assets						
Long-term assets	18	18	46	25	38	23
Mergers or acquisitions	31	49	36	38	17	36
Working capital	21	10	9	28	13	19
Subtotal	70	77	91	91	68	78
Restructuring						
Reduce short-term debt	7	9	0	0	8	5
Reduce long-term debt	23	14	9	9	7	16
Repurchase common	0[b]	0	0	0	0	0[c]
Redeem preferred	0	0	0	0	16	1
Subtotal	30	23	9	9	31	22
Total	100	100	100	100	99[d]	100

[a]Number of issues in parentheses.
[b]Unrounded percentage is 0.4375.
[c]Unrounded percentage is 0.189.
[d]Does not equal 100% due to rounding.

these traditional arguments, preferred stock is seen as having *(i)* a tax disadvantage compared to debt, *(ii)* no tax advantage compared to common, and *(iii)* a disadvantage in "flexibility" compared to common. In this view, debt has a tax advantage over preferred stock since interest payments on debt are tax deductible but preferred dividends are not. On the other hand, debt is less flexible than preferred stock in the sense that omission of the preferred dividend will usually have less serious consequences for the firm than omitting interest payments. Compared to common stock, however, preferred is viewed as being less flexible and as having no tax advantage since neither preferred nor common dividends are tax deductible. Consequently, in this traditional view preferred stock is something of an enigma and is a suitable financing vehicle only under special circumstances.[7]

Fooladi and Roberts [13] argue that this traditional viewpoint is too simple because it ignores the dividends-received tax deduction which exempts 70% of dividend income received by corporate investors. They demonstrate that in a Miller [18] equilibrium, firms with low tax rates will be induced to issue preferred stock to corporate investors with high tax rates who can take advantage of the dividends-received deduction. This inducement takes the form of a lower before-tax current yield on preferred stock than would be required of equally risky corporate debt. For example, high-quality Dutch auction rate preferred stock yields are typically less than 80% of the rates on commercial paper of similar duration and quality. For issuing firms with sufficiently low tax rates, this "pass-through" tax benefit in the form of a rate reduction outweighs the interest tax shield forgone by issuing preferred rather than debt. Elmer [10] extends the analysis of preferred stock in a Miller equilibrium by demonstrating that preferred stock is a potentially attractive financing alternative for firms with tax rates less than 0.8 of the aggregate expected corporate tax rate. Both studies imply that firms with below-average expected tax rates will have an incentive to sell preferred stock to a tax clientele of firms with above-average expected tax rates.

Tests of the Tax Hypothesis for the Sample as a Whole: Supply Side

The hypothesis to be tested is that, at the time of issuance, firms issuing preferred stock have lower tax rates than the average firm. In principle, the tax rate affecting the firm's decision to issue preferred stock is the firm's expected tax rate over the life of the instrument. Since the expected tax rate is unobservable, the average of the issuance year and the two previous years is used as an estimate of the expected effective tax rate, hereafter referred to simply as the firm's "tax rate." The primary test of the hypothesis is accomplished by comparing each firm's tax rate to the market median effective tax rate in the year of issuance. Additionally and of considerably less theoretical importance, a comparison of firm versus industry median effective tax rates is reported. Issuing firms' tax rates are also compared to the market and industry means.

[7] "[I]t is a puzzle why preferred stock is issued at all...," Copeland and Weston, [8, p. 480]. See also Ross, Westerfield, and Jaffe [21, p. 377].

The mean and median effective tax rates for each industry, and for the market as a whole, were computed for each of the seven sample years using COMPUSTAT. The mean and median tax rates for each industry were computed from the individual tax rates of all firms in the industry (2 digit SIC code). For the market as a whole, the mean and median tax rates were calculated from the population of all firms reported in COMPUSTAT.

The tax rates of the firms in this sample were collected from the footnotes of annual reports in the year preferred stock was issued. For the less than 3% of firms which failed to provide that disclosure, the effective tax rate was determined by dividing total income taxes by total pretax income for the year as reported in the annual report. A histogram of this distribution revealed significant departures from normality including an excess of values near the mean combined with severe negative skewness.[8] This observation was verified by performing three different tests of normality; a chi-square goodness of fit test, a skewness test, and a test of kurtosis [22, pp. 84–89]. The value of chi-square was 1,609, the coefficient of skewness was -1.2783 (over 15 standard deviations to the left of the mean), and the kurtosis value was 70.56 (3 is normal). One can conclude that the distribution is significantly skewed with very high positive kurtosis. The results of all three tests cause rejection of the hypothesis of normality at significance levels exceeding 0.001. Because of the severe departure from normality, the tax hypothesis must be tested primarily with nonparametric measures, specifically the sign test. Similarly, comparisons of firm tax rates to the medians of the market and industry tax rates will generally be more meaningful than comparisons to the means. Because of the large amount of positive kurtosis, the variance of the sample distribution is significantly greater than if it were normal [22, p. 89]. This biases the standard *t*-test against the tax hypothesis and in favor of the null. Because the direction of bias is known, the results of standard *t*-tests are reported in addition to the nonparametric sign tests.

Four sets of paired observations were tested: firm tax rate versus *(i)* market median tax rate, *(ii)* market mean tax rate, *(iii)* industry median tax rate, and *(iv)* industry mean tax rate.[9] The results are reported in Panel A of Exhibit 6. Note that the issuing firm's tax rate was lower than the median of the market in the year of issuance for 609 of 838 pairs (73%), and lower than the industry median for 524 of 838 pairs (63%). One-tailed sign tests test the hypothesis that the issuing firms' tax rates tend to be lower than the market and industry median tax rates. The pairs for both tests were significantly different at $\alpha = 0.0001$. Additionally, one-sided *t*-tests were computed. As shown in Exhibit 6, the results of the *t*-tests were highly significant and consistent with the sign tests. When firm tax rates were compared to the means of the industry and market tax rates, the

---

[8] Large negative tax rates are the result of low taxable earnings in a year in which a relatively large tax refund is reported.

[9] Beginning with the total population of 892 issues, we deleted 54 issues to preclude double counting firms which issued two different types of preferred stock in a given year. As a result, the tests of individual firm versus market tax rates and industry tax rates included 838 pairs.

EXHIBIT 6 RESULTS OF STATISTICAL TESTS OF THE TAX HYPOTHESIS: SUPPLY SIDE

	t-Test Results		Sign Test Results
Panel A. Comparisons of Issuing Firms' Effective Tax Rates Versus Market and Industry Tax Rates in the Year of Issuance for the Test Sample (838 observations)[a]			
Combined Industries (838 observations)			
609 firms (73%) < market median	14.08	(0.0001)	(0.0001)
524 firms (63%) < industry median	8.23	(0.0001)	(0.0001)
526 firms (63%) < market mean	9.06	(0.0001)	(0.0001)
529 firms (63%) < industry mean	7.88	(0.0001)	(0.0001)
Panel B. Comparisons of Issuing Firms' Effective Tax Rates Versus Market and Industry Tax Rates in the Year of Issuance for the Major Industry Groups			
Industrials (494 observations)			
348 firms (70%) < market median	9.64	(0.0001)	(0.0001)
320 firms (65%) < industry median	7.13	(0.0001)	(0.0001)
308 firms (62%) < market mean	6.22	(0.0001)	(0.0001)
307 firms (62%) < industry mean	5.83	(0.0001)	(0.0001)
Financials (255 observations)			
212 firms (83%) < market median	11.32	(0.0001)	(0.0001)
140 firms (55%) < industry median	2.89	(0.0050)	(0.1000)
191 firms (75%) < market mean	8.14	(0.0001)	(0.0001)
161 firms (63%) < industry mean	4.92	(0.0001)	(0.0001)
Utilities (89 observations)			
49 firms (55%) < market median	2.31	(0.0500)	(0.2000)
64 firms (72%) < industry median	5.45	(0.0001)	(0.0005)
27 firms (30%) < market mean	-1.94[b]	(0.0500)[b]	(0.0001)[b]
61 firms (69%) < industry mean	3.96	(0.0001)	(0.0005)

[a] An observation is defined as an issue by one of the sample firms in any one of the sample years. Thus a firm may be included more than once if it made issues in more than one of the sample years. However, to avoid double counting, a firm may not be included more than once in any given year. The difference between the total sample of 892 issues and the 838 issues included in the test sample is due to firms which made multiple issues in the same year.
[b] Significance is in the opposite direction of that predicted.

results were essentially identical to those obtained in comparisons against the medians.

In summary, the results are strongly supportive of the tax hypothesis. Nonetheless, it remains that 27% of the sample had tax rates equal to or greater than the market median. One can only speculate on the reasons for this cross-sectional variation, but it is likely that it can be at least partly explained by various "strategic" or "qualitative" factors. Perhaps chief among these are the strategic considerations surrounding the use of preferred stock to facilitate mergers and acquisitions. The survey respondents (see Exhibit 5) report using 36% of all preferred stock issues for this purpose. Other factors such as flexibility, preservation of debt capacity, signaling incentives, and attempts at market timing may also be relevant.

Tests of the Tax Hypothesis Across Industry Groups: Supply Side

In principle, the degree of industry regulation could affect a firm's capital structure decisions. One could argue, for example, that highly regulated firms might be less aggressive in their pursuit of tax benefits than less regulated, more competitive firms. One could also argue that regulated firms might be more willing to trade tax benefits for qualitative factors of primary importance to management, such as control of the firm. In either case, one would expect a weaker link between the firms' tax rates and the market median tax rate as the degree of regulation increased. In this sample there are substantial differences in the degree of regulation among the major industry groups with utilities being highly regulated, financials less highly regulated, and industrials essentially unregulated. To test for the existence of a "regulatory effect," the sample was partitioned into the three major industry groups and the sign and t-tests repeated as shown in Panel B of Exhibit 6. Issuing firms' tax rates are lower than the market median tax rates for each of the industry groups—specifically, for 70% of the industrials, 83% of the financials, and 55% of the utilities. They are also lower than the industry median tax rates for 65% of the industrials, 55% of the financials, and 72% of the utilities. All of these results are in the direction predicted by the tax hypothesis, all are significant using t-tests, and all but the utilities versus the market median are significant using the sign test.

Comparing firms' tax rates to the means of the market and industry tax rates, the industrials and financials are again significantly lower. Contrary to prediction, however, the utilities' tax rates are significantly higher than the mean of the market for 62 of 89 firms (70%). On the other hand, the utilities' tax rates are significantly lower than the mean of the utility industry for 61 of 89 firms (69%). The fact that utilities tend to be below their industry mean but above the market mean is explained by the fact that the utility industry average tax rate is higher than the market average rate in all seven years of the sample period.

The results are thus moderately supportive of the tax hypothesis for the utilities and strongly supportive for the financial and industrial firms which together constituted 90% of the sample. The mixed results for the utilities are indicative of a somewhat weaker link between tax savings and capital structure choice in that industry.[10] Viewed as a whole, the results strongly support the tax hypothesis.

Tests of the Tax Hypothesis: Demand Side

The second implication of the tax hypothesis is that firms which invest in preferred stock have higher tax rates than the average firm. Testing this hypothesis requires identifying a sample of firms holding investments in preferred stock. Currently, firms are not required to disclose the financial instruments in which

---

[10] This could be due to certain qualitative factors which are uniquely important to the utility industry. For example, Elsaid [11] makes the point that utility regulatory commissions commonly believe that "preferred stocks belong in every [utility] capital structure for 'balance'." If so, this could explain why even high tax rate utilities might desire to issue preferred stock.

they invest. Thus, the population from which a sample can be drawn is limited to firms which voluntarily disclose that information in their annual reports. If disclosed, investments in preferred stock are identified as either short-term or long-term. In accordance with GAAP, investments classified as short-term (or current) are expected to be liquidated within one year.

The test sample was limited to firms holding short-term investments. In principle, an investment decision is influenced by the stream of expected tax rates over the life of the investment. Because short-term forecasts have less error, on average, than long-range forecasts, the reported effective tax rate for the current year is a better predictor of the following year's tax rate than it would be a multiyear rate. Thus, limiting projections to a maximum of one year ahead achieves a more powerful test of the hypothesis. A sample of 117 reports of firms disclosing short-term investments in preferred stock was identified in NAARS for fiscal years 1983–1987.

A histogram of the effective tax rates of the sample of 117 investing firms revealed the same departures from normality as the distribution of tax rates for issuing firms. Standard tests of normality confirm significant negative skewness and high positive kurtosis, and cause rejection of normality at significance levels exceeding 0.001. Thus, although the results of standard *t*-tests are reported, the nonparametric sign tests are preferred. Again, it should be noted that the positive kurtosis biases the results of the *t*-tests against the tax hypothesis.

Arguably, when deciding to invest in a tax advantaged instrument, firms will consider the "marginal" tax rate, i.e., the tax rate that would be applicable to the firm's earnings in the absence of the tax advantaged investment. Again, this information is not required under current accounting standards but may be voluntarily disclosed. Of the total sample of 117 firms, 62 disclosed the effective average tax rate the firm would have faced had it not invested in tax-advantaged preferred stock. This rate is used as a proxy for the marginal tax rate. Although the marginal tax rate is presumably of greater importance in the decision to hold a short-term investment in preferred stock than the average tax rate, the hypothesis is tested using both measures. Consequently, four sets of paired observations are tested: two sets of paired observations of firm marginal tax rate versus market median and mean tax rates, and two sets of paired observations of firm average tax rate versus market median and mean tax rates. There are 62 observations on the marginal tax rate and 117 on the average tax rate.

The results of the tests using the firms' marginal tax rates are reported in Panel A of Exhibit 7. Note that the investing firm's marginal tax rate is higher than the median of the market in the year of issuance for 46 of 62 pairs (74%) and higher than the market mean for 54 of 62 pairs (87%). These results are in the direction predicted by the tax hypothesis and are significant at levels exceeding 0.0001 using the primary sign tests. The *t*-test results are positive, but not significantly so.

The comparisons reported in Panel B are similar to those of Panel A except that the firms' average tax rates are used rather than the marginal rates. Again, the results are in the predicted direction and the primary sign tests are highly significant at a greater than 0.0001. Although the *t*-value for the test against the

EXHIBIT 7 RESULTS OF STATISTICAL TESTS OF THE TAX HYPOTHESIS: DEMAND SIDE

	t-Test Results		Sign Test Results
Panel A. Comparisons of Investing Firms' Marginal Effective Tax Rates Versus Market Median and Mean Tax Rates For a Subsample of 62 Firms[a]			
Observed Tax Rates (62 firms)			
46 firms (74%) > market median	0.42	(0.350)[b]	(0.0001)
54 firms (87%) > market mean	1.26	(0.150)[b]	(0.0001)
Panel B. Comparisons of Investing Firms' Average Effective Tax Rates Versus Market Median and Mean Tax Rates For the Test Sample of 117 Firms			
Observed Tax Rates (117 firms)			
86 firms (74%) > market median	0.42	(0.350)[b]	(0.0001)
97 firms (83%) > market mean	2.11	(0.025)	(0.0001)

[a]Only 62 of the 117 firms in the sample provided sufficient information in their financial statements to calculate their marginal tax rates.
[b]Not statistically significant.

market median was insignificantly positive, the t-value for the test against the market mean was both positive and significant at α greater than 0.025. Altogether, the results of the demand side tests reported in Exhibit 7 provide strong support for the tax hypothesis.

Conclusion

Industry behavior on the supply side of the market for preferred stock is investigated and a number of changes are identified during the 1980s. The changes from previous patterns of industry behavior are so pervasive that it is useful to summarize the patterns that were not repeated during the 1980s: *(i)* utilities did not issue most of the straight fixed-rate preferred, *(ii)* financials did not generally issue adjustable-rate (variable dividend) preferred, and *(iii)* convertible preferred stock was not used primarily to finance mergers.

In sharp contrast to earlier periods, this study shows that industrials and financials dominated the market for preferred stock during the 1981–1987 period, with 60% and 30% of the total number of issues respectively. Utilities played a relatively minor role (10% of total issues). The advent of variable dividend preferred stock does not, by itself, account for the increase in the use of preferred stock by financials. The greatly increased participation of the financials is only secondarily attributable to the introduction of variable dividend preferred; it is primarily attributable to greatly increased use of fixed dividend preferred.

Strong support is provided for the tax hypothesis of preferred stock. Compared to market averages, firms issuing preferred stock tend to have significantly lower tax rates, and firms investing in preferred stock tend to have significantly higher tax rates. The survey results indicate that the majority of firms in each industry issued preferred stock to acquire assets—including mergers and acquisitions, which accounted for 36% of total issues. Specifically, 89% of financial issues and 66% of industrial issues were used to acquire assets. The remaining 11% of financial issues and 35% of industrial issues were used for financial restructuring. For industrials, these restructurings were predominantly leverage reducing.

References

1. M.J. Alderson, K.C. Brown, and S.L. Lummer, "Dutch Auction Rate Preferred Stock," *Financial Management* (Summer 1987), pp. 68–73.
2. D.V. Berger, "The Regulatory Environment and Capital Financing Alternatives for Banks and Thrifts," *Issues in Bank Regulation* (Spring 1988), pp. 3–6.
3. J.S. Bildersee, "A Review of Preferred Stock," *Financial Analysis Handbook*, 2nd ed., Homewood, IL, Dow-Jones Irwin, 1988.
4. R.A. Brealey and S.C. Myers, *Principles of Corporate Finance*, 3rd ed., New York, McGraw-Hill, 1988.
5. E.F. Brigham and L.C. Gapenski, *Financial Management: Theory and Practice*, 5th ed., Chicago, The Dryden Press, 1988.
6. W.J. Conover, *Practical Nonparametric Statistics*, 2nd ed., New York, John Wiley and Sons, 1980.
7. S.K. Cooper and D.R. Fraser, "The Boom in Bank Preferred Stock Issues," *The Bankers Magazine* (November/December 1983), pp. 73–77.
8. T.E. Copeland and J.F. Weston, *Financial Theory and Corporate Policy*, 3rd ed., Reading, Addison-Wesley, 1988.
9. H. DeAngelo and R. Masulis, "Optimal Capital Structure Under Corporate and Personal Taxation," *Journal of Financial Economics* (June 1980), pp. 3–29.
10. P.J. Elmer, "Miller Equilibrium in the Presence of Preferred Stock," Working Paper, The Federal Savings and Loan Insurance Corporation, 1988.
11. H.H. Elsaid, "The Function of Preferred Stock In the Corporate Financial Plan," *Financial Analysts Journal* (July/August 1969), pp. 112–117.
12. J.D. Finnerty, "Financial Engineering in Corporate Finance: An Overview," *Financial Management* (Winter 1988), pp. 14–33.
13. I. Fooladi and G. Roberts, "On Preferred Stock," *Journal of Financial Research* (Winter 1986), pp. 319–324.
14. S.C. Linn and J.M. Pinegar, "The Effect of Issuing Preferred Stock on Common and Preferred Stockholder Wealth," *Journal of Financial Economics* (October 1988), pp. 155–184.
15. B.M. Marr and R.G. Thompson, "Primary Market Pricing of Convertible Preferred Stock," *Quarterly Review of Economics and Business* (Summer 1985), pp. 73–80.
16. R.W. Melicher, "Financing With Convertible Preferred Stock: Comment," *Journal of Finance* (March 1971), pp. 144–147.
17. W.H. Mikkelson and M.M. Partch, "Valuation Effects of Security Offerings and the Issuance Process," *Journal of Financial Economics* (January/February 1986), pp. 31–60.

18. M. Miller, "Debt and Taxes," *Journal of Finance* (May 1977), pp. 261–275.
19. R. Nagle and B. Petersen, "Capitalization Problems in Perspective," in *Handbook for Banking Strategy*, R. Aspinwall and R. Eisenbeis (eds.), New York, John Wiley and Sons, 1985, pp. 293–316.
20. G.E. Pinches, "Financing With Convertible Preferred Stock, 1960–1967." *Journal of Finance* (March 1970), pp. 53–63.
21. S.A. Ross, R.W. Westerfield, and J.F. Jaffe, *Corporate Finance*, 2nd ed., Homewood, IL, Richard D. Irwin, Inc., 1990.
22. G.W. Snedecor and W.G. Cochran, *Statistical Methods*, Ames, IA, The Iowa State University Press, 1967.
23. L. Trigeorgis, "A Tax-Based Rationale for Issuing Preferred Stock: Conceptual Analysis and Empirical Evidence," Working Paper, University of Massachusetts, 1988.
24. D. Walter and P. Strasen, "Acquisition of Beatrice Companies, Inc.," *Taxes* (October 1986), pp. 628–633.
25. B. Winger, C. Chen, J. Martin, J. Petty, and S. Hayden, "Adjustable Rate Preferred Stock," *Financial Management* (Spring 1986), pp. 48–57.

Questions

1. Describe the characteristics of traditional (straight perpetual) preferred stock.
2. What is a convertible preferred stock? Exchangeable preferred stock? Payment-in-kind preferred stock?
3. Preferred stock offers a tax advantage to corporate investors but not to individual investors. For example, if Corporation A owns preferred stock (or common stock) of Corporation B and holds it for at least 46 days, then Corporation A may exclude from its taxable income 70 percent of the dividends received from Corporation B. This exclusion rule does not apply to interest earned on bonds or other loans.
   a. Suppose that Corporation A's marginal tax rate is 35 percent, and it receives $1,000 in dividends on a one-year $10,000 investment in preferred stock. Calculate Corporation A's tax liability, after-tax dollar return, after-tax rate of return, and effective tax rate applicable to the dividends.
   b. Repeat the calculations in Part *a* for $1,000 in interest instead of in dividends. Note the differences between your answers in Part *a* and Part *b*.
4. *Adjustable rate preferred stock (ARPS):* First issued in 1982 by Chase Manhattan and other companies, ARPS pays dividends tied to the rate on Treasury securities. If interest rates rise (fall), then the ARPS dividend is increased (decreased). Typically, the dividend rate is tied to the rate on long-term Treasury bonds and is reset every 13 weeks (quarterly).
   Dutch auction rate preferred stock (DARPS): First issued in 1984 by American Express, DARPS pays a dividend that is reset every 7 weeks (49 days) by a Dutch auction open to all investors. DARPS holders who want to sell offer their shares at par value, and buyers submit bids in terms of dividends they are willing accept during the next 7-week period. The dividend is then set (and paid by the corporate issuer) at the lowest level necessary to sell all the shares being offered.

What is the advantage to the shareholder of ARPS and DARPS in comparison to straight perpetual preferred stock?

5. By far, utility companies (electric, gas, water, and telephone companies) issued the majority of preferred stock during the 1970s. Did utility companies continue to dominate with new issues of preferred stock during the 1980s? What evidence supports your answer?
6. What type of preferred stock did industrial companies issue most during the 1980s? Answer this question for financial companies and for utility companies.
7. Describe the contents of Exhibits 4 and 5 regarding the use of proceeds from the issuance of preferred stock.
8. "The hypothesis to be tested is that, at the time of issuance, firms issuing preferred stock have lower tax rates than the average firm."
   a. What is the rationale for this hypothesis?
   b. Describe the evidence in Exhibit 6 supporting the hypothesis.
9. "The second implication of the tax hypothesis is that firms which invest in preferred stock have higher tax rates than the average firm."
   a. What is the rationale for this hypothesis?
   b. Describe the evidence in Exhibit 7 supporting the hypothesis.

Why Are So Many New Stock Issues Underpriced?

ANTHONY SAUNDERS

Each year hundreds of small firms approach the capital market to issue equity for the first time. These firms are usually growing so fast, or have so many profitable investment projects available to them, that traditional sources of funds (bank loans, retained earnings, and the owners' own equity) are often insufficient to finance their expansion.

Because of this need for finance at a crucial stage in their growth, it is important for these firms that the prices of their shares reflect the true value of company assets or growth opportunities. In particular, if their shares are sold too cheaply, these firms will have raised less capital than was warranted by the intrinsic values of their assets. In other words, their shares will have been "underpriced."

Considerable evidence shows that new or initial public equity offerings (IPOs) are underpriced on *average*. That is, the prices of firms' shares offered to the public for the first time are, on average, set below the prices investors appear willing to pay when the stocks start trading in the secondary market. That is, in the parlance of investment bankers, small firms appear to leave behind considerable "money on the table" at the time of a new issue.

Why small firms raise fewer funds in the new-issue process than the market indicates they should is a crucial public policy issue. Clearly, some degree of market imperfection or lack of competition could cause such an outcome. For example, if, by restricting commercial banks' participation in the market, the Glass-Steagall Act of 1933 has allowed investment bankers to enjoy a type of monopoly (market) power over new equity-issuing firms, then this would suffice to explain underpricing. Alternatively, underpricing may be the premium the issuing firm must pay for having little information about itself to offer potential investors. In that case, underpricing would have little to do with the regulatory structure of the investment banking industry.

At the time of this writing, Anthony Saunders was a professor of finance at New York University's Stern School of Business.

Source: Reprinted from *Business Review*, Federal Reserve Bank of Philadelphia, (March/April 1990).

Let's examine the reasons for IPO underpricing and evaluate the degree to which underpricing is due to Glass-Steagall restrictions. What is the evidence on the degree of underpricing of U.S. IPOs? What are the various explanations for underpricing? And what are the implications of these explanations, and of the associated empirical evidence, for commercial and investment bank regulation?

Evidence on Underpricing

In "firm commitment" underwriting ("firm" in that the investment banker guarantees the price), an investment banker (and his syndicate) will undertake to buy the whole new issue of a firm at one price (the *bid* price, or BP) and seek to resell the issue to outside investors at another price (the *offer* price, or OP). In doing so, the investment banker offers a valuable risk-management service to the issuing firm by guaranteeing to purchase 100 percent of the new issue at the bid price (BP). The return for the investment banker in bearing underwriting risk—that is, the risk that investors will demand less than 100 percent of the issue when it is reoffered for sale to the market—is the spread between the public offer price and the bid price (OP - BP) plus fees and commissions. (Here, and throughout this article, the term "investor" refers to those who buy shares through the investment banker at the offer price.) Thus, the investment banker's spread plus fees and commissions may be viewed as the *direct* cost of going public.

However, there is also potentially an *indirect* cost of going public, measured by the degree to which the issue is underpriced. For example, if the BP is \$5 per share and the OP is \$5.25 per share, then the underwriter's spread is 25 cents per share. However, suppose that on the first day of trading in the secondary market the share price (P) closes at \$7 per share. This indicates that the share has been underpriced in the new-issue process and that, potentially, the firm might have raised as much as \$7 per share had it been priced "correctly." This implies that the issuing firm has borne an additional *indirect* new-issue cost of \$1.75 per share (\$7.00 - \$5.25), because the investment banker has set the offer price below the price the market was willing to pay on the first day of trading.

Thus, more formally, the "raw" percentage degree of underpricing (UP) of an IPO can be defined as:

$$(1) \qquad UP = [(P - OP) / OP] \times 100$$

where:

OP = offer price of the IPO

P = price observed at the end of either the first trading day, week, or month

If UP is positive, the issue has been underpriced; if UP is zero, the issue is accurately priced; and if UP is negative, it has been overpriced. The expression for UP is also the expression for a percentage rate of return. Thus, equation (1) can be viewed as the one-day (or one-week or one-month) *initial* return on buying an IPO (that is, UP = R, the initial return on the stock).

Returns calculated by equation (1) are deemed raw returns. However, researchers also compute excess (market-adjusted) returns, as well. The reasons for this are easy to see. Given a lag between the setting of the offer price and the beginning of trading on an exchange (anywhere from one day to two weeks or more), the price observed in the market on the first day of trading may be high (low) relative to the offer price simply because the stock market as a whole has risen (fallen) over this period. Thus, in analyzing underpricing, reseachers need to control for the performance of the stock market in general. More specifically:

$$(2) \qquad R_m = [(I_1 - I_0) / I_0] \times 100$$

where:

R_m = return on the market portfolio

I_1 = level of the general market share index at the time of listing (first day, first week, or first month)

I_0 = level of the market share index at the time offer is announced

If R_m is positive, the market has been going up in the time between the setting of the offer price and the listing of the stock on the stock exchange. If R_m is negative, the market has been falling. Excess market or risk-adjusted initial returns (EX) can therefore be defined as:[1]

$$(3) \qquad EX = R - R_m$$

According to equation (3), underpricing occurs only when R is greater than R_m.

The findings of 22 studies that examine the degree of underpricing are summarized in the table on p. 501. Although the time periods, sample sizes, and ways of calculating initial returns (especially raw versus market-adjusted) differ widely across these studies, each finds underpricing on average. For example, studies that use a one-week period to calculate the difference between the offer price and the market price of an IPO find underpricing ranging from 5.9 percent to as much as 48.4 percent.[2]

Thus, an important empirical fact is that U.S. IPOs are underpriced on average, resulting in small firms raising less capital than is justified by the markets' ex post valuation of their shares.

---

[1] For a detailed discussion of excess returns, see Robert Schweitzer, "How Do Stock Returns React to Special Events?" this *Business Review* (July/August 1989) pp. 17–29. For IPOs, researchers adjust the initial return on the stock by deducting the return on the market. This is equivalent to assuming that a new IPO's returns move exactly with the market's. That is, they have a unit degree of systematic risk (or their β is 1). The reason for this assumption is that since IPOs have no past history of returns, one cannot estimate directly the IPO's β at the time of issue. The only researcher who has tried to address this problem was Ibbotson (1975), who developed an ingenious method of constructing synthetic βs for IPOs.

[2] It should be noted that these are one week's returns and are thus very large. These underpricing "costs" swamp the direct costs of a new issue, which are, on average, in the range of 2 to 5 percent of the issue's dollar size.

Why Are New Issues Underpriced?

Several reasons have been proposed in the institutional, finance, and economics literature as to why underpricing occurs. Although this article will not discuss all the proposed reasons, it concentrates on four views that have received much publicity. The first view attributes underpricing to "monopoly power" enjoyed by investment bankers. The second regards Securities and Exchange Commission regulations as the primary cause. And the third and fourth see underpricing as a problem of imperfect information among contracting parties—especially between investors and issuers.

The Monopoly Power of Underwriters

One possible explanation for pervasive underpricing is the monopoly power the investment banker enjoys over the issuer.[3] Given that commercial banks are barred from entering into corporate equity underwriting (a result of the Glass-Steagall Act, which effectively separated commercial banking from investment banking), investment bankers may have a degree of monopoly power that they use to earn "rents" by underpricing new issues. Of course, competition among investment banks would limit the extent of this monopoly power.

But how real is this monopoly power? Compared to U.S. commercial banks, U.S. noncommercial banking firms and foreign banks have always faced fewer restrictions on entry into investment banking. Moreover, thrifts also can enter investment banking. In recent years, for example, nonbank firms such as General Electric and Prudential have entered the investment banking industry via acquisitions, as has Franklin Savings Bank, a thrift. This potential competition presumably places a limit on the degree of monopoly power enjoyed by investment bankers.

In addition, foreign banks were not subject to Glass-Steagall regulations until passage of the International Banking Act of 1978. Even then, those already possessing investment banking powers had them grandfathered. The emphasis on investment banks is due to their traditional dominance of the underwriting market and to their potential economies of scope (cost savings from offering a combination of services) in extending to their underwriting customers a broader range of financial services.

If investment bankers have monopoly power over the new issuer, they might use it to increase both the spread between the offer price and bid price (the underwriters' spread) as well as the degree to which the offer price is set below the markets' true valuation (P). A monopolist investment banker might have the incentive to underprice, since by doing so he can increase the probability of being able to sell the whole issue to outside investors (thereby minimizing his underwriting risk) while earning a high investment banking spread (OP - BP) on the issue.[4]

---

[3] For a discussion of the reasons for and effects of investment bankers' potential monopoly power, see Ibbotson (1975) and Pugel and White (1984).

[4] Implicitly, this argument presumes that investment bankers are risk-averse. This is reasonable, given the private nature of many companies, their limited capital bases, and the potential for a large loss if they take a "big hit" (loss) on an underwriting. For example, many U.S. investment bankers suffered significant losses in underwriting an issue of British Petroleum shares at the time of the October 1987 stock market crash.

Clearly, if this was the prime reason for underpricing, it would tend to make a case for allowing commercial banks into the underwriting business. This argument would be based on the expectation that pro-competitive effects would reduce the average degree of underpricing.[5] But this argument would, of course, be tempered by the need to maintain safety and soundness of the banking system, which could be lessened if the spread (P - OP) is small enough to risk inability to sell the entire issue.[6]

Due-Diligence Insurance

A second reason given for why underwriters underprice IPOs is the fear of potential legal problems stemming from overpriced issues. Underwriters, along with company directors, are required to exercise "due diligence" in ensuring the accuracy of the information contained in the prospectus they offer to investors.[7] Since passage of the Securities Acts of 1933 and 1934, both underwriters and directors may be held legally responsible under SEC regulations for the accuracy of this information.

Investors who end up holding heavily overpriced issues may well have an incentive to sue the underwriter and/or the company directors for publishing misleading or incomplete information in the prospectus. The investors could contend they were misled into believing this was a "good" issue rather than a "bad" one. To avoid any negative legal effects, as well as adverse publicity and damage to reputation, a risk-averse underwriter may try to keep investors happy by persistently underpricing IPOs. Hence, some researchers believe that the legal penalties for due-diligence failures are what have created incentives for investment bankers to underprice.

The Problem of the "Winner's Curse"

The academic literature has paid a great deal of attention to a theory first advanced by Rock (1986) and extended by Beatty and Ritter (1986) and McStay (1987), among others. This theory considers underpricing as a competitive outcome in an IPO market in which some investors are viewed as informed while a larger group is viewed as uninformed. As a result, underpricing is directly related to the degree of information imperfection—or, more specifically, information asymmetry—in the capital market and to the costs of collecting information.

---

[5] A different monopoly-based argument, advanced in Baron (1982), is that investment bankers possess monopoly power through their private access to *information* about the likely size of the demand for a new issue. Since issuers are viewed as being relatively uninformed about the nature of this demand, they can easily be exploited by the investment banker. Indeed, since the issuer has no way of knowing ex ante the size of investor demand, the underwriter has an incentive to save resources on distribution and search ("shirking") by simply underpricing enough to ensure that the whole issue is sold. In this context, the presence of potential competitors, such as commercial banks, and the importance of maintaining a reputation might be viewed as potential controls on the investment bankers' temptation to shirk. This presumes, however, that commercial banks, if they entered into underwriting, have the same abilities to "place" (sell to investors) a new issue as investment bankers do. In reality, it might take commercial bankers a number of years to build up the same placement powers.

[6] Since P is not known with certainty, a small spread (P - OP) risks occasional negative spreads, in which case the underwriting firm suffers a loss.

[7] See, for example, Tinic (1988).

Both this theory and the one that follows view underpricing as a way of resolving the problem of costly information collection.

In Rock's model, there are two types of IPOs: good issues and bad issues. Informed investors, defined as those who expend resources collecting information on IPOs, will bid only for those issues that are good. (This search effort is assumed to allow the informed investor to assess exactly the true value of the IPO.) Those investors who are uninformed, however, will not engage in expensive search, but rather will bid randomly across all issues, good and bad. It is further assumed that informed investors are never sufficiently large as a group to be able to purchase a whole issue.

First, consider a good issue. In this case, both informed and uninformed investors will bid for the issue (the uninformed in a random manner). Because both groups bid for the issue, it is likely to be oversubscribed, so that any single *individual* bidder (informed or uninformed) will get fewer shares than he bid for. Thus, for good issues, uninformed investors get only partial allotments.

Next, consider bad issues. In this case, informed investors will not bid at all. The only bidders will be the uninformed. Moreover, owing to the absence of competing informed bidders, any individual bidder will more likely achieve his full allotment (or a higher probability of an allotment). That is, the uninformed bidder suffers from the problem of the "winner's curse": he achieves a large allotment for bad IPOs and a small allotment for good IPOs.

Rock's argument is that, because of the winner's curse, IPOs have to be underpriced on average so as to produce an expected return for the uninformed investor that is high enough to attract investment in IPOs regardless of whether the issue is good or bad.[8] That is, underpricing is a phenomenon perfectly consistent with competitive market conditions in a world of imperfect information flows. Thus, monopoly power is rejected as an argument explaining underpricing.

Underpricing as a Dynamic Strategy

In the most recent literature, underpricing is seen as a dynamic strategy employed by issuing firms to overcome the asymmetry of information between issuing firms and outside investors.[9] Implicitly, underpricing is viewed as a cost to be borne by the issuing firm's insiders to persuade investors to collect (or aggregate) information about the firm and in that way establish its true value in the secondary market. Moreover, the better the firm (a "good" issue), the more it will be underpriced relative to the bad issue.

Specifically, a good firm will underprice its issue to attract outside investors.[10] Investors (such as analysts) collect information about the firm and, in the secondary market, establish its true value above its offer price. The owners of

---

[8] Technically, the *conditional* expected return for the uninformed investor, across both good and bad issues, must be at least as great as the risk-free rate.

[9] See, for example, Chemmanur (1989) and Welch (1988).

[10] In these models, the investment banker plays a largely passive function, operating as an agent on behalf of the principal (the firm). The failure of the investment banker to take a more active role may be seen as a weakness of these information-based models.

the firm benefit from this strategy because once the true (higher) market value is established, the owners have an incentive to "cash in" by coming out with new (further) secondary offerings at the higher market price. Thus, the cost or losses of underpricing the IPO are offset by the benefits from cashing in on the secondary offering.[11]

By comparison, a bad firm—one that knows it is a bad firm—will have the opposite incentives. In particular, the firm may seek to price the IPO as high as possible, since it knows that once investors collect information and discover that it is a "bad" firm, its stock's price will fall on the secondary market.[12]

As in the Rock model, these types of dynamic-strategy models view underpricing as a phenomenon that is consistent with competition in a world of imperfect information among issuing firms and investors. The difference is that, here, IPO underpricing is viewed as a cost to be borne by good firms, which is offset by the revenue benefits from making a secondary ("seasoned") offering later on at a higher price.

Implications for Bank Regulation

What do these models imply for bank regulation and, in particular, the Glass-Steagall Act? If underpricing is indeed due to information imperfections in the capital market—especially between firms and investors—it is difficult to see how commercial banks' entry into underwriting will have much effect, unless these banks somehow collect more information and alleviate the degree of information imperfection in the market. Since the modern theory of banking views banks as major collectors and users of information, increased production of information about small firms may indeed be a benefit from repealing Glass-Steagall.

However, a better test of whether Glass-Steagall has undesirable costs is whether it confers monopoly power on existing investment banks that is reflected in the degree of underpricing. That is, what, if any, is the empirical evidence linking underpricing to the monopoly power of investment banks?

One implication of the monopoly-power hypothesis[13] is that an underwriter, because of his expertise and more precise knowledge of the issuing firm's true value, can save effort (shirk) by ensuring maximum sales through underpricing while still earning a high underwriting spread (OP - BP). However, even in a world of asymmetric information, presumably firms would learn that they are being exploited and, if competition exists, would switch to other underwriters. In contrast, monopoly power would imply that issuing firms would fare as well with one investment bank as with another and that underwriters could ignore all problems or considerations related to maintaining a reputation.

---

[11] Welch (1988) offers preliminary evidence that these issues that are more underpriced tend to follow up more quickly with a secondary (seasoned) offering.

[12] This is not to imply that the bad firms necessarily overprice. However, the theory has the *aggregate* implication that the greater the proportion of good to bad issues in the market, the greater the degree of underpricing on *average*.

[13] See Baron (1982), who developed a theory of investment banker monopoly power based on the inability of issuers to accurately monitor the investment bankers' effort in placing new shares with investors.

Beatty and Ritter (1986) have sought to test this reputation—monopoly power effect. That is, do investment bankers who heavily underprice in one period lose business from issuing firms in the next? Beatty and Ritter's results tended to confirm that the more an investment banker underpriced in one period, the greater his loss of business in the next—a result suggesting that monopoly power is temporary at best.

A second implication of the monopoly-power hypothesis is that the investment banker—to avoid risk—will have a greater incentive to underprice relatively risky issues so as to ensure maximum sales. For example, it can be argued that the more uncertain are firms' uses of the proceeds of the issue (for example, to pay off existing debt, to develop new projects, and so on), the riskier the issue. Or, alternatively, the more variable the after-market returns on an issue—measured by the standard deviation of returns over a period subsequent to listing on the stock exchange—the riskier the issue. Thus, we would expect underpricing to increase as the number of potential uses of proceeds, and the volatility of its (expected) price in the after-market, grows.

Beatty and Ritter (1986) found a positive relationship between number of uses of proceeds and underpricing; Ritter (1984) and Miller and Reilly (1987) found a positive relationship between the standard deviation of after-market returns and the degree of underpricing. Both these results are consistent with the monopoly-power hypothesis; however, it *must* be noted that both findings are also consistent with the competitive-market, information-imperfection "winner's curse" theory of Rock (1986).[14]

A third potential implication of the monopoly-power model is that the degree of underpricing should have been less prior to passage of Glass-Steagall—that is, the pre-1933 *average* degree of underpricing should have been less than the post-1933 average degree. In a recent study, Tinic (1988) tested the degree of underpricing in the period 1923–30 and compared it with the period 1966–71. He found that underpricing was higher in the 1966–71 period. While Tinic interpreted these results as consistent with the due-diligence-insurance hypothesis—that is, the passage of the Securities Act of 1934, which forced investment banks to underprice to avoid potential lawsuits—they are also consistent with the monopoly-power hypothesis. That is, in a period preceding Glass-Steagall (when commercial banks had greater power to underwrite corporate securities),[15] the degree of underpricing was less than in a period following the Glass-Steagall separation of powers.

A fourth implication of the monopoly-power hypothesis is that IPOs of investment banks (for example, Morgan Stanley going public) should *not* be underpriced, since the investment bank brings its "own firm" public. Looking at 37 IPOs of investment banks that went public in the 1970–84 period and participated in the distribution of their own issues, Muscarella and Vetsuypens

[14] That is, the greater the risk or uncertainty about the issue, the greater the cost of becoming informed and thus the greater the degree of underpricing required in equilibrium.

[15] This was particularly true in 1927–33, when commercial banks had the same powers as investment banks. Since technology and the structure of the financial services industry are continuously changing, a more valid test might have been to compare underpricing in the period *immediately following* passage of the Glass-Steagall Act.

Initial Returns, According to Various Studies

Study	Sample Period	Sample Size	Initial Returns 1 Week	1 Mo.
Reilly/Hatfield (1969)	1963–65	53	9.9%	8.7%
McDonald/Fisher (1972)	1969–70	142	28.5%	34.6%
Logue (1973)	1965–69	250	—	41.7%
Reilly (1973)	1966	62	9.9%	—
Neuberger/Hammond (1974)	1965–69	816	17.1%	19.1%
Ibbotson (1975)	1960–71	128	—	11.4%
Ibbotson/Jaffe (1975)	1960–70	2650	16.8%	—
Reilly (1978)	1972–75	486	10.9%	11.6%
Block/Stanley (1980)	1974–78	102	5.9%	3.3%
Neuberger/LaChapelle (1983)	1975–80	118	27.7%	33.6%
Ibbotson (1982)	1971–81	N/A	—	2.9%
Ritter (1984)	1960–82	5162	18.8%	—
	1977–82	1028	26.5%	—
	1980–81	325	48.4%	—
Giddy (1985)	1976–83	604	10.2%	—
John/Saunders (1986)	1976–82	78	—	8.5%
Beatty/Ritter (1986)	1981–82	545	14.1%	—
Chalk/Peavy (1986)	1974–82	440	13.8%	—
Ritter (1987)	1977–82			
Firm commitment		664	14.8%	—
Best efforts		364	47.8%	—
Miller/Reilly (1987)	1982–83	510	9.9%	—
Muscarella/Vetsuypens (1987)	1983–87	1184	—	7.6%

(1987) find an average degree of underpricing of *8 percent* on the first day of trading. At first sight this tends to contradict the monopoly-power hypothesis as the sole reason for underpricing; however, it could be argued that 8 percent underpricing is less than the median or mean underpricing found in the majority of studies listed in the table above and that monopoly power may offer a partial explanation for underpricing.

Nevertheless, the results favoring monopoly power as the major determinant of new-issues underpricing appear somewhat weak. Indeed, the evidence is largely consistent with the existence of competitive markets in which investors have incomplete or imperfect information about new firms. While new issues did appear to be *less* underpriced before Glass-Steagall (consistent with the monopoly-power hypothesis), evidence suggests that those investment banks that excessively underprice today lose future business from prospective issuing firms and that investment banks' own IPOs are also underpriced on average (although less so than those of other firms). The gains from allowing commercial banks to compete directly with investment banks for corporate equity underwritings may come less from creating more potential competition than from collecting, producing, and disseminating more information about small firms in the new-issue process. This conclusion suggests that allowing banks into investment banking activities may indeed bring about price changes that benefit the public; however, those changes may be smaller and occur for different reasons than once thought.

References

Baron, D.P. "A Model of the Demand for Investment Banking and Advising and Distribution Services for New Issues," *Journal of Finance* (1982) pp. 955–77.

Beatty, R., and J. Ritter. "Investment Banking, Reputation, and the Underpricing of Initial Public Offerings," *Journal of Financial Economics* (1986) pp. 213–32.

Block, S., and M. Stanley. "The Financial Characteristics and Price Movement Patterns of Companies Approaching the Unseasoned Securities Market in the Late 1970s," *Financial Management* (1980) pp. 30–36.

Chalk, A.J., and J.W. Peavy. "Understanding the Pricing of Initial Public Offerings," Southern Methodist University Working Paper 86–72 (1986).

Chemmanur, T.J. "The Pricing of Initial Public Offerings: A Dynamic Model With Information Production," mimeo, New York University (1989).

Giddy, I. "Is Equity Underwriting Risky for Commercial Bank Affiliates?" in I. Walter, ed., *Deregulating Wall Street* (New York: John Wiley, 1985).

Ibbotson, R.G. "Price Performance of Common Stock New Issues," *Journal of Financial Economics* 3 (1975) pp. 235–72.

Ibbotson, R.G. "Common Stock New Issues Revisited," Graduate School of Business, University of Chicago, Working Paper 84 (1982), unpublished.

Ibbotson, R.G., and J.J. Jaffe. "'Hot Issue' Markets," *Journal of Finance* 30 (1975) pp. 1027–42.

John, K., and A. Saunders. "The Efficiency of the Market for Initial Public Offerings: U.S. Experience 1976–1983," unpublished (1986).

Logue, D.E. "On the Pricing of Unseasoned New Issues, 1965–1969," *Journal of Financial and Quantitative Analysis* (1973) pp. 91–103.

McDonald, J.G., and A.K. Fisher. "New-Issue Stock Price Behavior," *Journal of Finance* (1972) pp. 97–102.

McStay, K.P. *The Efficiency of New Issue Markets*, Ph.D. thesis, Department of Economics, U.C.L.A. (1987).

Miller, R.E., and F.K. Reilly. "An Examination of Mispricing, Returns, and Uncertainty for Initial Public Offerings," *Financial Management* (1987) pp. 33–38.

Muscarella, C.J., and M.R. Vetsuypens. "A Simple Test of Baron's Model of IPO Underpricing," Southern Methodist University Working Paper 87–14 (1987a).

Muscarella, C.J., and M.R. Vetsuypens. "Initial Public Offerings and Information Asymmetry," Edwin L. Cox School of Business, Southern Methodist University, unpublished (1987b).

Neuberger, B.M., and C.T. Hammond. "A Study of Underwriters' Experience With Unseasoned New Issues," *Journal of Financial and Quantitative Analysis* (1974) pp. 165–77.

Neuberger, B.M., and C.A. LaChapelle. "Unseasoned New Issue Price Performance on Three Tiers: 1975–1980," *Financial Management* (1983) pp. 23–28.

Pugel, T.A., and L.J. White. "An Empirical Analysis of Underwriting Spreads on IPO's," Working Paper 331, Salomon Brothers Center for the Study of Financial Institutions, Graduate School of Business Administration, New York University (September 1984).

Reilly, R.K., and K. Hatfield. "Investor Experience With New Stock Issues," *Financial Analysts Journal* (September/October 1969) pp. 73–80.

Reilly, R.K. "Further Evidence on Short-Run Results for New Issue Investors," *Journal of Financial and Quantitative Analysis* (1973) pp. 83–90.

Reilly, R.K. "New Issues Revisited," *Financial Management* (1978) pp. 28–42.

Ritter, J. "The 'Hot Issue' Market of 1980," *Journal of Business* 57 (1984) pp. 215–40.

Ritter, J. "The Costs of Going Public," University of Michigan Working Paper 487 (1987a).

Ritter, J. "A Theory of Investment Banking Contract Choice," University of Michigan Working Paper 488 (1987b).

Rock, K. "Why New Issues Are Underpriced," *Journal of Financial Economics* 15 (1986) pp. 187–212.

Tinic, S. M. "Anatomy of Initial Public Offers of Common Stock," *Journal of Finance* 43 (1988) pp. 789–822.

Welch, I. "Seasoned Offering, Imitation Costs and the Underpricing of Initial Public Offerings," University of Chicago Working Paper (1988).

Questions

1. What is an IPO?
2. Textron Inc. issued 500,000 shares of common stock through investment bankers. The stock sold to the public for $35 a share, but Textron received $33.25 a share. Textron's out-of-pocket costs equaled $225,000.
   a. Calculate Textron's total flotation costs in dollars.
   b. Calculate Textron's total flotation costs as a percentage of gross proceeds (selling price).
   c. Calculate Textron's total flotation costs per share of stock issued.
3. Textron Inc.'s common stock (in Question 2) closed at $40 per share on the first day of trading in the secondary market.
   a. Calculate the ("raw") percentage degree of underpricing of the stock.
   b. Is the underpricing calculated in Part *a* part of Textron Inc.'s cost of going public? Explain.
4. Summarize the findings of studies on the underpricing of IPOs.

5. "Several reasons have been proposed in the institutional, finance, and economics literature as to why underpricing occurs." Describe each of the following four reasons:
   a. The monopoly power of underwriters.
   b. Due-diligence insurance.
   c. The problem of the "winner's curse."
   d. Underpricing as a dynamic strategy. (*Note:* In a *secondary offering*, company founders and other insiders sell ("cash in") their existing shares, issued sometime in the past.)
6. Which reason for underpricing (in Question 5) seems *least* reasonable to you? Explain.
7. Which reason for underpricing (in Question 5) seems *most* reasonable to you? Explain.

Does Dividend Policy Matter?

RICHARD A. BREALEY

Six years ago, Fischer Black, professor of finance at M.I.T., wrote an article entitled "The Dividend Puzzle." The puzzle referred to was that despite considerable debate and research, there is little agreement among economists, managers and investors about the stock price consequences of, and thus the corporate motives for, paying cash dividends. Does a high payout increase the stock price, reduce it, or make no difference at all?

Defining Dividend Policy

Part of the reason for this continuing controversy is that different people mean different things by dividend policy. So let me start by explaining what I mean by the term.

A company's dividend decisions are often mixed up with other financing and investment decisions. Some companies finance capital expenditures largely by borrowing, thus releasing cash for dividends. In this case, the higher dividend is merely a by-product of the borrowing decision. Other companies pay low dividends because management is optimistic about the company's future and wishes to retain earnings for expansion. In this case, the dividend is a by-product of management's capital budgeting decision.

It is therefore important to begin by isolating the effects of dividend policy from those of other financial management decisions. The precise question we should ask, then, is: "What is the effect of a change in cash dividends, given the firm's capital-budgeting and borrowing decisions?"

If we fix the firm's investment outlays, borrowing, and operating cash flow, there is only one source of additional dividend payments: a stock issue. For this

---

At the time of this writing, Richard A. Brealey was Midland Bank Professor of Corporate Finance and Director of the Institute of Finance and Accounting at the London Business School.

Source: From Bank of America *Journal of Applied Corporate Finance.*

reason, I define dividend policy as the trade-off between retaining earnings on the one hand, and paying out cash and issuing new shares on the other.[1]

We know that the value of the firm depends on a number of factors. It may be affected by the plant and equipment that it owns, how much debt it issues, how hard the managers work and so on. If we want to know whether dividend policy as such is important, we should hold these other factors constant and ask whether, given the firm's investments, capital structure and management incentives, the level of payout makes any difference.

No financial manager can avoid taking a view on this question. If you are involved in the company's dividend decision, you have an obvious interest in how that decision will affect your shareholders. If you are concerned with capital investment appraisal, you need to know whether the firm's cost of capital depends on its payout policy. (For example, if investors prefer companies with high payouts, management should be more reluctant to take on investments financed by retained earnings.) And, if you have responsibility for the pension fund, you will want to know whether it is better to invest more in high- or low-payout stocks.

Why Dividend Policy May *Not* Matter

There is now substantial agreement among academic economists that, as defined above, dividend policy is largely irrelevant apart from possible tax effects.[2] The reason for this, stated most simply, is that the money for new investments must come from somewhere. Once you have fixed on a sensible debt policy, any increase in dividends must be matched by a corresponding issue of equity. So management's choice, as we have observed, is between retaining earnings or simultaneously paying them out as dividends and issuing stock to replace the lost cash. To suggest that you can make shareholders better off by paying them money with one hand and taking it back with the other is rather like suggesting that you can cool the kitchen by leaving the refrigerator door open. In each case, you are simply recycling.

Of course, a higher payout could affect the share price if it was the only way that the shareholder could get his hands on the cash. But, as long as there are efficient capital markets, a shareholder can always raise cash by selling shares. Thus, the old shareholders can "cash in" on their investment either by persuading management to pay a higher dividend or by selling some of their shares. In either case there will be a transfer of value from old to new shareholders. Because investors do not need dividends to get their hands on cash, they will not pay higher prices for the shares of firms with a high payout. Therefore, firms ought not to worry about dividend policy.

---

[1] This trade-off may seem artificial at first, for we do not see companies scheduling a stock issue with every dividend payment. But there are many firms that pay dividends and also issue stock from time to time. They could avoid the stock issues by paying lower dividends. Other companies restrict dividends so that they *do not* have to issue shares.

[2] The irrelevance of dividend policy in perfect markets was demonstrated by Merton Miller and Franco Modigliani in "Dividend Policy, Growth and the Valuation of Shares," *Journal of Business* 34 (October 1961), 411–432.

Just as a high payout policy does not in itself raise firm value, so a low payout policy also cannot affect value. The argument is essentially the same. If you hold capital expenditure constant and pay lower dividends, then you will have more cash than you need. In the United States you can hand this cash back to the shareholders by repurchasing the shares of your own company. In countries where this is not permitted, you can hand the cash back by purchasing the shares of other companies.

Of course, all this ignores the costs involved in paying dividends and buying or selling shares. For example, if the company needs the cash, it is likely to be somewhat cheaper to retain it than to pay it out and make a stock issue. But these are matters of fine tuning and should not absorb large amounts of management time.

Some Common Misunderstandings

Some people find it difficult to accept the notion that, apart from tax considerations, dividend policy should not affect the value of the firm. For example, in the UK in 1975 the Diamond Commission received submissions from both the investment community and the trade unions about the effect of dividend control. The representatives of the investment community pointed out that the value of a share is equal to the discounted value of the expected stream of dividends. Therefore, they claimed, legislation that holds down dividends must also hold down share prices and increase companies' cost of capital.

The trade union representatives also thought that dividend policy is important. They argued that dividends are the shareholders' wages and so it was only equitable that the government's incomes policy should include control of dividends. Both sides ignored the secondary effects of dividend control. If a company raises its dividend, it must replace the cash by making a share issue. So the old shareholder receives a higher current dividend, but a proportion of the future dividends must be diverted to the new shareholders. The present value of these foregone future payments is equal to the increase in the current dividend.

Another common misunderstanding is the so-called "bird-in-the hand" fallacy. Dividends, it is suggested, are more predictable than capital gains because managers can stabilize dividends, but cannot control stock price. Therefore, dividend payments are safe cash in hand while the alternative capital gains are at best in the bush.

But, the important point to remember, once again, is that as long as management's dividend policy does not influence its investment and capital structure decisions, a company's *overall* cash flows are the same regardless of its payout policy. The risks borne by its stockholders are likewise determined only by its investment and borrowing policies. Thus, it seems odd to suggest that while dividend policy has no effect on the firm's total cash flow, it nevertheless can still affect its risk.

The actual effect of a dividend increase is not to decrease the fundamental riskiness of the stock, but to transfer ownership and, hence, risk from "old" to "new" stockholders. The old stockholders—those who receive the extra dividend and do not buy their part of the stock issue undertaken to finance the dividend—are in effect disinvesting: that is, their stake in the firm is reduced. They have indeed traded a safe receipt for an uncertain capital gain. But the reason their money is safe is not because it is special "dividend money," but because it is in the bank. If the dividend had not been increased, the stockholders could have achieved an equally safe position just by selling shares and putting the money in the bank.

The old shareholder who receives and banks his dividend check has a safer asset than formerly, whereas the new shareholder who buys the newly issued shares has a riskier asset. Risk does not disappear; it is simply transferred from one investor to another, just as it is when one investor sells his stock to the other.

A third common objection to the dividend irrelevance argument is that many investors for reasons good or bad like high dividends. This may well be the case just as many people like to own motor cars, television sets and so on. But it does not mean that you can get rich by going into the dividend-manufacturing business any more than you can do so by going into the car or television business. A high-payout policy will only increase the stock price if there are not enough high-payout companies to satisfy the clientele for such stocks.

Why Dividend Policy *Seems* to Matter

If there is such widespread agreement that dividend policy does not matter aside from the tax consequences, why do so many managers believe it to be important? The obvious explanation is that the economists have got it wrong again. But I suspect that the real reason is that the economists and managers are talking about different issues.

For example, although I have suggested that low-payout stocks sell for as high a price as high-payout stocks, I also believe that the stock price is likely to rise if the dividend is unexpectedly increased. In other words, *unexpected changes* in a company's dividend matter even though the expected *level* of dividends does not. The reason for this has mostly to do with how managements typically set dividend policy.

Studies of corporate dividend policy suggest that most companies have a conscious or, at least, some subconscious long-term target payout rate.[3] If management attempted to adhere to a target every year, then the level of the dividend would fluctuate as erratically as earnings. Therefore, they try to smooth dividends by moving only partway toward the target payout in each year. They also

---

[3] In the mid-1950s John Lintner conducted a series of interviews with corporate managers about their dividend policies. The results are presented in an article entitled "Distribution of Incomes of Corporations among Dividends, Retained Earnings, and Taxes," *American Economic Review*, 46:97–113 (May 1956). Lintner came to the conclusion that the dividend payout depends largely on two variables: the firm's current earnings and the dividend for the previous year (which in turn depends on that year's earnings and the prior year's dividend). The current dividend is thus generally a weighted average of past earnings, placing the heaviest weights on more recent years.

A more recent study by Eugene Fama and Harvey Babiak confirmed these results, demonstrating that the probability of a dividend increase depends largely on how consistently earnings have risen over the two or three years prior to the dividend change. See E.F. Fama and H. Babiak, "Dividend Policy: An Empirical Analysis," *Journal of the American Statistical Association*, 63:1132–1161 (December 1968).

take into account expected future earnings, as well as current earnings, in setting a long-run target. From long experience, investors are aware of this, and thus often interpret a large dividend increase as a sign of management's optimism about the company's prospects.

Thus, because unanticipated dividend changes convey information to the market about the outlook for profits, it makes sense to establish a reasonable set of investor expectations and to take these expectations into account when you decide on the annual payment.

A second reason that managers believe that the dividend decision is important is because they assume that it will affect the investment decision. In other words, they will say things like "If we pay this high dividend, then we won't have enough money to go ahead with our capital expenditure program." They are, therefore, implicitly rejecting the alternative of an equity issue. For example, many companies are reasonably tolerant of appropriation requests that can be financed out of retained earnings, but seem to impose much more stringent criteria on expenditure proposals that would involve a new issue of stock. In these cases the dividend decision feeds back on the investment decision and, therefore, it makes sense to take account of investment opportunities when setting the dividend level.

In both of these examples dividend policy appeared to matter. But in fact it was not the dividend policy as such that was important, but the company's investment policy and investors' expectations of future earnings.

Dividends and Taxes

The only serious challenge to those who believe that dividend policy does not matter comes from those who stress the tax consequences of a particular dividend policy.

If there were no taxes, investors would have no incentive to prefer one particular group of stocks. So they would hold well-diversified portfolios that moved closely with the market. But the fact that investors pay taxes at different rates on investment income provides an incentive for them to hold different portfolios. For example, the millionaire who is highly taxed on his dividend income has an incentive to slant his portfolio towards the low-payout stocks, even though this results in a less well-diversified portfolio. This extra demand by highly taxed investors for low-yield stocks will cause their prices to rise. As a result, tax-exempt investors such as pension funds will be induced to slant their portfolios towards the high-yielding stocks even though this causes their portfolios also to be less well-diversified. In between these two extremes is the investor with an "average" rate of tax. He has no incentive to slant his portfolio towards one particular group of stocks and will, therefore, invest in a well-diversified portfolio of high- and low-yielders.

The investor who pays tax at the average rate will be prepared to hold a well-diversified portfolio of both high- and low-yielders only if they offer him equal returns after tax.[4] But, if the returns are to be equal *after* tax, the high yielders must offer a higher return *before* tax. Thus, given two stocks which promise equal total returns (dividends plus capital gains) to investors, the stock that provides more of its return in the form of dividends will have a higher pre-tax expected return, and thus a lower stock price, than the one whose return is expected mostly in the form of capital gain.

The tax argument against high payouts is persuasive, but its advocates have so far failed to answer an important question: If generous dividends lead to generous taxes, why do companies continue to pay such dividends? Would they not do better to retain the earnings and avoid stock issues or, if they have excess cash, would it not be preferable to use it to repurchase stock? It is difficult to believe that companies are really foregoing such a simple opportunity to make their shareholders better off. Maybe there are offsetting advantages to dividends that we have not considered, or perhaps investors have ways to get around those extra taxes.

Merton Miller and Myron Scholes are among those who believe that the tax laws allow investors to avoid paying extra taxes on dividends.[5] For example, they point out that you can offset interest on personal loans against investment income. Such a strategy increases the risk of one's portfolio. But this increase in risk can be avoided or neutralized by channeling the borrowed funds through tax-exempt institutions like insurance companies or pension funds. As an example, one could eliminate taxes on investment income without any increase in risk by using the personal loan to pay the premiums on a life insurance policy.

It is hard to know how literally to take Miller and Scholes's argument. There is no doubt that wealthy people are aware of the tax advantages of saving through insurance policies and pension plans. But the "average" tax rate on dividends is clearly not zero. So the puzzle has not entirely gone away: If taxes on dividend income do reduce the value of high-payout stocks, why do firms pay such high dividends?

The Empirical Evidence

The obvious way out of such a dilemma is to look at the evidence and test whether high-yielding stocks offer higher returns. Unfortunately, there are difficulties in measuring these effects.

One problem is to disentangle the effect of dividend yield from the effect of other influences. For example, most economists believe that risky stocks offer higher expected returns, and many believe that small company stocks also do so. Researchers have developed techniques for removing the effect on return of

---

[4] Michael Brennan showed that two stocks with equal risk should offer the same expected returns net of the average rate of tax. This average tax rate is a complicated average whose weight depends on each investor's wealth and aversion to risk.

[5] See M.H. Miller and M. Scholes. "Dividends and Taxes," *Journal of Financial Economics*, 6 (December 1978) 333–364.

differences in risk, but there has been little attempt to disentangle the possible influences of yield and company size.

With the benefit of hindsight, we know some stocks have high yields because the dividend turned out to be higher than expected; others provided low yields because the dividend was lower than expected. Clearly what we want to measure is whether stocks that offer a higher *expected* yield also have a higher expected total return. To do that, however, it is necessary to estimate the dividend yield investors expected.

A third problem is that nobody is quite sure what is meant by a high dividend yield. For example, utility stocks are generally regarded as offering high yields. But are their yields high throughout the year, or only in the dividend month, or on the dividend day? Except at the time of the dividend payment, utility stocks effectively have zero yield and are thus perfect holdings for the highly taxed millionaire. The millionaire could avoid all taxes by selling the stock to a securities dealer just before the dividend date, and buying it back after. Since the securities dealer is taxed equally on dividends and capital gains, he should be quite content to hold the stock over the ex-dividend date. Thus, as long as investors can pass stocks freely between one another at the time of the dividend payment, we should not expect to observe any tax effect by dividends on stock prices. But if there are costs to avoiding taxes in this way, then any yield effect should become stronger as the ex-dividend day approaches.

A fourth problem is that most empirical studies have looked for a straight-line relationship between yield and return. But if there are any asymmetries in the tax system, that may not be the case. For example, if investors do not receive a tax refund on stocks that are sold short, there could be stocks traded only among millionaires and other stocks traded only by pension funds. In this case, there would be no single tax rate that clears the market and the relationship between yield and return would no longer be a straight-line one.[6] Stocks with above-average yields might be owned by pension funds, and priced to give the same expected pre-tax returns. By contrast, stocks offering below-average yields must all be owned by taxpayers, and priced to offer the same expected after-tax return.

Given these difficulties in measuring the relationship between yield and return, it is not surprising that different researchers have come up with somewhat different results. Table 1 summarizes the results of some of these empirical tests. Notice that in each of these tests the estimated tax rate was positive. In other words, over long periods of time, high-yielding stocks appeared to have offered higher returns, thus implying lower prices, than low-yielding stocks.

But if, at this point, the dividends-are-bad school can claim that the weight of evidence is on its side, the contest is by no means over. Not only are many of the empirical problems unsolved, but the standard errors in Table 1 show that the estimated tax rate is not always significantly different from zero.

---

[6] Michael Brennan, for example, in an unpublished working paper entitled "Dividends and Valuation in Imperfect Markets: Some Empirical Tests," argues that the relationship is not linear.

TABLE 1 Some Tests of the Effect of Yield on Returns

Test	Test Period	Interval	Implied Tax Rate Percent	Standard Error of Tax Rate
Brennan (1970)	1946–65	Monthly	34	12
Black & Scholes (1974)	1936–66	Monthly	22	24
Litzenberger & Ramaswamy (1979)	1936–77	Monthly	24	3
Litzenberger & Ramaswamy (1982)	1940–80	Monthly	14–23	2–3
Rosenberg & Marathe (1979)	1931–66	Monthly	40	21
Bradford & Gordon (1980)	1926–78	Monthly	18	2
Blume (1980)	1936–76	Quarterly	52	25
Miller & Scholes (1981)	1940–78	Monthly	4	3
Stone & Bartter (1979)	1947–70	Monthly	56	28
Morgan (1982)	1946–77	Monthly	21	2

Summary and Conclusion

It is difficult to summarize the dividend puzzle, and harder still to draw firm conclusions.

Almost no academic economist believes that paying out higher percentages of corporate earnings leads to higher stock prices. There is an important school which argues that taxes reduce the value of high-payout stocks. And, although there are unresolved problems of method, empirical tests of the issue to date provide tentative confirmation of an adverse tax effect on stock prices from higher dividends.

In setting the target payout, therefore, one should not dismiss entirely the tax argument against generous dividends. At the very least, management should adopt a target payout that, on the basis of its future capital requirements, is sufficiently low to minimize its reliance on external equity. In addition, the target payout should probably recognize that surplus funds can better be used to repurchase stock than to pay dividends.

There is little doubt, however, that sudden *changes* in dividend policy can cause dramatic changes in stock price. The most plausible reason for this reaction is the information investors read into dividend announcements. It is therefore important to define the firm's target payout as clearly as possible and to avoid unexpected changes in dividends. If it becomes necessary to make a sharp change in the level of the dividend, or in the target payout ratio, management should provide as much forewarning as possible, and take considerable care to ensure that the action is not misinterpreted.

References

Black, F., "The Dividend Puzzle," *Journal of Portfolio Management* 2 (Winter 1976).

Black, F. and M. Scholes, "The Effects of Dividend Yield and Dividend Policy on Common Stock Prices and Returns," *Journal of Financial Economics* 1 (May 1974), 1–22.

Blume, M.E., "Stock Returns and Dividend Yields: Some More Evidence," *Review of Economics and Statistics* (November 1980), 567–577.

Bradford, D.F. and R.H. Gordon, "Taxation and the Stock Market Valuation of Capital Gains and Dividends," *Journal of Public Economics* 14 (1980), 109–136.

Brennan, M.J., "Taxes, Market Valuation and Corporate Financial Policy," *National Tax Journal* 23 (December 1970), 417–427.

Hess, P., "The Empirical Relationship between Dividend Yield and Stock Returns: Tax Effect or Non-stationarity in Expected Returns," Unpublished Ph.D. dissertation.

Litzenberger, R.H. and K. Ramaswamy, "The Effects of Dividends on Common Stock Prices: Tax Effects or Information Effects?" *Journal of Finance* (May 1982), 429–443.

Litzenberger, R.H. and K. Ramaswamy, "Dividends, Short Selling Restrictions, Tax-Induced Investor Clienteles and Market Equilibrium," *Journal of Finance* 35 (May 1980), 469–482.

Miller, M.H. and F. Modigliani, "Dividend Policy, Growth and the Valuation of Shares," *Journal of Business* 34 (October 1961), 411–432.

Miller, M.H. and M. Scholes, "Dividends and Taxes," *Journal of Financial Economics* 6 (December 1978), 333–364.

Miller, M.H. and M. Scholes, "Dividends and Taxes: Some Empirical Evidence," *Journal of Political Economy* 90 (1982).

Morgan, I.G., "Dividends and Capital Asset Prices," *Journal of Finance* 37 (September 1982), 1071–1086.

Rosenberg, B. and V. Marathe, "Tests of Capital Asset Pricing Model Hypotheses," in H. Levy (ed.) *Research in Finance I*, Greenwich, Conn: JAI Press (1979).

Sharpe, W.F. and H.B. Sosin, "Risk, Return and Yield: New York Stock Exchange Common Stocks 1928–1969." *Financial Analysts Journal* (March/April 1976), 33–42.

Stone, B.K. and B.J. Bartter, "The Effect of Dividend Yield on Stock Returns: Empirical Evidence on the Relevance of Dividends," W.P.E.-76–78, Georgia Institute of Technology, Atlanta, Georgia.

Questions

1. How does the author define *dividend policy?*
2. In what way is the argument that dividend policy can increase shareholder wealth like trying to cool the kitchen by leaving open the refrigerator door?
3. Evaluate the following arguments for the importance and relevance of dividends:
   a. The value of a share of common stock equals the present value of future dividends. Therefore, if you reduce dividends, you also reduce share value.
   b. Dividend payments reduce the risk perceived by investors and thus increase share value.
   c. Many investors like dividends because they need the income to cover expenses. These investors bid up the stock price of companies that pay dividends.
4. Unexpected changes in dividends per share often cause a change in a company's stock price. Does this statement imply that dividend policy matters? Explain.

5. Why are the personal tax rates of a company's shareholders relevant to the company's dividend policy?
6. Transaction costs include: (a) the costs of investors buying and selling shares, and (b) the costs of companies paying dividends and issuing shares. In what way are these costs relevant to a company's dividend policy?

Why Companies Issue Stock Dividends

H. KENT BAKER AND AARON L. PHILLIPS

Researchers have long puzzled over why companies issue stock dividends. Conventional wisdom suggests that shareholders get no real benefits from such distributions. Stock dividends are accounting rearrangements of the owners' equity structure that reduce retained earnings by the dollar amount of the stock dividend. As Willens [12] notes, Section 305(a) of the IRS code generally exempts stock dividends from taxation, but the exceptions are broad. Although stock dividends increase the number of equity shares outstanding, they do not provide the corporation with new funds or the stockholders with any added claim to company assets. Theoretically, a firm's economic value remains unchanged because the corporate pie is simply cut into more pieces. If stock dividends are merely cosmetic changes, why do many firms continue to engage in such financial practices, particularly when they incur real costs in the process?

Our study provides further evidence about management views on issues and motives for distributing stock dividends. To date, the only other field study on stock dividends was published by Eisemann and Moses [3]. We examine only stock dividends because, as Lakonishok and Lev [7] note, such distributions are altogether different from stock splits. Furthermore, the characteristics of firms issuing stock dividends differ markedly from those of stock-splitting firms. Grinblatt, Masulis, and Titman [6] also conclude that the market interprets announcements about stock dividends and stock splits differently.

There are three major reasons for updating and expanding the Eisemann and Moses study. First, the body of theoretical and empirical research on stock dividends has greatly increased since the publication of the Eisemann and Moses

At the time of this writing, H. Kent Baker was the University Professor and Chair of the Department of Finance and Real Estate, and Aaron L. Phillips was an assistant professor of finance at the American University, Kogod College of Business Administration, Washington, DC.

Source: *Financial Practice and Education* (Fall 1993, pp. 29-37). Reprinted with permission.

study about 15 years ago. Specifically, researchers have set forth many hypotheses to explain why firms issue stock dividends and have provided empirical evidence supporting several of them. Awareness of this literature by managers may have influenced their views about stock dividends. A new study is needed to find out whether a gap exists between financial theory and managerial practice relating to stock dividends.

Second, the results of the Eisemann and Moses study apply only to New York Stock Exchange (NYSE) firms. Responses about issue statements and motives may differ significantly according to the characteristics of the firm or its stock dividend practices. For example, listed companies are generally larger and more mature than those traded on the over-the-counter market. Therefore, it may be inappropriate to generalize the findings of the Eisemann and Moses study beyond NYSE firms.

Finally, Eisemann and Moses base their findings on a limited sample and sample period. They received only 39 responses from the 80 surveyed firms that paid a stock dividend of less than 25 percent in 1974. Also, their classification of responses about the reasons firms issued a stock dividend is subjective. We improve upon their methodology by using a larger sample, a longer, more recent test period, and a more objective approach of identifying the motives for issuing stock dividends.

We address two major research questions. First, why do some managers support stock dividends? Second, do managerial views about the issues and motives for stock dividends differ with the firm's trading location (NYSE/Amex versus Nasdaq), the size of the stock dividend (< 10 percent versus 10 to < 25 percent), or the frequency of issuing stock dividends (regular versus occasional)? The Eisemann and Moses study examines the first question but not the second one.

In summary, our study is important because it adds new insights to our understanding of the stock dividend phenomenon, based on the opinions of practicing managers about these issues. The study also provides researchers with useful information for conducting further empirical investigations.

The paper has the following organization. Section I presents a brief review of the empirical literature on stock dividends and four hypotheses for issuing them. In Section II we describe the survey methodology and the respondent profile. Section III presents and analyzes the survey results and, where appropriate, compares and contrasts the findings with the Eisemann and Moses study. Finally, Section IV presents a summary and final conclusions and suggests several avenues for future research.

Research on Stock Dividends

Researchers have taken two complementary approaches to learn about stock dividends: using market data and surveying managers. The most popular approach is to quantify the reaction of the market as a whole. Empirical studies show that statistically significant abnormal returns accompany stock dividends on the announcement date. For example, Grinblatt et al. [6] confirm earlier work by Foster and Vickrey [5], Nichols [10], and Woolridge [13, 14], who find that stock prices, on average, react positively to stock dividend announcements. This real effect on shareholder wealth suggests that the market perceives stock dividends as conveying economic value. So far, there is no completely satisfactory explanation for such findings.

Researchers have advanced many hypotheses to explain potential motives for issuing stock dividends. Although these hypotheses are not mutually exclusive, they fall into four broad groups—signaling, liquidity, trading range, and cash substitution. The *signaling hypothesis* says that the announcement of a stock dividend conveys new information to the market. That is, managers can use stock dividends to signal good news or optimistic expectations to capital market participants. As company insiders, managers usually have better estimates of company prospects than do outsiders. Therefore, managers can convey their insider information to outside investors through their discretionary financial decisions.

Several empirical studies support the signaling hypothesis. For example, Grinblatt et al. [6], among others, find a positive share price response to stock dividend announcements. This evidence supports the view that investors infer favorable information about a firm's future prospects from these announcements. Doran and Nachtmann [2] and McNichols and Dravid [8] report that significant earnings increases follow the issuance of stock dividends. These results confirm the belief that stock dividends convey information about higher future earnings. Lakonishok and Lev [7] find that the announcement of stock dividends often signals an increased chance of a near-term cash dividend rise. Finally, Elgers and Murray [4] conclude that management's desire to signal optimistic expectations prompts them to issue small stock distributions.

These studies supporting the signaling hypothesis use different ways of defining stock dividends. The two most common ways are the accounting guidelines and the CRSP tape classification. The accounting guidelines require differential accounting treatments for large versus small stock dividends and recommend treating only stock distributions of less than 25 percent as stock dividends. Doran and Nachtmann [2] and Elgers and Murray [4] follow this approach. The CRSP classification uses the manager's own classification, regardless of whether the stock distribution is taken out of retained earnings. Grinblatt et al. [6] use both methods, but they limit their sample to stock distributions of 10 percent or more to avoid periodic predictable stock dividends. McNichols and Dravid use the CRSP classification, but they also require distributions of 10 percent or more. Lakonishok and Lev [7] use the CRSP tape classification.

The *liquidity hypothesis* suggests that stock dividends enhance liquidity by increasing the proportion of shares traded and decreasing bid-ask spreads. There is little empirical support for this hypothesis. For example, Murray [9] finds that firms undertaking a stock dividend experience both a short- and long-term decrease in proportional trading volume. He also reports that stock dividends do not affect percentage bid-ask spreads in the short or long run. These results are inconsistent with the notion that stock dividends improve liquidity. Lakonishok and Lev [7] find that average trading volume for their stock dividend sample is similar to that of their control firms in both the pre- and post-announcement period. However, they do note that the highest trading volume occurs during the announcement month.

A related hypothesis is the *trading range hypothesis*, which holds that stock dividends help to move a stock into a normal or optimal price range. Moving the stock into this range theoretically makes the market for trading in the stock wider or deeper by attracting more investors, which increases liquidity. Elgers and Murray [4] find that firms with low stock prices are more inclined to issue small stock distributions. They conclude that managers do not find small stock dividends useful tools to reduce high share prices. Lakonishok and Lev [7] also conclude that price is not a major motive for stock dividend distributions.

Finally, the *cash substitution hypothesis* says that managers can conserve cash by issuing a stock dividend as a temporary substitute for either existing or contemplated cash dividends. Firms may need to conserve cash because of limited financial resources due to cash flow difficulties or asset expansion requirements. Empirical studies provide little support for this hypothesis. For example, Elgers and Murray [4] find that a poor cash position is not a factor in the decision to issue stock dividends. Grinblatt et al. [6] report frequent association between stock dividends and simultaneous or subsequent cash dividend increases. Lakonishok and Lev [7] also find that large cash dividend increases often follow a stock dividend announcement. In practice, stock dividends do not appear to result in conserving cash.

The second approach to studying stock dividends is to probe the decision-making processes of managers through the techniques of behavioral science. Although many empirical studies have examined the phenomenon of stock dividends, only Eisemann and Moses [3] have approached the topic by surveying corporate officers. They examined two groups: (1) 80 NYSE firms that paid stock dividend of less than 25 percent in 1974 and (2) 89 NYSE firms that did not have a stock split or a stock dividend between 1970 and 1974. They received 39 responses from the first group and 58 responses from the second group.

Eisemann and Moses asked the respondents to indicate their level of opinion (agree, no opinion, disagree) on 17 closed-end questions. The stock dividend payers strongly agreed that stock dividends enable management to express their confidence in the firm, but most managers of firms not paying stock dividends disagreed with this view.

In their responses to an open-end question, the major reasons that stock dividend payers gave for issuing a stock dividend were historical company practice, conserving cash, and increasing the yield to stockholders. There were no practical differences in the importance attached to these motives. Managers of firms not paying stock dividends said their firms had not issued a stock dividend in recent years mainly because of high administrative costs.

In summary, non-survey research suggests little empirical support for the value of stock dividends for purposes other than signaling the market. The Eisemann and Moses study serves as a benchmark for comparing changes in management views about issuing stock dividends. The current study uses a behavioral approach to examine what motives justify the administrative costs of stock dividends.

Research Design and Respondent Profile

Sample and Survey Design

The full sample contained all firms that paid at least one stock dividend between 1988 and 1990—100 NYSE/Amex firms and 260 Nasdaq firms. The distribution of firms with stock dividends for 1988, 1989, and 1990 was as follows: 21, 34, and 45 for NYSE/Amex firms and 62, 96, and 102 for Nasdaq firms, respectively. The source of stock dividend firms was the CRSP Nasdaq and combined NYSE/Amex master files. Excluding non-U.S., takeover and bankrupt firms reduced the sample from 360 to 312.

We chose the 1988–90 period for two reasons. First, we wanted the study period to span several years to avoid any potential bias of using a single year. Second, we wanted a period long enough to provide a large sample size, but short enough to ensure getting someone knowledgeable about the firm's most recent stock dividend to answer the questionnaire. We do not believe that the choice of the period influenced the results.

The questionnaire had two parts. The first portion contained 15 closed-end questions on issues (identified by IS) drawn from the finance literature about stock dividends. Several questions are similar to those contained in the Eisemann and Moses [3] study. The questionnaire instructed respondents to indicate their level of disagreement or agreement with each question, using a seven-point semantic differential scale: -3 = strongly disagree, -2 = moderately disagree, -1 = slightly disagree, 0 = no opinion, +1 = slightly agree, +2 = moderately agree, and +3 = strongly agree. The second portion of the questionnaire contained seven questions about stock dividend decisions and four questions about the respondent's profile. Elgers and Murray [4] find managements have good self-insight into the factors that they consider in issuing stock distributions.

Several issue statements in the first portion of the questionnaire related to the four hypotheses for issuing stock dividends: (1) signaling hypothesis—stock dividends convey favorable information about the firm's future prospects (IS2), (2) liquidity hypothesis—stock dividends increase the number of the firm's shareholders (IS7), and trading volume increases immediately after stock dividend announcements (IS15), (3) trading range hypothesis—stock dividends adjust the firm's stock price to a preferred trading range (IS3), and (4) cash substitution hypothesis—stock dividends are a temporary substitute for cash dividends (IS5).

We sent a survey questionnaire and a cover letter to the highest ranking financial officer of each firm in early November 1991. Non-respondents received a follow-up survey and another cover letter one month later. The recipients were asked to give the survey, if necessary, to someone knowledgeable about their firm's most recent stock dividend decision. Of the initial 312 questionnaires mailed, only 299 questionnaires were delivered. Of these 299 questionnaires, 136 firms completed and returned them, giving a response rate of 45.6 percent.

We conducted several tests to find out whether characteristics of the 136 responding firms differed from those of the 299 firms receiving the questionnaire. The chi-square tests showed no significant differences between the two groups based on their trading location—Nasdaq, NYSE, or Amex. The 299 firms contained 201 Nasdaq, 50 NYSE, and 48 Amex firms, compared with 94 Nasdaq, 23 NYSE, and 19 Amex firms from the 136 respondents.

We also conducted tests on 17 financial attributes of the firms, using 1990 financial data drawn from the COMPUSTAT PC-Plus data base. The ten gross measures were: (1) total current assets, (2) total current liabilities, (3) total cash, (4) total long-term debt, (5) total assets, (6) depreciation, (7) annual net income, (8) earnings per share excluding extraordinary items, (9) year end stock price, and (10) year-end common shares outstanding. The seven financial ratios were: (1) current ratio, (2) cash to total assets, (3) cash to current assets, (4) long-term debt to total assets, (5) market value of equity to total assets, (6) net income to total assets, and (7) cash flow (net income plus depreciation) per share.

Tests for significant differences in the distributions included the t-test and two non-parametric tests, the Mann-Whitney U-test and the Kolmogorov-Smirnov test. These statistical tests showed the assumption of equivalent distributions could not be rejected for any items. Evidence concerning the 17 financial attributes suggests that the responding firms represented the broader population of firms declaring stock dividends.

An examination of the survey responses showed that the most recent stock dividend was at least 25 percent for 15 of 136 firms. The self-reported stock dividend sizes were consistent with the findings from CRSP. We constrained our sample by dropping these 15 firms from our analysis, for two reasons. First, we wanted to eliminate any possible bias caused by the differences between small (<25 percent) and large (≥ 25 percent) stock dividends found by some researchers. We used the accounting guidelines to exclude firms issuing stock splits in the guise of stock dividends. Second, we wanted to compare our results with those of the Eisemann and Moses study, which eliminated firms that paid a stock dividend of 25 percent or greater. The following analysis is based on 121 responding firms.

Respondent Profile

Based on the survey instrument, the respondent profile of the 121 firms shows that 77.5 percent of the respondents were involved in their firms' most recent stock dividend decisions. Most were chief financial officers or treasurers (62.2 percent) or presidents or chief executive officers (25.2 percent). The remaining respondents (12.6 percent) were corporate secretaries, investor relations managers, and others. The major business groups were financial (56.2 percent) and manufacturing (24.0 percent). No other business group amounted to 5 percent of the responses. The major trading locations of the stocks were 15.8 percent on the NYSE, 11.7 percent on the Amex, and 72.5 percent on the Nasdaq.

Most firms (62.4 percent) did not pay a stock dividend regularly (i.e., at least annually). The most common size stock dividends were 10 percent and 5 percent, representing 43.7 percent and 31.9 percent, respectively, of the respondents. Only 36.1 percent of the respondents said their firms had preferred trading ranges for their stock prices. Although the preferred range differed among firms, the average price ranged from about \$15 to \$24.

Survey Results

Combined Sample

Issue Statements about Stock Dividends

Exhibit 1 gives descriptive statistics on 15 closed-end issue statements about stock dividends. The statement with the highest level of agreement (95.0 percent) was that stock dividends have a positive psychological impact on investors receiving them (IS1). This finding is consistent with the views expressed in several textbooks. For example, Rao [11, p. 505] states: "... the majority of the arguments advanced rely on some sort of a psychological impact on investors receiving stock dividends." Cooley and Roden [1, p. 800] state: "... many financial managers believe that stock dividends and splits have a favorable psychological impact on investors." They also note that supporting evidence is scarce for the psychological impact.

The responses to several other statements appear consistent with the view that stock dividends have a positive psychological impact on investors. For example, over 68 percent of the respondents believed that stock prices generally react positively to stock dividend announcements (IS4). The results of empirical studies by Poster and Vickrey [5], Woolridge [13, 14], and Grinblatt et al. [6] support this view.

Most respondents (69.2 percent) also agreed that stock prices do not fully adjust to an occasional small (less than 25 percent) stock dividend (IS13). This view implies that corporate managers perceive small stock dividends as conveying economic value. Nichols [10] finds a positive, statistically significant adjustment in the stock dividend announcement month. However, this positive return is offset by downward adjustments over the following three months. Because full price adjustment does occur over time, this evidence does not support the reported beliefs that occasional small stock dividends convey economic value.

Another statement receiving a high level of agreement (70.6 percent) was that stock dividends are cosmetic changes that do not alter the firm's underlying risk and return characteristics (IS9). Apparently, many respondents perceived that investors are unaware of the cosmetic nature of stock dividends since they view them positively.

Of the four hypotheses about stock dividends, the signaling hypothesis received the most support. More than 78 percent of the respondents agreed that stock dividends convey favorable information about the firm's future prospects (IS2). Over half (54.6 percent) agreed with a statement of the trading range hypothesis, that stock dividends adjust the firm's stock price to a preferred trading range (IS3). Respondents had mixed views about statements of the liquidity (IS7 and IS15) and cash substitution (IS5) hypotheses.

EXHIBIT 1 MANAGEMENTS' VIEWS ON STOCK DIVIDEND ISSUES: COMBINED SAMPLE

Survey #	Issue	Disagree -3 -2 -1	No Opinion 0	Agree +1 +2 +3	Mean (Standard Deviation)	Rank
IS1	Stock dividends have a positive psychological impact on investors receiving them.	2.5%	2.5%	95.0%	2.14(1.07)	1
IS2	Stock dividends convey favorable information about the firm's future prospects.	9.2	12.5	78.3	1.33(1.46)	2
IS9	Stock dividends are cosmetic changes that do not alter the firm's underlying risk and return characteristics.	19.3	10.1	70.6	1.24(1.61)	3
IS4	Stock prices generally react positively to stock dividend announcements.	16.7	15.0	68.3	.90(1.41)	4.5
IS13	Stock prices do not fully adjust to an occasional small (less than 25%) stock dividend.	20.0	10.8	69.2	.90(1.59)	4.5
IS8	Stock dividends are more expensive to administer than cash dividends.	20.2	14.3	65.5	.86(1.68)	6
IS3	Stock dividends adjust the firm's stock price to a preferred trading range.	25.2	20.2	54.6	.61(1.68)	7
IS11	Shareholders expect stock dividends to continue once initiated.	34.2	7.5	58.3	.33(1.65)	8
IS12	The firm's stock price is negatively affected by discontinuing a policy of issuing regular stock dividends.	35.0	23.3	41.7	-.01(1.50)	9
IS15	Trading volume increases immediately after stock dividend announcements.	28.3	31.7	40.0	-.03(1.36)	10
IS7	Stock dividends increase the number of the firm's shareholders.	41.7	15.8	42.3	-.30(1.73)	11
IS14	Small (less than 25%) stock dividends can restrict the firm's ability to pay cash dividends by reducing its retained earnings.	49.2	15.0	35.8	-.46(1.76)	12
IS6	Stock dividends trigger reassessments of the firm's future cash flows.	43.7	30.3	26.1	-.49(1.53)	13
IS5	Stock dividends are a temporary substitute for cash dividends.	52.5	6.7	40.8	-.50(1.85)	14
IS10	Shareholders prefer stock dividends to cash dividends due to delayed payment of taxes.	52.9	20.2	26.9	-.58(1.65)	15

Note: Percentages may not total 100 due to rounding. A total of 120 of the 121 respondents gave their major trading locations as 19 NYSE, 14 Amex, and 87 Nasdaq. The seven-point scale was: -3 = strongly disagree, -2 = moderately disagree, -1 slightly disagree, 0 = no opinion, +1 = slightly agree, +2 = moderately agree, and +3 = strongly agree.

Comparing the results of our study and of the Eisemann and Moses study requires some caution, since several issue statements, though similar, are not identical. With this caveat, it can be said that both studies show that the respondents of stock-dividend-paying firms had similar views about a few issues. For example, about 70 percent of both groups agreed that stock prices do not fully adjust to an occasional stock dividend (IS13). Although most respondents agreed that issuing stock dividends conveys favorable information about the firm (IS2), the level of agreement was much higher in our study than in the Eisemann and Moses study (78.3 percent versus 64.3 percent). The two studies also differed widely in responses to the notion that issuing stock dividends increases the number of shareholders in the firm (IS7) and allows the firm to conserve cash (IS5). Stock dividend payers in the Eisemann and Moses study strongly agreed with these two issues (78.9 percent and 86.8 percent, respectively), but fewer than half our respondents expressed agreement (42.3 percent and 40.8 percent, respectively).

Motives for Issuing Stock Dividends

Exhibit 2 summarizes the most important motives (identified by M) for distributing stock dividends. Respondents selected the two most important motives for their firm's most recent stock dividend, from eight choices plus "other" and "don't know" options. Two motives clearly dominate the reasons the responding firms issue stock dividends. The most important motive was to maintain the firm's historical practice of paying stock dividends (M1). Almost 43 percent of the

EXHIBIT 2 MOTIVES FOR STOCK DIVIDENDS: COMBINED SAMPLE

		Importance			
Survey #	Motive	Primary (n = 112)	Secondary (n = 110)	Weighted Score	Rank
M1	Maintain the firm's historical practice of paying stock dividends	48(42.9%)	1(.9%)	97	1
M2	Signal optimistic managerial expectations about the future	26(23.2)	20(18.2)	72	2
M6	Increase trading volume	6(5.4)	18(16.4)	30	3
M3	Increase the total market value of the firm's stock	8(7.1)	8(7.3)	24	4.5
M9	Other	5(4.5)	14(12.7)	24	4.5
M5	Gain attention from the investment community	4(3.6)	14(12.7)	22	6
M8	Conserve cash	2(1.8)	13(11.8)	17	7.5
M4	Move the stock price into a better trading range	7(6.3)	7(6.4)	21	7.5
M7	Attract more investors	2(1.8)	11(10.0)	15	9
M10	Don't know	4(3.6)	4(3.6)	NA	NA

NA = Not Applicable

* The weighted score for each motive is calculated by multiplying the number of primary responses by 2 and the number of secondary responses by 1 and then summing the products.

respondents gave this as a primary motive. The second most important motive was to signal optimistic managerial expectations about the future (M2). No other primary motive accounted for even 8 percent of the responses.

Of the four hypotheses about motives for paying small stock dividends, the signaling hypothesis, represented mainly by M2, received the most support. The motive of maintaining the firm's historical practice of paying stock dividends (M1) is also a signaling motive. That is, investors may view discontinuing the payment of a regular stock dividend as a negative signal. Our results provide some support for the liquidity hypothesis (M6) and the trading range hypothesis (M4), but little support for the cash substitution hypothesis (M8).

Few respondents said that increasing the total market value of the firm's stock (M3) was their primary or secondary motive for issuing a stock dividend. The low ranking of this motive appears inconsistent with the widely cited normative goal of shareholder wealth maximization. However, several more highly ranked motives are likely to affect a firm's stock price. For example, maintaining the firm's historical practice of paying stock dividends (M1) may avoid the potentially negative impact on its stock price from stopping this practice. Also, signaling optimistic managerial expectations about the future (M2) is likely to increase market value. On the other hand, there is not universal agreement among practicing managers that their duty is to maximize shareholder wealth in every situation.

Comparing these results to the Eisemann and Moses [3] survey requires caution. For instance, they asked respondents to list the reasons why their companies issued a stock dividend and then subjectively classified the responses according to the perceived intent of the response. We asked the respondents to select the primary and secondary motives for their firms' most recent stock dividends from a list of motives. Thus, the studies used different approaches in trying to identify the motives for issuing stock dividends.

Although the motive of historical company practice is highly ranked in both studies, its relative importance is much greater in the current study. That is, there was virtually a tie among the top three motives in the Eisemann and Moses study, but in our study the importance of this motive clearly exceeds that of all others. Perhaps the most striking difference in the importance of motives between the two studies involves using stock dividends to conserve cash. Eisemann and Moses found in 1974 that conserving cash was a highly important reason for issuing a stock dividend. In our study, this motive ranked toward the bottom in importance.

Partitioned Samples

To gain further insight into managements' views about the issues and motives for stock dividends, we partitioned the sample according to three variables: trading location (NYSE/Amex and Nasdaq), frequency of issuing stock dividends (regular, i.e. at least one annually, and occasional), and size of the stock dividend (< 10 percent and 10 percent to < 25 percent). Both t-tests and chi-square tests were used to test for differences between the groups on their responses to the

15 issue statements. Because both tests consistently rejected the null hypothesis of no difference between the groups at the .05 level, we report only the results of the t-tests.

Trading Location

Partitioning the sample by trading location, which is a proxy for firm size and maturity, resulted in 33 NYSE/Amex firms and 87 Nasdaq firms. Because one respondent failed to answer the question on trading location, the resulting sample was 120, not 121, firms. The 19 NYSE and 14 Amex firms were combined into a single group because of the small sample size from each exchange. The characteristics of the NYSE/Amex and Nasdaq groups were similar in most respects. For example, these characteristics included the percentage of firms paying regular dividends, the frequency of issuing stock dividends since 1988, and the size of the firm's most recent stock dividend. The two groups differed on the firm's major business. Compared with the Nasdaq group, the NYSE/Amex group had a larger percentage of manufacturing firms (33 percent versus 19.5 percent) and a smaller percentage of financial firms (42.4 percent versus 62.1 percent).

Panel A of Exhibit 3 shows statistically significant differences between the NYSE/Amex and Nasdaq groups on only one issue statement. Respondents from the NYSE/Amex firms expressed a higher level of agreement on the statement that stock dividends are more expensive to administer than cash dividends are (IS8). The total cost of issuing stock dividends may be more expensive for NYSE/Amex than for Nasdaq firms because, on average, exchange-listed firms are larger and have more shareholders.

Exhibit 4 shows that both groups ranked the two most important primary motives (M1 and M2) in the same order. However, 56.7 percent of the NYSE/Amex group said that maintaining the firm's historical practice of paying stock dividends (M1) was most important, compared with only 37.8 percent for the Nasdaq group. The evidence suggests that managers have similar views about issues and motives for stock dividends, irrespective of their firms' trading locations.

Frequency of Stock Dividends

We divided the larger sample into 45 firms that regularly pay a stock dividend at least annually and 74 firms that do not. Only 119 of the 121 respondents answered the question needed to classify the firms by frequency of stock dividends. The characteristics of two groups are highly similar.

Panel B of Exhibit 3 shows statistically significant differences between the regular and occasional stock-dividend-paying groups on six statements. Not surprisingly, regular stock dividend payers are much more likely than occasional payers to agree that shareholders expect stock dividends to continue once initiated (IS11). They also show a higher level of agreement with the statement that the firm's stock price is negatively affected by discontinuing a policy of issuing regular stock dividends (IS12). In addition, regular stock dividend payers agree

EXHIBIT 3 Issue Statements with Significant Differences in Responses According to Trading Location and Frequency of Stock Dividends

Survey #	Issue		Disagree -3 -2 -1	No Opinion 0	Agree +1 +2 +3	Mean (Standard Deviation)	t-value
Panel A. Trading Location							
IS8	Stock dividends are more expensive to administer than cash dividends.	NYSE/Amex	6.1%	18.2%	75.8%	1.30(1.29)	2.13*
		Nasdaq	25.9	12.9	61.2	0.67(1.79)	
Panel B. Frequency of Stock Dividends							
IS11	Shareholders expect stock dividends to continue once initiated.	Regular	15.6	6.7	77.8	1.09(1.43)	4.31**
		Occasional	45.9	8.1	45.9	-0.16(1.60)	
IS12	The firm's stock price is negatively affected by discontinuing a policy of issuing regular stock dividends.	Regular	22.2	24.4	53.3	0.40(1.39)	2.40**
		Occasional	43.2	23.0	33.8	-0.27(1.53)	
IS13	Stock prices do not fully adjust to an occasional small (less than 25%) stock dividend.	Regular	6.7	15.6	77.8	1.27(1.21)	2.22*
		Occasional	28.4	8.1	63.5	.66(1.75)	
IS10	Shareholders prefer stock dividends to cash dividends, due to delayed payment of taxes.	Regular	37.8	20.0	42.2	-0.11(1.57)	2.66**
		Occasional	61.6	20.5	17.8	-0.86(1.44)	
IS6	Stock dividends trigger reassessments of the firm's future cash flows.	Regular	55.6	24.4	20.0	-0.89(1.67)	-2.36*
		Occasional	35.6	34.4	30.1	-0.22(1.39)	
IS5	Stock dividends are a temporary substitute for cash dividends.	Regular	62.2	8.9	28.9	-0.96(1.91)	-2.03*
		Occasional	47.3	5.4	47.3	-0.26(1.77)	

Note: Percentages may not total 100 due to rounding. The results are based on the following sample sizes: 33 NYSE/Amex and 85 Nasdaq, 45 regular and 74 occasional stock dividend payers. The seven-point scale was: -3 = strongly disagree, -2 = moderately disagree, -1 = slightly disagree, 0 = no opinion, +1 = slightly agree, +2 = moderately agree, and +3 = strongly agree.

* Significant at the .05 level.

** Significant at the .01 level.

more often with two other statements: stock prices do not fully adjust to an occasional small stock dividend (IS13), and shareholders prefer stock dividends to cash dividends due to delayed payment of taxes (IS10). However, regular stock dividend payers disagree more often with statements that stock dividends trigger reassessments of the firm's future cash flows (IS) and are a temporary substitute for cash dividends (IS5).

Exhibit 4 presents the two major motives for paying stock dividends for the two groups. Not surprisingly, the most important motive for firms regularly paying stock dividends is to continue this historical practice (M1). More than 65 percent of the respondents from this group gave historical practice as their firm's primary motive for issuing stock dividends. No other primary motive for this group amounted to even 10 percent of their responses.

The decision to continue paying stock dividends may stem from managers' concerns about shareholder expectations and the market's reaction to ending such distributions. As Exhibit 3 shows, 77.8 percent of the respondents from firms paying regular stock dividends agreed that shareholders expect stock dividends to continue once begun (IS1). Most (53.3 percent) also believed that dropping such a policy could negatively affect the firm's stock price (IS12).

For firms with occasional stock dividends, about 34 percent of the respondents said their primary motive was to signal optimistic managerial expectations about the future (M2). Although these firms did not pay stock dividends annually, maintaining the practice of paying stock dividends (M1) ranked a close second. These results clearly show that a firm's stock dividend pattern reflects managers' views about such distributions.

Size of Stock Dividends

Dividing the sample by size of stock dividends resulted in 62 firms whose last stock dividend was $<$ 10 percent and 57 firms whose last stock dividend was 10 percent to $<$ 25 percent. The sample size equaled 119 firms because two respondents did not answer the question about the size of their firm's last stock dividend. The major difference between the two groups was that 47.5 percent of firms with stock dividends $<$ 10 percent paid regular stock dividends, versus only 28.1 percent for the other group.

The chi-square tests and t-tests fail to reveal any statistically significant differences between the two groups on any of the 15 issue statements. Exhibit 4 shows that the two most important motives for issuing stock dividends were the same for the two size groups. However, 50.0 percent of the respondents from the small stock dividend group said their primary motive for paying this dividend was historical, versus 35.2 percent for the other size group. This finding is not surprising, because almost half the firms issuing small stock dividends had a practice of paying them regularly.

Summary and Conclusions

There is much speculation about the motives for issuing stock dividends. The current study provides further evidence from a managerial perspective about

EXHIBIT 4 MOTIVES FOR STOCK DIVIDENDS ACCORDING TO TRADING LOCATION, SIZE, AND FREQUENCY OF STOCK DIVIDENDS

Survey #	Primary Motive*	Trading Location				Frequency of Stock Dividends				Size of Stock Dividend			
		NYSE/Amex (n = 30)		Nasdaq (n = 82)		Regular (n = 43)		Occasional (n = 68)		< 10% (n = 62)		10% to < 25% (n = 57)	
		%	Rank	%	Rank	%	Rank	%	Rank	%	Rank	%	Rank
M1	Maintain the firm's historical practice of paying stock dividends.	56.7	1	37.8	1	65.1	1	27.9	2	50.0	1	35.2	1
M2	Signal optimistic managerial expectations about the future.	20.0	2	24.4	2	7.0	3**	33.8	1	19.0	2	27.8	2

* No other primary motive made up 10% or more of the responses.

** Tied with two other motives, namely, to increase the total market value of the firm's stock (M3) and to move the stock into a better trading range (M4).

these motives. Despite its limited scope, this study adds new insights to our understanding of the stock dividend question.

Before we present the conclusions, several limitations of the study warrant attention. First, the study does not directly test hypotheses about stock dividends, but simply reports managements' views about issuing them. A consensus does not make a hypothesis true or false, but it may provide insight about how managers view a certain hypothesis. Second, survey research has potential non-response bias, although the high response rate found in this study reduces this bias.

The results of the survey lead to several conclusions. First, managers strongly agree that stock dividends have a positive psychological impact on investors receiving them. The finding is significant because prior empirical evidence about this belief is scarce.

Second, of the four leading hypotheses for issuing stock dividends (signaling, liquidity, preferred trading range, and cash substitution), the signaling hypothesis receives the most support. Managers believe that stock dividends enable them to express their confidence in the firm's future prospects, suggesting that stock dividends may have some information content. Although this finding is consistent with other empirical evidence, we provide supporting evidence from a managerial perspective.

Third, the dominant motive for paying stock dividends is to maintain the firm's historical practice. Although Eisemann and Moses [3] reported the same motive almost 15 years ago, the importance of this motive has apparently increased over time. Some firms still continue to pay stock dividends because their managers are apprehensive about stockholder reaction to changing the firm's historical stock dividend practice.

Fourth, managerial views on issues and motives about stock dividends differ little in relation to the firm's trading location or the size of the stock dividend. However, managers of firms paying regular stock dividends and those paying occasional dividends display major differences in their views about certain issues and motives. Specifically, firms regularly paying a stock dividend are highly motivated to maintain this historical practice. They believe that shareholders expect stock dividends to continue once initiated and feel apprehensive about shareholder reaction to changing this practice.

There are several avenues for future research in the area of stock dividends. One extension of the current study is to survey shareholders to examine their views about receiving additional stock certificates and whether these views differ between individual and institutional shareholders. For example, a topic of particular interest is whether institutional investors avoid stocks paying frequent stock dividends because the handling cost makes such stocks unattractive. Another avenue of research is to survey firms to learn why they do not issue stock dividends. A third research topic is to find out whether the market responds differently to stock dividend announcements from firms having a policy of paying regular stock dividends and those paying occasional dividends. A final direction of research is to examine the market reaction to stopping stock dividends by firms that historically have paid them. This topic is particularly relevant given the importance that managers attached to the firm's historical practice of paying stock dividends.

References

1. P.L. Cooley and P.F. Roden, *Business Financial Management*, Chicago, IL, The Dryden Press, 1988.
2. D.T. Doran and R. Nachtmann, "The Association of Stock Distribution Announcements and Earnings Performance," *Journal of Accounting, Auditing and Finance* (Spring 1988), pp. 113–132.
3. P.C. Eisemann and E.A. Moses, "Stock Dividends: Management's View," *Financial Analysts Journal* (July-August 1978), pp. 77–80.
4. P.T. Elgers and D. Murray, "Financial Characteristics Related to Managements' Stock Split and Stock Dividend Decisions," *Journal of Business Finance and Accounting* (Winter 1985), pp. 543–551.
5. T.W. Foster and D. Vickrey, "The Information Content of Stock Dividend Announcements," *Accounting Review* (April 1978), pp. 360–370.
6. M.S. Grinblatt, R.W. Masulis and S. Titman, "The Valuation Effects of Stock Splits and Stock Dividends," *Journal of Financial Economics* (December 1984), pp. 461–490.
7. J. Lakonishok and B. Lev, "Stock Splits and Stock Dividends: Why, Who, and When," *Journal of Finance* (September 1987), pp. 913–932.
8. M. McNichols and A. Dravid, "Stock Dividends, Stock Splits, and Signaling," *Journal of Finance* (July 1990), pp. 857–879.
9. D. Murray, "Further Evidence on the Liquidity Effects of Stock Splits and Stock Dividends," *Journal of Financial Research* (Spring 1985), pp. 59–67.
10. W.D. Nichols, "Security Price Reactions to Occasional Small Stock Dividends," *Financial Review* (February 1981), pp. 54–62.
11. R.K.S. Rao, *Financial Management: Concepts and Applications*, New York, NY, MacMillan Publishing Company, 1987.
12. Robert Willens, "New Techniques Avoid Taxability Under Section 305 for Stock Dividends," *Journal of Taxation* (August 1988), pp. 98–101.
13. J.R. Woolridge, "Stock Dividends as Signals," *Journal of Financial Research* (Spring 1983), pp. 1–12.
14. J.R. Woolridge, "Ex-Date Stock Price Adjustment to Stock Dividends: A Note," *Journal of Finance* (March 1983), pp. 247–255.

Questions

1. In contrast to paying dividends with cash, a company may distribute new shares of stock to stockholders in the form of a stock dividend. With a stock dividend stockholders receive additional shares of stock in proportion to their current holdings. To illustrate the accounting treatment of stock dividends, consider the 10 percent stock dividend of Baker Corporation (BC), whose 100,000 $10-par-value shares trade for $25 per share. BC's equity accounts before and after the stock dividends are as follows:

	Before	**After**
Common Stock	$1,000,000	$1,100,000
Capital in excess of par	500,000	650,000
Retained earnings	3,500,000	3,250,000
Total	$5,000,000	$5,000,000

a. What is the rationale for the changes in BC's equity accounts? (*Hint*: Transfer $250,000—10,000 shares × $25—from retained earnings.)

b. Calculate BC's *before* and *after* book value per share.

c. Suppose you own 25 percent of BC's shares of stock. Calculate your total book value before and after the stock dividend. Did your total book value increase?

d. Estimate the price per share of BC stock after completion of the 10 percent stock dividend.

2. In what way is a 100 percent stock dividend similar to cutting a pizza pie into twice as many pieces?
3. Describe each of the following four hypotheses regarding stock dividends: signaling, liquidity, trading range, and cash substitution.
4. Describe the level of support provided by the survey results (in Exhibits 1 and 2) for each hypothesis in Question 3.
5. Interpret the survey results contained in Exhibit 3 regarding trading location and frequency of stock dividends.
6. Interpret the survey results contained in Exhibit 4 regarding trading location, frequency of stock dividends, and size of stock dividend.

PART
VII

Special Topics

Clarifying Marking to Market

ANN KREMER

Futures contracts seem to be very simple, but the simplicity is deceptive. Students, and probably also the general public, are often confused by specialized futures terminology, concepts and processes. This paper offers uncomplicated explanations of some of the terms and concepts. Then the paper demonstrates the process of marking to market using two easy examples, the first based on simplified data, and the second based on recent price quotations.

Probably the most confusing aspect of futures contracts is that, although the futures price was set when the contract was initiated, at delivery the *spot price* is exchanged between the buyer and the seller. How can a futures contract possibly be useful if the market's spot price is paid and received when the contract matures and the asset is delivered? The explanation is not simple: any difference between the original futures price and the final spot price has already been exchanged by adjusting the margin accounts of the buyer and seller. The original futures price is equal to the spot price at delivery plus or minus the total adjustments of the margin account.

Trade industry descriptions of hedging and speculative strategies with futures do not clear up this point. They seem to ignore margin adjustments, and describe strategies as if the original futures price is the price exchanged when the underlying good is delivered.

The daily adjustment of margin accounts and the resulting spot price at delivery are fundamental characteristics of futures contracts. The process of adjusting the margin accounts is called "marking to market" or "daily resettlement" of futures contracts. These seemingly elementary details, the source of bewilderment for students and for the investing public, are usually overlooked in textbooks and trade educational material. However, students can fairly easily grasp the concept of marking to market from the two consecutive examples given here.

There are also other characteristics of futures that are counterintuitive and perplexing to students. Some examples: Investors do not pay or receive cash

---

At the time of this writing, Ann Kremer was an assistant professor of finance at Michigan State University.

Source: *Journal of Financial Education* (Nov. 1991, Vol. 20, pp. 17–25). Reprinted with permission.

when they buy or sell futures. There are not one, but *three* kinds of "margin." The initial margin is not necessarily a cash deposit. The settlement price is often *not* the price of the last trade of the day.

Before considering the "marking to market" examples, students must understand the concepts of buying and selling futures, the three kinds of margins, and the forms of the margin deposits. Then they must be clear about how gains and losses are generated in futures positions. Finally, they can be introduced to the concept of marking to market, and given the two examples.

Futures Buyers and Sellers

The terms "buyer" and "seller" do not apply in their usual sense when we refer to a futures contract. A futures "buyer" has entered a legal contract promising to *buy* the underlying asset at a future date. The buyer does not pay cash when the contract is entered. A futures "seller" has entered a legal contract promising to *sell* the underlying asset at a future date. The seller does not receive cash when the contract is entered.

Three Kinds of Margin

To reduce the risk of default by one of the parties to the futures contract, the members of the Futures Exchange require a performance bond, called the margin, for each contract. The members of the Exchange have pledged their personal wealth to cover default losses to investors in futures contracts; this means that they are motivated to set margin deposits high enough to protect themselves from these losses. However, competition between several Futures Exchanges keeps margins low. What is a reasonable margin? It seems clear that the margin for a futures contract ought to reflect the riskiness of the futures price. In fact, studies have shown that futures margins respond quickly to changes in volatility of the futures price (see Chance [1991]).

The *initial margin* required of traders upon entering a futures contract is approximately the amount of expected price change during two days of trading. So we can conclude that the initial margin reflects the expected price volatility of the futures contract, and in fact this is so. For example, Treasury bill prices are less volatile than Treasury bond prices, and the initial margin for a $1 million Treasury bill futures position (one Treasury bill futures contract) is smaller than the initial margin for a $1 million Treasury bond futures position (ten Treasury bond futures contracts).

Individual investors deposit their initial margins with the broker. Brokerage firms who are members of the Futures Exchange combine the accounts of their customers and deposit margins with the Futures Exchange Clearinghouse. A member firm's margin deposit reflects the accounts of the firm's entire clientele.

When the futures price changes, all margin accounts are adjusted to compensate for the change. When the price change results in a loss to the investor, the margin account balance is reduced. When the change results in a gain, the margin account balance is increased.

If accumulated losses reduce the margin to a level which is the minimum margin allowed for that contract, called the *maintenance margin*, the trader receives a "margin call." A margin call is always bad news. The trader is required to deposit an amount of cash to bring the margin up to its initial level. The maintenance margin is usually about two-thirds of the initial margin, or roughly one day's normal price change for the contract.

The variable cash deposits that brokerage firms and individual investors make in response to margin calls are called *variation margin* and represent losses in the futures position.

Note that we have described three kinds of margin: the initial margin, the maintenance margin, and the variation margin.

The Forms of Margin Deposits

The initial margin is not necessarily required to be cash; it can consist of a portfolio of investments signed over to the broker. The broker will assign a value to this portfolio, for example, 50% of the market value of stocks, or 90% of the face value of Treasury bills. The assigned value must total at least the amount of the required margin deposit. If the market value of a customer's deposited securities falls below the required margin, the broker will give notice to firms or individuals to deposit more securities (or cash).

The brokerage firm member of the Futures Exchange also must maintain a margin account. The firm aggregates all of its clients' accounts, and deposits a margin with the Futures Exchange Clearinghouse representing the total of all positions of clients of the firm. The margin deposited with the Clearinghouse must be in cash, Treasury securities, or letters of credit from approved banks.

It makes sense for brokerage firms and individual customers to deposit securities rather than cash for their initial margin accounts. If the margin deposit consists of securities, the securities' owner, who is either the brokerage firm or the customer, continues to benefit from the securities' investment gains. On the other hand, if cash is deposited, the firm or customer receives no investment returns on the margin.

If losses from changes in the futures price are large enough to bring about a margin call, the variation deposit must be in cash. Cash is required because variation margin is not a performance bond, but represents losses incurred in the position.

Buyer's and Seller's Gains and Losses

The price of a particular futures contract changes in the market daily, and any change in the price changes the value of the contract to the buyer and seller. The amount of the change in price is immediately debited from the losing party's margin account and credited to the account of the party who gained. Here are the effects of futures price changes on the buyer's and seller's margin accounts:

The futures price rises: The buyer, who entered the contract when the price was lower, is better off by not having to pay this new higher price. The seller, who contracted earlier to accept the previous lower price, has lost. The amount of the seller's loss is deducted immediately (that day) from the seller's margin account, and added to the buyer's. The buyer may withdraw the gain if the margin account exceeds the initial margin requirement.

The futures price falls: The buyer, who will have to pay the higher price established earlier, loses by not being able to buy at this lower market price. The seller, who will sell at the higher original contract price, gains. The amount of the buyer's loss is immediately deducted from the buyer's margin account, and added to the seller's. The seller may withdraw the gain if the marginal account is higher than the initial requirement.

An easy way to remember who gains and who loses: the buyer of an asset gains if the asset's price rises after the purchase. Similarly, the futures contract "buyer" gains when the futures price rises. The seller (or short seller) of an asset loses if the price rises; similarly, the futures contract "seller" loses when the futures price rises.

The brokerage firm keeps accounts for all of its clients, and posts any gains or losses to their margin accounts daily. The Futures Exchange Clearinghouse keeps accounts for all members of the Futures Exchange, and posts their gains and losses daily.

Gains that raise a margin account above its initial level may be withdrawn immediately. When losses reduce a margin account below the maintenance margin level the trader receives a margin call, and must deposit variation margin to bring the account back to its *initial level.*

The futures contract price approaches the spot price as the maturity date approaches, until on the maturity date, the futures and spot prices are equal. Thus both buyer and seller expect that as time passes any difference between the futures price and the spot price will disappear.

The trade ("delivery") at the maturity of the futures contract is made at the maturity date futures price, which equals that day's spot price. At the time of delivery, the buyer's and seller's margin accounts are closed and repaid to them. The margin accounts usually are no longer at their initial level, because any differences between the original futures contract price and the spot price at maturity were entered into the margin accounts during the life of the contract.

Marking to Market

Each day at the close of trading, a settlement price for every futures contract is established by floor traders in the contract. The most active traders must agree on the settlement price, so it is not necessarily the price of the last trade. The prices of all open (or existing) futures contracts are adjusted to the new settlement prices. At the same time the margin accounts of buyers and sellers are adjusted to reflect their gains and losses from the day's price change.

By keeping the value of the contract at its current market price at all times, and adjusting the margin accounts, the broker and the members of the Futures Exchange are attempting to protect themselves from costs of default by the contract's buyers or sellers. For example:

Default during the life of the contract: If a losing party does not respond to a margin call immediately, the brokerage firm closes that side of the contract by offsetting it at the current market price. In effect, the broker takes over the defaulting trader's position and closes it. If the seller defaults, the broker, acting as the seller, offsets the contract by buying it, that is, by buying the same contract in the market. If the buyer defaults, the broker sells the contract in the market. The brokerage firm deducts its costs and losses from the defaulting trader's remaining margin deposit. Similarly, if a brokerage firm did not respond to a margin call from the Futures Exchange, the Exchange would close the firm's account in that day's market, at the market price.

Default at the maturity date: If either party should default at the maturity date, the broker (or the Exchange) is left with an obligation to buy or sell the underlying good at that day's market price, with the remaining party providing the opposite side of this exchange at the same price. If the defaulting party is the seller, the broker covers the seller's position by acquiring the good in the market (at the market price), delivering it, and receiving the market price. Similarly, if the buyer defaults, the broker receives the delivered good, pays the market price to the seller, and immediately sells the good (at the market price). The broker deducts its losses and costs of these transactions from the defaulting party's remaining margin deposit.

Margin accounts are adjusted daily, and customers have only a few hours (or less) to respond to a margin call. The maximum amount of the Exchange members' loss from a default is therefore one day's price change. Since the defaulting investor's margin had been above the maintenance margin level on the previous day, it is high enough to cover one day's ordinary price change. Therefore, customers' margins are large enough to cover the firm's predictable exposure. Chance [1991] notes that when volatility increases, the required margins also increase.

While the procedure of marking contracts to the current market price is intended to protect the members of the Futures Exchange, it also results in a stream of cash payments between the Exchange, the broker, and the parties to the contract. The initial margin is set somewhat higher than the maintenance margin, to cut down on the number of cash payments.

Marking to Market: Two Examples

Students can fairly easily grasp the concept of marking to market from two consecutive examples, the first using simplified data, the second using market price quotations.

Example 1 (Simplified Data)

Assume the initial margin is 2, maintenance margin is 1.5, and assume the fees, bid-ask spread, and any other transaction charges paid to the member of the Futures Exchange total k for each transaction. The cash flows and futures prices over time are given in Table 1. Time 3 is the delivery date.

TABLE 1 CASH FLOWS AND FUTURES PRICES: SIMPLIFIED DATA

	time 0	1	2	3	
Futures price	30.0	30.3	31.0	31.0	
					Net cash flows
Cash flows:					*(horizontal sum)*
Buyer	-2-k	+.3	+.7	-31+2	-30-k
Seller	-2-k	0	-1.0	+31+2	+30-k
Broker, etc.	+4+2k	-.3	+.3	-4	+2k

At time 0 the buyer and seller agree to a futures price of 30 for delivery of the underlying good at time 3. The Broker agrees to handle the contract for a fee of k from each party. The Broker insures its position by requiring each party to deposit a margin of 2. This amount is commonly 5% to 10% of the value of the contract. It covers approximately a 2-day change in the market price of the futures contract. The amount of margin is also affected by competition among brokers and among the several Futures Exchanges.

At time 1 the futures price for time 3 delivery has risen by .3. The seller has a loss of .3, and the buyer has a gain of .3. Since the maintenance margin is 1.5 and the initial margin deposit was 2, the seller does not need to deposit the amount lost, but the buyer is able to realize or withdraw the gain.

At time 2, the futures price for time 3 delivery has risen by .7. This time the seller is required to deposit the loss, to bring the margin back up to its original level of 2. The buyer is able to withdraw .7.

At time 3 the futures price has not changed, and equals the spot price for the underlying good. The good is exchanged at the spot price. The seller delivers the asset to the buyer, the buyer pays 31 and the seller receives 31. *Both also receive their remaining margin deposit at this time.*

If the buyer had not earlier withdrawn the gains, the buyer's margin would have risen to 3, compensating for the rise in the spot price and making the effective price of the good 30, the originally contracted price. Similarly, if the seller had not been required to deposit the loss, the seller's margin would have fallen to 1, compensating for the rise in price and making the effective price of the good 30, the originally contracted price.

The net cash flows for the buyer and seller, ignoring transaction costs, equal the originally contracted futures price. The net cash flow for the Broker, etc. is the sum of the two commissions.

Example 2 (Market Data)

Assume that transaction costs total $200, the initial margin is $3,000 and the maintenance margin is $2,200. Again, the delivery date is time 3. Note that the price is quoted in percent and 32nds of one percent of the face value. (We ignore the bond conversion factor, or assume it is 1.0.) Assume the buyer and seller withdraw gains and pay losses daily. Cash flows and futures prices are given in Table 2.

On day 3 the seller delivers the bond to the buyer, the buyer pays $98,281 and the seller receives $98,281. The buyer has also paid and the seller has also received a net amount of $94 on days 1 and 2.

In practice the buyer does not need to deposit the amount of the loss at time 1, because the loss lowers buyer's margin account to $2,625 which is still above the maintenance margin level. Similarly, in practice the seller probably would not withdraw a gain as small as $375. The price changes would simply be reflected in the margin accounts. Therefore, including the effects on margin accounts separately, it is more realistic to see the cash flows illustrated in Table 3.

The net cash flows for the buyer and seller equal the originally contracted futures price, minus transaction costs.

Note: If the seller withdraws the gain at time 1, the Broker finances this withdrawal, because the buyer is not required to deposit the loss at this time. The financing cost may be handled by requiring the seller to consider the withdrawal a loan and pay interest, or by setting commissions high enough to cover anticipated financing requirements.

To recapitulate the examples: When the price of the futures contract changes, the values of the contracts held by the seller and buyer change by equal

TABLE 2 CASH FLOWS AND FUTURES PRICES: MARKET DATA

	time 0	1	2	3	Net cash flows (*horizontal sum*)
Futures price	98-12	98-00	98-09	98-09	
Price in dollars	98,375	98,000	98,281	98,281	
Cash flows:					
Buyer	-3,200	-375	+281	-98,281+3,000	-98,375-200
Seller	-3,200	+375	-281	+98,281+3,000	+98,375-200
Broker, etc.	+6,400	0	0	-6,000	+400

TABLE 3 CASH FLOWS, FUTURES PRICES, AND MARGIN BALANCES

	time 0	1	2	3	Net cash flows (*horizontal sum*)
Futures price	98-12	98-00	98-09	98-09	
Price in dollars	98,375	98,000	98,281	98,281	
Cash flows:					
Buyer	-3,200	0	0	-98,281+2,906	-98,375-200
Margin account		-375	+281	-2,906	0
Seller	-3,200	+375	-281	+98,281+3,094	+98,375-200
Margin account				-3,094	0
Broker, etc.	+6,400	0	0	-6,000	+400

and opposite amounts. *If the price rises, the buyer gains and the seller loses. If the price falls, the buyer loses and the seller gains.*

In order to protect the members of the Futures Exchange from losses due to the default of either party, the *change* in value is charged to the losing party's margin account and credited to the gaining party's margin account. In effect, the gaining party receives part of the original futures price at the time that the market price of the futures contract changes, and the losing party pays part of the original price at the same time.

If the gaining party is the buyer, and the gain is NOT withdrawn from the margin account, the increase in the buyer's margin reduces the buyer's payment at the delivery date from the spot price to the level of the original contracted price. If the gaining party is the seller, and the gain is NOT withdrawn, the increase in the seller's margin increases the seller's receipts at delivery from the spot price to the level of the original futures price.

Similarly, if losses are small enough to avoid margin calls, a reduction in the buyer's margin account increases the buyer's cost at delivery from the spot price to the original futures price. A reduction in the seller's margin account lowers the seller's receipts from the spot price to the original futures contract price.

At the delivery date, time 3 in the examples, the futures price equals the spot price for the asset underlying the contract. The seller delivers the asset to the buyer, and the buyer pays the spot price to the seller. At the same time, the margin accounts are returned to both buyer and seller. For both parties, the spot price at delivery, plus the total changes in the margin account including any amounts added or withdrawn, is equal to the original futures contract price.

Conclusion

Trade and textbook explanations of hedging and speculative strategies with futures contracts seem to ignore the effect of the cash flows from marking to market. They describe strategies as if the original futures price is the price exchanged when the underlying good is delivered.

For many purposes, this assumption is valid. Often no margin calls are made during the life of the contract. When the good is delivered, the buyer pays and seller receives the spot price, and both are repaid the margin on the same day. The sum of the spot price and the total margin change equals the original futures price. In effect, on the delivery day the buyer pays the original futures price and receives the original margin deposit. The seller receives the original futures price and margin deposit.

However, during very volatile markets, investors may receive margin calls, and they should be prepared for this eventuality. They must be ready to respond to a margin call, either by paying their losses and closing the futures position, or by depositing sufficient cash to bring the margin up to its initial level.

The effect of marking to market is to protect investors, traders and the members of the Futures Exchange from losses due to the default of either the buyer or the seller. The parties have little exposure to unexpected catastrophic loss, since the margin accounts are adjusted daily to reflect losses already incurred.

A futures contract is closed, or offset, at the futures price on the closing date. If the contract is closed by delivery, the price is equal to that day's spot price. Any difference between the original futures price and the closing futures price has already been exchanged between the buyer's and seller's margin accounts. The net amount paid by the buyer and received by the seller, *that is, the sum of the closing price and total margin adjustments*, is the futures price set when the contract was initiated.

Bibliography

1. Chance, Don M., "The Effect of Margins on the Volatility of Stock and Derivative Markets: A Review of the Evidence," *Monograph Series in Finance and Economics 1990–2*, New York University Salomon Center (1991).

Questions

1. a. What is the primary difference between a *spot market* and a *futures market?*
   b. What is a futures contract?
   c. Identify several commodities on which you can trade futures contracts.
2. "Investors do not pay or receive cash when they buy or sell futures." Is this statement true? Explain.
3. Define the terms *initial margin*, *maintenance margin*, and *variation margin.*
4. Describe the role of the "Futures Exchange Clearinghouse."
5. Suppose that you buy a futures contract on a Treasury bill and your friend sells one. Later, interest rates rise. Who wins, you or your friend? Explain.
6. An investor's margin account for futures trading is *marked to market* each day. What happens each day to the investor's margin account?
7. Absolut Company owns a $10,000,000 U.S. Treasury bill maturing in 9 months. Absolut's financial manager was told that the T-bill must be sold in 6 months so that the company can invest in new equipment. How can the financial manager use the futures market to lessen interest rate risk?
8. Explain the examples of marking to market contained in Tables 1, 2, and 3.

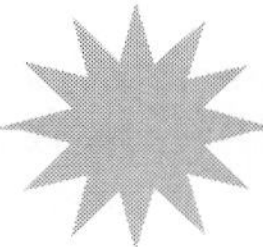

Interest Rate Swaps: A New Tool for Managing Risk

JAN G. LOEYS

Introduction

Sharp movements of interest rates in recent years have created serious problems for firms in which the maturity of their assets does not match the maturity of their liabilities. For example, some financial institutions and other corporations have long-term, fixed-rate assets financed with short-term liabilities. Such firms experience an earnings squeeze whenever market interest rates rise unexpectedly, because their cost of borrowing rises faster than the yield on their assets. As a result, many firms look for ways to reduce the sensitivity—or exposure—of their earnings to interest rate fluctuations. A recent technique that allows firms to hedge (reduce) this exposure is the "interest rate swap." Used first in the Eurobond market during 1981, interest rate swaps have taken the market by storm; and now the volume of interest rate swaps in the United States alone is close to $80 billion.

Why are interest rate swaps so popular? What are the advantages of this instrument over other hedging techniques, such as refinancing the firm's debt or purchasing interest rate futures? The answers to these questions require first an explanation of what interest rate swaps are and how they can be used to reduce interest rate risk.

What Are Interest Rate Swaps?

An interest rate swap typically involves two firms that want to change their exposure to interest rate fluctuations in opposite directions. For example, one firm has

---

At the time of this writing, Jan Loeys was a Senior Economist in the Macroeconomics Section of the Research Department of the Federal Reserve Bank of Philadelphia. The author is indebted to Charles Gibson for helpful comments.

Source: Reprinted from *Business Review*, Federal Reserve Bank of Philadelphia, (May/June 1985).

long-term assets that yield a fixed rate of return; but it also has liabilities with interest payments that fluctuate with market rates of interest (that is, floating rate liabilities).[1] This firm loses when interest rates rise unexpectedly, because the interest cost of its liabilities rises but the revenue from its (fixed-rate) assets remains the same. Conversely, this firm gains from an unexpected drop in interest rates. This sensitivity of a firm's net earnings to interest rate fluctuations is the firm's *exposure to interest rate risk.* The other firm involved in the swap faces the opposite situation: its assets yield a return that fluctuates with market rates, but the interest payments on its liabilities are fixed for a longer period of time. A rise in interest rates benefits this firm, because its revenues rise faster than its cost of borrowing; but a drop in market rates reduces its net earnings.

When two firms such as these have opposite interest risk exposures, one has the makings of a swap. In a typical swap the two firms get together—sometimes through an intermediary—and, in effect, exchange some of their interest payments. A firm with floating-rate liabilities essentially takes over some of the interest payments of a firm with fixed-rate liabilities, and in return the firm with the fixed-rate liabilities takes over some of the interest payments of the firm with floating-rate liabilities. For example, a firm that has liabilities on which the interest rate fluctuates with the 3-month Treasury bill (T-bill) rate could agree to pay another firm a fixed rate of 12 percent on an agreed upon dollar amount (principal) in exchange for a floating-rate payment of 50 basis points over the 3-month T-bill rate on the same principal. *In effect,* one firm converts the interest payments on its liabilities from a floating-rate to a fixed-rate basis, and the other converts its liabilities from fixed to floating rate. (For a more detailed discussion of the mechanics of swap arrangements, see HOW A SWAP WORKS.) Parties to a swap agree to make *interest payments* to each other—they do not actually swap liabilities, nor do they lend money to each other. Each firm remains responsible for paying the interest and principal on its own liabilities. Therefore, swaps do not appear on a firm's balance sheet; instead they are used to alter the exposure to interest rate risk implied by the balance sheet.

In just a few years, interest rate swaps have become very popular as a hedging instrument (see FROM ZERO TO $80 BILLION IN THREE YEARS). But why are firms using swaps rather than other more established hedging techniques, such as purchasing interest rate futures?

Swaps: Longer than Futures, but More Expensive

Futures are contracts that generate cash flows that can be used to reduce a firm's interest risk exposure. An interest rate futures contract is an agreement to buy or sell a certain financial asset, such as a T-bill, for a specific price at a specific date in the future. During the life of the futures contract, each time the market

[1] There are two types of floating-rate debt: one is a short-term liability that has to be refinanced frequently; the other is a long-term liability on which the interest rate fluctuates with the interest rate of a specific market instrument.

value of the asset falls (interest rates rise), the seller in the contract makes a profit, and receives cash, and the buyer takes a loss, and pays cash, and vice versa if the asset's market value rises.[2]

Consider again the case of a thrift institution that has long-term fixed-rate assets, like mortgages, that it funds with short-term liabilities, like certificates of deposit (CDs). If interest rates rise unexpectedly, this thrift will lose—it suffers reduced net earnings. But the thrift could hedge its interest rate risk with a futures contract to deliver (sell) a CD. Then, if interest rates rise, the market value of the CD falls, and the thrift receives a cash flow. This cash inflow offsets the reduced net earnings from the higher interest cost of the thrift's short-term liabilities. When interest rates *drop*, the futures contract produces a cash outflow, but this loss is offset by a lower interest cost on the thrift's short-term liabilities. By buying enough of these futures contracts, the thrift can, in principle, fully hedge its exposure to interest rate fluctuations.

One disadvantage of futures is that they are standardized contracts that exist only with certain specific delivery dates and deliverable types of financial instruments.[3] In particular, futures are available only for delivery dates at 3-month intervals out to about 2-1/2 years. This makes it impossible to hedge interest rate risk beyond 2-1/2 years.[4] Interest rate swaps, in contrast, are private contracts with virtually every aspect of the agreement open to negotiation. Consequently, a swap can be tailor-made to fulfill one firm's particular needs, assuming another firm can be found to fit the other end of the contract. This flexibility allows firms to set up long-term arrangements—most swaps have a final maturity of three to ten years—thereby filling the gap left by futures.

The ability to customize interest rate swaps does not come without its disadvantages. The lack of product standardization makes it more difficult to find another party and to negotiate a mutually agreeable contract. It also costs more to close out a swap contract if the need arises, than a futures contract position, which can be closed out readily. Apart from certain fixed costs of setting up an

---

[2] Cash flows are generated because the exchange where the contract is traded requires that both the buyer and seller in a futures contract post a certain margin. If the price of the underlying asset falls, the buyer has to deposit additional funds with the exchange to maintain the margin requirement, and the seller has his account credited by the same funds. Margins may consist of Treasury securities. For more details, see Howard Keen, Jr., "Interest Rate Futures: A Challenge for Bankers," *Business Review* (November/December, 1980), pp. 13–25; Mark Drabenstott and Anne O'Mara McDonley, "Futures Markets: A Primer for Financial Institutions," Federal Reserve Bank of Kansas City *Economic Review* (November 1984), pp. 17–23; and Nancy Rothstein (ed.), *The Handbook on Financial Futures* (New York: McGraw-Hill, 1984).

[3] The four delivery dates are March, June, September, and December. The deliverable assets are Treasury bills, notes, and bonds; Bank and Eurodollar CDs; Sterling CDs and Gilts; and Ginny Maes. However, there are no interest rate futures on the prime rate or on the London Interbank Offered Rate (LIBOR), although many firms have their cost of borrowing tied to either of these two rates. Firms that use, say, a T-bill futures to hedge their LIBOR-based borrowing are still exposed to fluctuations in the relation between the T-bill rate and LIBOR. Swaps, though, frequently have the same problem as it is difficult to find two firms with opposite exposure to the same market rate of interest (see the example in HOW A SWAP WORKS).

[4] As a practical matter, a firm that wants to hedge as closely as possible, say, a 5-year fixed-rate asset when only 2-1/2 year futures contracts are available, has to buy the contract with the longest available delivery date and then replace it every three months with the new 2-1/2 year contract. In this way, the firm can keep the delivery date of its futures contract as close to 2-1/2 years as possible. The firm will keep doing this until the remaining maturity of the asset reaches 2-1/2 years.

How a Swap Works

The following example is based on an actual transaction that was arranged by an investment bank between a large thrift institution and a large international bank; it is representative of many swaps that have been arranged since 1982. "Thrift" has a large portfolio of fixed-rate mortgages. "Bank" has most of its dollar-denominated assets yielding a floating-rate return based on LIBOR (the London Interbank Offered Rate).

On May 10, 1983, the "Intermediary," a large investment bank, arranged a $100 million, 7-year interest rate swap between Thrift and Bank. In the swap, Thrift agreed to pay Bank a fixed rate of 11 percent per year on $100 million, every 6 months. This payment covered exactly the interest Bank had to pay on a $100 million bond it issued in the Eurodollar market. Thrift also agreed to pay Bank the 2 percent underwriting spread that Bank itself paid to issue this bond. In exchange, Bank agreed to make floating-rate payments to Thrift at 35 basis points (.35 percent) below LIBOR. Intermediary received a broker's fee of $500,000.

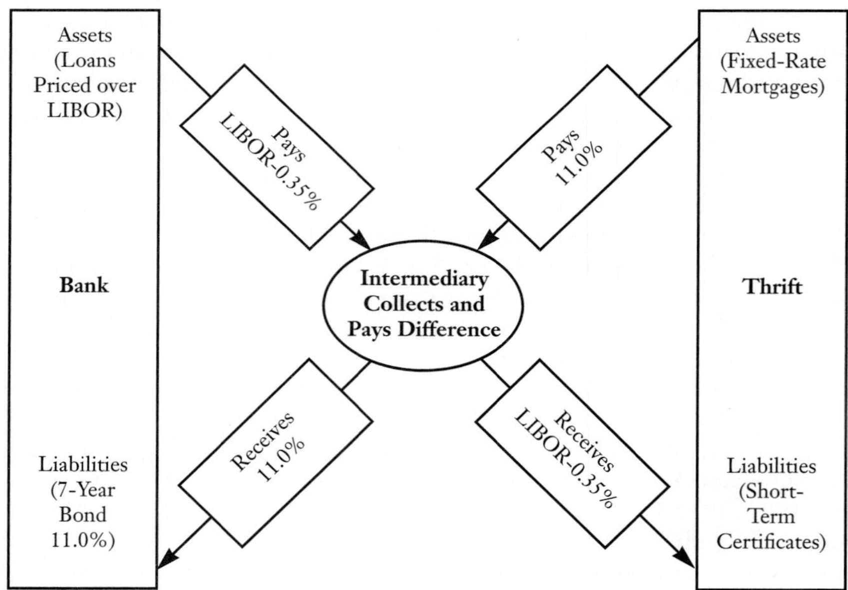

Twice a year, intermediary (for a fee) calculates Bank's floating-rate payment by taking the average level of LIBOR for that month (Col. 2), deducting 35 basis points, dividing by 2 (because it is for *half* a year), and multiplying by $100 million (Col. 3). If this amount is larger than Thrift's fixed-rate payment (Col. 4), Bank pays Thrift the difference (Col. 5). Otherwise, Thrift pays Bank the difference (Col. 6).

1	2	3	4	5	6
Date	**LIBOR**	**Floating-Rate Payment 1/2 (LIBOR - 0.35%)**	**Fixed-Rate Payment 1/2 (11%)**	**Net Payment from Bank to Thrift**	**Net Payment from Thrift to Bank**
May 1983	8.98%	—	—	—	—
Nov 1983	8.43%	$4,040,000	$5,500,000	0	$1,460,000
May 1984	11.54%	$5,595,000	$5,500,000	$95,000	0
Nov 1984	9.92%	$4,785,000	$5,500,000	0	$ 715,000
May 1985	8.44%	$4,045,000	$5,500,000	0	$1,455,000

The swap allows both Bank and Thrift to reduce their exposure to interest rate risk. Bank can now match its floating-rate assets priced off LIBOR with an interest payment based on LIBOR, while the fixed-rate interest payments on its bond issue are covered by Thrift. At the same time, Thrift can hedge part of its mortgage portfolio, from which it receives fixed interest earnings, with the fixed-rate payment it makes to Bank. However, the floating-rate payment that Thrift receives is linked to LIBOR while its cost of borrowing is more closely linked to the T-bill rate. Since LIBOR and the T-bill rate do not always move in tandem, Thrift is still exposed to fluctuations in the relation between LIBOR and the T-bill rate.

account with a trader and meeting regulatory requirements, the brokerage costs of initiating and eventually closing out a futures contract are 2 to 5 basis points. This is much lower than the arrangement fee of about 25 basis points that most swap brokers charge (not including additional fees for settling and guaranteeing the agreement).

Because swaps are agreements between private parties, they also have the disadvantage that one of the parties may default and thus be unable to continue the agreement. Although the other party has no principal at risk, it would again be stuck with an interest risk exposure. It could negotiate a new swap arrangement with another firm, but the terms of that agreement would depend on current market interest rates, which may be more or less advantageous to the firm. Default risk can be reduced by requiring collateral, standby letters of credit, or a third-party guarantee—all of which are costly.[5] Futures, on the other hand, are guaranteed by the exchange in which the contracts are traded and by the funds that both parties to a futures contract must hold on margin with the exchange.

To reduce the costs stemming from the customized nature of swaps, many intermediaries have started to standardize the contract terms of swap agreements,

[5] Often the third-party guarantee is provided by the intermediary who would be required to step in and take over the obligation of the defaulting party. So far, there have been no reports of defaults on a swap agreement.

From Zero to $80 Billion in Three Years

Interest rate swaps first emerged in the Eurobond market in late 1981.[a] Large international banks, which do most of their lending on a floating-rate basis, were involved in the first swaps so that they could use their fixed-rate borrowing capacity to obtain lower-cost floating-rate funds. Initially, the swapping partners consisted mainly of utilities and lower-rated industrial corporations that preferred fixed-rate financing. During 1982, the first domestic interest rate swap occurred between the Student Loan Marketing Association (Sallie Mae) and the ITT Financial Corp., with Sallie Mae making floating-rate payments to ITT. Since then, the market has grown tremendously; in 1984 about $80 billion in swap agreements were concluded.[b] Any large corporation can now use interest rate swaps as an instrument for asset-liability management.

Both investment banks and commercial banks have been active in arranging interest rate swaps. These intermediaries earn fees by bringing the different parties together, by acting as settlement agent (that is, collecting and paying the net difference in the interest payments), and by serving as guarantor of the agreement. Most intermediaries have recently gone beyond their initial role of merely bringing different parties together and function also as dealers. As a dealer, the intermediary is also the counterparty to each swap it "sells." That is, each party has an agreement only with the intermediary and is totally unaware of who might be on the other side of the swap. This arrangement allows the intermediary to sell one leg of the swap before selling the other and to work with an inventory of as yet unmatched swap agreements. The existence of dealers also facilitates an informal secondary market in swaps, where parties to a swap can sell their position to the intermediary or to another party, thereby increasing the liquidity of this instrument.

A typical swap involves a bond issue for $25 to $75 million with a 3 to 10 year maturity on one side, and a floating-rate loan on the other side. Initially, this floating-rate loan was priced at a fraction over LIBOR, the London Interbank Offered Rate. Recently floating-rate loans have also been using the prime rate, the T-bill rate, or other indices of the cost of short-term borrowing.

The most common type of swap is the one described above: a dollar fixed-rate loan swapped for a dollar floating-rate loan, otherwise called the "plain-vanilla" swap. However, several variations on this basic swap have emerged in the market. One such variation is a floating-to-floating swap where parties agree to swap floating rates based on different indices. For example, a bank with assets tied to the prime rate and liabilities based on LIBOR may want to swap the interest payments on its liabilities with payments on a prime-tied, floating-rate loan. Another type of arrangement involves currency swaps such as a swap of a sterling floating-rate loan for a dollar fixed-rate loan. For firms whose assets are denominated in a different currency than are its liabilities, this type of swap may be more appropriate. Finally, rather than exchanging interest payments on liabilities, swaps can also be used to exchange yields on *assets* of different maturities or currencies.

The interest rate swap market has proven to be very flexible in adjusting its product to new customer needs. This innovativeness all but guarantees that swaps will remain a permanent feature of international capital markets.

[a] For more technical and institutional details on interest rate swaps, see Carl R. Beidleman, *Financial Swaps: New Strategies in Currency and Coupon Risk Management* (Homewood, Illinois: Dow Jones-Irwin, 1985); and Boris Antl (ed.), *Swap Financing Techniques* (London: Euromoney Publications Limited, 1983).
[b] Since there are no official reporting requirements on swaps, estimates of the size of this market vary tremendously. The amount of $80 billion, as estimated by Salomon Brothers (see *The Economist*, March 16, 1985, p. 30, Table 16), appears to be somewhere in the middle.

such as the type of floating interest rate, repricing dates, and margin or collateral requirements.[6] As a result, interest rate swaps may become similar to futures contracts, but with longer periods available for hedging.

Given a choice, firms that want to reduce their exposure to interest rate fluctuations for up to 2-1/2 years may be better off with interest rate futures than with swaps because futures are less costly to use than swaps.[7] For longer-term hedges, interest rate swaps are a more appropriate, though relatively more expensive, hedging instrument.

Swaps: More Flexible and Cheaper than Refinancing

Rather than using complicated instruments such as swaps and futures, it may seem a lot less trouble for a firm to adjust its exposure directly by issuing liabilities (debt) with the pricing characteristics it desires. For example, a firm that has only floating-rate liabilities but now desires more fixed-rate liabilities, could buy back some of its floating-rate liabilities and issue fixed-rate liabilities instead; that is, it could refinance some of its liabilities. However, "sellers" of interest rate swaps claim that swaps may be less costly than refinancing for several reasons. One is that firms with lower credit ratings may have to pay relatively higher interest rates—that is higher quality spreads—in the fixed-rate market than in the

[6] For more details, see "Swaps: Managing the Future," *Euromoney* (October 1984), pp. 201–221; and "Making a Market in Slightly Used Swaps," *Institutional Investor* (November 1984), pp. 77–84.

[7] Firms could also use options in this case. An option is the right (rather than the commitment) to buy or sell an asset before a certain date in the future. Options are not discussed in this paper because a comparison of options with swaps is very similar to a comparison of futures with swaps. Options, like futures, are mostly standardized products, traded mostly on organized exchanges, and available only up to 2 years. However, certain over-the-counter options are increasingly available for longer periods.

floating-rate market. Thus, they claim, such firms should borrow in the floating-rate market and then swap, if they desire fixed-rate liabilities. Another reason is that swaps circumvent transactions costs associated with refinancing—such as legal fees, advertising, and regulatory restrictions—because swaps do not involve new borrowing; they only involve the exchange of interest payments on existing liabilities. To understand the advantages swaps can have over refinancing requires a closer look at these quality spread differentials and transactions costs.

Quality Spread Differentials

A quality spread is the premium that a borrower with a low credit rating has to pay over a borrower with a high credit rating. For example, during 1982 when interest rate swaps first became popular in the U.S., the quality spread between Aaa and Baa rated firms in the fixed-rate corporate bond market was over 2 percentage points, a post-war high.[8] At the same time, these quality spreads were less than 1 percentage point in the floating-rate market.

To see how interest rate swaps could exploit this apparent difference in quality spreads, consider an example typical of many of the early swaps. "Company" is a manufacturer whose assets yield a fixed rate of return. Company finances a major part of its assets by borrowing at a floating rate of 1 percentage point above the 3-month T-bill rate. Company prefers to finance its assets with a fixed - rate bond issue, but because of its low Baa credit rating it would have to pay, say, 16 percent.

On the other side is "Bank," a large international bank, with a portfolio of commercial loans on which it charges a rate based on the 3-month T-bill rate. Bank currently finances its portfolio by issuing CDs at 1/2 percentage point above the 3-month T-bill rate. Given its high Aaa credit rating it has the option of borrowing in the bond market at a fixed rate of 14 percent. Table 1 shows the different alternatives for the two firms. Note that the quality spread is 1/2 percentage point in the floating-rate market, and 2 percentage points in the fixed-rate market.

TABLE 1 QUALITY SPREAD DIFFERENTIALS

	Interest Rate on Liabilities	
Issued by	**Floating Rate**	**Fixed Rate**
Company (Baa)*	T-bill + 1.0%	16.0%
Bank (Aaa)*	T-bill + 0.5%	14.0%
Quality spread:	0.5%	2.0%

* Credit ratings are in parentheses. Baa is the lower rating.

[8] Aaa and Baa are credit ratings assessed by Moody's Investors Services, Inc., a major credit-rating agency. This rating system consists of 10 grades, ranging from Aaa (highest quality) to Baa (medium quality) to Caa (poor quality) to D (default).

If each simply wanted to match maturities, Bank would borrow in the floating-rate market at 1/2 percentage point above the T-bill rate and Company would borrow in the bond market at 16 percent. But both borrowers could reduce their cost of borrowing if Bank borrows at a fixed rate and Company borrows at a floating rate and they swap interest payments, with Company agreeing to pay Bank, say, an additional 1 percentage point. In effect, this means that Bank borrows at a 14 percent interest rate, pays Company the T-bill rate plus 1 percentage point (Company's borrowing cost), and receives payments from Company at a 15 percent interest rate. On net, Bank makes interest payments at the T-bill rate [14% + (T-bill rate + 1%) - 15%]. On the other side of the transaction, Company in effect borrows at the T-bill rate plus one percentage point, pays Bank a 15 percent interest rate, and receives payments from Bank at the T-bill rate plus one percentage point. On net, then, Company makes interest payments at a 15 percent interest rate [(T-bill rate + 1%) + 15% - (T-bill rate + 1%)].[9] As a result, Bank effectively borrows at the T-bill rate, better than it could do by itself, and Company borrows at a fixed 15 percent, less than the 16 percent it would have to pay if it had entered the bond market on its own. The source of this reduction in borrowing costs is the difference in quality spreads between the fixed-rate and the floating-rate market. By being able to borrow at a fixed rate through Bank, Company saves more than enough over its own fixed-rate cost of borrowing to compensate Bank for Company's higher (than Bank's) cost of borrowing in the floating-rate market (1/2 percentage point).

The reduction in borrowing costs made possible by these quality spread differentials has been a major selling point for swaps. These cost reductions may be more apparent than real, however. There is a lot of evidence that financial markets are efficient, and that pure arbitrage profits are not readily available.[10] Market efficiency suggests that the difference in quality spreads between fixed-rate and floating-rate markets—200 vs. 50 basis points in the example—reflects differences in risk to lenders in these respective markets. Indeed, the quality spread that is typically quoted does not refer to debt of the same maturity. The floating-rate debt that firms use as a basis for swaps is mostly short- to medium-term, while the fixed-rate debt consists of long-term bonds.[11] Debtholders consider *short-term* debt less risky than long-term debt because they have the option not to renew the debt if the firm looks shakier than anticipated.

---

[9] As explained in HOW A SWAP WORKS, only the *difference* between these two flows of payment actually changes hands. Unless the T-bill rate is above 14 percent, company pays the difference between 14 percent and the T-bill rate.

[10] For a survey of the evidence, see Thomas E. Copeland and J. Fred Weston, *Financial Theory and Corporate Policy*, Second Edition (Reading: Addison-Wesley, 1983).

[11] The floating-rate debt that firms use as a basis for a floating-to-fixed interest rate swap consists mostly of bank credit, commercial paper, certificates of deposits (CDs), and floating-rate notes (FRNs). More than 90% of commercial and industrial loans by U.S. banks are short term. Commercial paper usually has a maturity of 3 to 6 months, while most large negotiable CDs of financial institutions are for 6 months or less. Although FRNs have stated maturities of 7 to 15 years, almost all FRNs issued in the U.S. have covenants that give the holder the right to redeem the note at 3-year intervals, thereby reducing the effective maturity of these FRNs to 3 years. Some of the FRNs that do show large quality spreads usually give the issuer the option to exchange the issue for fixed-rate debt before a certain date. Thus, these last FRNs are more like fixed-rate bonds.

Therefore, debt-holders require smaller quality spreads on short-term debt than on long-term debt. The possibility that debt will not be renewed, however, makes issuing short-term debt rather than long-term debt more risky to *equity-holders*. Issuing short-term rather than long-term debt therefore merely shifts risk from debt-holders to equity-holders.[12] A firm that considers swapping the floating-rate interest on its short-term debt for a fixed-rate interest payment as an alternative to borrowing directly long term must take into account that the lower cost of borrowing produced by the swap comes at the cost of increased risk to the firm's equity-holders.

Quality spread differentials may seem to offer profit opportunities, and they may look like a good reason to use swaps instead of refinancing. But market efficiency suggests that true profit opportunities are likely to be short-lived at best, and that most of the time they are illusory. But there are more solid reasons why refinancing is more costly than interest rate swaps, and they are transactions costs and other non-interest costs (as opposed to interest costs in the form of high quality spreads).

Transactions Costs

Refinancing can take a lot of time, while a swap can be arranged within a few days. To refinance, a firm has to buy back its outstanding liabilities, which can be expensive, or wait until these liabilities mature. Then the firm must try to convince its regular lenders to provide a different type of funds. A thrift, for example, may have to expend much time, effort, and expense to convince its depositors of short-term funds to invest instead in long-term time deposits.

If a firm's regular customers are unwilling to provide, say, fixed-rate funds, the firm can look to alternative markets, such as the domestic or the Eurodollar bond market. Bond markets, however, are costly to use. Domestic bond markets, for one, are highly regulated. To issue a new domestic bond, a firm has to register with the Securities and Exchange Commission (SEC) and meet its disclosure requirements.[13] In addition, a prospective bond issuer is well-advised to obtain a credit rating from the major rating agencies, such as Moody's, or Standard and Poor's, which requires additional expense. The actual selling of a bond issue involves other costs such as advertising, legal fees, and an underwriting spread—that is, the difference between what the firm issuing the debt receives and the (higher) price that ultimate investors pay for the debt. This spread, which runs anywhere from 25 to 500 basis points and which averages about 80 basis points for investment grade debt, serves as payment to the underwriter (or underwriter's syndicate) for distributing the issue to the ultimate investors, and

---

[12] For a formal treatment of this issue, see Thomas Ho and Ronald Singer, "Bond Indenture Provisions and the Risk of Corporate Debt," *Journal of Financial Economics* (1982), pp. 375–406.

[13] Under SEC rule 415 firms can shortcut the normally lengthy registration procedure by filing a single registration statement covering securities they expect to sell from time to time within two years. These firms can then sell securities "off the shelf" whenever they choose. However, this procedure is only available to the largest and most creditworthy corporations.

for committing himself to buy that part of the issue that is not bought by the public at a given price.

As an alternative to the domestic bond market, a firm also can try the Eurodollar bond market. Eurodollar bonds are dollar-denominated bonds issued by international syndicates anywhere outside the United States. The Eurobond market has the advantage that it is almost totally unregulated (that is, there are almost no registration or disclosure requirements), so that issuing a bond does not take a lot of time. On the negative side, however, underwriting spreads on Eurodollar bonds are three to four times those on domestic bond issues. Also, because there are no disclosure requirements in Eurobond markets, investors are reluctant to lend to firms that do not have an excellent credit rating. Therefore, for relatively unknown firms the Eurodollar bond market is even less accessible than the domestic bond market.

The existence of interest rate swaps makes it possible for firms to borrow in the markets in which they have a comparative advantage rather than refinancing in markets in which they don't. These firms can then swap interest payments with firms that have a comparative advantage in another market to achieve the interest payments characteristics they desire. Comparative advantage can take the form of lower interest costs and lower transactions costs. Such lower costs can be the result of name recognition, an established retail network for issuing liabilities, government subsidies and regulations, or other attributes associated with borrowing or lending in certain markets. For example, international banks have the name recognition that allows them to borrow in the Eurodollar market. Domestic banks and thrifts, on the other hand, have the retail network and deposit insurance that give them a comparative advantage in attracting retail savings-type deposits. Interest rate swaps allow banks and thrifts to protect themselves against interest rate risk without having to give up the retail (short-term) savings market in which most of them specialize.

Summary

The high interest rate volatility of recent years has induced many firms to look for ways to protect their profit margins—to hedge—against interest rate fluctuations. A recent and popular technique is the interest rate swap, in which different parties *in effect* swap the interest rate payments on each other's liabilities. An interest rate swap typically allows a firm with floating-rate liabilities to exchange its floating-rate interest payments with another party for fixed-rate payments, thereby effectively acquiring a fixed-rate cost of borrowing.

In only a few years, interest rate swaps have become very popular hedging instruments because frequently they are better suited or less expensive than other hedging techniques, such as purchasing interest rate futures or refinancing the firm's debt. Because interest rate futures are standardized products traded on an organized market, they are inexpensive to use. But because of their standardization, they do not always meet a firm's specific requirements to hedge its interest rate risk exposure. In particular, futures have delivery dates only out to 2-1/2 years, while there is no such limit for swaps. Swaps are freely negotiated agreements between private parties, and, therefore, they can be tailor-made. But this customization makes swaps more expensive to use than futures.

Interest rate swaps can also be very useful when the high costs of entering a market as a new borrower make it too expensive for a firm to obtain directly the type of financing it needs to achieve its desired interest risk exposure. A firm may find that attracting fixed-rate financing in the bond market, for example, is very costly because of high underwriting fees, disclosure costs, or the high risk premium that relatively unknown borrowers may have to pay. An interest rate swap allows a firm to exchange interest flows in order to achieve the desired characteristics of its interest payments without changing the structure of its balance sheet. Interest rate swaps are thus an indirect way of entering financial markets in situations where firms find it very costly to obtain financing directly.

Questions

1. Company A and Company B have assets and liabilities described as follows:

Company	**Assets**	**Liabilities**
A	Fixed rate	Floating rate
B	Floating rate	Fixed rate

   Which company gains when interest rates rise unexpectedly? Explain.

2. Explain how Company A and Company B in the preceding question could benefit from an interest rate swap with each other.
3. Company A (in Question 1) could hedge its position by selling interest rate futures—say, a contract to deliver sometime in the future a Treasury bill. Then, if interest rates rise, the market value of the T-bill falls, and Company A makes a profit. This profit offsets the increased cost of Company A's liabilities. Explain how Company B can use interest rate futures to hedge its position.
4. What are the advantages and disadvantages of interest rate swaps in comparison to interest rate futures, for hedging purposes?
5. Company C pays 2 percentage points above the 3-month T-bill rate on its liabilities. It would prefer to finance its assets with a fixed-rate bond, but it would have to pay 18 percent. Company D pays 1 percentage point above the 3-month T-bill rate on its liabilities. Company D can issue fixed-rate bonds at 14 percent, if it so chooses. Describe an interest rate swap between Companies C and D wherein they both appear to benefit.

Hostile Takeovers and the Market for Corporate Control

Diana L. Fortier

"In recent years, the tender offer takeover has been praised and damned with a ferocity suggesting that the survival of capitalism is at stake. The truth, as in most disputes with substantial metaphysical content, is more prosaic." F.M. Scherer, *Journal of Economic Perspectives*, Winter 1988, pg. 69.

The market for corporate control—firms competing for the rights to manage their corporate resources—has become an increasingly important element of the corporate landscape. Mergers and acquisitions have increased every year since 1982, reaching an all time high of 3,336 net announced transactions in 1986. (See Table 1.)

Although contested tender offers—hostile takeovers—only account for a small fraction of all merger and acquisition activity, they involve large publicly traded companies with substantial market values across many industries. The $12.8 billion aggregate dollar value of 15 successful hostile takeovers in 1987 accounted for 7.7 percent of the total dollar value of the 972 mergers and acquisitions for which such data were disclosed. Moreover, the number of unfriendly takeovers was higher in each of the past three years than in any of the previous eleven years.[1]

Hostile takeover activity has a substantial impact on corporate behavior. Indeed, organizations involved incur substantial costs and devote much time to developing defensive or offensive strategies. Such battles may also impose large

---

At the time of this writing, Diana L. Fortier was an economist at the Federal Reserve Bank of Chicago.

Source: Diana L. Fortier, "Hostile Takeovers and the Market for Corporate Control," Federal Reserve Bank of Chicago, *Economic Perspectives*, Jan./Feb. 1989, Vol. XIII No. 1.

[1] Data on net merger and acquisition announcements are from *Mergerstat Review* 1978–1987. (Chicago: W.T. Grimm & Co.) Of the 2,032 net merger and acquisition announcements in 1987, there were only 972 in which the dollar value of the deal was disclosed.

costs on shareholders, creditors, management, employees, customers, and communities. These private and social costs of takeovers have recently spurred significant legislative interest in hostile takeovers and defensive tactics.[2]

This paper discusses the corporate control market by focusing on hostile takeovers as a mechanism for corporate control. It discusses the causes of hostile takeovers and the methods of defensive action by hostile takeover targets. It then analyzes their effects not only on the bidder and target shareholders but also on other stakeholders (e.g., management and employees). A final section reviews the evidence on the sources of takeover gains. Are such gains redistributions of wealth to one group at the expense of another or are they derived from improved efficiency. Finally, what does this evidence imply about the effect of hostile takeovers on social welfare?

Hostile Takeovers: Why Do They Occur?

Hostile takeovers, those opposed by the target's board of directors, became an "accepted" part of the corporate control market in 1974 with Morgan Stanley and Company's representation of International Nickel Company of Canada in its hostile takeover of ESB, Inc. In a hostile takeover, a bid is made directly to the shareholders of the target rather than to the target's management. The acquirer obtains the needed votes, gains control, and replaces existing management. But what factors need be present in the target and the bidder firms for hostile takeovers to occur?

Conflicts of interest between the target firm's management and shareholders lie at the root of the hostile takeover phenomenon. These conflicts result from the separation of ownership (shareholders) from control (management). Conflicts arise from management's desire to use the firm's resources to achieve outcomes that do not coincide with shareholders' interest, which is maximizing the net present value of the firm's future profits.

Economists term the lost profits arising from the separation of ownership and control, agency costs. Internal controls are generally sufficient to hold down these agency costs. But when agency costs become too high and internal controls, particularly the board of directors, have failed to protect the interests of shareholders from inefficient performance and non value-maximizing behavior of management, the firm is likely to become the target of a hostile takeover bid.[3]

---

[2] For instance, S. 1323 and S. 1324, 100th Cong. 1st sess. (1987)(amending Section 14 of the Securities Exchange Act of 1934, 15 U.S.C.).

"Securities Regulation, Hostile Corporate Takeovers: Synopses of Thirty-Two Attempts," United States General Accounting Office, March 1988, GAO/GGD-88-48FS, a study of 32 hostile takeover attempts in 1985 provides data indicating that, although financial-advisory-related service fees totaled approximately $60 million, this is only a minor fraction of the total value of the deals. Nonetheless, that data also indicate that in successful hostile takeovers, the target spent approximately twice as much as the bidder on such services.

[3] For a sample of papers dealing with the value maximization hypothesis, see Eugene F. Fama and Michael C. Jensen, "Organizational Forms and Investment Decisions," *Journal of Financial Economics*, Vol. 14, No. 1, (March 1985), pp. 101–119; Eugene F. Fama, and Merton H. Miller, *The Theory of Finance*, (Hinsdale, Ill.: Dryden Press, 1972), Chapter 2; and Paul Asquith, Robert F. Bruner, and David W. Mullins, Jr., "The Gains to Bidding Firms from Merger," *Journal of Financial Economics*, Vol. 11, No. 1–4, (April 1983), pp. 121–139. Andrei Shleifer and Robert W. Vishny, "Value Maximization and the Acquisition Process," *Journal of Economic Perspectives*, Vol. 2, No. 1, (Winter 1988), pp. 7–20, examine the failure of internal control mechanisms as one explanation of hostile takeovers.

Several factors can influence the level of agency costs. Often factors such as deregulation and increased competition create a need for valuation and restructuring of corporate assets in an effort to continue to maximize shareholder value. But sometimes current management fails to undertake the necessary steps to do so. New management without prior ties to employees or the community may be more objective and better able to adapt the firm's productive assets to its changing environment. Hostile takeovers are one way of effecting the necessary changes.[4]

Firms that are undervalued by the market, that is, there is a mismatch between realizable asset value and stock price, for whatever reason, are prime takeover targets. It is often argued that firms with managements that concentrate on long-term investments (e.g., research and development) at the expense of short-term earnings are susceptible takeover targets. The premise to this explanation of hostile takeovers is that markets are short-sighted and poor current profits lead to stock undervaluations which create favorable takeover conditions. Agency costs arise here as the market puts more emphasis on current cash flows and management places greater weight on future cash flows. However, evidence does not support this "myopic market" hypothesis.[5]

Significant amounts of free cash flow also contribute to agency costs. Free cash flow is that cash flow in excess of the amount required to fund all projects that have a positive net present value when discounted at the relevant cost of capital. With high levels of free cash flow, managers may seek to secure their own position by making inefficient low-return investments rather than paying out the free cash flow to shareholders in the form of dividends.[6] Yet, it may be difficult to distinguish this behavior from prudent investing that turns out to be less profitable than expected.

Agency costs may also explain why some companies choose to initiate hostile takeovers. Companies with significant cash flow and unused borrowing power may engage in unwarranted acquisition activity—paying significant premiums for targets to fulfill objectives other than value maximization. Acquisitions aimed at diversification, geographic expansion, or increased firm size may be pursued in

---

[4] Randall Morck, Andrei Shleifer, and Robert W. Vishny, "Characteristics of Targets of Hostile and Friendly Takeovers," in Auerbach, *Corporate Takeovers*, pp. 101–136 study the characteristics of hostile takeover targets and suggest that hostile takeovers occur in declining industries and those in a state of change, where management is slow to adjust to the changing environment for whatever reasons—e.g., to maintain their control or to protect employees from pay reductions or job eliminations.

[5] Michael C. Jensen, "Takeovers: Their Causes and Consequences," *Journal of Economic Perspectives*, Vol. 2, No. 1, (Winter 1988), pp. 55.; Randall J. Woolridge, "Competitive Decline and Corporate Restructuring: Is a Myopic Stock Market to Blame?," *Journal of Applied Corporate Finance*, Vol. 1, No. 1, (Spring 1988), pp. 26–36 finds that a myopic market is not to blame as "common stock prices react positively to announcements of corporate strategic investment decisions and the market appears to place considerable emphasis on prospective long-term developments in valuing securities." See also Bronwyn H. Hall, "The Effect of Takeover Activity on Corporate Research and Development," Alan J. Auerbach, ed., *Corporate Takeovers: Causes and Consequences*, (Chicago: University of Chicago Press, 1988), pp. 69–100; John J. McConnell and Chris J. Muscarella, "Capital Expenditure Decisions and Market Value of the Firm," *Journal of Financial Economics*, Vol. 14, 1985, pp. 523–553; and Jeremy C. Stein, "Takeover Threats and Managerial Myopia," *Journal of Political Economy*, Vol. 96, No. 1, (Feb. 1988), pp. 61–80.

[6] See Michael C. Jensen, "Agency Costs of Free Cash Flow, Corporate Finance, and Takeovers," *American Economic Review*, Vol. 76, No. 2, (May 1986, Papers and Proceedings, 1985), pp. 323–329.

order to further management's goals of self-entrenchment or "empire-building" rather than enrich shareholders. Thus, unwarranted acquisition activity not only explains why firms may become targets, but is also one explanation of bidder behavior in takeovers. This may also explain instances of negative returns to shareholders of acquiring firms—management benefits at the expense of shareholders.

Firms initiating hostile takeovers may also be victims of hubris. This "winner's curse" hypothesis asserts that takeovers may be motivated by the bidder's overestimation of the value of the target firm, when there may not be any true gains to be had.[7]

Defensive Tactics—The Target's Response

Whatever the cause of the hostile takeover attempt, a target or potential target must respond. Data in Table 1 indicate that only 25 percent of all targets are successful in remaining independent. Another 25 percent are saved from the hands of the hostile bidder but are acquired under friendly terms by a "white knight." The remaining 50 percent ultimately fall prey to the hostile acquirer.

Despite the fact that few targets are successful at fending off hostile suitors, there are several defensive measures available to boards, managements, and shareholders to assist them in their efforts to maintain an independent organization or current management.

The Best Defense

It is often said that the best defense is a strong offense. In the case of hostile takeovers a firm's best defense is the restoration of a closer relationship between asset values and share price. Thus, increased returns to shareholders or increased price/earnings ratios may be the most effective and direct "defensive" measure for an organization. Indeed, taking actions to increase the firm's value (e.g., selling underperforming units) before someone else takes over and does so may also achieve the results of increased stock prices and possible shareholder gains.

An evaluation of the firm's business strategies, ownership composition, and capital structure is a prerequisite to achieving these goals. Internal restructurings have a dual benefit of improving shareholder value through a more efficient allocation of resources and reducing the need to rely on other more costly takeover defenses.

Employee stock ownership plans (ESOPs) and leveraged recapitalizations or leveraged cash-outs (LCOs), are among the commonly used methods of restructuring a firm's capital and equity position and subsequently building its takeover

---

[7] Richard Roll, "The Hubris Hypothesis of Corporate Takeovers," *Journal of Business*, Vol. 59, No. 2, (April 1986), pp. 197–216.

TABLE 1 MERGER AND ACQUISITION STATISTICS[1]

				Contested tender offers							
		Total tender offers		Total contested		Successful offers[2]		Target remained independent		Acquired by white knight	
Year	Total mergers & acquisitions	#	% of col. 2	#	% of col. 3	#	% of col. 4	#	% of col. 4	#	% of col. 4
1978	2,106	90	4.3%	27	30%	13	48%	8	30%	6	22%
1979	2,128	106	5.0%	26	25%	8	31%	9	35%	9	34%
1980	1,889	53	2.8%	12	23%	3	25%	3	25%	6	50%
1981	2,395	75	3.1%	28	37%	13	46%	6	21%	9	33%
1982	2,346	68	2.9%	29	43%	17	59%	10	34%	2	7%
1983	2,533	37	1.4%	11	30%	7	64%	1	9%	3	27%
1984	2,543	79	3.1%	18	23%	10	56%	6	33%	2	11%
1985	3,001	84	2.8%	32	38%	14	44%	9	28%	9	28%
1986	3,336	150	4.5%	40	27%	15	38%	10	25%	15	37%
1987	2,032	116	5.7%	31	27%	18	58%	6	19%	7	23%
Ten year total	24,309	858	3.5%	254	30%	118	46%	68	27%	68	27%

[1]Data refer to net announcements (completed or pending transactions) or publicly announced formal transfers of ownership of at least ten percent of a company's assets or equity where the purchase price is greater than or equal to $500,000 and one of the parties is a U.S. company. Tender offer data refer to tender offers for publicly traded companies. Successful offers refer to both fully and partially successful deals.

[2]Offers still pending as of year-end are also included in these totals.

SOURCE: W.T. Grimm, *Mergerstat Review*, selected years.

defenses.[8] Both of these methods have a positive impact on shareholder wealth through an improved alignment of shareholder and management interests and shareholder tax benefits.

ESOPs change the equity structure toward a greater proportion ownership by employees. Also, ESOPs may improve takeover defenses because the trustees of the voting stock of the ESOPs are often controlled by management. LCOs, which require shareholder approval, increase firm leverage and management's proportional ownership. Efficiency and performance should improve under incumbent management as commitments to debt repayment reduce management's discretionary use of free cash flow. Hence, the agency costs of management/shareholder conflicts decline because default on debt service would have substantial negative financial impacts on management. In addition to increasing capital market scrutiny of the firm, the increased leverage also decreases the opportunity for a bidder to borrow against the assets of the firm to finance its acquisition.

Although size alone was once thought to be an effective takeover deterrent, it has become increasingly evident that it is no longer a reliable defense. Small firms may obtain acquisition resources for larger firms by issuing claims on the value of the target firm's assets, as with any other corporate investment. The ability to do this has been facilitated by the increase in financial market liquidity, particularly with increased acceptance of, and usage of, junk bonds.[9]

Antitakeover Amendments

Despite an excellent offense, protection from hostile takeovers may still be difficult without some other line of defense. There are numerous defensive mechanisms or "shark repellents" available through corporate bylaws and charter amendments. Not all of these provisions require shareholder approval. (See Box.)

Yet, as defensive tactics develop, so too do methods to render them ineffective. As a result, antitakeover amendments do not generally halt takeovers, rather they make them more difficult, more costly, more time consuming, and may also be harmful to shareholders. Basically, these defensive tactics impose conditions that must be met before control can be changed, whether by tender offer, merger, or replacement of the board. For example, shareholder rights plans dilute the equity holdings of the bidder and fair price amendments increase the cost of acquisition.

A study of hostile takeover attempts in 1985 indicates that the most often used defensive measures of targets in those cases were acquisition by a white

---

[8] For a series of articles discussing methods of and effects of corporate restructuring including Employee Stock Ownership Plans and Leveraged Cash-outs, see *Journal of Applied Corporate Finance*, Vol. 1, No. 1, (Spring 1988). For evidence of stock price reactions to capital structure changes generally indicating a direct correlation between changes in leverage and stock prices see Michael C. Jensen and C.W. Smith Jr., "Stockholder, Manager and Creditor Interests: Applications of Agency Theory," in E. Altman and M. Subrahmanyam, eds., *Recent Advances in Corporate Finance*, (Homewood: Richard Irwin, 1985), pp. 93–131.

[9] Although 30–40 percent of the junk bonds issued since 1985 have been used in acquisition-related financing, these junk-bond-financed transactions only accounted for approximately 8 percent of total merger financings in 1986, up from 4.3 percent in 1985. (*Mergers and Acquisitions*, 1987).

knight, recapitalization such as a stock buy-back, and litigation.[10] As noted earlier, leverage-increasing transactions such as recapitalization can diminish the attractiveness of the target by decreasing the ability of the acquirer to borrow against the assets of the target to finance the acquisition. LCOs also enhance takeover defenses by reducing the agency costs created when high levels of free cash flow are available. Litigation serves as a defense by increasing the costs and uncertainty of takeover and thus deterring bidders.

The ability of a firm to defend itself is also affected by its state of incorporation. The powers of firms, shareholders, and managers are controlled by state statutes that define and regulate corporations. (See Table 2.) The constitutionality of state restrictions on takeovers was supported by an April 1987 Supreme Court ruling.[11]

Also affecting the battle lines between bidders and targets are administrative and regulatory requirements. Tender offer disclosure, delay rules, and regulatory approval periods slow the acquisition process. This usually gives targets additional time to build defenses and often leads to increases in multiple and preemptive bidding and auction contests, all of which tend to decrease bidder returns by increasing target premiums.[12]

The Impact of Antitakeover Amendments

Several researchers have studied the impact of antitakeover amendments on targets' shareholders. Those amendments adopted by management without shareholder approval are in most cases found to be detrimental to shareholders. Although amendments requiring shareholder approval should be less likely to harm shareholders, about half of them have also been found to result in significant negative abnormal returns to target shareholders. (See Box.)

Among the most common defensive devices that require shareholder approval are fair price amendments, which have been found to have no significant effects on shareholders, and classified boards and supermajority clauses, both of which have been found to have significant negative impacts on shareholder

---

[10] GAO, Securities Regulation.

[11] Supreme Court of the United States, *CTS Corp. v. Dynamics Corporation of America*, 107 S Ct 1637(1987). Appeal from the United States Court of Appeals for the Seventh Circuit, No. 86–71. Argued March 2, 1987 and decided April 21, 1987. This decision reverses prior court trends and raises the possibility that state legislation may have a substantive impact on corporate control contests. The case upheld one form of takeover statute, the Indiana control share acquisition provision. For an invalidation of a state control share statute on constitutional grounds, see *RTE Corporation v. Mark IV Industries*, Civ. Action No. 88-C-378 (E.D. Wis.) May 6, 1988. Also see Lynn E. Browne and Erie S. Rosengren, "Should States Restrict Takeovers?" *New England Economic Review*, Federal Reserve Bank of Boston (July/August 1987) pp. 13–21, for a discussion of state antitakeover laws.

[12] Sanford J. Grossman and Oliver D. Hart, "Takeover Bids, the Free-Rider Problem, and the Theory of the Corporation." *Bell Journal of Economics*, Vol. 11, No. 1 (Spring 1980), pp. 42–64 discuss the ability of bidders to gain from takeover and Andrei Shleifer and Robert W. Vishny, "Greenmail, White Knights, and Shareholders' Interest," *Rand Journal of Economics*, Vol. 17, No. 3 (Autumn 1986), pp. 293–309 discuss the accumulation of shares prior to full disclosure.

The Williams Act, a 1968 amendment to the Securities and Exchange Act of 1933, Public Law No. 90-439, 82 Stat. 454 (July 29, 1968) as amended in 1970 Public Law No. 91-567, 84 Stat. 1497 (December 22, 1970) governs tender offers with disclosure, offer period and other procedural requirements, as well as antifraud provisions. It was intended to protect shareholders by allowing sufficient time and information to properly analyze a tender offer.

TABLE 2 PROVISIONS OF STATE CORPORATION LAWS IN THE SEVENTH DISTRICT

State	Effective date	Statute	Code
Illinois	1985	Fair price amendment Nonmonetary factors	Ill. Rev. Stat Chpt. 32, 7.85 & 8.85
Indiana	1986	Control share acquisitions Business combination	Ind. Code Ann. 23-1-43-(1-24)
Iowa	None	None	None
Michigan	1984	Fair price amendment	Mich. Comp. Laws Ann. 450.1775-1784
Wisconsin	1986 1987	Fair price amendment Anti-greenmail Business combination (sunset provision effective 9/10/91)	Wis. Stat. Ann. 180.725 & 180.726

Other states with the same provisions[1]
Fair price amendment: CT, FL, GA, KY, LA, MD, MS, NC, PA, VA, and WA
Business combination: AZ, DE, KY, MN, MO, NJ, NY, and WA
Control share acquisitions: AZ, FL, HI, LA, MA, MN, MO, NV, NC, OH, OK, OR, and UT
Nonmonetary factors: AZ, ME, MN, and PA
Anti-greenmail: AZ, MN, and NY

[1]The specific characteristics of these provisions may vary across different states.
SOURCE: *State Takeover Statutes and Poison Pills*, Robert H. Winter, Robert D. Rosenbaum, Mark H. Stumpf, and L. Stevenson Parker, Vol. 3 of *Shark Repellents and Golden Parachutes: A Handbook for the Practitioner.*

wealth. The poison pill, which does not require shareholder approval, has proven to be an effective and popular, yet controversial, defensive measure. However, its adoption has been shown to have significant adverse effects on shareholders.[13]

Why do shareholders approve amendments that may decrease shareholder wealth? Proponents of antitakeover amendments argue that such amendments are in the shareholders' interest by giving boards the power to ensure that the shareholder receives a fair price reflecting their maximum possible share of expected acquisition gains. Management, by acting as a negotiating agent for diffuse shareholder interests, is better able to hold out for the best price by reducing individual incentives to tender at too low a price. Of course, the composition of ownership will also affect the dispersion of shareholder interests. The greater

[13] For empirical evidence of the effects of defensive tactics and the market for corporate control see Greg A. Jarrell, James A. Brickley, and Jefrery M. Netter, "The Market for Corporate Control: The Empirical Evidence Since 1980," *Journal of Economic Perspectives*, Vol. 2, No. 1, (Winter 1988), pp. 49–68; Gregg A. Jarrell and Annette B. Poulsen, "Shark Repellents and Stock Prices, The Effects of Antitakeover Amendments Since 1980," *Journal of Financial Economics*, Vol. 19, No. 1 (Sept. 1987), pp. 127–168; John Pound, "The Effects of Antitakeover Amendments on Takeover Activity: Some Direct Evidence," *The Journal of Law and Economics*, (Oct. 1987), pp. 353–367; and Michael Ryngaert, "The Effect of Poison Pill Securities on Shareholder Wealth," *Journal of Financial Economics*, Vol. 20, No. 1–2, (January/March 1988), pp. 127–168.

Takeover and Defense Tactics*

There are numerous tactics for taking over corporations. Even more numerous are the modes of defense against takeovers. Following is a list of the major actions available to the offensive and defensive players of this increasingly popular enterprise, corporate takeover. The defensive tactics are grouped according to their impact on shareholder wealth, as indicated by research to date.

Takeovers

- ***Leveraged buyout:*** heavily debt-financed buyout of shareholder equity often by incumbent management.
- ***Merger:*** bidder negotiates with target management on the terms of the offer which is then submitted to a vote of the target's shareholders.
- ***Proxy contest:*** by a vote of the shareholders a dissident group tries to gain a controlling position on the board.
- ***Tender offer:*** bidder makes offer to shareholders for some or all of the target's stock.
  Friendly: offer supported by the target company's management.
  Unfriendly (hostile): offer opposed by target management.

Defensive Tactics

(Shareholder approval required)

No Impact or No Evidence of Impact on Target Shareholder Wealth

- ***Dual-class recapitalizations:*** restructure equity into two classes with different voting rights with the goal of providing management or family owners with voting power disproportionately greater than provided by their equity holdings under a one-share, one-vote rule; typical dual class firm is already controlled by insiders and the recapitalization may also provide needed capital without dilution of control and without harm to the stock value.
- ***Fair-price provision:*** a supermajority provision which applies only to nonuniform two-tier hostile takeover bids; insures that all shareholders selling within a certain time period receive the same price; the usual determination of fairness is the highest price paid by the bidder for any of the shares it has acquired in the target during a certain time period; has a low deterrence value and is not detrimental to stock values.
- ***Rights of shareholders:*** restricts rights of shareholders to vote on issues between annual meetings or at special shareholder meetings (e.g., only supermajority vote of the shareholders or the president of the board may call a special meeting).

Positive Impact

- ***Leveraged recapitalization or leveraged cash-out:*** a change in capital structure and equity ownership, retaining a publicly traded company; financial leverage is increased significantly as the company replaces the majority of its equity with debt so that a raider can not borrow against the assets of the firm to finance an acquisition; management (insiders) in essence receives a stock-split and proportional increase in ownership as all but inside shareholders receive a large one-time payout in cash or debt securities and continued equity interest in the restructured company.

Negative Impact on Target Shareholder Wealth

- ***Change state of incorporation:*** stringency of state antitakeover laws vary; may harm shareholders because it reduces takeover chances; may benefit states as they increase the likelihood of keeping jobs with strict state laws.
- ***Reduction in cumulative voting rights:*** increases management's ability to resist a tender offer but appears to reduce shareholder wealth. (Cumulative voting rights allow a group of minority shareholders to elect directors even if the majority opposes because each shareholder is entitled to cast a number of votes equal to the number of shares owned multiplied by the number of directors to be elected—thus one could accumulate votes for a particular director or group of directors.)
- ***Staggered directors or classified board:*** directors are broken into classes (usually three groups) with only one class being elected each year; works best with limit on number of board members; makes it difficult for a substantial shareholder to change all of the board at once without approval or cooperation of the existing board, but also makes any change of directors more difficult; also lowers the effectiveness of cumulative voting; has impact of significant negative abnormal returns.
- ***Supermajority clause:*** increases the number of votes of outstanding common stock needed to approve changes in control to two-thirds or nine-tenths from a majority of one-half (director must also be removed for cause); found to have significant negative stock-price effects around their introduction and on average they appear to reduce shareholder wealth; important to have an escape clause (provision allowing for simple majority vote) so that friendly offers are not also foreclosed; almost always combined with a lock-in provision.
- ***Lock-in provision:*** prevents circumvention of antitakeover provisions; most common provision requires a supermajority vote to change antitakeover amendments or limits the number of directors; has impact of a significant negative abnormal return.

(Shareholder approval not required)

Negative Impact on Target Shareholder Wealth

- ***Litigation by target management:*** a win by target may harm shareholders in that chances of acquisition may be lost or lowered—this may be reflected by a fall in share price, whereas the acquisition is likely to have increased share prices (examples: charges of securities fraud, antitrust violations, or violations of state or federal tender offer rules); delays control fight, yet also gives management time to find a friendlier deal.
- ***Shareholder rights plans or poison pills:*** do not require majority voting approval by shareholders; are triggered by an event such as a tender offer or by the accumulation of a certain percentage of target's stock by a single stockholder; trigger allows target shareholders with rights to purchase additional shares or to sell shares to the target at very attractive prices; can be cheaply and quickly altered by target management yet makes hostile takeovers very expensive by diluting the equity holdings of the bidder, revoking his voting rights or forcing him to assume unwanted financial obligations; different types include: flip-over, flip-in, back-end, and voting plans; generally harmful to stock values; judicial approval of certain types of plans (e.g., flip-in and back-end) is still not clear.
- ***Target block stock repurchases or greenmail:*** target repurchases, at a premium, the hostile bidders block of target's stock; often results in substantial fall in stock returns for the target or reduced shareholder value from foregone takeover potential as opposed to normally positive stock price effects of a repurchase of stock by a nontargeted firm; yet evidence indicates that a net positive stock price may result from the initial hostile bidder purchase (positive impact) to the target repurchase (negative effect); benefits returns for bidder firm shareholders; practice is controversial and has been challenged in federal courts, congressional testimony, and SEC hearings.

* For empirical evidence of the effects of defensive tactics and the market for corporate control see footnote 14 of the text.

the proportion of insider (management) stockholders, the more likely antitakeover amendments will be in the shareholders' interest.

According to this shareholder interest hypothesis, antitakeover amendments are a negotiating tool rather than a takeover deterrent. This argument seems to rest on the assumption that antitakeover amendments are ineffective at ultimately deterring takeovers. It suggests that the adoption of antitakeover amendments should have a positive impact on stock prices not because of the antitakeover amendment per se, but from the anticipation of ultimate takeover and positive returns. However, many of these antitakeover provisions have been found to decrease shareholder value, and research provides weak support for the shareholder interest hypothesis.[14]

Opponents of antitakeover amendments argue that management may abuse their veto power and act in their own interests at the expense of shareholders. They view such amendments as detrimental because they can entrench current management, reduce shareholder wealth by deterring tender offers and potentially valuable takeover bids, or reduce their share of the takeover premiums due to the acquirer's increased transactions costs as a result of the amendments. In general, they argue that such amendments have a negative impact on the efficient allocation of real capital in the economy. A fall in equity values resulting from adoption of antitakeover amendments would support the managerial entrenchment hypothesis.[15]

One way of dealing with, though not eliminating, this shareholder/management conflict of interest, is for the board to establish management compensation contracts with ownership stakes (e.g., stock options) to promote value-maximizing behavior by management.[16] Yet, boards often are not effective in controlling management behavior because the managers are able to create a board of directors loyal to management or with financial interests in maintaining existing management. Moreover, directors may lack sufficient information to determine the degree of value-maximizing behavior of management.

Ownership Composition

A firm's ownership composition also influences its defensive position. The percentage of institutional holdings and insider holdings affect the ability to get shareholder approval of antitakeover provisions. The lower the percentage of institutional holdings and the higher the percentage of insider holdings, the more likely antitakeover measures, particularly those with negative wealth effects, will obtain shareholder approval.[17]

---

[14] Scott C. Linn and John J. McConnell, "An Empirical Investigation of the Impact of 'Antitakeover' Amendments on Common Stock Prices," *Journal of Financial Economics*, Vol. 11, No. 4, (April 1983), pp. 361–399.

[15] Harry DeAngelo and Edward M. Rice, "Antitakeover Charter Amendments and Stockholder Wealth," *Journal of Financial Economics*, Vol. 11, No. 1–4, (April 1983), pp. 329–359 find weak support for the managerial entrenchment hypothesis.

[16] Kevin J. Murphy, "Corporate Performance and Managerial Remuneration: An Empirical Analysis," *Journal of Accounting and Economics*, Vol. 7, No 1–3, (April 1985), pp. 11–42 found a positive relationship between stock performance and managers' pay; and James A. Brickley, Sanjai Bhagat, and Ronald C. Lease, "The Impact of Long-Range Managerial Compensation Plans on Shareholder Wealth," *Journal of Accounting and Economics*, Vol. 7, No. 1–3 (April 1985) pp. 115–130; and Hassan Tehranian and James F. Waegelein, "Market Reaction to Short Term Executive Compensation Plan Adoption," *Journal of Accounting and Economics*, Vol. 7, No. 1–3 (April 1985) pp. 131–144 find introductions of incentive-based compensation programs cause stock price increases. The problem of management performance not achieving cost minimization and profit maximization at the expense of shareholders (absentee owners) was first identified by Adolf A. Berle, Jr. and Gardiner C. Means, *The Modern Corporation and Private Property*, 1932 (New York, New York: Macmillan, 1932).

[17] Jarrell and Poulsen, "Shark Repellents and Stock Prices." Today, institutional investors account for approximately 66 percent to 75 percent of equity ownership and trading compared to about 5 percent in the early 1960s.

Although inside holders have financial interests to protect, they also have careers to be concerned about. Thus, inside holders may trade-off wealth accumulation for greater corporate control. Data suggest that the greater the percentage of insider holdings of the hostile target the better the target's chances of remaining independent. Institutional holders also have large economic interests to protect; however, data do not suggest that relatively large shares of institutional holdings are indicative of greater takeover vulnerability.[18]

Also of importance is the percentage of low-stake uninformed shareholders. The costs of assessing antitakeover amendments are high for uninformed shareholders and incentives are relatively low for low-stake holders. Thus, such shareholders tend to vote with management under the assumption that voting more often with management than against them is more likely, in the long run, to yield greater shareholder wealth.

Effects of Hostile Takeovers and Policy Implications

The previous sections have presented the major elements of the hostile takeover battle and, as with any battle, there will be a winner and a loser. However, the effects of the battle go beyond the direct combatants. The remaining sections will discuss the impact of hostile takeovers on various stakeholders: shareholders, management, labor, and society in general. Although conclusive evidence on the net economic welfare impacts of hostile takeovers is elusive, arguments for and against them are not.

The Winners: Target Shareholders

Evidence from short-period merger event studies (covering the few weeks around a takeover announcement) clearly indicate that stockholders of target firms benefit by receiving positive abnormal returns—gains above those that would have occurred had the stock followed overall market movements. A recent study conservatively estimates the gain to target shareholders from takeovers of publicly traded companies between 1981 and 1986 to be 47.8 percent, or an estimated dollar value of $134.4 billion. Additionally, the average premium on all mergers and acquisitions in 1987 was 38.3 percent whereas the average for hostile takeovers that year was 42.7 percent.[19]

---

[18] GAO, Securities Regulation. 1985 data indicate that insider holdings averaged 21.8 percent for nine targets of unsuccessful takeover attempts and averaged 4.8 percent and 9.5 percent, respectively, for nine successful takeovers and seven targets acquired by white-knights. T. Boone Pickens, Jr., "Professions of a Short-Termer," *Harvard Business Review*, Vol. 64, No. 3, (May/June 1986), pp. 77 states that takeover targets from 1981–1984 averaged 22 percent institutional ownership compared to a market average of 35 percent.

[19] Bernard S. Black and Joseph A. Grundfest, "Shareholder Gains From Takeovers and Restructurings Between 1981 and 1986: $162 Billion is a Lot of Money," *Journal of Applied Corporate Finance*, Vol. 1, No. 1, (Spring 1988), pp. 5–15; Michael C. Jensen and Richard S. Ruback, "The Market for Corporate Control," *Journal of Financial Economics*, Vol. 11, No. 1–4, (April 1983), pp. 5–50; Roll, "The Hubris Hypothesis of Corporate Takeovers"; Jarrell, Brickley, and Netter, "The Market for Corporate Control: The Empirical Evidence Since 1980," *Journal of Economic Perspectives*, (Winter 1988), pp. 49–58; Michael Bradley, Anad Deasi, and E. Han Kim, "Synergistic Gains from Corporate Acquisitions and Their Diversion between the Target and Acquiring Firms," Working Paper, School of Business Administration, University of Michigan, 1987; and Asquith, Bruner, and Mullins, Jr., "The Gains to Bidding Firms from Merger."

Bidder Shareholders May Gain or Lose

For the acquiring firm, the results from the same studies are not so unequivocal. They indicate that on average there is no significant short-period effect, positive or negative, on shareholder returns, and, if anything, there is at best a slight positive impact on the acquirer's share value.[20] Evidence from longer-period event studies (one to three years) suggests that increases in target stock prices during takeovers overestimate the post-merger increase in firm value. Despite this overvaluation, recent research concludes that the average successful tender offer results in a statistically significant positive revaluation of the combined firm. Such increases have been fairly consistent over time. However, bidder gains have been diminishing over the last two decades while target returns have increased.[21] Thus, it appears that on average takeovers and mergers enhance shareholder value.

While it is concluded that mergers and acquisitions enhance shareholder value, this conclusion does not imply that such value is derived entirely, or at all, from increased efficiency (e.g., resource reallocation, removal of inefficient management, or economies of scale or scope).

Sources of Gain: Improved Efficiency or Wealth Redistribution

Although easily measured, shareholder gains do not provide an accurate measure of welfare gains. If takeover gains are a result of wealth transfers, then the increase in share prices overstates the efficiency gains of takeover. Shareholder gains must be weighed against the losses of other stakeholders such as management and employees.

As opponents of hostile takeovers argue, takeover gains result primarily from wealth redistributions: one stakeholder's gain—the target shareholder—is at the expense of another's economic loss—such as the target employee or bondholder. In the extreme, such takeovers are merely costly and disruptive restructurings of corporations that provide no social benefits. Preventing such takeovers would, it is argued, improve economic welfare.

---

[20] Jensen and Ruback, "The Market for Corporate Control" provides an extensive review of corporate control market studies and finds shareholders of acquirers do not lose; and Roll, "The Hubris Hypothesis of Corporate Takeovers" finds statistically insignificant results showing that acquirers, on average, do lose on bid announcements. Jarrell, Brickley, and Netter, "The Market for Corporate Control: The Empirical Evidence Since 1980" updates and confirms the earlier Jensen and Ruback (1983) study.

[21] In contrast to the earlier studies using aggregate data, Michael Bradley, Anand Desai, and E. Han Kim, "Synergistic Gains from Corporate Acquisitions and Their Division Between the Target and Acquiring Firms" study the gains and losses of matched pairs of bidders and targets from 1962–1984 and find a statistically significant synergistic gain of 7.5 percent created from tender offer combinations.

For empirical evidence on post-merger (long-run) negative returns and discussion on the issue, see F.M. Scherer, "Corporate Takeovers: The Efficiency Arguments," *Journal of Economic Perspectives*, Vol. 2, No. 1, (Winter 1988), p. 71; Jensen and Ruback, "The Market for Corporate Control," pg. 20; and Ellen Magenhein and Dennis C. Mueller, "On Measuring the Effect of Mergers on Acquiring Firm Shareholders," in John C. Coffee, Jr. et. al, eds. *Knights, Raiders and Targets*, (New York: Oxford University Press), 1988.

Proponents argue that takeovers provide net gains to society by reducing the agency costs related to management/shareholder conflicts, which, in turn, improve resource allocation and efficiency and encourages value-maximizing behavior. Thus, attempts to prevent a free corporate control market would have negative effects.

Overall, research is not conclusive on the sources of takeover gain and indicates that gains from redistribution as well as increased efficiency may be occurring. The sources of gain vary from deal to deal, from industry to industry, and from year to year. Studies have addressed the wealth transfer to target shareholders from target bondholders, government, and target labor.

One version of the redistribution theory asserts that the gain of one class of security holders comes at the expense of another. For example, bondholder values may decline as common shareholder values increase. This example may be more relevant to highly leveraged transactions in which corporate bond prices may fall and yields rise as increased leverage contributes to uncertainty about the acquirer's ability to service its debt. Despite some recent examples of such behavior related to leveraged buy-outs, studies of both mergers and leveraged buy-outs have failed to find consistent support for this theory.[22] Moreover, when such redistributions have occurred, the increase in shareholder value often more than offsets the fall in bond values. Thus, takeovers appear to result in net gains to investors as a group. In general, target shareholders' gains do not occur at the expense of either bidder shareholders or other classes of target or bidder investors.

The increase in shareholder value resulting from hostile takeovers could also be a redistribution from the government to shareholders. Hostile takeovers may generate tax savings without any underlying efficiency gain. Thus, government becomes another stakeholder in the takeover battle. But the evidence indicates that tax benefits have been only a minor force behind takeovers.[23]

Another form of redistribution espoused recently is that shareholder gains come at the expense of labor through long-term labor contract concessions which reduce employment or wages. Evidence from small firm acquisitions (not hostile takeovers) does not support assertions that acquisitions have an overall negative effect on labor in terms of lower employment and wages.[24] However,

---

[22] Debra K. Dennis and J. McConnell, "Corporate Mergers and Security Returns," *Journal of Financial Economics*, Vol. 16, No. 2, (June 1986), pp. 143–187; Kenneth Lehn and Annette B. Poulsen, "Sources of Value in Leveraged Buyouts," in *Public Policy Towards Corporate Takeovers*, (New Brunswick, NJ: Transaction Publishers), 1987; Paul Asquith and E. Han Kim, "The Impact of Merger Bids on the Participating Firms' Security Holders," *Journal of Finance*, Vol. 37, No. 5, (December 1982), pp. 1209–1228; and "Buyouts Devastating to Bondholders," *New York Times*, October 26, 1988.

[23] Alan J. Auerbach and David Reishus, "Taxes and the Merger Decision," in J. Coffee and Louis Lowenstein, eds., *Takeovers and Contests for Corporate Control*, (Oxford: Oxford University Press, 1987); D. Breen, "The Potential for Tax Gains as a Merger Motive," Federal Trade Commission Bureau of Economics, July 1987; and Lehn and Poulsen, "Sources of Value in Leveraged Buyouts."

[24] Andrei Shleifer and Lawrence Summers, "Hostile Takeovers as Breaches of Trust," in Auerbach, *Corporate Takeovers*, pp. 33–68; and Charles Brown and James L. Medoff, "The Impact of Firm Acquisitions on Labor," in Auerbach, *Corporate Takeovers*, pp. 9–32. In Bernard S. Black and Joseph A. Grundfest, "Shareholder Gains From Takeovers and Restructuring Between 1981 and 1986: $162 Billion is a lot of Money," on pg. 7 the authors notes that "Yago and Stevenson also find 'no evidence that unsolicited deals had systematically different effects than friendly transactions'."

hostile takeovers usually involve large organizations and create a fear that both explicit and implicit commitments by target management to labor will be broken following the takeover. A notable example is Carl Icahn's hostile purchase of TWA which resulted in improved management and shareholder premiums worth $300 to $400 million, but also resulted in wealth transfers to Icahn from three labor unions which one researcher valued at $600 million or one and a half times the takeover premium.[25] In this case, it would appear that shareholders gained principally at the expense of labor. The unanswered question is whether such labor concessions are simply wealth transfers or actually enhance efficiency.

Labor-related inefficiencies may result from the inability of management to respond appropriately to factors, such as technological developments, which decrease the demand for labor, or result from failure to deal successfully with a labor force that wields market power. In either case, these inefficiencies create conditions ripe for hostile takeovers, which in turn become the mechanism by which efficiency is enhanced. This does not mean that labor will always be a casualty in a hostile takeover battle. Takeover activity, and hence the fear of takeover, may be favorable to labor in that efficiency gains at potential target companies can lead to job preservation and greater long-run growth and employment.

Economic efficiency theories argue that net gains may occur from increases in economic efficiency achieved through major restructurings and better management of corporate assets. Takeovers can reduce agency costs and result in more efficient capital investments by subjecting the firm to the scrutiny of the capital markets and by reducing resources under management control. Benefits accrue when target shareholder wealth that had been appropriated to target management, employees, suppliers, or customers under non value-maximizing behavior is reallocated to target shareholders and the acquirer upon acquisition.

Business line financial data has been used to test the efficiency enhancement theory of takeovers by analyzing the *ex post* financial performance of acquiring firms. Two implications of the theory that takeovers increase efficiency due to improved management have been tested. First, the target's pre-takeover profits should be less than its industry peers', and second, *ceteris paribus*, post-takeover profitability should be relatively higher than pre-takeover profitability.

Examining these hypotheses, Scherer found that targets were slight underperformers relative to their industry norm, but that "operating performance neither improved nor deteriorated significantly following takeover," and "there is no indication that on average the acquirers raised their targets' operating profitability net of merger-related accounting adjustments."[26]

Generally, studies using accounting data to analyze post-takeover performance do not clearly support the economic efficiency theory of takeover gains. Unless this inconclusiveness can be attributed to measurement problems associated with the use of accounting data or the lack of coordination in the use of

---

[25] Andrei Shleifer and Lawrence Summers, "Hostile Takeovers as Breaches of Trust," pg. 50.

[26] Scherer, "Corporate Takeovers: The Efficiency Arguments," pp. 75–76; and David J. Ravenscraft and F.M. Scherer, "Life After Takeover," *The Journal of Industrial Economics*, Vol. 36, No. 2, (December 1987), pp. 147–156.

market and accounting data in analyzing shareholder gains and the sources of those gains, one must question whether there are any true wealth gains derived from the supposed improved management and efficiency subsequent to takeover.

While operational efficiencies may be elusive, it appears that financial market inefficiencies do create opportunities for takeover gains. If takeovers lead to the revaluation of undervalued firms, the cost of raising additional capital will be lower and more investment will take place. Several studies have tested the market undervaluation hypothesis. Evidence on it is mixed.

Empirical evidence using stock price data do not generally support the theory that target firms are victims of undervaluation. Stock prices of targets successful at fending off hostile bidders decline to approximately pre-bid levels. That is, the tender offer process does not reveal to the market significant new information about the intrinsic value of the target such that substantial price adjustments (increases) occur due to prior undervaluations of the target by the market. It is not merely the information generated from putting a firm into play, but the actual acquisition and expected gains that result in positive stock returns.[27]

However, an analysis of market valuation of large, multidivisional targets using business line financial data as well as market data provide somewhat different results. If the sum of the liquidation or replacement value of the firm's parts is greater than the market value of the firm as a whole then it is undervalued by the market. It is argued that this provides incentive for takeover by creating opportunities to improve performance and add value by divesting the target of certain units whose assets are more productively managed elsewhere. This has been the strategy in the recent takeovers of many conglomerates formed by previous diversification acquisitions.

Recent research suggests "that there is some undervaluation in the market as a whole, which can probably be attributed to underpricing of both multi-industry companies and small companies." Further, this undervaluation is proportional to the number of firm divisions and is more prevalent in certain industries and organizations with low institutional holdings.[28]

Conclusion

Although contested tender offers are a small fraction of all merger and acquisition activity, the target and bidder costs of fighting a hostile battle and the slight

---

[27] Michael Bradley, Anand Desai, and E. Han Kim, "The Rationale Behind Interfirm Tender Offers: Information or Synergy," *Journal of Financial Economics*, Vol. 11, 1983, pp. 183–206. Frank H. Easterbrook and Gregg A. Jarrell, "Do Targets Gain from Defeating Tender Offers?," *New York University Law Review*, 1984, Vol. 54, pp. 277–299 show that stock returns of targets of defeated hostile bidders fall to approximately pre-bid levels. Sanjai Bhagat, James Brickley, and Uri Lowenstein, "The Pricing Effects of Inter-Firm Cash Tender Offers," *Journal of Finance*, Vol. 42, 1987, pp. 965–986 find that increased valuations of target firms are too large to be explained solely by adjustments for prior undervaluations.

[28] See Dean LeBaron and Lawrence S. Speidell, "Why are the Parts Worth More than the Sum? 'Chop Shop,' A Corporate Valuation Model," *The Merger Boom*, Federal Reserve Bank of Boston, pp. 78–101; and Michael E. Porter, "From Competitive Advantage to Corporate Strategy," *Harvard Business Review*, Vol. 65, No. 3, (May/June 1987), pp. 43–59.

chances of targets remaining independent, as well as the attendant social costs of the fight, magnify the importance of understanding and dealing with the corporate control market.

A successful and profitable takeover depends on the extent to which the target firm is undervalued, the inefficiency of target management, the cost of overcoming the target's takeover defenses, the ability of the acquirer to transfer wealth from other stakeholders, and the ability of the bidder to divert some gains from the target shareholders.

Target shareholders are definite winners in the hostile takeover battle. Bidder shareholders, on average, have equal probabilities of gaining or losing and, at best, obtain modest gains.

However, the source and quantification of the gains to target shareholders remain elusive. Research does not provide clear support for the hypothesis that there are real efficiency gains from takeovers. Support for the several versions of the wealth redistribution theory is mixed. Wealth transfers are most likely to have negative effects on target management.

What is clear, however, is that net shareholder gains are not an accurate measure of welfare gains resulting from takeovers. Only with additional research can the social and economic welfare implications and policy directives regarding hostile takeovers be more precisely drawn.

References

Asquith, Paul, "Merger Bids, Uncertainty, and Stockholder Returns," *Journal of Financial Economics*, Vol. 11, No. 1–4, (April 1983), pp. 51–83.

Asqiuth, Paul, Robert F. Bruner, and David W. Mullins, Jr., "The Gains to Bidding Firms from Merger," *Journal of Financial Economics*, Vol. 11, No. 1–4, (April 1983), pp. 121–139.

Auerbach, Alan J., ed., *Corporate Takeovers: Causes and Consequences*, Chicago: University of Chicago Press, 1988.

Black, Bernard S., and Joseph A. Grundfest, "Shareholder Gains From Takeovers and Restructurings Between 1981 and 1986: $162 Billion is a Lot of Money," *Journal of Applied Corporate Finance*, Vol. 1, No. 1, (Spring 1988), pp. 5–15.

Browne, Lynn E., and Eric S. Rosengren, eds., "Are Hostile Takeovers Different," *The Merger Boom: Proceedings of a Conference held at Melvin Village, New Hampshire, October 1987*. Federal Reserve Bank of Boston, Conference Series; No. 31, pp. 199–229.

Browne, Lynn E., and Eric S. Rosengren, "Should States Restrict Takeovers?," *New England Economic Review*, Federal Reserve Bank of Boston, (July/August 1987), pp. 13–21.

Brown, Stephen J., and Jerold B. Warner, "Using Daily Stock Returns: The Case Of Event Studies," *Journal of Financial Economics*, Vol. 14, No. 1, (March 1985), pp. 3–31.

DeAngelo, Harry, and Edward M. Rice, "Antitakeover Charter Amendments and Stockholder Wealth," *Journal of Financial Economics*, Vol. 11, No. 1–4, (April 1983), pp. 329–359.

Eckbo, B. Espen, "Horizontal Mergers, Collusion, and Stockholder Wealth," *Journal of Financial Economics*, Vol. 11, No. 1–4, (April 1983), pp. 241–273.

Jarrell, Gregg A. and Annette B. Poulsen, "Shark Repellents and Stock Prices: The Effects of Antitakeover Amendments Since 1980," *Journal of Financial Economics*, Vol. 19, No. 1, (Sept. 1987), pp. 127–168.

Jarrell, Gregg A., James A. Brickley, and Jeffry M. Netter, "The Market for Corporate Control: The Empirical Evidence Since 1980," *Journal of Economic Perspectives*, Vol. 2, No. 1, (Winter 1988), pp 49–68.

Jensen, Michael C., "Agency Costs of Free Cash Flow, Corporate Finance, and Takeovers," Papers and Proceedings of the Ninety-Eighth Annual Meeting of the American Economic Association, New York, New York, Dec. 28–30, 1985, *The American Economic Review*, Vol. 76, No. 2, (May 1986), pp. 323–329.

Jensen, Michael C., "Takeovers: Their Causes and Consequences," *Journal of Economic Perspectives*, Vol. 2, No. 1, (Winter 1988), pp. 21–48.

Jensen, Michael C., and Richard S. Ruback, "The Market for Corporate Control: The Scientific Evidence," *Journal of Financial Economics*, Vol. 11, No. 1–4, (April 1983), pp. 5–50.

Linn, Scott C., and John J. McConnell, "An Empirical Investigation of the Impact of 'Antitakeover' Amendments on Common Stock Prices," *Journal of Financial Economics*, Vol. 11, No. 1–4, (April 1983), pp. 361–399.

Malatesta, Paul H., "The Wealth Effect of Merger Activity and the Objective Functions of Merging Firms," *Journal of Financial Economics*, Vol. 11, No. 1–4, (April 1983), pp. 155–181.

Mandelker, Gershon, "Risk and Return: The Case of Merging Firms," *Journal of Financial Economics*, Vol. 1, No. 4, (December 1974), pp. 303–335.

McConnell, John J., and Chris J. Muscarella, "Corporate Capital Expenditure Decisions and the Market Value of the Firm," *Journal of Financial Economics*, Vol. 14, No. 3, (Sept. 1985), pp. 399–422.

Palepu, Krishna G., "Predicting Takeover Targets: A Methodological and Empirical Analysis," *Journal of Accounting and Economics*, Vol. 8, No. 1, (March 1986), pp. 3–35.

Pound, John, "The Effects of Antitakeover Amendments on Takeover Activity: Some Direct Evidence," *The Journal of Law and Economics*, Vol. 30, No. 2, (October 1987), pp. 353–367.

Ravenscraft, David J., and F.M. Scherer, "Life After Takeover," *The Journal of Industrial Economics*, Vol. 36, No. 2, (December 1987), pp. 147–156.

Roll, Richard, "The Hubris Hypothesis of Corporate Takeovers," *Journal of Business*, Vol. 59, No. 2, (April 1986), pp. 197–216.

Scherer, F.M., "Corporate Takeovers: The Efficiency Arguments," *Journal of Economic Perspectives*, Vol. 2, No. 1, (Winter 1988), pp. 69–82.

Shleifer, Andrei, and Robert W. Vishny, "Value Maximization and the Acquisition Process," *Journal of Economic Perspectives*, Vol. 2, No. 1, (Winter 1988), pp. 7–20.

Stein, Jeremy C., "Takeover Threats and Managerial Myopia," *Journal of Political Economy*, Vol. 96, No. 1, (Feb. 1988), pp. 61–80.

Woolridge, Randall J., "Competitive Decline and Corporate Restructuring: Is a Myopic Stock Market to Blame?," *Journal of Applied Corporate Finance*, Vol. 1, No. 1, (Spring 1988), pp. 26–36.

Questions

1. Define the terms *tender offer*, *hostile takeover*, and *market for corporate control.*
2. Management Team *A*, consisting of 20 upper-level executives, currently runs AEC Company. When Management Team *B* takes over AEC Company, its total market value increases from $100 million to $150 million. What are some possible reasons for the increase in AEC Company's total market value?
3. Describe the potential role of each of the following factors in hostile takeovers: (a) agency costs in the target company due to the separation of ownership and control, (b) myopic market and the undervaluation of the target company's stock, (c) large amount of free cash flow generated by the target company, (d) large amount of free cash flow generated by the acquiring company, and (e) hubris of the acquiring company's management.
4. In what ways do ESOPs and LCOs defend against hostile takeovers?
5. Describe each of the following antitakeover amendments and indicate each one's impact on shareholder value: (a) dual-class recapitalization, (b) elimination of cumulative voting, (c) staggered directors, (d) poison pill, (e) supermajority clause, and (f) fair-price provision.
6. Are shareholders of the target company harmed by hostile takeovers? What evidence supports your answer?
7. Speculate on why the acquiring company's shareholders earn less in a hostile takeover than the target company's shareholders.
8. Explain why the acquiring company's bond holders might suffer from a decline in value in a hostile takeover. What does the evidence indicate?
9. Are any of the following groups likely to be economic casualties in a hostile takeover: (a) target-company executives, (b) employees, and (c) federal, state, and local taxing authorities? Explain.

The Cost of Restricting Corporate Takeovers: A Lesson from Switzerland

WERNER HERMANN AND G.J. SANTONI

Many people in management, labor, banking and Congress are alarmed about the recent increase in corporate takeovers. These people believe that the risk of a takeover is detrimental to the efficient management of corporations and not in the long-run interests of the owners (see insert on following page). As a result, they have advanced various proposals to restrict corporate takeovers.[1]

Others have a different view of takeovers, believing that restrictions of takeover activity will be harmful to shareholders' wealth. They argue that takeover activity is a simple manifestation of competition in the market for corporate control.[2] Furthermore, by inducing corporate management to weigh the effect of its decisions on the present value of the corporation (and, thus, share prices), this competition provides strong protection for the interests of all shareholders including those of "non-controlling" shareholders.[3] According to this view, the threat of takeovers is important to maintaining an efficient corporate sector.[4]

A recent change in Swiss commercial practice provides important new evidence about the consequences of restricting corporate takeovers. The Swiss

---

At the time of this writing, Werner Hermann was an economist at the Swiss National Bank and G.J. Santoni was a professor of economics at Ball State University. Santoni's research was supported by the George A. and Frances Ball Foundation. Scott Leitz provided research assistance.

Source: Federal Reserve Bank of St. Louis.

[1] These include restricting voting rights to those who have owned the stock for a minimum of one year, disallowing interest deductions from taxable income on certain types of bonds used to finance takeovers and a "sliding scale" capital gains tax rate that is lower the longer an asset is held before sale. In addition, there are at least five Senate and House panels that are planning to hold hearings on leveraged buyouts and other types of debt-financed takeovers. See Hershey (1988), Anders and Swartz (1988), Norris (1988) and Passell (1988).

[2] See Manne (1965), Manne and Ribstein (1988) and Jensen and Ruback (1983).

[3] See Manne (1965), p. 113.

[4] See Manne and Ribstein (1988), p. 29. Some have singled out an anti-takeover bill approved by the House Ways and Means Committee on October 15, 1987, as an important contributing factor to the stock market crash on October 19, 1987. See Ricks (1989).

Commercial Code in the past has allowed corporations to build effective barriers against takeovers. Many Swiss firms have taken advantage of this legal provision to protect themselves against foreign raiders. On November 17, 1988, Nestlé (by far the largest Swiss corporation) announced that it would allow foreign investors to buy a type of share that only Swiss citizens could hold until then. Since then, a foreign takeover of Nestlé has been possible, at least in principle.

Nestlé's announcement and the events surrounding it have important implications for U.S. proposals to restrict takeovers. This paper examines data on the share

Some Views On Hostile Takeovers

"You're going to have a bunch of highly leveraged companies that aren't going to be able to weather a financial storm."

J.L. Lanier, Jr., C.E.O.
West Point—Pepperell Inc.

"If it made sense to put the company together for economic strength in the beginning, then it certainly makes no sense to break it apart."

John De Lorean,
former General Motors executive

"I have to wonder if there's some kind of structural imbalance in the financial markets if the same package of assets broken into pieces are worth twice what the market puts on them when all together."

John R. Hall, C.E.O.
Ashland Oil Inc.

"People are questioning a whole series of this kind of activity, particularly in the light of all the foreign investment in this country. They're questioning the theory that many people are so enamored with—the whole 'me now,' big-hit generation of 28-year-old millionaires on Wall Street who haven't contributed to the country's economy. And a hell of a lot of people resent that."

Phillip J. Dion, C.E.O.
Del Webb Corp.

"How could it possibly help the company to be that much in debt? How does it help the employees? How can the company progress, how can they do research and development?"

Gino Pala, C.E.O.
Dixon Ticonderoga Co.

"There is no question that the Committee on Ways and Means will be looking at leveraged buy outs and mergers and acquisitions—and do something about it."

Dan Rostenkowski, Chairman
Committee on Ways and Means

prices of Nestlé and other Swiss firms around the November 1988 announcement date to analyze the effect of this sudden change in policy on shareholder wealth. If the data indicate that investors in Swiss stock generally benefited when restrictions against foreign takeovers were relaxed, current U S. proposals to limit takeovers are likely to be counterproductive in protecting shareholder wealth.

Stock Price Fundamentals

Since stock prices represent the market value of a firm, they play a significant role in the analysis of this paper. Therefore, it is important to understand how they are determined.

People value common stock for its expected return. Since investors may choose among broad categories of stock, the expected return on any particular stock must be equal to the expected return on other stocks of similar risk. For example, if a particular stock is expected to yield a relatively low return, investors will shun it, causing its price to fall and its expected return to rise until its yield is equal to that of similar stocks. The reverse holds for any stock with an expected return higher than other stocks of similar risk. An equilibrium exists when expected returns are equal across stocks with identical risk characteristics. The equilibrium return is called the required discount rate.

Equation 1 calculates the expected rate of return (r) from holding a share for one year assuming dividends (d) are paid at year end:[5]

$$(1)\quad E_t(r_{t,t+1}) = (E_tP_{t+1} + E_td_{t+1} - P_t)/P_t.$$

Equation 1 says that the expected return at time t of holding a share of stock from t to t + 1 is equal to the expected price of the stock at the end of the period (E_tP_{t+1}), plus the expected dividend (E_td_{t+1}), less the current price of the stock (P_t), all divided by the current price.

Equation 2 solves equation 1 for the current price by noting that the expected return equals the required discount rate (i) in equilibrium:

$$(2)\quad P_t = (E_tP_{t+1} + E_td_{t+1})/(1+i_t).$$

Equation 2 indicates that investors must forecast the price of the stock next period. What are the fundamentals of this price? In principle, the future price depends on the earnings of the company, dividend payments, and the required discount rate that investors expect to prevail over the life of the firm. If dividends are expected to grow at a constant annual rate (g) and the discount rate is constant, the calculation shown in equation 2 can be simplified as in equation 3:[6]

$$(3)\quad P_t = d_t(1 + g)/(i - g).$$

Equation 3 gives a relatively simple solution for the current stock price. For example, suppose the current dividend is $.98, the required discount rate is 12

---

[5] See Brealey (1983), pp. 67–72, and Brealey and Myers (1988), pp. 43–58.

[6] Brealey (1983), p. 69. The current price is defined by equation 3 only if the expected growth rate of dividends is less than the discount rate.

percent and the expected growth rate in dividends is 2 percent. Equation 3 indicates that a share of stock in this firm will trade at a price around $10[= $.98(1.02)/(.12 - .02)].

Takeovers and the Fundamentals

Equation 3 is a useful summary of the fundamentals that determine stock prices. It indicates that stock prices change when one or more of the fundamentals change. Furthermore, it is useful in contrasting the views of the proponents and critics of takeovers.

Critics of takeovers believe that competition for the control of firms adversely affects the fundamentals. For example, they argue that takeovers increase tension between management, labor and government to the detriment of future earnings and dividends; or that increases in the target's debt-to-equity ratio that accompany many takeovers increases the risk (and the discount rate) associated with the firm's expected earning stream; or that takeover threats force management to concentrate too heavily on projects that promise increased earnings in the near term at the expense of long-term research and development.

Others argue that the threat of takeovers improves the fundamentals on net because they induce management to use the firm's resources in ways that generate higher returns for the owners. They point out that the interests of management and shareholders can diverge and that it is costly for shareholders to monitor management's decisions. In the absence of strong competition from alternative management teams, the firm's managers, acting in their own interests, can capture a portion of the stream of earnings that would otherwise accrue to the shareholders. This may come in the form of high management salaries, large expense accounts, plush offices, lengthy vacations and other forms of shirking. Shirking affects the distribution of earnings between the firm's management and its owners. Furthermore, it may lower the stream of earnings generated by the firm. The cost associated with this type of behavior, called "agency cost," lowers the expected stream of dividends that accrue to shareholders and is reflected in lower share prices.[7]

The reduction in share price due to agency costs is a measure of the capital gain that could be obtained from a successful raid. According to this argument, competition among alternative management teams in the market for corporate control assures that agency costs are kept to a minimum, resulting in higher share prices for firm owners.[8] Thus, this theory suggests that takeover activity raises stock prices while the one mentioned earlier implies the opposite.

What evidence is there to support either view? Data on U.S. takeovers suggests that they raise stock prices.[9] The recent changes in the Swiss stock market should make Swiss data particularly useful in adding to this body of evidence.

---

[7] See Manne (1965), Manne and Ribstein (1988) and Alchian (1977), pp 227-58.
[8] See Manne (1965), p. 113, and Ruback (1988).
[9] See Jensen and Ruback (1983).

Swiss Stock Market Institutional Details

Registered, Bearer and Non-voting Shares

Swiss law allows corporations to issue several types of shares called bearer, registered and non-voting shares. Bearer shares are the equivalent of the typical common share issued by U.S. corporations. Ownership of a bearer share entitles the holder to the dividends and one vote at shareholder meetings. They can be transferred without restriction.

Registered shares differ from bearer shares in several important respects. For example, the purchase of a registered share entitles the buyer to dividends but does not grant the new owner the automatic right to vote at shareholder meetings. To obtain voting rights, the new owner must apply to be "registered" in the firm's book of shareholders. Until the new owner is registered, the voting right remains with the previous (and still registered) owner. Registration of the new owner, however, is not automatic. The corporate charter can summarily exclude certain investors from registration.[10] Furthermore, Swiss stockbrokers have declared publicly that they will refuse to exercise buy orders from clients that are unlikely to qualify for registration.[11] While registration is often restricted to Swiss citizens or institutions and, thus, can effectively prevent foreign takeovers of Swiss firms, this tool has been used to block Swiss raiders as well.[12]

A glance at the stock market page of a Swiss newspaper reveals that about a third of the Swiss corporations issue registered shares. Because these firms typically issue more registered shares than bearer shares, registered owners hold the controlling interest in the companies that issue both.[13] Coupled with the provisions regarding registration, this gives these Swiss firms iron-clad protection against hostile takeovers.

Besides registered and bearer shares, large companies issue securities that pay dividends but have no voting rights associated with them. Holders of these non-voting shares (participation certificates) have virtually the same rights as voting shareholders, apart from the right to vote.

Different Par Values

Dividend payments and the share of the firm's liquidation value that accrue to Swiss stockholders are proportional to the par value of the shares they hold. Both registered and bearer shares carry one vote. Swiss firms, however, are allowed to issue registered shares with lower par values than bearer shares. For example,

---

[10] See Horner (1988) and Foreman (1988). In the 1930s, this restriction was used to prevent takeovers of Swiss firms by firms in Nazi Germany. See "Shareholders, Who Are They?" (1989).

[11] See Horner (1988), pp. 70–71, and Foreman (1988).

[12] See Dullforce (August 9, 1988) and Wicks (August 2, 1988), who report on the takeover battle for La Suisse, a Swiss insurance company. In that case, the highest Swiss bidder for La Suisse withdrew his offer after the La Suisse board announced that it would refuse to register the bidder's shares.

[13] See "Shareholders, Who Are They?" (1989). For the number of shares issued of each type, see Swiss Bank Corporation, (1987).

let R be a registered share with a par value of \$50 while B is a bearer share with a par value of \$100. Both shares carry one vote but the expected stream of dividends generated by the registered share is one-half that of the bearer share. Other things the same, the registered share will trade at about one-half the price of the bearer share. Table 1 summarizes the participation rights of the different types of shares.

Nestling Up to Share Holders

To the surprise of many market participants, the common Swiss practice of discriminating against foreign investors was suddenly changed on November 17, 1988. Nestlé, the Swiss multinational foods group, decided to register shares of foreign investors. Nestlé had been repeatedly criticized for attempting to take over firms in countries outside Switzerland while being protected from foreign acquisition. In a release that accompanied the announcement, Nestlé's finance director explained that "there was a contradiction between being multinational in our behavior and national in our share control."[14]

Because of Nestlé's relative size, its decision was viewed as extremely important by market participants.[15] Since then, several other Swiss firms have made similar announcements.[16] Furthermore, the Swiss parliament is currently considering revisions to the commercial code that would make Swiss firms more accessible to outsiders. In part, such revisions have been prompted by Swiss shareholders who claim that they are adversely affected by anti-takeover rules. On the other hand, some Swiss citizens believe that hostile takeovers could harm Swiss companies and that management should be protected from raiders. Although the outcome of this debate is uncertain, the decision by Nestlé and other Swiss firms to liberalize shareholder registration marks a significant step in changing Swiss commercial practices regarding corporate takeovers.

TABLE 1 SWISS SHARES AND THEIR ENTITLEMENTS

	Participation	
Type of share	**Dividends**	**Voting**
Bearer	Yes	Yes
Registered	Yes	Upon registration
Non-voting	Yes	No

[14] A practical motivation for the decision was suggested by William Dullforce who commented that "Nestlé's access to capital markets was restricted by the differentiation between registered and bearer shares." See Dullforce (November 18, 1988).

[15] The value of Nestlé shares account for about 10 percent of the total Swiss stock market. See "Shareholders, Who Are They?" (1989), p.69.

[16] The most recent firm to make a similar announcement is Jacobs Suchard, a coffee and chocolate concern. See Wicks (June 22, 1988).

The theory of the market for corporate control suggests that impediments to takeovers are costly, which means that they reduce shareholder wealth. According to this theory, one consequence of reducing impediments to takeovers is that the capitalized value of the firm increases. To test this, data on Nestlé's share prices before and after November 1988 are examined. Since Nestlé's decision is viewed as having important consequences on the entire Swiss stock market, share price data on 44 other firms traded on the Zurich exchange are examined as well.[17]

The Swiss Evidence

To determine the effect of the loosening of voting restrictions on corporate shares in Switzerland, daily closing prices are analyzed at three points in time: the last trading days in December 1985, July 1988 and December 1988. The July 1988 date leads Nestlé's announcement by about three months to minimize the possibility that advance information about the forthcoming announcement might affect prices. The December 1988 date is the month immediately following the announcement month. The reason for choosing the December 1985 date is discussed below. The sample consists of nine firms that issue only bearer and non-voting shares, 21 firms that issue all three types of shares and 15 that issue only registered and bearer shares. A list of the firms appears in the appendix. The data are adjusted for differences in par values between different share types of the same company.

Did Registered Shares Trade at a Discount to Bearer Shares?

The first question examined is whether registered shares typically traded at a discount to bearer and non-voting shares of the same firm before November 1988.[18] Table 2 shows the ratios of the prices of registered to bearer and registered to non-voting shares for the same firm at three points in time: December 1985 July 1988 and December 1988.

The 36 firms in this sample differ in several respects. Some issue non-voting shares; others do not. In addition, some of the firms in the sample issue registered and bearer shares with the same par values while others issue these shares with different par values. Table 2 examines data on the price ratios while controlling for these differences.

Panel A of table 2 shows the mean of the ratio of registered to bearer share prices for the 21 companies that issue all three types of shares. The data are prices for the close of the last trading day of the month. The null hypothesis

---

[17] The Zurich stock exchange is the largest in Switzerland. More than 400 Swiss and foreign companies are listed on this exchange along with a much larger number of bonds.

[18] Some have argued that tax considerations and differential transaction costs imply that registered shares will sell at a discount to bearer shares. Since these factors did not change during the period analyzed, however, they cannot explain significant changes in relative share prices associated with Nestlé's decision to allow foreigners to purchase its registered shares.

TABLE 2 PRICE OF REGISTERED RELATIVE TO BEARER SHARES FOR SELECTED MONTHS

Panel A: Firms Issuing All Three Share Types With the Same Par Values

	Dates		
	12/85	**7/88**	**12/88**
Mean	.770*	.798*	.960
t-score	5.22	3.75	1.47
N = 21			

Panel B: Firms Issuing Only Registered and Bearer Shares With Different Par Values[1]

	Dates		
	12/85	**7/88**	**12/88**
Mean	.859*	.890*	.962
t-score	2.60	2.86	.98
N = 10			

Panel C: Firms Issuing Only Registered and Bearer Shares With the Same Par Values

	Dates		
	12/85	**7/88**	**12/88**
Mean	.767*	.799*	.870*
t-score	5.66	5.10	3.53
N = 5			

*Significantly different from 1.0 at the 5 percent level.
[1]Prices adjusted for difference in par values.

that the mean of the price ratios is one is rejected at a 5 percent significance level for the two dates before November 1988 but not for the December 1988 prices. The ratios for the December 1985 and July 1988 dates are indistinguishable in a statistical sense, suggesting that the discount on registered shares prevailed long before Nestlé's announcement.[19] This discount vanished, however, by December 1988.

The panel B data differs from the panel A data in two respects. The price ratios in panel B cover firms that issue only registered and bearer shares (no non-voting shares). Furthermore, the par values of each firm's registered shares are lower than the par values of the bearer shares for the firms in this panel. Since the stockholders of Swiss firms share dividends in proportion to the par values of the shares they hold, registered shares with lower par values than bearer shares should sell at a discount to bearer shares regardless of ownership restrictions on registered shares. To control for this "par value" effect, the registered share prices of the panel B firms are adjusted for differences in the par values.

The results shown in panel B are similar to the panel A results. The mean of the ratios of registered to bearer share prices is significantly less than one

[19] The discount is present in data extending back to December 1975.

before November 1988 but is statistically indistinguishable from one for the December 1988 data.

The data in panel C cover firms issuing only registered and bearer shares with the same par values. The results shown are similar to the panel A and B results for data before November 1988. The result for the December 1988 data differs, however. While the ratio of registered to bearer share prices is numerically higher for the December 1988 data than it was previously, it still is significantly less than one.

The Increase In Nestlé's Market Value

Table 3 shows the change in the market value of Nestlé shares from the end of July 1988 to the end of December 1988. As shown, the market value of Nestlé increased by almost 22 percent subsequent to its November policy change. Of course, this figure may over- or understate the change in value due to the policy change because other factors that affect stock prices may have changed.

To control for this, Table 4 shows the percentage changes in the prices of bearer and non-voting shares for the firms in our sample that do not issue registered shares. Since the Nestlé announcement pertained only to the treatment of

TABLE 3 THE CHANGE IN THE MARKET VALUE OF NESTLÉ: JULY 1988–DECEMBER 1988

Panel A: End of July 1988

Type of share	Price (in SFr)	Number of shares outstanding	Market value (millions of SFr)
Non-voting	1,315	1,000,000	1,315.00
Bearer	8,550	1,073,000	9,174.15
Registered	4,150	2,227,000	9,242.50
Market Value July 1988			19,731.20

Panel B: End of December 1988

Type of share	Price (in SFr)	Number of shares outstanding	Market value (millions of SFr)
Non-voting	1,320	1,000,000	1,320.00
Bearer	7,240	1,073,000	7,768.52
Registered	6,710	2,227,000	14,943.17
Market Value December 1988			24,031.69

Change in Market Value (millions of SFr) = 4,300.49
Percentage Change = 21.80%

TABLE 4 A PROXY FOR THE EFFECT OF OTHER FACTORS (CHANGES IN THE SHARE PRICES OF FIRMS THAT ISSUE NO REGISTERED SHARES)

Type of Share	Average percent change 7/88–12/88	t-score
Bearer	-7.97%	1.88
Non-voting	-9.20	2.00
N = 9		

registered shareholders, it is unlikely that the announcement would affect the share prices of firms that issue no registered shares. Changes in the prices of these firms between July and December 1988 can be used to proxy the effect of changes in other factors on Swiss stock prices.

The data in Table 4 indicate that the share prices of these firms did not rise from July to December 1988. While the point estimates of the average percentage change are negative in both cases, they are not significantly different from zero. Thus, these data suggest that other general influences did not raise or lower Swiss stock prices from July to December 1988. Consequently, the 22 percent increase in the market value of Nestlé can be taken as a "ball park" estimate of the rise in value associated with its change in registration policy.

The Nestlé Announcement and the Share Prices of Other Firms

The data in Table 2 suggest that the ratio of registered to bearer share prices rose from July to December 1988 for the 36 firms that issue both types of shares. The data in Table 5 show that the increase in this ratio resulted from a significant increase in the price of registered shares rather than from a decline in the price of bearer shares. This is important in evaluating whether the change in policy actually augments the shareholders' wealth. Any change that reduces the differences between the share types will cause their prices to converge even though stockholder wealth may not increase. For example, if the share prices converge because bearer and non-voting share prices generally decline while registered share prices remain unchanged, aggregate stockholder wealth will fall. If registered share prices increase while other share prices are constant, however, aggregate wealth will increase.

The data in Table 5 are consistent with the second case. Registered share prices increased by about 15 percent from July to December 1988 while changes in the prices of bearer and non-voting shares are not significantly different from zero. Again, the Table 4 data suggest that the increase in registered share prices is not due solely to other factors.

Conclusion

Recent experience with corporate takeovers has raised concerns that the capital of corporate shareholders is being held hostage by Wall Street power brokers.

TABLE 5 PERCENTAGE CHANGES IN SHARE PRICES: JULY–DECEMBER 1988

Type of share[1]	Average percent change 7/88–12/88	t-score	N
Registered	14.95%*	5.44	36
Bearer	-1.79	.71	36
Non-voting	.13	.03	21

* Significantly different from zero at the 5 percent level.

[1] Twenty-one of the 36 firms in this sample issue all three types of shares. Fifteen of the firms issue only registered and bearer shares.

Accordingly, various reforms designed to reduce takeover activity have been proposed.

This paper examines an economic theory that treats the control of a firm as a valuable asset. The theory suggests that takeovers represent trades of this asset in a market for corporate control and that such market competition provides strong protection for the interests of shareholders.

Data on the Swiss stock market are analyzed to determine whether restricting the market for corporate control affects stockholder wealth. Until recently, ownership restrictions on Swiss registered shares had prevented foreign citizens from competing for control of many Swiss firms. These restrictions were relaxed in November 1988. Data analyzed in this paper suggest that the registered share prices of firms rose by about 15 percent while the prices of bearer and non-voting shares were roughly constant following the relaxation. The data suggest that restricting competition in the market on corporate control can have serious adverse consequences on the wealth of shareholders. Since recent proposals to reform the takeover market in the United States intend to restrict this activity, they are likely to be counterproductive in protecting shareholder capital.

References

Alchian, Armen. *Economic Forces at Work* (Liberty Press, 1977).

Anders, George, and Steve Swartz. "Some Big Firms to Break Up Stock into New Securities," *Wall Street Journal*, December 5, 1988.

Brealey, R.A. *An Introduction to Risk and Return from Common Stocks* (The MIT Press, 1983).

Brealey, Richard, and Stewart Myers. *Principles of Corporate Finance* (McGraw Hill, 1988).

Burrough, Brian. "Circus-Like Takeover Contest for RJR Nabisco Inc. Brings Forth 2 New Bids of More Than $108 a Share," *Wall Street Journal*, December 1, 1988.

"CEOs React to RJR - and Ross Johnson." *Wall Street Journal*, December 2, 1988.

Dullforce, William. "Swiss Life Wins Battle for La Suisse," *Financial Times*, August 9, 1988.

———. "Nestlé to End Foreign Shares Discrimination," *Financial Times*, November 18, 1988.

———. "Nestlé Breaks Market Mould," *Financial Times*, November 22, 1988.

Foreman, Craig. "Nestlé Copycat Fears Cloud Swiss Stocks." *Wall Street Journal*, November 21, 1988.

Grossman, Sanford J., and Oliver D. Hart. "One Share-One Vote and the Market for Corporate Control," *Journal of Financial Economics* (January/March 1988), pp. 175–202.

Hershey, Robert D. Jr. "Congress Is Moving Closer to Weighing Buyout Curbs," *New York Times*, December 5, 1988.

Horner, Melchior R. "The Value of the Corporate Voting Right: Evidence from Switzerland," *Journal of Banking and Finance* (v. 12, 1988) pp. 69–83.

"Japan's Bias Against Domestic Mergers May Become Trade Issue, Tokyo Fears," *Wall Street Journal*, December 1, 1988.

Jarrell, Gregg A., and Annette B. Poulson. "Dual Class Recapitalizations As Antitakeover Mechanisms: The Recent Evidence," *Journal of Financial Economics* (January/March 1988), pp. 129–52.

Jensen, Michael C., and Richard S. Ruback. "The Market for Corporate Control: The Scientific Evidence," *Journal of Financial Economics* (April 1983), pp. 5–50.

Jensen, Michael C., and Jerold B. Warner. "The Distribution of Power Among Corporate Managers, Shareholders and Directors," *Journal of Financial Economics* (January/March 1988), pp. 3–24.

Manne, Henry G. "Mergers and the Market for Corporate Control," *Journal of Political Economy* (April 1965), pp. 110–20.

Manne, Henry G., and Larry E. Ribstein. "The SEC v. the American Shareholder," *National Review* (November 25, 1988), pp. 26–29.

Norris, Floyd. "A New Defense in Hostile Bids," *New York Times*, December 1, 1988.

Passell, Peter. "How to Defuse the Buyout Bomb," *New York Times*, December 7, 1988.

Ricks, Thomas E. "SEC Staffers Link '87 Crash to House Panel," *Wall Street Journal*, May 4, 1989.

Ruback, Richard S. "Coercive Dual-Class Exchange Offers," *Journal of Financial Economics* (January/March 1988), pp. 153–73.

"Shareholders, Who Are They?" *The Economist* (January 28, 1989), p. 69.

Stulz, René M. "Managerial Control of Voting Rights, Financing Policies and the Market for Corporate Control," *Journal of Financial Economics* (January/March 1988). pp. 25–54.

Swiss Bank Corporation. *Handbuch der Schweizer Aktien* (1987).

Wicks, John. "Suchard Lets Foreigners Own Registered Shares," *Financial Times*, June 22, 1988.

———. "Unprecedented Battle of La Suisse Suitors," *Financial Times*, August 2, 1988.

"Will Others Follow RJR as it Pioneers Megadeal Frontier?" *Wall Street Journal* December 2, 1988.

Appendix

FIRMS INCLUDED IN THE TESTS

Firm	Types of Shares Issued		
	Registered	**Bearer**	**Non-voting**
Elekrowatt		/	/
Fortuna		/	/
Gotthard Bank		/	/
Interdiscount		/	/
Pirelli		/	/
VP Bank Vaduz		/	/
Walter Rentsch		/	/
Zuercher Ziegeleien		/	/
Zellweger		/	/
Allusuisse	/	/	/
B.S.I.	/	/	/
Bank Leu	/	/	/
Bobst	/	/	/
Brown Boveri	/	/	/
Buehrle	/	/	/

FIRMS INCLUDED IN THE TESTS (CONT.)

Firm	Types of Shares Issued		
	Registered	**Bearer**	**Non-voting**
Ciba Geigy	/	/	/
Feldschloesschen	/	/	/
Georg Fischer	/	/	/
Haldengut	/	/	/
Jacobs Suchard	/	/	/
Konsumverein Zurich	/	/	/
Moevenpick	/	/	/
Nestlé	/	/	/
Sandoz	/	/	/
Schindler	/	/	/
Swiss Bank Corporation	/	/	/
Schweizer Rueck	/	/	/
Union Bank of Switzerland	/	/	/
Zurich Insurance	/	/	/
Globus	/	/	/
Accu-Oerlikon	/	/	
Charmilles	/	/	
Credit Suisse	/	/	
Crossair	/	/	
Frisco Findus	/	/	
Hermes	/	/	
Hero	/	/	
Huerlimann	/	/	
Mikron	/	/	
Usego	/	/	
Eichhof	/	/	
Holzstoff	/	/	
Hypo Brugg	/	/	
Sibra Holding	/	/	
Swissair	/	/	

Questions

1. Estimate the value of a share of common stock given the following information:
   - Expected cash dividend at the end of the year: $2.
   - Expected price per share at the end of the year: $50.
   - Expected (required) rate of return: 15 percent per year.
2. Use the dividend growth model to estimate the value per share of SMD's common stock. Investors expect SMD to pay a cash dividend of $1.50 one year from now. Investors expect dividends to grow 10 percent per year over the foreseeable future, and they require a 15 percent annual return on the stock.
3. Some critics argue against hostile takeovers, believing them to be detrimental to the long-run interests of shareholders. Others argue that just the *threat* of takeovers enhances shareholder wealth. Explain the arguments of these opposing groups.

4. Describe the three types of Swiss shares—bearer, registered, and non-voting.
5. What announcement did Nestlé make on November 17, 1988, and why was it important?
6. Did registered shares of Swiss companies typically trade at a discount to bearer shares prior to the Nestlé announcement? After the Nestlé announcement? Describe the evidence in support of your answers.
7. Describe the change in market value of Nestlé shares attributable to the change in registration policy.
8. What effect did the Nestlé announcement have on the share prices of other Swiss companies?
9. In your opinion, should the U.S. Congress pass laws to impede hostile takeovers? Explain.

Eclipse of the Public Corporation

MICHAEL C. JENSEN

New organizations are emerging in its place—organizations that are corporate in form but have no public shareholders and are not listed or traded on organized exchanges. These organizations use public and private debt, rather than public equity, as their major source of capital. Their primary owners are not households but large institutions and entrepreneurs that designate agents to manage and monitor on their behalf and bind those agents with large equity interests and contracts governing the use and distribution of cash.

Takeovers, corporate breakups, divisional spinoffs, leveraged buyouts, and going-private transactions are the most visible manifestations of a massive organizational change in the economy. These transactions have inspired criticism, even outrage, among many business leaders and government officials, who have called for regulatory and legislative restrictions. The backlash is understandable. Change is threatening; in this case, the threat is aimed at the senior executives of many of our largest companies.

Despite the protests, this organizational innovation should be encouraged. By resolving the central weakness of the public corporation—the conflict between owners and managers over the control and use of corporate resources—these new organizations are making remarkable gains in operating efficiency, employee productivity, and shareholder value. Over the long term, they will enhance U.S. economic performance relative to our most formidable international competitor, Japan, whose companies are moving in the opposite direction. The governance and financial structures of Japan's public companies increasingly resemble U.S. companies of the mid-1960s and early 1970s—an era of gross corporate waste and mismanagement that triggered the organizational transformation now under way in the United States.

At the time of this writing, Michael C. Jensen was the Edsel Bryant Ford Professor of Business Administration at the Harvard Business School.

The Privatization of Equity

The last share of publicly traded common stock owned by an individual will be sold in the year 2003, if current trends persist. This forecast may be fanciful (short-term trends never persist), but the basic direction is clear. By the turn of the century, the primacy of public stock ownership in the United States may have all but disappeared.

Households have been liquidating their direct holdings and indirect positions (through channels like mutual funds) at an unprecedented rate. Over the last five years, they have been net sellers of more than $500 billion of common stock, 38% of their holdings at the beginning of 1984.

Why have stock prices risen sharply despite this massive sell-off? Because there has been one huge buyer—corporations themselves. LBOs, MBOs, share repurchases, leveraged mergers and acquisitions, and takeovers have been contracting the supply of publicly held equity. In 1988, 5% of the market value of public equity (more than $130 billion) disappeared through these kinds of transactions, even after adding back all of the new issues brought to market during the year.

Of course, the risks and returns from the underlying corporate assets have not disappeared. To some extent they now reside in quasi-equity debt instruments like high-yield bonds, whose total market value exceeds $200 billion. But many of the risks and returns still exist as equity; they just take the form of large positions of privately held equity. The "privatization of equity" is now a central feature of corporate ownership in the United States.

Historically, public stock markets dominated by individual investors developed to a greater extent in the United States than in any other country. Broad public ownership offered managers a reasonably priced source of more or less permanent equity capital that could buffer the company against adversity in a way debt could not. Share ownership allowed individual investors to participate in equity returns and get the benefits of liquidity (because they could sell their shares) and diversification (because they could hold a small number of shares from many corporations).

The virtues of broad public ownership are not what they used to be, for managers or investors. One important factor is the emergence of an active market for corporate control. A capital structure consisting mostly of equity still offers managers protection against the risks of economic downturn. But it also carries substantial risks of inviting a hostile takeover or other threats to management control.

The role of the public market has also changed because investors themselves have changed. For decades, stock ownership has been migrating from direct holdings by millions of individuals to indirect beneficial ownership through large pools of capital—in particular, the huge corporate and governmental pension funds whose total value exceeded $1.5 trillion in 1988. These institutional funds, which now comprise more than 40% of total stock ownership, used to behave like large public investors. They kept diversified by retaining many different investment managers, each of whom traded an array of highly liquid public securities. But their investment philosophy has been evolving in recent years to include participation in a select number of private illiquid investments and private pools of equity capital. This new investment philosophy makes broad public markets less essential for institutions.

Large pools of capital such as pension funds and endowments don't really need the liquidity the public market offers. Liquidity serves two basic purposes. It allows investors to meet unexpected cash needs and to trade their stocks. Unlike individuals, the large funds can project their cash needs well into the future based on predictable factors such as employee demographics, life expectancies, and health trends. So they can take a long-term view of investment returns and keep their holdings in illiquid assets.

Fund managers are also realizing that trading is a tough discipline in which they hold little comparative advantage. Trading is a zero-sum game played in a fairly efficient market against equally talented rivals. Worse still, large funds face diseconomies of scale when executing trades. The larger a fund, the more difficult it is to trade quickly, based on transient information advantages. The very act of trading moves markets.

Still, these managers remain charged with generating returns in excess of passive benchmarks. Enter the market for private assets such as real estate, venture capital, and, more recently, the market for corporate control and restructurings. Instead of trading a large number of small, liquid positions, the funds can buy and own smaller numbers of large, illiquid positions in a form where they (or more likely, their agents) participate more actively with management in the control of the assets.

This alternative can be a positive-sum game; real changes in corporate policies can be a route to enhanced value. The very large funds also have a competitive advantage here. The larger their positions, the more actively they can participate in the ownership and management of the underlying assets. In the extreme, as with LBO funds, these changes can be dramatic. The LBO fund itself becomes the managing owner in partnership with company managers. In short, large institutional funds can behave more like owners and less like traders.

The same basic changes are at work in a wide variety of corporate recapitalizations where outside (or related) parties acquire large, relatively nontraded equity positions. Large pools of capital can participate in these private equity positions yet remain diversified by virtue of their own enormous size. Smaller funds and households cannot.

In the short run, this new investment philosophy has been, in the aggregate, a great success. Without the sobering influence of an economic contraction, the returns from these private investments have been very attractive. In the long run, the institutions' new philosophy is ushering

(Continued)

in a system of equity ownership dominated by "private positions" that resembles ownership systems in Germany and Japan. Individual investors in this system will increasingly be free riders on the coattails of a small number of very large private investors rather than the central feature of the financial markets.

—JAY O. LIGHT

Consider these developments in the 1980s:

- The capital markets are in transition. The total market value of equity in publicly held companies has tripled over the past decade—from $1 trillion in 1979 to more than $3 trillion in 1989. But newly acquired capital comes increasingly from private placements, which have expanded more than ten times since 1980, to a rate of $200 billion in 1988. Private placements of debt and equity now account for more than 40% of annual corporate financings. Meanwhile, in every year since 1983, at least 5% of outstanding value of corporate equity has disappeared through stock repurchases, takeovers, and going-private transactions. Finally, households are sharply reducing their stock holdings.[1] (See the insert, "The Privatization of Equity.")
- The most widespread going-private transaction, the leveraged buyout, is becoming larger and more frequent. In 1988, the total value of the 214 public company and divisional buyouts exceeded $77 billion—nearly one-third of the value of all mergers and acquisitions. The total value of the 75 buyouts in 1979 was only $1.3 billion (in constant 1988 dollars), while the 175 buyouts completed in 1983 had a total value of $16.6 billion. This process is just getting started; the $77 billion of LBOs in 1988 represented only 2.5% of outstanding public-company equity. (See the table, "Rise of the LBO.")
- Entire industries are being reshaped. Just five years ago, the leading U.S. truck and automobile tire manufacturers were independent and diversified public companies. Today each is a vastly different enterprise. Uniroyal went private in 1985 and later merged its tire-making operations with those of B.F. Goodrich to form a new private company called Uniroyal Goodrich. In late 1986, Goodyear borrowed $2.6 billion and repurchased nearly half its outstanding shares to fend off a hostile tender offer by Sir James Goldsmith. It retained its core tire and rubber business while moving to divest an array of unrelated operations, including its Celeron oil and gas subsidiary,

[1] Equity values based on trends in the Wilshire Index. Private-placement data from IDD Information Services as published in Sarah Bartlett. "Private Market's Growing Edge," *New York Times*, June 20, 1989.

> California-to-Texas oil pipeline, aerospace operation, and Arizona resort hotel. In 1987, GenCorp issued $1.75 billion of debt to repurchase more than half its outstanding shares. It divested several operations, including its General Tire subsidiary, to pay down the debt and focus on aerospace and defense. Last year, Firestone was sold to Bridgestone, Japan's largest tiremaker, for $2.6 billion, a transaction that created shareholder gains of $1.6 billion.

Developments as striking as the restructuring of our financial markets and major industries reflect underlying economic forces more fundamental and powerful than financial manipulation, management greed, reckless speculation, and the other colorful epithets used by defenders of the corporate status quo. The forces behind the decline of the public corporation differ from industry to industry. But its decline is real, enduring, and highly productive. It is not merely a function of the tax deductibility of interest. Nor does it reflect a transitory LBO phase through which companies pass before investment bankers and managers cash out by taking them public again. Nor, finally, is it premised on a systematic fleecing of shareholders and bondholders by managers and other insiders with superior information about the true value of corporate assets.

The current trends do not imply that the public corporation has no future. The conventional twentieth-century model of corporate governance—dispersed public ownership, professional managers without substantial equity holdings, a board of directors dominated by management-appointed outsiders—remains a viable option in some areas of the economy, particularly for growth companies whose profitable investment opportunities exceed the cash they generate internally. Such companies can be found in industries like computers and electronics, biotechnology, pharmaceuticals, and financial services. Companies choosing among a surplus of profitable projects are unlikely to invest systematically in unprofitable ones, especially when they must regularly turn to the capital markets to raise investment funds.

The public corporation is not suitable in industries where long-term growth is slow, where internally generated funds outstrip the opportunities to invest them profitably, or where downsizing is the most productive long-term strategy. In the tire industry, the shift to radials, which last three times longer than bias-ply tires, meant that manufacturers needed less capacity to meet world demand. Overcapacity inevitably forced a restructuring. The tenfold increase in oil prices from 1973 to 1981, which triggered worldwide conservation measures, forced oil producers into a similar retrenchment.[2]

Industries under similar pressure today include steel, chemicals, brewing, tobacco, television and radio broadcasting, wood and paper products. In these and other cash-rich, low-growth or declining sectors, the pressures on management to waste cash flow through organizational slack or investments in unsound projects is often irresistible. It is in precisely these sectors that the publicly held corporation has declined most rapidly. Barring regulatory interference, the public corporation is also likely to decline in industries such as

---

[2] For more analysis of the oil industry, see my article, "The Takeover Controversy: Analysis and Evidence," in *Corporate Restructuring and Executive Compensation* (Cambridge, Mass: Ballinger, 1989).

aerospace, automobiles and auto parts, banking, electric power generation, food processing, industrial and farm implements, and transportation equipment.

The public corporation is a social invention of vast historical importance. Its genius is rooted in its capacity to spread financial risk over the diversified portfolios of millions of individuals and institutions and to allow investors to customize risk to their unique circumstances and predilection. By diversifying risks that would otherwise be born by owner-entrepreneurs and by facilitating the creation of a liquid market for exchanging risk, the public corporation lowered the cost of capital. These tradable claims on corporate ownership (common stock) also allowed risk to be borne by investors best able to bear it, without requiring them to manage the corporations they owned.

From the beginning, though, these risk-bearing benefits came at a cost. Tradable ownership claims create fundamental conflicts of interest between those who bear risk (the shareholders) and those who manage risk (the executives). The genius of the new organizations is that they eliminate much of the loss created by conflicts between owners and managers without eliminating the vital functions of risk diversification and liquidity once performed exclusively by the public equity markets.

In theory, these new organizations should not be necessary. Three major forces are said to control management in the public corporation: the product markets, internal control systems led by the board of directors, and the capital markets. But product markets often have not played a disciplining role. For most of the last 60 years, a large and vibrant domestic market created for U.S. companies economies of scale and significant cost advantages over foreign rivals. Recent reversals at the hands of the Japanese and others have not been severe enough to sap most companies of their financial independence. The idea that outside directors with little or no equity stake in the company could effectively monitor and discipline the managers who selected them has proven hollow at best. In practice, only the capital markets have played much of a control function—and for a long time they were hampered by legal constraints.

Indeed, the fact that takeover and LBO premiums average 50% above market price illustrates how much value public-company managers can destroy before they face a serious threat of disturbance. Takeovers and buyouts both create new value and unlock value destroyed by management through misguided policies. I estimate that transactions associated with the market for corporate control unlocked shareholder gains (in target companies alone) of more than $500 billion between 1977 and 1988—more than 50% of the cash dividends paid by the entire corporate sector over this same period.

The widespread waste and inefficiency of the public corporation and its inability to adapt to changing economic circumstances have generated a wave of organizational innovation over the last 15 years—innovation driven by the rebirth of "active investors." By active investors I mean investors who hold large equity or debt positions, sit on boards of directors, monitor and sometimes dismiss management, are involved with the long-term strategic direction of the companies they invest in, and sometimes manage the companies themselves.

RISE OF THE LBO

	Public-Company Buyouts		Divisional Buyouts		
Year	Number	Average Value (In millions of 1988 dollars)	Number	Average Value (In millions of 1988 dollars)	Total Value of Buyouts (In billions of 1988 dollars)
1979	16	$ 64.9	59	$ 5.4	$ 1.4
1980	13	106.0	47	34.5	3.0
1981	17	179.1	83	21.0	4.8
1982	31	112.2	115	40.7	8.2
1983	36	235.8	139	58.2	16.6
1984	57	473.6	122	104.0	39.7
1985	76	349.4	132	110.1	41.0
1986	76	303.3	144	180.7	49.0
1987	47	488.7	90	144.2	36.0
1988	125	487.4	89	181.3	77.0

SOURCE: George P. Baker, "Management Compensation and Divisional Leveraged Buyouts," unpublished dissertation, Harvard Business School, 1986. Updates from W. T. Grimm, *Mergerstat Review* 1988. Transactions with no public data are valued at the average price of public transactions.

Active investors are creating a new model of general management. These investors include LBO partnerships such as Kohlberg Kravis Roberts and Clayton & Dubilier; entrepreneurs such as Carl Icahn, Ronald Perelman, Laurence Tisch, Robert Bass, William Simon, Irwin Jacobs, and Warren Buffett; the merchant banking arms of Wall Street houses such as Morgan Stanley, Lazard Fréres, and Merrill Lynch; and family funds such as those controlled by the Pritzkers and the Bronfmans. Their model is built around highly leveraged financial structures, pay-for-performance compensation systems, substantial equity ownership by managers and directors, and contracts with owners and creditors that limit both cross-subsidization among business units and the waste of free cash flow. Consistent with modern finance theory, these organizations are not managed to maximize earnings per share but rather to maximize *value*, with a strong emphasis on cash flow.

More than any other factor, these organizations' resolution of the owner-manager conflict explains how they can motivate the same people, managing the same resources, to perform so much more effectively under private ownership than in the publicly held corporate form.

In effect, LBO partnerships and the merchant banks are rediscovering the role played by active investors prior to 1940, when Wall Street banks such as J.P. Morgan & Company were directly involved in the strategy and governance of the public companies they helped create. At the height of his prominence, Morgan and his small group of partners served on the boards of U.S. Steel, International Harvester, First National Bank of New York, and a host of railroads, and were a powerful management force in these and other companies.

Morgan's model of investor activism disappeared largely as a result of populist laws and regulations approved in the wake of the Great Depression. These laws and regulations—including the Glass-Steagall Banking Act of 1933, the

Securities Act of 1933, the Securities Exchange Act of 1934, the Chandler Bankruptcy Revision Act of 1938, and the Investment Company Act of 1940—may have once had their place. But they also created an intricate web of restrictions on company "insiders" (corporate officers, directors, or investors with more than a 10% ownership interest), restrictions on bank involvement in corporate reorganizations, court precedents, and business practices that raised the cost of being an active investor. Their long-term effect has been to insulate management from effective monitoring and to set the stage for the eclipse of the public corporation.

Indeed, the high cost of being an active investor has left financial institutions and money management firms, which control more than 40% of all corporate equity in the United States, almost completely uninvolved in the major decisions and long-term strategies of the companies their clients own. They are almost never represented on corporate boards. They use the proxy mechanism rarely and usually ineffectively, notwithstanding recent efforts by the Council of Institutional Investors and other shareholder activists to gain a larger voice in corporate affairs.

All told, institutional investors are remarkably powerless; they have few options to express dissatisfaction with management other than to sell their shares and vote with their feet. Corporate managers criticize institutional sell-offs as examples of portfolio churning and short-term investor horizons. One guesses these same managers much prefer churning to a system in which large investors on the boards of their companies have direct power to monitor and correct mistakes. Managers really want passive investors who can't sell their shares.

The absence of effective monitoring led to such large inefficiencies that the new generation of active investors arose to recapture the lost value. These investors overcome the costs of the outmoded legal constraints by purchasing entire companies—and using debt and high equity ownership to force effective self-monitoring.

A central weakness and source of waste in the public corporation is the conflict between shareholders and managers over the payout of free cash flow—that is, cash flow in excess of that required to fund all investment projects with positive net present values when discounted at the relevant cost of capital. For a company to operate efficiently and maximize value, free cash flow must be distributed to shareholders rather than retained. But this happens infrequently; senior management has few incentives to distribute the funds, and there exist few mechanisms to compel distribution.

A vivid example is the senior management of Ford Motor Company, which sits on nearly $15 billion in cash and marketable securities in an industry with excess capacity. Ford's management has been deliberating about acquiring financial service companies, aerospace companies, or making some other multibillion-dollar diversification move—rather than deliberating about effectively distributing Ford's excess cash to its owners so they can decide how to reinvest it.

Ford is not alone. Corporate managers generally don't disgorge cash unless they are forced to do so. In 1988, the 1,000 largest public companies (by sales) generated total funds of $1.6 trillion. Yet they distributed only $108 billion as dividends and another $51 billion through share repurchases.[3]

Managers have incentives to retain cash in part because cash reserves increase their autonomy vis-à-vis the capital markets. Large cash balances (and independence from the capital markets) can serve competitive purpose, but they often lead to waste and inefficiency. Consider a hypothetical world in which companies distribute excess cash to shareholders and then must convince the capital markets to supply funds as sound economic projects arise. Shareholders are at a great advantage in this world, where management's plans are subject to enhanced monitoring by the capital markets. Wall Street's analytical, due diligence, and pricing disciplines give shareholders power to quash wasteful projects.

Managers also resist distributing cash to shareholders because retaining cash increases the size of the companies they run—and managers have many incentives to expand company size beyond that which maximizes shareholder wealth. Compensation is one of the most important incentives. Many studies document that increases in executive pay are strongly related to increases in corporate size rather than value.[4]

The tendency of companies to reward middle managers through promotions rather than annual performance bonuses also creates a cultural bias toward growth. Organizations must grow in order to generate new positions to feed their promotion-based reward systems.

Finally, corporate growth enhances the social prominence, public prestige, and political power of senior executives. Rare is the CEO who wants to be remembered as presiding over an enterprise that makes fewer products in fewer plants in fewer countries than when he or she took office—even when such a course increases productivity and adds hundreds of millions of dollars of shareholder value. The perquisites of the executive suite can be substantial, and they usually increase with company size.

The struggle over free cash flow is at the heart of the role of debt in the decline of the public corporation. Bank loans, mezzanine securities, and high-yield bonds have fueled the wave of takeovers, restructurings, and going-private transactions. The combined borrowings of all nonfinancial corporations in the United States approached $2 trillion in 1988, up from $835 billion in 1979. The interest charges on these borrowings represent more than 20% of corporate cash flows, high by historical standards.[5]

This perceived "leveraging of corporate America" is perhaps the central source of anxiety among defenders of the public corporation and critics of the new organizational forms. But most critics miss three important points. First, the trebling of the market value of public-company equity over the last decade means that corporate borrowing had to increase to avoid a major *de*leveraging.

---

[3] Calculated from Standard & Poor's Compustat file.

[4] Kevin J. Murphy, "Corporate Performance and Management Remuneration," *Journal of Accounting and Economics*, 1985, vol. 7, no. 1–3.

[5] Federal Reserve Board, Balance Sheets of U.S. Economy.

Second, debt creation *without retention of the proceeds of the issue* helps limit the waste of free cash flow by compelling managers to pay out funds they would otherwise retain. Debt is in effect a substitute for dividends—a mechanism to force managers to disgorge cash rather than spend it on empire-building projects with low or negative returns, bloated staffs, indulgent perquisites, and organizational inefficiencies.

By issuing debt in exchange for stock, companies bond their managers' promise to pay out future cash flows in a way that simple dividend increases do not. "Permanent" dividend increases or multiyear share repurchase programs (two ways public companies can distribute excess cash to shareholders) involve no contractual commitments by managers to owners. It's easy for managers to cut dividends or scale back share repurchases.

Take the case of General Motors. On March 3, 1987, several months after the departure of GM's only active investor, H. Ross Perot, the company announced a program to repurchase up to 20% of its common stock by the end of 1990. As of mid-1989, GM had purchased only 5% of its outstanding common shares, even though its $6.8 billion cash balance was more than enough to complete the program. Given management's poor performance over the past decade, shareholders would be better off making their own investment decisions with the cash GM is retaining. From 1977 to 1987, the company made capital expenditures of $77.5 billion while its U.S. market share declined by 10 points.

Borrowing allows for no such managerial discretion. Companies whose managers fail to make promised interest and principal payments can be declared insolvent and possibly hauled into bankruptcy court. In the imagery of G. Bennett Stewart and David M. Glassman, "Equity is soft, debt hard. Equity is forgiving, debt insistent. Equity is a pillow, debt a sword."[6] Some may find it curious that a company's creditors wield far more power over managers than its public shareholders, but it is also undeniable.

Third, debt is a powerful agent for change. For all the deeply felt anxiety about excessive borrowing, "overleveraging" can be desirable and effective when it makes economic sense to break up a company, sell off parts of the business, and refocus its energies on a few core operations. Companies that assume so much debt they cannot meet the debt service payments out of operating cash flow force themselves to rethink their entire strategy and structure. Overleveraging creates the crisis atmosphere managers require to slash unsound investment programs, shrink overhead, and dispose of assets that are more valuable outside the company. The proceeds generated by these overdue restructurings can then be used to reduce debt to more sustainable levels, creating a leaner, more efficient and competitive organization.

In other circumstances, the violation of debt covenants creates a board-level crisis that brings new actors onto the scene, motivates a fresh review of top management and strategy, and accelerates response. The case of Revco D.S., Inc., one of the handful of leveraged buyouts to reach formal bankruptcy, makes the point well.

---

[6] G. Bennett Stewart III and David M. Glassman, "The Motives and Methods of Corporate Restructuring: Part II," *Journal of Applied Corporate Performance*, Summer 1988.

Critics cite Revco's bankruptcy petition, filed in July 1988, as an example of the financial perils associated with LBO debt. I take a different view. The $1.25 billion buyout, announced in December 1986, did dramatically increase Revco's annual interest charges. But several other factors contributed to its troubles, including management's decision to overhaul pricing, stocking, and merchandise layout in the company's drugstore chain. This mistaken strategic redirection left customers confused and dissatisfied, and Revco's performance suffered. Before the buyout, and without the burden of interest payments, management could have pursued these policies for a long period of time, destroying much of the company's value in the process. Within six months, however, debt served as a brake on management's mistakes, motivating the board and creditors to reorganize the company before even more value was lost.[7]

Developments at Goodyear also illustrate how debt can force managers to adopt value-creating policies they would otherwise resist. Soon after his company warded off Sir James Goldsmith's tender offer, Goodyear chairman Robert Mercer offered his version of the raiders' creed: "Give me your undervalued assets, your plants, your expenditures for technology, research and development, the hopes and aspirations of your people, your stake with your customers, your pension funds, and I will enhance myself and the dealmakers."[8]

What Mr. Mercer failed to note is that Goodyear's forced restructuring dramatically increased the company's value to shareholders by compelling him to disgorge cash and shed unproductive assets. Two years after this bitter complaint, Tom Barrett, who succeeded Mercer as Goodyear's CEO, was asked whether the company's restructuring had hurt the quality of its tires or the efficiency of its plants. "No," he replied. "We've been able to invest and continue to invest and do the things we've needed to do to be competitive."[9]

Robert Mercer's harsh words are characteristic of the business establishment's response to the eclipse of the public corporation. What explains such vehement opposition to a trend that clearly benefits shareholders and the economy? One important factor, as my Harvard Business School colleague Amar Bhide suggests, is that Wall Street now competes directly with senior management as a steward of shareholder wealth. With its vast increases in data, talent, and technology, Wall Street can allocate capital among competing businesses and monitor and discipline management more effectively than the CEO and headquarters staff of the typical diversified company. KKR's New York offices and Irwin Jacobs' Minneapolis base are direct substitutes for corporate headquarters in Akron or Peoria. CEOs worry that they and their staffs will lose lucrative jobs in favor of competing organizations. Many are right to worry; the performance of active investors versus the public corporation leaves little doubt as to which is superior.

Active investors are creating new models of general management, the most widespread of which I call the LBO Association. A typical LBO Association consists of three main constituencies: an LBO partnership that sponsors going-private

---

[7] Stephen Phillip, "Revco: Anatomy of an LBO that Failed," *Business Week*, October 3, 1988.

[8] "A Hollow Victory for Bob Mercer," *Industry Week*, February 23, 1987.

[9] Jonathan P. Hicks, "The Importance of Being Biggest," *New York Times*, June 20, 1989.

transactions and counsels and monitors management in an ongoing cooperative relationship; company managers who hold substantial equity stakes in an LBO division and stay on after the buyout; and institutional investors (insurance companies, pension funds, and money management firms) that fund the limited partnerships that purchase equity and lend money (along with banks) to finance the transactions.

Much like a traditional conglomerate, LBO Associations have many divisions or business units, companies they have taken private at different points in time. KKR, for example, controls a diverse collection of 19 businesses including all or part of Beatrice, Duracell, Motel 6, Owens-Illinois, RJR Nabisco, and Safeway. But LBO Associations differ from publicly held conglomerates in at least four important respects. (See the illustration, "Public Company vs. LBO Association.")

1. *Management incentives are built around a strong relationship between pay and performance.* Compensation systems in LBO Associations usually have higher upper bounds than do public companies (or no upper bounds at all), tie bonuses much more closely to cash flow and debt retirement than to accounting earnings, and otherwise closely link management pay to divisional performance. Unfortunately, because these companies are private, little data are available on salaries and bonuses.

   Public data are available on stock ownership, however, and equity holdings are a vital part of the reward system in LBO Associations. The University of Chicago's Steven Kaplan studied all public-company buyouts from 1979 through 1985 with a purchase price of at least $50 million.[10] Business-unit chiefs hold a median equity position of 6.4% in their unit. Even without considering bonus and incentive plans, a $1,000 increase in shareholder value triggers a $64 increase in the personal wealth of business-unit chiefs. The median public-company CEO holds .25% of the company's equity. Counting *all* sources of compensation—including salary, bonus, deferred compensation, stock options, and dismissal penalties—the personal wealth of the median public-company CEO increases by only $3.25 for a $1,000 increase in shareholder value.[11]

   Thus the salary of the typical LBO business-unit manager is almost 20 times more sensitive to performance than that of the typical public-company manager. This comparison understates the true differences in compensation. The personal wealth of managing partners in an LBO partnership (in effect, the CEOs of the LBO Associations) is tied almost exclusively to the performance of the

[10] Steven Kaplan, "Sources of Value in Management Buyouts," *Journal of Financial Economics*, forthcoming.
[11] Michael C. Jensen and Kevin J. Murphy, "Performance Pay and Top Management Incentives," *Journal of Political Economy*, forthcoming.

PUBLIC COMPANY VS. LBO ASSOCIATION

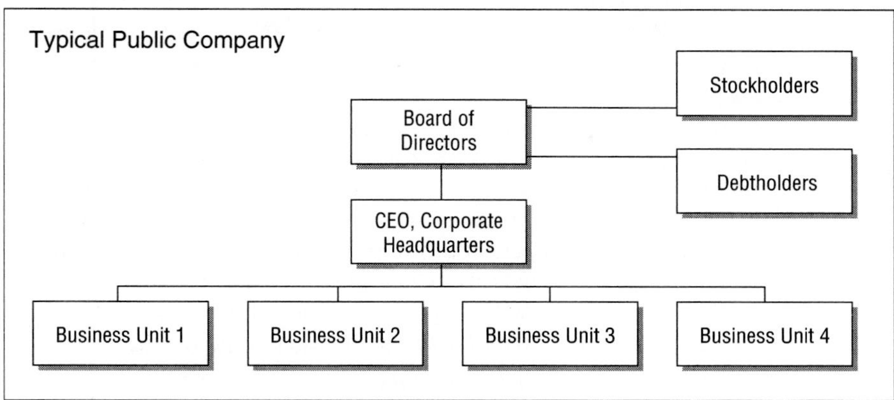

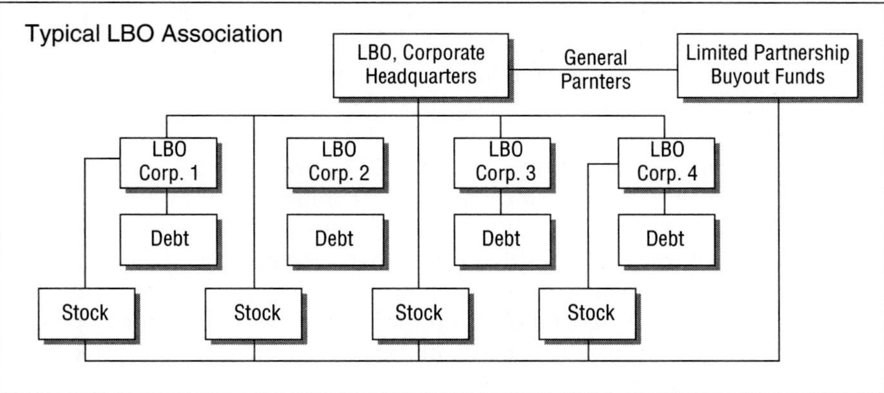

companies they control. The general partners in an LBO Association typically receive (through overrides and direct equity holdings) 20% or more of the gains in the value of the divisions they help manage. This implies a pay-for-performance sensitivity of $200 for every $1,000 in added shareholder value. It's not hard to understand why an executive who receives $200 for every $1,000 increase in shareholder value will unlock more value than an executive who receives $3.25.

2. *LBO Associations are more decentralized than publicly held conglomerates.* The LBO Association substitutes compensation incentives and ownership for direct monitoring by headquarters. The headquarters of KKR, the world's largest LBO partnership, has only 16 professionals

and 44 additional employees. In contrast, the Atlanta headquarters of RJR Nabisco employed 470 people when KKR took it private last year in a $25 billion transaction. At the time of the Goldsmith tender offer for Goodyear, the company's Akron headquarters had more than 5,000 people on its salaried payroll.

It is physically impossible for KKR and other LBO partnerships to become intimately involved in the day-to-day decisions of their operating units. They rely instead on stock ownership, incentive pay that rewards cash flow, and other compensation techniques to motivate managers to maximize value without bureaucratic oversight. My survey of 7 LBO partnerships found an average headquarters staff of 13 professionals and 19 nonprofessionals that oversees almost 24 business units with total annual sales of more than $11 billion. (See the table, "LBO Partnerships Keep Staff Lean.")

3. *LBO Associations rely heavily on leverage.* The average debt ratio (long-term debt as a percentage of debt plus equity) for public companies prior to a buyout is about 20%. The Kaplan study shows the average debt ratio for an LBO is 85% on completion of the buyout.

   Intensive use of debt dramatically shrinks the amount of equity in a company. This allows the LBO general partners and divisional managers to control a large fraction of the total ownership without requiring huge investments they would be unable to make or large grants of free equity. For example, in a company with $1 billion in assets and a debt ratio of 20%, management would have to raise $80 million to buy 10% of the equity. If that same company had a debt ratio of 90%, management would have to raise only $10 million to control a 10% stake. By concentrating equity holdings among managers and LBO partners, debt intensifies the ownership incentives that are so important to efficiency.

   High debt also allows LBO Associations and other private organizations to tap the benefits of risk diversification once provided only by the public equity market. Intensive use of debt means much of it must be in the form of public, high-yield, noninvestment-grade securities, better known as junk bonds. This debt, which was pioneered by Drexel Burnham Lambert, reflects more of the risk borne by shareholders in the typical public company. Placing this public debt in the well-diversified portfolios of large financial institutions spreads equity-like risk among millions of investors, who are the ultimate-beneficiaries of mutual funds and pension funds—without requiring those risks to be held as equity. Indeed, high-yield debt is probably the most important and productive capital market innovation in the last 40 years.

4. *LBO Associations have well-defined obligations to their creditors and residual claimants.* Most buyout funds are organized as limited partnerships in which the partners of the sponsoring LBO firm serve as

LBO Partnerships Keep Staff Lean

LBO Partnership	Year Started	Number of Professionals	Number of Nonprofessionals	Number of Business Units	Combined Annual Revenues (In billions of dollars)
Berkshire Partners	1986	14	6	15	$1
Butler Capital	1979	8	14	33	2.3
Clayton & Dubilier	1976	10	11	8	4.8
Gibbons Green van Amerongen	1969	6	7	12	5.3
Kohlberg Kravis Roberts	1976	16	44	19	58.7
Thomas H. Lee Co.	1974	15	12	25	8
Odyssey Partners	1950	19	39	53	N.A.

general partners. The buyout fund purchases most of the equity and sometimes provides debt financing. The limited partnership agreement denies the general partner the right to transfer cash or other resources from one LBO division to another. That is, all returns from a business must be distributed to the limited partners and other equity holders of that business. Such binding agreements reduce the risk of unproductive reinvestment by prohibiting cross-subsidization among LBO units. In effect, the LBO sponsor must ask its institutional investors for permission to reinvest funds, a striking difference from the power of public-company managers to freely shift resources among business units.

The management, compensation, and financial structures of the LBO Association square neatly with the rebirth of active investors. Institutional investors delegate the job of being active monitors to agents best qualified to play the role. The LBO partnerships bond their performance by investing their own resources and reputations in the transaction and taking the bulk of their compensation as a share in the companies' increased value.

To be sure, this delegation is not without its tensions. The fact that LBO partnerships and divisional managers control the LBO Association's small equity base but hold little of the debt creates incentives for them to take high-risk management gambles. If the gambles succeed, they reap large rewards by increasing their equity value; if their gambles fail, creditors bear much of the cost. But the reputational consequences of such reckless behavior can be large. As long as creditors behave rationally, an LBO partnership that tries to profit at the expense of its creditors or walks away from a deal gone sour will not be able to raise funds for future investments.

To date, the performance of LBO Associations has been remarkable. Indeed, it is difficult to find any systematic losers in these transactions, and almost all of the gains appear to come from real increase in productivity. The best studies of LBO performance reach the following conclusions:

LBOs create large gains for shareholders. Studies estimate that the average total premium to public shareholders ranges form 40% to 56%.[12] Kaplan finds that in buyouts that go public again or are otherwise sold (which occurs an average 2.7 years after the original transaction), total shareholder value increases by an average of 235%, or nearly 100% above market-adjusted returns over the same period.[13] These returns are distributed about equally between pre-buyout shareholders and the suppliers of debt and equity to the transaction. Prebuyout shareholders earn average market-adjusted premiums of 38%, while the total return to capital (debt plus equity) for buyout investors is 42%. This return to buyout investors is measured on the total purchase price of the LBO, not the buyout equity. Because equity returns are almost a pure risk premium, and therefore independent of the amount invested, they are very high. The median market-adjusted return on buyout equity is 785%, or 125% per year.

Value gains do not come at the expense of other financial constituencies. Some critics argue that buyout investors, especially managers, earn excessive returns by using inside information to exploit public shareholders. Managers do face severe conflicts of interest in these transactions; they cannot simultaneously act as buyer and agent for the seller. But equity-owning managers who are not part of post-buyout management teams systematically sell their shares into LBOs. This would be foolish if the buyout were significantly underpriced in light of inside information, assuming that these nonparticipating insiders have the same inside information as the continuing management team. Moreover, LBO auctions are becoming common; underpriced buyout proposals (including those initiated by management) quickly generate competing bids.

No doubt some bondholders have lost value through going-private transactions. By my estimate, RJR Nabisco's prebuyout bondholders lost almost $300 million through the downgrading of their claims on the newly leveraged company. This is a small sum in comparison to the $12 billion in total gains the transaction produced. As yet, there is no evidence that bondholders lose on average from LBOs. Evidence on LBOs completed through 1986 does show that holders of convertible bonds and preferred stock gain a statistically

---

[12] Yakov Amihud, "Leveraged Management Buyouts and Shareholders Wealth," in *Leveraged Management Buyouts: Causes and Consequences*, (Homewood, Ill.: Dow Jones-Irwin, 1989).

[13] That is, returns net of the returns that would normally be earned on these securities, given their level of systematic risk (beta) and general market returns.

significant amount and that straight bondholders suffer no significant gains or losses.[14]

New data may document losses for bondholders in recent transactions. But the expropriation of wealth from bondholders should not be a continuing problem. The financial community is perfecting many techniques, including poison puts and repurchase provisions, to protect bondholders in the event of substantial restructurings. In fact, versions of these loss-prevention techniques have been available for some time. In the past, bondholders such as Metropolitan Life, which sued RJR Nabisco over the declining value of the company's bonds, chose not to pay the premium for protection.

LBOs increase operating efficiency without massive layoffs or big cuts in research and development. Kaplan finds that average operating earnings increase by 42% from the year prior to the buyout to the third year after the buyout. Cash flows increase by 96% over this same period. Other studies document significant improvements in profit margins, sales per employee, working capital, inventories, and receivables.[15] Those who doubt these findings might take a moment to scan the business press, which has chronicled the impressive postbuyout performance of companies such as Levi Strauss, A.O. Scott, Safeway, and Weirton Steel.

Importantly, employment does not fall systematically after buyouts, although it does not grow as quickly as in comparable companies. Median employment for all companies in the Kaplan study, including those engaged in substantial divestitures, increased by nearly 1%. Companies without significant divestitures increased employment by 5%.

Moreover, the great concern about the effect of buyouts on R&D and capital investment is unwarranted. The low-growth companies that make the best candidates for LBOs don't invest heavily in R&D to begin with. Of the 76 companies in the Kaplan study, only 7 spent more than 1%, of sales on R&D before the buyout. Another recent study shows that R&D as a fraction of sales grows at the same rate in LBOs as in comparable public companies.[16] According to Kaplan's study, capital expenditures are 20%, lower in LBOs than in comparable non-LBO companies. Because these cuts are taking place in low-growth or declining industries and are accompanied by a doubling of market-adjusted value, they appear to be coming from reductions in low-return projects rather than productive investments.

Taxpayers do not subsidize going-private transactions. Much has been made of the charge that large increases in debt virtually eliminate the tax obligations of an LBO. This argument overlooks five sources of additional tax revenues generated by buyouts: capital gains taxes paid by prebuyout shareholders; capital gains taxes paid on postbuyout asset sales; tax payments on the large increases in

---

[14] L. Marais, K. Schipper, and A. Smith, "Wealth Effects of Going Private for Senior Securities," *Journal of Financial Economics*, 1989, vol. 23, no. 1.

[15] In addition to Kaplan, see Abbie Smith, "Corporate Ownership Structure and Performance," unpublished paper, University of Chicago, 1989. See also Frank R. Lichtenberg and Donald Siegel, "The Effects of Leveraged Buyouts on Productivity and Related Aspects of Firm Behavior," *National Bureau of Economic Research*, 1989.

[16] Lichtenberg and Siegel, NBER, 1989.

operating earnings generated by efficiency gains; tax payments by creditors who receive interest payments on the LBO debt; and taxes generated by more efficient use of the company's total capital.

Overall, the U.S. Treasury collects an estimated 230% more revenues in the year after a buyout than it would have otherwise and 61% more in long-term present value. The $12 billion gain associated with the RJR Nabisco buyout will generate net tax revenues of $3.3 billion in the first year of the buyout; the company paid $370 million in federal taxes in the year before the buyout. In the long term, the transaction will generate total taxes with an estimated present value of $3.8 billion.[17]

LBO sponsors do not have to take their companies public for them to succeed. Most LBO transactions are completed with a goal of returning the reconfigured company to the public market within three to five years. But recent evidence indicates that LBO sponsors are keeping their companies under private ownership. Huge efficiency gains and high-return asset sales produce enough cash to pay down debt and allow LBOs to generate handsome returns as going concerns. The very proliferation of these transactions has helped create a more efficient infrastructure and liquid market for buying and selling divisions and companies. Thus LBO investors can "cash out" in a secondary LBO or private sale without recourse to a public offering. One recent study finds that only 5%. of the more than 1,300 LBOs between 1981 and 1986 have gone public again.[18]

Public companies can learn from LBO Associations and emulate many of their characteristics. But this requires major changes in corporate structure, philosophy, and focus. They can reduce the waste of free cash flow by borrowing to repurchase stock or pay large dividends. They can alter their charters to encourage large investors or experiment with alliances with active investors such as Lazard Fréres' Corporate Partners fund. They can increase equity ownership by directors, managers, and employees. They can enhance incentives through pay-for-performance systems based on cash flow and value rather than accounting earnings. They can decentralize management by rethinking the role of corporate headquarters and shrinking their staffs.

Some corporations are experimenting with such changes—FMC, Holiday, and Owens-Corning—and the results have been impressive. But only a coordinated attack on the status quo will halt the eclipse of the public company. It is unlikely such an attack will proceed fast enough or go far enough.

Who can argue with a new model of enterprise that aligns the interests of owners and managers, improves efficiency and productivity, and unlocks hundreds of billions of dollars of shareholder value? Many people, it seems, mainly because these organizations rely so heavily on debt. As I've discussed, debt is crucial to management discipline and resolving the conflict over free cash flow. But critics, even some who concede the control function of debt, argue that the costs of leverage outweigh the benefits.

---

[17] Michael C. Jensen, Robert Kaplan, and Laura Stiglin, "Effects of LBOs on Tax Revenues of the U.S. Treasury," *Tax Notes*, February 6, 1989.

[18] Chris Muscarella and Michael Vetsuypens, "Efficiency and Organizational Structure: A Study of Reverse LBOs," unpublished paper, Southern Methodist University, April 1989.

Wall Street economist Henry Kaufman, a prominent critic of the going-private trend, issued a typical warning earlier this year: "Any severe shock—a sharp increase in interest rates in response to Federal Reserve credit restraint, or an outright recession that makes the whole stock market vulnerable, or some breakdown in the ability of foreign firms to bid for pieces of U.S. companies—will drive debt-burdened companies to the government's doorstep to plead for special assistance."[19]

The relationship between debt and insolvency is perhaps the least understood aspect of this entire organizational evolution. New hedging techniques mean the risk associated with a given level of a corporate debt is lower today than it was five years ago. Much of the bank debt associated with LBOs (which typically represents about half of the total debt) is done through floating-rate instruments. But few LBOs accept unlimited exposure to interest rate fluctuations. They purchase caps to set a ceiling on interest charges or use swaps to convert floating-rate debt into fixed-rate debt. In fact, most banks require such risk management techniques as a condition of lending.

Critics of leverage also fail to appreciate that insolvency in and of itself is not always something to avoid—and that the costs of becoming insolvent are likely to be much smaller in the new world of high leverage than in the old world of equity-dominated balance sheets. The proliferation of takeovers, LBOs, and other going-private transactions has inspired innovations in the reorganization and workout process. I refer to these innovations as "the privatization of bankruptcy." LBOs *do* get in financial trouble more frequently than public companies do. But few LBOs ever enter formal bankruptcy. They are reorganized quickly (a few months is common), often under new management, and at much lower costs than under a court-supervised process.

How can insolvency be less costly in a world of high leverage? Consider an oversimplified example on the following page. Companies A and B are identical in every respect except for their financial structures. Each has a going-concern value of $100 million (the discounted value of its expected future cash flows) and a liquidation or salvage value of $10 million. Company A has an equity-dominated balance sheet with a debt ratio of 20%, common for large public companies. Highly leveraged Company B has a debt ratio of 85%, common for LBOs. (See the illustration, "The Privatization of Bankruptcy.")

Now both companies experience business reversals. What happens? Company B will get in trouble with its creditors much sooner than Company A. After all, Company B's going-concern value doesn't have to shrink very much for it to be unable to meet its payments on $85 million of debt. But when it does run into trouble, its going-concern value will be nowhere near its liquidation value. If the going-concern value shrinks to $80 million, there remains $70 million of value to preserve by avoiding liquidation. So Company B's creditors have strong incentives to preserve the remaining value by quickly and efficiently reorganizing their claims outside the courtroom.

---

[19] Henry Kaufman, "Bush's First Priority: Stopping the Buyout Mania," *Washington Post*, January 1, 1989.

The Privatization of Bankruptcy

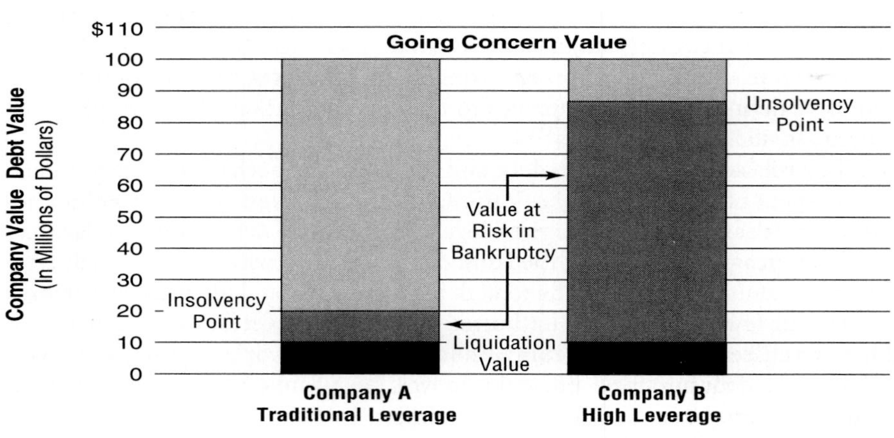

No such incentives operate on Company A. Its going-concern value can fall dramatically before creditors worry about their $20 million of debt. By the time creditors do intervene, Company A's going-concern value will have plummeted. And if Company A's value falls to under $20 million, it is much more likely than Company B to be worth less than its $10 million salvage value. Liquidation in this situation is the likely and rational outcome, with all its attendant conflicts, dislocations, and costs.

The evolving U.S. system of corporate governance and finance exhibits many characteristics of the postwar Japanese system. LBO partnerships act much like the main banks (the real power center) in Japan's *keiretsu* business groupings. The keiretsu make extensive use of leverage and intercorporate holdings of debt and equity. Banks commonly hold substantial equity in their client companies and have their own executives help them out of difficulty. (For years, Nissan has been run by an alumnus of the Industrial Bank of Japan, who became CEO as part of the bank's effort to keep the company out of bankruptcy.) Other personnel, including CFOs, move frequently between banks and companies as part of an ongoing relationship that involves training, consulting, and monitoring. Japanese banks allow companies to enter formal bankruptcy only when liquidation makes economic sense—that is, when a company is worth more dead than alive. Japanese corporate boards are composed almost exclusively of insiders.

Ironically, even as more U.S. companies come to resemble Japanese companies, Japan's public companies are becoming more like U.S. companies of 15 years ago. Japanese shareholders have seldom had any power. The banks' chief disciplinary tool, their power to withhold capital from high-growth, cash-starved companies, has been vastly reduced as a result of several factors. Japan's victories in world product markets have left its companies awash in profits. The development of domestic and international capital markets has created ready alternatives to bank loans, while deregulation has liberalized corporate access to these funds. Finally, new legal constraints prevent banks from holding more than 5% of the equity of any company, which reduces their incentive to engage in active monitoring.

Many of Japan's public companies are flooded with free cash flow far in excess of their opportunities to invest in profitable internal growth. In 1987, more than 40% of Japan's large public companies had no net bank borrowings—that is, cash balances larger than their short- and long-term borrowings. Toyota, with a cash board of $10.4 billion, more than 25% of its total assets, is commonly referred to as the Toyota Bank.[20]

In short, Japanese managers are increasingly unconstrained and unmonitored. They face no effective internal controls, little control from the product markets their companies already dominate, and fewer controls from the banking system because of self-financing, direct access to capital markets, and lower debt ratios. Unless shareholders and creditors discover ways to prohibit their managers from behaving like U.S. managers, Japanese companies will make uneconomic acquisitions and diversification moves generate internal waste, and engage in other value-destroying activities. The long-term result will be the growth of bureaucracy and inefficiency and the demise of product quality and organizational responsiveness—until the waste becomes so severe it triggers a market for corporate control to remedy the excesses.

The Japanese remedy will reflect that country's unique legal system and cultural practices. But just as hostile takeovers, LBOs, and other control transactions went from unacceptable behavior in the United States to a driving force in corporate restructuring, so too will they take hold in Japan—once the potential returns outweigh the costs and risks of challenging the corporate status quo.

Meanwhile, in the United States, the organizational changes revitalizing the corporate sector will create more nimble enterprises and help reverse our losses in world product markets. As this profound innovation continues, however, people will make mistakes. To learn, we have to push new policies to the margin. It will be natural to see more failed deals.

There are already some worrisome structural issues. I look with discomfort on the dangerous tendency of LBO partnerships, bolstered by their success, to take more of their compensation in front-end fees rather than in back-end profits earned through increased equity value. As management fees and the fees for completing deals get larger, the incentives to do deals, rather than good deals, also increases. Institutional investors (and the economy as a whole) are best served when the LBO partnership is the last member of the LBO Association to get paid and when the LBO partnership gets paid as a fraction of the back-end value of the deals, including losses.

Moreover, we have yet to fully understand the limitations on the size of this new organizational form. LBO partnerships are understandably tempted to

[20] Average (book value) debt ratios fell from 77% in 1976 to 68% in 1987. Given the 390% increase in stock prices over this period, market-value debt ratios fell even more dramatically. Figures calculated from the NEEDS Nikkei Financials file for all companies on the First Section of the Tokyo Stock Exchange.

increase the reach of their talented monitors by reconfiguring divisions as acquisition vehicles. This will be difficult to accomplish successfully. It is likely to require bigger staffs, greater centralization of decision rights, and dilution of the high pay-for-performance sensitivity that is so crucial to success. As LBO Associations expand, they run the risk of recreating the bureaucratic waste of the diversified public corporation.

These and other problems should not cloud the remarkable benefits associated with the eclipse of the large public corporation. What surprises me is how few mistakes have occurred thus far in an organizational change as profound as any since World War II.

Questions

1. An LBO (leveraged buyout) is called an MBO (management buyout) if the investors are the target company's managers. Characterize the nature of an LBO.
2. "The public corporation is not suitable in industries where long-term growth is slow, where internally generated funds outstrip the opportunities to invest them profitably, or where downsizing is the most productive long-term strategy." The author argues, however, that the traditional corporate form—dispersed public ownership and professional managers—is a viable option for growth companies with profitable investment opportunities greater than internally generated cash. Defend these propositions.
3. The potential conflict of interest between corporate managers (agents) and shareholders (principals) is often referred to as an *agency problem*.
   a. Identify several potential conflicts of interest that might result from this agency relationship.
   b. Organizational theorists claim that the behavior of corporate managers is controlled (to some extent) by product markets, internal control systems, and capital markets. Explain how each of these three factors help to resolve the agency problem.
   c. Having successfully defended against a noted corporate raider's tender offer, Goodyear chairman Robert Mercer described the raider's creed as follows: "Give me your undervalued assets, your plants, your expenditures for technology, research and development, the hopes and aspirations of your people, your stake with your customers, your pension funds, and I will enhance myself and the dealmakers." What is Mr. Mercer's complaint? As a Goodyear shareholder, would you place more confidence in Mr. Mercer or the raider Sir James Goldsmith?
4. "Corporate managers generally don't disgorge cash unless they are forced to do so. In 1988, the 1,000 largest public companies (by sales) generated total funds of $1.6 trillion. Yet they distributed only $108 billion as dividends and another $51 billion through share repurchases."
   a. What are the incentives for corporate managers to retain excessive cash balances in lieu of payment to shareholders?
   b. A corporation's *free cash flow* is the amount in excess of that required to finance all capital projects with positive net present values. In what way do high debt levels resolve the struggle over free cash flow?
   c. "Equity is soft, debt hard. Equity is forgiving, debt insistent. Equity is a pillow, debt a sword." Interpret the meaning of this quotation.

5. The author describes an LBO Association as consisting of three major constituencies: an LBO partnership, company managers, and institutional investors. Compare and contrast the organizational structure of a typical corporation with that of a typical LBO Association. (See the illustration.)
6. Evaluate the advantages of a typical LBO Association along the following dimensions: management incentives, centralization of management, financial leverage, and obligations to capital suppliers.
7. Describe the evidence that supports the following conclusions on LBO performance:
   - LBOs create large gains for shareholders.
   - Value gains do not come at the expense of other financial constituencies.
   - LBOs increase operating efficiency without massive layoffs or big cuts in research and development.
   - Taxpayers do not subsidize going-private transactions.
   - LBO sponsors do not have to take their companies public for them to succeed.
8. Suppose that you plan to interview a sample of corporate executives on the perils of LBOs. Speculate on your expected findings.
9. In your opinion, do LBOs serve a useful function in corporate America? Explain.

Is Corporate Bankruptcy Efficient?

FRANK H. EASTERBROOK

Corporate bankruptcy has two functions: (1) to deliver the penalty for failure by forcing a wrapping up when a business cannot pay its debts and (2) to reduce the social costs of failure. When a business fails, the legal process writes off claims that have become uncollectible, turns out managers and others responsible for the debacle, and pays the claims for which assets remain. Bankruptcy or a private substitute such as a workout succeeds when this happens quickly (before good money is thrown after bad) and with low transactions costs. Because the process of paying some claims and extinguishing others can lead to a race to carve up the carcass, which may still have a positive cash flow, bankruptcy combines a stay of self-help with a collective forum for the resolution of competing claims. Like the separation theorem of finance, the bankruptcy process divorces decisions about the optimal deployment of assets from decisions about the claims to those assets. If it works well, assets continue to be devoted to their most productive uses.

Bankruptcy certainly writes down claims, and Gilson (1990) finds that it leads to sanctions in the managerial labor market as well. Is the cost worth incurring? Every study of bankruptcy shows it to be expensive, as it is bound to be given creditors' incentives to stake out competing claims to whatever wealth remains. Weiss (1990) measures costs approximating 3% of the assets in the bankruptcies of substantial firms. Other estimates run between 3.4% and 21% for smaller firms. [See White (1989), collecting studies.] In the process, Weiss finds, bankruptcy courts refuse to enforce some claims in the order provided by contract, despite the 'absolute priority rule'. (Carrying a grandiose name, the rule means only that contractual allocations of priority in distribution are to be honored.)

On top of these direct costs are losses from inefficient uses of assets during or after the process, or in anticipation of it as parties maneuver for position. Gilson, John, and Lang (1990) find that private restructuring is superior to

---

At the time of this writing, Frank H. Easterbrook was a judge for the United States Court of Appeals for the Seventh Circuit, Chicago, IL.

Source: *Journal of Financial Economics* (1990, pp. 411–417). Reprinted with permission.

bankruptcy. Does this damn the bankruptcy process, or does it show only that people choose restructuring when that is cheaper and choose bankruptcy when the legal process holds the advantage in cost?

The Weiss and Gilson-John-Lang papers raise the question: why is there corporate bankruptcy? If it is costly, either in absolute terms or compared with private alternatives, and does not enforce contractual entitlements, what's the point? One alternative is an auction. After a firm enters bankruptcy, and the automatic stay prevents dismemberment of the assets, the business could be sold as a going concern to the high bidder. This process would yield a pot of cash to be distributed according to contractual entitlements (as modified by statutes implementing other rules, such as priority for taxes or $2,000 of wages per employee). If the assets are worth more when broken up or melted down, the buyer will redeploy them appropriately; the auction yields the highest value available from any future use. Law could assure the buyer that no claims arising out of the firm's activities before the sale would be honored (other than against the proceeds). Bids then would reflect the full value of the assets, and sunk costs would be disregarded.

Auctions are common in moving assets to their best uses, whether they be auctions for art or for offshore oil fields or for targets of tender offers. Investment banks specialize in running auctions for entire corporations, ending in mergers or tender offers or leveraged buyouts. Markets for corporations and their divisions appear to be reasonably thick. Some nations (Germany, for example) auction the whole firm as the first recourse in a corporate bankruptcy. In the United States an auction of the firm is the normal way of disposing of the assets of failed banks, making it seem all the more odd that auctions are rare for other kinds of corporations. Banks to one side, the normal process of bankruptcy calls on a judge to entertain arguments from lawyers and investment bankers, attach a value to the firm's assets, and then dole out interests in the assets determined to exist.

Think what you want about the ability of investment banks and auctions to generate 'accurate' values for whole corporations, it is hard to believe that judges relying on lawyers will be more accurate. Bidders risking their money have every reason to spend the optimal amount to value the assets; those who estimate accurately will prosper, and others will fail. Money generally is wielded by the financially astute. Competition leads to decent (though not perfect) pricing. Judges lose nothing if the value they attach to the firm is inaccurate, and they win the praise of those who would have lost out if the guess had been more astute. Judges are neither selected for ability to value assets correctly nor selected-out on account of poor business judgment. In any contest of real prices (in auctions) against hypothetical prices (in court), real prices will be more accurate. No wonder Baird (1986) has strongly questioned whether corporate bankruptcy makes sense when a cheaper alternative lies at hand. Other scholars, although not taking up a hue and cry for auctions, have proposed methods of increasing the role of market forces in valuing both corporate assets and the claims against them [e.g., Bebchuk (1988), Roe (1983)].

Corporate bankruptcy without auctions or other market valuation devices has been with us for some time. Modern corporate bankruptcy is an outgrowth of the equity receivership, a collective proceeding filed by creditors. Although these often ended in auctions they were thought cumbersome and were replaced by common consent by a statute that does not require auctions.

The Federal Deposit Insurance Corporation turned to auctions of failed banks as a cheaper alternative to acquiring and eventually reselling the banks' assets, showing the evolution toward auctions is possible. Yet nothing of the kind happens today with other businesses in or out of bankruptcy. Private debt restructurings rarely involve auctions. When creditors meet outside of bankruptcy to readjust claims, they use the same devices they are apt to employ if they meet in court. Sometimes they arrange to sell the firm as a unit, but this is uncommon. And when creditors draft legislation to present to Congress, their agenda does not include a demand that judges put corporate debtors on the block. The Bankruptcy Code of 1978 is largely what creditors wished it to be. No surprise, for corporate bankruptcy is a process of resolving claims among creditors, with few competing interests. Although judicial decisions concerning this code sometimes lead to loud demands for change (demands usually satisfied), there is no comparable demand for a larger volume of auctions.

Enduring legal institutions endure either because they are efficient or because they redistribute wealth to concentrated, politically effective interest groups. (Laws also may have moral bases, but these are unlikely explanations for the rules governing corporate bankruptcy.) Market versus hypothetical valuation in bankruptcy has no redistributive effect. Who would be the winners and losers? There may be winners and losers in particular cases (a violation of the absolute priority rule transfers wealth to the holders of the junior debt), but such transfers *ex post* do not imply transfers *ex ante*, given responses to known rules.

Suppose current bankruptcy law always falls harshly on junior, unsecured debt, more harshly than a more efficient auction rule that raised larger sums would do. This does not transfer wealth from unsecured claimants to secured claimants; it extinguishes wealth without creating winners and therefore without creating political support. And although such a law creates losers given that a firm becomes a debtor in bankruptcy, it does not create losers *ex ante*. Unsecured creditors will charge more for money, emerging no worse off across their portfolio of loans. The losers will be not the unsecured creditors but the superior firms (and their investors), which must pay the higher price of capital. Investors in these firms—including both secured and unsecured creditors—would be better off if the legal rule were more efficient. So too if existing rules fall harshly on secured creditors by disregarding the absolute priority rule and by indulging optimistic judicial valuations that allow unsecured creditors and equity investors to obtain more than their contractual shares. Again prices adjust, and the anticipation of redistribution *ex post* means that there is none *ex ante*.

It is at all events unrealistic to suppose that suppliers of capital fall naturally into groups such as secured lenders, unsecured lenders, and equity investors. People have portfolios of investments, and even though some institutions (such as banks) cannot purchase some instruments (such as stock), financial intermediaries are not themselves winners and losers. Real persons supply the capital, and their portfolios are or readily can be diversified across kinds of investment. If an inefficient rule raises the price of unsecured debt, both prices and portfolios will adjust. No one gains *ex ante*, and all creditors (potentially) lose.

The remaining interest group is lawyers. Bankruptcy laws were drafted not by the creditors but by their lawyers. Agency problems are everywhere; maybe the bar figured out how to feather its own nest through extended proceedings at the expense of all creditors' interests. Such an explanation works, however, only if the bankruptcy bar is closed; free entry would dissipate any rents. Entry is not hard. Lawyers may take up bankruptcy practice freely, and many have done so. Large law firms have greatly expanded their bankruptcy departments in recent years, while other departments such as antitrust have melted away. Because entry is possible, and large financial intermediaries have their own teams of lawyers to monitor the work of legislative drafters, rent-seeking is not a plausible explanation of the failure of bankruptcy law to auction off corporate debtors. This leaves efficiency as the likely explanation.

Many people find it hard to believe that the judicial system ever operates with lower transactions costs than markets. Baird (1986) expresses justified skepticism on this score. Yet consider that Weiss's (1990) measurements of the cost of corporate bankruptcy, the best now available, show costs significantly less than those entailed in taking a corporation public. Ritter (1987) finds that the costs of a firm-commitment offering average 14% of the gross proceeds, with a range of 9.3% for placements exceeding $10 million to 19.5% for those of less than $2 million. Private debt placements are less costly, but a bankruptcy auction is more like the sale of equity—for the debtholders in bankruptcy have the residual claims, and the failure of the firm to pay its debts implies substantial risk concerning the success of its future operations. High variability means high costs of sale, for potential buyers rationally spend more evaluating the firm's prospects and determining whether changes can improve them. Variability is especially high when the value of a firm is linked closely to its managers' human capital. Managers of firms going public or involved in LBOs usually promise to stay and often are tied by golden handcuffs—stock, often subject to formulaic buy-sell agreements (the departing manager gets only book value for the stock); if the manager is allowed to sell the stock, any diminution in value attributable to the manager's departure will be reflected in the lower price realized. Managers of firms in bankruptcy are not tied to the firm in this fashion (their stock probably is worthless), and as Gilson (1990) shows, are likely to depart.

Auctions of bankrupt firms may well be more costly than IPOs. Although, as Baird (1986, pp. 137–138) observes, flourishing and failed firms may hire the same investment banks to sell the assets, different people set the reservation price and decide when to sell. The residual claimants, who bear the costs of the auction and collect the marginal dollar of receipts, have the right incentives to make decisions about timing and minimum price. When a firm is sound, the equity investors hold the residual claims and make the decisions through the managers. The fabled conflict between debt and equity claimants is a last-period problem. See Easterbrook (1991). When the firm is in default, the managers may still be in control, but the equity claimants they represent no longer hold the residual claims. If the firm's prospects are volatile, shareholders will want the managers to delay, in the hope of selling when the price is high. On average, however, delay will be costly. Equity claimants have reason to wait too long and to set unrealistic reservation prices, for their claims are worthless unless something unexpectedly good happens. Immediate sale at a realistic price wipes them out; debt claimants bear any erosion of value during a delay, yet have fixed claims and so do not realize the full gain if things turn out well. This is the standard conflict between debt and equity claims, and as usual is substantially aggravated during times of financial distress, when the equity claim is worth little.

A bankruptcy judge could cure the problem by assigning to the residual claimant not only the right to run the auction but also the obligation to do so within a short time. But this is not possible until the bankruptcy process begins, and managers, knowing that court means a prompt end to their powers, may delay inefficiently before commencing the case [White (1989, pp. 149–150)]. What's more, how does a judge identify the residual claimant when there are several layers of debt? To do this the judge must know the firm's value—yet the superiority of market over judicial processes in pricing the firm's assets is the impetus for holding an auction. It is not particularly useful to have *both* a judicial and a market valuation process for the same corporation. This means that the court should not itself try to run an auction; how is a judge to set a reservation price intelligently? Not by hiring an investment bank to determine a 'fair price' for the assets. Small changes in assumptions about the discount rate and the income stream produce spectacular differences in bankers' estimates of value [Bebchuk and Kahan (1989)], and the judge has no way to evaluate the wisdom of the bankers' assumptions. If instead of trying to value the assets the judge invites one group of investors to buy the entitlement to resell the firm as a unit, this is an auction by another name, and it does not solve the question who is to determine timing and reservation price.

In comparing the costs of market and judicial valuation, it is important to understand that bankruptcy values the claims as well as the assets. A substantial portion of the measured costs of bankruptcy would exist even if the assets were sold immediately, and the judge dealt only with a pot of cash. Proceedings such as the Manville and Robins bankruptcies were devoted principally to determining the value of contingent claims held by persons injured by the firm's products. Other cases require valuation of the costs of cleaning up toxic wastes, or of contentions that the debtor committed fraud. Whether the debtor can recover payments made to creditors before bankruptcy (preferences), whether a given debt arises out of a valid contract, and so on, are questions that must be answered by a court even if all assets turn to cash on day one. It is beneficial to resolve in a single forum the extent and priority of all claims to the firm's wealth. Here lie the principal costs of the process, making the comparison between bankruptcy and IPOs unduly favorable to IPOs. If bankruptcy does well even in such a comparison, it is understandable why there has not been an outcry for a better way.

Bankruptcy is a backup. When auctions are superior, creditors will arrange for them in or out of bankruptcy; when they are more expensive, the legal system supplies the method of writing down investments. All investors gain from an agreement to use the more efficient method. Holdouts may prevent the realization of gains from choosing the superior method, and because there are many creditors, holdouts could be a serious problem. Yet the 1978 code makes it hard for a small number of creditors to hold out. The code allows a class to compromise its claims by majority vote (two-thirds by value). That rule influences the bargains that can be struck outside of bankruptcy. Solitary holdouts no longer may play the role of spoilers, so it is more likely that creditors as a group will be able to take advantage of superior nonbankruptcy alternatives. When we see creditors resort to bankruptcy, they are telling us that the legal process is superior to market methods available to them.

Consider another possibility: the absence of auctions in bankruptcy may be attributable not to any comparative advantage of the legal process but to the infrequent bankruptcy of public corporations. Current legal processes may be adequate for closely held firms but inferior for larger entitles. Now that bankruptcy of well-known firms (Texaco, Eastern Airlines, Federated Stores) is more common, creditors may demand a change in the statute. A competing explanation is that bankruptcy of large firms is more common because with the 1978 code bankruptcy became more attractive in comparison with other devices for dealing with financial distress: workouts, mergers, and so on. I am not so sure that bankruptcy of public corporations *is* more common; railroad bankruptcies in particular have hogged judicial time for more than 100 years. But if it is, an efficiency explanation is at least as attractive as an oversight explanation. Survival will distinguish the two, and it will be interesting to see whether in the coming decades the law moves toward a preference for market over judicial valuation of corporate assets.

References

Baird, Douglas G., 1986, The uneasy case for corporate reorganization, *Journal of Legal Studies* 15, 127–147.

Bebchuk, Lucian Arye, 1988, A new approach to corporate reorganizations, *Harvard Law Review* 101, 775–804.

Bebchuk, Lucian Arye and Marcel Kahan, 1989, Fairness opinions: How fair are they and what can be done about it?, *Duke Law Journal* 1989, 27–53.

Easterbrook, Frank H., 1991, High-yield debt as an incentive device. *International Review of Law and Economics*, forthcoming.

Gilson, Stuart C., 1990, Bankruptcy, boards, banks, and blockholders, *Journal of Financial Economics.*

Gilson, Stuart C., Kose John, and Larry H.P. Lang, 1990, Troubled debt restructurings: An empirical study of private reorganizations of firms in default, *Journal of Financial Economics.*

Ritter, Jay R., 1987, The costs of going public, *Journal of Financial Economics* 19, 269–281.

Roe, Mark J., 1983, Bankruptcy and debt: A new model for corporate reorganizations, *Columbia Law Review* 83, 527–602.

Weiss, Lawrence A., 1990, Bankruptcy resolution: Direct costs and violation of priority of claims, *Journal of Financial Economics*, this volume.

White, Michelle J., 1989, The corporate bankruptcy decision, *Journal of Economic Perspectives* 3, 129–151.

Questions

1. *Bankruptcy* is a legal declaration of financial distress that places the company under court supervision. What is the purpose of bankruptcy?
2. Under the *absolute priority rule*, common shareholders receive nothing until senior claimants are completely satisfied. However, the rule may be broken in practice. What incentives do senior claimants have to agree to payments to common shareholders when not required by law?
3. Identify examples of *direct* and *indirect* costs of bankruptcy.
4. In what way would an auction assist a bankruptcy judge? What decisions remain after the auction?
5. "Enduring legal institutions endure either because they are efficient or because they redistribute wealth to concentrated, politically effective interest groups...Market [auctions] versus hypothetical valuation in bankruptcy has no redistributive effect. Who would be the winners and losers?" Explain the arguments against the redistribution of wealth—caused by existing bankruptcy practices—among creditors and to lawyers.
6. What is the relevance of the cost of IPOs (initial public offerings) in the discussion of bankruptcy efficiency?
7. In your opinion, are judicial valuations of corporate assets in bankruptcy more efficient than auction valuations? Explain.

Bankruptcy as a Deliberate Strategy: Theoretical Considerations and Empirical Evidence

WILBUR N. MOULTON AND HOWARD THOMAS

Over the past decade, since the implementation of the Bankruptcy Reform Act of 1978, there has been a growing perception that deliberate bankruptcy can be used by managers as an effective strategy for dealing with financial distress. In a recent article in this Journal by Flynn and Farid (1991: 73) state 'Chapter XI (sic) can be used as a strategic alternative to realign the organization with its strategic competencies with a higher probability of reemerging from bankruptcy as a revitalized organization.' We believe that this view is oversimplistic and overoptimistic.[1] In this paper we will present evidence that bankruptcy reorganizations are not a simple matter, and that the probability of successful outcomes is low. A critical difference between Flynn and Farid's view and ours revolves around the issue of managerial control. The complexity of the bankruptcy process severely limits mangerial control, which in turn makes the achievement of reorganization objectives difficult.

The first part of this paper will deal with the costs and benefits of bankruptcy process, the second part will provide empirical data on the extent to which bankruptcy reorganizations are successful, and the final part will use materials

---

At the time of this writing, Wilbur N. Moulton taught at the College of Business Administration at the University of Toledo, Toledo, OH. Howard Thomas taught at the College of Commerce and Business Administration at the University of Illinois, Champaign, IL.

[1] The article by Flynn and Farid (1991) also suffers from their use of titles and provisions of the old Bankruptcy Act, which was replaced by a new Bankruptcy Code under the Bankruptcy Reform Act of 1978. A standard source for legal information on the Bankruptcy Code and Rules is the *Collier Bankruptcy Manual* (King, 1981). A good source for financial and accounting information is *Bankruptcy and Insolvency Accounting*. 3rd ed. (Newton, 1985 and Supplements).

from the first two parts to reflect on the possibilities and limitations of bankruptcy as a deliberate strategy. In presenting our views we will not attempt to make a point-by-point critique of Flynn and Farid, but rather we will attempt to identify important points on which we share their views and those on which we differ.

Much of the following discussion is directed toward providing a counterpoint to the bankruptcy propositions of Flynn and Farid (1991), but it is not limited to that particular point of view. Our conclusions are based in part on our own empirical research, and in part on the pioneering work on bankruptcy by D'Aveni (1989a, 1989b), Hambrick and D'Aveni (1988), and more recent work by Bradley and Rosenzweig (1992), Gilson (1989, 1990), Weiss (1990), White (1989), Wruck (1990), and others. We also want to stress that our conclusions are based on studies of bankruptcy and reorganization of relatively large, publicly-traded firms, and may have limited applicability to small businesses or entrepreneurial ventures.

Bankruptcy as a Deliberate Strategy

It is not possible to evaluate the benefits of any public policy or business strategy without explicitly or implicitly defining the objectives of the policy or strategy, and in the case of conflicting objectives, without setting priorities among the objectives. The primary purposes of bankruptcy are the rehabilitation of debtors, the protection of creditors, and the promotion of the general welfare. These are worthy purposes, and bankruptcy has stood the test of time as a useful public policy in the United States and around the world. It is difficult to evaluate the magnitude and distribution of the costs and benefits of the bankruptcy process, but in the following sections we highlight some important issues for a diverse set of stakeholders.

Benefits of the Bankruptcy Process

Flynn and Farid (1991: 64) never explicitly define the objectives they urge managers to pursue, but they seem to implicitly equate organizational survival with success. For example, they write: 'The expectation is that these firms emerge from this protection to fulfill contractual relationships.' Similarly, Bradley and Rosenzweig (1992) and many other lawyers (*ABI Newsletter*, 1992) contend that Congress, in writing the Bankruptcy Reform Act of 1978, believed that in cases of financial distress the general welfare was usually best served by corporate reorganizations under the control of incumbent managers. This belief was based on the assumptions that the causes of financial distress were largely exogenous, and that corporate assets and employment tended to be firm-specific. On this basis the primary benefits of bankruptcy should be organizational survival and asset preservation. However, a statement of intent provides no assurance that the objectives will be achieved. In the empirical section of this paper we present evidence that these objectives are frequently not achieved.

Neither the protection of creditors nor the promotion of the general welfare is recognized as a benefit of bankruptcy in Flynn and Farid (1991), although others (Jackson, 1986; Bradley and Rosenzweig, 1992) give both objectives high priority. In fact the advantages to owners and managers which Flynn and Farid seek to achieve can come only at the expense of others.

Costs of the Bankruptcy Process

If bankruptcy provides the benefits attributed to it, it would be unrealistic to assume that those benefits are costless. A major weakness in the Flynn and Farid (1991) study is the lack of any consideration of bankruptcy costs. While the authors do recognize that an attempted reorganization may not succeed, or the firm may emerge with diminished assets, their primary emphasis is on organizational survival.

Bankruptcy has both direct and indirect costs. Direct costs are primarily administrative and include such items as professional fees, court costs, document preparation, and communications with investors and creditors. Existing research estimates of the direct costs of the debtor firms are in the range from 3 percent of liabilities for large firms that were reorganized to more than 20 percent for small firms that were liquidated (Weiss, 1990; White, 1983).

The indirect bankruptcy costs for both debtors and creditors are almost certainly larger than direct costs, but they are much more difficult to estimate. Increases in the costs of doing business may arise from reduced bargaining power over suppliers, higher interest rates for lines of credit, and an inability to enter into long-term commitments of any sort.

Bankruptcy costs are not limited to financial costs. Bankruptcy has always had a stigma associated with it (Sutton and Callahan, 1987), although some contend that the stigma has been diminished in the current environment (Sherman, 1991). In his study of management turnover in 69 bankrupt firms Gilson (1989) found that 71 percent of the senior managers turned over during the 4-year period centered on the bankruptcy filing date, and every senior executive departing a bankrupt firm either left the executive labor market or moved to a subordinate position in another firm. Much of the Flynn and Farid (1991) agenda focuses on reducing stigma effects, but again the evidence suggests that those efforts will not be very successful.

Intentional or Strategic Bankruptcies

The Bankruptcy Code clearly distinguishes between voluntary bankruptcies initiated by the debtor and involuntary bankruptcies initiated by creditors, but any other classification is a matter of perception. Any voluntary bankruptcy is by definition 'intentional', although the action may be taken to avoid any involuntary petition by creditors. It has been popular for a number of years to label certain bankruptcies as 'strategic', but there is no generally accepted definition of 'strategic bankruptcies.' The general implication is that a bankruptcy is strategic if it is initiated by one stakeholder at the expense of others (Delaney, 1992). D'Aveni's

(1989a) and Flynn and Farid's (1991) 'intentional bankruptcies' fit this description, but they focus rather narrowly on managerially-initiated bankruptcies. As Delaney points out, strategic bankruptcies can also be initiated by creditors. The common element in most examples of 'strategic bankruptcies' is at least the perception that they are invoked to deal with a single problem, such as labor contracts or product liability claims. Alternately a creditor may initiate bankruptcy to protect an individual claim at the expense of other creditors. However, in any case a single large claim can severely affect the interests of a wide variety of stakeholders as the firm seeks to allocate the costs of a settlement of that large claim.

The enthusiasm for strategic bankruptcy has developed with little evidence to its value, even as a survival mechanism. Not only is there a lack of systematic data, but the anecdotal evidence is largely limited to a few cases, most notably the 1983 Continental Airlines bankruptcy. Continental Airlines did use bankruptcy to unilaterally reject its labor contracts, but that occurred before the Bankruptcy Act was amended in 1984 to provide more protection for employees. Manville and A. H. Robins, both of which were driven into bankruptcy by product liability claims, have also been cited as additional cases of strategic bankruptcies. As we will discuss in greater detail in the results section of this paper, both met with limited success.

Timing of Bankruptcy Filings

Discussions about the effect of the timing of bankruptcy presents problems equally difficult as those about intentionality. Flynn and Farid (1991) conclude on the basis of theory and anecdotal data that accelerated filing is generally preferred to delayed filings under conditions of high adversity and low slack, conditions which make bankruptcy imminent.

Sirower (1991) has shown, using event studies, that bankruptcy filing increases shareholder returns, at least in the short run, and he concludes that bankruptcy can be an effective strategy for troubled firms. However, no information was provided about how long the firms had been in decline or how critical their financial condition had become, so one cannot say whether the filings were early or late. All of which is to suggest that in an efficient market investors are aware of the firm's decline, and the primary uncertainty is the timing of the managerial response. The results are consistent with the general observation that in most adverse circumstances (such as divestments and accounting adjustments) the market values action over inaction. However, it should be noted that the market does not always reward bankruptcy filings. In the case of the Texaco-Pennzoil dispute, the market value of Texaco and Pennzoil both declined by over 10 percent the day after Texaco filed for bankruptcy.

The question of whether to accelerate or delay bankruptcy filing obscures a more fundamental dilemma. Bankruptcy is a costly and painful experience, which any rational firm would prefer to avoid, but like many curative processes, if the action is inevitable, prompt action is preferable to delay. As D'Aveni (1989b; 1135) writes, 'Using tactics to delay bankruptcy may be a useful strategy if there is any hope for improvement in any of the regulatory, economic or competitive conditions facing the firm.' The circumstances under which Flynn and Farid (1991) recommend delayed filings can be seen as circumstances in which there is still a possibility that bankruptcy can be avoided. What are seen by outside observers as delayed filings are probably failed attempts to avoid bankruptcy. Although the situation is complicated by the diversity of their interests, the same conclusion can be drawn about involuntary filings by creditors.

Our discussion about the timing of bankruptcy filing to this point has been based on an overall firm perspective, but, in practice, timing may be determined more by stakeholder preferences than by concern for the firm's wealth maximization. Stakeholder preferences will be determined not only by their wealth calculations, but also by their risk preferences. Well-secured creditors, whom one would expect to be risk-averse, may well prefer early bankruptcy, and perhaps even liquidation. However, managers, whose interests may be only marginally affected by the extent of overall firm wealth preservation, may prefer high-risk survival strategies to early bankruptcies (Kahneman and Tversky, 1979). Given managers' control over both information and action, delayed filings may represent opportunistic behavior on their part rather than pursuit of firm wealth preservation.

Now that we have addressed the conceptual problems in Flynn and Farid, the validity of their analysis and recommendations remains to be questioned. To that end, we next present the results of an empirical study of 73 bankruptcy reorganization cases.

Empirical Evidence

Data Collection

As part of a continuing research project on business failure we have collected data on the reorganization attempts of a sample of 73 publicly-traded firms which filed bankruptcy under Chapter 11 of the Bankruptcy Code in the period from 1980 through 1986. Financial and other service companies (SIC Code 6000 and higher) and regulated public utilities were excluded from the sample. In selecting the sample, two additional requirements were (1) that the firm was on the Compustat files with complete annual report data for 6 years prior to filing for bankruptcy, and (2) that the firm had entered formal bankruptcy proceedings after January 1, 1980, the first full year after the effective date of the Bankruptcy Reform Act of 1978. All of the firms were listed on national stock exchanges prior to their bankruptcy: 24 on the NYSE, 23 on the ASE, and 26 on NASDAQ. All 73 cases were voluntary bankruptcies filed as Chapter 11 Reorganizations. Some, but not all, of the reported liquidations followed conversion to Chapter 7 Liquidation cases. No known bankruptcy within the study period was excluded on any basis other than not meeting the data requirements described above.

The reorganization data were collected from many publicly available sources, including *Compustat, Standard & Poor's Corporate Reports, Moody's Manuals, Ward's Directory, The Wall Street Journal,* and firm annual reports and 10-Ks.

Postbankruptcy information was difficult to obtain for many of the firms, particularly the smaller ones. Many of the smaller firms were delisted by the stock exchanges when they filed for bankruptcy, and, in some cases, prior to the filing. When the firms were delisted, they were usually also dropped from the common reporting services, such as Standard and Poor's and Moody's.

Bankruptcy Reorganization Outcomes

At the present time (September 1992) 72 of the 73 firms have completed the bankruptcy process, with only LTV Corporation still in bankruptcy.[2] The earliest reorganization was completed in 1980, the same year as the earliest bankruptcy. The time required for reorganization varied from 6 to 83 months with an average of 27 months.

The reorganization outcomes were classified according to the following four categories:

1. *Successful reorganizations:* firms which maintained their corporate identities, continued as publicly traded firms on national stock exchanges, and had postreorganization assets of more than 50 percent of prebankruptcy levels.
2. *Partially successful reorganizations:* firms which maintained their corporate identities, but which failed to meet one or more of the other qualifications stipulated for classification as successful reorganizations.
3. *Mergers or acquisitions:* firms which were publicly reported as being acquired by previously existing firms.
4. *Liquidations:* firms which were publicly reported as liquidated or which had no identifiable successor business.

Classifying the successful reorganizations was unambiguous, but classifications according to the other three categories were frequently problematic. Some of the reorganizations classified as partially successful were technically liquidations in which assets were transferred and the business continued by a new firm created for that purpose. In those cases in which there was a clearly identified new successor company, the outcome was classified as a reorganization.

The firms studied and their outcomes are listed in the Appendix. The outcome classifications were based on the circumstances surrounding the firms at the end of the reorganization process. Later events and current status, to the extent that they are known, are shown in the Notes section of the Appendix table. Of the 72 bankrupt firms, only 44 (61%) were reorganized, and of those 44 only 15 emerged with more than 50 percent of their prebankruptcy assets. Of the 15

[2] At the time this paper was written LTV Corporation was still in bankruptcy. Based on available reorganization plan projections the reorganization will meet our criteria for classification as successful, but the case was not used for any of the quantitative analyses.

that were reorganized with more than 50 percent of prebankruptcy assets, the postbankruptcy assets averaged 92 percent of prebankruptcy assets. Of the 29 that were reorganized with less than 50 percent of prebankruptcy assets the postbankruptcy assets averaged 24 percent of prebankruptcy assets. Three of the 15 firms whose reorganizations were classified as successful, and 6 of the 29 classified as partially successful, have suffered repeat bankruptcies. Only 6 of the 15 firms originally classified as successful reorganizations, and 12 of the 29 partially successful reorganizations, continued to meet the original success criteria in 1992.

Bankruptcy Reorganization Outcome Predictors[3]

Given the outcome results, the next logical question is what factors determine those outcomes or can be used to predict the outcomes. Potential predictors of reorganization outcomes were identified using a number of variables and a range of statistical techniques including ANOVA with Tukey comparison of means and stepwise multidiscriminant analysis techniques. The variables which showed statistically significant mean differences were used as predictors in multivariate discriminant analysis. Among the variables tested only *size* and the *rate of decline* exhibited significant differences between outcome groups. Insignificant results were obtained using financial performance measures (both univariate ratios and multivariate bankruptcy prediction scores), length of time in bankruptcy, and other variables. The natural log of total assets at the end of the last fiscal year before bankruptcy proved to be the best measure of size with an overall ANOVA F value of 6.88 ($p < 0.001$). The liquidated firms with a mean of $59 million in assets were significantly smaller than the firms in the other three groups, and there were no significant differences among those groups. Other size-related measures, such as sales, were closely correlated with total assets and gave significant, but slightly inferior, results.

The second significant predictor of bankruptcy outcomes was the *rate of decline of the failing firm*. The rate of decline was measured by counting the number of years in which the firm had a negative net income during the 6 years prior to bankruptcy, based on the assumption that the larger the number of losing years the slower the decline. The number of years ranged from zero to six. The overall ANOVA F value was 6.37 ($p < 0.001$). The Tukey comparison of means based on ANOVA indicated that firms which were liquidated had significantly more years of negative net income than firms in the other three groups, and there were no significant differences among those groups. What we have defined as rate of decline can also be seen as a measure of lingering (Flynn and Farid, 1991) or downward spirals (Hambrick and D'Aveni, 1988). After identifying asset *size* and *rate of decline* as significant variables, we then used multiple discriminant analysis to predict outcomes. The overall prediction accuracy of 51.4 percent was not impressive, but the discriminant function was highly significant: Wilk's lambda = 0.66, $F(6, 134) = 5.09$ ($p < 0.0001$).

---

[3] Detailed information on the data and statistical analyses are available from the first author.

The results observed can be compared with broader based data reported by the Administrative Office of the United States Courts (American Bankruptcy Institute, 1991). Their report estimated that only 17 percent of the approximately 144,000 Chapter 11 filings from 1980 to 1987 would result in a confirmed reorganization plan. If those 17 percent suffer the same attrition rate after reorganization as the firms in our sample, the long-term success rate will fall below 10 percent. Their estimate of bankruptcy duration was 21.6 months compared to our finding of 26.6 months. In our study bankruptcy duration was significantly correlated with asset size (r = 0.544, $p < 0.0001$). Obviously, their large sample included many small firms, so the higher probability of reorganization and the longer duration of bankruptcy in our study of large firms is further evidence for our observed *size effects.*

Discussion

The results clearly contradict Flynn and Farid's (1991) assumption that a firm which files for bankruptcy under Chapter 11 has a high probability of achieving the joint objectives of survival and asset preservation. Only 44 firms out of 72 were nominally successful in reorganizing, but two-thirds of those retained less than 50 percent of their assets on completion of the reorganization process. Furthermore, measuring success in the year a firm emerges from bankruptcy is only the beginning of the story. Reorganized firms remain weak and many continue to decline. Only 18 of the 44 reorganizations classified successful or partially successful have been able to continue to meet the success criteria after reorganization.

Large firms had a better chance of reorganizing than small firms for both positive and negative reasons. With their large and varied assets they are better able to survive substantial losses and decreases in size than small firms. Large firms are more likely to have some successful businesses that can serve as the core for the reorganized firm, and to have assets that can be sold to provide cash for operating continuing businesses. Also, their very size makes liquidation or acquisition less likely. Whereas some investors may be willing to risk acquiring small bankrupt firms or buying their assets, few investors have, the resources to acquire billion-dollar bankrupt firms. Acquisitions and mergers of very large firms may also be constrained by antitrust considerations.

While we have no systematic information on the bankruptcy costs of the firms in our sample, low payouts to creditors and the decline in assets between filing and reorganization provide evidence that bankruptcy costs, both direct and indirect, are substantial. The worst case for indirect costs comes to firms that suspend their operations during the reorganization process. Braniff Airways conducted no flight operations during its reorganization and emerged with only 7 percent of its prebankruptcy assets. Continental Airlines, which was quite similar in size and bankruptcy performance, resumed operations within a week and increased its assets by 37 percent during reorganization. However, neither firm regained its financial health and both suffered repeat bankruptcies.

As pointed out in the introductory part of this paper, the common element in most examples of 'strategic bankruptcies' is the perception that they are invoked to deal with a single problem, such as labor contracts or product liability claims. However, we found that firms that filed for bankruptcy to resolve a single problem had about as much difficulty in reorganizing as firms suffering more general distress. Continental Airlines used bankruptcy to unilaterally reject, its labor contracts, but it had other serious financial problems. Although Continental was reorganized with its assets intact, repercussions of its bankruptcy strategy contributed to its continuing decline and its second bankruptcy four years later. While Frank Lorenzo retained control of Continental through the first bankruptcy, his reputation became a major factor in Continental's second bankruptcy, as well as in Eastern Airlines' bankruptcy following its acquisition by Continental, and he was ultimately driven from the industry. In at least two product liability cases, bankruptcy proved to be relatively unsuccessful. A. H. Robins, which had incurred huge product liabilities for the Dalkon Shield, was unable to reorganize and was acquired by American Home Products. Manville was reorganized only after its management was ousted and most of its ownership was transferred to the asbestos liability claimants. Manville is now under going a non-bankruptcy restructuring largely motivated by a desire to reduce its bankruptcy stigma.

The Flynn and Farid (1991) strategy recommendations are clearly debtor biased; they are recipes for maintaining managerial control. They are also consistent with the doctrine that the primary obligation of managers is to maximize shareholder wealth. We believe that is too narrow a view of managerial responsibility, especially for firms in which shareholder wealth has been extinguished before the bankruptcy filing. Even if the motivation were proper, we believe that the proposed strategies are based on unrealistic assumptions about the bankruptcy process. Most importantly they are overly optimistic about the probability of reorganization. They are also unrealistic about the extent of managerial control during bankruptcy. For example, it is unrealistic to expect that a firm could conceal a bankruptcy filing or that 'Chapter XI provides a business with an opportunity to solve a financial crisis with little intervention from the courts or creditors' (Flynn and Farid, 1991: 64). A very different perspective has been expressed by Sol Stein, founder and CEO of Stein and Day Publishers, who describes the bankruptcy of his firm in the following terms, 'For the leaders of business trapped in it, Chapter 11 is the twentieth-century equivalent of the eighteenth-century pillory, a dehumanizing, inefficient public spectacle' (Stein,1989:303). Fundamentally corporate bankruptcy is a legal process for ensuring that all claimants are treated fairly when the resources of the firm are inadequate to meet the claims on it in full, and when the individual claimants cannot reach a mutually satisfactory resolution of these claims. The Bankruptcy code provides that, once bankruptcy is declared, all actions by management and creditors are under the jurisdiction of the bankruptcy court, a matter of public record, and subject to review by all interested parties. As a result, managerial control may be severely limited, and the narrow objectives of strategic bankruptcy are unlikely to be achieved.

While our evidence clearly demonstrates the low success rate of bankruptcy, it provides little direct evidence on the question of bankruptcy timing. Flynn and Farid (1991) conclude, on the basis of theory and anecdotal data, that accelerated filing is generally preferred to delayed filing under conditions of high adversity and low slack, conditions which make bankruptcy imminent. In our study we found that firms with longer histories of decline were more likely to be liquidated than those with shorter periods of decline, but it is not clear that the timing of the filings was a critical factor. Slow declines appeared to be associated with environmental stress, while more rapid declines were associated with firm-specific events. This evidence, reinforced by the case evidence, suggests that the critical issue is not the relative advantages of early vs. delayed filing, but rather that bankruptcy is the strategy of last resort. The hope that bankruptcy can be avoided overrides the knowledge that delay will only make reorganization more difficult, if bankruptcy becomes inevitable.

If bankruptcy is a costly mechanism for resolving conflicts over the assets of financially distressed firms, then negotiated settlements should be less costly. In complex cases with multiple creditors, negotiated financial restructurings (Gilson, John, and Lang, 1990) and liquidations (Kim and Schatzberg, 1987) may be lower-cost alternatives, but they may be difficult to achieve. A recent development is the 'prepackaged bankruptcy,' in which the reorganization plan is negotiated with major creditors before the bankruptcy filing (Light, 1991; Morgenstern and Rubin, 1991; Saggese and Ranney-Marinelli, 1991). This reduces the cost and duration of the reorganization process and retains the advantages of legal bankruptcy. Bradley and Rosenzweig's (1992) widely discussed proposals for bankruptcy reform are designed to similarly shorten the process, but they take a much harsher position on limiting equity holders' control and on the early ousting of incumbent managers.

If there are less costly alternatives, the question becomes why do firms choose bankruptcy? The answers are the same as for any use of coercive action in conflict resolution: the threat must remain credible, the conflicting parties may misinterpret each other's intentions and actions, and psychological factors, such as pride, take precedence over economic rationality. These considerations would appear to be most pertinent in single-issue bankruptcies, such as the Texaco case. In complex cases with multiple stakeholders, the application of an external set of rules and procedures under the jurisdiction of a neutral third party, the Bankruptcy Court, facilitates conflict resolution and reduces opportunism. An important element of those rules is the freeze on all unilateral actions by creditors once bankruptcy is declared. After the bankruptcy declaration, reorganizations require a lower level of unanimity than voluntary restructurings, in which a minority claimant may be able to block an entire restructuring. They also require broader and more uniform distribution of information than voluntary restructurings. In addition, bankruptcy may have tax advantages, and it may allow the preservation of a corporate charter, which may have value even without a productive set of assets.

Conclusions

Every bankruptcy case represents some form of business failure that is costly to all stakeholders, although those losses are not evenly distributed. Legal bankruptcy is a settling-up process designed to equitably allocate those losses using a well-established and publicly-controlled process, but the process is costly and time-consuming with a relatively low probability of successfully rehabilitating the bankrupt firm. Cooperative settling up processes, especially those that avoid legal bankruptcy, minimize the losses associated with failure, yet legal bankruptcy may remain the best defense against uncooperative, opportunistic stakeholders.

With regard to the timing of bankruptcy filing, we take the position that bankruptcy is a costly strategy and should be avoided whenever possible. However, if it cannot be avoided, accelerated filing is preferable to delayed filing. We believe these propositions are true for both debtors and creditors. The dilemma for decision makers is determining when the costs and risks of avoiding bankruptcy outweigh the costs of bankruptcy. Understanding the strategic decision in this way should encourage all stakeholders to accept more negotiated costs to avoid bankruptcy.

From a broader perspective, we believe that a proper understanding of the bankruptcy process and of the costs and benefits bankruptcy will assist all participants in the process of finding strategies that will maximize value preservation and reduce the pain for all. We believe that cooperative models are more socially responsible and, in the long run, more profitable than the adversarial model presented by Flynn and Farid (1991).

References

American Bankruptcy Institute (1991). *Bankruptcy Statistical Information*, American Bankruptcy Institute, Washington, DC.

American Bankruptcy Institute (May 1992). 'ABI roundtable: Should Chapter 11 be scrapped', *ABI Newsletter*, **XI**, pp. 1–8 (insert).

Bradley, M. and M. Rosenzweig (1992). 'The untenable case for Chapter 11', *The Yale Law Journal*, **101**, pp. 1043–1095.

D'Aveni, R.A. (1989a). 'The aftermath of organizational decline: A longitudinal study of the strategic and managerial characteristics of declining firms', *Academy of Management Journal*, **32**, pp. 577–605.

D'Aveni, R.A. (1989b). 'Dependability and organizational bankruptcy: An application of agency and prospect theory', *Management Science*, **35**, pp. 1120–1138.

Delaney, K.J. (1992). *Strategic Bankruptcy: How Corporations and Creditors use Chapter 11 to Their Advantage.* University of California Press, Berkeley, CA.

Flynn, D.M. and M. Farid (1991). 'The intentional use of Chapter XI: Lingering versus immediate filing', *Strategic Management Journal*, **12**, pp. 63–74.

Gilson, S.C. (1990). 'Bankruptcy, boards, banks, and blockholders', *Journal of Financial Economics*, **25**, pp. 355–387.

Gilson, S.C. (1989). 'Management turnover and financial distress', *Journal of Financial Economics*, **25**, pp. 241–262.

Gilson, S.C., K. John and L.H.P. Lang (1990). 'Troubled debt restructurings', *Journal of Financial Economics*, **27**, pp. 315–353.

Hambrick, D.C. and R.A. D'Aveni (1988). 'Large corporate failures as downward spirals', *Administrative Science Quarterly*, **33**, pp. 1–23.

Jackson, T.H. (1986). *The Logic and Limits of Bankruptcy Law*, Harvard University Press, Cambridge, MA.

Kahneman, D. and A. Tversky (1979). 'Prospect theory: An analysis of decision under risk', *Econometrica*, **47**, pp. 263–291.

King, L.P. (ed.) (1991). *Collier Bankruptcy Manual*, Matthew Bender, Albany, NY.

Kim, E.H. and J.D. Schatzberg (1987). 'Voluntary corporate liquidations', *Journal of Financial Economics*, **19**, pp. 311–328.

Light, L. (29 April 1991). 'Quickie bankruptcies: Speed isn't everything', *Business Week*, pp. 72–73.

Morgenstern, P.D. and K.L. Rubin (July/August 1991). 'The prepackaged bankruptcy: Restructuring troubled credit', *The Secured Lender*, **47**, pp. 24, 26.

Newton, G.W. (1985). *Bankruptcy and Insolvency Accounting* (3rd ed.), Wiley, New York (and Annual Supplements).

Saggese, N.P. and A. Ranney-Marinelli (1991). *A Practical Guide to Out-of-Court Restructurings and Prepackaged Plans of Reorganization.* Prentice Hall Law and Business, Englewood Cliffs, NJ.

Sherman, S.P. (3 June 1991). 'Bankruptcy's spreading blight', *Fortune*, pp. 123–132.

Sirower, M. (1991). 'Bankruptcy as a strategic planning tool', *Best Papers Proceedings: Academy of Management*, Miami Beach, FL, pp. 46–50.

Stein, S. (1989). *A Feast for Lawyers: Inside Chapter 11: An Exposé*, M. Evans and Company. Inc., New York.

Sutton, R.I. and A.L. Callahan (1987). 'The stigma of bankruptcy. Spoiled organizational image and its management', *Academy of Management Review*, **30**, pp. 405–436.

Weiss, L.A. (1990). 'Bankruptcy resolution: Direct costs and violation of priority of claims', *Journal of Financial Economics*, **27**, pp. 285–314.

White, M.J. (1989). 'The corporate bankruptcy decision', *Journal of Economic Perspectives*, **3**(2), pp. 129–151.

White, M.J. (1983). 'Bankruptcy costs and the new bankruptcy code', *Journal of Finance*, XXVIII, pp. 477–488.

Wruck, K.H. (1990). 'Financial distress, reorganization, and organizational efficiency', *Journal of Financial Economics*, **27**, pp. 419–444.

Appendix: Bankrupt Firms and Outcomes

SUCCESSFUL REORGANIZATIONS (n = 15)

Firm	Bankruptcy In	Bankruptcy Out	Present status
AM International Inc	1982	1984	NYSE
Continental Airlines Inc	1983	1986	ASE, bankrupt again 1990
Data Access Systems Inc	1983	1984	NASDAQ
Leisure Dynamics Inc	1983	1983	Acquired by Coleco 1986
Lionel Corp	1982	1985	ASE, bankrupt again 1991
Manville Corp	1982	1989	NYSE
Phoenix Steel Corp	1983	1985	Private
Poloron Products Inc	1981	1983	OTC
Revere Copper & Brass Inc	1982	1985	Private (Revere Copper Co.)
Robintech Inc	1983	1984	No record 1991
Salant Corp	1985	1987	NYSE, bankrupt again in 1990
Storage Technology Corp	1984	1987	NYSE
UNR Industries Inc	1982	1986	NASDAQ
Wheeling-Pittsburgh Steel	1985	1991	NYSE
Wickes Cos Inc	1982	1984	Private (WCI Holdings, Inc.)

PARTIALLY SUCCESSFUL REORGANIZATIONS (n = 29)

Firm	Bankruptcy In	Bankruptcy Out	Notes, Present status
Amfesco Industries Inc	1985	1988	Bankrupt again 1989 (New American Shoe Company)
Anglo Energy Ltd-cl A	1983	1986	ASE (Nabors Industries)
Argo Petroleum	1986	1987	NASDAQ (Fortune Petroleum Co.)
Berry Industries Corp	1984	1986	No record 1991
Bobbie Brooks Inc	1982	1983	NASDAQ
Braniff International Corp	1982	1983	Bankrupt again 1989 and 1991
CS Group Inc	1982	1983	Bankrupt again 1989
Charter Co	1984	1987	NYSE
Continental Steel Corp-Del	1980	1982	Bankrupt again 1985
Cook United Inc	1984	1986	Bankrupt again 1987
Eastmet Corp	1986	1988	No record 1991
Flame Industries Inc	1983	1985	No record 1991
Garland Corp-Cl a	1980	1980	Private
Gilman Services Inc	1982	1985	No record 1991
Global Marine Inc	1986	1988	NYSE
K-TEL International	1984	1986	OTC
Marion CORP	1983	1986	No record 1991
Mclouth Steel Corp	1981	1984	NASDAQ, (MLX Corp.)
MEGO International	1982	1983	OTC

(Continued)

Partially Successful Reorganizations (n = 29) (continued)

Firm	Bankruptcy In	Bankruptcy Out	Notes, Present status
Mesta Machine Co	1983	1984	NYSE, (Mestek Inc)
Mobile Home Industries	1984	1986	No record 1991
Morton Shoe Cos Inc	1982	1983	No record 1991
Nucorp Energy Inc	1982	1985	NASDAQ
Pathcom Inc	1981	1983	No record 1991
Richton International Corp	1980	1981	NASDAQ
Rusco Industries Inc	1982	1983	Bankrupt again 1983
Smith International Inc	1986	1987	NYSE
Tacoma Boatbuilding Inc	1985	1989	NYSE
White Motor Corp	1980	1983	NASDAQ, (EnviroSource Inc)

Acquired by Other Firms (n = 12)

Firm	Bankruptcy In	Bankruptcy Out	Notes, Present status
Altec Corp	1983	1985	Acquired by Gulton Industries
Beker Industries	1985	1988	Acquired by NuWest Industries
Commodore Corp	1985	1986	Acquired by Great American Mgt. and Invest Inc.
KDT Industries INC	1982	1984	Acquired by Ames Department Stores (also bankrupt)
MGF Oil Corp	1984	1987	Acquired by Southmark
National Shoes Inc	1980	1985	Acquired by Shoecliff Corp.
Robins (A.H.) CO	1985	1989	Acquired by American Home Products
Saxon Industries	1982	1985	Acquired by Paper Company of America
Solomon (SAM) Inc	1980	1982	Acquired by Service Merchandise Co.
Steelmet Inc	1983	1985	Acquired by Elg Haniel Metals Corp.
Stevcoknit Inc	1981	1983	Acquired by J.P. Stevens
Towle Manufacturing Co	1986	1987	Acquired by First Republic Corp.

Liquidations (n = 16)

Firm	Bankruptcy In	Bankruptcy Out
Advent Corp	1981	1982
Auto-Train Corp	1980	1981
Barclay Industries	1981	1984

LIQUIDATIONS (n = 16) (CONTINUED)

Firm	Bankruptcy In	Out
Berven Carpets Corp	1983	1985
Branch Inds	1984	1986
Capitol Air Inc	1984	1985
Cooper-Jarrett Inc	1981	1985
Crompton Co Inc	1984	1987
Glover Inc	1980	1981
Good (L.S.) Co	1980	1980
Lynnwear Corp-cl A	1981	1983
Magic Marker Corp	1980	1981
Sambo's Restaurants	1981	1985
Tobin Packing Co Inc	1981	1984
Transcontinental Energy	1984	1985
Upson Co	1980	1984

Notes: Successful reorganizations: firms that emerged from bankruptcy with their original corporate identity, whose stocks were traded on the NYSE, ASE, or NASDAQ, and retained more than 50 percent of their bankruptcy assets. Partially successful reorganizations: firms that emerged from bankruptcy with their original corporate identity, whose stocks were traded on the NYSE, ASE, or NASDAQ, and retained less than 50 percent of their pre-bankruptcy assets. Unsuccessful reorganizations: all other firms. Present Status: Current stock exchange (OTC indicates local or regional stock exchanges) or as reported in Wards Directory (1991).

Questions

1. *Chapter 11* of the Bankruptcy Act of 1938 (as amended) addresses reorganization, the means for a debtor to restructure debts so that creditors will be treated fairly. *Chapter 7* deals with liquidation, selling the debtor's assets and distributing the cash proceeds among the creditors. Would you expect any differences between companies that file under Chapter 11 versus those that file under Chapter 7? Explain.
2. Manville Corporation's bankruptcy petition in 1982 was intended to let it grapple with $2.5 billion of asbestos-related lawsuits. At the time of filing, the company had a net worth of $1.1 billion. Texaco filed a bankruptcy petition in 1987 to protect itself from a judgment of more that $10 billion awarded to Pennzoil as a result of Texaco's $10.1 billion acquisition of Getty Oil in 1984. Texaco was found guilty of tampering with a merger agreement between Getty and Pennzoil. At the time of filing, Texaco had $34 billion of total assets and $13.7 billion of net worth. Why did Manville and Texaco file petitions for bankruptcy? After all, each company had a sizable net worth—that is, total assets exceeded total debt.
3. Which type of bankruptcy cost, direct or indirect, would you expect to be larger in most cases? Explain.
4. What are the primary differences among voluntary, involuntary, and strategic bankruptcies?
5. Explain whether it is better to accelerate or delay a bankruptcy filing from the viewpoint of well-secured creditors. Of shareholders. Of corporate executives. Of low-level employees.

6. Answer the following true-false questions based on the authors' empirical study:

    T F The time required for reorganization varied from 6 to 83 months with an average of 27 months.

    T F A.H. Robins' bankruptcy resulted in a successful reorganization.

    T F Most of the bankruptcies were filed under Chapter 11.

    T F Most of the Chapter 11 bankruptcies were successful.

    T F Small companies with a slow rate of decline tend to be Chapter 7 bankruptcies.

    T F Small companies tend to be in bankruptcy proceedings longer than large companies.

7. Sol Stein, Founder and CEO of Stein and Day Publishers, describes the bankruptcy of his company as follows: "For the leaders of business trapped in it, Chapter 11 is the twentieth-century equivalent of the eighteenth-century pillory, a dehumanizing, inefficient public spectacle." Do you think Mr. Stein's castigation of Chapter 11 is appropriate? Explain.
8. Since Chapter 11 bankruptcies are so costly, why don't claimants simply negotiate appropriate settlements?

The Globalization of World Financial Markets

Bruce G. Resnick

The term "globalization" has become the business buzzword of the eighties, and it appears likely to be the key word for describing business practices into the 1990s. The word globalization indicates international integration. It causes one to visualize firms obtaining raw materials from one national market and financial capital from another producing goods with labor and capital equipment in a third, and selling the finished product in yet other national markets.

In particular, the eighties have brought a rapid integration of international capital markets. Corporations obtain financing from major money centers around the world in many different currencies to finance their global operations. Global operations force the treasurer's office to establish international banking relationships, place short-term funds in several currency denominations, and effectively manage foreign exchange risk. Additionally, investors have begun to take advantage of the better performance potential from internationally diversified portfolios of financial assets. This article will trace the development of the global financial markets and describe the major security groups, their uses, and some emerging trends.

Background

The underlying economic implication of globalization is that profitable market opportunities exist for those with the necessary expertise. For this to be true, imperfections or inefficiencies in national product markets, factors of production, or financial markets must exist. This implies that national markets are to a degree segmented from one another even if they are locally efficient. National

---

At the time of this writing, Bruce G. Resnick was an associate professor of finance at the Indiana University School of Business. The author is grateful for comments on earlier drafts by Larry Davidson, Robert Jennings, and the guest editor, Robert Klemkosky.

Source: Reprinted from *Business Horizons,* November–December 1989.

market segmentation can persist because of a number of factors: language barriers, legal restrictions, a lack of relevant investment information, excessive tariffs or transaction costs, discriminatory taxation, political risks, and exchange rate uncertainty. If the costs of overcoming these barriers are high enough to prevent profitable international business, markets will remain segmented and the benefits arising from international trade and investment will not be captured.

Such severe segmentation is not the case, however, as is suggested by the volume of world trade and by large multinational corporations (MNCs). *Forbes* in 1988 listed the 100 largest U.S. MNCs. To qualify for the list, a corporation had to generate foreign revenues of at least $1 billion in 1987. Most of the firms are household names—Exxon, IBM, Ford, Coca-Cola, and General Electric. Many derived more than 40 percent of their total sales revenue from foreign operations and had 25 percent or more of their total assets overseas. Similarly, *Fortune* (1988) published a list of the world's 50 largest industrial corporations ranked by 1987 sales revenue. Thirty of these firms are foreign and have a major presence in the U.S. product markets—Toyota, Daimler-Benz, Volkswagen, Nestlé, Samsung, Bayer, and Honda, for example.

The growing ability of MNCs to capture market share in foreign product markets illustrates the globalization process. Aggregate statistics, however, provide a fuller and clearer picture of the extent of globalization. During the ten-year period ending in 1988, Americans increased their investment overseas by about 180 percent. During the same period, foreigners increased their investment in the United States by about 380 percent. At the end of 1988, foreign assets in the U.S. totaled $1,786 billion. Of this, $329 billion was direct investment. Of the remainder, most was invested in financial assets: U.S. corporate bonds, U.S. government securities, and claims on U.S. banks. By comparison, U.S. assets abroad registered $1,254 billion. Of this total, $327 billion was direct investment, $604 billion was in bank loans, and $157 billion was investment in foreign bonds and stocks.

These numbers tell an interesting story about the degree of globalization. First, since 1985 the U.S. has been a net international debtor nation. Second, the U.S. has about the same direct investment abroad as there is foreign direct investment in the U.S.; however, the investment is not evenly distributed. The lion's share is captured by three nations: the United Kingdom ($102 billion), Japan ($53 billion), and the Netherlands ($49 billion). On the U.S. side, three-quarters of direct investment abroad is in developed countries. The largest amount ($61 billion) is in Canada, followed by Great Britain ($48 billion) and West Germany ($22 billion). Investment in Japan accounts for only $17 billion. Direct investment by MNCs has contributed to the globalization of product and factor markets.

Of more importance, perhaps, is the flow of portfolio investment in financial assets and the amount of bank lending overseas revealed by the figures. This is important because inefficiencies in financial markets can be arbitraged much more rapidly that imperfections in product markets. Indeed, one of the major trends of the eighties has been the increasing integration of the international capital markets, caused in part by the recent liberalization of some domestic capital markets.

The globalization of product, factor, and financial markets promises to continue into the nineties. Japan has promised to adopt a more globalized economic posture. As this unfolds, the yen will play an increasing worldwide role as an international currency, in keeping with Japan's strong economic stature. Wider use of the yen will also require Tokyo's capital markets to develop greater depth and diversity, as have New York's in response to the the worldwide use of the dollar. Additionally, the nineties will bring major changes to Europe. In 1992, Europe is scheduled to create a single market. Barriers to the free flow of trade, capital, and people among the 12 members of the European Community (EEC) are to be eliminated. Ideally, Western Europe hopes this move will strengthen its economic position relative to the U.S. and Japan; it will also provide the opportunity for each country's markets to equalize in strength and operational efficiency. The potential is certainly there. Western Europe shares a common culture, a high level of education, and a high standard of living. On the other hand, deep-rooted nationalism is centuries old; even staunch Europeanists, who believe Europe will succeed in creating a unified trading market, are skeptical of the chances that Europe will be able to reach the political unity necessary to become a major global economic power. Nevertheless, 1992 will be another step along the path of globalization. This is especially true for the capital markets. In preparation for 1992, "... some 400 banks and finance firms across Europe have merged, taken shares in one another, or cooked up joint marketing ventures to sell stock, mutual funds, insurance, and other financial instruments" (Reimer, et al. 1988). Moreover, major financial institutions from the U.S., Japan, and Switzerland are establishing their own operations to capture a piece of the action.

As business becomes more global, changes in the chief executive suite will take place. Today's corporate CEO has typically started out in finance and has been trained as an accountant. He has worked his way up through a divisional controller's office, to running the division, then to the top job. The global manager of tomorrow will likely have an undergraduate liberal arts degree, a joint M.B.A./technical degree, and will have started out in research. He will have traveled extensively, be fluent in at least one foreign language, and will have held several different positions. According to Ed Dunn, corporate vice-president of Whirlpool Corporation, the global corporate chief "must have a multi-environment, multi-country, multi-functional, maybe even multi-company, multi-industry experience" (Bennett 1989).

The Eurocurrency and the Euroloans Markets

An early factor in the growth of international investment, and the world economy in general, was the development of the Eurocurrency market. A Eurocurrency is a dollar or other freely traded currency deposited in a bank outside the country of origin. The Eurocurrency market encompasses those banks that seek deposits and make loans of foreign currency.

The origin of this market can be traced back to the late fifties and early sixties, when a number of Soviet-bloc countries had accumulated a large stock of dollars as a result of trade in gold and commodities with the U.S. and European countries. Because of anti-Soviet and anti-communist sentiment in the United States, the Soviets were afraid of depositing these funds in the U.S. where they could be seized. The French bank the Soviets chose had the telex address EURO-BANK. In time, all offshore dollar deposits came to be referred to as Eurodollars, and the banks that accepted these deposits and made loans from them became Eurobanks. An Asian version of this market operates out of the money center banks of Singapore, Tokyo and Hong Kong.

The size of the Eurocurrency market has grown rapidly. In the ten-year period ending in 1987, total net deposits have increased from $478 billion to $2,377 billion. Dollar-denominated deposits account for the largest share of the market—66 percent at the end of 1987. In dollar terms of roughly $1,569 billion, this compares with a total figure of $2,376 billion held domestically in the U.S. by commercial banks and thrift institutions in savings, time, and demand deposits.

The rapid growth of this market stems in part from the demand for U.S. dollars as an international currency, in part from the lack of government regulation, and in part from the tremendous flows of "petrodollars" into international banks from the Oil Producing Export Countries during the mid-seventies and early eighties. Eurodollar deposits are not subject to Federal Reserve reserve requirements. Consequently, the deposit rate is typically higher and the borrowing rate lower compared with U.S. domestic rates.

The growth of Eurocurrency deposits has facilitated Eurodollar loans. These are made on a floating-rate basis, with the base rate being the London Interbank Offer Rate (LIBOR). LIBOR is the market rate at which a Eurobank would be willing to place a dollar deposit with another Eurobank. Commercial loans are priced at LIBOR plus a margin dependent upon the credit-worthiness of the borrower. Eurodollar and other Eurocurrency loans have helped foster international trade and short-term investment.

LIBOR, not a household word at present, soon could become one. During 1988, several U.S. lenders began issuing adjustable-rate mortgages linked to LIBOR instead of domestic indices, such as the one-year Treasury-bill rate. The push for this came from foreign banks and thrift institutions that buy mortgages in bulk and desire having assets linked to the LIBOR base they pay to raise money. LIBOR-linked loans are not a large part of the market at present, but it is estimated they could climb to 20 percent of new adjustable rate mortgages within three years.

U.S. banks currently cannot accept foreign currency deposits. However, the Federal Reserve has decided to allow foreign currency deposits effective December 31, 1989. This change should facilitate trade for small firms doing business overseas; a foreign currency deposit can be used to hedge the risk of a depreciating dollar. For the same reason, it should also prove helpful to small investors who are planning to invest in retirement or mutual funds overseas.

The International Bond Market

The international bond market gives borrowers, including multinational and domestic corporations, sovereign governments, governmental organizations and financial institutions, a source for medium and long-term funds. It also gives investors a way to diversify their portfolios over several currencies. The market can be broadly broken into Eurobonds and foreign bonds. Eurobonds are bonds denominated in one or more currencies other than the currency of the country in which they are sold. In contrast, foreign bonds are denominated in the currency of the country in which they are sold; the issuer, however, is from another country. For example, bonds denominated in yen, but sold by a Japanese firm outside of Japan, would be classified as Eurobonds—more specifically, Euroyen bonds. If the same Japanese company issued dollar-denominated bonds to investors in the U.S., they would be considered foreign bonds— more specifically, "Yankee" bonds. Many foreign bonds have colorful nicknames; foreign bonds sold in Japan are "Samurai" bonds; foreign bonds sold in the United Kingdom are "Bulldogs."

The international bond market is exceedingly large. At 1985 year end, the total nominal value of international bonds outstanding was equivalent to $499 billion, or about 8 percent of the $5,933 billion value of the entire world bond market. New issues in 1985 and 1986 were, respectively, $164.5 and $221.5 billion. The market, however, slipped after 1986 (for reasons to be discussed shortly) and registered a total of $175.6 billion in 1987.

In recent years the Eurobond segment has accounted for more than 80 percent of the total of new issues. Most trading in Eurobonds is conducted in London. The Eurobond market began in the early sixties and has grown much more rapidly than the foreign bond market. This growth is attributable to several unique features. Eurobond issues are not subject to the regulatory authorities of the country in whose currency they are denominated. Consequently, Eurobond issues can be brought to market more quickly and with less disclosure than would be required by, say, the U.S. Securities and Exchange Commission (SEC). This gives the issuer greater flexibility to take advantage of favorable market conditions. Eurobonds also offer favorable tax status. They are usually issued in bearer form, meaning the owner's name and residence are not on the bond certificate; holders desiring anonymity can thus receive interest payments without revealing their identity. Additionally, interest on Eurobond not generally subject to an income withholding tax. These two features facilitate tax avoidance and, as one might guess, tax evasion.

Because of their unique features, investors are willing to accept a lower yield from Eurobonds than from securities of comparable risk but lacking the favorable tax status. Nevertheless, name recognition of the borrower and an impeccable credit rating are important to successful issuance in the Eurobond market. The lower yield translates into a cost savings for the borrower. Historically, for example, highest-quality Eurodollar bonds could be issued at a lower rate than the market yield on similar maturity U.S. Treasury bonds.

The largest part of the Eurobond market has historically been and remains today Eurodollar bonds. In 1982, more than 85 percent of the value of new issues was dollar denominated. This figure fell to about 40 percent in 1987, a main reason for what has been termed the slump in the Eurobond market. Examination of the statistics suggests this decline is primarily a dollar problem. Between 1986 and 1987, new issues of non-dollar Eurobonds increased from $69.7 billion to $83.8 billion; Eurodollar bonds declined from $118.1 to $56.7 billion. One reason for the decline in new issues of Eurodollar bonds is the dollar's weakness over the last couple of years. When foreign investors wish to diversify out of dollar denominated assets, the Eurodollar bond market will be one of the first hit. Other reasons relate to regulatory changes in the U.S. making domestic dollar bonds relatively more attractive. In 1984, the U.S. withholding tax on interest paid to foreigners was repealed, thus neutralizing a feature of the favorable tax status for Eurodollar bondholders. This eliminated some of the cost savings to Eurodollar bond issuers, as the yield demanded by investors in top-ranked issues increased to a level in excess of the Treasury yield. Additionally, in 1982 the SEC introduced shelf registration, which allows firms to register securities and sell them to the investing public for two years after registration. This increased the flexibility and ease of issuing domestic bonds, making the market more competitive with the Eurobond market.

Because of the recent weakness of the dollar, other currencies have gained an increased share of the Eurobond market—particularly the Japanese yen. Facilitating this were two actions by the Japanese government. In 1984, it relaxed regulations to allow Japanese financial institutions to participate in the placement of Euroyen bonds issued by private non-Japanese corporations. Without the participation of local financial institutions, an off-shore issue will fail. Additionally, in 1985 Japan eliminated the withholding tax on interest paid to foreign bondholders by Japanese corporations. Both of these moves have been interpreted as efforts by Japan to open its capital markets and show a willingness to make the yen a major international currency. New issues of Euroyen bonds increased from less than a quarter billion dollars in 1983 to $23.1 billion (a 16.5 percent share of the Eurobond market) in 1987.

Also growing in the Eurobond market are issues denominated in the European Currency Unit (ECU) of the European Monetary System. The ECU is a composite (often called a "cocktail" or "basket") of nine Western European currencies that are pegged to one another but float against the dollar. Euro-ECU bonds offer the safety of currency diversification to borrowers and investors, particularly within the European Monetary System, and a hedge against a depreciating dollar. In 1987, Euro-ECU bonds accounted for about 5 percent of new Eurobond issues.

Most Eurobond issues are fixed-rate bonds. However, floating-rate notes (FRN) have become a substantial portion of the market, especially in periods of volatile interest rates. The coupon on Euro-FRN issues is indexed to some variable interest rate and adjusted periodically. Numerous variations exist. The largest part of the FRN market segment has been for dollar-denominated bonds, which are typically indexed to the six-month LIBOR. Obviously, the interest rate risk of Euro-FRNs is minimal, as they will always be priced close to par value. Floating-rate issues are attractive to borrowers with floating-rate assets and to investors desiring an investment with little price variability.

Perhaps the primary reason for the growth in the Eurobond market over the past few years has been a technique known as the swap. A swap is a financial transaction in which one party agrees to exchange with the other the interest obligations of the respective issues or, carrying it further, the entire debt service obligations (principal and interest). A swap allows the parties to raise funds under one interest rate structure or currency, and swap to another. It has been estimated that 70 percent of Eurobond issues are swapped. A swap allows the parties to arbitrage the comparative advantage each may have, perhaps because of name recognition in different currency or market segments. The swap produces a cost savings for each party and, in the case where currencies are swapped, the potential for reducing long-term transaction exposure if cash inflows are denominated in the same currency as the debt service obligations

The secondary market for Eurobonds has historically lacked depth. However, in recent years the increased number of financial institutions trading Eurobonds for their portfolios has increased its depth, making its liquidity second only to that of the U.S. domestic bond market. This is important to investors because of the recent increased volatility in the bond and currency markets. Previously, under more stable conditions, investors were willing to hold bonds to maturity. Long maturity issues, in particular, still experience some liquidity problems.

The Eurobond market, although presently in somewhat of a slump, is by no means on its deathbed. As long as advantages continue to exist for both borrowers and investors, this market will remain a major segment of the international capital markets. Nevertheless, it seems safe to predict that yen and ECU-denominated issues will gain in market share relative to dollar-denominated issues as the yen becomes a major international currency and preparations are made for 1992.

The International Market for Equities

For years the idea of placing shares in foreign equity markets has been attractive to corporate financial managers. However, the equity markets have, to a great extent, remained outside the globalization process of international financial markets. Typically, the parent firm of a MNC would issue shares in the home market and wholly own foreign subsidiaries, or issue equity shares in a foreign national market, but only to finance the local subsidiary in the country. For these reasons, the globalization of the primary equity markets has lagged behind that of bonds, and in terms of comparative development, it is where the Eurobond market was in the 1960s. Nevertheless, new developments in global communications technology, deregulatory changes in national markets, and a greater awareness by investors of the benefits of international portfolio diversification have rapidly accelerated the integration of secondary equity markets during the 1980s.

Favorable macroeconomic conditions and good growth prospects in a number of countries have caused the market value of the world's equity markets to increase dramatically in recent years. Between 1976 and 1986, world market capitalization increased more than 300 percent from $1,371 billion to $5,642 billion. In order of market size, the five largest national equity markets at the end of 1986 (in billions of U.S. dollars) were the U.S. ($2,203), Japan ($1,746), U.K. ($440), West Germany ($246) and Canada ($166). Particularly good growth in Japan, coupled with an appreciating yen, has caused the Japanese market to grow spectacularly when measured in dollar terms. In 1984 it was $617 billion, versus $1,593 billion for U.S. equities; by early April 1987 it had claimed the number one position, with a value of $2,688 billion versus $2,672 billion for the U.S. market. In general, the large size of the national equity markets suggests opportunities for investors to construct well-diversified international equity portfolios.

Facilitating this opportunity are a number of deregulatory measures recently taken in major national markets. One important change made in 1985 by the Tokyo Stock Exchange was to create ten new seats and admit as members to six of these ten its first foreign brokerage firms. Four of these firms were American: Merrill Lynch, Goldman Sachs, Morgan Stanley, and Citicorp's London-based affiliate, Vickers da Costa. Membership will allow these firms, and the two European firms admitted, to better serve European, American, Mideastern and Asian investors desiring to take positions in Japanese securities. For foreign firms without membership, opportunities are limited. Nonmember firms must develop relationships with Japanese firms or attempt to buy existing seats from small Japanese firms. Membership will provide the opportunity to handle large block trades for Japanese institutional investors. However, this portion of the business may develop slowly; the Big Four of Japanese securities houses—Nomura, Daiwa, Nikko, and Yamaichi—have long, close ties with Japanese financial institutions.

Indeed, Nomura is a competitive force to be reckoned with around the world. It is Japan's most profitable company, with assets of $372 billion, in comparison to Citicorp's $204 billion and Merrill Lynch's $55 billion. With Japan's enormous current account surpluses, the country has become the world's major source of capital, and Nomura is adept at placing investments around the globe. It employs 12,000 people in 38 investment offices in 21 countries. With the exception of New York (to date at least), Nomura has been able to establish a commanding presence in many national securities markets.

Perhaps the most celebrated deregulatory change in recent years occurred in London on October 27, 1986, and is known as the "Big Bang." On that date, as on "May Day" in 1975 in the U.S., the London Stock Exchange (LSE) eliminated fixed brokerage commissions. Additionally, the regulation separating the order-taking function from the market-making function was eliminated. Moreover, in February of 1986 the LSE began admitting foreign corporations as full members of the exchange. In contrast to Japan and the U.S. (by the Glass-Stegall Act), Europe allows financial institutions to perform both investment banking and commercial banking functions; hence London affiliates of foreign commercial banks were eligible for membership to the LSE. These changes were designed to give London the most open and competitive market in the world. Facilitating this is the ideal time zone of London—its geographic location allows it to be the middle link for 24-hour trading between markets in the Far East and New York. Because of the deregulatory changes and the attraction of the London market, foreign financial institutions jumped at the opportunity and rushed to set up operations. As one might guess, volume increased dramatically and profit margins were sliced razor thin. With the October 1987 market correction, trading volume slumped, reducing the profitability of many firms. It now appears that many firms may have expanded their operations too rapidly. Some players will certainly close up shop, and others will scale back or consolidate. Nevertheless, the "Big Bang" is not the "Big Bust" that others have described. The changes made in London will yet prove to be a major factor in further integrating the world's capital markets.

Similar changes to those in London took place in Canada in 1987, and some call it the "Little Bang." On June 30 the Canadian equivalent of the Glass-Stegall Act was eliminated, allowing financial institutions to participate in both commercial and investment banking. Additionally, in 1988 foreign financial institutions were allowed to acquire 100 percent ownership of Canadian brokerage firms in Ontario (the securities industry is regulated by provinces in Canada). Canadians desired these changes to allow its securities industry to participate in the increasing globalization of financial markets. And as mentioned before, 1992 will facilitate the integration process when EEC countries open their borders to the free flow of goods, people, and money.

A trend strengthening the integration of international equity markets is the increasing number of firms listing their stock in foreign stock markets. At the end of 1986, the Tokyo Stock Exchange was trading 55 foreign equity issues from nine countries. Over 500 foreign issues trade on the London Stock Exchange. In the U.S., the shares of about 550 foreign firms are traded. Only about 100 of these are listed on the organized exchanges; the remainder are traded over the counter.

Initiating dual or multiple listing (or trading) can provide many potential advantages for a corporation. To do this the firm must meet the foreign securities market regulations and those of the stock exchange. Foreign listing provides a MNC with a form of advertising for its product brands in the foreign market. Additionally, foreign listing raises the profile of the firm in the foreign capital markets, easing the way for it to raise future financing in foreign national markets. Also, there is some academic evidence that dual listing reduces the firm's cost of capital. The risk to the firm's management of a hostile domestic takeover may also be reduced when equity ownership is diversified internationally.

In the United States, the trading of foreign equity is usually and most conveniently accomplished by means of American Depository Receipts (ADRs). ADRs are special shares of the foreign equity priced in dollars. They are negotiable certificates issued by a U.S. bank representing the underlying foreign shares, which are deposited with the bank's overseas affiliate or custodian. A single ADR represents some multiple of the underlying shares packaged so it will trade at the appropriate price range in the U.S. market. ADRs can be converted to the underlying shares or vice versa. Consequently, arbitrage will cause an ADR to sell for the same price as the equivalent number of underlying foreign shares after exchange rates and transaction costs have been accounted. Dividends are passed through the custodian to the investor in dollars. ADRs, however, do not provide voting rights to the investor. ADRs are either "sponsored" or "unsponsored." Sponsored ADRs are created at the request of the foreign firm desiring to have its stock traded in the U.S. Unsponsored ADRs are created by a U.S. financial institution reacting to U.S. investor demand for trading in the equity of a foreign firm.

Multiple listing of equity shares has helped integrate the world's equity markets; nevertheless, globalization in the sense of the debt markets is a long way off. Only recently have U.S. firms started to sell parts of new issues of equity overseas. The most cited example is Black and Decker, who in 1985 issued 8.5 million new shares. Two million of those were sold to European investors. These "Euro-equity" issues, as they have been dubbed, totalled $1.2 billion in 1984 and $3.5 billion in 1985. The Euro-equity market was expected to double its volume in 1986, but its size is minute compared to the Eurobond market. Perhaps as more firms' shares are listed on foreign stock exchanges, they will consider Euro-equity placements when the need for new equity financing arises. The initial evidence is that Euro-equity issues lower placement costs and bring in a larger, diverse group of investors.

Because national equity markets are not completely integrated, movements between prices of shares traded in different national equity markets are on average not as highly correlated with one another as they are between shares traded in the same national market. Indeed, recent academic evidence documents a strong country factor in correlation coefficients. The less correlated national markets are, the better the opportunities for investors to reduce systematic portfolio risk (for a given level of expected return) through international diversification.

Both individual and institutional investors have become somewhat aware in recent years of the potential benefits internationally diversified portfolios can provide. At present there are at least 50 U.S.-based international mutual funds that invest a significant portion of their assets in foreign securities. New sales of these funds exceeded $7 billion in 1986. This represents more than a threefold increase over the previous year. U.S. pension fund managers are also starting to get into the international action. In 1988, out of approximately $2 trillion in total assets, $60 billion, or 3 percent, was invested abroad. It is projected that by the year 2000, pension funds under management will total $6.3 trillion, of which at least 20 percent will be invested in international markets. Nevertheless, even among portfolio managers, stocks have largely remained outside the globalization trend. It is estimated that shares of about 200 major MNCs are traded in significant volume around the world, and even with these stocks the trading is primarily done in the domestic equity markets.

Further integration of the world's equity markets should occur as investors become increasingly aware of the benefits of international diversification. In the most comprehensive study to date, recent academic evidence has shown that over the ten-year period ending 1986, ten out of 13 U.S.-based international funds had a greater reward-to-variability ratio than the typical domestic portfolio as measured by Standard & Poor's 500 Index. However, the results were mixed over equal-length subperiods of five years. Over the first, all international mutual funds outperformed the U.S. market; in the second subperiod slightly less than half did. Nevertheless, even for the second subperiod it was shown that for more than 80 percent of the funds, some combination of the international fund and investment in the U.S. market would have provided superior performance than solely investing in the U.S. market. This is evidence that global diversification can provide the U.S. investor with beneficial gains.

The Foreign Exchange Market

For international trade in goods and investment in financial assets to occur, a market for foreign exchange must exist, since each country has a different currency. As succinctly stated by Eiteman and Stonehill (1989), "The foreign exchange market provides the physical and institutional environment in which foreign exchange is traded, exchange rates are determined, and foreign exchange managment is implemented." The underlying purpose of the market is to transfer purchasing power from one currency to another. In the broadest sense, the market encompasses the spot and forward markets and the markets for futures and options on foreign exchange.

Since the final collapse of the fixed-rate, gold exchange standard (known as the Bretton Woods system) in early 1973, the international monetary system under which the world operates is loosely classified as a free-floating, or flexible, exchange rate system. Under this type system, each country's currency price in other currencies is determined by the market forces of supply and demand. More accurately, the system allows the world's major currencies (dollar, British pound, yen) to float versus one another, with periodic central bank intervention in an attempt to adjust relative currency values. It is a system of the monetary union characterized by the ECU—where nine EEC currencies are pegged to one another but float against others—and of pegging currency value to a strong currency or currency composite by many less developed countries.

The floating of major currencies and the increased globalization of business have caused the market for foreign exchange to increase in volume and volatility in recent years. The exact size of the market is difficult to determine, but it is by far the largest and, most likely, one of the most efficient financial markets in the world. One estimate put average daily trading volume at $425 billion in 1987, up from $300 billion in 1986 and $150 billion in 1984; current estimates range up to $1,000 billion per day (Stern 1988; Shapiro 1989). By comparison, the largest single day's volume on the New York Stock Exchange was $21 billion on October 19, 1987, the day of the crash.

The foreign exchange market is not a specific physical place; it is the network of international banks that trade currencies with one another and the foreign exchange brokers and dealers who facilitate these trades. This network spans the globe and is open somewhere in the world 24 hours a day. Primary trading centers are London, New York, and Tokyo. Other major trading centers are Sydney, Hong Kong, Singapore, Frankfurt, Zurich, Paris, San Francisco, and Los Angeles. Communication with one another is via computerized dealing systems, telephone, telefax, and telex machines.

Banks, acting as dealers, trade currencies with their corporate and individual clients to help them conduct foreign currency transactions. These trades form the retail or client market. Banks also trade with one another to adjust their inventories of foreign currency (correspondent bank balances in foreign banks) for retail transactions as well as for speculation and arbitrage. Interbank transactions form the wholesale or interbank market, involving transactions of a million or more currency units. A 1986 Federal Reserve study indicated that almost 87 percent of all bank foreign exchange transactions were wholesale trades. Banks (when acting as dealers) and foreign exchange dealers profit by buying foreign currency at the "bid" price and reselling at a higher "ask" price. Because of the many competitors in the market the bid-ask spread is very narrow, attesting to the efficiency of the market. Retail customers are not charged a commission; the bid-ask spread is slightly larger than it is in the wholesale market. When acting as speculators, banks attempt to profit by changes in exchange rates. A typical $5 million position can earn substantial profit if the rate changes by only a small amount. A bank trading room may conduct hundreds of trades in a single day. Many large international banks operate trading rooms around the globe in several money centers to service their corporate clients on a 24-hour basis. They also better maintain speculative positions around the clock through trading partnerships. The foreign exchange operations can be extremely profitable for a large international bank. In 1987, Bankers Trust earned $593 million from currency trading, Citicorp earned $453 million, and Chase Manhattan showed $232 million.

Some investment banking houses have recently joined the action. It is estimated that Morgan Stanley and Goldman Sachs earned about $50 million each from speculative foreign exchange market trading in 1987. Many large MNCs have their own trading rooms and trade in the wholesale market. These are cost centers when the MNC conducts its own foreign exchange transactions and profit centers when taking speculative positions. Central banks and treasuries also trade in the wholesale market to acquire or spend foreign exchange reserves and intervene in the market's determination of exchange rates.

A transaction in the spot market involves almost immediate delivery of foreign exchange. (This market is not the same as the bank note, or cash market for small transactions with which many vacationers are familiar.) A spot exchange rate represents the current price of one currency in terms of another. Spot transactions account for about 60 percent of interbank transactions.

A forward trade is a contract involving delivery of foreign exchange at some future date. Typical delivery dates are one, two, three, six, and twelve months into the future. However, intermediate dates and, especially for major clients, contracts with maturities longer than one year are available. The forward exchange rate is the contractual price for delivery of foreign exchange on the delivery date. It may be higher or lower than the spot rate, depending upon whether the market anticipated the foreign currency to appreciate or depreciate in value relative to the currency used for quotation. Forward contracts allow for hedging the volatile exchange rates that exist under a free-floating international monetary system. MNCs, for example, can lock in the purchase price of foreign exchange needed to meet a forthcoming liability by the forward buying of foreign currency. Further, the sale price of foreign exchange to be received in future can be locked in by the sale of a forward contract.

Similar to forward contacts are futures contracts, which allow for the future purchase or sale of foreign currency. Futures contracts differ, however, from forward contracts in that the terms of the contract (face amount and maturity) are standardized. They are also traded on organized futures exchanges. The largest futures exchange for foreign exchange is the International Monetary Market (IMM) division of the Chicago Mercantile Exchange. Contracts currently trade for the British pound, Canadian dollar, West German mark, Swiss franc, French franc, Japanese yen, Australian dollar and ECU. Since 1985 interchangeable contracts have traded on the Singapore International Monetary Exchange (SIMEX), thus allowing more global trading. The IMM and SIMEX also trade a Eurodollar interest rate futures contract based on three-month LIBOR. The contract helps MNC treasurers and international banks hedge interest rate risk. In 1987 it unseated the U.S. Treasury bond contract to become the U.S.'s most highly traded futures contract. Other, non-interchangeable, currency and Eurodollar futures contracts are traded on the London International Financial Futures Exchange.

Options also provide a means of hedging foreign exchange risk. A call option allows the purchase of a certain amount of foreign exchange at a contractual exchange rate over a specified period of time. A put option provides for the sale of foreign exchange. Unlike forward and futures contracts, an option contract does not have to be exercised if the spot price of foreign exchange is more favorable to the option holder than the contractual exchange rate. A premium must be paid to purchase an option, however. Standardized exchange-traded options on the same currencies as the IMM futures contracts became available in 1982 when trading began at the Philadelphia Stock Exchange. Other exchanges throughout the world also trade currency options. Additionally, international banks offer over-the-counter currency options with tailor-made terms to their commercial customers. And, the IMM offers exchange-traded options on its currency futures contracts.

All of the international financial markets have grown extensively in the eighties, as business has become more global and national markets have become more integrated. Many new securities exist today that were not present as little as a decade ago. Further developments should be expected in the nineties and into the next century as continued integration takes place.

References

G. Andrews, "U.S. Lenders Tie Mortgages to London Interbank Rate," *Wall Street Journal,* August 3, 1988.

A. Bennett, "Going Global: The Chief Executives in the Year 2000 Will Be Experienced Abroad," *Wall Street Journal,* February 27, 1989.

E.S. Browning, "Tokyo Bourse Grants Seats to 6 Foreigners," *Wall Street Journal,* December 2, 1985.

B. Burrough, C. Forman and K. Graven, "Global Traders: How Merrill Lynch Moves Its Stock Deals All Around the World," *Wall Street Journal,* November 9, 1987.

D.K Eiteman and A.I. Stonehill, Chapter 10 *Multinational Business Finance,* 5th ed. Reading, Mass.: Addison-Wesley, 1989).

C.S. Eun and B.G. Resnick, "Estimating the Correlation Structure of International Share Prices," *Journal of Finance,* December 1984, pp. 1311–1324.

C.S. Eun and B.G. Resnick, "Exchange Rate Uncertainty, Forward Contracts, and International Portfolio Selection," *Journal of Finance*, March 1988, pp. 197–215.

C.S. Eun, R. Kolodny and B.G. Resnick, "U.S.-Based International Mutual Funds: A Performance Evaluation," working paper, University of Maryland and Indiana University, May 1989.

W.R. Folks and R. Aggarwal, Chapter 2, *International Dimensions of Financial Management* (Boston: PWS-Kent, 1988).

Forbes, July 25, 1988, pp. 240–250.

C. Forman, "U.K. Stock Mart Becomes Bloody but Not Good Show," *Wall Street Journal*, April 20, 1989.

Fortune, August 1, 1988, pp. D1–D4.

M. Givant, "Global Assets will Surge," *Pensions & Investment Age*, July 11, 1988.

K.E. House, "The '90s and Beyond: Europe's Global Clout is Limited by Divisions 1992 Can't Paper Over," *Wall Street Journal*, February 13, 1989.

R.I. Kirkland, Jr., "Outsider's Guide to Europe in 1992," *Fortune*, October 24, 1988, pp. 121–125.

S. McMurray, M. Winkler and M. Kanabayashi, "Endless Dealing: U.S. Treasury Debt Is Increasingly Traded Globally and Nonstop," *Wall Street Journal*, September 10, 1986.

R.A. Melcher, W. Glasgall, and B. Reimer, "Big Bang: Big Bust, Big Lessons," *Business Week*, March 6, 1989, pp. 38–39.

A. Merjos, "Investors' Ticket Abroad: American Depositary Receipts are Growing in Popularity," *Barron's*, April 30, 1984, pp. 24 and 26.

H. Miyamoto, "Japan Takes Big Strides to Globalize its Markets," *Barron's*, June 22, 1987.

K. Muehring, "The Looming Battle in International Equities," *Institutional Investor*, October 1986, pp. 318–326.

A. Murray and P. Duke, Jr., "Fed Ruling Will Allow Banks to Take Foreign-Currency Deposits," *Wall Street Journal*, January 4, 1989.

G. Putka, "British Jitters: London's Exchange Braces for Big Bang Set to Occur Monday," *Wall Street Journal*, October 24, 1986.

G. Putka, P. Truell, and M. Winkler, "Unsettled 'City': London Financial Mart Quakes as First Phase of Deregulation Nears," *Wall Street Journal*, February 28, 1986.

C. Rapoport, "Will the Yen Push Aside the Dollar?" *Fortune*, December 5, 1988, pp. 155–160.

B. Reimer, R.A. Melcher, J. Templeman, and W. Glasgall, "The Moneymen Can't Wait for the Starting Gun," *Business Week*, December 12, 1988, pp. 72–73.

F.L. Riveria-Batiz and L. Riveria-Batiz, *International Finance and Open Economy Macroeconomics*, (New York: Macmillan, 1985), p. 89.

B. Rudolph, "Yen Power Goes Global," *Time*, August 8, 1988, pp. 26–29.

M.R. Sesit and C. Torres, "What if They Traded All Day and Nobody Came?" *Wall Street Journal*, June 14, 1989.

A.C. Shapiro, *Multinational Financial Management*, 3rd ed. (Boston: Allyn and Bacon, 1989), p. 672.

B. Solnik, Chapter 6, *International Investments*, (Reading, Mass.: Addison-Wesley, 1988.)

R.L. Stern, "(Dangerous) Fun and Games in the Foreign Exchange Market," *Forbes*, August 22, 1988, pp. 69–72.

D. Wessel, "U.S. Debt to Rest of World Increased by 40% to $532.5 Billion Last Year," *Wall Street Journal*, June 30, 1989.

P. Widder, "Foreign Brokers Ready to Blast off in Toronto," *Chicago Tribune*, June 22, 1987.

B. Wysocki, Jr., "Invading Japan: Foreign Stockbrokers Compete for Business in the Tokyo Market," *Wall Street Journal*, October 16, 1986.

Questions

1. What factors account for segmentation among national product markets and national financial markets? Explain.
2. If national product markets and national financial markets were either perfectly integrated or severely segmented, then profitable opportunities in global investments would be lessened. Explain why the extreme opposites of integration and segmentation reduce profitable opportunities in global investments.
3. Which national markets are likely to be more segmented, product or financial? Explain.
4. Define the term *Eurocurrency* and describe its origin.
5. What is a floating-rate Eurodollar loan based on LIBOR?
6. a. Describe the difference between a *Eurobond* and a *foreign bond.*
   b. Identify each of the following bonds as a Eurobond or a foreign bond: Yankee bond, Euroyen bond, Samurai bond, Bulldog bond, and Euro-ECU bond.
7. Which financial market is more segmented, the international bond market or the international equity market? What accounts for the difference?
8. What are ADRs and what role do they play in the secondary equity market?
9. What is meant by the term *foreign exchange market*? Where is this market located? Explain.
10. Match the item in Column A with its closest counterpart in Column B. Use each item only once.

A	B
a. Spot market	____ SIMEX
b. Forward market	____ MNC
c. Futures market	____ LIFFE
d. Appreciate	____ Negotiated contract
e. Depreciate	____ ECU
f. Chicago Mercantile Exchange	____ Decrease in price
g. Coca-Cola	____ IMM
h. Option	____ Cash mark
i. Australia	____ Increase in price
j. Cocktail	____ Standard contract
k. London	____ Call
l. Singapore	____ Dollar

Japan's Corporate Groups

Hesna Genay

In recent years, the Japanese economy has come under close scrutiny as the liberalization of both financial and nonfinancial international markets gained momentum and Japanese companies proved themselves to be successful competitors. The differences and similarities between the industrial structures in Japan and the U.S. are of interest to regulatory bodies as well as to companies that compete with Japanese companies in the international markets.

One distinctive feature of the Japanese economy that attracts considerable attention is the existence of well-diversified industrial groups, called keiretsu. The complex relationship among firms within these groups is characterized by cross-ownership of equity, close ties to the group's "main bank" (which provides the majority of the firm's debt financing), and product market ties with the other firms in the group.

Although such industrial groups are not unique to Japan (Germany, Korea, Spain, and France have similar industrial groups), Japan's corporate groups are larger. Furthermore, Japan, as the second largest trading partner of the U.S., attracts more attention and criticism. For example, during the Structural Impediments Initiative talks at the beginning of this year, the "main bank" system in Japan with its "captive" customer base was criticized for acting as a nontariff barrier, restricting entry by foreign competition.

These and similar criticisms of the keiretsu assume that its main function is to limit the activities of group firms' competitors. The results of recent studies, however, indicate that Japan's industrial groups provide other important services to their members. Therefore, understanding the characteristics of the keiretsu system has important implications for the competitiveness of American firms.

This study compares Japanese keiretsu and independent firms in terms of their ownership structure, assets, earnings per share, stock returns, dividend payments, and equity-related bond issues. The results point to significant differences

---

At the time of this writing, Hesna Genay was an economist at the Federal Reserve Bank of Chicago. The author would like to thank Herbert Baer for his helpful comments.

Source: Hesna Genay, "Japan's Corporate Groups," Federal Reserve Bank of Chicago, *Economic Perspectives*, Jan./Feb. 1991, Vol. XV No. 1.

between these types of firms. In addition, the study explores the implications of these differences for the U.S.

The Six Groups and Their Characteristics

The history of large industrial groups in Japan can be traced as far back as the 17th century. For around 300 years until the end of World War II, the Japanese economy was dominated by ten large industrial groups, called zaibatsu.[1] Companies belonging to these large conglomerates were vertically integrated and owned by families or holding companies. Although members of the zaibatsu spanned a wide range of industries, the most powerful tended to be banks and trading companies, which controlled the financial operations and the distribution of goods in the groups.

After World War II, under the direction of the Allied Occupation Forces, the zaibatsu were dissolved and the equity held by the controlling families was distributed to the, public. During the restructuring of the Japanese economy in the 1950s and early 1960s, some of the old zaibatsu associations emerged in a new form, called keiretsu, and other new keiretsu were formed.

Today there are six major keiretsu in Japan: Mitsui, Mitsubishi, Sumitomo, Fuyo, Sanwa, and Dai-Ichi. The first three are continuations of the pre-war zaibatsu, while the last three groups were newly formed.[2] The nature of the keiretsu relationships differs somewhat from the relationships among zaibatsu companies. Unlike the zaibatsu companies, keiretsu firms are not owned by one holding company or family. Furthermore, the keiretsu are characterized by significant crossholdings of equity among members. While zaibatsu companies were vertically integrated, with the holding company or the family standing at the top of the hierarchy, the major keiretsu firms are related through customer/supplier relationships and ownership of each other's equity.

A common feature of the old zaibatsu and the new keiretsu is the central role of financial institutions, city banks in particular.[3] These institutions provide the majority of the group firms' bank loans and also hold significant amounts of equity in the member firms. In addition, the trading companies of the groups continue to play a major role in the distribution of goods and coordination of new ventures in overseas markets.

---

[1] The ten groups are Mitsui, Mitsubishi, Sumitomo, Yasuda, Nissan, Asano, Furukawa, Okura, Nakajima, and Nomura.

[2] The newer groups, however, include some of the companies from the former zaibatsu. For example, some of the Yasuda zaibatsu companies belong to the Fuyo group and Furukawa group companies are associated with the Dai-Ichi group.

[3] The Japanese financial system is highly compartmentalized into groups that traditionally have segmented business activities. There are four types of banks: city banks, long-term credit banks, trust banks, and regional banks. City banks supply short-term capital to large companies and have limited deposit activity. Long-term credit banks, on the other hand, provide long-term loans to business and raise funds through debentures. Regional banks provide funds to small to medium-size enterprises and have the most extensive retail deposit network. Trust activities are provided by the trust banks that also provide long-term credit to companies. For a detailed description of the Japanese banking system, see Federation of Bankers Associations of Japan (1989).

Description of Sample Firms

There are 471 companies in the sample; 361 keiretsu firms and 110 independent firms. Firms belonging to the six keiretsu were identified by the information given in *Industrial Groupings in Japan 1988/1989*, *Japan Company Handbook, Spring 1989*, and Nakatani (1984). The Mitsui, Mitsubishi, Sumitomo, Fuyo, Sanwa, and Dai-Ichi groups have 66, 65, 64, 56, 59, and 51 companies, respectively. The sample of independent firms was obtained from a random sample of all companies listed in the Tokyo Stock Exchange (TSE), First Section in 1989 after firms identified as keiretsu companies were eliminated. The total sample size represents approximately 40 percent of all companies listed in TSE First Section.

Similarities between the pre-war zaibatsu and today's keiretsu also exist in their personnel and management ties. Major member firms strengthen their ties with affiliates by exchanging top management and directors. In addition, each group has a Presidential Council that meets every month to exchange information and resolve disputes that may exist among member firms.

One feature that distinguishes keiretsu from industrial groups in many other countries is the scope of their business. Keiretsu firms are not concentrated in one or two industries; instead, in each group, such industries as chemicals, machinery, food, transportation equipment, and communications are well represented.

Given these general features of keiretsu firms, what are some of the specific characteristics that differentiate them from other companies in Japan? This study examines the financial aspects of a sample of keiretsu and independent firms (see box) to answer this question. The particular questions that are addressed include: How does the structure of equity ownership differ between keiretsu and independent firms? Are there significant differences between these firms in terms of their size, earnings, stock market performance, and the issues of equity-like bonds? Are the characteristics of financial firms, which are subject to a greater degree of regulation and government guidance, different from those of nonfinancial firms? In addition, particular attention is paid to the period from 1986 to 1989 to determine whether the rapid deregulation and internationalization of Japan's financial markets affected keiretsu firms differently from independent firms. In the last section, the implications of the results presented here are discussed in view of the earlier studies on keiretsu companies and their economic role.

The Financial Characteristics of Keiretsu and Independent Firms

Members of keiretsu have strong financial ties. Table 1 shows the percentage of equity owned by the top ten shareholders of firms in each group in 1989, where shareholders are classified either as members of one of the six keiretsu or as independents. For keiretsu firms, the amount of equity owned by other firms in the same group (for example, percentage of stock of a Mitsui firm owned by other Mitsui firms) ranges from 14.8 percent for the Dai-Ichi group to 26.5 percent for the Sumitomo group. Moreover, this percentage is much greater than that owned by any one group outside each keiretsu. Although the table indicates that the six keiretsu hold equity in one another, there is no evidence to suggest that these cross-holdings play an economic role. For example, while the other five keiretsu own more than 22 percent of a typical Mitsui firm, it is not clear that their role is the same as the one played by the shareholders who are affiliated with the Mitsui group.

Table 1 also shows that the Mitsui, Mitsubishi, and Sumitomo groups, direct descendants of the pre-war zaibatsu, have stronger equity ties than the Fuyo, Sanwa, and Dai-Ichi groups, which were formed after the war. Finally, an analysis of ownership from 1979 to 1989 reveals the same basic pattern as in Table 1.[4]

The central role of financial institutions in keiretsu firms is reflected in their ownership of equity in other member companies. Table 2 presents the percentage of equity owned by each group's shareholders who are also members of the same group and is broken down by financial and nonfinancial firms (for example, financial shareholders of Mitsui company that are also Mitsui group members).

In each group, holdings by financial firms are significantly smaller than holdings by nonfinancial investors; however, financial shareholders are more pervasive than nonfinancial shareholders. The disparity between the amount of shares owned by financial and nonfinancial investors probably results from the fact that the majority of financial investors are banks, which are allowed to hold a

TABLE 1 KEIRETSU'S STRONG EQUITY TIES

	Percent of shares owned by top 10 shareholders, 1989					
Shareholder	**Mitsui**	**Mitsubishi**	**Sumitomo**	**Fuyo**	**Sanwa**	**Dai-Ichi**
Mitsui	25.50	3.61	3.45	4.31	3.21	4.31
Mitsubishi	4.02	24.60	3.38	4.63	4.07	4.48
Sumitomo	3.53	3.53	26.51	4.04	3.47	4.03
Fuyo	5.47	3.72	3.84	17.24	3.22	4.28
Sanwa	5.15	4.89	5.02	4.59	18.61	5.02
Dai-Ichi	4.16	4.37	5.48	4.90	8.51	14.84
Independent[a]	9.17	8.74	8.55	12.66	12.18	15.43
Same Group[b] / Independent	0.81	0.85	0.89	0.49	0.54	0.40

SOURCE: *The Japan Company Handbook* (1979–1990).

[a] Investors that do not belong to any of the six keiretsu groups.
[b] The ratio of the amount of shares owned by firms in each group to the amount of shares owned by independent firms.

[4] See Genay (1990), where all the analyses here were also carried out for the years 1979 and 1984.

TABLE 2 WITHIN-GROUP OWNERSHIP OF EQUITY AND DEBT

	Equity				Debt
	Nonfinancial firms' ownership of other firms in the same group		Financial firms' ownership of other firms in the same group		Loans to other firms in the same group
Keiretsu	(% of total shares)	(number of companies owned)	(% of total shares)	(number of companies owned)	(% of total loans)
Mitsui	22	69	11*	170	29
Mitsubishi	15	68	15	212	33
Sumitomo	22	72	12*	182	25
Fuyo	15	32	12	155	28
Sanwa	17	35	10*	142	23
Dai-Ichi	15	42	7*	86	19

SOURCE: *The Japan Company Handbook* (1979-1990).

NOTE: *Indicates cases where the percentage of equity owned by financial shareholders is different from that owned by nonfinancial shareholders at the 5 percent significance level.

maximum of 5 percent of the equity of any one company.[5] As was the case in Table 1, the structure of ownership by financial and nonfinancial investors is very stable over time; the percentages reported in Table 2 are not very different from those in 1979 or 1984.

In addition to being the major shareholders of group firms, affiliated financial institutions also are the single largest source for the group firms' loans. In 1989, keiretsu financial firms made between 19 percent (Dai-Ichi) and 35 percent (Sumitomo) of the loans to their member firms. As before, the three groups that are the historical extensions of the former zaibatsu, Mitsui, Mitsubishi, and Sumitomo, on average have stronger debt ties than the newer groups.

Comparison of the Performance of Keiretsu and Independent Firms

Are the differences in the ownership structures of keiretsu and independent firms reflected in their performance? In particular, are these firms significantly different from each other in terms of their size, earnings, dividends paid, and stock market performance? Table 3 provides data on these variables and their statistical significance for the sample of keiretsu and independent firms. Financial and nonfinancial firms are examined separately because financial firms operate under stricter regulation and government guidance.

As the table indicates, nonfinancial keiretsu firms are larger than nonfinancial independent firms, as measured by their total assets. Although the asset growth

[5] For each group, the number of top ten shareholders that are banks is 104, 118, 110, 98, 91, 50, and 161 for the Mitsui, Mitsubishi, Sumitomo, Fuyo, Sanwa, Dai-Ichi, and Independent groups, respectively.

TABLE 3 FINANCIAL PERFORMANCE

	Nonfinancial		Financial	
	Keiretsu	**Independent**	**Keiretsu**	**Independent**
Average total assets (*in billions of yen*)				
1977-1989	319.3*	109.5	9,458.7	6,085.6
1977-1981	254.5*	85.7	5,003.0	3,758.6
1982-1985	332.5*	117.1	9,592.3	6,328.9
1986-1989	407.8*	183.3	16,292.3	9,581.5
Average annual change in total assets (*percent*)				
1977-1989	7.22*	8.72	16.35*	12.39
1977-1981	6.80	7.86	14.69**	10.83
1982-1985	5.40	5.92	18.43*	11.81
1986-1989	8.87	9.92	16.34	14.95
Average level of earnings per share (*in yen*)				
1976-1989	16.69	24.29	28.63	37.73
1976-1980	14.67*	23.61	21.77	30.14
1981-1985	17.21*	26.01	25.01	32.16
1986-1989	18.72	23.57	41.73	55.02
Average annual stock returns (*percent*)				
1977-1989	22.72	23.00	22.92	21.06
1977-1980	17.67*	10.02	4.91	2.10
1981-1985	14.87	14.60	31.07	25.27
1986-1989	37.22*	44.91	31.13	34.59
Payout ratios[a] (*percent*)				
1980-1989	47.77	39.99	34.47	34.22
1980-1984	46.04	42.51	40.84	37.13
1985-1989	49.48	37.46	28.11	31.21
Price-earnings ratios[a] (*in yen*)				
1980-1989	58.88	58.34	56.17*	41.97
1980-1984	28.75	27.41	34.88*	23.06
1985-1989	89.90	89.33	77.45**	61.31

SOURCE: *The Japan Company Handbook* (1976-1990); *Handbook on Stock Prices* (1976-1990).

[a] The denominator of these ratios is the five-year moving average of earnings per share.
* Denotes cases where keiretsu firms are different from independent firms at the 5% significance level.
** Denotes cases where keiretsu firms are different from independent firms at the 10% significance level.

rates among nonfinancial keiretsu and independent firms did not differ significantly in any one subperiod, during the overall period from 1977 to 1989, nonfinancial keiretsu firms grew at a slower rate than nonfinancial independent firms.

In contrast, total assets of financial keiretsu and independent firms are not significantly different, yet the growth rates do differ. Except for the period from 1986 to 1989, the assets of keiretsu firms increased at a greater rate. Furthermore, for both keiretsu and independent firms, nonfinancial firms had significantly lower growth rates, as well as lower levels of assets, than financial firms.

The differences between financial and nonfinancial firms can be attributed to the scope of businesses in each type of firm and the central role of financial institutions in the keiretsu. First, nonfinancial firms cover a wider range of businesses than financial firms so that the shocks they are subjected to are more varied. On the other hand, financial companies are subject to the same types of shocks, which tends to make them more uniform than nonfinancial firms. Second, the close, long-term ties between keiretsu financial institutions and other members of the group may play a role in their asset expansion. As the nonfinancial companies of the group grow, the demand for funds by these companies may result in asset growth for the financial firms. The results of a study by Dohner, Lowrey, and Terrell (1990) support this hypothesis. They compare the activities of keiretsu and independent banks that operate in the U.S. They find that lending in the U.S. by keiretsu banks is sensitive to Japan's GNP, while it is not for independent banks. It is likely that keiretsu banks are sensitive to Japan's GNP because of the demand for loans by their "captive" clientele, the other keiretsu firms.

Table 3 also shows that while earnings of nonfinancial keiretsu companies in general are significantly lower than earnings of nonfinancial independent firms, there are no significant differences in earnings between financial keiretsu and independent firms.

Comparing financial and nonfinancial firms within keiretsu and independent groupings does reveal significant differences. Within keiretsu, the earnings of financial firms were significantly higher than the earnings of nonfinancial keiretsu firms during the overall period, as well as the 1986–1989 subperiod. For independent companies, the earnings of financial firms were significantly higher than those of nonfinancial firms only during the 1986–1989 period. These results suggest that financial firms benefitted more from the deregulations that took place in the late 1980s than nonfinancial firms. Given that most of the liberalization occurred in the financial markets, it is not surprising that earnings of financial firms experienced greater growth than those of nonfinancial firms.

In addition, the data presented in Table 3 show that during the whole period from 1977 to 1989, there are no significant differences in the stock returns of keiretsu and independent firms—financial or nonfinancial. But an interesting pattern emerges in the subperiod comparison. From 1977 to 1980, keiretsu nonfinancial firms had significantly higher returns than independent firms. These differences disappeared in the period from 1981 to 1985 and reversed their pattern in the 1986–1989 period. During the bull market of 1986–1989, when the Nikkei 225 index rose from 13,113 to 38,916, nonfinancial keiretsu firms had significantly lower returns than independent firms. In effect, since 1981 the stock prices of independent nonfinancial firms appreciated more than the stock prices of keiretsu firms.

Table 3 also shows that the price-earnings (p-e) ratios of keiretsu financial firms are significantly higher than those of independent financial firms. There are two possible reasons for higher price-earnings ratios of keiretsu firms. First, if keiretsu financial firms have more extensive shareholdings than independent firms, then their stock prices would reflect not only the value of the firms' ongoing operations but also the value of any equity they hold. The stock prices of firms with more extensive equity holdings would capitalize the earnings of companies that they own stock in, resulting in higher p-e ratios. Second, the earnings of keiretsu financial firms may be expected to grow faster. In that case, the stock prices and the p-e ratios would reflect the higher growth potential of these firms.

To sum up, nonfinancial keiretsu firms are larger companies that have slower rates of growth and lower earnings than nonfinancial independent firms. On the other hand, financial keiretsu firms are comparable in size to financial independent firms, but have higher asset growth rates. Moreover, financial keiretsu firms have higher price-earnings ratios then independent financial firms. There are also significant differences among financial and nonfinancial firms within the keiretsu and independent groups. In general, financial firms are larger, faster growing companies with higher earnings than nonfinancial firms.

The Corporate Bond Market

During the 1980s there have been several developments in the Japanese bond markets that have the potential to weaken keiretsu ties. Until the late 1970s, regulations severely restricted the size of the corporate bond markets in Japan. Consequently, banks were the major source of external funds for corporations. The pattern of financing, however, has changed in the 1980s.

Beginning with the relaxation of interest rate ceilings on corporate bonds in 1978, the government has steadily loosened many of the restrictions that made it difficult to raise capital in the bond markets. Probably the most important deregulatory move was in 1983 when firms were allowed to issue unsecured bonds.[6] Since 1981 Japanese firms also have been permitted to issue warrant bonds that give the investor the option to buy the company's stock at the "exercise price" during a specified period of time.[7]

During the 1980s Japanese firms also gained greater access to the offshore debt markets. Regulations requiring government permission before issuing foreign bonds were removed. Consequently, funds raised overseas as a proportion of total funds raised in the capital markets increased from approximately 26 percent in 1980 to 55 percent in 1986. As Japanese firms started to issue bonds in the overseas markets in increasing numbers, the government relaxed the restric-

---

[6] Prior to 1983, all bond issues had to be collateralized by the assets of the issuing firm. Furthermore, the banks guaranteed all of the issues and were forced to buy all outstanding bonds at par in cases of reorganization.

[7] The warrants on these bonds have been detachable since 1985, although the secondary market for them is small and illiquid.

tions on the issuance of domestic bonds to attract some of the issues back to Japan.[8]

As a result, the percentage of funds raised in the bond markets, both domestically and overseas, increased from 58 percent of all funds raised in the capital markets in 1980 to 84 percent in 1987. The largest increases were in the issues of convertible and warrant bonds; the share of these equity-related bonds in all bond issues increased from 34.4 percent in 1980 to 84.6 percent in 1987.

At the same time, corporations reduced their bank borrowings. Hoshi, Kashyap, and Scharfstein (1989) report that total bank borrowing by keiretsu firms as a proportion of total debt decreased from 93 percent in 1977 to 88 percent in 1986. During the same period, the proportion of borrowing from group firms decreased from 31 percent to 29 percent of total bank borrowing.

The liberalization of financial markets in Japan during the 1980s and the resulting changes in corporate behavior might have direct implications for the keiretsu system. The decline in the importance of bank loans, coupled with the increase in the convertible and warrant bond issues, has the potential to weaken the strong keiretsu ties. First, the reduction in bank loans from group banks means that one of the most distinctive features of the keiretsu ties is loosened. Second, if convertible and warrant bonds issued by the keiretsu firms are purchased by investors outside the keiretsu system, then as the warrants are exercised, the cross-holdings of shares among keiretsu firms are diluted. If, on the other hand, these bonds are purchased by the members of the keiretsu, then the equity ties among keiretsu firms would not be altered. In that case, keiretsu firms would be changing the composition of their debt portfolio without weakening their group ties. The equity holdings of keiretsu firms over the past five years indicate that there has not been a significant decline in their equity ties.

Another interesting question is: Who benefited the most from the deregulations that took place in the bond markets? Table 4 indicates nonfinancial independent firms issued more bonds, as a percentage of assets, than nonfinancial keiretsu firms. For convertible bond issues, the differences were significant in all periods; for warrant bond issues, the differences were significant in all periods except for the 1980–1984 period. In contrast, there are no significant differences among financial keiretsu firms and financial independent firms with respect to their average issues of convertible and warrant bonds.

The Economic Role of Keiretsu

Industrial groups played an important role in the rebuilding of the Japanese economy after WW II. Group banks were the major source of funds for member firms when capital was in short supply. Trading companies were instrumental in the overseas expansion of group firms by obtaining imported raw materials and developing overseas markets for group firms. In other words, the industrial groups were important in developing Japan's infant industries during a period

---

[8] For a concise description of the issue requirements, see Karp and Koike (1990) and Kaneko and Battaglini (1990).

TABLE 4 CONVERTIBLE AND WARRANT BOND ISSUES (PERCENT OF ASSETS)

	Nonfinancial		Financial	
Average issues	**Keiretsu**	**Independent**	**Keiretsu**	**Independent**
Convertible bonds				
1976-1989	19.20*	20.27	1.85	2.05
1976-1979	6.78*	7.75	0.00	0.00
1980-1984	4.24*	6.39	1.55	0.00
1985-1989	8.25*	11.23	0.32	0.47
Warrant bonds				
1980-1989	13.70*	20.69	2.55	1.69
1980-1984	2.92	2.66	1.63	1.62
1985-1989	7.37*	10.98	1.36	.98

SOURCE: *The Japan Company Handbook* (1976-1989), and *The 1989 Handbook on Bonds and Debentures* (1989).

NOTE: These figures are normalized by total assets of the firm.
*Denotes cases where keiretsu firms are different from independent firms at the 5% significance level.

when the Japanese economy was highly regulated and was isolated from the international markets. Today, Japan is one of world's strongest economies and Japanese companies are some of the most competitive in their field. Therefore, it is unlikely that the current economic role of keiretsu is the same as it was during the high growth period.

The keiretsu system can play three possible roles. First, the keiretsu system may be a cartel-like organization that limits competition. Group firms may act in concert to maximize joint profits and earn monopoly rents. For example, they may organize a network of buyer-supplier relationships and differentiate between group firms and outsiders in their business deals. Such a cartel-like organization requires a high degree of coordination and enforcement, since some of the firms would be hurt by the arrangement, at least some of the time.

The keiretsu system may also serve to diversify industry-specific shocks. In a group where members are from a wide range of industries and hold each other's equity, the costs of a negative industry-specific shock would be shared by all firms in the group, minimizing the cost to any one company. If keiretsu firms minimize the costs of such industry-specific shocks, then their earnings will be more stable. Managers of firms may prefer more stable earnings if their performance is judged not only on the level of earnings but on their variance also. Furthermore, volatile earnings, through the uncertainty they create, may lead to higher transaction costs for the firm.

Finally, the results of recent studies indicate that the keiretsu system may play an important role in reducing costs associated with capital market imperfections. In perfect capital markets, all agents would have the same information so that they can write enforceable contracts that are contingent on all possible actions of the agents. In reality, however, some agents are better informed than others which increases the cost of transactions. The agency theory of firms, for example, predicts that shareholders of a leveraged firm have incentives to transfer wealth from debt-holders to themselves by taking on excessively risky projects.[9] Recognizing the potential for transfer of wealth, debtholders would require a higher return on their investment; that is, they would raise the cost of capital to borrowers.

Kim (1990) shows that in a financial system where debtholders can also hold equity, the optimal contract between a firm and its creditors is one that comprises both debt and equity holdings. With the optimal contract, creditors can monitor the activities of the firm more effectively. Through their role as shareholders, creditors can be better informed about the decisions of the management. In addition, if lenders hold equity, then the incentives for wealth transfers by other shareholders are reduced, since the lender would share the benefits of any such transfer.

Prowse (1990) presents evidence on the effectiveness of the keiretsu system in reducing agency costs. He argues that the financial organizations in keiretsu avoid agency costs by taking both equity and debt positions in group firms. Prowse finds a strong correlation between variables that proxy for measures of agency costs (such as R&D expenditures and amount of assets that are not tied up in fixed plant and equipment) and the amount of wealth invested in group firms in the form of equity and debt. Prowse's results also indicate that agency costs are reduced to a greater extent in Japan than in the U.S.

In addition to the incentive problems emphasized by the agency theory, there are information asymmetries between managers of a firm and investors in the market, a capital market imperfection first emphasized in Myers and Majluf (1984). Sometimes, the managers, who are better informed about the prospects of the firm, may feel that the equity of the firm is underpriced. Such information asymmetries, along with potential conflicts of interest between debtholders and shareholders, would raise the cost of external finance relative to internal sources of funds. In such instances, a firm's investment would be highly sensitive to its cash flow.

The results of two recent studies show that the keiretsu system may be effective in circumventing such problems associated with information asymmetries. Hoshi, Kashyap, and Scharfstein (1990a) examine the investment behavior of keiretsu firms and independent firms. The authors find that investment by independent firms is more sensitive to liquidity than investment by keiretsu firms, suggesting that information asymmetries are important and that industrial groups are effective in avoiding problems associated with such capital market imperfections.

In a second study, Hoshi, Kashyap, and Scharfstein (1990b) analyze the investment behavior of keiretsu firms that recently loosened their ties with the group's main bank. They find that investment by these firms has become more sensitive to cash flow since they left the group. This result supports the authors' earlier conclusion that a keiretsu firm's ties with its "main bank" may mitigate information problems.

---

9 See Myers (1977) and Jensen and Meckling (1976).

Furthermore, the data on bonds in Table 4 offer additional support. If independent firms are more cash constrained than keiretsu firms because they lack the close ties to the group banks, then it is not surprising that independent firms issue more bonds. It is likely that before the deregulation of the bond markets, the cost of funds for independent firms was higher. So they had more to gain from deregulation and took better advantage of it.

Hoshi, Kashyap, and Scharfstein (1990c) also examine the role of the keiretsu system in ameliorating the problems of member firms that are in financial distress. They argue that transaction costs in renegotiating the terms of financial instruments, information asymmetries, and free-rider problems among the different claimholders (suppliers, customers, and so forth) all work to exacerbate the cost of financial distress. The authors point out that the ties among keiretsu firms may help reduce the costs of distress. Since group banks hold both equity and debt in affiliated firms, they may not have the same information problems as debtholders of unaffiliated firms. In addition, the financial institutions of keiretsu hold the majority of the group's debt. The concentration of debt among a small number of investors reduces the transaction costs of renegotiating. Furthermore, cross-holdings of equity among member firms that also have product market ties may reduce free-rider problems. Hoshi, et al. (1990c), analyze investment and sales in financially distressed keiretsu and independent firms to determine the costs of financial distress. They find that investment and sales of keiretsu firms are higher than those of firms that have dispersed claimholders. This result also holds true for independent firms that have small numbers of debtholders.

Given that Japan's "main bank" system provides important services to its members, what are the implications for the U.S.?

There are explicit and implicit restrictions on the ability of American firms to form groups like keiretsu. The most explicit restriction is the Glass-Steagall Act, which separates commercial and investment banking. The Act prohibits American banks from owning equity for their own accounts. (Although Article 65 of Japan was explicitly patterned after the Glass-Steagall Act, it allows a Japanese commercial bank to own up to 5 percent of any one company's equity.) Likewise, regulations limit the types of stock the large institutional investors, such as insurance companies and pension funds, can own.

Furthermore, there are implicit costs if debtholders of U.S. firms actively participate in the management of a company. For example, under U.S. law, creditors that participate in the management of a company lose their priority in the bankruptcy proceedings.[10] Similarly, creditors that are involved in the management of a company may be held liable for the actions of the management. These implicit costs may limit the ability of American banks to monitor the activities of the management.

Because of U.S. laws that impose explicit and implicit costs for holding both debt and equity in a firm, U.S. firms tend to face higher costs of debt and are likely, therefore, to have lower debt-equity ratios than Japanese firms in general,

[10] See, for example, Prowse (1990) p. 10.

and keiretsu firms in particular. During the 1980s, however, the patterns of financing have been changing for both countries. Increasingly, firms in the U.S. rely on private capital markets, where the ownership of equity is concentrated in a few institutions or manager/owner/creditors of leveraged buy-outs. In addition, American firms increasingly prefer private placement of their debt, as opposed to going directly to capital markets, which concentrates the debt of these firms in the hands of a few bondholders.

Japanese firms, by contrast, have been moving away from concentrated bank loans toward diffuse bond financing. However, it is not clear that the trend toward increased bond financing during the 1980s has led to the weakening of keiretsu ties. Furthermore, the form of financing is still changing in both countries. During the first ten months of 1990, the stock prices in Tokyo (as measured by the Nikkei 225 index) have declined by approximately 36 percent. At the same time, Japanese issues of equity-related bonds have declined significantly and, for the first time since 1986, the level of bank loans have increased.

Conclusions

This study examined the differences between Japanese firms that are affiliated with the six major industrial groups called keiretsu and those that have no group affiliations. The results showed that keiretsu firms own a significantly higher percentage of group shares than independent firms. The financial institutions of the groups, which in 1989 supplied 28 percent of the total bank loans to group firms, were major shareholders in the other group firms, typically holding 21 percent of equity.

The study also found significant differences between nonfinancial keiretsu and independent firms with respect to their size (keiretsu firms are larger than independent firms), earnings (nonfinancial independent firms had significantly higher earnings per share), and stock returns. In effect, during the 1980s, the role of the independent firms in the Japanese economy has been increasing.

Moreover, the financial firms in each group display characteristics different from those of nonfinancial companies. Although asset size was similar between keiretsu and independent financial firms, keiretsu firms had significantly higher asset growth rates. In addition, financial keiretsu firms had significantly higher price-earnings ratios than financial independent firms.

The data also showed that within each group there are significant differences between financial and nonfinancial keiretsu firms. In general, financial firms are larger, faster growing companies with higher earnings.

The data on the convertible and warrant bond issues of these firms showed that keiretsu firms have been less quick to take advantage of the deregulation in these markets than independent firms.

In contrast to the popular belief that the only role of the keiretsu system is to restrict competition, the results of other studies reviewed here indicate that the keiretsu system, with its close financial ties among members, is effective in mitigating the agency costs and problems associated with asymmetric information. It is likely that the keiretsu system plays an important role in explaining the differences in the financial and investment behavior of Japanese and American firms.

References

Aoki, Masahiko. 1988. "The changing nature of industrial organization." In *Information, incentives, and bargaining in the Japanese economy.* Ed. by M. Aoki. New York: Cambridge University Press, pp. 204–257

Association of Bond and Debenture Underwriters. 1989. *The 1989 Handbook on Bonds,* Tokyo.

Dodwell Marketing Consultants. 1988. *Industrial groupings in Japan 1988/89.* Tokyo.

Dohner, Robert S., Barbara R. Lowrey, and Henry S. Terrell. 1990. "The impact of industrial affiliation on the lending activities of the U.S. offices of Japanese banks." Board of Governors of the Federal Reserve System. Mimeo.

Federation of Bankers Associations of Japan (Zenginkyo). 1989. *The banking system in Japan.* Tokyo.

Genay, Hesna. 1990. "The financial characteristics of Japanese keiretsu firms." Federal Reserve Bank of Chicago. Mimeo.

Ishizaki, Masao (ed.). *Handbook on Stock Prices,* 1976–1989. Tokyo.

Hoshi, Takeo, Anil Kashyap, and David Scharfstein. 1990(a). "Corporate structure, liquidity, and investment: evidence from Japanese panel data." *Quarterly Journal of Economics.* Forthcoming.

———. 1990(b). "Bank monitoring and investment: evidence from the changing structure of Japanese corporate banking relationship." In *Asymmetric information, corporate finance, and investment.* Ed. by R. Glenn Hubbard. Chicago: University of Chicago Press. Forthcoming.

———. 1990(c). "The role of banks in reducing the costs of financial distress in Japan." NBER Working Paper No. 3435. Cambridge.

Jensen, Michael C., and William H. Meckling, 1976. "Theory of the firm: managerial behavior, agency costs, and ownership structure." *Journal of Financial Economics* 3, pp. 305–360.

Kaneko, Yoshiki, and Luca Battaglini. 1990. "Yen-denominated convertible bonds." In *The Japanese bond markets.* Ed. by Frank J. Fabozzi. Chicago: Probus Publishing Company, pp. 381–422.

Karp, Edward W. and Akira Koike. 1990. "The Japanese corporate bond market." In *The Japanese bond markets.* Ed. by Frank J. Fabozzi. Chicago: Probus Publishing Company, pp. 353–380.

Kim, Sun Bae. 1990. "Modus operandi of lender-cum-shareholder banks." Federal Reserve Bank of San Francisco. Mimeo.

Myers, Stewart C. 1977. "Determinants of corporate borrowing." *Journal of Financial Economics* 5, pp. 147–175.

Myers, Stewart C., and Nicholas S. Majluf. 1984. "Corporate financing and investment decisions when firms have information that investors do not have." *Journal of Financial Economics* 13, pp. 187–221.

Nakatani, Iwao. 1984. "The economic role of financial corporate grouping." In *The economic analysis of the Japanese firm.* Ed. by Masahiko Aoki. Amsterdam: Elsevier Science Publishers, B.V., pp. 227–265.

Prowse, Stephen D. 1990. "Institutional investment patterns and corporate financial behavior in the U.S. and Japan." Federal Reserve Board. Mimeo.

Toyo Keizai Shimbun. 1976–1989. *Japan company handbook.* Tokyo.

Questions

1. What is the difference between the terms *keiretsu* and *zaibatsu?* Also, identify the six major keiretsu and ten major zaibatsu and note any overlap.
2. Contrast Japan's "main bank" system to the relationship between U.S. banks and their corporate customers.
3. Describe the crossholdings of equity among keiretsu, as shown in Table 1.
4. Describe the Keiretsu financial firms' within-group ownership of equity and debt. (See Table 2.)
5. Compare *nonfinancial* keiretsu and independent firms along the following dimensions: average total assets, average annual change in total assets, average level of earnings per share, average annual stock return, payout ratio, and price-earnings ratio. Now compare *financial* keiretsu and independent firms along the same six dimensions.
6. During the 1980s the Japanese government reduced restrictions on its corporate bond market by allowing firms to issue foreign bonds without permission and by easing the issuance of domestic bonds. In addition, the government instituted the following changes:

Year	Regulatory Change
1978	Relax interest rate ceilings on corporate bonds.
1981	Allow firms to issue bonds with warrants.
1983	Allow firms to issue debentures.

   Explain the implications of liberalizing bond regulations for the keiretsu system.

7. "In contrast to the popular belief that the only role of the keiretsu system is to restrict competition, the results of other studies reviewed here indicate that the keiretsu system, with its close financial ties among members, is effective in mitigating the agency costs and problems associated with asymmetric information." Describe the theory and the evidence in support of this conclusion.